BURR, HAMILTON, AND JEFFERSON

BURR, HAMILTON, AND JEFFERSON

A Study in Character

ROGER G. KENNEDY

OXFORD
UNIVERSITY PRESS

2000

OXFORD
UNIVERSITY PRESS

Oxford   New York
Athens   Auckland   Bangkok   Bogotá   Buenos Aires   Calcutta
Cape Town   Chennai   Dar es Salaam   Delhi   Florence   Hong Kong   Istanbul
Karachi   Kuala Lumpur   Madrid   Melbourne   Mexico City   Mumbai
Nairobi   Paris   São Paulo   Singapore   Taipei   Tokyo   Toronto   Warsaw

and associated companies in
Berlin   Ibadan

Published by Oxford University Press, Inc.
198 Madison Avenue, New York, New York 10016

Oxford is a registered trademark of Oxford University Press

Library of Congress Cataloging-in-Publication Data
Kennedy, Roger G.
Burr, Hamilton, and Jefferson: a study in character/
Roger G. Kennedy.
p.   cm.
Includes bibliographical references and index.
ISBN 0-19-513055-3
1. Burr, Aaron, 1756–1836.   2. Jefferson, Thomas, 1743–1826.
3. Hamilton, Alexander, 1757-1804.   4. Character—Political aspects—
United States Case studies.   5. Reputation (Law)—United States
Case studies.   6. Statesmen—United States Biography.   7. Statesmen—
United States—Conduct of life.   8. United States—Politics and
government—1775–1783.   9. United States—Politics and
government—1783–1865.   I. Title.
E302.5.K46   1999   973.4' 6' 0922—DC21   99-22453

Text set in Baskerville
Design by Adam B. Bohannon

1 3 5 7 9 8 6 4 2

Printed in the United States of America
on acid-free paper

For Frances, Ruth, and Rob

"I wish there was a war."

(Alexander Hamilton to Edward Stevens, November 17, 1769)

"You are not afraid of a little salt water, are you? This makes an adventure of it. This is the fun of the thing. The adventure is the best of it all."

(Aaron Burr to his companions
crossing New York harbor in a storm, about 1830)

"Those whom I serve have never been in a position to lift up their voices against slavery . . . I am an American and a Virginian and, though I esteem your aims, I cannot affiliate myself with your association."

(Thomas Jefferson to Jacques Pierre Brissot de Warville
of Les Amis des Noirs [Friends of the Blacks], 1788)

Contents

Acknowledgments, xv
Preface, xvii

PART ONE
Character and Circumstance, 3

CHAPTER I

Character ➤ Gentlemen ➤ Hotspur and Bolingbroke ➤ Sacrificial Suicide
Pretensions to Character ➤ The Chesterfieldian Fallacy ➤ Candor

7

CHAPTER 2

Circumstance ➤ Party and Faction ➤ Emulation, Rivalry, and Ambition
The West and Slavery ➤ The Character of Burr

21

CHAPTER 3

The Fatal Twins ➤ Burr, Hamilton, and the Consolations of Religion
Hamilton and the Consolations of Home ➤ Pain and Wrath

33

CHAPTER 4

I Wish There Was a War ➤ Staff Work ➤ The Cincinnati and Thomas
Jefferson ➤ Colonels Burr, Hamilton, and Jefferson ➤ Where Is Jefferson?
John Marshall, Thomas Jefferson, and the Question of Character

44

CHAPTER 5

Politics, Love, Learning, and Death ➤ The Women ➤ Burr and Washington
A Hypocrite or a Dangerous Man? ➤ Oaths and Other Words to Be Kept
Dueling Founders ➤ Dr. Cooper Eavesdrops

56

CHAPTER 6

Fascination ➤ Jachin and Boas ➤ Equal and Opposite
Assisted Suicide ➤ The Code

75

PART TWO
Character Tested by Slavery and Secession, 87

CHAPTER 7

The Civil Rights Movement of the 1790s and the First Jim Crow Period
The Fourteen-Year Campaign ➤ Good Company ➤ Religion, Conviction,
and Abolition ➤ The Manumission Society ➤ The Presence of Washington
Burr, Hamilton, Jefferson, the French, and the Blacks ➤ The Center Holds:
Burr, Jay, and Moderation ➤ Removal: Red and Black

89

CHAPTER 8

Misdemeanors in Kentucky and Tennessee ➤ Secession, Filibustering, and
James Wilkinson ➤ Washington Copes with Secession ➤ The French Incite
Secession and Filibustering ➤ George Rogers Clark: Frustrated Filibuster

111

CHAPTER 9

Filibustering as Policy, Glory, or Adventure ➤ Wilkinson and Wayne
Hamilton and Wilkinson ➤ Hamilton's Will ➤ Strict Construction
Burr and Disunion

127

CHAPTER 10

Washington, Western Pennsylvania, and Secession ➤ Erring Sisters and Their
Siblings ➤ Albert Gallatin and Secession ➤ Riots and Reaction ➤ Braddock's
Field and Washington's March ➤ A Tempest in a Teapot? ➤ Georges Collot
Burr, Gallatin, and the Election of 1800 ➤ Gallatin Attempts to Keep Two Friends

147

CHAPTER 11

Character, Economic Interest, and Foreign Policy ❧ The Quasi-War and the
Black Speech ❧ Private War and Private Embarrassments

172

PART THREE
In the Wake of the Hurricane, 183

CHAPTER 12

Clamor and Retreat ❧ Sanctuary ❧ The Truxtons ❧ The General
The Biddles Come to the Rescue

185

CHAPTER 13

Southern Hospitality ❧ Gin, Green Seed, and Empire ❧ Patriotic Gratitude
and Yankee Ingenuity ❧ The Attractions of Florida ❧ The Presences of
History ❧ Three Generations of McIntoshes and Slavery ❧ Family
Southern Communications

195

CHAPTER 14

Fort George ❧ Don Juan McQueen ❧ Bowles, Slavery, and McQueen
John Houstoun McIntosh ❧ Caballing in the Carolinas with the Scots
Virginia Complications

214

PART FOUR
The Great Valley, 231

CHAPTER 15

Burr and the Middle Ground ❧ Among the Stockbridges
Joseph Brant

233

CHAPTER 16

"A Country of Slaves" ❧ Turning Oglethorpe Around ❧ Seminole Carondelet
and Servile Insurrection ❧ Militia Matters ❧ Calming Mr. Jefferson

242

PART FIVE
The Expedition, 255

CHAPTER 17

Intentions, 1800–1805 ❧ Absurd Reports ❧ The Manic Burr Goes West
On to the Hermitage, New Orleans, and the Clergy ❧ Casa Calvo, Grand Pré,
Morales, and Recruiting ❧ La Chaumiere du Prairie ❧ Wilkinson's Fidelity
Wilkinson's Estimates ❧ Jefferson Recomputes the Odds

257

CHAPTER 18

Whose Valley? ❧ A Garden with a Past ❧ Burr's Lost Paradise
Empire, Sanctuary, and Speculation

283

CHAPTER 19

Mr. Jefferson's Colleagues ❧ Neutral Ground ❧ In the Shoes of Thomas
Adam Smith ❧ George Morgan for the Prosecution ❧ John Adams and the
"Lying Spirit" of the Virginians ❧ Meanwhile, in Bruinsburg
Captain Hooke

292

CHAPTER 20

The Thinking Part of the People ❧ The Jury Convenes at Jefferson College
Senator Plumer Reports ❧ The Charge of Filibustering ❧ Mr. Jefferson's
Private Armies and the Opinion of Another Jury ❧ The Mississipi Federalists
Silas Dinsmoor ❧ Robert Ashley ❧ Thomas Rodney and Old '76
John McKee

305

CHAPTER 21

The Wheeled Cell and the Trial ❧ Rousing the Neighborhood
Benjamin Hawkins ❧ The Case of Bollmann ❧ Elijah Clarke and His Trans-
Oconee Ruins ❧ Fort Wilkinson

333

CHAPTER 22

Precedents and Justice ❧ Recalling a Real Rebellion
Consolation Prizes ❧ French Accessories

347

CONTENTS

CHAPTER 23
Groundsprings of Wrath ❧ West by Southwest ❧ Cherchez les Femmes
359

POSTSCRIPT
John Quincy Adams, Harriet Beecher Stowe, and Other Women ❧ James
Parton Attempts a Rescue ❧ The Falling Man ❧ Adams, Abolition, and
Jefferson ❧ Adams and Jefferson ❧ The Worst and the Best
371

Appendix: Biases and Apologies, 389
Notes, 395
Bibliography, 435
Index, 453

Acknowledgments

After nearly sixty years of writing for publication, and asking others to help improve what I publish, I have accumulated so many debts to so many that I cannot sort out to which subset gratitude is owed for their aid in bringing this work, which has only a decade of thought in it, to its present state. All books after the first one are sequels. This one certainly is. Its origins go back a long way, probably requiring acknowledgment to F. Scott Fitzgerald, whose vitality as editor of my school newspaper, that distinguished publication *The Now and Then*, sustained it long enough for me to succeed him as editor after a lapse of fifteen years or so, permitting me an early opportunity to nurture a penchant for prose and an ambition to publish my own. I have thanked specific scholars for specific contributions to this work in the end notes to the text where those contributions can most readily be observed.

I do have to say, however, that without the kind but firm attention given by my editor, Thomas LeBien, to my original sprawling mass of material, only a portion of which wound up within these covers, there would be no book here for you to read.

And without the genuine courage of Peter Onuf in assembling first-rate scholars, young and old, in Mr. Jefferson's Charlottesville, my inquiry into the interactions among the Sage of Monticello and his contemporaries would have been much impoverished. We did not agree on much of anything, but it was great fun, and I learned a lot. The heart of the scholarly enterprise has two lobes: the encouragement of fresh appraisals of old data, and new research. Not all such appraisals or research are done by university scholars. It was a joy to me, after many years of working to improve the quality of scholarly work in museums and in national parks, in historical societies and by independent scholars, to find in Virginia an academic institution more dedicated to learning than to institutional definition. Henry Adams would be pleased. Winston Churchill might be amused. As an independent scholar, I am not only grateful but impressed.

Preface

Before we go farther, I'd like us to have a talk. I do not intend to delay you for long, and only to offer a little consumer protection. The author has a point of view, a way of thinking about the lives of public men and women that arises from fifty years living either in government or near government, reporting on government, or writing about governments past. Over those years, life has informed me that the established reputation of many public persons, living and dead, is rarely congruent with their true character. I recall my mentor Eric Severeid saying of one such person, "There is less there than meets the eye." But that is not all that needs to be said, for often there is more, especially among those whom history, or journalism, have dismissed as failures. Aaron Burr is the central figure in this book because his character was better than his reputation. Though unquestionably a failure, his role in our history was larger than the credit he has received.

The term "spin control" is modern, but the practice to which it refers is ancient and constant in all political systems. Reputation is a cocoon of many threads, some of them spun around themselves by the characters within, some gathered from others, whether solicited or unavoidably attached by controversy. Appraisals of character require unwinding such cocoons, to examine each strand for authenticity. Any undertaking of that sort must be energized by the unwinder's own needs and guided by the unwinder's own sense of justice. No one embarks on a study of Burr, Hamilton, and Jefferson without preconceptions about them, and few without passionate preconceptions. That is why a candid declaration of bias is important at the outset.

Certainly their contemporaries had strong opinions about each, and we have learned to heed those judgments. In this book we will attempt to ascertain the emotional stimuli leading to the views expressed of them by George Washington, John Jay, John Marshall, John Adams, Albert Gallatin, John Quincy Adams, and Harriet Beecher Stowe, among others. But always we will try to ground ourselves in what they said of each other, which can tell us as much about the person talking as about the person talked about. They were there onstage simultaneously, within hearing, touch, sight, and assessment of each other.

We cannot judge any one of our protagonists by some absolute standard. We must take them as fellow humans; they were flawed, as we are. Burr was imperfect; so were Hamilton and Jefferson. Though some readers might sense in that assertion a desire to bring the rest of the Founders down to Burr's level, leveling is not inherent in a determination that all be judged by the same standards. Applying those standards may leave some people very much more exalted than others. Nor is either qualitative homogenization or leveling the necessary consequence of a strong sense that sin is ubiquitous. On the contrary, sin may be present in all humans without its being distributed equally. Democracy is based upon the premise that none are so wise or pure as to be trusted to govern without constraint, and none so lacking in wisdom or purity as to be left out of the governing process.

A measure of wariness about the perfection of anyone, even heroes who found republics, leads to history as reappraisal. The impulse to correct injustice can bubble forth even from those who have themselves been lucky in public life, because they know about injustice better than most: they have had attributed to them virtues they did not in fact possess, and therefore grow as wary of big reputations as of small—that is, they do so if they share our conviction that politics is an extension of morality.

There are many lucky public men and women who do not regard such a conviction as naive. Lucky or unlucky, most public people intend to leave the world better for their having breathed its air and trod its turf. I write of their intentions, not necessarily of their effects, for along with sin there is evil in the world, and most of us are from time to time overwhelmed by evil, from inside or out. Conceding, as I do, that my general belief in moral intentions of public people may be both credulous and unsusceptible of proof, nonetheless I am convinced that the three Founders selected for discussion in this book were moral men, serious about leaving a beneficial legacy.

Naive or not, this opening letter is here to tack my intentions and objectives upon the door. I write of the character, the circumstances, and the reputations of three Founders in the hope that lessons useful to the present may be drawn from such a study. Aaron Burr is, for me, central to this discussion. I hope by it to hasten his return from the exile on that shadowy periphery to which Jefferson consigned him.

The sources of the biases of which I spoke at the outset are set out in the autobiographical appendix at the back of the book, out of the way of readers who want to get on with the story, or who enjoy doing their own ferreting out of an author's preconceptions.

One further note, addressed to those readers who have traveled with me before. In the course of these many years, we have gone together to some of the places, subjects, and people revisited here. Some of my earlier books record judgments which now seem to me foolish, so I have tried to make corrections in these pages, while reaffirming other judgments which seem more important now than they were when first offered. In order to admit error and to reassert truth, I have cribbed a paragraph here or there from earlier works. Endnotes admitting this pillage may strike some as shameless cross-touting, but better that than leaving a mistake without acknowledgment—or worse, eschewing mention of something germane merely because it has been mentioned once before. As in those earlier works, I have changed archaic spelling and punctuation in quotations to make them more comprehensible to modern readers except when the archaism makes a point as such. Now—let us set forth on our voyage.

BURR, HAMILTON, AND JEFFERSON

PART ONE
Character and Circumstance

In which we will attempt to assess the characters of Thomas Jefferson, Alexander Hamilton, and Aaron Burr, taking account of their reputations and of the experiences within which their characteristic predispositions hardened into maturity. As their circumstances tested what that maturity had become, their reputations swirled before and after them in the winds of public opinion, like loose cloaks. Finally, in Burr's case, the reputation was flung away from the man and lay upon the ground, inert, while the man went on through thirty more years of life.

While their circumstances affected them, these powerful characters altered those circumstances, thereby altering as well the lives of millions of others. It may seem odd to include Burr in the company of world-shapers, but the conclusion drawn from our character studies is that he belongs with Hamilton and Jefferson at center stage in the drama of the founding of the American Republic. There can be no full biography of Thomas Jefferson or Alexander Hamilton that leaves Burr out. He functioned as a sort of Black Hole, largely invisible in most accounts of the period, but acting with sufficient force upon the more celebrated heavenly bodies as to make their behavior inexplicable without taking account of him. Otherwise unaccountable twistings and bendings, advances and withdrawals, anxieties, exertions, and affinities and oppositions can then be better explained.

Our subject is character, and its relationship to reputation; throughout the fifty years in which Jefferson and Burr were national figures (some of those years merely living out their declining energies), their contemporaries expressed doubts about the character of them both. There was something in them that induced many who knew them not to trust them—though many upright men trusted each. It is remarkable that Hamilton escaped that sort of skepticism, for he was no more consistently straightforward or truthful than they. That was probably a matter of demeanor: Hamilton, at once trustworthy and unreliable, seemed less devious than Jefferson or Burr; the former was often described as sly, and the latter as a rogue.

The character of each of these great men was first severely tested in the Revolutionary War of 1775–83, in which all three achieved the rank of colonel. Burr was a hero; Jefferson was not; after being eclipsed by the dashing Burr, Hamilton served unheroically as a staff officer until, at Yorktown, in 1783, at the very end of the war, he persuaded Washington, his commander and sponsor, to let him lead a charge.

Jefferson became President of the United States in 1800, having restored his reputation from his wartime governorship of Virginia by successes as a diplomat in Paris and as Secretary of State. Hamilton was briefly a congressman and brilliantly a Secretary of the Treasury under Washington and was killed in a duel by Burr in 1804. Burr had been attorney general of New York, senator, and Jefferson's Vice President. After a failed effort to be elected governor of New York, the duel, and a failed filibuster in the Mississippi Valley, Burr was proclaimed by Jefferson in 1806 to be engaged in treason. Though unsuccessful in finding a court to convict Burr of that charge, Jefferson drove him into exile in 1808.

Having disclosed the bare chronology of our story, let us anticipate some of the conclusions drawn at the end of this work. All three of our characters were on occasion noble, generous, and touching in their willingness to express their affections. All were ambitious, though neither Burr nor Hamilton had Jefferson's mastery of the means to satisfy ambition. Was Hamilton, then, a success, like Jefferson, or a failure, like Burr? The answer each of us gives to that question depends largely upon the weight we give to reputation, to demeanor, and to circumstance, as well, in judging character. Taking circumstance into consideration means judging each other not so much by whether we win or lose but by how we play the cards we are dealt, without thereby conceding to the view that cards ordain outcomes. We have observed how some people seem to affect their circumstances as much as circumstances affect them, thereby reinforcing the folk wisdom of expressions such as "making their luck." Since life is not entirely fair, many admirable card-makers are not lucky—there are fortune's favorites and fortune's victims.

Thomas Jefferson was one of the former, and also a very great man, quite possibly the most intelligent of our Presidents. As a writer, he has had an irresistible appeal to historians, whose profession, after all, is writing. His flaws were those of character, not of competence. His failings, like those of both Hamilton and Burr, can best be assessed in the light of the conviction, stated earlier, that politics is an extension of morality.

I

Character

The problem for historians assessing the character of Thomas Jefferson is that they have too much accessible information. As to Aaron Burr, they have the opposite problem; after his trial, his exile, and the loss of his beloved daughter and grandchild, he made no significant effort to present his own case, while Alexander Hamilton, in his final hours, made an effort to set things straight, but only in anticipation of death, and so desperately that not even his most admiring friends accept his self-disclosure as reliable.

The three had very little good to say for each other. Except for his confessions on the night before he died, Hamilton allocated much of the energy of his final year to the destruction of Burr's reputation. After Hamilton's death, Jefferson used the full powers of the presidency to finish that work. Hamilton had charged debauchery and mendacity. Jefferson added treason. Neither, it may be noted, accused Burr of mean-spiritedness, cruelty, or vindictiveness, probably because at the time such assertions would have injured their case against him. The gentry acquainted with the three knew better.

The allegation of treason upon which Jefferson's presidential indictment of Burr centered was three times put to juries. None of the three reached agreement with Jefferson. Considering all this, the wonder is how little Burr had to say for himself. Even after Hamilton and Jefferson forced him out of politics, he still refused to explain, from his point of view, why they had been so eager to do so. If he wished posterity to think well of him, it would have been better had he thought well enough of it to engage it in a conversation. Without turning upon those who made charges against him, he merely wrote:

> I fear I have committed a great error; the men who knew their falsity are dead, and the generation who now read them may take them for truths, being uncontradicted. I admit I have committed a capital error, but it is too late to repair it.[1]

Perhaps it is not too late. But it will require a great deal more work than doing equivalent justice to Jefferson. Knowing that historians build with paper, the bibliographer and Sage of Monticello saved and arranged every paper that might demonstrate his character as he wished posterity to assess it. The mere listing of his correspondence runs for more than six hundred pages, and he provided eighteen thousand copies of his outgoing correspondence through the use of the polygraph machine he invented. Because the process was slow, mechanical, and burdensome, we can be certain that not a word in those eighteen thousand reproduced letters was unconsidered. Neither is there anything among the twenty-five thousand incoming letters he kept on file that would unbecome him; nor did he offer any comfort to admirers of either Burr or Hamilton in the accounts of his conversations with them in his *Anas*.

Burr lingered on until 1836, still unwilling to provide for history those documentary conveniences upon which it depends. He did retain much useful material, but his best chronicler, his daughter, and all his crucial papers were lost at sea. (His second choice as biographer, his son-in-law, was so overcome by grief after his wife's death that he commenced a descent into an early grave.) With Hamilton dead and Burr mute, Jefferson's self-asserted character has occupied the field. He has had critics, but however skeptical they may have been, much of their work must depend upon material he selected for their use.

Burr, Hamilton, and Jefferson were leery of the opinions of any large number of persons. Hamilton and Burr did not approve of what Burr called Jefferson's "Jacobin leveling principles." They knew their man well enough to doubt that Jefferson was at heart any more promiscuous in his democratic instincts than they. Yet both suspected that he would pretend to be so, despite his shrinking from exposure to people to whom he had not been introduced. Hamilton tried electioneering, once, was ridiculed, and recoiled. Burr was willing to meet with the leaders of Tammany but not to go either to their clubhouse or to the streets.[2]

In an oratorical age, Jefferson never made an audible public oration—*never*. He was willing to step onto his portico to acknowledge the adulation of welcoming committees who would greet him on his return to Monticello, but that was that. He delivered two inaugural addresses as President. They read well, but we are solemnly informed by those present that neither could be heard. Hamilton and Burr were both audible as public speakers, though their audiences never exceeded the company of gentlemen. When he came before the Constitutional Convention, Hamilton essayed a six-hour instruction so deadening to his hearers that it induced a weary adjournment. Burr was better; his farewell to the Senate, in 1804, was one of the most affecting public addresses delivered between those of Patrick Henry and the advent of Daniel Webster. Perhaps that was because those affected were men of his own sort, to whom he affirmed their self-estimation as persons set aside to govern because they were not ordinary.

Gentlemen

We need no reminding that Hamilton was charged with "aristocratical" ideas, though in fact his principles were more mercantile than aristocratic. Burr's chosen placement in society was demonstrated by his retort to a young lawyer who rose in a courtroom in Jamaica, Long Island, seeking to inflame the crowd against him:

> I learned in the Revolution, in the society of gentlemen, and I have since observed, that a man who is guilty of intentional bad manners, is capable of crime.[3]

There is more in this than the pride of a single officer. It tells us how "a society of gentlemen" thought of the nature of the Revolution itself. The affronted gentry did not rise against custom, king, and country for light or specious reasons. The affront to them was to the principles of their class—a class Aaron Burr entered by "birth, parentage, and descent," according to John Adams. Adams went on to emphasize a point essential to our story, that Burr sustained his status when his military record displayed "the character of a knight without fear, and an able officer."[4]

In that character, he might have made a great career as a demagogue if that had been his nature. Burr was, however, trained in a fastidious mode of public discourse that became natural to him after a terrible childhood. He eschewed that noisy righteousness of indignation that even then was becoming an American characteristic. As the descendant of evangelists, Burr might have been fitted to sustain the emotional pitch of the Revolution, but because his every expansive instinct was extinguished in his youth, he did not possess the capacity to gush. His life oscillated only between a modernized and secularized pursuit of Puritan example and a cool, aristocratic reaction against it.

Burr came of a tradition of scholars and clerics, leavened by merchants accounted gentlemen, but without Cavalier pretensions. Like the Adamses, they might own houses beyond the city limits, but they would have thought it silly to search in the attic for heraldic shields. It is crucial to recognize that such people thought first of conscience and only then of honor. "Southern honor" did not always shadow southern conscience; when a man thinks of himself as a descendant of Cavaliers, he is not likely to think like a Roundhead. In tight places, class and sectional interest do sometimes conflict with individual conviction, and in tight places Aaron Burr chose the latter. So, in fact, did Hamilton, who inherited no class nor section.

Hotspur and Bolingbroke

Hamilton was the Hotspur among the periwigs, as Jefferson was the Bolingbroke.* They were different in character, and they were also different in manner. Hamilton was accounted to be more sincere, but that was because he seemed so, for Jefferson shared with Burr a cool, covered demeanor which even so early as 1800 was thought by Amer-

*Readers of Shakespeare's *King Henry IV* recall Harry Percy (Hotspur) as the earl of Northumberland's impetuous heir who participated in the Revolution of 1399 to seize the throne from Richard II and to install upon it the cool, farseeing Henry of Lancaster, known as Bolingbroke for his place of birth in Lancashire. Bolingbroke and Hotspur fell into dispute over some Scottish prisoners and fought it out at Shrewsbury, where Hotspur was killed.

icans to be incompatible with candor. Hamilton made public professions of religious fervor; Jefferson and Burr did not. But we must be cautious about making a romantic of Hamilton just because his oratorical style was rapturous. He was, in fact, a calculating man, nearly as calculating as Jefferson. Burr was the romantic, though his personal style was covered and his literary mode drier than Jefferson's.

Jefferson was a landed gentleman, American style—that is to say that he owned both real estate and "personalty" in the literal sense. In modern parlance: He owned persons. Burr, the scion of men of the Book and the Cloth, had no awe for the landed gentry. Hamilton had a tenuous connection to Scottish lairdship; his putative father was not, in fact, a "peddler" but a decayed gentleman who had descended to trade. Since that gentleman had deserted him, he early made the choice for trade writ large among a class of men making the transition from trade toward manufacturing. His determination introduced him to their way of thinking, in particular to their aversion toward dependence upon larger merchants and toward any monopoly not their own. He was the natural advocate of home industries, providing a patriotic reason for protecting them, for clearing their traffic lanes, and for taxing farmers to subsidize them. Unlike Jefferson, he correctly perceived the danger that, having declared political independence, the United States would lapse into a neocolonial dependence upon British manufactures, as, indeed, the South did.

In Hamilton's world of contract and purchased alliances, keeping your word, or honoring your contract, is the primary gauge of character, and he was never (so far as we know) guilty of a deliberate lie. That is not to say that he always spoke the truth. A deliberate lie is different from an impetuous declaration of something which, in a cooler moment, one may admit to have been untrue. Hamilton was guilty of yielding to transitory truths of the moment, as he was guilty of yielding to sexual opportunities of the moment. His psychiatrist grandson was right: His faults were those of an impetuous nature.

Burr's lies were to foreigners, concerning politics, and perhaps to creditors concerning money, though it is possible that neither he, nor Jefferson, nor Hamilton, three chronic debtors, deliberately stated an untruth to those they owed. Not one died solvent, and all three failed to make promised payments, but they may have thought they might pay when they said they would. As to political mendacity, Jefferson's breaches of pledged word cannot be said, like Hamilton's, to have been the rotted fruit of impetuosity. From the circumstances, it is apparent that, each time, he meant to lie. Yet those who admire Burr as much as the other two must admit that many who knew them all thought him to be the shiftiest, the least reliable, and the most devious. There is no ready explanation for this, because the written record of their actions, comparatively, does not bear this impression out. Yet it cannot be denied as prevailing widely at the time. Hamilton and Jefferson did nothing to dissuade anyone of its truth, but they cannot justly be said to have created it. Burr may have delighted in giving such an impression when it cost him little to do so, for neither he nor anyone else could have anticipated that in 1804 and again in 1807 the game of politics would become deadly. He and Hamilton engaged in a duel to the death in 1804, and Jefferson brought him to trial on a hanging offense in 1807.

Sacrificial Suicide

Burr became Vice President of the United States in 1800 despite Hamilton's having turned the full force of his excoriative skills from John Adams toward Burr. Thomas Jefferson was the beneficiary of Hamilton's work on Adams and was again indebted to Hamilton in 1804 when, by dying, he weakened Burr. The price was very high, but the result was devoutly desired; Hamilton only disdained Adams, while his feeling for Burr was deeper than hate.

As early as 1800, Hamilton was writing his friends that he could do no "better than withdraw from the scene. Every day proves to me more and more that the American world was not made for me." What other world was there? So—how to make an exit? "For some time past," Hamilton told those at his bedside as he lay dying, he had known "that my life must be exposed to that man." Why? Henry Adams hazarded an answer: "Instead of killing Burr, [Hamilton] invited Burr to kill him." Another historian, Douglas Adair, took Hamilton's admission that he had been guilty of maligning Burr to be a step toward expiation, so that death at Burr's hands would become "an act of repentance." That is certainly how his religious contemporaries took it, and they sainted him for it.[5]

In 1978, four psychological biographers discussed the matter and concluded that Hamilton had committed suicide, "using Burr as an instrument," having projected upon Burr his failures as man and leader. Burr became his own "evil self," to be entrapped into taking them all—Hamilton the protagonist, Hamilton the projected evil one, and Burr the adversary—*all* down with a single shot.[6]

And what if Hamilton thought he was going to die soon enough anyway? It is possible that his life was coming to an end, or that he thought so. His physician, Dr. Hosack, reported that he was unable to treat Hamilton's wound with "all those remedies which are usually indicated on such occasions" because "his habit was delicate and had been lately rendered more feeble by ill health, particularly by a disorder of the stomach and bowels."[7]

Whether he thought of himself as sacrifice or hero or instrument of fate, Hamilton wrote his farewell documents to establish his own character and to destroy Burr's. Hamilton needed to make himself a victim—a Christian victim.

Let us see how he sought to establish his character, and Burr's as well. As our tale unfolds, the reader can then juxtapose what Hamilton said of himself with what his actions tell us. It will then be a great convenience that, because of the precision with which his projection mechanism operated, we can judge both him and Burr by what he said of Burr. Let us begin with what he wrote of himself.

I think it proper to make some remarks explanatory of my conduct, motives and views. I was certainly desirous of avoiding this interview. . . . My religious and moral principles are strongly opposed to the practice of dueling. . . . I am conscious of no *ill will* [Hamilton's emphasis] to Col. Burr, distinct from political opposition, which I trust has proceeded from pure and upright motives. . . .

. . . my animadversions on the political principles, character, and views of Col. Burr . . . have been extremely severe. . . . In proportion as these impressions were entertained with sincerity, and uttered with motives and for purposes which might appear to me commendable, would be the difficulty (until they could be removed by evidence of their being erroneous) of explanation or apology. . . . It is not my design, by what I have said, to affix any odium on the conduct of Col. Burr, in this case. He doubtless has heard of animadversions of mine, which bore very hard upon him; and it is probable that as usual they were accompanied with some falsehoods. He may have supposed himself under a necessity of acting as he has done. I hope the grounds of his proceeding are such as ought to satisfy his own conscience.

I trust at the same time, that the world will do me the justice to believe that I have not censured him on light grounds, nor from unworthy inducements. I certainly have had strong reasons for what I may have said, though it is possible that in some particulars, I may have been influenced by misconstruction or misinformation. It is also my ardent wish that I may have been more mistaken than I think I have been, and that he, by his future conduct, may show himself worthy of all confidence and esteem, and prove an ornament and blessing to the country.

As well because it is possible I may have injured Col. Burr, however convinced myself that my opinions and declarations have been well founded, I have resolved . . . to throw away my first fire. . . . It is not, however, my intention to enter into any explanations on the ground—Apology from principle, I hope, rather than pride, is out of the question. To those who, with me, abhorring the practice of dueling, may think that I ought on no account to have added to the number of bad examples, I answer that my *relative* [his emphasis] situation as well in public as private, enforcing all the considerations which constitute what men of the world denominate honor, imposed upon me (as I thought) a peculiar necessity not to decline the call. The ability to be in future useful, whether in resisting mischief or effecting good . . . would probably be inseparable from a conformity with public prejudice in this particular.[8]

Hamilton did not offer this document to Burr, or to anyone who might have spoken to Burr of it before the duel. The apology was to be posthumous. Whatever Hamilton intended, it was not to avert a fatal encounter. A man who writes in this way is engaged in defining himself, correcting thereby what he fears he has, until then, conveyed about himself. In Hamilton's case, the image he might most have desired to erase was himself-in-Burr, as he had depicted Burr to others. Anyone who knew them both could readily hold up a mirror to Hamilton when he presented his projection of evil as Burr—his doppelgänger, his other. What he said of Burr was true of himself.

(1) He is in every sense a profligate, a voluptuary in the extreme. . . . His very friends do not insist upon his integrity.

(2) He is without doubt insolvent for a large deficit. . . .

(3) He must therefore from the necessity of his station have recourse to unworthy expedients. These may be a bargain and sale with some foreign power . . . and probably, to enlarge the sphere—war.

(4) He has no pretensions to the Station [the presidency] from service [in the Revolution] . . . He . . . gave indications of being a good officer; but without having had the opportunity of performing any distinguished action. . . . In civil life, he has never projected nor aided in producing a single measure of important public utility. . . .

(7) He is of a temper bold enough to think no enterprise too hazardous and sanguine enough to think none too difficult. . . .

(8) Discerning men of all parties agree in ascribing to him an irregular and inordinate ambition . . . he will in all likelihood attempt an usurpation.[9]

And, finally, with the most astonishing self-deception about the perils of self-revelation, Hamilton said of the circumspect Burr: "He has held very vindictive language respecting his opponents."[10]

Pretensions to Character

When in 1800 Hamilton had done with John Adams, Adams was finished as a leader of the Federalist party, and Hamilton was left to choose whether, among the survivors, more was to be feared from Jefferson or from Burr. His conclusion was that "Jefferson is to be preferred. He is by far not so dangerous a man; he has pretensions to character." As if instantly to offer a parody of what pretensions to character might permit, he proceeded to urge other Federalists of character "to throw out a lure for him [Burr], in order to tempt him to start for the plate, and then lay a foundation in dissension between the two chiefs." Thus, having dissembled just enough, or lied just a little, the Federalists could snap shut the trap and leave their opponents divided and weakened.[11]

"Pretensions to character." What might those be? Is pretension something different from possession? Jefferson's response to Hamilton's charges was that his accuser was "a man whose history, from the moment at which history can stoop to notice him, is a tissue of machinations against the liberty of the country . . . not only a monarchist, but for a monarchy bottomed on corruption."[12]

Corruption was incompatible with "character," as these men used the term. Our use of the term "integrity" reminds us that for them a person of character manifested a harmonious wholeness out of which correct behavior ensued. Character did not necessarily require goodness of heart, nor was a person of character expected to be generous. Generosity expressed something beyond character, a quality the eighteenth century admired and called "liberality." After 1800 or so, as too much amiability or generosity came to provoke apprehension, "liberality" fell from fashion. Saving (a bourgeois virtue) replaced benign expenditure (a characteristic of feudal chieftains), and reinvestment replaced potlatch. As Burr learned to his sorrow, too much liberality became a sign of bad character. This transition can be observed in what was said of Burr by Hamilton, by Hamiltonians, by Jefferson, and by a host of others. Hamilton, Jefferson, Madison, and Monroe all died bankrupt after lavish expenditure upon their own comfort and upon expensive country houses, in the English fashion. While Jefferson was generous to his friends, Burr was munificent. This was one of the ways in which he was becoming an anachronism.

Bankruptcy had been commonplace among gentlemen and merchants in the founding generation. Financial mismanagement carried nothing of the onus it carries today, nor did improvidence in providing for oneself. Gentlemen were not thought lacking in character merely because they left to their heirs only debts. The emergent century, however, brought with it, after the economic confusions of the 1790s, a saving-and-investing society, looking forward to Ebenezer Scrooge rather than backward to Charles James Fox. Aaron Burr had no place in a society in which character was defined among the middle class as abstinence from expenditure they could afford, and among the workers as a willingness not to ask for more than they might then spend. The sphincter replaced the open palm as the preferred portion of a good citizen's anatomy.

The emergent middle class coupled its crabbed avoidance of philanthropy to a boisterous expression of religious conviction. Burr was "liberal" in the eighteenth-century sense, as "liberalism" in the nineteenth century came to mean approval of the free play of market forces, without distortion by generosity. Though middle-class people who professed that sort of liberalism found Burr's kind condescending and vaguely irresponsible, they talked much of religion, while Burr did not. To the day he died, he was coy about public pronouncements of his moral motivation and of its religious grounding. Hamilton could be generous, too, but hardly to the point of liberality, in part because he had generated a large and expensive brood, which had first call upon his resources. Like the business men he served, however, he thought it necessary to profess "pure and upright motives," asserting publicly his "religious and moral principles." Jefferson instructed posterity as to his religious views by way of his own scissors-and-paste Bible but, during his lifetime, was as coy as Burr and as indisposed to the noisier forms of religious expression.

Burr's coyness was, as he said, a great mistake in spin control. Hamilton's effusions were wiser, and Jefferson's addresses to coming generations cleverer still. Had Hamilton survived the twelfth duel he provoked, we can be confident that we would have heard a good deal more about his "principles."

The Chesterfieldian Fallacy

The character of Aaron Burr lies hidden from us by clouds of false witness borne against him by his political opponents, behind his own persistent refusal to explain himself, and obscured by certain platitudes about him composed even by those who thought themselves his friends. His first biographer to be trained as a historian, James Parton, set adrift the notion that "Chesterfield was not a more consummate Chesterfieldian than Aaron Burr." To support this assertion, Parton, eloquent but careless, offered only a sentence in a letter to Burr from his wife, in which she discounted the utility of Chesterfield as a guide to the young, along with other fashionable preceptors of the day, such as Rousseau and Voltaire. As if in the belief that good manners cloak a bad heart, many subsequent biographers seeking such a heart in Burr have cited Parton, implying or assuring us that Burr disagreed with his wife. For example, Nathan Schachner, otherwise an admirable guide through this thicket, tells us that Chesterfield, Rousseau, and Voltaire guided Burr's education of their daughter after the death of his wife, despite her wishes.[13]

If this were true, we might deduce from it not only that Burr was a Chesterfieldian but also that he had little respect for his wife's intellect and preferences. In truth, however, there is not a single reference to Chesterfield in all his hundreds of instructions to their child. Nor did he adopt for his own behavior the most obvious of Chesterfieldian characteristics, which Dr. Johnson singled out as an insolent lack of kindness or "consideration." Both Burr and his wife knew that the *Letters of Chesterfield* were amusing but useless as instruction. They were written in a vain attempt to school Philip Stanhope, Chesterfield's dull, loutish, shambling though amiable, bastard son, in the behavior necessary to gain favor in the corrupt court at Versailles.[14]

The callous admonitions of Chesterfield did not supervene the precepts of Epictetus, Marcus Aurelius, or Plutarch in setting the moral standards of the classically trained Burrs. At her parents' insistence, their daughter Theodosia gained fluency in both Latin and Greek before she was twelve, and was assigned to read the classics as Plutarch would have them read: for moral instruction. Burr bestowed upon her the calm Aurelian spirit, not the waspish tone of Chesterfield, in setting forth his own maxims of good behavior in adversity:

> Receive with calmness every reproof, whether made kindly or unkindly; whether just or unjust. Consider within yourself whether there has been no cause for it. If it has been groundless and unjust, never the less bear it with composure, and even with complacency. . . . We must learn to bear such things; and let me tell you, that you will always feel much better, much happier, for having borne with serenity the spleen of anyone, than if you had returned spleen for spleen.
>
> You will, I am sure, my dear Theodosia, pardon two such grave pages from one who loves you, and whose happiness depends very much on yours.[15]

Candor

When David Reisman discovered "sincerity" in the 1950s, the irony was new, but the phenomenon was not. Alexander Hamilton may not have possessed a "sincere tie," but he had a "sincere suit" and a very "sincere voice." Hamilton was impetuous in large matters, but he was deliberate in details, skilled in the rhetoric of dress and behavior that, as any actor knows, can immeasurably improve the effect of mere language. It was well for Jefferson to have been so masterful in prose, for he had to rely so much upon language. He utterly lacked a theatrical sense.

In the company of others, Hamilton was charming, effusive, effulgent, and apparently candid. Burr was always covered, always apparently scheming. Benjamin Henry Latrobe wrote that Burr's demeanor belied his nature, dissembling his "benevolence," as if he wished to seem *less* benevolent, *less* passionate, *less* candid, and *more* devious than he actually was. As a result, it became conventional to attribute to him a diabolical cleverness even before the duel with the saintly-seeming Hamilton, even before the "conspiracy" of which he was charged by Jefferson.[16]

Yet no one who knew them both, or studied them both with any care, accepted as authentic either an angelic Hamilton or a Satanic Burr. Dr. Allan Hamilton, the first professionally trained psychiatrist to examine the two in retrospect, quoted with approval the conclusion of one of his grandfather's most admiring biographers, Frederick Scott Oliver: "Lovers of Hamilton and of a settled order . . . have drawn the picture of Burr which is accepted in history books. It is only natural that the shadows have been overblackened." But Burr himself had provided the shadows. Latrobe lamented his persistent refusal to emerge from them to contend for the sunlight with the apparently openhearted Hamilton:

> Mr. Hamilton had more apparent frankness and candor, with less actual benevolence; Colonel Burr, more discretion and command of himself, with the most generous and liberal mind. Of Colonel Burr, numerous proofs of the most disinterested benevolence are known. Not a single instance of munificence is known of Hamilton.[17]

Trying to be fair, with Allan Hamilton's assent, Oliver could only bring himself to write:

> Strictly he was an immoral citizen, because he flouted the sanctity of contract and gave away upon an impulse what was already

hypothecated to others. But at least he did not spend upon himself. . . . He gave because he could not resist appeals, because he could not help giving. . . . His charity was of the heart, spontaneous, promiscuous, and usually misdirected. . . . In his old age the habit amounted to a mania.[18]

Now, after another ninety years have passed, is it truly "too late" for a person to be thought sane if given enthusiastically to liberality and to adventure? I do not think so. Instead, it seems to me, it is high time to restore Aaron Burr to the Pantheon of the Founders.

2

Circumstance

Aaron Burr saw more of the world than any of the other Founders. His adventures took him as far as Quebec, the Missouri, the verge of the Gulf of Mexico, Jacksonville, and Mobile. His misadventures brought him to Stockholm, London, Paris, Edinburgh, and Amsterdam. Like Washington and Jefferson, Burr took an active interest in American antiquity, and he shared with them a capacity to observe and record natural history, but the tone of his commentary differs from theirs. His sympathies were more inclusive than Hamilton's or Jefferson's, and his style was more personal than Washington's. He treated people of African descent as respectfully as Europeans, and, alone among the Founders, Burr had Indian friends. With Hamilton and John Jay, he was among the leaders of the battle to end slavery in New York. And, as we shall see, his protofeminism required more of him than his wearing an amulet of Mary Wollstonecraft during most of his adult life. But such a symbolic act, so long sustained, "signifies," as he might have said.

Our protagonists now begin to lead us out of libraries and onto the land. Beyond their verandas lay their cultivated countrysides, for all three were intensely physical—tactile—men, eighteenth-century patrons of architecture, of horticulture, and of landscape design. All three loved their country houses. Jefferson's Monticello is more famous than Hamilton's disgracefully bereft Grange and Burr's now obliterated Richmond Hill, but any full sympathy for the three requires us to pay attention to these places as well. Hamilton's estate, where he made his notes on natural history, lay upon the upper escarpment of the island of Manhattan; it can only be seen today ambiguously, truncated and cabined in a back lot in upper Manhattan, disgracing the Congress of the United States, the City of New York, and the National Park Service. But when it was where it belonged, Hamilton and his friend Dr. David Hosack created about it a landscape including tropical shrubbery, where, Hamilton said, a "Creole" might feel at home. Hamilton was not, however, by nature a homebody. He settled for retirement to The Grange only after he was twice denied the opportunity to start life anew in the West, at the head of an army.[1]

It does not seem that Hamilton shared the interests of Washington, Jefferson, and Burr in American antiquity. Burr visited the Ohio Valley mound country and speculated about its architecture—which we know to have been created in Roman times—in letters to his daughter. Washington had preceded him and paid tribute to the Indian architecture by building two mounds to frame his westward view at Mount Vernon. Jefferson completed the Palladian plan of Poplar Forest, his second country house, by placing mounds where, in the Veneto, the dependencies would be. It is possible, indeed probable, that in Burr's case no such new construction was necessary. *The AIA Guide to New York* says that the house he purchased at Richmond Hill, in New York City, had been constructed on top of "its 100-foot-high mound near today's intersection of Charlton and Varick Streets." That could mean that New York, like Cincinnati, St. Louis, Lexington, and Pittsburgh, had ancient earthen structures beneath its European buildings. Burr acquired the twenty-six-acre estate in 1797 and wrote his daughter regularly of his progress in damming its stream to create a little lake and in setting about it trees and bushes, no doubt from the same nursery from whence Hamilton drew plant material for The Grange. Hosack was friend to them both.[2]

Thomas Jefferson prided himself on being a good guide to his "country," Virginia, offering in his *Notes* accounts of its flora, fauna, and politics. From him we learn that his Piedmont is not a lazy, subtropical countryside. It is abrupt. It snows there. Life can be as harsh as it is in Maine. Nor was Jefferson any drawling dilettante; he was severe in his demands upon himself and upon others, including his two hundred slaves. He had them shear off the entire mountaintop at Monticello, so that the villa he placed upon this platform was visible for twenty miles from the lowlands.

Party and Faction

Jefferson was a Man of Will. He shaped not only a mountain but a nation, refusing to brook obstacles physical or personal.

Burr and Hamilton were fourteen years younger than Jefferson—too young to have played a role in the declaring of independence, though both served in the ensuing war, as Jefferson did not. Soon after the Peace of Paris, in 1783, he recovered from a failed wartime governorship of Virginia to reestablish, in France, a reputation as diplomat. He did not have a role in the making of the Constitution, which was underway at home, though he was careful not to join publicly in James Monroe's opposition to it. George Washington noted the difference and brought Jefferson home to be Secretary of State, balancing Hamilton, who took office as Secretary of the Treasury. (Monroe got his Secretaryship of State, but only after waiting a quarter of a century.)

At the time, Burr was busily practicing law in New York. He was no more active in the battle for ratification of the Constitution than Jefferson. Hamilton dealt himself out of the process of Constitution-making after a display of his famous temper in May of 1787, departing the convention after only a two-week stint. Later, however, he returned, to make a speech to which we will refer in its context, and, with John Jay and James Madison, created, in The *Federalist Papers*, the most compelling possible argument for a document he admitted to be flawed.

Neither Hamilton nor Jefferson served throughout Washington's two terms (1788–96), but, while they were in office, both made use of their time to begin the organization of those who agreed with them in clusters that later evolved into political factions—and only factions, not parties. We cannot justly assess the career of any of them, especially

Burr's, unless we steadfastly refuse to apply to this period modern ideas of "party" or of "party loyalty." The Federalists and Republicans never developed into parties in the early twentieth-century sense of that term. To illustrate the point, we may note that Burr's debut on the national scene occurred in 1792, when a five-to-one majority of those designated as Federalists in the New York legislature chose him for the U.S. Senate over Hamilton's father-in-law, Philip Schuyler.

After his resignation from Washington's cabinet, Jefferson went into opposition to the President and to Washington's successor, John Adams. Hamilton managed to sustain his filial relationship to Washington, but after Adams was elected President, in 1796, he moved into subfactional disputation against the President within their Federalist alliance, splitting the Federalists by his virulent personal attack upon Adams just before the election of 1800. Meanwhile, Burr, whose natural métier was coalition-building, sustained understandings with Federalist friends such as John Jay, Jonathan Dayton, and Stephen van Rensselaer, as well as with the anti-Federalists allied with Jefferson, including De Witt Clinton and Robert L. Livingston. None of these New York "Republicans" constrained themselves by any burdens of consistent support for each other, confounding those who wish all politics to be ideological.

Jefferson did not extend to any of these non-Virginians the faintest glow of affection, though only in the case of Burr did his cool indifference toward politicians outside his circle turn toward hate. By his own account this began to occur as early as 1792, though its first provocation occurred in 1794. Burr was necessary to Jefferson's election as President in 1800. So the Sage of Monticello asked Albert Gallatin to convince Burr to become his running mate, though hardly his soul mate, a task Gallatin reassigned to his father-in-law, Commodore James Nicholson, who was also Burr's friend. Nicholson did the job, but Jefferson's animus toward his Vice President of necessity erupted in 1802 and became ferocious in 1806.

It is likely that the contest in law and politics between Hamilton and Burr eventuating in their famous duel was already gnawing at Hamilton well before 1792. For twenty years thereafter, Burr did not acknowledge the depth of Hamilton's hatred for him. Yet he came to their final resolution full of the wrath of a man who has finally admitted what he has denied even to himself: that he is hated.

Emulation, Rivalry, and Ambition

Why is so much more of this book devoted to Burr than to either Hamilton or Jefferson? Because a reevaluation of the character of Burr is necessary to piece out an informed estimate of the others. Why did Hamilton find Burr at once so hateful and so fascinating? Why did Gallatin abandon Burr, who, more than any other man, provided him with an American political career? What was it in Burr, a heroic and effective military officer, which made him anathema to Washington? What was it about Burr which led the Sage of Monticello, generally so admirable a man, to become careless about due process? Why was Burr so infuriating as to lead Jefferson to expend his moral capital in rewarding and protecting from justice traitors and scoundrels, merely because they could help in his vendetta against Burr?

The explanations offered by Hamilton and Jefferson of their own behavior are credible only if we accept as well their characterization of Burr. If we conclude that they are not wholly to be trusted as judges of him, we may, as well, have reason to question what they said were their own motives in dealing with him. For example, in 1808, Jefferson wrote that "for myself, even in his [Burr's] most flattering periods of the conspiracy, I never entertained one moment's fear." Why then were fleets and armies, and the militias of three states, arrayed toward a paltry and lightly armed force of less than seventy, and the nation left ill prepared to repulse its serious enemies? Why were government funds used to encourage testimony of doubtful veracity against him? Why, after dispersing Burr's young friends, did Jefferson not declare victory? Burr was in custody. Why could the President of the United States not bless the scene with a magisterial wave of the hand and get on with life?[3]

There is something wrong with that statement of Jefferson's. He reiterated it to Dupont de Nemours with the wrinkle that no one who was wholly rational could have seriously assessed Burr's enterprise in the West, in 1806, as a threat to the Union. But that was exactly what Jefferson's presidential proclamation said at the time. Are we to infer from this that he did not believe what he told the nation, as its President? Did he not mean every word of it, while the fever was on him? Did he not fear this man as a force greater than a mere adventurer? Had he not sent messages instructing American ministries in Paris, London, and Madrid to root out Burrites?

Even after the Richmond Trial of Burr, in 1807, even after Burr's western friends had abandoned him, his political organization had exploded, and he was himself hopelessly bankrupt, Jefferson ordered his lawyers to seek to impeach Chief Justice John Marshall, who had presided over Burr's trial, for no worse crime than setting Burr free. And he demanded that none of several hundred witnesses who had been summoned to Richmond should depart without submitting an affidavit of his testimony, which was "now more important than ever!"[4]

> The criminal is preserved to become the rallying-point of all the disaffected and worthless of the United States, and to be the pivot on which all the intrigues and conspiracies which foreign governments may wish to disturb us with, are to turn. If he is convicted of the misdemeanor, the judge must in decency give us respite by some short confinement of him.[5]

Did Jefferson not assess Burr as a fearful force? It seems that he did, and with considerable justification—from his point of view. So powerful had Burr's presence been among them that, despite all Jefferson was able to do against him in 1807, after Burr returned from exile in 1812, John Adams inquired: "Colonel Burr; Attorney General Burr; Senator Burr; Vice President Burr; almost President Burr. . . . What is to be his destiny?"[6]

Such a man must have had somewhat more vitality even in defeat than the traditional picture conveys—more "credibility," as the current phrase would have it. Let us then, in deference to John Adams, attend to his use of words and follow his implicit injunction to listen to the opinions expressed of Burr by others, especially by others who like Adams had themselves experienced "emulation, rivalry, and ambition," the themes within which Adams considered the careers of Burr, Jefferson, and Hamilton.

The American whose histories and novels best deal with these themes from the inside of politics is Henry Adams, great-grandson of John and grandson of John Quincy Adams. "I will volunteer for Burr," Henry Adams announced to his publisher, and for more than a year he devoted himself to producing Burr's biography. Then something happened. Adams seems to have been overwhelmed by the weight of received wisdom, or perhaps he merely tired of responding to the disdainful inquiries of his colleagues. In any case, he abandoned his biography, though confessing to a residual admiration of Burr as an "ideal scamp" and beguiling "scoundrel." But he did acknowledge that the key to understanding the relationship of Jefferson to Burr was Jefferson's agent against him, James Wilkinson. That was an important lead.[7]

When Adams wrote, there were things hidden even from one so diligent among the archives as he, evidence proving Wilkinson to be worse, and thus Burr to be better, than Jefferson's appraisal of them. Between 1892 and 1898, after Adams had abandoned his Burr project, the clinching evidence of Wilkinson's treason and insubordination, and of Burr's innocence of much of what was set against him by both Jefferson and Wilkinson, was discovered by two graduate students, Walter Flavius McCaleb and Isaac Joslin Cox. They bicycled fifteen hundred miles across bandit-ridden northern Mexico, finding in dusty provincial archives clue after clue to the perfidy of Wilkinson. Following those clues, we can construct a narrative of the imperial and racial politics of the Spanish borderlands that explains why it was so important for Jefferson to rid himself of Burr.

The West and Slavery

The contest between Hamilton and Burr was for dominance in New York. When, in 1804, it became manifest to Burr that both he and Hamilton had lost by the duel, and that there was no place for him in the East, where the political landscape had been polluted by their animosity, he turned to the West. Hamilton had aspired to a western career, but his own actions in robbing the Federalists of the presidency in 1800 had deprived him of any chance to serve those ambitions. Jefferson had been building his own base beyond the mountains since the 1770s, and in 1800 he possessed the presidency which Hamilton had denied Adams.

This political grappling has so occupied our attention that we have given insufficient attention to the degree to which, while it was going on, slavery was contaminating the West. The prize was poisoned while Jefferson, Hamilton, and Burr were in contention for it. George Washington, who preceded the others in his attention to the West, sent both indentured servants and slaves to work his lands on the Ohio and Kanawha, anticipating the efforts of his adoptive grandson George Washington Parke Custis to show by competing work gangs at

Arlington House that slavery was not necessarily the only way to get hot work done.

After the Revolution, as Washington moved toward an active opposition to slavery, he was a busy man, unable to attend to his interests and experiments in the West, though by then he knew its contours better than any other Founder. Albert Gallatin knew western Pennsylvania, a corner of it, but that was all. Washington had learned to be a soldier there during the 1750s, upon the very terrain on which he and Hamilton put down the Whiskey Rebellion forty years later. When he completed his presidency in 1796, he planned to return to the Ohio Valley as a venerable civilian. But his eight-year tour of duty as a revolutionary commander and his eight more years as President had absorbed his mature energies. When he was finally free for postpresidential travel, he was too tired to make his Grand Tour from Pittsburgh to Detroit, on to St. Louis, and down the great river to New Orleans. During his remaining two years, he was only able to imagine what might be seen past the mounds he built at Mount Vernon to frame his western view.

Two years before Washington's death in 1799, Hamilton began dreaming of a new start in the West and laying plans to lead an army to wrest the lower reaches of the Mississippi Valley from Spain. After killing Hamilton in 1804, Burr succeeded to these ideas, modified into a two-stage design. First, he said, he and his friends would situate themselves within the United States, on a tract now straddling the Louisiana-Arkansas border. Then, when the inevitable war broke out with Spain, they would conquer Mexico, or at least Texas.

Two crucial questions now arise: What would be the nature of a western power base managed by Burr, or by Hamilton? What would be the place in it of slavery? It is astonishing how little recent attention has been given to this inquiry, for between 1784 and 1820 the future of slavery in the West was repeatedly debated. In 1784, Jefferson proposed that inherited human servitude be eliminated west of the Appalachians after 1800. He did not press the matter, but a few years later the Northwest and Southwest Ordinances divided the region into two systems at the Ohio River, one composed of *territories* open to slavery, the other not. As we shall see, the Northwest Ordinance as drafted by Jefferson did not preclude the organization of slave *states* north of the Ohio River. The problem of slavery arose again each time a Western *territory* was organized by Congress or a state formed its constitution. The outcome was not a foregone conclusion in Ohio, Indiana, Illinois, Kentucky, Tennessee, Arkansas, and even Mississippi. We will have reason to give special attention to the debates convulsing the U.S. Senate in 1805–6, while Burr was in the West and the Hillhouse Amendments made inescapable a decision as to the future of slavery and the slave trade in Louisiana. As we shall see, his record as an emancipator in New York made him dangerous to owners of or traffickers in slaves.

That discussion will be part of our consideration of the positions taken on this central question in American history by our protagonists. They were all slaveowners at one time or another. Jefferson held several hundred at his death and in his will freed only a handful. At *his* death, Burr did not own any. Hamilton may have owned one, an elderly house servant. His will does not discuss the matter, but there is no doubt that he, like Burr, opposed the institution of slavery and did all he could to eliminate it.

Hamilton grew up with the peculiar institution. His first employment was in the office of a planter and slavetrader on the island of St. Croix. He had been born on Nevis, an even tinier sugar island in the West Indies. Through the sponsorship of Thomas Stephens, a planter and slaveowner (who may have been his father), and Stephens's mercantile agent, Nicholas Cruger, he was given first a home, then employment, then rudimentary tutoring by a Princeton graduate, after which he was force-fed on college requirements in a school operated by kinsmen of Burr and finally sent to what is now Columbia University. It is probable that Stephens and Cruger also provided him with the clothing and pocket money of a gentleman-student. Otherwise there is no easy explanation for his being presentable enough to qualify as a gentleman-officer, and thus to find his second, and essential, sponsor: George Washington.

With Washington's aid he entered the mainstream of colonial life, found a useful marriage, and established himself as a lawyer in New York. Thereafter, in the law and politics, he vied with Burr, who, like Jefferson, was gentleman-born, with a cozy small fortune. Burr had the most distinguished antecedents of the three, being the son, grandson, and great-grandson of celebrated clergymen, two of whom were college presidents. Of our three principals, only Burr sprang from a tradition of opposition to slavery, and only he had family connections with the Mississippi Valley. Among Burr's kinsmen and antecedents were missionaries to the Indians, including his grandfather the great Jonathan Edwards. Others had been speculators in land as far as Florida and Natchez. He went after them over the mountains in 1804 and visited the West in each of the next two years. In 1806, Jefferson charged his former Vice President with treason, which caused Burr to be apprehended by federal agents and brought home in custody in a rolling cell.

Four juries failed to find Burr guilty of any crime or misdemeanor. But the power of Jefferson's reputation, of Jefferson's army, navy, and Department of Justice, of Jefferson's political organization, and of his allies among the southern slaveowners, who had good reason to want Burr out of the way, was coordinated with the efforts of admirers of Hamilton, who felt Burr had murdered their leader, to drive Burr out of American political life. He went into exile in Europe. Though he returned four years later and lived on into the 1830s, he was dead politically in 1808.

The Character of Burr

The explanation for all this lies in the character of Burr. Everything we thought we knew about the character of Jefferson, the character of Hamilton, and the springs of their political actions must be reexamined with Burr in mind. The history of abolition in New York cannot be told without him, nor can we comprehend the grouping of forces in that state which ultimately produced the rise to power of Martin Van Buren and the formation of the Whig party without placing Burr at its watershed. Let us ask once more: What was his character? What did he bring to the contest with Hamilton for control of New York, and to the contest with Jefferson for the Lower Mississippi Valley?

David Mattern, an editor of the Papers of James Madison at the University of Virginia, suggested, during a vetting by a group of his peers of an early draft of this work, that its main theme is an expansion of the following passage I had written more than a decade ago:

> Thomas Jefferson saw the Hispanic possessions falling from "feeble" hands "piece by piece." The question was: would those pieces fall into the hands of the United States or into the clutches of the perfidious British? Or of Napoleon? Or someone else of

Napoleonic aspirations and Napoleon's indifference to nationality? The carcass of the Spanish empire lay exposed. The scent of
carrion . . . brought forth from the United States a succession of
adventurers, chief among whom was Aaron Burr. . . . Burr was a
man of the mettle to succeed to the empire of Cortez by the
methods of Cortez.[8]

Let us reconsider that last line. Is it true? Is it not a better assessment
of our principal characters to conclude that Alexander Hamilton was
the analogue to Cortez among the Founders? Hamilton was a born
scrapper. Burr was not. He avoided unpleasantness. When we consider
the drama of Cortez winning an empire in Mexico, we think not of
Burr but of Hamilton. And when we consider how Cortez kept that
empire, we do not think of Burr but of the absence, among his Spanish
competitors, of anyone as clever as Jefferson. Jefferson's success against
Burr would not have been so easy against an opponent of the mettle
of Cortez, or even of Hamilton. But Burr failed repeatedly to exert
himself at crucial moments.

When Burr was still in his twenties, and still a military hero, he
himself identified that quality which kept him from the ranks of the
conquistadores. He was recovering from wounds suffered during the
Revolutionary War. During one of his fits of depression, he wrote a
friend that he was too much given to "volatility," too much "inclined
to *hypo*" [Burr's emphasis]. Dr. Allan Hamilton found the same pattern
in his grandfather, "alternating depression on one hand and gaiety on
the other," and pointed out that a manic depressive is likely to miss
essential opportunities in the great game of politics on an imperial
scale. Steadiness, composure, settled purpose, and a constant readiness
to pounce are the requirements of statesmanship. These qualities Thomas Jefferson possessed. Burr and Hamilton did not. The biography
of Aaron Burr is an anthology of missed opportunities. Probably that
was largely because he did not make or keep to plans, except tactically,
and therefore was never quite ready to move when an opening appeared. Even when he was purposeful he lacked a strategic sense. It is
not strange that he did not write theses; he probably did not have any.
He had feelings, however, and they were remarkably generous among
politicians.[9]

Hamilton, unlike Burr, was a man of large ideas, coherently synthesized into grand schemes. But he either overreached or failed to reach

at all when gripped by his primary passion, which was envy. It is difficult to recall any other American statesman so incapacitated by resentment. That is a grave deficiency, for statesmanship requires a steady compass as well as a good set of binoculars. It also requires companions. A statesman must know how to find parallel interests with others of near-equal ability. He must be able to partner. Hamilton could not do that. Burr could.

And as for Jefferson—he was a master of parallelism. He remains the Favored Founder for good reason. He is a figure as multifaceted and fascinating as a Picasso portrait. A master of general concepts and a literary craftsman, he had a lifelong interest in the management of the opinions of posterity. Jefferson was a philosopher of politics, capable of holding a large idea in his head for decades, able to turn it about, formulating and reformulating it, until it emerged in the most powerful language composed by any American leader before Abraham Lincoln.

The wonder of Jefferson the politician is that, unlike many literary people, he was adept at intrigue beyond the level of a university department. He could think on a global scale yet move within the nice mechanical tolerances of local politics. Though he could take the long view, he was also a ruthlessly effective tactician, capable of deploying the cleverest of his contemporaries without their perceiving what he was doing. No other American President has with such virtuosity combined the roles of theoretician and practitioner of politics.

At the end of the War for Independence, Burr was a hero and Jefferson was not. Twenty-five years later, Jefferson was a hero and Burr was not. That is our story. Its defining events occurred within the compass of four years, from the duel with Hamilton, in 1804, to the treason trial in Richmond—Burr's duel with Jefferson—in 1808.

The Fatal Twins

Never was there a possibility that Alexander Hamilton would be President. He received not a single vote in the electoral college in any election. In 1800, Aaron Burr received as many votes as Thomas Jefferson. He might have negotiated his way to the presidency, quite constitutionally, had he exerted himself to do so. He had a loyal following in his own party, and a sufficient number of Federalist electors preferred him to Jefferson. As it was, he did not respond to their urging, never departing from an insistence that the electorate intended Jefferson to be President. This part of the story is familiar, but the brilliance of its familiarity has left in the shadow the significance of the votes given him by many who wanted him to be President, as they had desired in the two preceding presidential elections. He received many electoral votes in 1792 and 1796, when he stood alone, and in competition with Jefferson. In 1796, for example, the vote was John Adams 71, Jefferson 68, and Burr 30.*

*Burr's electoral votes in 1796 came as follows: from Pennsylvania 13 (Jefferson 14); from Maryland 3 (Jefferson 4); from Virginia 1 (Jefferson 20); from North Carolina 6 (Jefferson 11); from Kentucky 4 (Jefferson 4); from Tennessee 3 (Jefferson 3). The totals were Jefferson 68, John Adams 71, Burr 30, George Clinton 7, and, among others, John Jay with 5.

The highest national offices to which Alexander Hamilton was elected were his two separate terms in the Continental Congress—one in 1782 and the other in 1788. He did win election to the New York Assembly in 1787, but no one took him seriously as a candidate either for the presidency or for the governorship of New York. What was Hamilton's disqualification? It did not arise from his having been "foreign born"; he met the necessary residency requirement by the middle 1790s. No, Hamilton's problem was his character: He had a propensity for that sort of candor which is only occasionally forgiven in a friend, and never in a candidate. Even those who loved him deplored the presence of something less admirable beneath his candor. His pride and passion sometimes soured into a mean-spirited disdain for those like Jefferson and Burr who enjoyed crowds as little as he, but who summoned sufficient respect for the *idea* of a republic to make careers requiring the approval of the crowd.

There is an anecdote which illustrates the difference of temperament between Burr and Hamilton as they adjusted to the rise of democracy: After his return from exile in Europe in 1812, Burr settled into a practice of law in New York, where, during the 1820s, younger members of the gentry were wont to deplore the consequences of what Burr himself had called Jefferson's "Jacobin . . . leveling principles." One day the discussion in his chambers was about the "expounders of the Constitution," probably because many people at the time were fascinated by John Jay's contention against James Madison that the Founders had intended to permit Congress to regulate the interstate commerce in slaves.[1]

> At the moment a noisy crowd of electioneering Democrats were passing. Burr, who had stood silent for some time with his hands behind him . . . pointed to the mob, and said: "*They* are the expounders of the Constitution!"[2]

From the beginning, Burr became the organizer and deployer of crowds, though he was no more of a hobnobber than Jefferson. As we noted earlier, this master of Tammany never set foot within its clubhouse. Hamilton could not bring himself to court popular favor; he got so far as the grandstand, so to speak, but remained within what we might now call the "owners' booth." In 1795, he attempted a reasoned public defense of a treaty with Britain and was pelted with stones by a mob. He responded by declaring that he was "ready to fight the whole 'detestable faction' [the Democrats] one by one." He was a great one for challenges, but Edward Livingston dismissed his threats as more becoming to "a street bully." That was not fair. It was only that he was unprepared for the Age of Livingston—and of Jefferson.[3]

The death of George Washington in 1799 deprived Hamilton of his sponsor; he withdrew from the stage for the wings, where he continued to coach others. Though he had the intellect and interest for politics, he had not the temperament for it. To his credit, when he retired he had the good sense not to go from government into the practice of law in the national capital. He was not one of those made to grow old in the Federal City, where proximity, but not access, to power makes for geriatric dyspepsia.

Jefferson escaped that affliction because he had access to power for another decade after leaving the presidency, and after that, even when he was very old, power came to him, at Monticello. His fourteen years of seniority to Hamilton and Burr provided him an early start: He was deeply practiced in the devices of power before they graduated from college. When they were twenty, he was thirty-four, already among the Virginia Burgesses, already demonstrating that he could maintain a sanitary distance from the voters while managing others so adeptly that office was repeatedly offered him.

Individual persons did not much interest Thomas Jefferson. His skill lay in mobilizing coincident interests into coalitions among *types* of people. That does not make him the founder of the American party system, though his Postmaster General, Gideon Granger, created the spoils system. Both were amply rewarded for their ingenuity.

Burr, Hamilton, and the Consolations of Religion

Oratory is ephemeral. Immediate in its effects, it evaporates quickly. Sometimes, as in the case of a Gettysburg Address, a speech has a literary by-product, but none of Burr's orations were of that sort. His farewell left the Senate of the United States shocked and remorseful. For ten minutes, it was said, the chamber was silent except for the sound of weeping. Yet even the farewell lies today as lifeless upon the recorder's page as the famously witty sermons of Burr's contemporary

Sydney Smith. Burr had a gift for the trenchant phrase, yet he never attempted to compete as essayist or theoretician with Jefferson, Hamilton, Jay, or Madison.

Why was that? Probably because he was the son, nephew, and grandson of theologians, and, as people so situated often do, he steadfastly refused to advertise his piety. In this refusal to follow Hamilton's example, rending his garments in accordance with the increasingly fatuous religiosity of the nineteenth century, Burr remained an eighteenth-century gentleman. He was no more successful in curbing his wit than was an even later anachronism, Adlai Stevenson, with similar results. Neither Stevenson nor Burr was thought sincere. Something serious was lost in his wit, however. As a witty man, he eschewed sentiment and thus lost the power of persuasion by which his Grandfather Edwards had restored feeling to an American Protestantism grown somewhat stale and crabbed. Edwards's emphasis was not upon fear, though his famous sermon on "sinners in the hands of an angry God" might have left some fearful. His theology was, instead, based upon love.

Aaron Burr might have been another man had his grandfather lived to help him believe that such a theology was compatible with a realistic appraisal of human nature. But his theologian grandfather and father, and his theologically eloquent mother and grandmother (herself the daughter of a theologian), died, one after another, after each one had assured him of a loving God and an intentional universe. They had thus failed him as a child, and so had their religion. He was ever thereafter unconsolate—not bitter, nor complaining, but unwilling to trust much in persons and not willing at all to trust in ideology. As he revealed on his deathbed, he did not wish to be once more disappointed at that marrow of his being where theology resides. As he was dying, his kinsman Judge Ogden Edwards induced him to accept the presence of a Reformed Dutch clergyman, who inquired if he wished to ask God's pardon through the intercession of Jesus Christ. "To which he said, with deep and violent emotion, 'on that subject I am coy.' "[4]

Alexander Hamilton was not coy on the subject of religion. He made use of it, politically, long before he brought it into the final apologia before his duel. Burr's skepticism about the profundity of Hamilton's conversion at that time may be excused somewhat by Hamilton's having organized the Christian Constitutional Society in 1802 and having gotten himself elected as its president general. Politics and religion were always closely linked for him; in 1791, after Burr's defeat of Philip Schuyler—and thus of Hamilton—and his election to the Senate, Hamilton wrote that he felt "a religious duty to oppose Burr's career."[5]

A *religious* duty. What a peculiar locution. To understand what may have brought that word to Hamilton's mind in a political context, we may turn to John Adams. Like Burr, Adams was trained for the ministry and knew envy to be a sin. Nonetheless, he complained that Burr had religious advantages, coming to him from "birth, parentage, and descent." Adams did not use the terms "religious" and "parentage and descent" as Hamilton might. For Adams, "descent" from Protestant divines would raise greater expectations than would a lineage of lairds. Puritans who were ennobled by the cloth would merely be distinguished by the ermine, as Adams noted while reflecting upon Burr's advantages of religion—or at least of residual theocracy—over either Hamilton or himself:

> That gentleman was connected by blood with many respectable families in New England. He was the son of one president, and the grandson of another president of . . . Princeton University; the idol of all Presbyterians in New York, New England, New Jersey, Pennsylvania, Maryland, Virginia, and elsewhere.[6]

As we shall see, Burr did not rely upon Presbyterians alone. He was also successful in forging alliances with the Roman Catholic clergy in Canada and, thereafter, in New York, in Louisiana, and possibly even in Mexico. As the Irish Catholics rallied around this man who retained the affections of the Presbyterians, Hamilton might well have been led to the word "religious" in association with his resentment of Burr even if he had not approached their duel in such confusion in his own religious life.

The assessment of Hamilton's character by Benjamin Henry Latrobe took account of the discordance between his practices and his much-proclaimed faith. Hamilton made much of his religious aversion to dueling, yet, wrote Latrobe, "was shot on the very spot . . . where his son had fallen in a duel to which his father advised him, and when brought home wounded sent for a bishop to administer the sacraments to him to prepare him for death. Even the papers he left behind breathe piety and resignation; and his object was accomplished, for after his death he was canonized."[7]

Hamilton and the Consolations of Home

Who was this man, who achieved such public greatness, but whose private nature baffled and infuriated those who admired, and loved, him most? How did he come to be what he was when he told them his career was at an end and went to Weehawken? His childhood, like Burr's, was without parents. But Burr had at least the comfort of other people's assurances that he could be proud of the departed. Hamilton was one of two boys born, according to the judgment of a divorce court, as "obscene children" to a disgraced woman who was herself the daughter of disgrace. His grandmother Mary Fawcett had deserted her husband. With her daughter Rachel, she went to the Danish-ruled island of St. Croix, where her older daughter had married one of the sons of the Lytton family, proprietors of a plantation called The Grange. Apparently Mary Fawcett expected the Lyttons to take them in, but though they accepted Mary, they rejected Rachel. She was forced into a marriage of convenience with a merchant-planter named Lavien, by whom she bore a legitimate son, Peter.

Four years later, Lavien had Rachel arrested and jailed for adultery. Friendless but not always alone, she remained for a time on St. Croix and then fled to Nevis. Either on St. Croix or on Nevis, a tiny island ruled by Britain, she took up with James Hamilton, as vagrant as herself and her mother. Though Hamilton was by then somewhat degenerate, he came of good stock; he was the fourth son of a minor Scottish laird, whose decaying stone fortress was coincidentally also called The Grange. Rachel Fawcett Lavien bore her second and third sons, Alexander and James, on Nevis. It is impossible to prove who Alexander's father was, or if Alexander and James Hamilton, who treated each other as brothers, had the same father.

Lavien finally sued Rachel for divorce on the ground that she had "gone elsewhere and begotten several illegitimate children." The Danish court granted the divorce, proscribing any subsequent marriage and requiring that any property she may have held should go not to her bastard sons but to Lavien and then to Lavien's son, Peter. Rachel, having been formally declared a fallen woman, was abandoned by Hamilton. She returned with her boys to the Lyttons on St. Croix, and this time they took her in.[8]

In July 1769, Peter Lavien was found dead in a pool of blood, allegedly a suicide. Under the terms of his will, his small estate went to a black woman and their son. His father died a few weeks later. His illegitimate half-brother Alexander was twelve. Then, out of Rachel Lavien's past, there appeared Thomas Stevens, a planter of St. Croix, who took the orphaned boy into his own household. It already contained his own son, Edward, who was fourteen and became Alexander's lifelong friend. Throughout the lives of the two, their astonishing resemblance gave rise to gossip that they were half-brothers. Sometimes gossip is true: Henry Cabot Lodge, in his biography of Hamilton, provided the testimony of James Yard, Edward Stevens's brother-in-law, who asserted that Thomas Stevens was Alexander Hamilton's father, though Edward Stevens made light of the idea. Lodge also recorded the statement of Secretary of State Timothy Pickering that he could not tell Stevens and Hamilton apart, though he knew them both intimately. The corespondent in Lavien's suit against Rachel for adultery has not been identified. On a small island, the governor of which was Thomas Stevens's brother-in-law, such candor might have appeared unseemly; Stevens was a rich man and already married.[9]

Whatever their relationship may have been, Thomas Stevens was kind to Alexander, providing him an education under the Princeton-trained Reverend Hugh Knox and finding him an apprenticeship in a merchant's office. There, it may be surmised, he began to feel an affiliation with merchants rather than with planters—such as the Lyttons, the Laviens, or, for that matter, the Jeffersons.

In the back office of that merchant a proud young man, deprived of his small estate by a "legitimate" half-brother, worked on his ledgers, trapped in that "condition . . . to which my fortune condemns me." Thirty years later, the Honorable Alexander Hamilton, just retired as Secretary of the Treasury, named his own house on upper Manhattan The Grange. Like the Stevens plantation headquarters, it was galleried in the West Indian manner, and there he wrote that he felt himself to be a "Creole," at home. Finally, at home. His mother had died at the Lyttons' Grange—a fact which may have been of considerably more psychological importance than the happenstance that the Scottish Hamiltons had a Grange as well, in spite of his natural preference for the lairdly Scottish association. We may hope that he was finally reconciled to his mother. In 1771, her disgrace, and his, had still been raw as the frail and abandoned bastard wrote two little poems. The first was an ode to church weddings: "Love is doubly sweet/in wedlock's holy bands." The second began: "Coelia's an artful little slut . . . she must have her will."[10]

In 1773, when he was sixteen, Alexander Hamilton was sent after Edward Stevens to the mainland colonies to find respectability—and surely to resent it. The Rev. Dr. Knox saw to it that he went where any Princetonian knew respectability could be found—in the circle of the Edwardses and Burrs. Knox had been a student of Aaron Burr Senior and had been ordained by him. (The College of New Jersey was located in Princeton and later became Princeton University.) Since by the elder Burr's standards Hamilton's education had been too spotty for admission to Princeton, Knox and Stevens remitted him for polishing to the school in Elizabethtown (now Elizabeth), New Jersey, established by Burr's son-in-law, Tapping Reeve, and attended by Aaron Burr the younger (our Aaron). (Burr was at the school at the time, doing some extracurricular reading, but there is no record of his impressions of Hamilton.) While Hamilton was a student there, the Academy was governed by Francis Barber, who, like Reeve, had married into the Edwards-Burr clan. But even after this remedial respectability, Hamilton was refused entry to Princeton, from which Burr graduated in 1772.

Hamilton came to the mainland—for something Burr already possessed. As he came ashore, there, as always thereafter, was Burr. Always, before him, there fell the shadow of a man not himself—not quite. Burr was also five feet, six or seven inches tall, slight of build, with narrow shoulders, and roughly the same age: Burr was born on February 6, 1756; Hamilton on January 11, 1757. Burr! The son, grandson, and great-grandson of eminent men. Burr! At the Academy at Elizabethtown graduating a year before him. Burr! Famous at Princeton before Hamilton left Columbia. Burr! Hero of the Quebec campaign before Hamilton had heard a cannon fired. Burr! Major before he was made captain. Burr! Aide to General Washington before him. And, always, so beautifully and expensively tailored.[11]

Though the fatal twins were in body much alike, in aspect they were not. Indeed, had Hamilton been taller, it would have been striking how much his coloring was like that of Jefferson. They were Celts, with fair skin tending to freckle, sandy hair, and blue eyes—Hamilton's were almost violet. Hamilton said of himself that he was "not handsome"; his forehead protruded, his nose was narrow, prominent, and sharp, his chin a knob.[12]

Burr was of largely East Anglian blood, sallow, and with eyes so dark as to be often described as a brilliant black. Like Hamilton, he had a problem nose; it was "rather inclined to the right." His "ears [were] so small as to be almost a deformity," so he wore his hair long on the sides to cover them. In later years, like many another man tending to baldness, he compensated for what was gone from the front by letting it grow behind, sweeping the surplus forward. The eighteenth century was permissive about what people did with hair; his forward sweep was given a dash of elegance with a small shell comb.[13]

Burr said of himself that he was "a grave, silent, strange sort of animal, inasmuch that we know not what to make of him." What a "strange" way to speak of oneself, unless, of course, one were intent upon being sure that the animal kept protected his vulnerable parts.

Pain and Wrath

Is misfortune comparable? Is pain? Does a broken leg hurt more than a broken thumb, or a home broken by desertion hurt more than one broken by death? Aaron Burr bore a great name, but during his formative years, he bore misfortunes nearly as crushing as Hamilton's. He, too, had been an orphan. Father, mother, grandfather, and grandmother were torn from him by death before he was four years of age. One after another, they took him into their arms, gave him warmth, and left him. Each time, after trusting, he was deserted and handed on to someone else. The lesson, repeated four times, was that no one could be counted upon. After embrace and assurance of love there was, after fumbling talk of the consolations of the faith—cold.

Burr did not offer himself readily thereafter, nor was the curse upon him expiated. Whenever he permitted himself to love, and to contemplate the joy of loving tomorrow, his beloved was torn from him. He married a woman already suffering from cancer. They had three children, two of whom died in childhood. Then his wife died. He transferred what capacity for intimate love he had left to his surviving daughter and to his grandson. The boy died young, and Theodosia Burr disappeared at sea.

The term "childhood trauma" comes to mind when we reflect upon the early lives of both Hamilton and Burr. Hamilton came hot from youth and grew in wrath. Burr emerged from childhood having learned to be cold, or to seem to be. There is ample evidence in human experience that rejection by parents, or their disappearance, makes for an unwillingness to trust again. Desertion or rejection has often produced careers like those of Don Juan, Burr, and Hamilton.

Burr was as coy about giving himself away in public display of emotion as in public display of religious fervor. He dropped the mask only rarely: In 1804, there was the occasion at Weehawken. In 1807, he burst into frustrated tears after finding no one to rescue him from Jefferson's lynching party. And in the 1830s, when a very old man, he went with a youthful admirer to the scene of his duel with Hamilton, where he was overcome with recollected anger.

One hundred and six years after his grandfather's death at Weehawken, Dr. Allan Hamilton set himself to reanimating the field of force which drew Burr to Hamilton and Hamilton to Burr, in wrath, mutual fascination, and a kind of hideous intimacy. They knew each other very, very well. Perhaps that is why over sixteen years they could cooperate and contend as the principal trial attorneys in a city of only twenty-five thousand people, without exchanging a harsh word, until one of them killed the other. Until a few months before their fatal duel they insisted that they were friends, and they dined in each other's houses. Yet if anything is certain in this story, it is that when they raised their weapons against each other, their fascination had become hatred. We suggested earlier that Hamilton saw in Burr everything he feared most in himself. When he fired, he was consumed by his loathing of a projected person—as much himself as Burr. Having forfeited a series of occasions—four at least—in which he might honorably have avoided killing or being killed, in the end he arranged to have Burr kill him.

Full of self-loathing, Hamilton made certain that Burr would come to the killing ground. He made certain as well that Burr would have every reason to believe that their long contest of love and hate could only be resolved there. If Burr did not kill Hamilton, Hamilton would use his special pistols to kill Burr. Though calculation might have brought them to Weehawken expecting only a ritual expiation of their differences, Burr and Hamilton were by that time so gripped by their antipathy that the arms that raised their pistols were not controlled by calculation.

It has been the conviction of the Hamilton family and of Hamilton's admirers that he threw away his first shot. Perhaps he did. No one knows, nor is it likely that he himself either knew his last-second intention at the time or recalled it in his shock and pain afterward. So it is in the writing of history. We never know anything with absolute certainty; certainly we do not know when the "fascination" between the two became lethal—if, indeed it did. When did *Hamilton* first begin to "fascinate" *Burr?* Dr. Hamilton suggested that event occurred just before the end, as the necessary precondition *toward* that end. If that is so—and I think it is—Burr experienced a horrified acknowledgment of hate.[14]

Those who have never been hated may have difficulty empathizing with Burr. But those who have, and who felt that hatred to be undeserved, can understand why Burr did not throw away his shot.

4

I Wish There Was a War

Hamilton and Burr became defined, as men, in the presence of violence. For both of them, military experience brought a sudden eminence. Revolutions do that. Burr, no doubt, would have found adventure somehow, and fellow adventurers among his kinsmen and Princeton classmates, but it is unlikely that Hamilton, the threadbare foreigner, would have had a political career without the associations made during his career as a soldier. Hamilton needed a patron, and in the Revolution he got one.

When Hamilton was thirteen, he wrote his friend Edward Stevens from his desk in the slavetrader's office on St. Croix: "I wish there was a war." He got his wish before he was twenty. As he entered his Revolutionary service, he was described as "a mere boy with small, delicate and slender frame . . . with a cocked hat pulled down on his eyes." When a captain of artillery, he marched "behind his cannon, patting it every now and then as if it were a favorite toy." At the same age and stage of *his* military career, Burr was said to be "a mere stripling . . . with a . . . slender form, and a youthful face, . . . possessed [of] a power of prolonged exertion, and a capacity for enduring privation, that were wonderful in a youth of nineteen. His courage was perfect; he never knew fear. . . . He was a good horseman, a good helmsman, a tolerable fencer and a decent shot."[1]

As we noted earlier, Burr arrived at Washington's headquarters with his reputation already made. His famous deeds in the Canadian campaign were so pictorial that images of the young Burr hung on schoolroom walls as recently as my own youth—"Little Burr" in the snowstorm, in his tricornered hat, under fire before the walls of Quebec, struggling to carry back to the American lines the body of General Richard Montgomery, his mortally wounded commander.

He had led men outfitted at his own expense six hundred miles across Maine in winter—six hundred hideous miles of frozen swamp, icy streams, wind-crusted snow, and rocky portages. The other Revolutionary picture we saw on our schoolroom walls showed us George Rogers Clark slogging across the frozen prairies on his way to surprise the British at Vincennes. We knew Maine in winter to be a greater challenge than Indiana, and we imagined that Burr was selected as Montgomery's aide, with the rank of captain, as much for his endurance as for his heroism.

By the end of 1779, he enjoyed another kind of fame, spread through the gossiping army: After Montgomery's death, he had refused the same post under Benedict Arnold. Thirty years later, many a surviving veteran of the Canadian campaign resented Thomas Jefferson's use of words to condemn Burr which sounded to them much like those Burr had written of Arnold:

> [He] is ready for any deeds of valor; but has not a particle of moral courage. He is utterly unprincipled, and has no love of country or self-respect to guide him. He is not to be trusted anywhere but under the eye of a superior.[2]

Staff Work

Burr put his life at risk to be a good staff officer for Montgomery and later served admirably as aide to Israel Putnam, "my good, old general." Neither he nor Hamilton, however, was happy with that sort of assignment. Burr was especially unfitted for it, having grown up with too much authority on the male side, rather than too little. Burr lasted as a subordinate to George Washington only six weeks. "Burr, the electric Burr, the born soldier, the most irrepressible of mortals, found himself sinking into the condition of a *clerk!*'' To Washington, clerks were necessary, as they are to all great men. The General was unforgiving to anyone unwilling to subordinate personal preference to patriotic duty—defined by Washington, as by most Great Men, as duty to him. We cannot enter his mind, but it is safe to say that he never forgave Burr for using his father's friendship with John Hancock to secure more active employment under Putnam, where he broke mutinies, drilled troops, defeated British probes, confounded Tory plots, and added to his own reputation, rather than Washington's.[3]

At one juncture during the confused defense of the city of New York, Burr and Hamilton were in the same arena, giving rise to legends that Burr saved Hamilton's life. The truth may be less romantic: Burr led a trapped brigade to safety after its commander, Henry Knox, had given up. Knox protested, refusing to believe escape possible, so Burr simply walked off with the troops, leaving Knox to follow, puffing and blowing. Hamilton was with Knox, as an artillery commander. In Burr's dust, Hamilton did his best to save his guns but suffered the humiliation of losing one of them to the British, along with his own baggage.

The New York campaign did little for the reputation of either Hamilton or Washington, and Burr did not help restore them. Having made an enemy of Knox, he did not dissemble his view that Washington was "a bad general . . . [though] honest, [a] weak man." An echo came from Hamilton, who would only say that "the general is a very honest man" and that "his competitors have slender abilities and less integrity." That was true. But, as Hamilton noted, Washington's political position was too strong for even the best of "competitors" to challenge, and, therefore, no ambitious young man should cross him. "His popularity has often been essential to the safety of America, and is still of great importance to it. These considerations have influenced my past conduct respecting him, and will influence my future."[4]

Hamilton had learned that lesson painfully. Soon after Burr left Washington's "family," Hamilton replaced him. After four years' service, he put his career in jeopardy by keeping Washington waiting— Hamilton said "not two minutes;" Washington said ten. Washington dressed him down. Hamilton took his departure, as Burr had done— but with a characteristic difference. Burr told no one. Hamilton provided his side of the story to the rest of the staff. When Lafayette told

Washington what Hamilton had said, the General replied that he would have told him the story himself, "had it not been for the request of Hamilton, who desired that no mention might be made of it. Why this injunction to me, while he was communicating it himself, is a little extraordinary." But he forgave him, and when Hamilton demanded a command at Yorktown, he got it.[5]

Hamilton paid for that opportunity on the installment plan—four years of clerkship on a larger scale, clerkship to a general rather than a slave-merchant, while Burr added to the glory earned at Quebec and New York and, at the same time, added to the list of impertinences Washington could lay against his name. Burr and his patron, Israel Putnam, were associated with the Yankee wing of the army, whose leader was Horatio Gates. In the fall of 1777, Washington repeated his failure to defend New York, and Philadelphia was lost. At nearly the same time, Gates and Daniel Morgan scored the Revolution's first major victory at Saratoga, surrounding and capturing "Gentleman Johnny" Burgoyne's army. Voices were heard among what was called at the time the Conway Cabal that Washington should be replaced by Gates. While Putnam's camp was full of this murmuring, Hamilton was sent into that camp by Washington to ask for speedy reinforcements. Gates temporized to the point of insubordination; Putnam pouted with Burr at his side. Hamilton wrote Washington that he doubted that Putnam "will attend to any thing I shall say, notwithstanding it comes in the shape of a positive order." Exasperated, he wrote a thoroughly Hamiltonian letter to Putnam:

> I speak freely and emphatically, because I tremble at the consequences of the delay that has happened. . . . My expressions may have more warmth than is altogether proper, but they proceed from the overflowing of my heart. . . . How the non-compliance can be answered to General Washington you can best determine.[6]

Hamilton's rage did not abate when Putnam sent Burr and his command down to join Washington. Two years later, in South Carolina, Gates's incompetence was revealed as he suffered disastrous defeat at Camden. A galaxy of talent had made him victor of Saratoga, but at Camden neither Putnam nor Daniel Morgan nor Benedict Arnold was there to guide him. Hamilton gloated: "Was there ever an instance of a general running away, as Gates has done, from his whole army? Was there ever so precipitate a flight? . . . I have always believed him to be far short of a Hector or a Ulysses. All the world, I think, will begin to agree with me.''[7]

Hamilton and Burr were both drawn into the next phase of Washington's effort to hold together an army bedeviled by sectionalism and personal rivalries. General Charles Lee succeeded Gates as his bête noire. At Monmouth, in the summer of 1778, conflicting orders from Washington and Lee confused the army, and many died. Burr's command was left cruelly and unnecessarily suspended, in midcharge, by an order from Washington. Burr's horse was shot from under him, and his second in command was killed. Lee had done worse damage, and Hamilton had to rally the troops Lee had misdirected.

Washington had Lee court-martialed. Hamilton took Washington's part, testifying against Lee, and his friend Henry Laurens challenged Lee to a duel, in which Hamilton served as Laurens's second. Burr exchanged friendly letters with Lee, whom he thought to have been unfairly treated.

Burr served nearly four years in the front lines, and three more in occasional confidential missions. Recuperating from wounds and illness, he was in New Haven when Arnold reappeared as a British general ravaging the coast. Burr summoned a contingent of Yale students to repel the British, becoming that hero in Connecticut he remained to the end of his career.

The Cincinnati and Thomas Jefferson

Two linked assertions appeared earlier in these pages that may now be amplified: that at the end of the War for Independence, Burr was a hero and Thomas Jefferson was not, and that Jefferson's unheroic status emerged from his failed wartime governorship of Virginia.

Jefferson's political education began in 1769 as a member of the Virginia House of Burgesses. He was twenty-six. In 1775, when he was thirty-two and of prime military age, the Burgesses ceased to function as a colonial legislature amid a clamor for war and independence. Jefferson and Richard Henry Lee went to Philadelphia at the end of the year to deliberate upon the means by which the colonists might assert their rights and were not laggard in pushing for a violent outcome. Lee drafted a Declaration of Independence but, like John Adams, recognized that there was a genius of language among them. The final words of the Declaration were Jefferson's.

Thereafter, Lee and Jefferson went separate ways; Lee became an officer in active service, while Jefferson did not, to Lee's disgust—and subsequently to the disgust of Lee's biographer Charles Royster, who began describing Jefferson as untrustworthy and also as a coward. So we cannot be surprised when even so good a scholar as Royster falls into making extreme statements such as this: "Neither Jefferson nor any other signer of the Declaration of Independence served in the Continental Army during the Revolutionary War."[8]

That may be correct in a very strict sense, but though correct it is not fair. The surprise in Jefferson's military behavior is not that he was *typical* of the Signers but that he was an exception among them. This was recognized by those who organized the Order of the Cincinnati, who did not limit their own definition of service to the Revolution to those who had been officers in the Continental Army. Many of the Signers—Jefferson excepted—*did* put themselves at risk in battle, and others who did not have battlefield service were later offered status as either original or honorary members of the Society of the Cincinnati. In the latter catagory were Samuel Adams of Massachusetts, Benjamin Franklin of Pennsylvania, Benjamin Harrison of Virginia, Robert Morris of Pennsylvania, William Paca of Maryland, and James Wilson of Pennsylvania. Jefferson was not offered original or honorary membership in the society. As we review his war record, we can see why.[9]

Colonels Burr, Hamilton, and Jefferson

Having set his match to the fire, Jefferson returned to Virginia in September 1776 and took his seat in the House of Delegates. The war engulfed Boston, New York, Philadelphia, Charleston, and Savannah, but things remained fairly tranquil in Virginia, where Jefferson served as a model legislator. In the words of a biographer of John Marshall, Senator Albert Beveridge:

> Jefferson was in the State Legislature . . . starting such vital reforms as the abolition of entails, the revision of the criminal code, the establishment of a free school system, the laying of the legal foundations of religious freedom.

In short, Jefferson was sowing the seeds of liberalism in Virginia. But it is only human nature that breasts bearing the storm of war should not have thrilled in admiration of this civil husbandry. It was but natural that the benumbed men at Valley Forge should think the season early for that planting of State reforms, however needful, when the very ground of American independence was cold and still freezing with patriot misfortune and British success.[10]

In December 1777, George Washington's defeated army, with Aaron Burr, John Marshall, and Alexander Hamilton in its ranks, dragged itself into winter quarters on a windswept ridge between a little creek valley where an ironworks had been, Valley Forge, and the bluffs overlooking the Schuylkill. Washington later recalled that "you might have tracked the army from White Marsh to Valley Forge by the blood of their feet." Thousands were without either shoes or blankets. Amputation of frozen legs and fingers was common. The quartermaster's department having collapsed, food supplies ran short. Beweeviled flour was mixed with water, squeezed flat, and cooked on hot stones for "fire cake," three times a day. The water was "hard to drink," one soldier reported, "so many a dipping and washing it which made it very dirty and muddy." "Putrid fever," typhus, and smallpox spread through the camp. The hospitals were so crowded that "four or five patients die on the same straw before it was changed." One Virginia regiment lost 37 of its 40 men to disease.[11]

Into such a regiment during the preceding springtime, in April 1777, Jefferson had sent one Strother Jones, "by nature," wrote the Sage of Monticello, "well principled, for war bold, honorable and modest; but he is young and will need the fatherly hand of some one to lead him through the mazes of military delicacy and duty." Aaron Burr, in Valley Forge, might have led Strother through the "mazes of military delicacy" if he found the young man alive. But Burr was busy with a different reality. He had been in the army since July 1775. He had survived the bitter march to Quebec and the more bitter defeat before its walls. He had seen Washington driven from New York and New Jersey. He had commanded a regiment and gained a reputation not only for courage under fire but also for stern discipline in camp.

As seditious talk was heard in the army, Burr was directed to take command of a mutinous unit at the outermost extension of the American defenses. He commenced enforcing discipline.

A portion of the most worthless became restless, and were determined to rid themselves of such a commander. Colonel Burr was notified of the contemplated mutiny, in which he would probably fall a victim. He ordered the detachment to be formed that night (it being a cold, bright moonlight) and secretly directed that all their cartridges should be drawn, so that there should not be a loaded musket on the ground. He provided himself with a good and well-sharpened saber. He knew all the principal mutineers. He marched along the line, eying the men closely. When he came opposite to one of the most daring of the ringleaders, the soldier advanced a step, and leveled his musket at Colonel Burr, calling out—"Now is your time, my boys." Burr, being well prepared . . . anticipating an assault, with a celerity for which he was remarkable, smote the arm of the mutineer above the elbow, and nearly severed it from his body, ordering him, at the same time, to take and keep his place in the line. In a few minutes the men were dismissed . . . [and] no more was heard of the mutiny.[12]

Little was heard of Jefferson, at the time, either, but for other reasons. He was at Monticello, serving from time to time as county lieutenant for Albemarle County. As Colonel Jefferson, he "had to do much paper work in connection with the militia." He was also disturbed from "the philosophical pursuits of which he was so fond" by the recruitment of "a band of domestic musicians. . . . He had a gardener, a weaver, and a stone cutter, however, and hoped to secure a vigneron. He believed that in cultivated Italy or France his correspondent [a young Italian, Giovanni Fabroni] might find for him men of these useful trades who could also perform on the French horn, the clarinet, the hautboy, or the bassoon. The letter was captured by the British. Jefferson did not get his musical workmen from Europe."[13]

Where Is Jefferson?

Dumas Malone, who provided us with this charming account of Jefferson's activity in 1778, assures us that "his contemporaries did not blame him for not being in the Continental Army. Entirely apart from his family obligations, his greater usefulness in the public councils was obvious." Not to everyone, it seems. His failure to extend his service to "public councils" beyond those of Virginia was noted. Why were he and George Mason not serving with the Continental Congress, Washington inquired of Mason: "Let this voice . . . call upon you, Jefferson, and others." Washington wrote home that if Virginia's "best and ablest men" did not take up arms, at least they should take up the national work in national "councils." They "must not slumber nor sleep at home in such times of pressing danger—they must not content themselves in the enjoyment of places of honor or profit in their Country [Virginia] while the common interests of America are moldering and sinking into irretrievable . . . ruin, in which theirs also must ultimately be involved."[14]

Here was a foreshadowing of later differences between Federalists and Republicans. Thenceforward, Washington, Marshall, Hamilton, and Lee shared the conviction that "the States, separately, are too much engaged in their local concerns." So, from Valley Forge, Washington wrote: "[I]n the present situation of things, I cannot help asking—Where is Mason—Wythe—Jefferson?"[15]

Malone described as "fanciful" Beveridge's "surmise that the question 'Where is Jefferson' was echoed among the 'shivering soldiers and officers.' " To which Beveridge replied:

> If Washington would so write, is it not likely that the men would so talk? For was not Jefferson the penman who had inscribed the Declaration of Independence, for which they were fighting, suffering, dying? Just as to John Marshall's army experience the roots of the greatest of his constitutional opinions may clearly be traced, so the beginnings of his personal estimate of Thomas Jefferson may be as plainly found in their relative situations and conduct during the same period.[16]

This does not seem too fanciful: John Marshall had served in the Revolutionary Army since the carnage at Great Bridge, when he was barely twenty. His "personal estimate of Thomas Jefferson" must have been somewhat tinctured by the differences in their responses to Virginia's proclamation that it meant to fight to be free. In any case, that opinion was well formed by the time Jefferson completed his first, and relatively tranquil, term as a war governor, having abandoned his paperwork colonelcy in 1779. Marshall was still a footsoldiering lieuten-ant of twenty-five when Jefferson, at thirty-seven, was reelected in 1780.

Malone tells us that "the character of Jefferson's last eight months as governor . . . was determined by military events over which he had little or no control." The British, who had not mounted a threat since Great Bridge, appeared on the coast at the end of 1780 and began serious invasions from the seacoast, and overland from the south, early in 1781. Malone tells us that "the fates pursued Jefferson into the depths of the forest, and the feeble government collapsed. . . . [I]t was brought low by attrition and inanition at the time, and Jefferson him-self, though struggling valiantly, had already appeared as the sport of circumstance."[17]

The British cavalry under Colonel Tarleton chased Jefferson from Monticello, over Carter's Mountain, and into the depths of the forest, where he ceased to struggle valiantly. Indeed, he ceased to govern, though Malone has explained that it "would be nearer the truth to say that the government abandoned him rather than that he aban-doned the government, but there must have been people then, as there were more thereafter, who believed he had abdicated in utter impotence."[18]

John Marshall, Thomas Jefferson, and the Question of Character

The winter of 1778–79 at Valley Forge tested the characters of those who endured it, just as the winter of 1780–81 tested Jefferson and the Virginians who had remained at home. Washington's companions pre-sumably were warmer and better fed at the upper reaches of the mil-itary hierarchy than at the lower; Washington slept more comfortably than staff officers such as Alexander Hamilton or James Monroe, who, in turn, lived better than line officers such as John Marshall and Aaron Burr. And, then, there were the hovels of the enlisted men. Thomas Jefferson was most comfortable of all, and was not forgiven for that comfort by many of the Cincinnati, who lay in wait for him, or, to be more precise, for his reputation, thereafter. They were infuriated when Jefferson, in 1796, dared to use military metaphors in attacking the reputation of Washington and those of his officers who had become Federalists.

The Sage of Monticello had been too sage to permit himself to disparage the General directly, but he did write a letter to his Florentine friend, Philip Mazzei, which Mazzei translated into Italian, published in French, and broadcast to the world, in which reference was made to persons who had been "Samsons in the field" but in peacetime had been "shorn by the harlot England." The Cincinnati remembered that Jefferson himself had been anything but a Samson in the field, and Marshall let it be known that "the morals of the author of the letter to Mazzei cannot be pure."[19]

Three years later, as the quirks of the unamended electoral college system produced the tie between Jefferson and Burr for the presidency, Hamilton permitted hatred to overcome mere aversion and entreated Marshall to endorse Jefferson. Marshall replied:

> To Mr. Jefferson . . . I have felt almost insuperable objections. His foreign prejudices seem to me totally to unfit him for the chief magistracy of a nation which cannot indulge those prejudices without sustaining deep and permanent injury. In addition to this solid and immovable objection, Mr. Jefferson appears to me to be a man who will embody himself with the house of Representatives. By weakening the office of president, he will increase his personal power . . . diminish his responsibility, sap the fundamental principles of the government.[20]

Jefferson had made much of his devotion to the legislative branch while it might be controlled by his party and the presidency was in the hands of Washington and John Adams. He demonstrated soon enough that he had no intention of "weakening the office of the president" when he filled that office. Marshall could not have anticipated that, however. All he had to go on was Jefferson's record as governor.

Hamilton was in no mood to debate such niceties. He was after Burr. So he wrote Marshall again, unpacking his usual trunkload of charges against Burr. Marshall would only reply:

> Your representation of Mr. Burr, with whom I am totally unacquainted, shows that from him still greater danger than even from Mr. Jefferson may be apprehended. Such a man as you describe is more to be feared. . . . Believing that you know him well, and are impartial, my preference would not be for him, but I can take

no part in this business. I cannot bring myself to aid Mr. Jefferson.[21]

"Totally unacquainted" with Burr? They had both been at Valley Forge, which was not the Grand Canyon.[22]

The exchange between Marshall and Hamilton in 1800 occurred after Hamilton had destroyed the competitive position of John Adams for the presidency and produced the opportunity for both Jefferson and Burr. Having done so, he sought to reduce the list yet again through his assaults upon the reputation of Burr. He did not have to bring Marshall around, because Burr took himself out of contention. Though Marshall's objections to Jefferson were shared by enough Federalists to make Burr President, Burr did not negotiate arrangements with the Federalists; Jefferson did, and became President.

In the next chapter, we will tell how they all came to such a pass, and then how, in 1804, Hamilton succeeded in the task he set out for himself in 1800. He eliminated Burr from the competition, but at the ultimate price. The field was Jefferson's by the summer of 1804. Or so it seemed. But Burr had one more campaign in him.

Politics, Love, Learning, and Death

The chief difficulty of comparative biography, for anyone foolish enough to attempt it, is that it does not admit of experiment. It is not a science. Life does not provide tests in which like conditions are repeated. However, since the task before us is not so ambitious as comparative biography, only the observation of contemporaries as they interacted, we need not contend with science but merely raise questions, as we go along, as to how one or another of our protagonists might have responded to circumstances in which another found himself. We may ask, at the same time, whether or not the first may have created those circumstances for the second.

We have been observing Aaron Burr and Thomas Jefferson as they responded to circumstances created in large measure by Alexander Hamilton, as Hamilton removed John Adams as an impediment to Jefferson's ascent to the presidency and stood in the way of any contention for that eminence by Burr. It was as if they were climbing a mountain together, as if Hamilton kicked Adams down an icy slope, let Jefferson pass, and then stood athwart the trail with an ice ax in his hand, ready for Burr. Now we should double back to the base of the

ascent, to see how Jefferson, Hamilton, and Burr handled certain complexities of the route bringing them to the crisis of 1800.

In 1784, the embarrassments of Virginia's wartime government retreated behind the glorious tableau of the Virginian commander-in-
chief receiving the British surrender at Yorktown, on Virginia soil. A
somewhat subdued Thomas Jefferson returned to the Congress as
Hamilton and Burr turned to the practice of law. The two New Yorkers
were evenly matched, though with entirely differing styles. Hamilton's
fervent nature flowed into a romantic courtroom demeanor and into
rhetoric described as exalted, flowing, and rapturous. Burr was cool,
terse, and convincing. The two young men often displayed their respective skills as cocounsel in celebrated cases, in the sponsorship of
rival banks, and in politics.

Jefferson served only six months in Congress before he left for his
mission to France, but they were the occasion for him to respond to a
proposal by David Howell of Rhode Island and draft his famous, failed
Ordinance of 1784. It was a grand gesture, which not only would have
banned slavery in all territories relinquished by the states west of the
Appalachians after 1800 but would also have required that any governments, temporary or permanent, established there should remain
forever a part of the United States. The first part of this proposal has
received most commentary, including some skepticism by those who
note that Virginia was selling slaves full-tilt into the West; that its primary market, Kentucky, was not included in the prohibition because
it remained part of Virginia until 1792; that the prohibition would not
take effect until the selling and the creation of new plantations had
gone on for sixteen more years; and that there was no suggestion as
to the means by which slavery would be abolished.

The second part, however, is considerably more important, because,
as Dumas Malone has pointed out repeatedly (though no one seems
to be listening), it would have made secession illegal—except, one
supposes, in Kentucky, but that is a quibble. Did Jefferson intend such
an outcome? Or was this an idea of Howell's, to which he acceded
because he knew that no part of the resolution would pass anyway? As
it was, he carried no other Virginian with him, and only one other
vote, from North Carolina's antislavery mountains, came along. Jefferson expressed regret that the ordinance failed but, as Malone also
pointed out, did not try again on either point. He had nothing to do

with either the prohibition of slavery in territories north of the Ohio or the fugitive slave provision of the Northwest Ordinance of 1787, for he was still in Paris when it was discussed and passed.

Jefferson remained abroad until October 1789. Burr, meantime, was serving in the New York Assembly and became attorney general of New York just as Jefferson returned to be integrated into the first administration of George Washington as Secretary of State.

Hamilton served in the Continental Congress in 1783 but after one term returned to the law. In 1786, he returned to the national stage in a leading role at the Annapolis Convention, came back to New York for a term in the Assembly in 1787, and then rose steadily in the esteem of his countrymen with his speech to the Constitutional Convention, his coauthorship of *The Federalist,* and his successful fight to secure New York's adoption of the Constitution in 1788.

Hamilton was, therefore, an eminent young man in his early thirties in April 1789. When the first Washington administration was organized, he became Secretary of the Treasury, balancing Jefferson, who had refurbished his character by a successful term as a diplomat in Paris and was a fully mature forty-six. Burr was not "ministerable" in the French sense (qualified for a cabinet office) because of his opposition to Washington during the Revolution.

The Women

Jefferson's wife died in 1782, after ten years of marriage. Martha Wayles Skelton had been a widow, and none of Jefferson's biographers, even the resourceful Fawn Brodie, has been able to tell us much about her—from the solitary letter remaining to us in her hand or the accounts of their contemporaries—beyond the general impression that she was handsome, musical, and frail. Four of their children died in infancy.

In the same year as the death of Jefferson's wife, 1782, Burr was married to Theodosia Bartow, a widow ten years his senior, who had already borne five children. She died of cancer in 1794.[1] Only one of their children survived, their daughter Theodosia. Her character emerges from their large and fervent correspondence. She was confident, well connected, well read, beautiful even after a burn scarred her face, witty, worldly, and full of expectations of him.

Hamilton's Elizabeth was an heiress, the daughter of an upstate squire, Philip Schuyler, with Livingston and van Rensselaer connections. She was plain, straightforward, loyal, and neurasthenic, endured his flagrant and frequent infidelities, and lived to the brink of the Civil War. Several of Burr's biographers have repeated the saw that "the Clintons had power, the Livingstons had numbers, the Schuylers had Hamilton." They had Hamilton—indeed they did—but he had them as well. The Schuylers acquired their genius, while Hamilton acquired the Schuylers, and with the Schuylers, legitimacy.[2]

Philip Schuyler held a seat in the U.S. Senate thanks to his ponderous rectitude and the presumed control by his friends of the upper house of the New York legislature, which selected senators. It was expected that the seat would stay in the hands of Hamilton's father-in-law, but, in 1792, a strange thing happened on the way to the Senate: Twelve of the sixteen members of the upper house voted for Burr instead, and, as Hamilton wrote, "his eyes were opened at last to the true nature of Burr."[3]

While she lived, Theodosia Burr endorsed and enlarged her husband's predisposition to accept women as peers—the Edwards women were formidable as well—and led him to organize his feelings into a protofeminist position on female education. That, in turn, brought them to propose a role for women in government that was novel even in New Jersey, where women voted in 1790. Unlike Jefferson's and Hamilton's, Burr's character was molded by the love of a woman of immense force and intelligence. Theodosia drew forth from him all that was most admirable; he had already been a heroic soldier, but she made of him an adventurer of the intellect. There were many military heroes in those times, but she asked more of Burr than physical courage and endurance. To satisfy her, he must set forth into unknown emotional territory amid the tempests of feeling between men and women, venturing where none other of the Founders dared go—except, perhaps, for Albert Gallatin.

He was, as suggested earlier, predisposed to do so. When a friend first told Burr of Mary Wollstonecraft's *Vindication of the Rights of Women*, he wrote his wife that he had "made haste to procure it, and spent last night, almost the whole of it, in reading it. Be assured that your sex has in *her* an able advocate. It is, in my opinion, a work of genius. She has successfully adopted the style of Rousseau's Emilius [Emile]; and her comment on that work, especially when it comes to female education, contains more good sense than all the other criticisms upon him I have seen put together."[4]

Wollstonecraft was an Anglo-Irish lady who was moved by the two revolutions—in France and in America—to believe that there might be a third. She and her future husband, William Godwin, urged men and women to reconsider their relationships, rebalancing their relative power positions toward equal rights and equal education. Mr. and Mrs. Burr agreed with Mr. and Mrs. Godwin, though all four wondered why they found so few true colleagues of the soul: "Is it owing to ignorance or prejudice," wrote Burr, "that I have not met a single person who has discovered or would allow the merit of this work?"[5]

As Burr's character blossomed in the radiance of his wife and mentor, he suggested a test of the theory that males were superior to women in ability, proposing a "fair experiment" to determine when, exactly, it was in childhood development that "male superiority becomes so evident. . . . [B]oys and girls [were already being educated] . . . in much the same way until they are eight or nine years of age, and it is admitted that girls make at least equal progress with boys; generally, indeed, they make better." That admission need not be made grudgingly, wrote Burr, for "women have souls!"[6]

Neither Hamilton nor Jefferson married a woman who evidenced such force of character and independence of view. Women did not vote in Virginia, and Jefferson stood in the way of such an eventuality, opposing "systematized schooling" for them, admitting them to the University of Virginia or permitting them to attend "public meetings with men." Even after his exposure to Maria Cosway and the philosophical women of Paris, he wrote George Washington from France in 1788, deploring their influence upon the French governing class and rejoicing that "in our country" that "influence . . . fortunately for the happiness of the sex itself, does not endeavor to extend itself . . . beyond the domestic line."[7]

Jefferson's letters of instruction to his daughters are much like Hamilton's to his: They condescend, and thus are strikingly different from Hamilton's to his sons, and Jefferson's to the young men in whom he took an interest after his own son died in infancy. Burr's letters to his daughter Theodosia are not like either Jefferson's or Hamilton's. They graduate from straightforward instruction, when she was very young, to comradery, when she was beyond twelve or so, but they never patronize.

As Jefferson's opinions upon women's education and assembly in public show, the views of our protagonists as to the education of females led directly to their opinions as to women's proper role in government. It was earlier suggested that Albert Gallatin may have shared some of Burr's views about women's rights because Gallatin, too, had a sprightly and intellectual wife, Hannah Nicholson, who also took an interest in public affairs. She was the daughter of a friend and political ally of Burr's, who raised her to be a New York woman. (Even in 1790, that meant something different from a southern belle. There were many able females born and living south of the Mason-Dixon Line, but their opportunities for education and for exposure to the world were much restricted from those of their counterparts in the North.) It is likely that Gallatin was induced by Hannah to "remember the ladies" when Jefferson was forming his government in 1800. That had been the injunction of Abigail Adams to her husband in 1776, as John Adams, Jefferson, and the other Signers were preparing to declare American independence. Adams called his wife "saucy" for her suggestion.

Twenty-four years later, Jefferson responded thus to Gallatin: "Th. J. to Mr. Gallatin. The appointment of a woman to office is an innovation for which the public is not prepared nor am I."[8]

It is not odd that women respected Burr. He respected them. Perhaps that is why Abigail Adams sought to convince her husband that if either Jefferson or Burr was chosen to replace him in 1800, Burr was to be preferred as "the more bold, daring, and decisive."[9]

He was bold. His daring was so notorious that it was asserted that he planned to make his daughter "Empress" of his western colony of the Ouachita. The allegation was, of course, ludicrous, but it is true that he endeavored to provide her with an education fit for an empress. She was taught Hebrew, Latin, Greek, Spanish, French, botany, natural history, and the classics of political theory. When she became a woman, he gave her his portrait of Wollstonecraft to remind her of the *Vindication* he had used as a primer for her education. And—beyond Wollstonecraft—there were others; Theodosia should "read with avidity and prepossession every thing written by a lady."[10]

It was not easy for her to do so. The conventions of their time so trivialized the possibilities for young women that Burr told his wife that he feared their daughter might not be strong enough to assert her full character. Then, he wrote, she might become "a mere fashionable woman, with all the attendant frivolity and vacuity of mind." If that were to happen, though she were "adorned with grace and allurement, I would earnestly pray God to take her, forthwith hence."[11]

By 1804, Burr's apprehensions were gone. On the night before his duel with Hamilton, Burr wrote his daughter:

> Having written my will, and given my private letters and papers in charge to you, I have no other direction to give you on the subject but to request you to burn all such as, if by accident made public, would injure any person. This is more particularly applicable to the letters of my female correspondents.
>
> ... I am indebted to you, my dearest Theodosia, for a very great portion of the happiness which I have enjoyed in this life. You have completely satisfied all that my heart and affections had hoped or even wished. With a little more perseverance, determination, and industry, you will obtain all that my ambition or vanity had fondly imagined. Let your son have occasion to be proud that he had a mother. Adieu. Adieu. A. Burr.[12]

Burr had said some years earlier that he hoped, by Theodosia, "to convince the world [of] that [which] neither sex appear to believe—that women have souls." Though she did not disappoint him, life—and death—did. In July 1812, her only child, Aaron Burr Alston, died, at the age of eleven. The death of their hope and their pride struck them just as Burr returned from exile to "that country which," he feared, "might reject me with horror." Though he found old friends who did not reject him, and though he was able to start his life again, it became apparent that Theodosia was suffering from the same kind of painful cancer which had killed her mother. On December 30, 1812, she took ship from South Carolina to New York. The vessel disappeared in a storm off the North Carolina Banks. With her to the depths went all those documents which her father had hoped she might use to compose proper biographies of her mother, her father, and herself.[13]

Burr and Washington

In 1791, Aaron Burr had taken his seat in the Senate. Hamilton was already in the national capital, serving as Washington's principal adviser. Henry Knox was the President's counsel on military matters. With those old foes arrayed at his front, Burr's back was also exposed, for in New York, the Clintons and Livingstons had found him to have ideas of his own. The miracle is that he got as far as he did.[14]

In 1793, the mutual antipathies between Burr and Washington were inflamed by a report that the new senator had leaked to the press an account of a discussion held in secret session of Washington's appointment of William Short to negotiate a treaty with Spain. In fact, the secretary of the Senate, Samuel Otis, was the guilty party, but Burr did enter the subsequent squabble about whether or not the "advice" of the Senate to the President extended to judgments as to whether or not the Chief Executive could name his own emissary to the Hague without Senate confirmation. Burr introduced a motion denying that power to Washington, and John Adams was forced to cast a vice presidential tiebreaker. John Jay wrote Washington that Burr's motion gave him "much concern," but not enough, it seems, to terminate Jay's friendly feelings for him. Washington took it harder, telling Jay it was "only the prelude . . . to what is intended to follow, as occasions present themselves."[15]

In 1794, Colonel (now Secretary of the Treasury) Hamilton reminded General (now President) Washington of how he felt about Colonel (now Senator) Burr. Despite the recommendations of the Republican caucus, in which even the Virginians joined, the President declined to make Burr minister to France. If they could make trouble for Short, he could make trouble for Burr. Washington gave as his reason that he "was not assured" of Burr's integrity, echoing Hamilton's statement that "Mr. Burr's integrity . . . is not unimpeached."

Just before Washington's death in 1799, there was a postscript: John Adams had become President—except as to those matters in which Washington still took an interest, including the army. When Congress agreed that Adams might appoint a set of brigadier generals, Burr's name came up. Washington instructed Adams to reject him, this time asserting that he was too much given to intrigue. Instead, Washington forced Hamilton's appointment as a major general, second in command only to himself. Adams fumed but could not refuse, telling his diary that Washington had made "the most restless, impatient, artful, indefatigable and unprincipled intriguer in the United States, if not in the world . . . second in command under himself . . . [But said he] dreaded an intriguer [Burr] in a poor brigadier!"[16]

Three years earlier, in 1796, Burr had lost his Senate seat to

Federalist opposition organized by Hamilton, but in 1800 Burr returned the favor by defeating Hamilton's proxy for the governorship, his brother-in-law. Stephen van Rensselaer. Burr backed George Clinton and won, perhaps because so much of Hamilton's energy was expended at the time in averting the possibility that Burr might become President.

On December 26, 1800, Hamilton told Gouverneur Morris that "with Burr I have always been personally well. But the public good must be paramount." On December 27, Hamilton assured James Bayard of Delaware that Burr was "a voluptuary by system. . . . No engagement that can be made with him can be depended upon. . . . To contribute to the disappointment and mortification of Mr. Jefferson, would be, on my part, only to retaliate for unequivocal proofs of enmity; but in a case like this, it would be base to listen to personal considerations. . . . I dine with him [Burr!] but lately."[17]

James Bayard was an American gentleman, justifying that appellation by lineage, character, and behavior. Hamilton chose his words to appeal to Bayard's stiff rectitude, knowing that the lesser Federalists would follow Bayard's lead, and as the proprietor of Delaware's lone vote, he could tip the balance. (The Bayards were Huguenot descendants of a sister of Peter Stuyvesant, gentry who had divided into New Jersey and Delaware branches.) Hamilton knew Bayard to be beyond platitudes and sought to sway him by implicitly acknowledging that they all, all these Founders, knew ambition; it was only *extreme* and *irregular* ambition that might be culpable. Bayard was known to be a devoted husband, and, though Hamilton was not, perhaps Bayard might read something into the word "profligate" which might lead him to believe Burr was something worse.

A Hypocrite or a Dangerous Man?

The circumstances drawing forth both Hamilton's excoriations of a man with whom he dined and was "personally well" was provided by a quirk, since remedied, in the constitutional provisions for the election of the President and Vice President. Jefferson and Burr were nominated by a coalition of interests and followings, concerted in an understanding that Jefferson was to be the top of the ticket. Since he and Burr received the same number of electoral votes, the resolution of the tie went to the House of Representatives, where each state had a single vote, whatever might be its population or number of representatives. This provided a glorious opportunity for Federalist mischief. Surely, suggested Harrison Gray Otis, they should not scruple too much, for excessive delicacy might "omit or misdirect an effort which might be beneficial to the country, [and] preserve the Constitution." Feigning an inadequate personal knowledge of Burr, whom he had known for more than a decade (and, in this, following the course taken by John Marshall), Otis asked Hamilton to set aside his personal animus against Burr for the sake of the Constitution: "I presume that honor and duty will sanction every endeavor to preserve it, even by an ineligible instrument."[18]

The indications of haste in the draft of Hamilton's answer tell us more about Hamilton than about Burr:

> If Jefferson and Burr come with equal votes to the House of Representatives, the former ought to be preferred by the [struck: House of Representatives] Federalists. Mr. Jefferson is respectably known in Europe—Mr. Burr little and that little not advantageously for [strike-out] a President of the United States.—Mr. Jefferson is a man of easy fortune.—Mr. Burr, as I believe, is bankrupt beyond redemption unless by some *coup* at the expense of the public and his habits of expense are such that wealth he must have at any rate.—Mr. Jefferson is a man of fair character for probity.—Very different ideas are entertained of Mr. Burr by his enemies and what his friends think, you may collect from this anecdote—A lady said to Edward Livingston ironically "I am told that Mr. Burr will be President. I should think it very well if I had not [struck: been told] learned that he is a man without property."—"Let him alone for that," replied Edward,—"If he is President four years, he will remove that objection."—Mr. Jefferson, though too revolutionary in his notions, is yet a lover of liberty and will be desirous of something like orderly government.—Mr. Burr loves nothing but himself—thinks of nothing but his own aggrandizement—and will be content with nothing short of permanent power [struck: and] in his own hands.—No compact, that he should make with any [struck: other] passion in his [struck: own] breast except ambition, could be relied upon by himself.—How then should we be abler to rely upon our

agreement with him? Mr. Jefferson I suspect will not dare much. Mr. Burr will [*inserted in margin*: dare everything in the sanguine hope of affecting every thing.]

If Mr. Jefferson is likely from predilection for France to draw this country into war on her side—Mr. Burr will certainly endeavor to do it. . . . This portrait is the result of long and attentive observation on [*sic*] a [*strike-out*] man with whom I am personally well—and in respect to whose character I have had peculiar opportunity of forming a correct judgement. By no means, my dear sir, let the Federalists be responsible for his elevation,—In a choice of evils, let them take the least—Jefferson is in my view less dangerous than Burr.[19]

Jefferson was "less dangerous" because he "will not dare much." This was Hamilton's line against Jefferson: He was pusillanimous. But in order to head off Burr, Hamilton suggested that Jefferson's very weakness was in the national interest: Though he might not be "very mindful of truth . . . and a contemptible hypocrite," he was better than Burr, the "most unfit and dangerous man in the community . . . profligate . . . voluptuary . . . [and] bankrupt." Besides, as a "hypocrite," Jefferson might make a deal.[20]

We ought—still to seek some advantages from our situation. It may be advisable to make it [*strike-out*] a ground of exploration with Mr. Jefferson or his confidential friends and the means of obtaining from him some assurances of his future conduct.[21]

Hamilton then listed "three essential points for us to secure," and secure them the Federalists did from Mr. Jefferson's confidential friends. The Federalists could be satisfied that there would be no "Revolution of 1800," though Jefferson proclaimed to the world that there would be, and afterward that there had been. Bayard assured Samuel Smith that he would tip the balance for Jefferson if "I had the assurance" on necessary points, and, on the following morning, Smith returned, saying that "he had seen Mr. Jefferson, . . . and was authorized by him to say that the Federalist requirements corresponded with his views and intentions." Bayard then brought over the pivotable electors to support Jefferson rather than Burr, on the thirty-sixth ballot.[22]

Oaths and Other Words to Be Kept

In scores of seminars, scholars have disputed two questions: First, did Burr in 1800 seek by clandestine means to negotiate a transaction like that successfully consummated by Jefferson? Jefferson may have thought he did, for he said so often enough. Second, did Jefferson break his word and intervene against Burr in the New York gubernatorial election of 1804?

Answering the first question, Federalists and Republicans whose record for truth was good, including Bayard, Robert Goodloe Harper, Caesar Rodney, and Samuel Smith, testified that Burr had abstained from any such effort. The Federalists among them knew that the portrait of Burr presented by Hamilton was of his own shadow-self, a picture that would have been more compelling had he criticized Burr for qualities *not* conspicuously his own—for example, qualities such as irresoluteness or being pathetically credulous beneath a cynical demeanor. In the end it did not matter, because the Federalists had Jefferson on the "essentials," and Jefferson had the presidency.

Why, then, were so many of their contemporaries ready to believe the worst of Burr. Was this, for Burr, a tragedy of manner? Was he simply out of date? Probably. The quietly self-assured among them, taking Burr's aristocratically cool view of the proper demeanor for a public man—Jay, Gallatin, Bayard, Harper, John Adams, and Gouverneur Morris—remained to the end unwilling to join the jackal pack. This is a matter to which we must of necessity return.

In 1804, Jefferson corroborated Hamilton's description of *his* character. Solemnly he assured Burr, face to face, that he would not get in his way to the governorship, repeating that assurance to Burr's running mate, Oliver Phelps, and encouraging Gideon Granger to repeat it once more to William Van Ness—the phraseology of all three assurances was the same. Yet, as the campaign was drawing to a close, Jefferson, flanked by Attorney General Levi Lincoln (a northern Republican), received at his residence two New York congressmen, Beriah Palmer and Thomas Sammons, and told them that they might go forth to tell the Republican organization that the previous report of his conversation with Phelps had been somewhat truncated. Jefferson asserted that he had gone on to say something which, when they heard of it, was new to Phelps, Van Ness, and Burr:

Remember, Mr. Phelps, that I do not consider the *Little Band* [Burr's closest adherents] as making any part of the real Republican interest.[23]

It was the eleventh hour. Burr protested, but the newspapers blazoned forth Palmer and Sammons's account of their discussion with Jefferson. Jefferson did not repudiate their tale. Nor did Granger. Nor did Lincoln. Burr lost. The cobelligerency of Jefferson and Hamilton against Burr was successful.[24]

Despite what Hamilton had said of him, the character of Burr was, however, not the determining factor. Pure political power produced the outcome. Federalists, such as John Jay and Stephen van Rensselaer, and Republicans, such as the younger members of "Manor Branch" of the Livingston family, supported Burr, though Chancellor Robert R. Livingston joined the Jeffersonians and the Clintons against him. Edward Livingston, the chancellor's younger brother, never deserted Burr, and, in 1803, John Armstrong, Chancellor Livingston's brother-in-law, wrote that Burr had "the most industry, the most talent, and the most address" of all the vice presidential candidates, including George Clinton.[25]

Dueling Founders

After the gubernatorial election was lost, Burr was showing signs of abandoning his forbearance in the face of Jefferson's duplicity and Hamilton's false witness. He had challenged Hamilton's brother-in-law, John Barker Church, for remarks about his integrity, at the intersection of his private and public character, alleging that Burr had taken a bribe in a transaction in which he and Hamilton were both involved. Burr declined to respond with an attack upon Hamilton, whose behavior was as vulnerable—it is most unlikely that either took bribes, though the Schuyler-Hamilton-Church clan did benefit from the matter considerably more than Burr did. On the dueling ground, Church apologized.[26]

A year later, Hamilton's son Philip, named after his grandfather, had paid the ultimate price for the family's assault on Burr's honor; he died in a duel with a Republican, George Eacker. Still, as Burr and Hamilton dined in each other's houses, Hamilton twice more apologized, promising no further provocations. This was his way: In 1797, he had made a notorious appearance on the doorstep of James Monroe, to call him a liar. Burr was then Monroe's confidant and assured him that Hamilton "would not fight!" He might provoke. He might challenge. But he would not fight.[27]

Burr proved himself right by negotiating a settlement on Monroe's behalf. That was made easier after it was learned that the real breach of gentlemanly behavior had not occurred within Monroe's control. Monroe had been one of three congressmen to whom, in 1793, Hamilton had presented the sordid details of an adulterous relationship with Mrs. James Reynolds. All three had solemnly pledged to keep the matter secret. Monroe admitted that he had extended the circle of confidentiality by shipping his notes to "his friend in Virginia . . . and declared upon his honor that he knew nothing of their publication until he arrived in Philadelphia from Europe" in 1797. Jefferson had passed them along to his paid character assassin, James Callender.[28]

Hamilton did not press the matter by challenging Jefferson, who, after all, had only betrayed Monroe's confidence, and Monroe needed Jefferson more than Jefferson needed Monroe. It is worthy of note, however, that the affair began when the anti-Hamilton faction threatened an impeachment proceeding against him for conduct in the Treasury in which Reynolds was a party, and that it was to escape such a proceeding that Hamilton was forced to acknowledge that his intimacy with the Reynoldses was with the wife, not the husband. When we are all done with our story, we may keep this matter in mind, for whatever else may be laid against Burr, no legislature ever thought his conduct so dubious as to threaten impeachment.[29]

What if? What if Hamilton had not become sick of the entire subject by 1797? What if he had added Jefferson to the other men with whom, according to Joanne Freeman, he involved himself in "affairs of honor": the Rev. William Gordon (1779), Aedanus Burke (1790), John Francis Mercer (1792–3), James Nicholson (1795), Maturin Livingston (1795–96), Monroe (1797), John Adams (1800), Ebenezer Purdy and George Clinton (1804), and Burr (1804). There was another dueling opportunity for Hamilton, but only as a second for his friend John Laurens, who challenged General Charles Lee during the Revolution.[30]

Violent means of settling questions of honor were part of the culture of the class to which Hamilton clung; his sons Philip and James were duelists, and his brother-in-law Church had almost professional standing, having killed at least one opponent in England with his special set of pistols. The appeal to trial by combat was widespread even in John Adams's New England, where we might not expect it among Puritans with no pretensions to Cavalier status.

In his old age, Adams was willing only to say that "without entering into any moral, political or religious discussion of the subject of private [combats] and individual administration of justice," he did not think a *judge* should engage in a duel. Perhaps recalling that he had placed that amiable Federalist Bushrod Washington upon the U.S. Supreme Court knowing that Washington had fought his own duel, he added that "I cannot but lament, that the sacred solemn [benches] of justice should exhibit perpetual [exemplifications] of the practice before the people. This is not conformable to the policy even in Europe, where dueling is not carried to such deliberate and malicious excess as it is in America."[31]

"Public opinion" still urged a duel upon the New York Federalist Congressman Berent Gardenier in 1808; he was called out on the floor of the House of Representatives by three Democrats, of whom the best shot was George W. Campbell of Kentucky, who nearly killed Gardenier on the dueling ground at Bladensburg, Maryland. On the Virginia side of the Potomac there was a killing field where two members of the Mason clan contended at close range with shotguns. Henry Clay fought his most famous duel there, contending with John Randolph of Roanoke in 1826. Clay had been badly wounded in an earlier duel with his and Burr's Federalist archopponent in Kentucky, Humphrey Marshall.

Aside from De Witt Clinton, Monroe, Hamilton, Clay, Randolph, and Burr, other famous duelists included Horatio Gates, William Harris Crawford, Thomas Hart Benton, Andrew Jackson, Stephen Decatur and—the man who killed him—James Barron, Walpole, Pitt, Wellington, Canning, Grattan, Fox, Sheridan, Jeffrey, Wilkes, Disraeli, Lamartine, Thiers—and Lachlan McIntosh, who, as we shall see, had ample provocation to call out the Signer Button Gwinnett, whom he killed. Not a bad list.

Jefferson and Madison had expressed their view of dueling in 1797, when Monroe, like Hamilton, considered challenging Adams. Monroe, they concluded, had been provoked but was relieved of the necessity of taking on Adams because Adams was "an old man and the President." Madison had written with disapprobation of the decision of Roger Griswold to substitute a congressional investigation for a duel. Griswold had been affronted by Matthew Lyon of Vermont—Lyon spat on him. Said Madison: "If Griswold be a man of the sword, he should not have permitted the step [the investigation] to be taken. . . . No man should reproach another for cowardice, who is not ready to give proof of his own courage."[32]

Though Madison presented a very small target, it is not recorded that he ever felt required to offer such a proof; nor did Jefferson, though he did make a slighting reference to Albert Gallatin's unwillingness to provoke Randolph of Roanoke. Noting the fissure between Jefferson's expectations of others and his own behavior, Henry Adams concluded that "if Mr. Jefferson thought that his Secretary of the Treasury wanted moral courage to speak out at the risk of personal danger, there is no more to be said so far as concerns Mr. Jefferson."[33]

As arbiter of all such matters, George Washington took a thoroughly realistic view. Good behavior in peacetime was bad behavior during a war. During the Revolution, Nathaniel Greene brought a court of inquiry against Captain James Gunn for selling a horse to the army. Gunn subsequently retired to a plantation in Georgia, advertising himself as a heroic member of the Cincinnati. Then a grateful Georgia legislature brought Greene to the scene with the gift of that plantation where Eli Whitney later produced the cotton gin for Greene's widow. To Gunn, Greene was an insufferable remonstrance. Acting through an intermediary, he challenged on the ground that he had been unfairly condemned. Greene turned to Washington for advice, and was given it:

> [It is] my decided opinion that your honor and reputation will stand . . . perfectly acquitted for the non-acceptance of his challenge, [and] . . . your prudence and judgement would have been condemned by accepting it; because, if a commanding officer is amenable to private calls for the discharge of his public duty, he has always a dagger at his heart, and can turn neither to the right not the left, without meeting its point.[34]

As derisively as Burr rejected De Witt Clinton, Greene refused to treat Gunn as worthy of his attention. Gunn threatened. Greene retorted: "I always wear pistols and will defend myself," but he would not dignify the challenge.

Gentlemen had to be ready to duel. Hamilton's consciousness of such requirements was intense, as class consciousness usually is among those whose status is precarious. (The most common incentive to class consciousness—having nothing else of which to be proud—was not his problem.) Why was Burr, then, forbearing for so long? His passivity is remarkable; only the fundamental "coyness" of that "silent creature" can explain it. He had seen to it that when Hamilton wrote something foolish about John Adams it was published to the world, with the result that both Adams and Hamilton lost credibility. But he apparently kept himself from giving much thought to what was said about him until it actually cost him the governorship in 1804. Up to that time, he did very well despite the worst Hamilton could do. He was busy getting on with life, politics, and his continual efforts to get rich enough to give money away in larger amounts.

Dr. Cooper Eavesdrops

Into the eerie, contrived, fragile, and unstable silence created by Burr's forbearance, the *Albany Register*, in April 1804, printed a letter from an upstate clergyman, Dr. Charles D. Cooper, gossiping to a friend that he had been present at a meeting of Hamilton with other eminent Federalists, at the home of Cooper's father-in-law. After dinner and much wine, Hamilton launched into his customary philippic against Burr—but with certain embellishments as to Burr's *private* character. When his copy of the *Register* reached Schuylerville, Hamilton's father-in-law scented trouble. Men died for attacks on private character.

Schuyler wrote Cooper, entreating him to admit that Hamilton had not gone so far as to say something about Burr's private character, but Cooper, delighting in the attention of the great, not only refused to withdraw what he had said but added Hamilton's death sentence. Responding to Schuyler, he asserted that he "could detail to you an even more despicable opinion which General Hamilton expressed of Mr. Burr." This "private" letter was "stolen," as Cooper may have intended, and published.[35]

More than three weeks later, Burr, apparently still appraising his opponent as the person about whom he wrote Monroe in 1797, requested a *private*—not *public*—denial from Hamilton that he had used the terms Cooper reported. Surely Hamilton would, once again, withdraw his hasty words. The secondhand, vague term "despicable" could be brushed aside. Hamilton could assert, as he did later—but too much later—that he had not said anything one gentleman might not say of another. The witnesses were likely to add their hasty agreement, for they were Federalists who did not wish to admit that Hamilton had stooped to private malice. Even after the duel, none of them was willing to step forward even to defend what Hamilton had said, offering truth as a defense.

Burr drafted a request that Hamilton cleanse the record, with a "general" denial, "so as wholly to exclude the idea that rumors derogatory to Col. Burr's honor have originated with General Hamilton or have been *fairly* [Burr's emphasis] inferred from any thing he has said."[36]

Hamilton responded at length, asking Burr to tell *him* what *Cooper* could have meant that *he* had said, and adding the ritual challenge: If Burr could not do that, he would "abide the consequences." Burr replied that he asked only that Hamilton disavow "uttering expressions or opinions derogatory to my honor," requiring a catalogue of years of derogations and entering the zone of provocation under the dueling code. Hamilton responded through his second, Nathaniel Pendleton, that if Burr were to draft "a letter . . . properly adapted . . . he would be able to answer consistently with *his* [Hamilton's] honor." Then, at long last, the concession "that the conversation to which Doctor Cooper alluded, turned wholly on political topics, and did not attribute to Col. Burr, any instance of dishonorable conduct, nor relate to his private character."[37]

According to the editors of the Hamilton Papers, the first draft of Hamilton's reply, "presumably dictated by Hamilton," had read as follows:

General Hamilton says he cannot imagine to what Doctor Cooper may have alluded unless it were to a conversation at Mr. Taylor's in Albany last winter, (at which Mr. Taylor he and General H— were present) General H—cannot recollect distinctly the particulars of that conversation so as to undertake to repeat them, without running the risk of varying or omitting what might be deemed important circumstances. The expressions are entirely forgotten, and the specific ideas imperfectly remembered; but to the best of his recollection it consisted of comments on the political principles and views of Col. Burr, and the results that might be expected from them in the event of his election as governor, without reference to any particular instance of past conduct, or to private character.[38]

Hamilton then suggested that—while Burr was drafting his version of what Hamilton asserted he could not himself remember of his own comments—Burr might also prepare his own catalogue of specific charges levied by Hamilton against him over the preceding fourteen years, and to which he had objection. Then, Hamilton wrote, he could decide which he wished to affirm and which he would admit to being unfair. Thus a major general and former Secretary of the Treasury suggested that the Vice President of the United States compile a compendium of allegations for what was in effect a public record, a detailed indictment of himself, in the full glare of public attention, of which a magnanimous review would be made, reserving to himself a judgment as to whether or not in each instance it was a transgression of the code of gentlemanly discourse.[39]

It is often left unsaid, in reviews of this situation, that this was not a reciprocal shouting match. Burr had made no attacks upon Hamilton, except that Hamilton had unfairly attacked his personal honor. There was considerably more he might have said, but for more than a decade all belligerent language had come from one of the parties. Burr was not blameless. There were grounds for some of Hamilton's charges. And there would have been no duel had Burr withdrawn in sackcloth to a monastery. As it was, however, he declined to do so. Acting as a gentleman of his time might be expected to behave, he left them both without an exit, except a ritual—or, beyond ritual, an actual—duel, stating that he was "obliged to conclude that there is, on the part of Mr. Hamilton, a settled and implacable malevolence; that he will never cease, in his conduct toward Mr. Burr, to violate those courtesies of life. . . . [T]hese things must have an end."[40]

Burr challenged.

Hamilton accepted.

6

Fascination

[There is] . . . a species of fascination and affection—distinct as it were from another self—that becomes so hateful and insupportable, that destruction is the only relief.

(Dr. Allan Hamilton on his grandfather's feelings for Aaron Burr)

What was that "fascination" to which Allan Hamilton referred?[1] The word was brought to the subject before us by Hamilton himself, writing of Burr that "his address was pleasing, his manners were more, they were *fascinating* [my italics]." What can this mean? What is "fascination?" Clinically, it is being powerfully drawn by the gravitational force of oneself, in projection. And in Hamilton's case that projected self was a person whose "ambition is unlimited," whose "sole spring of action is an inordinate ambition." Burr's ambition! That from a man who had written of himself: "The love of fame [is] the ruling passion of the noblest minds." Burr was not given to passion; Hamilton was; yet he wrote of Burr: "He is of a temper to undertake the most hazardous enterprise." That is exactly what John Adams said of Hamilton.[2]

Ambitious. Passionate. And "bankrupt beyond redemption," wrote this man who left his wife nothing but a mortgaged house and a worthless claim on Ohio River property—property which happened to be a few hundred yards from Blennerhasset's Island, where Burr's treason occurred, according to Jefferson. Most astonishing, Hamilton wrote that Burr was forced into sharp practice because of a need to provide for a large and demanding brood! Burr had a single surviving child, while Hamilton kept his wife pregnant until she had borne him eight children.

As noted at the outset of our discussion, Hamilton contended that his discourses about Burr were limited to their *public* differences but admitted in his last letter to his wife (and posterity) that Dr. Cooper had been correct: "On different occasions I . . . have made very unfavorable criticisms on particular instances of the private conduct of this gentleman."[3]

What were these charges of "instances of . . . private conduct" that were so heinous as to require expiation in blood? What exactly did Hamilton say? No one knows, because it was in no one's interest to reveal precisely what it was. But there was a pattern of projection in Hamilton's charges. Self-disgust is the propellant of projection. Loathing of the other is its consequence. Projection is not hypocrisy, though it looks like it. It is seldom conscious, as hypocrisy is, by definition. And one may be a hypocrite in total isolation, while projection requires a screen—a person projected upon. Therefore the hypocritical Hamilton indicted by Latrobe for prating "of religion, and order, and [who] went to church from the bed of the wife of his friend," was distinct from the projecting Hamilton, who behaved as "an insatiable libertine" while insisting that Burr was the "profligate," the "voluptuary in the extreme."[4]

Many writers, including several novelists, have assumed that the references to Burr's private character referred to his sexuality. This is not necessarily the case: "Private matters" could have included financial probity or untruthfulness. Leaving to fiction further speculations, we can assert with confidence that the voluptuary Hamilton was charged with "incest" by John Adams, presumably referring to his notorious flirtations with his wife's sister, Angelica Church. Adams wrote of Hamilton's "fornications, adulteries, and his incests . . . [required by] a superabundance of secretions which he could not find whores enough to draw off." Mrs. Church flirted with both her brother-in-law Hamilton and with Burr, directly, repeatedly, and in writing. On one occasion, she wrote to her sister, the plain and perpetually pregnant Elizabeth, "I love him very much and if you were as generous as the Old Romans you would lend him to me for a little while." Flirting with Angelica Church was, however, everybody's diversion; Jefferson wrote to her—and probably behaved toward her—as he did toward Mrs. Maria Cosway, the Anglo-Italian woman of the world with whom he had a romance in Paris, who was married at the time, it may be noted.[5]

An astonishing amount of prurient curiosity has been lavished in speculation as to what Hamilton said against Burr that might justify Cooper's term "despicable." All such inquiries begin by assuming that Cooper was speaking the truth—that Hamilton had, in fact, said of Burr something new, and worse, than what he had said of him often before. Each of us must make his or her own mind up about that. It is quite likely that Cooper was lying, though many a salacious paragraph has been dumped into the abyss between Hamilton's first denial that he had said *anything* of Burr's private character and his later admission to his wife that he had in fact said much about it. There was, however, nothing new in that. For years, Hamilton had projected upon Burr his own sexual and financial profligacy, and regaled the world with his projections. He did not need to add anything to these charges to justify Burr's finally calling him out for them. It was Burr's response that was new.

Why should we believe Cooper's delighted report that he had heard "something more despicable"? He was eager to destroy Burr's chances of election. Leaving afloat the implication that there was something truly "despicable" "to say of him" would serve that purpose. Implication-leaving is a primary tool of irresponsible political discourse, and, as the literary history of this passage demonstrates, once started, speculation aroused reverberates forever. Once reverberating, there was no incentive for any of the Federalists present to bother to stop it. None of them would bear the risk of death by duel. Besides, many of them, by that time, wanted Burr politically dead more than they wanted Hamilton politically or even personally alive.

Jachin and Boas

There were many lurid stories circulating about sexual competition among these three, though Jefferson was not so frequently mentioned as the other two. It was said that Hamilton had wooed Theodosia Burr before Burr—but these stories probably confused him with James Monroe, who did. Others, later, asserted that Burr was the lover of Mrs. Reynolds and "set Hamilton up" with her; Burr had been her lawyer, but Hamilton's own account of his adulterous affair with her demonstrates that he needed no prompting. Even Mrs. Jumel, whom Burr married when he was in his seventies, was said to have been among Hamilton's collection of extramarital flings. We will return, later, to an inquiry into the reasons for the durability of Hamilton's charges against Burr's private life, and of Jefferson's charges against his public life, despite the array of jury verdicts and evidence against those allegations. Here we merely note that the adulterous Hamilton and the adulterous Jefferson (both admitting to having fallen from virtue in this respect) are to this day regarded by many as paragons, while Burr is set down in standard texts as a philanderer.

Latrobe, having reflected that Hamilton "went to church from the bed of the wife of his friend," wondered why he was treated as if he were Burr, who "carried unhappiness into no man's family; seduction was no part of his plan of pleasure; and yet he was abused for his libertinism more than Hamilton, for he was not a . . . hypocrite." It was not that Burr was less sexually active—they were "both inordinately addicted to the same vice," but Burr was not, said Latrobe, exploitive.[6]

These thoughts arose as Latrobe was at work upon the interior design of a chamber in the U.S. Capitol, thinking of monumental sculpture. Writing his foreman, Latrobe went on:

> If ever you get into the East Indies in consequence of the transmigration of your soul into a Hindu rajah, provided the British leave any of them alive, you will see little Hamilton and little Burr standing in the temple of Lingam (the Hindu Priapus), like the columns of Jachin and Boas in the temple of Solomon, in eternal and basaltic erection without fruition, for their sins.[7]

The symbolic language was exact: Their nature was priapic. But Burr was fastidious. Though they were both short in stature and slight of build, perhaps Burr was not so proud of anatomical disparities as was Hamilton, who, as he contemplated marriage, wrote John Laurens a letter bold even by the standards of wartime comradery and eighteenth-century sexual candor. Laurens was authorized to impart to any eligible lady that Hamilton was remarkable for his "*size* [Hamilton's emphasis], make, quality of mind and *body* [again, Hamilton's emphasis]. . . . In drawing my picture you will no doubt . . . do justice to the length of my nose, and don't forget that I . . . [five words crossed out]."[8]

Hamilton's pride, and his friends' understanding of its somewhat primitive origin, was expressed in a letter to him, in French, from Edward Stevens, referring to Hamilton's physical "grandeur." Stevens's mysterious missive fell into the hands of British intelligence and was presented to the commander of their forces in New York, Sir Henry Clinton. It baffled him. He had not grown up with Hamilton.[9]

Edward Stevens was Hamilton's intimate in youth, and John Laurens his wartime partner. Toward them and his other friends, Hamilton expressed his affection with the ardency that later flowed into his "rapturous" courtroom speeches—and into antipathies as fervent, and fervently stated.

Equal and Opposite

Hamilton, the man of passionate affection, was also given to passionate antipathy; as to Burr, envy wore channels into his psyche until it became a fascination "settled and implacable." Burr's reciprocal animosity settled in more slowly, and he did not appear to be fully conscious of it until the spring of 1804. Then, at a dinner of the Order of the Cincinnati, it could no longer be denied. Amid their fellow officers of the Revolution, comrades and colleagues, came the provocation.

Dr. Hamilton gave this account of the evening:

> Hamilton entertained the company with a song, and . . . Burr, who was present, was observed to be silent and gloomy, gazing with a marked and fixed earnestness at Hamilton during this song. It is not difficult to believe that this was one of those cases when one man breeds in the other a species of fascination and affection—distinct as it were from another self that becomes so hateful and insupportable, that destruction is the only relief.[10]

A song is communication on pitch, using a voice different from that of ordinary speech; its effects are often more intense for that reason. As anyone can verify by observing audiences as they experience the art of "master singers," song can set loose the contents of the unconscious, with consequences wonderful or appalling. Alexander Hamilton sang of death that night, concluding with this stanza.

> We're going to war, and when we die
> We'll want a man of God nearby;
> So bring your Bible and bring your drum.

This man of Bibles and drums had said thirteen years earlier that he had a "religious" reason for bedeviling one whom he called his friend. He had dined with Burr's family, and after the goodnights had been exchanged, had gone home to his desk, with Burr's wine still on his breath, to compose invectives against his host and "friend." As we have noted, he wrote on the night before their duel that he was "conscious of no *ill will* to Col. Burr, distinct from political opposition," yet that his "animadversions on the political principles, character, and views of Col. Burr . . . have been extremely severe." And so they were; was Hamilton's self-deception so complete that he could be conscious of no ill will toward a man he charged with dishonesty, profligacy, Caesarian ambition, and Catalinian conspiracy? In such perplexity, Hamilton chose to deliver his invitation—or provocation—at a dinner among comrades, men who had known them both when friends and foes wore different uniforms, and when gentlemen knew how to die.

Assisted Suicide

We have suggested earlier that Hamilton deliberately provoked Burr into a duel in a desire either to kill his evil twin, his doppelgänger, or, by being killed, to kill Burr's career. The question remains: why did Burr accommodate? Several times before, he had induced Hamilton to make private apology for derogation of his character, as one gentleman to another, and even at the end expressed regret that a statement made on an earlier occasion might still be circulating "to the prejudice of Colonel Burr," though it had been "long since explained between Colonel Burr and himself."[11]

In the spring of 1804, however, Burr came to the end of his patience. He had lost the vice presidency, lost the gubernatorial election, and suffered intolerable public and private abuse. Having threatened to "call out the first man of any respectability concerned in the infamous publications'' written by James Cheetham, whom he believed to be encouraged by Hamilton, he was ready to listen to a song of death.[12]

When one is strained, disappointed, destabilized, and vulnerable, one may come to feel a vehement interest in someone like oneself, someone constant in his attentions, even if those attentions arise in hate. Burr finally could allow himself to feel the terrible wonder that *that* was how it was for Hamilton, and had been. In the song, the lightning arced and illuminated before him, that fusion of person and projection which is often the target for a murder. That negative pole had been there all along, awaiting enough accumulation of electricity to perform its incendiary function. After the duel, Burr took to referring to ''my friend Hamilton—whom I shot.''[13]

> ''Was Hamilton a gentleman,'' asked a foreigner once in Burr's hearing. Burr resented the question, and replied with hauteur: ''Sir, *I* met him.''[14]

Burr revisited the scene of the duel when he was in his seventies, ''to oblige a young friend, who wished to see a spot so famous.'' According to James Parton, this was the ''one occasion on which he spoke of the duel seriously and eloquently.''

> As he talked, the old fire seemed to be rekindled within him; his eye blazed; his voice rose. . . . He was moved to the depths of his soul: the pent-up feelings of twenty-five years burst into speech. . . . All the way home he still spoke of the olden times, and seemed to renew his youth, and live over again his former life.[15]

The Code

No one who has tried the experiment of revisiting a scene of passion, disaster, or great joy after twenty-five or fifty years can doubt that Parton was correct about how important the place itself was in releasing Burr's ''pent-up feelings.'' Parton was apparently citing the testimony of that youthful companion and, through him, of Burr himself. How else would he know that, on that May morning, Burr's anger ''rekindled'' as he recalled how often ''he had forborne and forborne, and forgiven and forgiven, and even stooped to remonstrate.'' Had that remonstrance been made before or after Hamilton sang to Burr his death song? When had Burr resolved that there was "no choice but to slink out of sight . . . degraded and despised, or meet the calumniator on the field and silence him?"[16]

Ordinarily, there were other choices. Ordinarily, dueling was a fool's game, but a game nonetheless, of dare and counterdare, twist and spin. Seldom did it become a ritual dance of death in the Age of Reason, in which Burr and Hamilton came of age. It was a time infatuated with clockwork toys turning upon pivots, and its duelists were like automata of chivalry. Mechanically the challenger advanced, spoke, and then retreated onto his rotating carnival plate, always knowing how to stop the dance. *Twelve times* Alexander Hamilton entered the ritual. Twelve times! And never had he fired or been fired upon. Burr was a duelist only once before, and in a ritual exchange the only casualty was a coat button. Duels and the threat of duels were "demonstrations of manner, not marksmanship; . . . intricate games of dare and counter-dare, ritualized displays. . . . Each man's response to the threat of gunplay bore far more meaning than the exchange of fire itself. . . . Regardless of whether or not shots were fired . . . ritualized negotiations constituted an integral part of a duel."[17]

However, in May 1804, one such game became a contest to kill. In 1829, Burr told his interviewer at Weehawken that he had thought Hamilton "would not fight . . . [He] would slander a rival, and not stand to it unless he was cornered." But he was cornered, as much by himself as by Burr, who recalled Hamilton's face as looking "like a convicted felon . . . oppressed with the horrors of conscious guilt." That *hypocrite*, exclaimed Burr "with infinite contempt," that *voluptuary*, had written on the evening before the duel a document that read "like the confessions of a penitent monk."[18]

Hamilton had trapped himself. He could only be certain of saving his life if he avoided the duel, and thus lost his public life, which he saw as his "ability to be in future useful . . . in those crises of our public affairs which seem likely to happen." However little store he put in the opinions of the crowd, he required the approbation of gentlemen, and gentlemen dueled. He must duel, too, for a fight with Burr "would probably be inseparable from a conformity to the prejudice [among gentlemen] in this particular."[19]

When he wrote these words, Hamilton, sitting coolly in his study, manifestly did not assume that the duel would be to the death—or did not want those who read his words to think he made that assumption.

Either explanation would do, and neither tells us what was impelling his actions on the morning of the duel.

Nor could Burr "slink away." William W. Van Ness, his second, explained: "What would have been the feelings of his friends?—they must have considered him as a man, not possessing sufficient firmness to defend his own character, and consequently unworthy of their support.—While his enemies . . . would, to all the other slanders propagated toward him, have added the ignominious epithet of coward."[20]

On the morning of July 11, 1804, Hamilton, Burr, their seconds, and Dr. Hosack were rowed across the Hudson to the rocky shore of New Jersey. They climbed to the wooded shelf where Philip Hamilton had died. The seconds swept it clean of fallen branches.

Whatever he may have said to his wife about his intentions, Hamilton performed a series of deliberately provocative actions to ensure a lethal outcome. As they were taking their places, he asked that the proceedings stop, adjusted his spectacles, and slowly, repeatedly, sighted along his pistol to test his aim. Strange, that gesture. He had selected the weapons and knew things about their qualities unknown to historians until the 1970s.

The pistols had been made specially in England for his brother-in-law, John Barker Church. After the affair on Weehawken Heights, they were returned to him. They did not reappear until 1930, and then only long enough for them to be securely stowed, without examination, in the vaults of the Chase Manhattan Bank. In 1976, at the request of the U.S. Bicentennial Commission, they were removed and given for study to Merrill Lindsay, a firearms expert. Lindsay found that they hid a concealed set of hair triggers. When those triggers were set, an informed and experienced user could fire with less pressure from the finger than was required with conventional pistols, and faster than his opponent, using the other, unset pistol in the pair. They also carried "weighted bronze fore-ends, adjustable front and rear sights and a .54 caliber bore. While some of these features could be found on a cased pair of gentleman's pistols, none would appear on a proper set of dueling pistols."[21]

Burr had one of those pistols in his hand during his duel with Church. He might have learned, then, of the hair trigger, but he had no opportunity to practice with them, and Hamilton, instructed by Church, did. In testimony given later, Hamilton's second, Major Nathaniel Pendleton, asserted that as the two principals and two seconds were standing about, Pendleton asked whether or not Hamilton wanted the hair trigger set. Hamilton replied, "Not this time," and then set about his adjustments of his sights and glasses. Having issued that final threat, he fired. Did he "throw his shot away"? His bullet passed over Burr's head. Did Burr mean to inflict a fatal wound? How can anyone know? What if Burr had missed? What if Hamilton had shot twice in the air? What if Burr had then thrown his second shot away? Would they then have been able to arrange a purging common statement that all was now forgiven? The answers each of us gives to these questions depend upon whether or not we think we know what each of the two intended at each moment in this drama. What was the "intention" of either? "Intention" is a literary, not a psychological, term. As any trial lawyer knows, it cannot be discussed without qualifying which millisecond one has in mind.

For my part, I think Hamilton went to the killing field consciously weighing several alternative courses of action and consciously hoping that Burr would be yet another of those he had provoked who would let him off. The best evidence that his unconscious imperative was toward assisted suicide is that every action he took on the field was provocative. To those provocations Burr responded.

The first shots were fired by very angry men, men possessed by a need and a counterneed to extirpate a projected evil.

Hamilton fired as his arm was arcing down toward his target. His bullet passed not far over Burr's head. Was the hair trigger actually set, as Lindsay suggested? Might Pendleton have done so, in error? If so, he could never thereafter admit it. Or was the verbal exchange between Hamilton and Pendleton rehearsed and intended to deceive? "Not this time," Hamilton said. But did he and Pendleton have an understanding that whatever he said the hair trigger would be set?— This was an even worse thing to confess. Could it be that Hamilton squeezed it prematurely, before he had Burr in his sights? All Burr knew was that Hamilton had, in his dramatic provocations, indicated that he meant to fire accurately. And Burr returned the fire.

Hamilton had written, in his apologia, "I have thoughts *even of* [my emphasis] reserving my *second* [my emphasis] fire, and giving a double opportunity to Colonel Burr to pause and reflect." Or a double opportunity for Burr *not* to pause but, having reflected, to shoot to kill. At ten paces! No wonder Hamilton looked "oppressed with the horrors of conscious guilt!" He had a set of trick pistols.* But he could not make up his mind to kill or be killed. Perhaps in his confusion, being the one to be killed and the one doing the killing had become two parts of the same person. Which was he? Which the other?[22]

His confusion of purpose—and of target—was apparent in another set of actions, at variance with all the foregoing, which occurred before the firing began. When the seconds cast lots to determine the firing position, Hamilton won—but chose to face the sun. It was as if Hamilton wanted at once to be sure that Burr did not reconsider, and that Burr would also have every advantage in the killing. Yet as Hamilton swung down his arm. What? Did another part of his troubled brain take over, and control his arm?

Burr "heard the ball whistle among the branches, and saw the severed twig above his head." The smoke of Hamilton's shot cleared. Burr took his own aim, at the abdomen, where the heavy caliber bullet would prevent Hamilton's firing another round. If Burr's bullet had struck an inch or two higher or lower, the doctors later found, Hamilton might have survived. Yet Hamilton knew what he had done. As he lay bleeding on the ground: "This is a mortal wound, doctor!"[23]

Hamilton was borne to his boat and recovered consciousness enough to say "my vision is indistinct." When his sight had cleared somewhat, his eye fell upon his pistol, lying outside its case, and he said: "take care of that pistol; it is undischarged and still cocked; it might go off and do harm;—Pendleton knows that I did not intend to fire at him."[24]

Hamilton's words in the boat were spoken as he tried to turn his head to look at Dr. Hosack. In shock, bleeding internally from a terrible wound, Hamilton summoned the energy to present an argument to his last jury, trying to persuade Hosack that he had not meant to fire. Under such circumstances, human memory does not accurately recover data recently stored. The gun was *not* still dangerous. It *had* been fired. Hamilton's actual intentions at the moment of firing were

---

*One competent writer has suggested that they were not trick pistols "unless Burr did not know about the hair trigger" and that both Burr and Van Ness "seemed to know about the hair trigger in advance." The trickiness was there, in the hidden contrivance, and in the fact that Burr could not have the experience of working with it in advance, while Hamilton and Church possessed the weapons. And I have found no evidence that Burr knew of the existence of the trick, though he had held one pistol in his hand during his duel with Church. If he commented on it, I have not found the comment.

probably lost to him, as they are to us. His feelings for Burr had been tearing at him so long that it is likely that when he came to Weehawken love, hate, and conscience still contested with each other and with the imperative to do what a gentleman should do and, finally, what posterity would approve.

Burr went home and awaited the news. When he heard that Hamilton had died, he went into a profound depressive lassitude. Bedeviled by the calumnies of both the Jeffersonians and the Hamiltonians, harassed by creditors who had run out of patience with his improvidence, he operated below the level of calculation, on a kind of autopilot, guided into his past, toward military glory.

"I wish there was a war," Alexander Hamilton had written thirty-six years earlier, a war to purify the ignoble past, to resolve all uncertainties, to simplify life. So it was for Burr in 1804. He turned backward from the killing ground, where friend fired upon friend with ambiguous intention, toward a good, clear, simplifying war against somebody unknown, someone with whom he had not shared wine and food and song. Some Spaniard, perhaps.

PART TWO

Character Tested by Slavery and Secession

We have come to 1804, the year in which the enemies of Aaron Burr, despite their differences with each other, gathered against him and drove him from the center of American public life to its fringes. As they harried him forth, they tested his character and revealed more of their own.

In 1803, Thomas Jefferson forced Burr out of the vice presidency, then entered into a cobelligerency with Alexander Hamilton to finish him off. Together they chivvied forward a coalition of New York politicians to defeat Burr in his attempt at election as New York's governor. They succeeded. It was a vicious campaign. In the summer, Hamilton and Burr fought their fatal duel, and, after Hamilton's death, Burr made ready for his first desperate sortie into the Spanish and Indian borderlands.

To this point in our story, we have focused upon character, assessing each of our protagonists as he emerged upon the national stage. In Part Two, we retrace our steps through the 1780s and 1790s, to see what we have missed by our narrow focus. Just beyond our range of vision, all along, have been broader circumstances: slavery and secession.

The Founding Fathers faced quandaries posed by both—from the beginning, and even before the beginning, of the Republic. And, in their responses, each of our protagonists affected the trajectory traced by these powerful determinants of American history. Because of what was done, and not done, between 1775 and 1804, the American polity lost the opportunity truly to create a New Order in the Universe, and the time came closer when slavery and secession would bring the nation to Civil War. We begin this part of our discussion with Chapter Seven, which deals with the civil rights movement of the 1790s, in which Hamilton and Burr, together with John Jay, took the lead in New York. Lamentably we must follow that story with its aftermath, the first Jim Crow period, having much in common with that which came a century later, including disenfranchisement and legalized resegregation. Some historians do not like the application of phrases like Jim Crow, or civil rights movement, grounded in one period, to events in another, but in these two cases, there is more to be gained by the shock of similarities—and lost opportunities—than in a little loss of hermetic pressure.

Separatism among the former colonies of Great Britain which declared their independence in 1775 began before there was a United States. In this sense, secession preceded Union. Jefferson, Hamilton, and Burr reacted in distinct ways to that threat, as we shall see in Chapters Eight, Nine, and Ten.

They differed as well in their response to slavery. The ideal of a New Order in the Universe proclaimed by the Founders in their Great Seal was incompatible with the ownership of one human by another. Most of the Founders acknowledged that incongruity: To use the sort of homely metaphor introduced into their councils by Benjamin Franklin, they had cut into that apple, and they all saw the worm. Their New Order was conceived in liberty. It was dedicated to the proposition that all men are created equal. But it was contaminated by slavery, and not just in the South. Slavery was an American institution, as important to the economies of Dutch farmers on the Hudson and to merchants of Newport, Bristol, and New York as to planters along the Santee and merchants of Charleston, Beaufort, and Savannah. That being the case, as the character of each of our protagonists was tested by their responses to threats of secession, they were also required to demonstrate their seriousness of moral purpose by the degree to which they exerted themselves toward shrinking the power and extent of slavery. All three asserted their intention to do so, on moral grounds. In Part Two we shall see how they behaved.

Jefferson was in his late fifties in 1800; Hamilton and Burr, in their early forties. Their characters were formed; now let us assay their metal in their responses to slavery, secession, and to the racial currents running beneath the surface of American foreign policy.

The Civil Rights Movement of the 1790s
and the First Jim Crow Period

> When you come hither you must send for Frederic, and open your whole heart to him. He loves me almost as much as Theodosia does; and he does love you to adoration.
>
> (Burr to Theodosia, writing about a Negro slave in their service, January 27, 1804, *Letters*, p. 171)

> [John Jay would] only have the smallest prospect of success . . . [because] his popularity was lost, or totally absorbed in consequence of his exertions . . . in favor of manumitting the slaves.
>
> (Van Gaasbeck to Burr in 1792, *Burr Papers*, Vol. I, p. 104; Burr declined to run against him.)

No one can justly say that it was easy for Aaron Burr, Alexander Hamilton, or John Jay to struggle toward the abolition of slavery in New York. Their long-sustained and arduous endeavor tested their characters; slavery was as deeply entrenched in New York as in Virginia, and probably more profitably. Despite the heroic efforts of the abolitionists and of the blacks themselves, there were still slaves in New York until the outbreak of the Civil War. From the 1840s onward, its harbor was once again thriving upon an illicit slave trade. Among its manufacturers, "Cotton Whigs" saw their economic interest as intertwined with that of the South. Therefore, it is small wonder that when the South seceded in 1861, the mayor of New York proposed in his State of the City Address that the city secede as well, taking Long Island with it. The new state of Tri-insula, so created, would remain neutral in the Civil War, and the port would prosper on blockade-running, as it had in 1812. Though the secession scheme foundered, proslavery gangs, inflamed by Tammany, disrupted the war effort with race riots and antidraft riots. Even after the Union victory in 1865, the New York Democrats resisted the Fifteenth Amendment to the U.S. Constitution, requiring equality of suffrage.

The battle against race-based slavery and race-based discrimination began in New York at the White Plains Convention of 1776, at which the colony's revolutionaries gathered to create their new government, guided toward abolition by John Jay and Gouverneur Morris. Though Jay and Morris were joined in the fight by Hamilton and Burr at the end of the 1780s, slavery was so deeply ingrained in the culture of the Hudson Valley that a map drawn showing concentrations of servitude per capita in the United States in 1800 as graded shades from white to black, county by county, would show the region from Peekskill to the sea in a density of darkness equaled only by the region around the Chesapeake in Virginia and Maryland, and by tidewater South Carolina and Georgia.

Burr entered into his first working alliance with the Federalists during the 1790s to free New York's slaves and to protect refugee slaves from recapture by slave-stealing gangs operating on the streets of New York. This chapter describes the campaign for emancipation in which Burr and the Federalists were joined by the free blacks concentrated in the Federalist precincts at the tip of Manhattan Island and, even then, in Harlem. It is true that there was political benefit to Burr, Jay, and Hamilton in finding support in those free black precincts, but there was greater cost in alienating the votes of the city's slave-merchants and the slaveholding farmers and planters upstate.

A concurrence of moral purpose united Burr, Hamilton, Jay, Gouverneur Morris, and Rufus King, until Morris retired from the U.S. Senate in 1802, Hamilton was killed in 1804, and Burr exiled in 1808. Only then did the balance swing toward their opponents. Jay and King were virtually alone in their generation in keeping up the fight, and even they were unable to resist the power of the rising racist democracy. Free blacks were systematically deprived of the franchise. Finally, just as emancipation was complete, so was disenfranchisement.

Let us return to our atlas of slave-density maps, turning back to pages covering the process by which that density became so dark in New York. In the seventeenth century, the Hudson River Valley under Dutch rule had a higher proportion of black slaves to white settlers than did Virginia at the time. In the early eighteenth century, there were 3,400 white families in Dutchess County, New York, holding 1,360 slaves. Many white families in New York City—some estimates say 43 percent—owned slaves, while along the Hudson, *swarten* did the heavy, hot work. Even after the Revolution of 1776–83, Dutchess County retained a higher proportion of slaves than did western Virginia, while New York, as a whole, had a higher proportion of slaves than North Carolina—a higher proportion than any of the "slave states" of Maryland, Delaware, and Missouri had in 1860. In 1790, there were *areas* of New York in which blacks made up a larger proportion of the population than they did in Kentucky or Tennessee when those two *territories* were admitted as slave territories, and a larger proportion than in the slave *states* of North Carolina and Delaware.[1]

Further, when blacks sought freedom in New York, the ripostes of the slave power were as merciless as anywhere in the South. After a rebellion in 1712, blacks were deprived of night-schooling. After another, in 1741, thirty-four men and women were burned alive or hanged. The pressure to manumit continued, however. Freed blacks became more numerous and politically important as they were joined by others who had, in effect, manumitted themselves. Fleeing the patroonships, they found sanctuary in the Catskills, intermarrying with the Indians. (Their descendants are still there.)

The presence of so many people of African descent in the city of New York and along the Hudson River aroused a countervailing force. A working agreement emerged between the southern slaveholders and the New York interests headed by the Clintons and Livingstons. In 1790, the Livingston clan held thirty-five slaves, and Livingston kin thirty more. Many of these were the residual products of the family's importing activities that had contributed greatly to the tenfold increase in the number of slaves in the province from 1698 to 1771; Philip Livingston's family alone had accounted for the importation of 219 Africans. There was a pause in importation during the Revolution, and thousands of slaves escaped to freedom by accompanying the British evacuation of New York at the war's end—for them, it was, indeed, a revolution. Those who remained in New York soon discovered that until the Manumission Society was organized, things had gotten worse, not better, for blacks. Despite the efforts of Burr, Hamilton, and Jay, the slave importers were busy. There was a 23 percent increase in slaves and a 33 percent increase in slaveholders in New York City in the 1790s.[2]

As Chancellor Livingston discussed high Republican politics at Arryl (R. L.—Robert Livingston) House, visiting Virginians could be perfectly comfortable. Four Negro boys padded barefoot about his breakfast table, and there were another eleven about the house and grounds. There were many reasons why the Virginians felt comfortable with the chancellor, preferring him to Burr as the New Yorker of choice for Vice President in 1795. And there were reasons other than his economic theories that the planters abhorred the abolitionist Hamilton.

The Fourteen-Year Campaign

Both Burr and Hamilton took the proposition that all men—black or white—were created equal. (As we shall see, Burr insisted that women, too, were equal, while Jefferson refused to extend the principle of equality beyond white men.)

In 1779, Hamilton composed a little essay on race. In his first draft, he wrote of Negroes that "their natural faculties are perhaps as good as ours." Thinking it over, he crossed out the word "perhaps" and inserted instead "probably." Later, he tried again: A first draft said that slaves were "bound by the laws of degraded humanity to hate their masters," but in the final version, he scratched out the word "degraded" and inserted "injured" instead.[3]

It is a melancholy coincidence that Hamilton's liveliest modern biographer, James Thomas Flexner, denigrates his commitment to freeing the slaves, and so does Burr's, Milton Lomask. In two volumes of biography, Lomask provides a total of one and a half paragraphs to the entire record of Burr's abolitionism.

Burr, like Hamilton and many other contemporaries, never seems to have felt any compulsion to adjust practical conduct to personal conviction. Burr inveighed frequently against slavery . . . but from time to time both men owned slaves. Burr's battle for instant emancipation came to naught. . . . As Governor George Clinton and his advisers well knew, the upstate landowners, big and small, were not yet ready for emancipation.[4]

That is far from the full story. Burr and Hamilton *did* "adjust their . . . conduct to personal conviction." Otherwise, they would not have secured the support of free blacks. Skeptical for good reason, they, like whites, could read the newspapers. The Federalists had been their best hope from 1776 onward; it was no secret that Rufus King, not Jefferson, first proposed that there be no slavery in the Northwest Territories, and only Burr, among the Republicans of the first generation, was noticeable for his exertions on their behalf. That was why he was celebrated in an editorial in the *Liberator* by William Lloyd Garrison on January 8, 1858, as being the proponent of immediate abolition fifty years earlier.[5]

It was probably Hamilton who brought his father-in-law around; by 1789, Philip Schuyler had come a long way from the Saratoga battlefield, where he apologized that he had been forced to recruit free blacks. In the late 1780s, the apologies were over. Schuyler was among the leaders who sought the votes of free blacks and endeavored to bring freedom to more of them. New York finally agreed to abolition in 1799, as a result of a long campaign led by Burr as leader of the Republicans in the legislature and by Jay as governor. When the chroniclers tell us that freedom was voted by a predominantly Federalist Assembly "on an almost straight party vote of sixty-eight to twenty-three," the "almost" is a badge of courage for Burr. In 1785, his proposal for immediate emancipation had been defeated by a vote of 33 to 13, but he persisted over the next fourteen years, against a coalition of slaveholding landowners, slave-working farmers, and artisans fearing black competition. The fight was not won in 1799, but the course was set.

A fourteen-year fight is a gauge of character. And, when it is fought together with another ambitious man, for agreed moral purposes, it becomes difficult to believe that that man is ferociously bent upon your destruction. How could Burr have believed that of Hamilton? They had not only served as occasional cocounsel in the courtroom. They had been colleagues in a long battle to achieve an ideal.

Good Company

Just as we need Burr to understand Hamilton and Jefferson, the Burr-Jay common front in racial politics (like the Burr-Gallatin linkage to which we next turn) informs us more accurately about these men than what was said of them by those with a reason to derogate them. Through the refracting lenses of these relationships, we may discern much of importance about their opponents. In particular, we may discern why Thomas Jefferson had so much in common with the Clinton and Livingston factions with which he came into alliance in order to eliminate Burr.

From 1776 onward, John Jay developed his own ways of coping with the moral imperative of the principle that all men are created equal, while at the same time demonstrating, in his behavior toward Jefferson, Hamilton, and Burr, how he assessed the responses of these three to that imperative. He avoided the mannerisms in Burr which appeared to suggest an unwillingness to curry favor by effusiveness—an unwillingness to trust often provokes the reaction that a person so coy must be untrustworthy. Instead, Jay was infuriatingly, but reassuringly, condescending.

The upright Jay, like the conscientious Albert Gallatin, found Burr acceptable as a friend. Does that not suggest that we be wary of accepting what was said of Burr by Jefferson and Hamilton? Gallatin and Jay were exemplars of "a school of rigid self-disciplinarians and high-minded men who invested the foundation of American nationality with a peculiar mantle of righteousness and dignity." How could men of that sort have seen anything in Burr to admire if, in truth, he was "worthless . . . shallow . . . superficial . . . bad, unscrupulous, tricky . . . and utterly devoid of any moral sense," as described by Henry Cabot Lodge in his adulatory biography of Hamilton?[6]

Jay knew Burr at first hand, yet he was no more deterred from friendship with him by what Alexander Hamilton said than he might have been had he read Lodge. Jay, Burr, Hamilton, and Jefferson inhabited a world in which paid character assassins were set against each of them. Jay probably read with an admiring smile, much as we might, what one of these hired guns, James Cheetham, set in print on April 28, 1804. Cheetham expressed outrage that Burr had entertained "a considerable number of gentlemen of color—upwards of twenty [at a] . . . ball and supper" at his residence. It is remarkable that as much attention has not been given to Aaron Burr's dinner parties as to the occasion on which Theodore Roosevelt welcomed Booker T. Washington to the White House, and Eleanor Roosevelt's habitual entertainment of people of color in her home.[7]

Religion, Conviction, and Abolition

The root system of the Jay-Burr alliance in matters of race can be traced to their common religious background. Among clockwork deists, contemptuous of traditional Christian religious practice, and abolitionist only out of convention, Burr, Jay, and Jay's wife grounded their racial views in their religious faith, the faith of Burr's Edwards cousins and antecedents.

John Adams pointed us in this direction (in his acerbic way) by writing of Burr, his fellow student of theology, that he was "the son of one president, and the grandson of another president of . . . Princeton University; the idol of all Presbyterians in New York, New England, New Jersey, Pennsylvania, Maryland, Virginia, and elsewhere."[8]

The "Presbyterian party" in New Jersey was led by Governor William Livingston (Burr called him Billy), the father-in-law of Jay, and a more radical Livingston than those of the "Manor" line on the other side of the Hudson. The "Presbyterian party" inclined to the views of Timothy Edwards, Burr's foster father, who was dismissed from his pulpit for advocating an end to slavery, and of Burr's uncle Judge Pierpont Edwards, who had made himself persona non grata in Connecticut by his intransigently abolitionist views. Burr and Jay thus shared a tradition that was more important than partisan differences.

Jay has been described as a prig, and Burr as an accommodating politician, and some biographers, apparently drawing their impression of Aaron Burr from what was said of him by Hamilton and Jefferson, have expressed puzzlement that he and Jay were friends and frequent allies. How could the candid, humorless, virtuous, grave, and dutiful Jay be so obviously fond of the morally veiled, apparently cynical, witty, adventurous, and erratic Burr? Yet we think of Jay when we read Burr's self-description of 1812, that he was "a grave, silent, strange sort of animal, insomuch that we know not what to make of him." An equivalently Aurelian privacy had been noted in Jay as a young man when he was said to be "serious," "grave," and "sedate" and wrote of

95

himself as having been made "staid" by a mixture of "bashfulness and pride." Burr refused to play to the crowd, drawing down the anathema of the same sort of critics as the historian who wrote of Jay as being "as weirdly impressive as a walking statue, over whose irritable nature, unquenchable vanity, and iron contempt there lay a quite persuasive veneer of gentle and conciliatory manners."[9]

Burr and Jay did not make themselves accessible to the public or to posterity, and the manner of their deaths lacked the drama of Hamilton's. They had no illusions that democracy, because capacious, should be expected to be generous, or because open, to be wise. True, they were habitually "grave" as to matters they found "serious," and most serious of all to them was the composition of the American polity, the New Order for which they labored. They did not wish it to be divided into sections, to be ruptured by anarchy, or riven by racial cleavages. Jay wrote somberly of what might be expected of the perfectability of human nature and the virtue of the multitude. Burr agreed but contented himself with gentle mockery of the illusions of Jefferson's "Jacobin leveling principles."

The affinity of Jay and Burr began under circumstances in which two other men might have begun to hate each other. In 1792, for the first time, the upstate Federalists urged Burr to accept their support to run against the Clintons as candidate for the governorship of New York. Without an adequate knowledge of Burr's views as to slavery, Peter van Gaasbeck, an Ulster County Federalist, pressed him to enter the lists because Jay would "only have the smallest prospect of success. . . . [H]is popularity was lost, or totally absorbed in consequence of his exertions . . . in favor of manumitting the slaves." Van Gaasbeck mistook his man, and his man's feeling for both Jay and what Jay stood for. Burr declined to run against him; George Clinton did, the race card was played, and Clinton won.[10]

Burr was, however, assigned the task by his "party" of disputing Jay's claim to having won the tightly contested election, but did so with sufficient grace that when the canvassers, in the end, determined that the governorship had once more been won by Clinton, Jay declined to be offended. Burr had done his legal best for his client but had also made known that he had not supported Clinton in the election. In 1795, van Gaasbeck's Ulster County Federalists actually nominated Burr against Jay; once again he declined the contest, and this time Jay was elected.

The Manumission Society

Alexander Hamilton came as a self-constructed character to the position in which Aaron Burr and John Jay found themselves naturally, through their lineage and their childhood training. Hamilton is therefore even more to be admired. It is sad that James Thomas Flexner, otherwise also to be admired, felt emboldened to write of Hamilton's "personal conviction" with regard to slavery without searching sufficiently for evidence of that conviction. How can a historian be confident of what was in another man's heart? But Flexner wrote that Hamilton "was not seriously wrung by the plight" of Nicholas Cruger's slaves and that

> when a citizen of New York, after the Revolution had been won, he never went beyond what was expected of a member of his circle in that vaguely abolitionist city. As secretary of the Society for the Promotion of the Manumission of Slaves, he signed a petition urging manumission, but he himself owned, bought, and sold house slaves for himself and his friends. . . . His opposition was, in sum, extremely mild for a man of his combative temperament. Hamilton actively crusaded for many things in his life; abolition was not one of them.[11]

We will come, at the very end of this book, to an equivalently bold assertion about the contents of Burr's "heart" offered by John Quincy Adams, and to Adams's later implicit repentance for such boldness, under extraordinary circumstances.

Flexner deepened his error by seeking to convince his readers not only that Hamilton was callous as to slavery but also that the Manumission Society was a tabby cat. What are we told by those who have studied the matter carefully? Dr. McManus tells us that as a "real working organization" it circulated petitions, awarded prizes for tracts which it printed and distributed, sponsored lectures and orations, and, most important of all, exposed violations of the laws against the slave trade by placing watchers to report purchases and to spot ships known to participate in the trade. Its lawyers, such as Hamilton and Burr, processed thirty-six cases of unlawful enslavement as legal counsel for blacks.[12]

No one who has experienced the reaction of merchants to a civil rights boycott, or that of newspaper owners to the loss of advertising revenue, would dismiss as trivial the risks taken by Burr, Hamilton, and Jay in organizing "boycotts against . . . merchants . . . and newspaper owners . . . involved . . . in the trade. . . . The Society had a special committee of antislavery militants who visited newspaper offices . . . to remind publishers of the unwisdom of accepting advertisements for the purchase or sale of slaves. Another committee kept a list of persons who either participated in or invested in the slave trade . . . and urged [members] to boycott anyone listed." Even without specific personal experience with boycotts, we know that action of this sort requires character. A general knowledge of the human heart instructs us that racism is deeply rooted, and a general knowledge of the politics of the 1790s, or of the 1990s, tutors us that bland smiling politicians do not tackle the rooting out. That requires more than "what was [or is] expected."[13]

Leon Higginbotham, the first great black jurist to review the record of Aaron Burr, judged him to have been the "leader" of the "militant group of antislavery representatives." To McManus's list, Higginbotham added the success of these militants in winning thirty-four of the thirty-six cases they litigated and their establishment of schools to teach black children their rights, as well as academic and vocational subjects.[14]

For fifty years, Jay remained an ardent and constant foe to slavery. After proposing abolition in New York in 1775, after organizing the Manumission Society a decade later and joining Burr in the long fight for emancipation in the New York state government, he was still in the fight as late as 1819. In his last public action, he entered the Missouri debate to support the position that the Constitution provided Congress with the right to regulate interstate commerce in slaves, as well as to terminate the traffic in slaves from overseas after 1808. As noted earlier, Jay's position brought him into conflict with James Madison, his old partner in *The Federalist Papers*, who took the view that slavesellers could not, and should not, constitutionally be prevented from disposing of their surplus human property to the lands of the West.[15]

The Presence of Washington

In that West, brooding over the Ohio Valley and the route to New Orleans that he had once dreamed of pursuing in his old age, awaited the specter of George Washington. What sort of West was it to be? Washington had views on this matter, and the Madison of 1819 was not in accord with those views. Washington has been present through- out our tale, as he was in the nation's life: the most imposing figure in American politics from 1775 until his death twenty-four years later. One came into his presence with diffidence, but, having checked our ties and hair, let us come somewhat closer to him. Let us at the same time bring into that presence our three leading characters, so that we may observe how each of them acted toward him and toward the prob- lems Washington selected in his final years as worthy of his considered attention. Among those problems were secession and slavery.

Washington died in 1799, leaving to Jefferson the Louisiana Pur- chase, by which a second chance was provided for nation-making. West of the Appalachians, beyond the fixed sway of slavery, there might be— if not a New Order in the Universe—then a Renewed Order. Had Washington lived, it is likely that he would have insisted upon another try for a racially inclusive republic. His view of Negro slavery had evolved and brought him toward agreement with Hamilton, Burr, and Jay rather than with Jefferson, Madison, and Monroe. That is what Washington meant in saying to Edmund Randolph that if the North separated from the South on the issue of slavery, he had made up his mind "to move and be of the northern." Where in the North that might have been is indicated by a letter he wrote not long before his death to his former officers who dwelt in the slave-free Northwest Ter- ritory, telling them he longed to settle with them but was too old and infirm. Manasseh Cutler, their leader, had invited Washington and Hamilton to join them at Marietta, where a new start could be made without slavery. "In order to begin right, there will be no wrong habits to combat, no inveterate systems to overturn—there is no rubbish to remove."[16]

But, of course, the rubbish had accumulated in overwhelming bulk. By 1820, slavery had claimed half the Louisiana Purchase. The differences among these Founders as to the applicability of the prin- ciples of the Declaration of Independence to the western territories began to emerge after 1784, when Jefferson made his effort to limit the spread of slavery beyond the Appalachians. Three years later, the final version of the Northwest Ordinance, written, though not initiated, by Jefferson, prohibited slavery in *territories* organized north of the Ohio River, but it did not extend to cover those areas when they became organized as *states*. Then they could do what they willed.

When Kentucky was admitted to the Union in 1792, it adopted a slaveowners' constitution by a narrow margin, over the fervent opposition of many taking their lead from Gallatin, Hamilton, Burr, and Jay. After another debate on the question, Tennessee came into the Union on the Kentucky model in 1796, despite resistance from the area of East Tennessee that held out for the Union in 1861 and from the Northern Federalists.

In 1798, the Mississippi Territory was organized under the terms of the Northwest Ordinance but *without* its prohibition of slavery. Once again, there was an explosion of debate. George Thacher of Massachusetts attempted to reinsert that inhibition. Once again, the slave power prevailed, though East Tennessee had as few slaves as West Arkansas, which resisted the entry of that territory under a slaveowners' constitution. The Hillhouse Debates of 1806 reopened the question when a reenergized opposition to the spread of slavery sought to bring it to an end in the Louisiana Purchase. Those debates occurred as the abolitionist Burr was himself arousing the anxieties of the slaveowners in Louisiana, and while the senior officials of the Spanish empire on the western boundaries of the Purchase were reasserting royal policies aimed at destabilizing the Anglo-American slave system. Burr was dead politically, Jay was out of office and getting old, and neither John Quincy Adams nor Albert Gallatin was yet wholly free of subservience to the planters.

Amid all this rubbish, in 1820, James Madison directed the full force of his magnificent lawyer's intellect into the argument that Jay was wrong and that, though Congress had the power to intrude into free states to recover escaped slaves, it could not intrude into slave states to halt the interstate commerce in humans. Madison's partner, Thomas Jefferson, had moved far from his positions of 1784 and 1787. Then he had urged Congress to forbid slavery beyond the Appalachians and, when that effort failed, endorsed a congressional ban on slavery north of the Ohio River. Now, like Madison, he denied to Congress the power to keep slavery out of Missouri.

This debate of the 1820s appears in these pages because it was fought over the intentions of the Founders in the 1780s. There was no doubt that one kind of interstate commerce in slaves had been squarely placed within the regulatory power of Congress by the insistence of the slaveowners, the commerce in slaves who were captured by bounty hunters in free states and territories and returned to their owners. The Constitution had set forth the basis for a fugitive slave law in Article IV, Section II(2), and Article VI of the Northwest Ordinance of 1787, written concurrently, made the matter specific. Fugitives *anywhere* might "be lawfully reclaimed by their masters," and the slaveowners took that to mean that the officials of the invaded state could be forced by federal law to cooperate with slavehunters.

It was a matter of mobility versus portability. According to the slaveowners' argument, Congress was to oppose slaves escaping, and thus being moved of their own volition. Portability at their masters' behest was quite another matter. As to that, Madison could brook no interference from Jay. Perhaps he recalled that on November 9, 1802, Jefferson, still President of the United States and still professing to deplore both slavery and the traffic in slaves, wrote Governor Drayton of South Carolina asking him to issue a permit to Jefferson's son-in-law Thomas Mann Randolph so that a coffle of Virginia-owned slaves could pass across South Carolina to a market in Georgia. South Carolina by that time, however, wished to monopolize the Georgia market, and Drayton refused, adding that he was acting evenhandedly because he had declined a similar request from Wade Hampton.

Character is effected by circumstance. That is certain. By 1802, Jefferson was already caught in a situation in which he held his own child, or children, as slaves and knew full well that his fellow Virginians were selling children away from their parents. More than 13 percent of the slaves they shipped to the Louisiana firm of Franklin and Armfield, to work in the killing cane fields, were children taken from their mothers.

Sometimes, on the other hand, character effects circumstance. So it was for Burr and Hamilton in their antislavery work; they did not separate their theoretical principles from their personal convenience. Burr did both legal and political work for the Manumission Society, when he could ill afford the time or the animosities he aroused. Hamilton did likewise, and commenced his participation by proposing that all members free their own slaves and accepting the chairmanship of the society's Committee on Ways and Means—meaning, in this instance, not the finance committee but, instead, the group charged with finding better tactical methods to achieve justice for people of African descent. "They [slaves] are men," he had said, "though degraded to the condition of slavery." They might be treated as property in the South, but "they are persons known to the municipal laws of the states which they inhabit, as well as the laws of nature."[17]

Burr, Hamilton, Jefferson, the French, and the Blacks

It was no accident that Jefferson wrote his *Notes on Virginia* in French; he wished to establish his character among the antislavery *philosophes*. It is one of the modest tragedies of his life that he did not pass that test after those Frenchmen found an unattractive dissonance between what he said were his convictions and what he did. Hamilton won a higher grade, though Jefferson was wont to treat his rival as having a fixed and irrational antipathy to all things French. In fact, Hamilton corresponded with his most intimate friends in their language, made use of French architects (the Mangin brothers) for his own require-ments, sustained friendships with many French officers, especially with Lafayette, and, in the early years of the French Revolution, supported close relations with the moderate governments established just after the fall of the monarchy. There were many reasons for this, among them that Hamilton and the leaders of these governments agreed as to the desirability of abolishing slavery and as to many of the ways and means of doing so.

As violence increased in France under the Jacobins, and despotism returned with Napoleon, bringing reimposition of slavery in the French West Indian possessions, Hamilton turned away from France. Jefferson did so as well, but only after a decade had passed—and, dur-ing that decade, considerable traffic with Napoleon, whom Hamilton abhorred. In the 1790s, those moderate French revolutionaries averse to both tyranny and slavery, whose leader was Brissot de Warville, learned how different were Hamilton's racial politics from those of Jefferson.

Brissot was a professional journalist who came to America ostensibly to pursue investments made in Ohio for a family foothold to be oc-cupied by his brother-in-law. Actually, however, he was engaged in or-ganizing abolitionist lodges in cells similar to those of the Freemasons. Some members called themselves Les Amis des Noirs (Friends of the Blacks), while others merely described themselves as members of the League of Franco-American Friendship.

Hamilton endorsed this aspect of Brissot's work; Jefferson did not, but, as we shall see, chose to assist him in another. The Friends of the Blacks shared membership and objectives with the New York Manumission Society, of which Hamilton had become president. Brissot was entranced by Hamilton (though he mistook him to be a decade older than he was), describing him as "firm and . . . decided . . . frank and martial. . . . Washington. . . . had great confidence in him, and he well merited it."[18]

It was largely through the influence of Brissot that Hamilton was made an honorary member of the French National Assembly. Though Jefferson was the American representative in Paris, that honor never came to him. It seems that he disappointed Brissot, who had returned to France to lead a moderate but abolitionist government. Apparently assuming that Jefferson would wish to join Les Amis des Noirs, in accordance with the view of slavery offered in the *Notes on Virginia*, Brissot had made the invitation. Jefferson declined: "Those whom I serve have never been in a position to lift up their voices against slavery. . . . I am an American and a Virginian and, though I esteem your aims, I cannot affiliate myself with your association." He then refused to support the proposals of Les Amis in the National Assembly that the slaves held in the French possessions in the West Indies be set free.[19]

"I am an American and a Virginian." Jefferson did not apparently detect any tension between the two self-definitions. Do we? Are we not permitted to feel a chill as he permitted himself to be defined in this way? Many of his best biographers have felt none, regarding this as merely a statement of a practical politician.[20]

Vats of ink have been poured out in efforts to penetrate into the psyche of Thomas Jefferson to determine what he calculated to be the limits of practicality and what he did by preference, out of racial prejudice. We have little to add to what has already been written, even after the recent disclosure of another anomaly: his relationship to Sally Hemings within the scope of his relationship to people of color. Having noted his willingness to settle for what "the people I represent" expected of him, we can read with greater understanding his letter to the Abbé Henri Gregoire, dated February 25, 1809, written twenty-two years after the *Notes*, in which he was willing to acknowledge that blacks were "*gaining* daily in the opinions of nations, and hopeful *advances* . . . *towards* their re-establishment on an equal footing with the other colors in the human family":

Be assured that no person living wishes more sincerely than I do, to see a complete refutation of the doubts I have myself entertained and expressed on the grade of understanding allotted to them by nature, and to find that in this respect they are on a par with ourselves. My doubts were the result of personal observation on the limited sphere of my own State, where the opportunities for the development of their genius were not favorable, and those of exercising it still less so. I expressed them therefore with great hesitation; but whatever be their degree of talent it is no measure of their rights . . . On this subject they are gaining daily in the opinions of nations, and hopeful advances are making towards their re-establishment on an equal footing with the other colors of the human family."[21]

Jefferson went only so far as to admit that the abbé had supplied him with "many instances . . . of *respectable* intelligence in that race of men, which cannot fail to have effect in *hastening* the day of their relief." But he did not announce the arrival of that day, else his letter would long since have been inscribed upon some cenotaph or other. He and the slaveowners of New York saw matters alike.

After Burr's removal of Hamilton from the scene, and Jefferson's removal of Burr, the way was open to that slaveowning faction in New York to delay emancipation, to deprive blacks of the franchise, and to burnish their connections with the southern planters. From 1800 to 1820, blacks lost the right to vote in New York, whether they had been newly freed or had been free for generations. During the first Jim Crow period, New York developed devices put to use in the South ninety years later, accompanied by equally populist rhetoric. Property requirements were reduced for whites and raised for blacks. Blacks attempting to vote—though not whites—had to meet a burden of proof. In Alabama in 1950, they had to prove they were not illiterate. In New York in 1815, they had to prove that they were not slaves: "Inspectors at the polls . . . presumed as slaves all black men who could not prove their freedom by sufficient evidence."[22]

Into this climate advanced Gideon Granger of Connecticut. (When we come to Granger's determinative role in swinging Jefferson into militant opposition to Burr's western ambitions, we will observe his success in playing upon the racial fears of southern planters. He had rehearsed that role in the racial politics of New York.) Though

Granger's partner, De Witt Clinton, had joined the Manumission Society when he was very young, after 1800 he and Granger concertedly appealed to the racist fears of white artisans. They were especially successful among the recent Irish immigrants, who, after the Alien and Sedition Acts, had good reason to regard the Federalists as their enemies. Derisive songs were set for marching bands, with titles such as "Federalists with Blacks Unite," and orators were heard at Tammany crying against former slaves—mostly former house servants—as "dependent, and unfit" to vote because they would merely ape the political opinions of their former masters. That was the meaning of catchphrases such as "family autocracy." As the suffrage was extended to all white males, the triumphant party of Jefferson, in its reincarnation as the party of Clinton, Martin Van Buren, and Andrew Jackson, celebrated democracy by removing the franchise from all but a handful of blacks.[23]

While Burr was busy in Washington, two of those who had followed him, the unspeakable Matthew L. Davis and Samuel Swartwout, sachems of Tammany, accommodated the drift of "the party of the small tradesman [who] wished to see no competition from Negroes at the polling place or the work bench." Federalist slaveowners were much more likely to manumit their blacks than were Democratic Republicans. In Brooklyn; for example, "five of the thirteen Federalist candidates in 1810 were men who had set free their slaves, while there was but one among their opponents."[24]

The Center Holds: Burr, Jay, and Moderation

Their Federalist opponents were not shy about pointing out that the welcome given by Clinton Democrats—George and De Witt Clinton Democrats—to new immigrants from France, Ireland, and northern Europe was corrupted by their arranging that the newcomers would have no competition from blacks. Brissot and other Frenchmen had observed the onset of that pattern in the early 1790s. In 1810, some of them who had escaped the guillotine and Napoleon's firing squads welcomed the threadbare and hungry Aaron Burr to Paris because he had steadfastly desisted from joining in the currying of favor with political refugees from Europe at the expense of those whose ancestors had been brought to America from Africa in chains. Constantin-

François Chasseboeuf, comte de Volney, was often Burr's guest at Richmond Hill between 1795 and 1798, while he hid from the Terror. He had already been to the Middle East, for, like his political colleague Brissot de Warville, he was a professional travel writer. His reputation was first established with fervid accounts of the Near East: It was very anciently settled, full of magnificent architecture, and worthy to be occupied only by the French.

After the Terror abated, Volney returned to France, equally convinced of the virtues of the Mississippi. The French on the Nile could cut off the British from the short route to India, but in North America they might reconstruct a French empire, albeit with a difference: It could be a refuge for blacks as well as whites. Short of that, the United States could be influenced to open its doors to French ideas while offering a better life to the blacks already there.

The opportunity for a French-sponsored multiracial polity in North America was missed, in part because the party of Jefferson, while Francophile, was dominated by slaveowners. The Federalists, while open to integrating blacks into American society, resisted integrating immigrant Jacobins and Irish revolutionaries, responding to the rush of refugees from political turmoil in France and the Irish who fought on the losing side of the failed rising in 1798 by passing the Alien and Sedition Acts. Though all men might have been created equal, all were not equally welcome in the New Order in the Universe. Hamilton and Jay could only watch with chagrin as their more intransigent colleagues aroused the anger of the newcomers by delaying as long as possible the right of immigrants to participate in the American polity. The Alien Acts were ostensibly directed against Jacobin agents from France but were also intended to retard the voting power of Irish Catholics.

Fear of foreigners is a particularly ugly aspect of a nation of immigrants, and it has been as present in the United States as racial fear—whether the members of the other race were newly arrived or not—and for as long. Behind the scenes, Aaron Burr worked things out with Governor Jay. As several New England states, governed by radical Federalists, sent Jay proposals that he was required to present to the predominantly Federalist New York legislature, Jay gravely handed them alternately to the Assembly and the Senate, where they were picked off, one by one, by Burr and his lieutenants.

Then, in 1798 and 1799, came the Jeffersonian Kentucky and Virginia Resolutions, ostensibly in retort to the Alien and Sedition Acts.

While Aaron Burr found means to weaken the implementation of the acts through arrangements with Jay, Jefferson and Madison turned to extreme measures, though, characteristically, Jefferson hid his hand, concealing his authorship of the nullification resolutions put forward by his friends in Kentucky, some of whom had been issuing secessionist threats since 1793. In a second set of Kentucky Resolutions, Jefferson put into national currency the concept that when majority rule, as manifested in actions of the Congress, produced something not to the liking of one state or another, the "rightful remedy" was "nullification." If there were any doubt of his meaning, he wrote Madison that, if driven to nullification, a state "determined . . . to sever . . . [itself] from that union we so much value, rather than give up the rights of self government which we have reserved," could secede from the Union. That language blazed across the sky in 1832, when Jefferson's authorship of the Kentucky Resolutions was revealed, and remained smoldering until it blazed forth once again in 1861 and left the South in ashes.

Madison's Virginia Resolutions were a little milder: "In case of deliberate, palpable, and dangerous exercise of other powers not granted by the said contract [the Constitution] the states . . . are in duty bound to interpose for arresting the progress of the evil." Duty bound to oppose the Alien and Sedition Acts, the Kentuckians urged other states to join "in declaring these acts void and of no force."[25]

In 1799, Burr took it to be his duty to inform Jefferson, the likeliest presidential candidate of his party, that nullification would not find a favorable hearing in the New York legislature: "Under circumstances so inauspicious, I have not thought it discreet to urge a determination in either house." When he was required to act for the Republicans in presenting the Kentucky and Virginia Resolutions, he did so with as little enthusiasm as Jay had shown in the opposite case. New York joined nine other states in remonstrating against Jefferson's proposals.[26]

The Alien Acts were coupled to the Sedition Acts, which criminalized criticism of the government, especially by such foreign-born pamphleteers as Thomas Paine. As waves of immigration swept upon American shores after the Irish risings of 1798 and the successive revolutions in France, the extreme Federalists—though not Hamilton or Jay—espoused the view that the newcomers should be kept silent and unfranchised until they had been thoroughly housebroken.

Hamilton by then was too far advanced in his projective pathology to find common cause with Burr, but the reciprocal trust established between Burr and Jay persisted well after the Alien and Sedition Acts and the Virginia and Kentucky Resolutions had evaporated. As the election of 1800 was hanging suspended, in the tied vote among the electors between Jefferson and Burr, Hamilton turned to desperate measures. In order to stop both Burr and Jefferson in one unconstitutional action, he proposed to Governor Jay that he call the lame-duck Federalist legislature into session, redistrict the state retrospectively, and substitute a new set of electors. It was a bad idea but not a crazy one: A majority of the voters in the United States probably favored the reelection of John Adams, despite Hamilton's defection.

Jay laid Hamilton's message aside, noting that it was merely "a measure for party purposes, which I think it would not become me to adopt." His sense of what would not become him had much in common with what Burr thought "not . . . discreet!" Political life was moving beyond the range of what both regarded as decency for gentlemen of their character, but, for a time, Burr and Jay held the middle ground against the excesses of their factions.[27]

Their mutual confidence had expressed itself in 1796 as Burr chose Jay to be his confidant in discussing western possibilities that we will review in the next chapters, but its most poignant expression came in 1804, when Jay supported Burr's candidacy for the governorship of New York, infuriating Alexander Hamilton. Burr's lieutenant in that election, Peter Jay Munro, Jay's nephew and foster son, wrote simply, without apparent surprise, that "Gov. Jay will vote for you and Mr. Phelps—he is as decidedly and openly with us as we could wish."[28]

Removal: Red and Black

There was utter consistency in the position of Thomas Jefferson on racial matters, a consistency equal to but opposite to that of Jay and Burr. They took the position that the United States should provide for the inclusion of free blacks in the mainstream and refused to join the cry that the Indians must be removed from their ancestral lands. Jefferson was on the other side. His policy for both blacks and Indians was that they should be "removed." Blacks, if freed, should be shipped to Africa or to Haiti. There was no place for them, whether free or slave, on the same continent with whites. If they were set free and not removed, wrote Jefferson, "all the whites south of the Potomac and Ohio must evacuate their states, and most fortunate those who can do it first." On another occasion he wrote: "Nothing is more certainly written in the book of fate than that these people are to be free; nor is it less certain that the two races, equally free, cannot live in the same government."[29]

This view was not required of a "man of his time," or even of a Virginian of his time. Among Virginians, George Washington not only freed his slaves but endowed them to continue to live in Virginia. David Meade took his slaves to Kentucky but freed them there, as Edward Coles did in Illinois and Thomas Worthington did on his way to Ohio. St. George Tucker was only one of the leaders of Virginia to advocate freeing slaves and permitting them to emigrate to Kentucky or elsewhere in the West, a different concept from forced deportation outside the United States. In 1816, the Kentucky Abolition Society proposed that Congress set aside "vast tracts of unappropriated lands . . . [as] suitable territory . . . to be laid off as an asylum for all those Negroes and Mulattoes who have been, or those who may hereafter be, emancipated within the United States." The Kentucky proposal may sound to some like a South African Homeland, but there is a large difference. The Homelands were places white South Africans could do without, and land in Kentucky was quite agreeable.[30]

A strengthening of Western constituencies by men whose record on racial matters was like that of Hamilton, or Jay, or Burr, was a noisome prospect to the Jeffersonians. It is not necessary to prove that Burr or Hamilton would have freed the slaves of Louisiana had their military expeditions produced a new power base for either along the Mississippi or Ouachita; we cannot penetrate so far as that into the world of might-have-been. It is enough to know that slavery was being disputed in the West and that along the southern and western borders of the United States, toward which both Hamilton and Burr proposed to lead expeditions, both Indians and blacks were already in opposition to the spread of the slave system.

An underground railroad ran south and west before it ran north, organized and operated by black people long before the birth of Harriet Beecher Stowe. Its destination was not Canada but Spanish Louisiana and Florida. In 1804 and again in 1806–7, it was asserted that

Burr intended to raise a black army. Hamilton might have stimulated the same ferocious response had he actually gotten so far as Natchez; his record, from the point of view of the slaveowners, was even worse than Burr's: Only twenty years earlier, in 1779, Hamilton and John Laurens had promised freedom and free land to blacks who served in the Revolutionary army. This was especially worrisome to planters along the Spanish border, because the generals and admirals serving the King of Great Britain had announced intentions to welcome slaves who chose to free themselves by escaping the Americans, just as the King of Spain had promised emancipation to those who departed the British dominions—as we will see. Hamilton and Laurens went on to propose that three thousand Negro troops be armed in South Carolina and Georgia.

Washington was skeptical, but in 1782 he assented to the formation of a "Black Corps" and began the slow progression toward manumission which ultimately led him to free his slaves and to endow them to remain in Virginia. For this implication that a multiracial society was possible, Washington was charged with irresponsibility to his class and section; resident free blacks, like resident Indians, would impede a policy of removal.

(As we have noted, Laurens died in one of the last skirmishes of the Revolutionary conflict. With him died one of the last opportunities for South Carolina's slaveowners to redeem themselves before the cotton gin created a surge in demand for slave labor in the West. Eighty years later, in the last months of the Civil War, Robert E. Lee agreed to a Black Corps for the Confederacy, also coupled to free land and emancipation of those who agreed to serve.)

Misdemeanors in Kentucky and Tennessee

Two charges were laid against Aaron Burr by Thomas Jefferson in the winter of 1806–7. Both had been defined in 1794, a year in which the American Union was severely tried. Jefferson's first allegation was that Burr had been guilty of planning an expedition against the possessions of Spain, a nation with which the United States was at peace. This would have been a misdemeanor, violating George Washington's Neutrality Law of 1794. In the course of that year, two distinct changes were made in American jurisprudence: Peacetime treason received its first definition, in a federal court in Pennsylvania, and a presidential proclamation was codified into law.

By that time, a Dutch word for pirate, *vrijbuiter*, had become reused as "freebooter" by the sixteenth-century Englishmen, who had suffered from the depredations of Dutchmen in little "free boats," to cover land piracy of a political sort. It then passed through the French *flibustier* and the Spanish *filibustero* to become employed by Americans as "filibuster," meaning overland piracy by private armies. There is some irony in the fact that the term is often used to describe the activity Jefferson asserted to have been contemplated by Aaron Burr, a man most unlikely to use his military prowess to serve the slaveowners:

Purloining other people's *time* in a legislature became known as "filibustering" after the 1840s and 1850s, the great age of slaveowning expansionists such as William Walker, who sought to extend the plantation system into Latin America by force of arms.

This chapter deals with activities from 1770 until 1794, largely in Kentucky and Tennessee, that led Washington first to issue an executive order against filibustering and then to cause it to be proscribed by statute. Washington wished to stop the French-sponsored attacks upon British shipping that had been based in American ports and also to prevent French-sponsored filibustering against Spanish Florida and Louisiana. It was appropriate for Jefferson in 1806 to look to Burr's activities on those two frontiers in search of a law under which he might be prosecuted. It is also appropriate for us to note that those provisions of Washington's law applicable to Burr in 1806 applied just as well to Hamilton in 1798 and to a series of filibusters sponsored by Jefferson and his successor, James Madison, from 1786 through 1812. Jefferson was willing to encourage filibusters when they were led by men he chose or approved. Both Hamilton and Burr were not among those men, but they nonetheless contemplated private adventures against Spain and in very bad company.

So much for misdemeanors. The second charge against Burr was treason, also defined in 1794, under circumstances to which we turn in later chapters. Over the two decades before Jefferson ordered Burr to be taken into custody early in 1807, charges of treason—a hanging offense—had been laid several times in Kentucky and Tennessee against disgruntled or ambitious former officers of the Revolution. There had been efforts to separate the settlements of the West from the Union, as several of these officers anticipated the actions of the Confederate states in 1861. In some cases, sedition was coupled to plans of filibusters in the direction of Florida and Louisiana. Treason and filibustering were sometimes associated, sometimes not. Through French agents of sedition, the secessionist-filibusters of Kentucky and Tennessee were linked to the insurgents of Pennsylvania charged in 1794 with treason, but otherwise these two bodies of dissidents had so little in common that we will treat them separately.

The law of peacetime treason was formulated in the instructions given juries trying the Whiskey Rebels of Pennsylvania because Washington and Hamilton saw to it that those juries had prisoners to be tried. Jefferson did not approve of the actions by the President and by

Hamilton in his role as commander of the American army. Albert Gallatin, who in 1794 became a secondary but essential figure in our story, barely escaped trial for treason. He thereafter turned to Burr for support, which Burr offered, and thereby further embittered his relationships to Washington and Hamilton.

Character being our topic, it is incumbent upon us to delve into the legitimacy of the indignation evidenced by Jefferson in 1806–7 and into Gallatin's tepid assistance to him against Burr. How deeply were they offended by filibustering? How much were all these great Founders devoted to the ideal of "neutrality" and to the integrity of the Spanish possessions—and, for that matter, to the integrity of the Union itself?

In 1807, Jefferson attributed to Burr an intention to lead a separation from the Union of the states and territories lying west of the Appalachians. Our story turns around the act of allegation as much as it does the truth or falsity of the charge. For that reason, we will review the earlier record of Jefferson and of his principal witnesses against Burr with regard to filibustering and to secessionist plots, to determine how clean were their hands. Because James Wilkinson was chief among those witnesses, we will focus upon him, to ascertain how he was able to seduce Jefferson, Hamilton, and Burr by playing to the characteristic frailties of each. To reach so close as that to them, he had to rid himself of George Rogers Clark and Anthony Wayne.

Secession, Filibustering, and James Wilkinson

The Kentucky and Tennessee stories are to be told first because the threat of secession in those states commenced earlier than in Pennsylvania and lasted longer.

Separatism and secession are not quite the same thing. There had been separatism in the West before there was a United States from which to secede. In the 1770s, the people who had driven the Indians from the region around the headwaters of the Tennessee River set themselves apart from North Carolina in a peculiar protogovernmental entity calling itself the Watauga Association. Only in the twentieth century was their rickety handiwork elevated by Theodore Roosevelt and George Bancroft to the status of "the Republic of Watauga."[1]

By 1784, Watauga had transmogrified into "the State of Franklin," with James Sevier as a filibustering governor with continuing imperial ambitions toward the lands of the Creeks and Cherokees. These ambitions commended themselves neither to the Indians nor to the Spaniards nor to the states of the seaboard. Adventures in Alabama might induce an expensive war against Spain. Yankee merchants had no stake in a Mississippi open to the exports of Watauga-Franklin, and, if Spain were provoked, their own trade with Europe and the West Indies would be disrupted. Accordingly, Congress declined to encourage the Wataugans. Angrily, Sevier changed the name and status of his domain once more, to Frankland, and informed the Spanish governor of Louisiana, Esteban Rodriguez Miró (sometimes spelled "Mero") that, under the right terms, Frankland's citizens would consider "a more interesting connection"—the "protection" of Spain. These intentions were signaled to North Carolina, still nominally responsible for its subsidiary, Frankland, and its legislature was agreeable to naming the Nashville Basin "the Mero District."

(It is probable that Sevier never really meant to secede from the Union, only from North Carolina—as Vermont seceded from New York. But the Wataugan threat was taken very seriously.)

In 1786, the United States was still a loose confederation, subject to dismemberment. Don Diego de Gardoqui arrived in Philadelphia to represent Spain in the United States, with a program to produce that result. His chosen device in dealing with the amorphous American state was Spain's control of the mouth of the Mississippi, at New Orleans, and of the delta of Tombigbee. Since produce of the American West could only reach world markets if those effluents were kept open, and since the preconstitutional American confederation lacked the power to open them, Gardoqui set about to convince the westerners that their interests would be best served by casting their lot with Spain. Spanish agents approached the citizens of Kentucky and Tennessee with the promise that if they would separate from the Union and join their settlements to the Spanish dominions, they would have free access to the sea.

James Wilkinson scented opportunity. Gathering a shipment of tobacco and hogs, he descended upon New Orleans, where he was paid an extravagant price for his crop and for his oath of fealty to the Spanish crown. He then returned to Kentucky full of ideas for a convention of its aggrieved citizens to achieve Gardoqui's plan. His paymaster was Thomas Power, an Irish adventurer trained for the priesthood and subsequently for those devices useful in frontier espionage such as hiding shipments of silver, to be used for bribes, in hogsheads covered by tobacco or clothing.

Wilkinson was a contemporary of Hamilton and Burr, born in 1757. He had been with Burr and Arnold in Canada; currying favor with the latter, he gained a lieutenant colonelcy ahead of his contemporaries. Arnold passed him along to Horatio Gates, the victor at Saratoga, and Wilkinson became a junior partner to Gates and the Franco-Irish soldier of fortune Thomas Conway in their cabal against Washington. On a mission between members of the conspiracy, Wilkinson took part in a drinking bout with James Monroe and another aide to General Lord Stirling, William McWilliams. Full of himself, full of wine, and full of pride, Wilkinson boasted of the contrast between the ragtag force at Valley Forge and the exuberant, victorious army of the north, with its delightful plan to displace Washington as commander-in-chief.

Monroe and McWilliams sobered up and hastened to Washington with the news. Washington told Conway what he had heard. Conway remonstrated with Wilkinson, who denied everything. Conway believed him, and so did Gates, who claimed that his private views could have been communicated only if Alexander Hamilton had rifled through his papers while he was out of the room. Stirling next confronted him, on the basis of what Monroe and McWilliams had reported. Gates knew where the blame really lay, charged Wilkinson with violating his confidence, and awaited a challenge. Wilkinson obliged, but Gates relented.

They all descended upon Valley Forge. Things simmered down, though Wilkinson had done much to destroy the morale of the officers there present, and in the summer of 1778 another exchange of hot words brought him and Gates finally to a dueling ground. Wilkinson's second was Hamilton's brother-in-law John Barker Church who knew a lot about dueling. Wilkinson shot three times. "Satisfaction" was declared, but Wilkinson thought it prudent to retire from the army. In July 1779, however, he was back in the army as clothier-general. His record was no better in that office; he escaped conviction for stealing but was relieved of his command in 1781.

A decade later, Wilkinson was in Kentucky, still in the dry goods business but now on his own. Discredited as an officer of the Continental Army, twice cashiered, already known by many in the West to be in the pay of Spain, he was taken up by Alexander Hamilton, with that condescending cynicism which was his least admirable character-istic. The Secretary of the Treasury urged Washington (who had be-come President in 1788) to overlook Wilkinson's character and repu-tation and to launch him once again upon a military career, arguing that Wilkinson was popular among the militia on the frontier and that all he seemed to desire was command of the dispirited garrison at Fort Washington.

It appears that Hamilton accepted the view of Thomas Marshall, chief of the western Federalists:

> I considered him [Wilkinson] dangerous to the quiet of Ken-tucky, and perhaps her safety. If the commission would not secure his fidelity, it will at least place him under control, in the midst of faithful officers, whose vigilance will render him harmless, if not honest.[2]

It was only the first occasion on which Hamilton's propensity to think himself worldly-wise led him to the error made by Franz von Papen in recommending to old Marshal Hindenberg that Adolf Hitler might be evil, but he could be useful. Hamilton was a better man than von Papen, but a good man may do much evil when convinced that he can use evil to serve good ends. There was no mystery as to Wilkin-son's character when Hamilton dealt with him until 1800, when Burr took him up thereafter, or when Jefferson, after 1805, made him the primary agent of both his campaigns to drive Aaron Burr out of public life.

Back in the regular army, Wilkinson gloated to his Spanish paymas-ter that he had received advancement from "an incompetent Secretary of War, an ignorant Commander-in-Chief, and a contemptible Union." Gathering his supporters, including Judge Harry Innes, Wilkinson did all he could to serve Spain by taking Kentucky out of that "contempt-ible Union." In September and October 1788, in Danville, John Brown led the Kentuckians in discussions of the means by which the Missis-sippi might be opened, culminating in a resolution that "measures should be taken . . . [both] for obtaining admission of the district as a separate and independent State of the Union, and[to secure] the nav-igation of the Mississippi, as may appear proper . . . *or* to do and ac-complish *whatever* on a consideration of the state of the district *may* in their opinion promote its interests [emphasis supplied]."[3]

This was as far as things could be pushed. A majority of the delegates proved to be as interested in statehood within the United States as in free navigation, a conclusion that Brown accepted—or so he wrote James Madison, and, in any case, he thereafter ceased to participate in secessionist schemes. Wilkinson, chagrined, wrote Miro for a land grant of 600,000 acres within the Spanish possessions and at the same time opened negotiations with the British. In January of the next year, the vortex of secessionism shifted from Kentucky to Tennessee, as Governor Sevier reopened *his* discussions with the Spaniards.

Washington Copes with Secession

At this juncture, George Washington demonstrated once again his versatility in finding means to save the American Union. He had won a revolution, had presided over the production of a constitution, and now defined the nature of the presidency. An army was required to put down a rebellion in Pennsylvania, but subtler means would do in Kentucky and Tennessee. Washington, unlike Jefferson, did not develop an intelligence system to serve the presidency domestically. But he had a considerably more useful kinship network. Dr. David Stuart of Fairfax County, Virginia, had married the widow of Martha Washington's son, John Parke Custis, who had been adopted by Washington as his own son and heir. On January 22, 1789, Stuart published in Washington's newspaper, the *Alexandria Gazette*, a report from Kentucky detailing the events in Danville during the previous fall, emphasizing Brown's role and urging immediate retaliatory action. Thomas Marshall confirmed the information and (a little late) added that he was now convinced that Wilkinson was a paid agent of Spain.[4]

Marshall's recollection was further confirmed by Judge John Allen: At the Danville Convention, Brown and Harry Innes *had* advocated separating Kentucky from Virginia and forming "a government independent of her and of the *general government* [emphasis supplied] and to form connections where they should find it most beneficial to her interest," which could only have been Spain.[5]

Moving swiftly, Washington moved to accommodate the ambitions of the leaders of the West. Virginia ceded her claims to Kentucky and Tennessee to the "General [then General Washington's] Government." William Blount (see below) was made governor of Tennessee. Sevier received command of the militia around Knoxville, Wilkinson got his commission in the regular army, Harry Innes was made judge of the federal district court, and John Brown went to the U.S. Senate. However, neither Wilkinson and Innes, in Kentucky, nor Blount, in Tennessee, was done with conspiracy and secessionism.

In December 1794, the President felt it wise to send out to Kentucky the enormously corpulent and enormously persuasive attorney general of Virginia, James Innes, brother to Harry. James Innes was said to be as mesmerizing an orator as Patrick Henry. Sad to say, he spoke extempore and unrecorded. After service as rector of the College of William and Mary, he had been captain of the Williamsburg volunteers, raising a regiment and serving beside Washington and the French at Yorktown. He married early, and the marriage seems to have been an extraordinarily happy one. (The Inneses' daughter, Ann, married Peyton Randolph of Wilton, a cousin of Thomas Jefferson.) Renowned for his appetite and good humor, he grew so rotund that he could not "ride an ordinary horse or sit in a common chair, and usually meditated in his bed or on the floor," which shook when he moved, and it was said his eloquence would "shake the human mind." Perhaps it was his bulk that kept him from racing after the highest office. Though he defeated John Marshall for election as attorney general of Virginia, he refused Washington's offer of the Attorney Generalship of the United States and John Adams's request that he become minister to France in 1797.[6]

In 1785, Harry Innes had moved across the mountains to take up *his* duties as Virginia's attorney general for its western district, now Kentucky. In Kentucky's first constitutional convention, Innes supported a provision abolishing slavery, which almost won—"almost" once again. Though on the side of the angels as to slavery, Harry Innes fell under the spell of Wilkinson. In 1787, he wrote to Edmund Randolph, governor of Virginia (later Burr's counsel in his trial in Richmond):

> I am decidedly of the opinion that this western country will, in a few years, revolt from the union, and endeavor to erect an independent government; for under the present system, we can not exert our strength, neither does Congress seem disposed to protect us.[7]

At the end of December, James Innes managed to work his way out of a carriage and assumed control of Frankfort, capital city of the newly admitted state of Kentucky—until then James Wilkinson's town. Wilkinson had laid it out and, on borrowed money, had given it its squirely seat: his weatherboarded, log-framed mansion house at the corner of Wilkinson and Wapping streets, in which the legislature met. Lexington was also the seat of Wilkinson's joint operations with Harry Innes. They had been partners, in effect, for the three years since Wilkinson had been back in the regular army. In 1791, Wilkinson placed his overt financial affairs in the care of Judge Innes, with instructions to dispose of land to relieve debts owed by Wilkinson to his partner, Peyton Short. Short's brother, William, was Jefferson's intimate friend; their brother-in-law was Henry Harrison. These were splendid associations for Wilkinson and his Spanish clients, but James Innes had the trumping card. He informed Governor Isaac Shelby of Kentucky that there was no need to go to the inconvenience of separation, because negotiations would be shortly undertaken in Madrid to open the port of New Orleans—and that the emissary to Madrid would be Jefferson! The post was offered, and though Jefferson turned it down, the effect upon his followers had been achieved.

With patronage and diplomacy, the secessionists were mollified. Pinckney's Treaty, in 1796, opened the Mississippi again. Kentucky remained in the Union; Harry Innes broke from Wilkinson to the extent of rejecting further Spanish solicitations. Secessionism should no longer "be countenanced," he wrote; "the Western people had now obtained the navigation of the Mississippi, by which all wishes are gratified." Innes even had the grace to join George Nicholas in putting a formal terminus to their dalliance with Spain: "We will not be concerned, either directly or indirectly, in any attempt that may be made to separate the western country from the United States." This time they apparently meant it.[8]

The French Incite Secession and Filibustering

The French next took up the game. Spanish sedition of the Americans in Kentucky was succeeded by French sedition, and, though secession was to be its outcome, its ultimate consequence was to be filibustering turned against Spain. After his return from America, Brissot published a report on what he had seen in the Mississippi Valley, regretting that France had lost it to Spain in 1762 and offering the suggestion that, since Spain was unworthy of such an endowment, France should take it back. When his party came to power in France in 1789, Brissot proposed a grand design: Edmond-Charles Genêt was to go to the United States with a fourfold assignment. He was to stir up French-inclining separatism in the West. He was to recruit, in the American territories, troops to take Louisiana from Spain and return it to France. Another set of Americans was to be assembled to conquer Florida under the tricolor flag of France, and appropriate quarters were to be found in the West for a deposed Louis XVI, after Brissot arranged his escape from the guillotine.

All such romantic notions withered after the Brissotins lost power to the Jacobins. Brissot, the King, and Marie Antoinette went to the guillotine. Many American towns were named Marietta to memorialize both her and the exploded dream that the French might carry forward a gentleman's rebellion like their own. As emissaries appeared, bloody-handed, from the Jacobin regime, Hamilton recalled that "it was from . . . [the King], the then sovereign of the country, that they [the Americans] received those succors . . . so important in establishing their independence and liberty." It would hardly be "consistent with a decent regard" for the decapitated monarch for the American administration to receive representatives of those with the blood of Louis on their hands.[9]

> A struggle for liberty is in itself respectable and glorious. When
> conducted with magnanimity, justice and humanity it ought to
> command the admiration of every friend to human nature. But
> if sullied by crimes and extravagancies, it loses respectability.[10]

A French government without "respectability" was not one to which the Federalists owed any wartime loyalty, especially if that government meddled in American internal affairs to weaken further the fragile American Union. When the Jacobins went to war with England, Hamilton led the Washington administration out of a French alliance toward a resumption of amity with Britain. Jefferson had not been so affronted as Hamilton or Washington by the Terror and wrote to James Monroe that Hamilton was willing to present "our breach to every kick which Great Britain may chose to give it."[11]

Kicks from France were another matter. Though the King was dead, Genêt came to the United States anyway, with sedition and conquest, rather than sanctuary for a king, as his agenda. At Charleston, South Carolina, this rash, vainglorious young man came ashore in gold epaulets, flowered cravat, and satins, carrying with him a commission as major general in the armies of the French Republic for the Virginian hero of the Revolution, George Rogers Clark.

George Rogers Clark: Frustrated Filibuster

And a true hero he was. Clark is sometimes coupled to Daniel Boone as if they were both rude, illiterate, bear-skinning frontiersmen. In truth, Clark was a Piedmont gentleman. His manor was Castle Hill, a few miles from the Jeffersons' Shadwell. Clark received a good Piedmont classical education at the hands of Dr. Robertson, in Newtown, along with James Madison, Edmund Pendleton, Harry Innes, and John Taylor of Caroline (a Virginia plantation, not, in this instance, a woman's name.)

It is true that Clark refused to spell as others spell, but what is that to set beside his athletic prowess? Standing above six feet, redheaded, black-eyed, he was prodigiously strong, crafty in wood lore, and committed to serving Jefferson and Kentucky—not Virginia, which did not accord him sufficient respect, nor a United States that barely existed for him and for many other frontiersmen.

In 1775, Clark's Kentuckians organized themselves as the Transylvania Colony, solemnly notifying the Continental Congress of their independence and their determination to stand aside from any revolution against the King. In the course of the next winter, some changed their minds, but, after Virginia failed to reward them with arms and equipment, Clark responded by threatening that Transylvania would remain independent and neutral unless Virginia did better. It was in that context that we should read his famous statement that "a country that is not worth defending is not worth claiming." What Virginia would not defend, it could not claim: "Put up or shut up!"

The British, Tories, and Indians attacked the Transylvanians' stockades, burnt out their newly planted cornfields, and hewed down their young apple trees. Clark could not long endure being pent up in stockades. His natural style was attack. So, in 1778, he exploded westward with a little army and went all the way to Cahokia, across the Mississippi from St. Louis. Clark's rediscovery of the medieval ruins at Cahokia occurred while he was encamped beneath its mounds, preparing the Spanish and French citizens of St. Louis and Cahokia to defend themselves against the British and Indians. When the attackers arrived, Clark led the defenders to a victory as remarkable as Andrew Jackson's at New Orleans in 1815. Immediately thereafter he began planning that riposte which became the most famous campaign of the Revolutionary War in the West, immortalized in engravings of Clark's men slogging through the slush of drowned prairies on the way to the British post at Vincennes. Like the depictions of Burr in the snowstorm before the walls of Quebec, these were reminders of proud moments in a conflict in which, until the very end, American officers had more experience in salvaging remnants of defeated armies than in achieving brilliant strokes. Burr's rescue of Montgomery's body is a symbolic statement of the first. Clark's capture of Vincennes and its commander, Colonel Henry Hamilton, is the equivalent of the second.

After his victory at Vincennes, Clark might have returned southward to Kentucky to relieve refugee-thronged forts besieged by the British and Indians. But Governor Jefferson required him instead to take his little army northward, toward the British base at Detroit, away from Kentucky. In explanation, one of Jefferson's admirers, Anthony Marc Lewis, has written that the governor had concluded that "the Old Dominion must play a lone hand at any cost! . . . [Therefore he] risked very briefly the very security of Kentucky."[12]

Displaying the farseeing ruthlessness of a Winston Churchill, Jefferson gave Clark two assignments: He was to worry the British at Detroit and to cut off any movement westward of the forces of Pennsylvania. That, Jefferson wrote privately to Clark, would "have an important bearing ultimately in establishing our [Virginia's] northwestern boundary." In America's prenational phase, both Virginia and Pennsylvania had declared their independence of Great Britain, and they often proceeded independently of each other. Jefferson instructed Clark to take "your expedition up the Wabash" rather than to cooperate in joint maneuvers with Pennsylvanian commanders appointed by Washington. Though the commander of the armies of the Continental Congress was, by birth, a Virginian, he was already an American. According to the Pennsylvanians, their leaders, Edward Hand, Daniel Brodhead, and George Morgan, were not treated as allies by Jefferson because they were also "investors in land schemes with the Pennsylvania interests."[13]

Jefferson gave Washington a different explanation: Clark could not join any "joint expedition" with the Pennsylvanians because "these two officers [Clark and Brodhead] cannot act together." He neglected

to inform Washington that he had ordered Clark *not* to "act together" with Brodhead or that he *had* ordered him to give assurances
to the slaveholders of St. Louis, Cahokia, Kaskaskia, and Vincennes
that they need not worry about their human property if Virginia were
the occupying power. Pennsylvania Quakers were notoriously opposed
to slavery.[14]

No broader patriotic scruples stood in Brodhead's way, for *his* President was President (that was his title) Reed of Pennsylvania, to whom
he wrote: "Should our State determine to extend its settlements over
the Allegheny River I should be happy to have an early hint of it because it would be in my power to serve several of my friends." In
Pittsburgh four hundred partisans of Virginia signed a petition for
Brodhead's removal, on the grounds that he was "actuated by motives,
selfish and interested and his views are totally confined to land, manors
and mill seats."[15]

During the Revolution, common perils required common military
action among people who had not yet formed a nation. Some, who
experienced the binding force of suffering together, surviving mortal
danger together, and feeling the thrill of a triumphant charge together, became natural nationalists—one might even say federalists.
Others, whose association had been more distant and more considered, were not ready to relinquish their sense of invidious apartness.
In the first category were those, such as Hamilton and Washington,
who became fierce in their insistence that no chances be taken with
the Union. In the second were several men of noble qualities who in
this regard had a higher tolerance of risk.

As soon as peace was concluded with the British, in 1783, Clark was
asked by Jefferson to undertake another mission. He was to return to
Cahokia and then to set forth up the Missouri Valley, on a Virginian
version of the exploration Jefferson nationalized—though without
abandoning his insistence upon Virginians in the lead—as President.
Then, in 1803, Clark's brother William and Meriwether Lewis undertook the project he had declined in 1783, while no happier with Virginia than with Pennsylvania. As suggested earlier, the United States
did not exist for him. The Constitution had not yet brought forth an
executive; Congress was unable to govern, to pay its debts, to defend
its frontiers, or to protect its shipping. The British were in smug occupancy of forts well within American territory, some of them conquered by Clark himself but relinquished to a federal government

which failed to prevent British reoccupation. Virginia was so negligent in repaying his wartime expenses that Clark turned to freshwater piracy against Spanish shipping. Somewhat later, turning from offense to defense, and from the United States to Spain, he wrote the Spanish authorities that he would abandon buccaneering and turn to them, in future, in return for a commission to defend Kentucky against the Indians. "No property or person is safe under a . . . weak and infirm" American government.[16]

In 1786, though without a Spanish commission, Clark attempted a campaign against the Wabash tribes on his own, but the militia mutinied, probably encouraged to do so by Wilkinson's gossip that Clark was often drunk at midday and, when sober, was supplying a private army with stolen goods. There was truth in the first instance but probably not in the second. He had "greatness of . . . mind," wrote Jefferson, who professed himself "the more mortified at the cause which obscures it. . . . [C]ould it be surmounted, his lost ground might yet be recovered."[17]

Alcoholism was the endemic infirmity of what has been truly called "an alcoholic republic." When George Washington reviewed possible commanders for the forces of the United States in the West, in 1792, he found that two of the five major generals on the list were alcoholic. He turned to a third, Anthony Wayne, "whether sober or a little addicted to the bottle I know not." Poor befuddled Clark, estranged from Virginia and rebuffed by Spain, turned in the early 1790s to the French, assuring them that he could take Louisiana from the Spaniards:[18]

> I can raise an abundance of men in this western country . . . who have repeatedly fought, obtained laurels. . . . I can by my name alone . . . raise 1500 brave men. . . . I can take the whole of Louisiana for France. If France will be hearty and secret in this business—my success borders on certainty.[19]

However hearty France might have been for his success, those who heard him slur his commands and saw him uncertainly walk the parade ground were not. Clark had volunteered to come to Europe to assist revolutionary France. Several other Americans actually went, but Thomas Paine saw no reason to waste Clark on Flanders. Paine, an Irish emigré, was living and pamphleteering in Paris, and he had better uses for Clark. Paine convinced the French government that if Clark would diminish his intake of alcohol he was just the man to lead the Americans against Spain, which had allied itself with Britain. In exchange for a general's commission, excitement, and the hope of glory, Clark agreed to set up in America's—and Virginia's—trans-Appalachian territories an independent western state under French protection while his kinsman Elijah Clarke, with another commission as a general in the armies of France, added Florida to the possessions of the French Republic. (Elijah Clarke's patronymic is generally spelled that way by historians, though not by himself—he used "Clark." Historians, however, myself included, have trouble enough keeping apart kin who are also coadjutors and contemporaries, so "Clarke" it is.)

After a triumphal progress from Huguenot Charleston, South Carolina, amid choruses of the brand-new anthem "La Marseillaise," Genêt finally arrived in the capital. Intoxicated with adulation, he disclosed his plans to Jefferson, who as Secretary of State had been admonished by the President to bear in mind his primary obligation. Cabinet officers were told they should not encourage Genêt, or anyone else, to organize invasions of Spain, or of any other territories or nations with which the United States was at peace. Instead, Jefferson failed to warn Washington of the French plots to which he had become privy and assisted Genêt in dispatching their mutual friend the botanist André Michaux to the West. Michaux went with letters of introduction from Jefferson, carrying Clark's French commission along with his botanical instruments. Research could be done along the way, so any qualms felt by the Secretary of State were, it seems, overwhelmed by the prospect of advancements in science.[20]

Ignited by Wilkinson and Innes, Kentucky was ablaze. The remonstrance of the Danville Convention was sent to the Congress, complaining that the United States had neglected western interests and had treated the overmountain people with contempt. After the grievances were stated came the threat: "If the general government will not procure [relief] for us, we shall hold ourselves not answerable for any consequences that may result from our procurement of it."[21]

Having spread his seeds, Michaux set out for Philadelphia, detouring the Tennessee settlements under the influence of Blount and Sevier. Blount preferred a British to a French alliance, while Sevier was considering autonomy under the sovereignty of Spain.

Meanwhile, on the eastern seaboard, Genêt had begun outfitting the brigantine *Little Democrat*, to attack New Orleans. When it was ready, it went to sea in the face of a direct order from Washington; on its test voyage it assaulted British shipping and brought its prizes into Delaware Bay. On September 15, 1793, Washington convened his cabinet; Genêt was ordered to be recalled to France. Though some Northern Francophiles objected, the slaveowners of the South did not. They had learned from refugees from the revolution in Haiti that Genêt was among Les Amis des Noirs.

As the French Revolution entered another and bloodier phase, Genêt prudently declined to accept the death sentence implied in returning to France and retired to Long Island. He married George Clinton's daughter and became a potato farmer.

George Rogers Clark was left behind to face James Wilkinson, who used the threat of an attack upon New Orleans by Clark to make himself necessary to the Spaniards. They were not driven into panic, for by then Clark was a sad case, drunken and easily derided, an old soldier fading away, leaving a space that might have been filled by either Anthony Wayne or James Wilkinson. The marvel is that before Thomas Jefferson turned to Wilkinson he managed to escape any opprobrium for his sponsorship of Clark, the hero turned embarrassment. They had had a long association.

Our first scrutiny has been of Jefferson's hands. There can be no doubt that he never sought to separate West from East; the language of his proposed Ordinance of 1784 shows that he did not welcome separatism, though his defenders admit that Kentucky was excepted from the prescriptions against secession in that ordinance and that Kentucky was where most of the problem lay at the time. Did Jefferson encourage others in secessionist activity when he could please them at little risk of an actual rebellion? The answer to that is cloudier, though he was remarkably shy of *discouraging* secessionist talk on the part of Kentuckians well within the reach of his influence. While Secretary of State, in 1793, he assisted French agents of sedition to go to secession-prone Kentucky and Tennessee and failed to provide timely warning of their purposes to the government of that territory.

In the next chapter, we will complete our review of the background of the misdemeanor charge of filibustering laid against Burr in 1806. Then, in Chapter Ten, we will observe Jefferson after he left the government on January 5, 1794, providing comfort, if not aid, to an insurrection in western Pennsylvania which had a secessionist component.

9

Filibustering as Policy, Glory, or Adventure

Secretary of State Thomas Jefferson learned from Citizen Genêt on July 5, 1793, that French agents of sedition were headed for Kentucky. He did not get around to saying so to Governor Shelby of Kentucky until October, though he wrote himself—and posterity—a memorandum in July that he had told Genêt that "enticing officers and soldiers from Kentucky to go against Spain, was really putting a halter around their necks, for . . . they would surely be hung, if they commenced hostilities against a nation at peace with the U.S." Genêt did not remember it exactly that way:

> He [Jefferson] gave me to understand that he thought a little spontaneous irruption of the inhabitants of Kentucky into New Orleans could advance matters; he put me in touch with several deputies [congressmen] of Kentucky, notably with Mr. Brown, who, convinced that his region would never flourish as long as the navigation of the Mississippi were not free, adopted our plan with as much enthusiasm as an American can manifest.[1]

Jefferson had taken an oath of office to a United States government led by a President who had made clear his opposition to filibustering irruptions anywhere. Unless the Secretary of State was uncharacteristically naive about the purposes of Genêt and Michaux, his biographer Dumas Malone was being too kind when he wrote of Jefferson's fiduciary lapse that he "came dangerously near conniving with the Frenchman." Not only did the secretary delay warning the officials of Kentucky that they were about to receive a carrier of the virus of separatism to which that state was already prone. When Clark coupled separatism to filibustering against Spain (Jefferson's charge against Burr in 1806), Jefferson would only say that the risk of hangings in Kentucky would diminish if Clark's men quietly packed their weapons, moved stealthily down the Mississippi, and assaulted New Orleans. If that filibuster were to get underway, Jefferson indicated, he "did not care what insurrections should be excited in Louisiana."[2]

That was an authentic bit of Jeffersoniana. Though the new federal system was unstable and its central government frail, if his constituent frontiersmen wished to turn to secession, or to filibustering, they were free to express themselves in accordance with what Hamilton and Burr called Jefferson's "Jacobin leveling principles." Though in 1794 the Jeffersonians charged Hamilton with an intention to organize a putsch against democratic government, recycling that allegation against Burr in 1806, neither of them gave aid or comfort to separatists, though the ambitions of both did, in fact, include filibusters upon the Spanish possessions.

Hamilton in 1798 and Burr in 1806 insisted that they would prefer to take up arms against Spain only after the United States had declared war. In extreme circumstances, however, either might have anticipated that formality, incurring what might be called the off-sides penalty of a misdemeanor charge. That was what George Rogers Clark planned to do, what John Sevier, William Blount, and Elijah Clarke (see below) did, and after them, Sam Houston and John C. Frémont.

Jefferson and James Madison professed to be shocked at Burr's assembling men to populate his colony in the West with the clear anticipation that in the event of hostilities they and he would be in the vanguard. It is absurd to expect Jefferson and Madison to look upon the military rehabilitation of a war hero and political opponent with the solicitude they displayed toward filibusters they themselves sponsored. But their professions of dismay about Burr's threat to Spain are unconvincing to those who recall their smug silence in the face of the proclaimed purposes of Clark, Clarke, Sevier, and Blount and Madison's support of Reuben Kemper, John Houstoun McIntosh, George Mathews, and Fulwar Skipwith once Burr was out of the way.

We do not have space here for a complete chronicle of the Jeffersonians' program of sponsored filibusters, but we can trace its origin back to 1790, even before Genêt reported Jefferson's encouragement of irruption into the Spanish domains. In that year, Jefferson drew upon his classical learning to pounce upon the failure of the Spanish colonial service to take sufficient heed of the lessons of Roman history. The governors of Spanish Louisiana, Texas, and Florida recapitulated a device the Romans had attempted and found disastrous: bringing barbarians within the gates in the hope that they would defend the city against other barbarians.

As we shall see, the use of "auxiliaries" failed to protect St. Augustine and Fort Miro any better than Rome. Jefferson needed only the faintest hint to apply Roman lessons to American possibilities; as Secretary of State he recommended, and as President set in motion, a system of sponsored colonization, by which the colonists accepted the invitations of the Spanish authorities, assembled critical mass, declared independence, and then united themselves to the sponsoring state. This is the story of McIntosh's East Florida Republic, of Skipwith's West Florida Republic, of the Texas of the Austins and Houston, and of Frémont's California. Jefferson's system might be called amoebic imperialism, but his was deeply plotted and amoebas merely do what comes naturally.

We can imagine this marvelously shrewd Secretary of State, in 1790, releasing his polygraph long enough to rub his hands in glee as he wrote George Washington that the governor of Spanish Florida had been so imprudent as to invite "foreigners to go and settle in Florida."[3]

> This is meant for our people. . . . It will be the means of delivering to us peaceably, what may otherwise cost us a war. In the meantime we may complain of this seduction of our inhabitants just enough to make [the Spaniards] believe we think it very wise policy for them, and confirm them in it. This is my idea of it.[4]

Three years later, still Secretary of State, Jefferson merely added what seemed a fillip: that the Americans might wear French uniforms. There was, of course, a risk: The seduction of independence might supersede the seductions of loyalty to either the sponsoring power or the receiving one, and the North American continent might become balkanized into little warring border states. Even after a number of them actually cropped up, such as Watauga-Franklin, the Trans-Oconee Republic, and the Free State of Muskogee, Jefferson did not appear to be much bothered by the possibility that another set of Roman precedents might become relevant and the Mississippi or Oconee be crossed as portentously as the Rubicon—unless one of those free states were led by Aaron Burr.

The French uniforms were important. On November 15, 1793, Jefferson's Kentucky kinsman George Nicholas wrote James Madison: "France may be induced to join us in procuring what . . . our government wants inclination and spirit to obtain for us." Taking account of the possibilities of French sponsorship, John Breckinridge, who later became Jefferson's Attorney General, warned that "the Mississippi we must have. If the government will not procure it, we will procure it for ourselves."[5]

Jefferson did not rebuke Breckinridge, Genêt, or Michaux, but, in March 1794, Washington did. Perhaps recalling Jefferson's suggestion, four years earlier, of a filibuster by stealth in Florida, and his more recent complicity with Michaux and Genêt, the President issued a proclamation to preclude the activity Jefferson had thought might lead to "hanging" in Kentucky. Washington did not propose the halter as a deterrent, but he did forbid American citizens from "invading and plundering the territories of a nation at peace with the United States." Congress made the proclamation law in the Neutrality Act of November 1794. This was the statute to which Jefferson turned in indicting Aaron Burr in 1806. There is piquancy in the fact that such a tool became available to him primarily because of Washington's disquiet with the filibustering activities of Jefferson's former agent, George Rogers Clark.[6]

Wilkinson and Wayne

Clark's rival and successor in the service of Thomas Jefferson, James Wilkinson, was capable of soliciting more than one engagement. Since his reemployment by the U.S. Army, he had supplemented his paycheck as an American general with gold from Spain. It was probably during the pivotal year, 1794, that Wilkinson extended his palm toward the British. He went to that trouble after rejecting an offer of twenty thousand acres from the French party, through Clark's brother-in-law, Doctor James O'Fallon, provided he helped them conquer it from Spain. He thought it over, as he wrote a friend on February 14, 1791:

> O'Fallon is here making wonderful exertions; has engaged General Clark to command his troops, and has made extensive contracts for provisions, Negroes, horses, etc. The company offered me 20,000 acres as a compliment, but I finally rejected it.[7]

Self-abnegation was not Wilkinson's strong suit, but his life was becoming complicated even by his standards. One day, a Spanish agent was murdered on his way to him with three barrels of silver, as well as dispatches in Spanish sewn into the decedent's coat. When the murderers were apprehended, they sought to exchange the dispatches for leniency. The judge in the case was Harry Innes, who rushed the prisoners beyond risk of exposure to trial in Kentucky, sending them to Wilkinson under an armed guard commanded by Captain Zebulon Pike. Pike, later famous for exploration, was then notoriously as much one of Wilkinson's men as Innes. Requiring an interpreter for private interrogation in Spanish, Pike found one. After his questioning they were declared guiltless and sent on, once more under guard, to the Spanish authorities in New Madrid. Pike's chosen interpreter was Wilkinson's paymaster from those authorities, Colonel Thomas Power.

The guard, selected by Pike and commanded by Innes's brother-in-law, was, however intercepted on orders from Anthony Wayne. Wayne and Wilkinson had been rivals in war, and rivals as well for the hand of the lady who finally married Wilkinson—Ann Biddle. Wilkinson may have wished to rid himself of Wayne before, but now he had a better reason.

Washington had placed Wayne over Wilkinson. Wilkinson's response was to send out letters which went beyond insubordination to sedition:

> I owe so much to my feelings and to professional reputation, that I cannot consent to sacrifice the one, or to hazard the other, under the administration of a weak, corrupt, minister [Henry Knox, Secretary of War] or a despotic, vainglorious, ignorant general.[8]

A man of Wilkinson's vanity will do much to prevent the "hazard" of his "professional reputation," as he had shown the Spaniards seven years earlier:

I hope it may never be said of me, with justice, that in changing my allegiance from the United States of America to the honorable Court of Madrid, I have broken any of the laws of nature or of nations, nor of honor and conscience . . . [T]he policies of the United States having made it impossible for me to obtain this desired end under its government, I am resolved to seek it in Spain.[9]

It appears that in 1794 Wilkinson had made himself available to yet another client, for in October one British agent reported to another: "I have received an easy letter from General Wilkinson, which I forward to you in this packet, lest I too may become suspected of having an improper correspondence." As this "easy letter" was followed up, it was arranged that there would be delays in the delivery of military supplies to the American army led by Wayne, and, if that army could still press on, its commander would be assassinated. Wayne was not deterred, and, as Timothy Rusche tells the tale:[10]

The attempt on Wayne's life occurred when Wayne was at Fort Adams. While he was sleeping, a tree fell on top of his tent. The tree smashed through the tent and severely injured Wayne's knee and loins. Wayne . . . [wrote] in a letter . . . that he was . . . only saved by a stump diverting the blow. From that day on, Wayne needed help to mount his horse. . . . The many clues Wayne had of the conspiracy's existence were not enough to give Wayne anything but a strong suspicion. . . . However, upon the return of . . . Robert Newman, Wayne was able to see the full extent of his enemies' plan.[11]

The full extent of Wilkinson's villainy also became apparent, for he was engaged in his fourth known conspiracy with an enemy to defeat an army under his own command. He had arranged for the ambushing of one of his own detachments in Tennessee by the Creeks. In 1806, he notified the Spanish authorities that his own troops were advancing across Texas. Most astonishing, a year earlier he sent a force including his own son on a mission against which he stimulated a Spanish attack—though it is possible that he had arranged for his son to be sent out of harm's way just before it. Wilkinson's tactics against Wayne in 1794, the first of these and not the last, are the most germane to our story; they demonstrate most horridly his willingness to use extreme measures. His attempts to "cut out" Aaron Burr on the way to Natchez, and to have him dry-gulched there when the "cut-out" failed, were not known until years later, but a man who knew his methods against Wayne emerged from the shadows in Richmond in 1807.

Robert Newman had been Wayne's quartermaster and intelligence agent. While on the latter duty, he was picked up by the British. Pretending to be a deserter, he offered to assist Matthew Elliot, a British representative in the Miami villages, and soon discovered that Elliot's brother Robert was working with Wilkinson. There was frequent communication between Wilkinson and both Elliots.[12]

According to Newman, the British espionage system, headed by Major Littlehales, expected that if the Indian war could be kept going without a victory by Wayne, Wilkinson might succeed to him and bring the whole Ohio Valley back into the British empire: the Indians were mere "tools or creatures, to trouble the frontier, in order to prevent a dissolution of the Army until things . . . are in order, for the 'Happy Event.' "[13]

Newman made good his escape back to the American lines, still claiming to be a deserter. He was not safe until he could reach Wayne, and he fell into real danger when, on the way, he was picked up by men reporting to Wilkinson, who had him interrogated by Philip Nolan. Though Nolan was still, at this stage, thought to be Wilkinson's agent, he was detoxifying himself and apparently did not warn Wilkinson that Newman was *not* a deserter but, instead, was "employed by . . . Wayne. . . . He insists that he served the army." Though the British were becoming suspicious that "Newman must have been sent in for some sinister purpose" and was "not the character he represents," before these suspicions reached Wilkinson, Newman succeeded in reaching jail. Wayne was his only visitor, and Newman emerged free of any desertion charge, smiling, self-assured, and bearing a pad of brand-new currency. Wayne had what he needed to deal with Wilkinson. Or so he apparently believed.[14]

Wilkinson had reason to expect the worst. Wayne held the murderers of Power's courier; he had heard from Newman. We do not know what Wayne told Secretary of War Knox, or what Knox told Hamilton and Washington. All we do know is that, despite everything they knew, Washington asked Wayne to work something out with Wilkinson and was referring to Wilkinson as "that vile assassin." Wayne, who had an Indian war to fight, replied that "[if] the true interests of my country [required me] to accommodate . . . with Wilkinson, I most certainly would have made the attempt in compliance with the President's wishes. But it is impossible—for I have a strong ground to believe that this man is a principal agent, set up by the British and Democrats of Kentucky to dismember the Union.[15]

Yet Hamilton, and after him Jefferson, had this man promoted, and Burr entered into partnership with him! Wilkinson was given an inadvertent reprieve by a man who disliked him even more than Wayne did: George Rogers Clark. Clark and Wayne had once been colleagues, but Wayne was no more a friend to French sedition than to that of the British or Spaniards. Wayne got wind of the fact that one of Clark's deputies, Colonel John Montgomery, had begun raising troops and preparing invasion craft in Ohio and Kentucky. U.S. troopers swept down upon Montgomery's base and destroyed his boats—in the river ports where Burr's little fleet was destroyed at the equivalent moment in 1806.

That took care of Clark's expedition against New Orleans. Now, finally, Washington agreed to put Wilkinson on trial. Knox had been succeeded as Secretary of War by Timothy Pickering, who wrote Wayne that "Newman's information has . . . confirmed ideas of [a] certain character which have destroyed all confidence in him." Then, on December 15, 1796, before the trial was held, Wayne died, apparently of natural causes.[16]

His associates among the former officers of the Continental Army were busy in those years. In 1797, Senator William Blount of Tennessee substituted the British, Canadians, and Indians for Clark's French as logistical supporters of a run at Spanish New Orleans. Blount made the mistake of entrusting an incriminating letter to a courier; his purposes were discovered, and he was forced out of the Senate. Neither he nor John Sevier was tried under Washington's Neutrality Act of 1794, and after escapes from state jurisdictions in true Zorro style (see below), they were both elevated to the highest offices of their states. In 1799, it was Alexander Hamilton's turn. Hamilton did not propose a British expeditionary force but only a commitment by the British to have a fleet standing by at sea while he and a pickup army descended the Mississippi to the same destination, and no one seems to have thought him guilty of anything worse than vaingloriousness. No rumblings of prosecution under Washington's Neutrality Act were levied at him, either.

Hamilton and Wilkinson

We now approach the nadir of Alexander Hamilton's career. In 1798–99 he descended to the level of James Wilkinson; Burr's turn to choose Wilkinson as partner came four years later, and Jefferson's two years after that. In the first years of the decade, Hamilton had brought forward the career of this separatist and traitor by convincing George Washington to return Wilkinson to the regular army. Worse judgment was to come, after John Adams succeeded Washington as President in 1796. Hamilton's military ambitions had been made to seem ridiculous by the failure of the Whiskey Rebels to give him a fight. Out of office, Hamilton buzzed about, a contentious and unwelcome presence on the fringes of the Adams administration. Through back channels to several of Adams's cabinet officers, especially the Secretary of War, James McHenry, he extracted offices and policies from the President by invoking the name of Washington, who glowered down upon them from Mount Vernon. Hamilton was able to deny a second military career to Burr, in spite of the prospect that the absence of Burr from the list opened the way for Wilkinson, of whom he wrote:

> [Though] some doubts [!] have been entertained of him . . . yet he . . . is a man of more than ordinary talent, of courage and enterprise . . . and will naturally find his interest, as an ambitious man, in deserving the favor of the government; while he will be apt to become disgusted, if neglected, and through disgust may be rendered really what he is now only suspected to be.[17]

Wilkinson's dependence upon the Spanish payroll was hardly a secret; yet the old man at Mount Vernon wearily agreed. Adams was advised to give Wilkinson the commission, on the ground that it would "feed his ambition, soothe his vanity, and, by arresting discontent, produce the good effect you contemplate."[18]

McHenry wrote that he was astounded by Hamilton's proposal to promote him:

Until the commercial pursuits of this gentleman with an expectation from Spain are annihilated, he will not deserve the confidence of the government. . . . I require this caution on good grounds.[19]

Casting prudence aside, Hamilton was swept into the current of Wilkinson's imperial drama: New Orleans, denied to Clark and France, would be taken by an American army with Hamilton in command and Wilkinson at his elbow. After New Orleans was saved from France, they would advance against Mexico.

The rapid increase of our Western country is such, that we must possess this outlet. Whatever interests may be opposed to it. . . . Our territories must have that outlet. . . . The unity of our empire . . . requires that we should annex . . . all the territory east of the Mississippi, New Orleans included.[20]

Hamilton besieged Adams with proposals not to wait for an offer to sell New Orleans from either Spain or France, but to assemble the hardy pioneers, snap up the Crescent City, and present Napoleon a fait accompli. French policy was known to link Louisiana to Haiti, viewing the former as the source of food supplies to the latter. The Americans might reverse the polarity: If the scene of the Quasi-War were shifted to the Mississippi, a naval strategy might then be developed to defend both Louisiana and Toussaint's Haiti.

As Hamilton and Wilkinson were conspiring, Burr was winding up his service in the U.S. Senate and preparing to shift his political base to the New York Assembly. At this juncture, Jefferson wrote Burr his carefully constructed "esteem" letter of June 17, 1800. One of its most delicious implications was that he and Aaron Burr agreed with regard to the geopolitics of the Mississippi Valley. Amid Jefferson's apparent ramblings on the state of intrafactional politics in New York and the nation, there was the implication that if Federalist policy led into a full-scale, declared war with France, the nation would be powerless to resist a French reacquisition of Louisiana from Spain. Should that happen, Jefferson wrote Burr, the "future fortunes" of the United States "will be in the air." Did he know of Hamilton's plan to take those "future fortunes" into his own hands? Was he so prescient as to consider the possibility that Burr might do likewise?[21]

As Jefferson wrote, Hamilton was deep in consultation with Wilkinson about Florida and Louisiana. By August 1798, Hamilton informed Rufus King that he knew exactly how to resolve Jefferson's dilemma: The federal forces might be too weak for the job, but he could assemble a volunteer army to march through Mississippi Territory to New Orleans. At the head of this "land force . . . the command . . . would very naturally fall upon me." It would be, he wrote King, "the most grand and glorious project in all the world."[22]

It would also be a violation of Washington's Neutrality Law of 1794. The United States was still at peace with Spain, but Hamilton may have consoled himself that Spain was an ally of France, which was in a quasi-war with the United States, and if New Orleans were transferred by Spain to France and there was *then* a declaration of war, an assault on New Orleans would become both glorious and legal.

For such a strained sequence of possibilities, the diminishing political capital of Alexander Hamilton was expended. After meetings with Wilkinson in New York, his dreams of glory expanded: "We should certainly look to the possession of the Floridas and Louisiana, and we ought to squint at South America." In this manic mood, Hamilton wrote a group of Venezuelan patriots, asking that the little fleet they were assembling at Philadelphia be prepared to carry an American expeditionary force to Louisiana.[23]

After Spanish resistance in Louisiana had been eliminated, Hamilton would establish "a government for the liberated territory agreeable to both the co-operators"—the other being the Venezuelans. What sort of government? Probably a junta, of the sort Hamilton had proposed for Haiti, with Hamilton in the place of Toussaint. Then the Venezuelans could expect assistance from both a Hamiltonian Louisiana and Toussaint's Haiti.[24]

There was nothing sudden or spontaneous in Hamilton's association with Wilkinson; it had been growing in intimacy for more than a year when Wilkinson, apparently for the first time, inserted into their discourse that idea which thereafter polluted it, and with which the traitor-general later convinced Jefferson to charge Burr: that a march on New Orleans to open the mouth of the Mississippi might be coupled to the separation of the western states from the eastern.

In August 1799, Wilkinson slyly mentioned that conjunction to Hamilton, as if to tease out of him any ambition to become an independent sovereign: "Under such circumstances would it be indecorous should I express my apprehensions that we repose in false security, and that if we are not seasonably aroused, the dismemberment of the union may be put at hazard?'' Here was the Danville Convention's primary proponent of dismemberment decorously disguising solicitation as admonition. Having hazarded his suggestion to Hamilton, Wilkinson characteristically threatened his Spanish employers with the possibility that Hamilton might take it up and asked a higher subsidy to prevent its success.[25]

Hamilton remained so enraptured by the prospect of another army to lead to glory that, accompanied by Wilkinson and acting with no more authority than as commander of the army and without the approval of the President, he assembled John Adams's cabinet without John Adams, at a "retreat" in Trenton and asked the British minister to remain conveniently on call in nearby Philadelphia. On October 10, 1799, they were surprised when Adams, who had been thought to be prostrated by a cold, rose from his bed to recover his government from Hamilton. Adams did not mince words, to which, he later reported, Hamilton reacted by striving to explain himself, and "never have I heard a man talk more like a fool."[26]

In Adams's vehemence, Hamilton scented a reversal of the administration's support of Toussaint and a sellout to the French. That was unfair. The President was turning its policy by only ninety degrees, from hostility toward neutrality. Despite Hamilton's threat that an agreement with Napoleon would "increase our internal differences," Adams proceeded with negotiations for a truce.

The agony of Hamilton's final, angry, frustrated years began that day in Trenton. He had been bemused by Wilkinson, as Burr was bemused in 1804, and as Jefferson was in 1806. In Hamilton's case, alliance with Wilkinson led only to the brink of disaster. Burr was carried over the brink, and Jefferson saved himself. Or—in the judgment of informed posterity—did he? In 1801, during his joint venture with Napoleon against Toussaint, Jefferson had been warned repeatedly by his representative in London, Rufus King, that Bonaparte intended to move on from Haiti to Louisiana. Finally, in 1802, the President gave credence to King's reports, as confirmed by intelligence that the French were provisioning an army to occupy Louisiana and that Napoleon had proclaimed an intention to hold it against all contenders. Jefferson instructed his minister in Paris to inform the French government that an attempt to seize Louisiana would be answered with force.

There is on the globe one spot the possessor of which is our natural and habitual enemy. It is New Orleans, through which the produce of three-eighths of our territory must pass to market, and from its fertility it will ere long yield more than half our whole produce. . . . France, placing herself at that door, assumes to us an attitude of defiance.[27]

Jefferson was even willing to suggest that the French threat in the Mississippi Valley would force the Americans into "marriage" with the British fleet. "Now, now," one can imagine Napoleon's foreign minister, Charles-Maurice de Talleyrand-Perigord, murmuring as he read such language from a man he knew well—"now, now"—*that* marriage could not be expected on this side of the gates of Hell. Some show of action would be required, for, as Monsieur Pichon, Talleyrand's man in Washington, was well aware, "if he [Jefferson] acts feebly, he is lost among his [western] partisans; it will be then the time for Mr. Burr to show himself with advantage." So Jefferson blustered to the British ambassador that with the Royal Navy to back him up he might be "obliged to resort to force, [and] . . . throw away the scabbard."[28]

Hamilton's Will

After the Trenton gathering, Hamilton went home with two tasks in mind. The first was to protect himself from contamination by the secessionist company he had kept. On October 31, he prepared a memorandum to Wilkinson (we do not know whether or not it was sent): Among "the citizens of the Western country, as far as your agency may be concerned, you will do every thing to foster goodwill and attachment toward the government of the United States. A firm and cordial union is certainly the vital interest of every part of our country." Every part. Even in Kentucky, among the sellers of goods through New Orleans.[29]

Hamilton's second self-assignment was the composition of his fifty-page paean of ambition denied. Though formally an excoriation of Adams, and politically an effort to replace him in the presidency by Charles Cotesworth Pinckney, it was transparently a statement of his frustration that someone other than himself occupied the President's chair: Adams was, he wrote, not only "excessively vain and jealous" but also "ignobly attached to place." Between Alexander Hamilton and "place" were Jefferson, Adams, and Burr; against all three he charged the faults he saw in his own mirror.[30]

Jefferson was described by Hamilton as "crafty and persevering in his objects . . . not scrupulous about the means of success, nor very mindful of truth . . . a contemptible hypocrite." Yet, lest the presidency be captured by Burr, the ultimate lightning rod for his jealousy, Hamilton fought to secure it for Jefferson, having cleared the way for him by the destruction of Adams. As that unlucky man wrote: "If the single purpose had been to defeat the President, no more propitious moment could have been chosen." The election was close enough anyway, but with Hamilton's denunciation cracking away Federalist support in marginal districts, Adams could not win. Having deprived Adams of the presidency and himself of a further career, still furious and not yet repentant, Hamilton prevented Burr from becoming governor of New York, then goaded him into their fatal duel.[31]

Afterward, the hearse deposited its burden in the cemetery and the horses returned to the livery, to be groomed for the next mortuary occasion, as the widow and the bereaved children remained to be consoled and the lawyers turned to their postmortem inquiries. Three days after Hamilton's death, his executor, Oliver Wolcott, wrote James McHenry that "Genl. Hamilton left a will in which all his property . . . is vested in trustees for the payment of his debts: this property consists almost entirely of real estate, chiefly new lands."[32]

The "new lands" turned out to be represented by five shares in the Putnams' Marietta colony in Ohio. Like Washington earlier, and like Burr only a year later, Hamilton apparently hoped that in the West there might be a place for a new life. Sad to say, those shares were found to be of little value. Mrs. Hamilton had an inheritance, however, and lived to be ninety-seven, in comfortable circumstances, hating the Virginians her husband hated, and hating Burr even more.

Strict Construction

Two years before Hamilton's death, the Federalists had their own flirtations with secession. They got there by a peculiar route—following the course of a carom shot. Just before the stroke of midnight at the

Portrait bust of Aaron Burr, statesman, appearing in the United States Capitol among those of the other vice presidents. COURTESY OF U.S. SENATE COLLECTION.

Thomas Jefferson, sage and statesman, in 1805; portrait by Rembrandt Peale. COURTESY OF THE LIBRARY OF CONGRESS, LC-USZ62-10044.

Alexander Hamilton, probably a good image of his actual aspect, by James Sharples. NATIONAL PORTRAIT GALLERY, SMITHSONIAN INSTITUTION, WASHINGTON, D.C.

Alexander Hamilton, the idealized version, by John Trumbull. NATIONAL PORTRAIT
GALLERY, SMITHSONIAN INSTITUTION, WASHINGTON, D.C. GIFT OF HENRY CABOT LODGE.

Aaron Burr In Youth, by Gilbert Stuart. FROM THE COLLECTIONS OF THE NEW JERSEY HISTORICAL SOCIETY.

Rembrandt Peale portrait of George Washington, as Founding Father. NATIONAL PORTRAIT GALLERY, SMITHSONIAN INSTITUTION, WASHINGTON, D.C. TRANSFER FROM THE NATIONAL GALLERY OF ART; GIFT OF ANDREW W. MELLON.

A popular and imaginary image of Aaron Burr recovering General Armstrong's body under fire at Quebec, by C. H. Stephens.

Theodosia Burr Alston as young matron, by Charles Balthazar Julien Fevret de Saint-Memin.

Aaron Burr's residence at Richmond Hill, New York, situated upon a now-obliterated hill in the West Village, previously the residence of John Adams. ENGRAVING BY C. TIEBOUT.
© COLLECTION OF THE NEW-YORK HISTORICAL SOCIETY, NEW YORK CITY

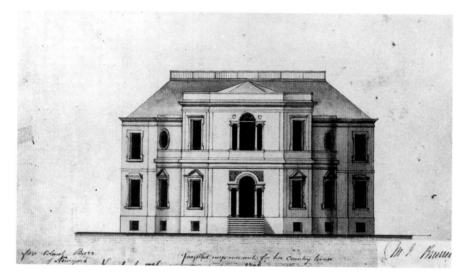

Brunel's design "for Colonel Burr of New York," of a "projected improvement for his country house," Richmond Hill, 1796. COURTESY OF MR. AND MRS. STEPHEN HURST.

Marc Isambard Brunel, one of the artists and architects sponsored by Burr, later celebrated as the engineer of the Thames Tunnel. ENGRAVING BY CHARLES BALTHAZAR JULIEN FEVRET DE SAINT-MEMIN. NATIONAL PORTRAIT GALLERY, SMITHSONIAN INSTITUTION, WASHINGTON, D.C. GIFT OF MR. AND MRS. PAUL MELLON.

John Jay, statesman, judge, and friend to Aaron Burr, by Gilbert Stuart and John Trumbull.
NATIONAL PORTRAIT GALLERY, SMITHSONIAN INSTITUTION, WASHINGTON, D.C.

A popular and imaginary version of the Burr-Hamilton duel at Weehawken, New Jersey.

Hamilton's The Grange, his estate in upper Manhattan, near the Cloisters, by George Hayward. © COLLECTION OF THE NEW-YORK HISTORICAL SOCIETY, NEW YORK CITY.

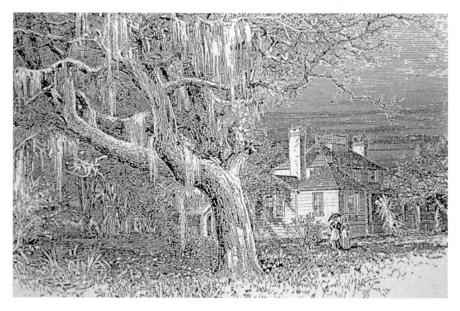

The McQueen-McIntosh house at Fort George as it appeared in 1872, from *Harpers Magazine.*

Commodore Thomas Truxton, friend to Hamilton and Burr, who refused to testify falsely against Burr. COURTESY OF THE NEW YORK PUBLIC LIBRARY.

Joseph Brant as noble savage in 1786, by Gilbert Stuart. NEW YORK STATE HISTORICAL ASSOCIATION, COOPERSTOWN, NEW YORK. COURTESY OF RICHARD WALKER.

An early nineteenth-century image of the earthworks explored by Aaron Burr in Marietta, Ohio. COURTESY OF THE OHIO HISTORICAL SOCIETY.

end of the administration of John Adams, they had proposed to fill the federal judiciary with judges of their own persuasion, arguing that the West, "this vastly expansive, growing country" settled by frontiersmen of "restless spirit," would otherwise fall into anarchy.

As soon as the Jefferson administration came into power, it set about to reverse that process. There would be no more judges. According to the Federalists, the rule of law required judges, and without the rule of law the West would degenerate into anarchy like that to which the Jeffersonians had been so complaisant during the Whiskey Rebellion. Uriah Tracy and James Bayard proclaimed that those committed to a strong judiciary must be "willing to spill their blood to defend" it. Roger Griswold of Connecticut was so shaken as to take up the cry for secession where the *anti-Federalists* had left it. If the Union was without law, as they wanted law to be, the next step, said men of Griswold's thinking, would be the "general dissolution of the Union." John Adams was moved to write that what Jefferson had done in "ambition . . . and revenge will snap the strongest cords of our Constitution."[33]

The parties were crossing over each other. Jefferson and Madison had asserted a strict-construction interpretation of the Constitution in the 1790s, as they sought to dissuade George Washington from approving Hamilton's National Bank. But strictness about federal power became less appealing as power flowed steadily toward the slaveholding South. Jefferson admitted that his acquisition of Louisiana was unconstitutional; he talked of getting it approved through a retroactive constitutional amendment, but never got around to it. This vast augmentation of the scope of slavery's dominion led the Federalists to reverse roles and to couple strict construction—contending that Louisiana had been unconstitutionally purchased—with threats of secession. By 1804, their rhetoric echoed language employed by the South Carolinians and Georgians during the Constitutional Debates of 1787–89. During the Louisiana Debates of 1804, James Hillhouse, leader of the antislavery forces, spoke of his role "*while* I am the representative of a state which is *yet* a member of the Union."[34]

Griswold, having concluded that "the only remedy is separation," sought out Burr. He was thought to be vulnerable since he had just been forced out of the vice presidency and was seeking Federalist support to become governor of New York. Griswold reported to Rufus King that his mission was to determine whether or not Burr would "agree and pledge himself . . . if he becomes governor [that] New York may be united with the Northern [New England] states in the project of separation." He left disappointed. Burr would agree only that "the Northern states must be governed by Virginia, or govern Virginia," and that he would govern "in a manner satisfactory to the Federalists." But that was all.[35]

Rebuffed by Burr, the Federalists, now in fact acting as anti-Federalists, went underground until the humiliations of the United States during "Mr. Madison's War" of 1812 confirmed all their earlier scoffing about Virginian rule. Griswold and the others, moved as much by aversion to incompetence as by aversion to slavery, angry at lost trading opportunities with Britain, and shamed by Jefferson and Madison's bringing their country into cobelligerency with the tyrant Napoleon, organized their Hartford Convention in 1814. Contrary to the impression conveyed in some texts, they scrupulously eschewed any further talk of secession, turning their attention instead to the insufficiencies of the Madison administration's support of their war efforts. It is noteworthy that Madison himself relied upon the residual Burrites in New York, led by Robert Swartwout, to keep New York solidly behind his efforts to survive the indignities of the war long enough to permit Gallatin to negotiate a respectable peace with Britain.

One wonders whether or not Madison felt a twinge when writing Swartwout, in January 1815, authorizing him to use Treasury funds and to raise volunteers to resist either a British invasion or a rebellion from within. Burr may well have been with Swartwout when this missive arrived, for he was often in Swartwout's house. He had been given refuge there three years earlier, when he returned from the exile into which he had been sent by Jefferson and Madison.[36]

Burr and Disunion

Burr had gone into that exile charged by Jefferson with having sought to divide the Union and setting himself up as a caudillo in the West. The charge has stuck because the accuser was Jefferson, and because Jefferson was President. Washington and Adams had taught the public to believe Presidents. We inquire elsewhere into the likelihood that Jefferson believed in his own charges, though he found no jury to accept them. The question for us here is whether or not we should believe Jefferson, though his allegations are repeated year after year, accompanied with little more evidence than a general assertion that Burr was a bad character, or the assertion that Burr, in exile, in effect pled guilty by proposing that France support a revived separatist scheme.

We can understand better much of the detailed story that lies before us if we accept the invitation offered by this reference to what Burr did or did not say in 1810 about what he intended in 1806. We will have skipped ahead of the detailed evidence, but we will get a glimpse of Burr's character when it was most severely tested. His Paris years were his worst. We will come back to them at the very end of our tale, but let us here take up the challenge offered by his severest critics and determine whether or not he clarified during those years what he was doing while he was still a force in American politics fearsome to Thomas Jefferson.

Is it true that he corroborated the charge that he was willing to dismember the Union by offering to do so with Napoleon's support? It is not true. Burr did not provide any such corroboration. Quite the contrary. What he said in Paris was wholly consistent with a record of steadfast loyalty to the American Republic, in wartime and in peace, in good times and bad.

Let us examine that record, as it culminated with his negotiations with the French. As others were in complicity with the French plots of the 1790s and wept for the failure of the Whiskey Rebellion, as William Blount conspired with Britain and John Sevier with Spain, as Harry Innes and James Wilkinson encouraged the Kentucky separatists and Thomas Jefferson said nothing, Burr never took Jefferson's acquiescent posture toward separatism. In 1804, when it was the Federalists' turn, he rebuffed them. Jefferson, on the other hand, was a centrifugal force while out of power, invented the doctrine of nullification, and ultimately came to espouse a strong central government only when he was President.

Though Burr failed to provide a treatise of his views on secessionism, every statement he made on the subject indicates that he shared with Hamilton a steadfast allegiance to a strong central government. Besides, he was a gentleman, and he gave his word to other gentlemen, such as William Henry Harrison, Henry Clay, and Andrew Jackson, that he had never had any intention to sever the Union or to set himself up as chief of state of a severed portion. At the very end of his life, as he approached death, he repeated that assurance.

It has been asserted that he did not mean what he said, having said it only when it was easy to do so. That is not true. He affirmed that position in extremis, when he gave an extensive interview to the French secret service on the subject. He was in Paris, in exile, in 1810, having every reason to encourage the French to think he might lead a separatist movement under their aegis, reinvigorating a concept proposed by General Georges Collot (see below). Burr was known to have been willing in 1806 to tell the British, French, or even the Spaniards what they wanted to hear about his plans, when all he wanted from any of them was money to attack Mexico in the event of war, but he would not sell himself to Napoleon—ever—if that meant dismembering the Union. Before his trial and after it, he made a distinction between adventuring, to the brink of misdemeanor, and treason. The reports filed by the French secret service between the tenth and the thirteenth of March 1810 reporting their failure to seduce Burr provide the clearest expression of Burr's response. The French were seeking to draw him into a discussion of how "the division of the United States into two or more governments entered into the view of Great Britain and Spain," but

> Mr. A. B. does not see these powers as having had any other object other than the odious one of putting the country into disarray. He does not see what interest a power that is not at war with the United States could have in disuniting it. He has none himself, nor has he any desire to see one carried out.[37]

The French concluded that "of all the different plans that Mr. Burr believes practicable, the one to which he clings the most is the independence of Florida." His argument for French assistance toward such an outcome, through "an expedition into the [Spanish] Floridas" was that it would keep these provinces out of the hands of the British. "The first result . . . would be the declaration of their independence; a more remote result, but one that the geographical position of this section would render inevitable, would be the joining of the Floridas to the United States."[38]

That does not sound like a separatist scheme. Indeed, it sounds more like an accretist one. Nonetheless, M. Roux, an eager junior intelligence officer ("one of the employees of this ministry," according to his superior officer, the duc de Cadore), indicated that Burr had been willing to consider a separation of Louisiana. However, Cadore, observing that none of those notes were "signed or initialed by him [Burr] to indicate his approval of . . . [their] contents," cautioned the Emperor not to take them any more seriously than "the rumor which has spread of communications directed against his own country." Having heard "that he was accused of having made" such communications, "Mr. B. has come back" and, putting himself at even greater risk of being held in further house arrest, or worse, "limited himself to repeating what he had said before, and that he spoke only of the Floridas and Canada." These were provinces held not by the United States but by nations with which it was about to go to war. No secessionism there, either.[39]

Here are the sections of the March 13 notes kept in the files of the French secret service relevant to Burr and East *and* West Florida:

> The plans Colonel Burr submits to His Majesty . . . are to have some colonies of America declared independent. . . . His aims can be limited to the Lucayes Islands (the Bahamas) or extended to the two Floridas and to New Mexico.
>
> Pensacola would be the center of his operations. . . . He has had an understanding with the most influential men. The inhabitants of the Georgias and the western United States whose rivers have their mouths in Florida would be equally favorable to a change that would allow them freedom of trade. . . . It was in those areas that he had already succeeded in making numerous levies for an invasion of Mexico two years ago, when the United States government stopped him in his plans.
>
> The first result of the expedition to the Floridas would be the declaration of their independence; a more remote result, but one that the geographical position of this section would render inevitable would be the joining of the Floridas to the United States.[40]

None of the provinces against which Burr was said to "aim" were then parts of the United States; Pensacola was in Spanish Florida. There was no suggestion that "the inhabitants of the Georgias," etc., were to be encouraged in separatist schemes in order to achieve "freedom of trade." When Burr reopened his discussions with Cadore, as to Canada, he only did so to induce the French to help him take the Floridas, because, from there, he might be willing to lead an invasion of Canada—after all, he had invaded Canada once before. "In Florida he would make his preparation for this expedition. . . . Without the

Floridas no success could be attained at all, not in Mexico, or in Jamaica, or in Nova Scotia."[41]

Only witnesses suborned by money or favors for the Richmond Trial testified to any inconsistency between the intentions expressed by Burr in Paris in 1810 and what he had said in the West in 1805 and 1806. And there is further corroboration in his having shared his ideas with John Jay. Is it credible that Jay would encourage anyone to dismember the Federal Union? Yet his biographers inform us that "as early as 1796," Burr laid out for Jay his western plans, in "various conversations . . . in reference" to the Spanish dominions, probably Louisiana and Texas. Burr "expressed his views" of those provinces, "which, he said, he could revolutionize and take possession of." Expressing his opinion that it was "not impracticable," Governor Jay replied that the boldness of the project would contribute to its success. John Jay would never have endorsed the idea if it had carried with it any prospect of a division of the United States.[42]

As early as 1796, Jefferson had inaugurated his program of filibustering by stealth. Two years later, Hamilton began his final effort to find glory, in a military expedition against the Spanish possessions. Burr's adventure was a decade off—and by that time utterly "impracticable."

10

Washington, Western Pennsylvania, and Secession

In the early spring of 1794, Talleyrand, once a bishop and stockjobber, then an ambassador, managed to bribe Danton, who, as minister of justice of one of the bloodier regimes in French history, was able to decide who would live and who would die. All Talleyrand required was Danton's personal signature on a permit to leave the country, which he received, and on the strength of which he found himself spending thirty-eight days at sea, bored for lack of witty companions, until he arrived in the estuary of the Delaware, with Philadelphia promising more amusement. He bore a letter of introduction from Lord Shelborne to George Washington and thus to the new Secretary of the Treasury, Alexander Hamilton. After the departure of Thomas Jefferson at the turn of the year, Hamilton was the government's chief theoretician; contrary to all canards, he liked Frenchmen—even bishops.

Washington thought it prudent to decline the pleasure of meeting Talleyrand, thereby losing any chance for the kind of immortality conveyed in the memoirs of men of wit, but Hamilton did not, and the two became cronies. That may or may not have been for the reasons given by Duff Cooper in his biography of Talleyrand, but Cooper's view of our three protagonists has the virtue of a perspective not often encountered in American accounts of the period:

> In default of meeting Washington, he made friends with . . . the most remarkable man in the whole of that continent[,] Hamilton, . . . whom Talleyrand could both love and respect. They . . . both . . . despised sentimental twaddle whether it poured from the lips of a Robespierre or a Jefferson. The terrorist sobbing over humanity or the slave owner spouting about freedom were equally repulsive to these two practical statesmen. . . . But while the Frenchman became a byword for lack of principle in an unprincipled age, the American had principles for which he would have died. While Talleyrand saw in politics a path to riches, Hamilton would sooner have picked a pocket than made a penny out of his political position. . . . Years afterwards [in 1810] Aaron Burr, who had killed Hamilton in a duel, left a card upon Talleyrand in Paris. The major-domo was instructed to inform Monsieur Burr when he called again that over Talleyrand's mantelpiece there hung the portrait of Alexander Hamilton.[1]

Actually, Talleyrand knew both Hamilton and Burr, whose guest he was frequently at Richmond Hill, and who had been his business partner in speculations in Pennsylvania lands as recently as 1797. His refusal to see Burr was less principled than Washington's refusal to see him, since all that Burr was seeking was an exit visa, though perhaps he knew that Burr lacked the means to secure it as Talleyrand had managed to escape the Terror in 1794.

Duff Cooper's view of things may be annoying, but it is all of a piece with the convention among some biographers of relying upon Talleyrand's assessments of the Americans he met during his own exile, often deploying the portrait-over-the mantelpiece vignette as a prelude to Talleyrand's judgment of Napoleon, Fox, and Hamilton as "the three greatest men of our epoch" and his statement that if he "were forced to decide among the three, . . . [he] would give without hesitation the first place to Hamilton."[2]

Washington had not deigned to see him, so we must take that into account. Would we not add Washington's name to the list of great ones? Indeed, would we not give him first place in greatness among Americans of the time?

Washington led the armies which gave his country independence, launched that independence as presiding officer over its Constitution-making, served as its first chief executive, and, in that bitter year of 1794, with Talleyrand watching, sustained the Union. As soon as the Revolution had been won, the colonists we customarily call frontiersmen erupted across the Appalachians out of the original thirteen states and into the West. Many doubted, at the time, that the nation could be held together over so vast a territory, or that any republic could be stretched to double itself between the mountains and the Mississippi. Washington did not doubt, or, if he did, he kept his doubt to himself while he created the first extensive republic in the history of human-kind.

Hamilton and Burr echoed that confident affirmative. Madison and Jefferson were not so sure, repeatedly indicating a willingness to acquiesce in a division of the Union on the perforation of the peaks of the Appalachians. As we have noted, both Hamilton and Burr were asked to consider schemes to divide New England, or New England plus New York, from the Union, and both refused. Hamilton's view, as expressed to Washington in August 1792, was that neither the western nor the Yankee separatists—neither Republicans nor Federalists—should be encouraged:

> It is certainly much to be regretted that party discriminations are so far geographical . . . , and that ideas of a severance of the Union are creeping in both North and South. In the South it is supposed that more government than is expedient is desired by the North. In the North, it is believed that the prejudices of the South are incompatible with the necessary degree of government and with the attainment of the essential ends of national union. In both quarters there are respectable men [Washington knew who they were], who talk of separatism as a thing dictated by the different geniuses and different prejudices of the parts.[3]

Washington and Burr came to know what lay in the West better than any of the other Founders. Washington had surveyed the ridge and valley province between the Blue Ridge and the Ohio watershed in 1749, 1750, and 1752, had made his first military expedition into the "Western Waters" in 1753, had suffered his first military defeat there at Fort Necessity in 1754 and his second with Braddock in 1755, and had enjoyed his first small victory in the entourage of Forbes and Bouquet three years later. Washington's first Mississippi Valley investments were made in 1763, and those in the Ohio Valley explored by him in 1770 and again in 1784. No other President before Andrew Jackson knew so much of what lay beyond Pittsburgh and the Cumberland Gap. Washington owned a total of nearly seventy thousand acres in the West—a small spread compared to Burr's claim on 270,000, but, on the other hand, Washington's titles were good.

At Valley Forge, Washington had talked with his officers about his western investments, encouraging those who could to consider setting their own stakes in the Ohio Valley, offering the dream of Cincinnatian colonies within a nation extending as far as the Mississippi. At the end of his life he was still talking of an expedition to Detroit and then to New Orleans. His portage-seeking, when he first met Gallatin, was part of his binding together of the new nation of which he was the undeniable leader. The Appalachian Highlands were abrasive, threatening to sever the primitive land communications between the Ohio Valley and the eastern seaboard. The westerners, said Washington, "have no other means of coming to us but by a long land transportation and unimproved roads . . . the worst . . . ever trod by man or beast," so steep, a woman traveler reported in 1787, "that the horses seem ready to fall backwards."[4]

If, however, the routes could be improved so that a system of portages and canals would make it as easy to ship flour, whiskey, and corn eastward upstream as southward down the Ohio and Mississippi, "how astonishingly our exports will be increased. [And] . . . from a political point of view . . . how necessary it is," Washington wrote, "to apply the cement of interest to bind all parts of it [the nation] together, by one indissoluble band—particularly the middle states with the Country immediately back of them—for what ties let me ask, should we have upon those people." How necessary, indeed, because the immense energies of the West must be released: it was a "new and rising empire . . . one of the most fertile countries in the globe."[5]

Washington's search for portage routes and his laying out of canals sprang from the same urgency that led him and Hamilton to put down the Whiskey Rebels in Pennsylvania and to do all he could to see to it that the Westerners had access to the sea through New Orleans. A canal system between the Ohio and Potomac valleys would, he hoped,

> open a wide door, and make a smooth way for the produce of that Country to pass to our markets. . . . [C]ommercial connec-

tions of all others, are most difficult to dissolve. . . . The Western Settlers . . . stand as it were upon a pivot—the touch of a feather would almost incline them any way—[looking] down the Mississippi . . . [they see their goods may be] glided gently down the stream.[6]

Goods might glide gently downstream toward the Spaniards, but Washington did not want western loyalties to glide with them. Therefore he took steps to pry loose any impediments to the trade, in order to retain the loyalties. While the waters of the Mississippi flowed untroubled to the Gulf, everything floating upon them, every craft of any size bearing hides, grain, indigo, rice, whiskey, or lumber, could be stopped by Spanish intervention. Imperial policy formulated in Madrid determined the value of Indiana pork, Kentucky tobacco, and Tennessee whiskey. This was the primary problem of foreign policy for the western half of the United States until the Louisiana Purchase.

Erring Sisters and Their Siblings

Across this political landscape in the 1780s and 1790s, Thomas Jefferson soared. And where did his "touch of a feather" alight?

In 1776, Virginia asserted western dominions extending to the Mississippi and Lake of the Woods, an immensity so vast that Jefferson proposed that it might best be divided into separate, independent units: In "the western and northern extent of this country . . . new colonies . . . [shall be] established on the same fundamental laws as [Virginia] . . . and shall be free and independent of this colony and of all the world."[7]

Though by 1789, Virginia and the other states claiming western lands had ceded them to the federal government, Jefferson did not alter his views. He wrote Madison from Paris that if the settlers of the Mississippi Valley were to "declare themselves a separate people, we are incapable of a single effort to retain them"; they could not be forced back into the Union. "Our citizens can never be induced . . . to go there to cut the throats of their own brothers and sons."[8]

A year later, Jefferson wished bon voyage to Kentucky:

[Though] every measure should be taken, which may draw the bands of union tighter . . . [still,] if they see their interest in separation, why should we take side with our Atlantic rather than our Mississippi descendants? It is the elder and the younger son differing.

Whether we remain in one confederacy or form into Atlantic and Mississippi confederacies, I believe it not very important to the happiness of either part . . . and did I now foresee a separation at some future day, yet I should feel the duty & the desire to promote the western interests as zealously as the eastern.[9]

Jefferson did not know those "western interests" at first hand. He was not inclined toward personal exploration, never traveling so far west as his father, who penetrated the pinnacles of the continental divide now marked by the Appalachian Trail. Madison did not claim even that breadth of knowledge, for he never ventured beyond the ridge which he saw from the portico at Montpelier. In 1787, Jefferson wrote Madison: "I never had any interest Westward of the Allegheny; and I never will have any. But I have had great opportunities of knowing the character of the people who inhabit that country." Really?[10]

Astonishing as it now seems to us, Jefferson's complaisance in the face of a shattering Union persisted for a time even when he himself was President. As late as 1803, he wrote: "His policy was still as diffident as that of James Buchanan in 1858: God bless them both, and keep them in the union, if it be for their good, but separate them, if it be better." One may imagine Alexander Hamilton's response had Jefferson's polygraph made a copy of this for him.[11]

And what might John Jay have thought? He had encouraged Burr to seek a new career in the West in 1796, when Jay was back in the governorship of New York after a long succession of frustrations attempting his own program for the West. It is unthinkable that Jay would have tolerated for a moment an acquiescence "in separation." After a decade laboring to extricate from Spain rights to the navigation of the Mississippi through diplomacy, he might well have encouraged a person of a different disposition, like Burr, to attempt it by force. Jay had given up his Spanish negotiations by November 1794, turning instead to the British, with whom he worked out the evacuation of the posts they had retained in the Northwest Territory despite the requirements of the treaties of 1783. He had proposed that the United States give up, in exchange, its Revolutionary alliance with France—

the France of the Terror, with which Britain was once again at war, not being the France of Louis XVI.

Jay's failure to open the Mississippi by diplomacy did not endear him to the westerners, who charged him with caving in to Spain, or to the Jeffersonians, who alleged that he had betrayed their friends the French. Burr did not go ahead at the time, probably because Thomas Pinckney, who took Jay's place in Europe, seemed for a while to have succeeded where Jay failed. The Spanish monarchy suddenly expressed a desire to reach an understanding which would permit the obstreperous westerners to ship their salt pork to market through New Orleans. Soon, however, rumors flew that Spain was not in earnest and was, instead, considering returning Louisiana to France to relieve the pressure for more painful concessions.

The rumors were correct. In the secret Treaty of Basel in 1795, Spain concluded a separate peace with France; it was followed by the secret Treaty of San Ildefonso in October, 1800, in which it was agreed that Louisiana would go back to France (from which it was received by Spain in 1762), an arrangement confirmed, again in secret, by the Treaty of Aranjuez on March 21, 1801. Meanwhile, relations between France and the Federalist administration degenerated into undeclared war at sea—Mr. Adams's Quasi-War. Now it was Hamilton who threatened to take New Orleans by force. In the West Indies, the Quasi-War produced bloody decks and shattered hulls. Burr, Jay, and Hamilton, once more in agreement, convinced New York's legislature to appropriate funds to fortify the mouth of the Hudson against the French, and all three took part in the supervision of the work.

This maneuvering revealed Burr to be willing to cooperate with the Federalists and to be lukewarm toward France. Neither position endeared him either to the Francophile Virginians or to the Livingstons, who, in the largest family building campaign before the onset of the Vanderbilts, were, at the time, laying up a series of villas along the east bank of the Hudson, employing French architects or using plans sent mail-order from Paris.

Burr's aberrations from Republican discipline and taste might have been enough, but he added his abolitionist alliance with Hamilton and Jay, as well as that peculiar insistence upon the intellectual equality of blacks and women to white males, for which Mr. Jefferson had said "the public is not prepared nor am I." And worse. All along, he had the irritating habit of reminding his contemporaries of European ancestry that there were Indians, such as Joseph Brant and the Stockbridge chiefs, who had to be included in planning for the future of the North American continent.

Worse yet, as the 1790s wore along, Aaron Burr exacerbated his relationship with Jefferson by being unwilling to inveigh either *against* John Jay's handling of the Federalists' Alien and Sedition Acts or *for* Jefferson's countermeasures, the Kentucky and Virginia Resolutions. Charged with being in cahoots with the Federalists, so prickly was his nature that he failed to solicit the benefits of reconciliation with the Federalist leaders, Washington, Hamilton, or John Adams. Still, he seemed to take perverse pleasure in irritating Washington, whose monumental sense of self did not permit such liberties. Washington, always proud and nearly always solemn, understood politics very well. He was especially clear as to his own role in stabilizing the raw, untested, fissiperating republic that had made him its President. Chief among his assets as general and as President was gravitas. As colonel and in his earliest actions as senator, Aaron Burr had offended against both Washington's pride and his grave utility. Burr made things worse by pitting himself against both Washington and Hamilton in an obstreperous defense of his fellow senator Albert Gallatin.

Albert Gallatin and Secession

Gallatin was so closely linked to the Whiskey Rebellion in western Pennsylvania that, as late as 1813, after his own reconciliation with Jefferson, John Adams persisted in calling the rebellion "Gallatin's Insurrection," and Uriah Tracy of Connecticut rose in Congress to remind his colleagues that Gallatin's Revolutionary service had been most obscure and that in peace he had been all too free with French-accented criticism of George Washington the President. The people of Connecticut, said Tracy, "were not of a stamp to dance around a liberty pole today and curse their government, and [then], upon hearing of a military force, sneak into a swamp. . . . I cannot be thankful to that gentleman for coming all the way from Geneva to give Americans character [meaning to deride them] for pusillanimity."[12]

When he first came to the Senate, Gallatin was unpopular with the southerners, being considered an abolitionist from Pennsylvania, as Burr was known to be an abolitionist from New York. Burr had been

Gallatin's friend from their first acquaintance, during the abolitionist 1780s, and made that friendship indelible in the contest for Gallatin's Senate seat and the tortured negotiations prior to the election of 1800. As late as 1804 or even 1805, Gallatin shuttled irresolutely between Burr and Jefferson before making his painful final choice for Jefferson after Burr's duel with Hamilton. Though Gallatin's most recent biographer, Raymond Walters, is correct that his "loyalty to the attractive adventurer brought him embarrassment and annoyance," it also brought him ten years of political advantage and, he himself said, a great deal of joy.[13]

The Burr-Jay connection in New York politics overlapped and succeeded the Burr-Gallatin connection. One is tempted to bundle them together as the French connection, for Jay was proud of his Huguenot descent, and Gallatin never lost his French accent. There was, however, a difference between the two that produced crucial political consequences: Jay was born in New York, and Gallatin in Geneva.

The former event occurred in 1745, the latter in 1761, fifty years after the birth of Rousseau. Gallatin came to the United States in 1780, canoed the rivers of Maine, served in a little frontier fight during the Revolution, tutored at Harvard, and emigrated to western Pennsylvania. As we focus on his political progression through the period in which he and Burr moved in parallel, we must anticipate his better-known later career, in which, under Jefferson's aegis and within Jefferson's penumbra, he emerged as Hamilton's successor as the nation's preeminent expert on finance. Gallatin served as Secretary of the Treasury under Jefferson and Madison and became under their successors a diplomatic success in Europe. In the 1840s, resuming an antislavery position in which he and Burr found common cause until 1799, he joined a morally revivified John Quincy Adams in a campaign against the spread of slavery.

Gallatin's political career began in 1784, when he gave up the only bed in his log cabin in the Appalachian Mountains to George Washington, who was seeking routes across the Alleghenies. Gallatin, though willing to relinquish his cot to an older man—and a general—erred in telling the great man how simple it was to find portages. Like Burr, he was too obviously clever in Washington's presence when it would have been better to be deferential. Both Burr and Gallatin had the problem of invidious intelligence. Gallatin made things worse by being clever in a French-Swiss accent, going so far as to permit himself caustic comments on Anglo-Saxon persons and institutions. When he was serving in the Congress and opposed a Federalist proposal, a Federalist representative from Connecticut arose to assure the House "that there was American blood enough in the House to approve this clause and American accent enough to pronounce it."[14]

Gallatin was the sloppiest of the Founders, neglecting his teeth and hair, notoriously given to wearing his clothes beyond a sanitary date and postponing repairs about his elbows and knees. But he was very bright, and his esteem for the intelligence of Thomas Jefferson was great. In 1798, he moderated his principles of racial equality to accommodate the objectives of the plantocrats as they starved out the republic of Toussaint Louverture on Haiti. In 1806, when Jefferson turned on Burr, Gallatin went silently along, providing vouchers from the Treasury to pay the agents sent against the old friend.

Characteristically, Burr refused to speak ill of Gallatin, recalling to others only their joint intellectual interests. In 1808, when Burr was in London, he congratulated Pierre-Etienne-Louis Dumont on his translations of two of Jeremy Bentham's most esoteric essays on economics into French, seeking an introduction to Bentham. "No one in the United States," wrote Burr, "appreciated [Bentham's] ideas except himself [Burr] and Albert Gallatin . . . who was the best head in the United States." Burr and Bentham became acquainted, and Burr became a resident in Bentham's house, where their discussions of economics led Bentham to write that there was "very good evidence of analogy between his [Burr's] ideas and mine." And, one assumes, those of Gallatin as well.[15]

Gallatin was surely admirable, a loving and a lovable man. He shared a rare affection for Jefferson with James Madison. (It is one thing to esteem such a man, quite another to be fond of him.) And so long as they lived, both Burr and Jefferson retained a genuine affection for Gallatin. When Jefferson was eighty, he wrote Gallatin, "I shall love you forever, and rejoice in your rejoicing, and sympathize with your evils. God bless you and have you ever in his holy keeping!" As I have suggested elsewhere, "this letter should be required reading for those who believe they understand all there is to understand about Thomas Jefferson."[16]

Gallatin's constituency in western Pennsylvania was largely comprised of Scotch-Irish Presbyterians—Burr's natural following as well—of whom John Smilie, Gallatin's first American political mentor, was a leader. With Smilie, Gallatin took part in the Harrisburg convention of 1788, which annoyed Washington and Hamilton by urging that Pennsylvania only accept the U.S. Constitution if it were much amended. Gallatin led those demanding changes and took the view, chilling to all good Federalists but not to Jefferson, that the American Union would become too big for true representative government if it were extended further than its borders of 1783. Both he and Jefferson reversed that position in 1802.

Gallatin was elected for the first time to the Pennsylvania Assembly in 1790 and reelected thereafter for each session through 1794. By Pennsylvania custom, he was permitted to serve in both the U.S. House and the U.S. Senate. He would have saved himself much trouble if he had not tried to do so.

Riots and Reaction

It was a troublesome time in western Pennsylvania. In 1786, a state excise tax collector had been attacked in Washington County, seat of which was the city of Washington, the core of resistance to excises whether state or federal. Only a decade earlier, excises on tea and stamps had provoked riots—called tea parties. After these riots of the 1770s had come independence, which some described as secession from the British empire. In 1791, as soon as the westerners heard of Hamilton's proposal to set a similar tax upon their chief cash crop, whiskey, they sent a remonstrance, composed by Gallatin, to Congress. Reminding the easterners of Boston harbor and 1775, they warned that the same measure might provoke the same result and would be, therefore, "subversive of the peace, liberty and rights of the citizen."[17]

Congress, goaded by Hamilton, went ahead anyway and passed the Whiskey Tax in March 1791. Assembling in the town of Washington, with Gallatin acting as clerk, the Pennsylvanians renewed their remonstrances and passed a resolution urging all citizens to shun anyone who tried to collect the excises. Gallatin, later the nation's chief taxing official, confessed a few years later that the "sentiments" of the Washington convention "were not illegal or criminal; yet they were violent, intemperate and reprehensible." His role in bringing them forward was, he admitted, his "only political sin."[18]

That expression gives us pause. He was admitting a miscalculation;

that was all, using hyperbole to diminish its sinfulness. As we pause, we may consider what he might have said at the end of his life, reflecting upon his Black Speech (see Chapter Eleven), or his silence as slavery expanded into the West, or his equally profound silence when, as Jefferson's Secretary of the Treasury, he found money for the government of which he was a part to use the means it did against Aaron Burr, his protector of the 1790s. These circumstances tested Gallatin's character far more than his role in the tax revolt in the 1790s. He could not then have known that within a decade he would himself be Secretary of the Treasury, when the taxes he raised were for the purpose of buying Louisiana and financing the War of 1812 against Great Britain. What if the money had been for another war against France, like that of 1798, when he opposed expenditures to fight it? What if the purchase had been of Lower Canada from Britain?

Leaving to further rumination these central questions, we may return to 1792, when President George Washington responded to the resolutions submitted over Gallatin's signature: "I shall exert all the legal powers with which the executive is invested, to check so daring and unwarrantable a spirit." His Secretary of the Treasury, Mr. Hamilton, saw at once the gravity of the threat to public order, the affront to Washington personally, and the opportunity for military adventure. He drafted for the President a tough proclamation, vowing action against anyone who obstructed the enforcement of the law.[19]

Washington, perhaps advised by Hamilton, determined to smoke out Jefferson, sending him a copy of the draft for review at Monticello. The Sage sidestepped the traps, blandly suggesting minor modifications. Out of the fray, he wrote the President that he was "sincerely sorry to learn that such proceedings had taken place." Gallatin was not so prudent. Further exposing himself to retribution, he saw to it that those who had expressed the strongest antiadministration sentiments were hidden away from the federal marshals who came after them with writs.[20]

Washington talked privately of calling out the militia but did not do so until the phrase "Jacobin plots" acquired an uglier meaning. At the end of January 1793, the French decapitated Louis XVI, and gentlemen in Philadelphia spoke of Gallatin as being a Jacobin. It did not help matters when he wrote to a friend that in France "enthusiasm" had produced "an energy equally terrible and sublime."[21]

Twenty-seven days after the death of the King of France, Albert Gallatin was elected to serve Pennsylvania in the U.S. Senate. Two weeks after that, he was married to Hannah Nicholson.

Only a few minutes after Gallatin was sworn in, on December 2, 1793, his contest with the administration of George Washington and Alexander Hamilton recommenced. Vice President John Adams reported to the Senate that a petition had been received asserting that Gallatin could not meet the Senate's nine years' citizenship requirement, and Gallatin was not much slower in reopening his side of the feud. Excise taxes had brought him there, and excise taxes he would continue to oppose. Now he had parliamentary weapons, tried-and-true for all legislative oppositions to administrations of which they disapprove: He asked Hamilton to produce, with his handful of Treasury employees, detailed schedules of reports of revenues and expenditures for each of the preceding years. These reports were not easily completed, and they were not finished on February 10, 1794, when the Federalists finally contrived to have Gallatin expelled from the Senate.

Gallatin was deprived of his seat because nativist Federalists found that he had not quite satisfied the Constitution's residency requirements. His accent did not help, nor did the hoisting of liberty poles that winter all across western Pennsylvania. Ignoring both accent and poles, Burr, in one of his greatest speeches, derided the nativists as representing a nostalgia for some Anglo-Saxon Peaceable Kingdom that never was—certainly not in New York or Pennsylvania. Burr's ironic style was equally natural to Gallatin, who redeployed his arguments five years later in the struggle over the Alien and Sedition Acts.

Braddock's Field and Washington's March

On July 15, 1794, a U.S. marshal was fired upon and his house set afire; he returned fire at his besiegers, killing one and wounding six. On July 28, the radicals called a mass assembly at Braddock's Field, where Washington won his first laurels in war. The crowd was told that they would soon have an opportunity to display *their* "military talents," and off they marched to occupy Pittsburgh.[22]

One chronicler of these events, Judge Henry Brackenridge, estimated the crowd at Braddock's Field as from five to seven thousand; it was the largest public assembly since the Revolution, and very dangerous. On August 14, 1794, at Parkinson's Ferry, another mob assembled and heard a resolution proposed that "the western country [would] repel any hostile attempts that may be made against the rights of the people." Gallatin was present and talked them out of passing this deliberate provocation, but they did raise a six-starred flag. Six. That was especially threatening to Washington (and should have been to Jefferson), for only four of the seditious counties lay in Pennsylvania. Two of the stars represented those counties in Virginia (now in West Virginia) lying along the western slopes of the Appalachians and deeply engaged with the secessionists.

On August 23, Hamilton published the first of a series of public letters, signed "Tully," charging that "the insurgents . . . are . . . hostile to the peace, unity, and indivisibility of the United States" and that their leaders were using the agitation over whiskey "to cover the commencement of a more extensive plan" to break "the counties over the mountains from the Union." For the first time in American public discourse, Hamilton placed the threat of nullification preliminary to secession. As "Fenno," he adumbrated the principle, later affirmed by Abraham Lincoln in 1861, that when a group of citizens (by implication, a state government) sought "to rejudge and reverse" a federal law, they thus rendered that law "a nullity," and the federal government could not permit this to happen.[23]

There were more tarrings and featherings. Men were killed on both sides. West of the mountains, the national legal system ceased to be effective. On September 25, Washington called out the troops and, with Hamilton riding beside him, as Secretary of War as well as Secretary of the Treasury, set forth across the autumn-yellowing ribs of Pennsylvania, following an ancient Indian track now covered over, much of the way, by the Pennsylvania Turnpike and U.S. Highway 30.

The brigades that marched past Washington in review in 1794 comprised a larger army than he commanded against the British between 1776 and 1783—nine thousand infantry and three thousand cavalry. Did the old gentleman not recall, as he traversed one granite defile after another, one narrow valley after another, that this was the way he had taken with Braddock, against the French, forty years earlier? As Hamilton turned his attention to rounding up those he took to be responsible for the insurrection, sparing "no effort to secure evidence to bring Gallatin within the pale of an indictment," did Washington recall occupying that brash young man's cabin in 1784, at a place his Virginia militia were passing once again?

There were those on the march who will figure elsewhere in our tale in quite other roles: Alexander Dallas rode with the Philadelphia gentleman's cavalry. It was Dallas who told Gallatin that "a list" was "handed about the army . . . of the names of those persons who were to be destroyed," of which Gallatin's "was one of the most conspicuous." After another decade, in 1804 Dallas offered Aaron Burr sanctuary in Philadelphia. Yet another decade passed, and in 1814 Dallas, apparently forgiven his aberration, succeeded Gallatin as Secretary of the Treasury.[24]

A Tempest in a Teapot?

In November 1794, Gallatin made every effort to moderate the rhetoric of the rebels and removed his name from those likely to fall before Paterson's definition of treason by repudiating all exhortations toward either nullification or secession. To his credit, Hamilton acknowledged that the "list" which Dallas had seen had been compiled before he had had adequate opportunity to hear of the moderates' efforts to restrain the violence of the mob. Until then, only the indictments against them by their political enemies had been heard: "Had we listened to some people," Hamilton said, "I do not know what we might have done."[25]

This was apparently the moderate course preferred by most of his constituents, for he was reelected to the Pennsylvania Assembly and, at the same time, elected to the U.S. Congress. The Assembly into which Gallatin took his place was no longer so friendly to him as that before the election. Once again he was rejected from a seat to which he had been elected, this time on the basis that his election was invalid because his district was in a state of insurrection when it was held. Out went Gallatin again, but his district promptly returned him in a fresh election. Once back in Washington, he assumed the leadership of the opposition.

During the Whiskey Rebellion, other outbreaks of violence against the central government flared in Kentucky and South Carolina. How serious was the threat to the Union? How justified were the actions taken by Washington and Hamilton to repress it? Gallatin's most recent biographer, Dr. Walters, tells us that David Bradford, who led the radicals, "dreamed of himself as the George Washington of a new western republic," and it seems that Washington himself agreed, for he charged the Bradfordites with "treasonable acts." That sort of language was not used by him lightly, and when he pardoned other Whiskey Rebels, he declined to pardon Bradford. Those with sympathy for secessionists have found it useful to argue that Washington was overreacting in 1794, just as Lincoln, in their view, overreacted in 1861. To them, the Whiskey Rebels were proto-Confederates; they denigrate Hamilton to score a carom shot on Abraham Lincoln.[26]

Those of us who believe that Washington was correct, that there was a genuine crisis of 1794, also are drawn to the conclusion that in that crisis Jefferson was not useful to his country. On December 28, 1794, scenting political advantage, he wrote Madison:[27]

> [O]ur militia returned from the westward. . . . [T]hough the people let them pass quietly they were objects of their laughter, not of their fear; that one thousand men could have cut off their whole force in a thousand places of the Allegheny; that their detestation of the Excise Law is universal, and has now been associated to it a detestation of the government; and that a separation [of the western people] which was perhaps a very distant and problematical event, is now near and certain, and determined in the mind of every man.[28]

In accordance with this view of things, the Jeffersonians responded to Washington's efforts to sustain the union by securing from the Virginia House of Delegates a condemnation of Governor Henry Lee for bringing the Virginia militia into Washington's army. As a further remonstrance against Lee's rallying to the federal cause, they declared the office of governor vacant.

Latter-day Jeffersonians, such as Claude Bowers, have suggested that the Whiskey Rebellion was a "tempest in a teapot," a pleasant afternoon's diversion—but, they are prone to add, a politically useful one. According to Bowers, Jefferson made use of the occasion to build support for his "Revolution of 1800," condemning Hamilton's "plans for the political suppression of the 'mob' " as "aristocracy" riding "with a drawn sword" upon "democracy." David Bradford, the secessionist, depicted by Bowers as a patriarch surrounded by "old men who had fought for American independence" and "young men all bronzed by the weather." Bowers pictures Jefferson as encouraging Bradford and his "men of no particular importance . . . to think in terms of politics," as the Sage looked northward down the slopes of Monticello to observe "their growing power with complete approval."[29]

Washington viewed them differently, believing that the Union was in peril. As we now recall, his informed assessment was that "the Western Settlers . . . [stood] as it were upon a pivot—the touch of a feather would almost incline them any way."

Georges Collot

Hamilton's appearance at the head of the army to prevent the secession of western Pennsylvania, and perhaps Kentucky as well, brought the charge by the Jeffersonians that he was planning a putsch, an accusation reused against Burr in 1806, though in that case the coup d'état was asserted to have depended upon a slave uprising not likely in western Pennsylvania, where there were few blacks to arouse. Jefferson may have feared a Hamiltonian putsch in 1794; he said he did. He may have feared a Burrite putsch in 1806; he said that, too. But in 1794 he also said that he took satisfaction from the possibility that "one thousand men could have cut off [Hamilton's] . . . whole force in a thousand places of the Allegheny," an odd thing for a former Secretary of State to consider happily since that force was the U.S. Army, commanded by George Washington. It was as if he were, indeed, a little bit Jacobin and had been conversing with the same military experts who, two years later, convinced General Collot that the Whiskey Rebellion had offered a great opportunity for Jacobin insurrection and secession.[30]

Collot had been despatched in March 1796 to see if there was any further hope of secessionism in Pennsylvania and, while he was on the ground, to survey the Ohio and Mississippi for sites to fortify, should the people of "the counties over the mountains from the Union" become willing to separate under French auspices. As Collot passed the bluffs at the mouth of the Wabash, he noted that they could be held against an attack coming upstream and pointed out that the Pennsylvania insurgents could "have blocked up the passages of the Alleghenies against the federal army [coming along Braddock's Road from the east], by seizing these defiles, and stationing their principal force at Bedford ... [and] perhaps have determined the inhabitants between the Alleghenies and the Susquehanna to take an active part in their resistance."[31]

Collot lamented lost possibilities. "Had the chiefs of the insurrection of 1794 been soldiers, or had they any military knowledge of these mountains, they might, with the troops under their orders—they had more than eight thousand men at their disposal, all excellent light infantry ... have added to the flags of independent nations of the Western Hemisphere the six-starred standard they raised atop their liberty poles."[32]

By the time Collot went into the Mississippi Valley, two years had passed since the Whiskey Rebellion; the threat of French-encouraged secession had also abated in Kentucky. Though Albert Gallatin was back on the national stage and pooh-poohing the significance of French plots, and though Collot carried to the West a letter of introduction from Burr (presumably influenced to do so by Gallatin), John Quincy Adams, then in his Federalist phase, wrote his father on August 3, 1797, that the presence of such a trained officer showed that the French were still contemplating the juncture of an expeditionary force with Western rebels to dismember the Union.

Burr, Gallatin, and the Election of 1800

Where had Burr been all these years? For part of the time, in the U.S. Senate, and after that doing his work of manumission in the New York Assembly. In the winter of 1792, as a freshman senator, he made frequent use of the State Department archives in order to find original documents for use in the composition of an account of foreign policy decisions reached in the course of the Revolution and, in general, to deepen his knowledge of foreign affairs. Though Secretary of State Jefferson had initially given Burr permission to do so, he appears to have had second thoughts, for a curt note was sent by him to Burr saying that "it has been concluded that it would be improper to communicate the correspondence of existing ministers." This appears to have been the first use of the "don't embarrass living persons" rule, which was especially pernicious in combination with the Senate's habit of doing its serious business in secret. The files, like the Senate, were closed.[33]

Two years later, after the Genêt Affair, the American ministry to France became open; Gouverneur Morris had been clever one time too many at the expense of the ragtag *arrivistes* assuming power there. Morris became elegantly, satirically, non grata; it was obvious that he must be replaced. Burr wanted the post. He was still seeking to broaden his knowledge of foreign affairs, though he could hardly hope to rival Jefferson. For the first time, though not the last, Hamilton and Jefferson then ranged themselves against him. Hamilton used his influence upon Washington, who responded to a recommendation of Burr from the Republican caucus that he would not give any important post to anyone "in whose integrity he had not confidence." The post went to James Monroe.[34]

Jefferson's hand was hidden, but not completely. Theodore Sedgwick observed to Jonathan Dayton that though the Republicans in the Congress coveted "the aid of his [Burr's] character and talents," he was defeated by "insidious machinations" within that party. "And wherefore was it that they preferred Monroe to him? Had they more confidence in Monroe's talents? They are not so stupid. In his integrity? No. But they knew the one would and the other would not condescend to act as their tool. They doubtless respect Burr's talents, but they dread his independence of them."[35]

There it was. Burr's political obituary, a little early. Two years passed. In the presidential election of 1796, Burr performed upon a pledge to produce presidential electors from New York, Pennsylvania, and elsewhere for Jefferson. In return for this, the Virginians were to deliver to him half their own and others from their dependencies, North Carolina and Kentucky. They broke that pledge, providing only one vote out of the promised twenty of their forty-two, throwing away another fifteen to Samuel Adams as a sort of derisive gesture. The North Carolina Republican organization took its lead from Jefferson and delivered to him eleven votes, scattering their second choices amid a miscellany, including one for George Washington, who was not running. Nonetheless, six North Carolinians went for Burr, as did one voter from Virginia.

In the spring of the following year, however, Burr remained a power. The election of 1800 was now three years away. Jefferson computed his necessities, chief among them carrying New York City and Burr's stronghold in the Yankee districts of upstate, without which there could be no winning coalition. Gallatin was dispatched to New York to assist the Virginian and Pennsylvania delegations in assessing whether Burr or George Clinton would better serve to bring New York into the Republican column as vice presidential candidate. Clinton was getting older and had been a vehement anti-Federalist, opposing the Constitution as drafted. He would garner no marginal Federalist support. Burr had taken no part in the ratification controversy and had a following among moderate Federalists. His virtues became even more apparent after Hamilton did such a useful job putting a machete into John Adams's following. Even more Federalists could then be persuaded by Burr to shift to the Republican ticket. Three quarters of a century later, Adams's grandson Henry made considerable use of the report sent back by Gallatin as one of his sly devices to smuggle a little Burrist sentiment into his history of the Jefferson Administration. Adams cited with evident approval Gallatin's appraisal that "the New York Republicans were divided into three factions, represented by the Clinton, Livingston, and Burr interests; and among them there was . . . little difference in principle or morals." Adams attributed to "a politician as honest and an observer as keen as Albert Gallatin" an inclination "to Burr as the least selfish of the three."[36]

If that is what Gallatin believed, it is an arresting antidote to later derogation of Burr's character, even though his judgment was no doubt colored by Burr's support during Gallatin's emergence onto the national scene after the Whiskey Rebellion. Commodore James Nicholson agreed, it seems, for he wrote his son-in-law that "Burr is the most suitable person and perhaps the only man. Such is also the opinion of all the Republicans in this quarter; their confidence in A. B. is universal and unbounded."[37]

Setting aside whatever apprehensions he might have harbored because of Burr's opinions as to slavery and the role of women in public life, Jefferson summoned Gallatin and Nicholson to bring Burr around. After the temperature was warmed, Jefferson felt safe in writing Burr directly, "recalling" himself to Burr's "memory," or lapse of memory, one assumes, "and . . . evidencing my esteem for you."[38]

Burr responded coolly, but the campaign of solicitation continued. On Jefferson's behalf, Gallatin asked Nicholson of New York to offer Burr the vice presidency. Nicholson answered that Burr had "no confidence in the Virginians; they had once deceived him, and are not to be trusted." But the vice presidency has its charm, if only as a space-platform to the stars. Burr was, as Andrew Jackson had said, "as easily fooled as any man I ever knew." So Burr accepted Gallatin's assurances that Jefferson's "esteem" was genuine.[39]

Burr did his duty. New York was delivered. But, to the surprise of everyone, Jefferson was confronted once again with the unhappy possibility of a tie between him and Burr. That possibility had led to the breaches of promise in 1796 and to the last-minute reduction of Burr's Virginia and North Carolina electors. On December 15, 1799, he wrote another of his man-to-man letters to Burr, suggesting that this time it would be an elector from Tennessee who might switch his vote from Burr to Gallatin, "not from any indisposition towards you, but from extreme reverence to the character of Mr. Gallatin." How touching! And were there no available Jefferson electors for that testimonial?[40]

Recalling 1796, Burr let him cook. That was another of his mistakes. As John Marshall observed of Jefferson, "Every check on the wild impulse of the moment is a check on his own power, and he is unfriendly to the source from which it flows." That put the matter mildly. The Sage was careful not to express any unfriendliness to the esteemed Senator Burr while the election of 1800 hung in the balance, though on one occasion Burr apparently thought it wise to send a shot across his bow; "it was so obvious," he wrote, that, in the circumstances, "the most malignant spirit of slander and intrigue would be busy, that without any inquiry, I set down as calumny every tale calculated to disturb our harmony. My friends are often more irritable and more credulous; fortunately I . . . pronounce to be a lie everything which ought not to be true."[41]

There is a distinct possibility that at one stage Gallatin took the risk of expressing that preference for Burr over Jefferson shared with Abigail Adams and John Marshall, two other sagacious judges of character: On the third of February, Gallatin sent Burr a letter now lost—or, more likely, deliberately destroyed. It came after he had laid the necessity of choice in a tied election before two advisers. One of them, Peter Townsend, told their mutual acquaintance Benjamin Betterton Howell that they counseled Gallatin to urge Burr to come to Washington "without a moment's delay" to seize the prize, which Gallatin did. According to Howell, Townsend joined in urging Burr to "lose not a moment, [which] he agreed [not] to do . . . but at the critical moment his heart failed him . . . [and] he remained in Albany and wrote letters."[42]

The "hypo" disease—Burr's manic disability—apparently set in, for Gallatin's letter found him immobilized, a self-pinioned adventurer. Burr replied to Gallatin that he would have nothing to do with a "usurpation" by the Federalists, whether in his favor or against both him and Jefferson, and that Edward Livingston was authorized to impart to Gallatin his views of the matter. Livingston also preferred Burr, but not at the cost of constitutional process and possible civil war. But Burr gave us a clue to his mood in the language he used, saying he would have no part in "all timid temporizing projects." As Milton Lomask noted: "It is interesting that Burr should have given such prominence to the words 'timid' and 'temporizing.' "[43]

Livingston later testified that Burr shared his own adamant opposition to any such ideas. Burr explained his inaction on a computation which, it turned out, underrated his standing and overrated Jefferson's: "J. would have 10 or 11 [states'] votes on the first trial." When the vote was taken in the House of Representatives, "J." had only eight.[44]

Even after that vote, Burr refused to accept the urging of Nicholson and Gallatin to negotiate with the Federalists, who then turned to Jefferson, who pointedly bypassed Gallatin to choose Samuel Smith of Maryland as *his* negotiator. It was a painful affront, for Smith and Gallatin had been long at odds. It was becoming obvious that there were some things Jefferson did not like to ask Gallatin to do, and he was left out of the subsequent deal-making that brought Jefferson the presidency.

On May 8, 1848, Gallatin wrote Henry Muhlenberg, a Pennsylvania colleague, that he did not know until "after the publication [in the 1820s] of the correspondence" between Jefferson, Madison, and Monroe, on February 15 and 18, 1801, that they planned to meet Federalist "usurpation" by calling a new constitutional convention. "That Mr. Jefferson had ever thought of such a plan was never known to me . . . and I may aver that under no circumstances would that plan have ever been resorted to or approved by the Republican party." The inner circle had been extended to include Monroe, Madison's rival, but Gallatin still lay outside it. Perhaps it was just as well, for, in ignorance, he was able to tell Burr that reports of Jefferson's transaction through Smith were false. Burr seems to have believed him.[45]

Gallatin Attempts to Keep Two Friends

If this account differs somewhat from that offered by biographers of
Jefferson, it is because the character of Burr which so attracted Jay and
Gallatin is absent from those works. With that character restored, how-
ever, one can understand the Burr who accepted an assurance from
Jefferson, to his injury, in 1796, and who accepted another, by way of
Gallatin, in 1800, nonetheless was sufficiently naive to ask Gallatin to
ask political favors of Jefferson after the election controversy was over.
He was, it is true, Vice President. He had, it is also true, made possible
Jefferson's presidency. He had a right to ask—or so both he and Gal-
latin seemed to think.

On most patronage matters, Burr dealt with the President's northern spoilsman, Gideon Granger. Burr started with Granger with his
most important request, the placement of his future biographer (and
betrayer) Matthew Livingston Davis in the post of naval officer for the
port of New York. Granger either tried and failed to get Jefferson's
assent or did not try; he was turning to De Witt Clinton, who had no
love for Burr. Next, the Vice President enlisted Gallatin, who with
equal naiveté wrote Jefferson that Burr had a few appointments coming
because he was supported by a "large majority" of New York Republicans—adding that assurance of Burr's being "the least selfish" of the
three New York factions quoted earlier and recommending Davis as "a
man of talent, . . . quickness, and correctness, . . . strict integrity, un-
tainted reputation, and pure Republican principles." No answer. Davis
was importunate and made an uninvited call at Monticello, where he
was told that "nothing has been determined." Six months later, the
Davis appointment still lay in limbo. Jefferson appears to have enjoyed
goading Burr into that activity he described in his private *Anas* as badg-
ering him for patronage. Frustrated, Burr wrote Gallatin that the President used a tone toward him that was "so commonplace [patronizing]
that I would prefer any other answer to this only *request* which I ever
made."[46]

Gallatin was in an unhappy position. He was Jefferson's Secretary of
the Treasury. Burr was his friend and had been his sponsor; they
agreed both as to the pernicious effects of slavery where it was already
rooted and as to the importance of preventing its spread. Gallatin remained, however, a good "team player," avoiding public mention of
his differences with Jefferson during the eight years in which he served

him. As soon as Jefferson was out of office, however, Gallatin pointedly informed William Henry Harrison, a Virginian who took the planters' line as to the introduction of slavery into Indiana when it became a state, that "I *was and still am* decidedly opposed to the introduction of slavery into any part of the Union where it does not exist or can be checked [emphasis added]."[47]

In 1804, when Gallatin heard of the duel with Hamilton, he called it a "catastrophe," not so much because Hamilton was a loss, or because the means by which he was lost were deplorable; "the duel, for a duel, was certainly fair." His regret was that Burr had not anticipated the reaction. It should have been obvious that his enemies' "unquenchable hatred" and what Gallatin called "Federal policy" would combine "in producing an artificial sensation much beyond what might have been expected, and a majority of both parties seems disposed . . . to deify Hamilton and to treat Burr as a murderer."[48]

"Federal policy" could either be read as Federalist policy or, as we would read it today, as the policy of those in control of the federal government. Either way, it was bent upon the elimination of Burr as a political force, and from that moment onward, Gallatin was increasingly forced to make his choice for Jefferson. Immediately after the duel, however, when Burr arrived back in Washington to preside over the trial of Justice Chase, Gallatin was even more attentive to Burr than were Jefferson and Madison. At the beginning of 1805, after Burr had been dumped as Vice President in favor of George Clinton but was still serving out his term, Jefferson and Madison needed his favor in their effort to use the Chase trial to purge Federalists from the Supreme Court (see below), but it is likely that Gallatin's repeated dinners with Burr at the time were genuine expressions of friendship. In 1805–6, after Burr had made his first expedition to the West and tongues were wagging of his nefarious plans there, the Gallatins still treated him with courtesy.

But only with courtesy.

Burr felt the chill. Writing Gallatin from Philadelphia on July 31, 1806, he asked only diffidently for information about the Bastrop Tract, upon which he planned to establish his western colony. Burr knew Gallatin had that information, for he and Jefferson had secured it from Meriwether Lewis. Burr asked for guidance as to "what channels" he might use as a private citizen to obtain such knowledge; "would a letter from you to any person, facilitate the research? These inquiries are made without apology, presuming that the subject of them cannot be considered as a breach of state secrets." He then went on to put another inquiry, which he could not have expected to be answered since it clearly fell into the state secret category: Had General Wilkinson resigned "or been removed from the office of governor of Louisiana—and if so, is his successor named or agreed on?" And he added poignantly, "If this be deemed out of order, the error must be ascribed to the influence of former habits."[49]

We may all hope that no old friend writes us asking a favor, knowing we have chosen to cut that friend off, and reminds us of "the influence of former habits."

II

Character, Economic Interest, and Foreign Policy

Jeffersonian foreign policy differed from Federalist foreign policy in its inclination toward France rather than Britain. That was true as to Jeffersonians and Federalists north and south. There were, however, sectional differences within both parties arising from the presence of the slave-driven economy of the South. It was not just France to which the southern Jeffersonians clung, it was, after 1796, France as the power most intent upon keeping intact the slave economy of the Western Hemisphere, of which the plantation South of North America was the northernmost extension. Napoleonic France and Jeffersonian America were united in seeking to restore race-based slavery to Haiti and other islands in the West Indies.

Some of the inhabitants of those islands had taken seriously the words of the Declaration of Independence and the first French statements as to the Rights of Man and had declared themselves free. Jefferson's quasi-alliance with Napoleon to put them back in slavery offended the moral precepts of many Federalists, such as Alexander Hamilton. It was also contrary to the economic interests of the merchants of the port cities, who wished to trade with any West Indian, of any color, who had products to exchange with American manufactured goods.

So it was that slavery had its foreign as well as its domestic implications. American slavery carried overhead, like the perpetual cloud over a volcano, the threat of secession and the division of the Union. European powers interested in weakening the United States, especially France and Spain, sought frequently to precipitate storms from that cloud. Thus slavery and secessionism were known to be the twin infirmities of the early American Republic by the Founders. They judged each other, as we may judge them, by their responses to both.

In the three years preceding the election of 1800, the struggle to restrict slavery in the North united Aaron Burr, Alexander Hamilton, and John Jay. Albert Gallatin was no longer in the front line in that endeavor and, instead, took a prominent role in the attacks by the Jeffersonians upon the Federalists' foreign policy, joining in the Virginians' assaults upon spending to increase the navy deployed in the West Indies against the French and in the Federalists' quasi-alliance with Toussaint. Gallatin may or may not have shared the Virginians' antipathy to a republic of former slaves. It may have been enough for him, smarting after Washington and Hamilton's campaign in Pennsylvania, and their successful effort to deprive him of his seat in the Senate, that the naval program was Federalist and an offshore expression of their "anti-Jacobin" program. Gallatin earned undying fame in the 1840s for pointing out that the government of the United States had a foreign policy dictated by the imperatives of race as to Indians and the dark-skinned population of Mexico. Forty years earlier, however, he failed to make the same point as to the efforts of the Jeffersonians first to cripple the navy in its support of Toussaint and then, when they had assumed power, to assist the French in their effort to reimpose slavery on Haiti.

Burr was not in the national capital during these years and took no significant part in these debates. Therefore he cannot be charged with complicity in the race-based foreign policy of his party, nor did he assist the Jeffersonians in expanding the range of the slave-based plantation system into the West. It is, however, also fair to charge against him that he, like Gallatin, failed to resist that expansion by joining in the Federalists' efforts to require that all new territories enter without slavery. Perhaps it was obvious to him, as it is to us, that the commercial policies of the Federalists did not require a moral dimension, for they could afford to be indifferent to race, while race played an essential part in the marketing plans of the planters. That was because they had surplus slaves to sell.

We can only guess that had Burr understood that the economic imperatives of the planters were incompatible with the moral imperatives of those opposed to slavery, he might have better understood why he was putting himself at such risk of the wrath of the expansionists in 1805. After the planters' original slave corps of Indians had died off, white indentured servants were found not to be competitive in price to imported Africans if one deducted from the price of a slave his or her marketable progeny. With each purchased slave, the buyer got that slave's descendants free of further charges. Sales of these progeny into interstate commerce became important in the planters' calculus. These transactions explained much—though not all—about the militant foreign policy of the Virginia dynasty toward the Spanish borderlands, in the same way their desire to deter further slave revolts explained their policy toward the West Indies.

The threat of France or Britain—though hardly Spain—to the Republic was real. Removing that threat was important. It was also important that much of the borderlands were underlain by fertile soil that might become plantations and, as plantations, markets for slaves. The foreign policy of the Virginians was a complex of motives, but the export policy of the Tidewater and Piedmont planters was simple: It was determined by the need to sell slaves. For that, the chief requirement was that more land be put under cultivation by slaves, both in the Floridas and in Louisiana.

Virginia was the nation's principal exporter of slaves. The expansion of the market for slaves required rupturing the southern and southwestern boundaries of the United States. There were other reasons for such expansion, chief among them the necessity to protect access to the sea for the products of the West, but the western Federalists were as interested in that as the Republicans.

Even in Virginia itself, the Federalists were willing to discuss manumission and compensated abolition as late as the 1820s. A convention then met to reallocate distribution of seats in the state legislature, at which Federalists from western Virginia sought to repeal the three-fifths rule favoring slaveowners. In Connecticut, New York, Virginia, North Carolina, South Carolina, and Georgia, Republicans more often than Federalists voted to support the maintenance of slavery, and, in the Congress, the Republicans encouraged the domestic trade in slaves to a much greater degree than did Federalists.

Aaron Burr was distinguished by his refusal to accommodate either of these tendencies in his own party. But not doing something is hardly the highest of recommendations in a time when too much was going wrong by narrow margins. Slavery did not have to win the battles of the 1790s and the first two decades of the following century. But it did. Hamilton did not live long enough to be tested by the sharpest of those tests. Neither Burr nor Jefferson earned much of posterity's admiration for his role thereafter.

The Quasi-War and the Black Speech

At the end of the 1790s, the United States and France engaged in what President John Adams called a quasi-war. The French had sent their navy into West Indian waters to deny to Toussaint supplies provided by American merchants, to whom this trade was more important than the color of the customers. American warships responded, and a full-scale naval war ensued.

Hamilton was the chief defender of Toussaint's regime in the councils of the American government, and, characteristically, his ardor went beyond the norms of political behavior. When he had an enemy, such as Burr, he was unreconcilable, even unto death. For an ally such as Toussaint, nothing was too much: He provided the draftsmanship for Toussaint's constitution for Haiti, carefully balancing the interests of blacks, mulattoes and whites. At long distance, he served as Toussaint's economic adviser, and he persuaded Secretary of State Timothy Pickering to send Edward Stevens to serve as the American emissary to Haiti.

In 1799, Jefferson wrote to Burr seeking his aid in preventing "free commerce with . . . the cannibals of the terrible republic . . . and free ingress and intercourse with their black brethren in these states." This was rather tactless. Burr's views on slavery were well known, and so were his efforts to draw electoral support from free blacks in New York. To his credit, Burr gave Jefferson no encouragement. To our frustration, he did not explain why.[1]

Perhaps one reason was his aversion to Napoleon, a tyrant of prodigious talent, crippled by the racist prejudices of a Corsican bourgeois. Lusting for world empire and disdainful of persons of a skin color darker than that of the green olives of his native island, he sought to batten once again upon the colonies of France the most execrable of slave systems since Roman times. It is well to recall, from the biography of Georges Collot, that it had been Napoleon's intention to supply the sugar economy of Haiti with food and hides brought to it from a reoccupied Louisiana. His double strategy would be covered by the desperate measures taken by the colonial powers of the Caribbean, Britain, Spain, Holland, and Denmark to answer black-led revolts.

All those powers agreed with the administration of Thomas Jefferson that nowhere was repression more urgent than on Haiti, where Toussaint had led the creation of the second nation to achieve independence from the colonial powers in the New World. (This is the conventional way to put the matter, though there were, of course, many independent nations remaining from the pre-European world.) After Napoleon was defeated by Toussaint and by tropical disease, there was no longer an attraction to him to renew a French Empire in the Americas.

Four years after the six-starred flag of western Pennsylvania had gone up, Albert Gallatin still complained that "the Federals call me a Frenchman, in the French interest, and forsooth in the French pay!" None of those charges was true, unless one sets down "the French interest" as that sort of sympathy which may bend a man's judgment. Burr affirmed that same sympathy, and his continuing propensity to court George Washington's displeasure, by wrapping his arm around Gallatin's shoulders in 1794. The two remained partners, corresponding after Gallatin was demoted to the House of Representatives and Burr to the New York Assembly.[2]

They did not see alike, however, as to the moral implications of the Quasi-War against France in 1797–99, which was a war fought in alliance with a government composed largely (though not exclusively) of people of African descent. During those two years Burr was distant in New York. In the national capital, Gallatin, at Jefferson's behest, led the Republicans of the House to resist every effort by the Adams administration to sustain the strength of the Haitian regime of Toussaint Louverture.

While Burr, Hamilton, and Jay were fortifying New York against the French, the American navy was not only interposed as the first line of defense against any foreign invader but was also supporting Toussaint. The Federalists sought further appropriations for the navy. Gallatin and Jefferson opposed them and went on to propose the end of all that trade with the blacks the navy was protecting. Thus it was that Gallatin's sentimental loyalty to France and his hopes for its revolution were reinforced by his growing friendship with Jefferson, and thus it was, also, that he was led into the deepest error of his political life. His "sin" of support for the Whiskey rebels was relatively trivial by comparison to his "Black Speech."

Jefferson had told James Monroe as far back as 1793 that he feared that "all the West India islands will soon remain in the hands of people of color," and that American policy should be to do all that might be done to prevent political contagion from them. "We may expect . . . black crews and supercargoes and missionaries thence in the southern states; and when the leaven begins to work" there would be "bloody scenes which our children, certainly, and possibly ourselves (south of the Potomac) [would] have to wade through."[3]

Jefferson's apprehensions were not groundless, as recent scholars have found in their inquiries of French agents at work in Richmond during the rebellion of the Blacks led by Gabriel Arthur in 1800. Yet resistance to domestic insurrection did not necessarily require abandonment of the Federalists' efforts to work out a respectful alliance with the Haitian people. A realistic, though not necessarily idealistic, analysis might be expected of someone who had Gallatin's record. But when exposed fully to Jefferson's influence, he made judgments leaving the French free to do what they willed in the Caribbean. And was willing to use racial fear for political ends.

Gallatin's Black Speech began with an echo of Jefferson's invocation of fear of blacks. Haiti had a "black population. . . . [T]he interest will be wholly black . . . [T]he General [Toussaint] is black, and his agent here is married to a black woman in this city." Admitting that Toussaint "had behaved well to Americans," Gallatin was also generous enough to reiterate his own long-term commitment to "an abolition of slavery when it could be properly effected." In the meantime, however, he asserted a duty to stress to the House that Hamilton's arrangements with Toussaint were with those who had abolished slavery for themselves. "It will be with a black population we must treat." Gallatin had once told the world that the French revolutionaries represented "mankind against tyranny." In 1798, however, mankind on Haiti constituted "a whole nation of freed slaves," who, if permitted to remain at large, would "throw so many wild tigers on society."[4]

Lest such a catastrophe occur, Jefferson, as soon as he became President, dismissed Edward Stevens and replaced him with Tobias Lear, who could be expected to follow orders. Shortly thereafter, Toussaint was kidnapped to France, where he died in prison. His successors, refusing to concede victory to the French, cried out for American aid. Though it no longer came, they reduced the invaders to a few entrepôts in the west and to that eastern portion of the island once held by Spain. At this juncture, Jefferson directed Lear to send American commerce to the French-held ports. On February 7, 1802, Lear, doing his best despite the imperatives of both business and conscience, wrote Secretary of State Madison: "I find great difficulty in persuading some of the captains & other Americans to conduct themselves in a friendly manner to the French." These same "captains & others" had lost sons and brothers in these waters to French privateers and naval vessels operating out of those same ports during the Quasi-War. After Jefferson turned against them, these captains girded themselves for a resumption of hostilities in 1803–4, though, this time, without the assistance of the U.S. Navy.[5]

Private War and Private Embarrassments

While he occasionally indicated some anxiety lest Napoleonic recolonization spread beyond Haiti, Jefferson did not relent in his efforts to starve out the Black Republic, though that put his administration at odds with the U.S. Navy and also with the West Indian merchants. Both the naval officers and the merchants had more at stake than trade.

All politics cannot be explained by economic analysis. If it were so, we could avoid all assessment of character. But those judgments cannot be eschewed, though the demons howl: "That's a value judgment!" Without judgments grounded in morality one can no better judge character than one can anticipate behavior without considering all that is done out of affection or animosity.

Economic analysis is insufficient to explain, for example, the fracturing of the system of political alliances formed during the first decade of the American Republic. Observe, if you will, the behavior of the merchants of the ports such as Baltimore, Norfolk, and even

Charleston, exporting the products of slave states to the West Indies after a decade of interaction with the former slaves of Haiti and St. John. Sympathy and affection may be found even among commercial people. And, aboard the vessels of the navy, there were many who had not only found friends in the ports of these islands but had also seen shipmates maimed and killed by the French. People such as these did not cheer the appearance on the horizon of a fleet bearing French armies bent upon reimposing slavery upon those islands.

Jefferson did not have such experiences. He may have had theoretical objections to slavery, but he objected more strenuously to power in the hands of former slaves. Freedom, as he knew, is contagious. In March 1804, he proposed to the British minister that the American government join with the European imperial powers in "an agreement not to suffer the former [slaves] to have any form of navigation whatsoever or to furnish them with any species of arms or equipment." In November he sent a message to Congress deploring "commerce with certain ports and countries" (a characteristically fastidious locution) and urged that the navy now be deployed to protect the *French* from the *American* merchants' "private war," rather than protecting American trade from French privateers. Many southern states passed laws forbidding immigration from Haiti. Printers were jailed for publishing the Haitian declaration of independence. In Virginia itself, after the risings under Gabriel Arthur and Sancho, both encouraged by news from the Caribbean, the legislature required that blacks who were freed by their masters must leave the state within one year.[6]

The U.S. Navy was now deployed to help the European powers restore slavery to Haiti. Under the Federalist regime, the Americans had been on the other side, while their minister in London, Rufus King, attempted to create a refuge for former slaves in the British West African colony of Sierra Leone. King was replaced by James Monroe in the summer of 1803, and these efforts were terminated by Jefferson, who explained that both West Africa and Haiti were too "unsettled" to be appropriate depositories for spirited blacks. Douglas Egerton, the historian who has most recently and carefully reviewed these diplomatic exchanges, justly comments that "this . . . was a little disingenuous. . . . Much of Saint Domingue's 'unsettled' condition was due to the actions of the president."[7]

Napoleon attempted to restore to Haiti a notoriously cruel system of servitude, "a restoration to which Jefferson provided aid and comfort." The opponents to slavery had lost any significant voice in the councils of the national administration and could do little more than to prevent the consequences of that policy from being brought to the streets of New York. Slaveowners driven out of their plantations by Toussaint and his successors arrived in American port cities by the hundreds, many with ample fortunes. They urged local fugitive slave laws to require the return to them of former slaves who had escaped from Haiti, sometimes as sailors in American merchant vessels, and could be found walking freely about the streets. Hamilton and Jay, in New York, responded by reenergizing the Manumission Society to prevent the reenslavement of Haitian blacks. A standing committee of the society had succeeded in setting free "a respectable portion of these unfortunate beings," but Hamilton was dissatisfied with its vigor. Explaining to his wife that it was urgent, he obtained a special meeting on September 23, 1801, and had himself appointed to draw up a plan for action; he remained active in the reenergized society until his death.[8]

Quite aside from the obligations of morality which these men of good character felt toward refugee slaves, they shared a view of the character of the former owners. As Gallatin put it: "A more ignorant and depraved race of civilized men did not exist. . . . Give them slaves and let them speak French (for they cannot write it) and they would be satisfied."[9]

Deferring to pressure from such people, from their powerful lobby in Paris, and from the government of Napoleon, Jefferson issued an embargo on trade with the Haitian rebels. Eighteen years later, Gallatin responded to an inquiry as to any recollection he might have of an American administration permitting another nation to induce it to "restrict the commerce of their citizens," answering: yes. The Jefferson administration "had, on one occasion, passed a temporary law forbidding the trade with San Domingo; but the act was much disapproved, had not been renewed, and would not be admitted as a precedent." His account of this interchange is to be found in a letter to John Quincy Adams—who was then beginning that transition which ultimately brought him to the *Amistad* case, at Gallatin's side, in the 1830s.[10]

Gallatin wrote to Adams that "the principal motive for passing" the embargo was "the apprehension of the danger which at the time (immediately after the last massacre of the whites there) might on account of our numerous slaves, arise from the unrestricted intercourse with the black population of that island." After Adams's death, Gallatin joined with Abraham Lincoln, in the 1840s, in resistance to the Mexican War, which he described as a campaign further to extend the sway of slavery.[11]

Aaron Burr responded to Jefferson's embargo, but characteristically so laconically that the record of that response is exceedingly difficult to discern. When the "starving-out embargo" was put to a test in the Senate in 1805, Burr was presiding as enough Republican senators broke ranks and joined the Federalist opposition to produce a tie. Among them was Adams, who on this occasion abandoned his acquiescence to Jefferson's policy and added his vote to that of the other senator from Massachusetts, Timothy Pickering, Toussaint's most consistent supporter in the Senate. The Jeffersonians had arranged that the onus for proposing the embargo should fall upon George Logan of Pennsylvania, a Quaker, who was heard to say that nonviolence required avoiding any trade with Haiti that the French might be disposed to interrupt violently. Dark-skinned people might starve to death while compassionate Americans consoled themselves that there had been no bloodshed. Jefferson's son-in-law John W. Eppes of Virginia announced himself as delighted to accept support from such an unexpected quarter. Otherwise he and his friends might have had to "pledge the Treasury of the United States, that the Negro government should be destroyed."[12]

The peculiar Quaker-planter alliance was equal in power to the Federalists and merchants, providing Burr with an opportunity to break the tie as the presiding officer of the Senate. Break it he did, voting, as he often had in New York, with the Federalists, for the Blacks and with his conscience. The bill got no further until the full power of Jefferson's presidency was rallied behind it. When it went to the House of Representatives, the Republicans lined up to produce a two-to-one majority, leaving no other option to antiadministration Virginians such as John Randolph, John Clopton, and the Federalist Joseph Lewis but to avoid the vote. After Burr ceased to occupy the vice presidential chair and no longer presided over the Senate, a somewhat adjusted bill went to the Senate, which Jefferson signed into law. As Burr, in his New York office, read reports of this maneuvering, he had the satisfaction of knowing that he had loosened for a time, at least, the slaveowners' noose around the neck of the black government of Haiti. That time was crucial. Slavery never was restored to the island, although, in economic isolation and virtually under blockade, it declined into poverty.[13]

PART THREE

In the Wake of the Hurricane

In which we follow Aaron Burr through the Southland to Florida, in the summer of 1804, as he tested two possibilities. The first was composing a party from segments of the Federalist and Republican constituencies estranged from Thomas Jefferson in Virginia, the Carolinas, and Georgia. As early as 1792, Burr had received southern votes in the electoral college for the presidency. Increasing numbers of southern electors supported him in 1796 and 1800. His son-in-law, Joseph Alston, was a power in South Carolina, and so was Thomas Sumter, the husband of Burr's adopted daughter. Two other magnates of that state, Wade Hampton and Pierce Butler, were his political allies. He had family ties to the McIntoshes and Houstouns of Georgia, and many friends among the Order of the Cincinnati of all the southern states. He had been well received in a reconnaissance of the South in 1802. In 1804, his support even in Virginia turned out to be greater than he expected.

Burr's second possibility was abandoning political life in the United States to establish himself in Spanish Florida.

As Burr explored the South, slavery was receiving a sudden, unexpected renewal of its role in the agriculture of that half of the nation. While the North slowly and painfully reduced reliance upon the overseer's lash as a primary device in the management of labor, the cultivation of upland cotton by slaves swept across the South. The past of southern agriculture was represented by Jefferson and Butler, its future by Hampton and Andrew Jackson. Jefferson's tobacco economy of Virginia was in decline, and, with it, Butler's indigo, rice, and Sea Island cotton agriculture of the Carolina and Georgia coasts. Hampton's zealous development of the cotton gin and his engrossment of hundreds of acres of land south and west of the Appalachians opened the way for thousands of lesser planters to move westward. Political power shuffled westward, too, along with coffles of slaves from the exhausted soil of the seaboard states to the "new lands" of the Southwest. Those lands were not new, but their owners were, for as the Indians were forced out and the blacks forced in, the Age of Jefferson gave way to the Age of Jackson.

As the power center of the American Republic shifted from east to west, Aaron Burr seemed to recognize that shift, drawn by its energy from East Florida toward Louisiana and Texas. In Florida and Georgia, cotton had been a luxury product grown on plantations like Butler's, on the shore; Hampton, more than anyone else, made it economic to move the plantation system upland, where the comb-gin made it possible to turn green-seed, short-fiber bolls into a commercial crop. By the time of Burr's death in 1836, upland cotton was already demonstrating its dominance of the economy of the South from the fall line to the Rio Grande.

Burr's effort to find an arena for his energies in East Florida, in 1804, was fruitless. He did not succeed in recruiting the partners he sought, nor, it seems, did he find compatible those who were most eager to wrest the cotton-producing uplands and the rice plantations of the shore from the Spaniards. In 1810, these eager expansionists, led by John Houstoun McIntosh, were recruited by the Jeffersonians to lead private filibusters against the Spanish possessions—in clear violation of that Neutrality Law of 1794 under which Burr was prosecuted in 1807.

12

Clamor and Retreat

As soon as it became known on the streets of New York that Alexander Hamilton had been killed by Aaron Burr, the Vice President's political enemies raised a great clamor. Leading the pious pack were the Clintons, with some of the Livingstons close behind, professing to be appalled at dueling and suddenly full of admiration for the fallen hero. Their conversion to nonviolence had come suddenly, for the Livingstons were renowned duelists, and only two years earlier De Witt Clinton had exchanged five shots with Burr's friend John Swartwout, complaining, "I don't want to hurt him, but I wish I had the principal here—I will meet him when he pleases." Burr declined to gratify Clinton's wish, but less than a year later Burr's kinsman Senator Jonathan Dayton of New Jersey did call Clinton out on the floor of the U.S. Senate. This time Clinton declined to fight. Dayton was a crack shot.[1]

(In 1796, Edward Livingston wrote that Hamilton had failed to take up his cousin Maturin Livingston's offer to respond to Hamilton's boast that he was ready to fight the whole Republican faction, one by one. In 1798, as if to take *his* faction up on it, Brockholst Livingston fought a Federalist, James Jones, in a duel on Weehawken Heights—

and, like the dueling Justice Bushrod Washington, went on to serve on the U.S. Supreme Court.)

As the summer of 1804 exfoliated, so did hypocrisy. Juries were impaneled and then reempaneled in New York, where Hamilton died, and in New Jersey, where he had been mortally wounded. From scores of pulpits, tear-drenched obituaries were delivered by men who had treated him with scorn a few weeks earlier. Jeffersonians joined with Hamiltonians and Clintonians in solemn processions of mourning. The irritatingly cool, covered, enigmatic Burr had permitted himself an act of passion. Suddenly he was vulnerable. Even the dueling cavaliers of Virginia joined the auto-da-fé. Though there had been no true revolution in 1800, after 1804 there was a sharp increase in cant.

Burr became bewildered and fell into the error of perception characteristic of embattled depressives: He felt himself an outcast, and acted as if he were until he had lost his opportunity to counteract the campaign of disparagement against him. Though the duel with Hamilton was far from sufficient to eliminate Burr from American public life, his next duel, with Jefferson, was fought over a larger ground, with more complex weapons.

Though there was much noise from preachers and the minions of the Clintons, Jefferson did not quickly show his hand, and the dueling gentry south and west of New England were slow to execrate Burr for dueling. The Federalists among them felt the loss of Hamilton, but they did not blame Burr for the manner of his death: At Hamilton's funeral, Gouverneur Morris refrained from playing Antony. "Colonel Burr ought to be considered in the same light as any other man who has killed another in a duel." Morris had his opportunity to dissuade Hamilton from fighting, but neither he nor John Jay nor Matthew Clarkson attempted to do so. Morris recorded that Clarkson had then said to him: "If we were truly brave we should not accept a challenge; but we are all cowards." To which Morris added: "The tears rolling down his face gave strong effect to the voice and manner with which he pronounced this sentence. There is no braver man living, and yet I doubt whether he would so brave the public opinion as to refuse a challenge."[2]

When Burr told his friends of the duel, they responded reassuringly, and he wrote his son-in-law that it was "the opinion of all considerate men here, that my only fault has been in bearing so much and so long.

... All men of honor must see with disgust the persecutions which are practiced against me."[3]

Apparently, it did not then occur to Burr that the "opinion of all considerate men" as to dueling was changing, and that the sheer drama of a duel to the death between a Vice President and a former Secretary of the Treasury would change it even more rapidly. Codes of courtly violence had never been of much interest in the mercantile Northeast, and the world was being conquered by tradesmen. Whether Puritan or Quaker or merely commercial, burghers thought little of armored men, courtly love, and trials by individual combat. As Mark Twain has instructed us, tinkering mechanics out of Connecticut were extinguishing the world of chivalry.

Sanctuary

New Jersey might have seemed safe, for it was his home state, where his father and grandfather had led the educational, religious, and political establishment. "Billy" Livingston and the current governor, Joseph Bloomfield, were old friends, and Senator Jonathan Dayton and former Senator Aaron Ogden were his kinsmen. But the jury of Union County, in which the duel had taken place, was persuaded to indict him for murder.

Then why not go to the Alstons, in South Carolina? Protected in the ample accommodations of the Alstons' plantations at Georgetown or in their summer quarters in the Santee Hills, within the scope of the Alstons' political power, he might have rallied his supporters and built a new base. Killing a man in a duel was hardly heinous to Georgians and South Carolinians. He could be safe there. After his first confident communiqué to the Alstons about the duel, Burr came to recognize that "the event of which you have been advised has driven me into a sort of exile, and may terminate in an actual and permanent ostracism." His depression deepened, and he had difficulty even in responding to Theodosia's anxious inquiries: "You must not complain or find fault if I omit to answer, or even to write. Don't let me have the idea that you are dissatisfied with me a moment. I just can't endure it. ... Your letters amuse and console me. Continue to write with this reliance, and without the expectation of pay in kind."[4]

An embarrassed father seldom wishes to lay his burdens upon a daughter whose respect, more than any other living being's, he wishes to sustain. Offering a multitude of unconvincing excuses, Burr refused to go to the Alstons. The orphaned boy who, forty years before, had been sent to live with relatives would not impose again. Never, never, that again. *Acquaintances* might have to put up with him, but they were not *family*. "I have no faith in the climate of your mountains," he wrote, "surrounded as they are by noxious swamps." That was most unconvincing, and knowing she would see it so, and be hurt, he added: "God bless and preserve thee."[5]

Into the marshes he would go, into the realm of the shadows and the indistinct, where remonstrances were few and expectations vaguer, a marshland where only a few sandbanks and Indian shell middens elevated sweating slaves above the bogs and paddies during the deadly summer. Even the coastal towns were notoriously malarial, though they had been drained of swamps and built on dunes to catch any vagrant breeze. "Charleston I shall at this season most certainly avoid." Shame was more to be feared than malaria; worst of all was that form of shame felt as imposition.[6]

Had Burr not been so frantic and so fearful of imposing, he might have found time to consider his course more thoroughly, and with better advisers. He did not need to go beyond the pale. But until he found himself acceptable to others in Georgia and Florida, he was too proud to ask the Alstons and their friends to come to his side.

He had to get through New Jersey to the port of Philadelphia, or to New Castle, in Delaware, for a vessel to take him southward. He required friends who knew about such things, and that is why he found himself at breakfast with Commodore and Mrs. Thomas Truxton.

The Truxtons

During the night of July 21, 1804, Burr was rowed eighteen miles by moonlight, out from Manhattan across the Upper Bay into the succession of creeks and tidal estuaries dividing Staten Island from New Jersey. Sleep was difficult for him, though he lay with his head pillowed on a coat in the stern of the longboat. In the morning—it was Sunday—he ordered the boat brought to rest amid the eddies of Arthur Kill, where they would be out of sight of the veranda of the villa of Commodore and Mrs. Truxton until the Truxtons might conclude their breakfast.

After an hour or so, Burr sent his mulatto valet, Peter Yates, to announce his presence—and to allow the Truxtons to turn him away if they desired to do so. They did not so desire. Instead they summoned a fresh breakfast for Burr, his companion, Samuel Swartwout—and, one assumes, in the servants' quarters for Peter Yates. On a sunny Sunday morning, Burr received his first reassurance that all the world was not united against him.[7]

During the ensuing week, two military heroes went to considerable inconvenience to demonstrate that fact. First of the two was Truxton (1755–1822), the most celebrated American captain of the Quasi-War against France concluded only three years earlier. The second was Jean Victor Marie Moreau, who had been, next to Napoleon, the most famous leader of the French Revolutionary armies. Both happened to be residing along the route of Aaron Burr's escape.

Thomas Truxton was born near Hampstead, on Long Island. During the Revolutionary War, he was a successful privateer. Afterward, having invested his swag in trade goods, he acquired a merchant vessel and in 1786 took it on the first voyage from Philadelphia to Canton and back again, laden with silks and spices. After selling them, he was richer yet, rich enough to provide Mrs. Truxton with the villa upon the veranda of which they breakfasted with Burr. Their New Jersey shore was still green and sweet, sluiced by streams of fresh water from the highlands purified in passage through a hundred miles of sandy plain.

Only after taking his seat as a manor laird did Thomas Truxton enter formally into the U.S. Navy, and when he did so, in 1794, he did not enter quietly. Truxton forced the navy to accept his iron sense of discipline, embodied in the service's first set of manuals. He was not a subtle man: Bluff, proud, and restless, he could not abide hypocrisy. In command of the *Constellation* off Alexander Hamilton's home island of Nevis, in 1799, Truxton's assignment was to protect American shipping against French privateers, in accordance with the foreign policy of Hamilton and Timothy Pickering.

Truxton came upon the French frigate *Insurgente*, which had been harassing American trade, and forced it to surrender. The French captain came aboard protesting that "our two nations are at peace," despite a long record of depredations against American merchantmen. Truxton would only reply: "You are my prisoner," and had him led below. "The French Captain tells me," he reported to his superiors, "I have caused a war with France, if so I am glad of it, for I detest things done by halves."[8]

On February 1, 1800, spoiling for "another touch at these Frenchmen," Truxton sighted *La Vengeance*, with fifty-four guns to his thirty-eight, and gave chase. The French were carrying thirty-six Americans and much loot captured while the "two nations" were "at peace" and wished to avoid a fight. After five hours of long-distance cannonading, Truxton forced *La Vengeance* to strike its colors. This was the last major battle of a conflict which had been by that time formalized by a declaration of war from the French side (by way of their governor of Guadeloupe), though not from the American. The American squadron including the *Constellation* had been in battle in support of Toussaint's land forces, eliminating first a fleet of small craft assembled by the French and Toussaint's Haitian opponents, and then quieting the shore defenses which had slowed Toussaint's advance. In effect, Truxton commanded Toussaint's high-seas fleet. After the Jefferson administration reversed Hamilton's foreign policy, Truxton resigned from the navy.

That is how he and Mrs. Truxton were able to provide Burr breakfast on that February morning in 1804. Truxton was hospitable but candid, informing his visitor at the outset that he had esteemed Hamilton as "an invaluable friend, statesman, and soldier[;] . . . as a politician, I had admired him always, and, in fact, loved him as a brother."[9]

Regretting, it seems, his heavy-handedness, Truxton told Burr that "at the same time," he had always had "an unfeigned and sincere regard for . . . [him] and that while I regretted the past event, I . . . gave him a hearty welcome, as I should have done for Colonel Hamilton, had the fate of their interview been reversed, and he had made me a visit."[10]

Perhaps Truxton also recalled that in 1802 he had assured Burr that he wished to see him succeed Jefferson as President, adding, even-handedly, the admonition that to secure that office he would have to "take care of Alexander Hamilton [,] King—Pinckney and Paterson—besides all those at the heads of departments."[11]

As recently as March 1804, Burr had received another letter from Truxton. Apparently the word was spreading that Jefferson had broken his word to Burr and was using his machine to keep Burr from the governorship of New York. Truxton warned him against the machinations of the Virginians, writing on March 19 that he sent his "best wishes for your health and success . . . against the shafts of all your enemies under whatever name or names."[12]

In Richmond, three years later, Truxton was called as a government witness and had his opportunity to respond to those enemies. With his career at stake, he freely admitted that Burr had asked him to command his volunteer fleet for an invasion of Mexico. But asked if Burr proposed to divide the nation, Truxton replied that instead he had sought . . .

to give liberty to an enslaved world, and establish an independent government in Mexico. . . . I told him there would be no war. . . . He said . . . that if he was disappointed as to the event of war, he was about to complete a contract for a large quantity of land on the Washita; that he intended to invite his friends to settle it; that in one year he would have a thousand families of respectable and fashionable people, and some of them with considerable property: that it was a fine country, and that it would have a charming society, and that in two years would double the number of settlers; and that being on the frontier he would be ready to move when ever a war took place.[13]

There, from the mouth of an old seadog, truth-teller and foe to calumny and rumor, *there* is the best statement of the nature of the famous "conspiracy" of Aaron Burr. He had nothing to gain, for he had declined Burr's invitation, having inquired whether or not it had the explicit sanction of Jefferson's administration; Burr had given a candid response in the negative, and, in the summer of 1806, Truxton sent to President Jefferson a detailed plan to discourage what he thought to be a foolish undertaking on Burr's part. When Truxton told the jury that Burr had never said anything "about dismembering the Union, or seizing New Orleans," he scuttled any possibility that he might again be given a command at sea by the Virginia Dynasty.[14]

Truxton, the seadog, refused to be swept along by the lynching spirit loosed against Burr in 1804, nor would he be budged by Burr's enthusiasm for the West in 1806. A year later, that same steadfastness reappeared in the face of the onslaught of Jefferson's legal team at Richmond. On that Sunday morning in New Jersey, having unburdened himself to his guest, Truxton asked Burr to accept a show of support by spending the night under his roof, and on the following morning, his own carriage carried Burr across the brown stubble of New Jersey's wheat fields to Cranbury.[15] Burr disembarked less than ten miles from Princeton.

The General

From Cranbury, someone conveyed Burr to the Delaware River ferry at Bristol. Journalism could not discover where the Vice President spent the next three days before he emerged in Philadelphia, where he spent the first night in the home of Alexander Dallas, the U.S. Attorney, later Secretary of the Treasury, and, in 1794, the reporter to Albert Gallatin that he had been singled out for punishment among the Whiskey Rebels. Dallas never bothered to explain his hospitality; journalism reported that with the U.S. Attorney manifesting friendship, Burr "had the hardihood to show himself in the streets."[16]

Where did he spend those three days before he arrived in Philadelphia? It is likely that he repaired to the residence of General Moreau, a quiet place where he spent the summer of 1806. Moreau had settled himself in exile in Morrisville, six miles upstream from the Bristol ferry, on the Pennsylvania side of the Delaware. A man of Burr's kidney, Moreau became a key figure in Burr's subsequent recruitment of French military officers for his western adventures.

Moreau had commenced his military career as the organizer of a free corps of law students in Rennes—his title was provost, not general—in street battles against the *noblesse* and their hired thugs. He served in Flanders beside the Venezuelan liberator Francisco de Miranda and became a general at thirty-one, in 1794. He was given command of the Army of the Rhine-Moselle, leading it twice across the Rhine. In 1799, while Napoleon was in Egypt, the Russians and Austrians swept across northern Italy, and Moreau had to manage a graceful retreat for the outnumbered French. He had been growing increasingly discontented with the corrupt and incompetent Directory then in power and joined with Napoleon in the coup d'état of 18 Brumaire. But with the naiveté of a Burr, he then posted off again to the northern front to rally the French, leading his army once again across the Rhine, to his most celebrated victory, at Hohenlinden, in December 1800.

Like Burr, Moreau lacked the instinct to grasp the prizes of victory. Burr might have made himself President in 1801; for Moreau the moment had come a little more than a year earlier, in September 1799, as he was dining with the Abbé Sieyès. Word was brought to them that Bonaparte had landed from Egypt and was riding for Paris. Moreau turned to Sieyès, who had the power to make him dictator, and said: "There's your man. He will manage your coup d'état much better than I."[17]

Bonaparte came to power. Moreau's ambitious Creole wife, furious at Napoleon's ascendancy over her husband and jealous of Napoleon's wife, another Creole, organized a "Club Moreau" and blundered into intrigues with the Royalists. Moreau had no love for Napoleon or for Josephine, but he hated the Bourbons and accepted banishment rather than fight it out with the Bonapartes. So he took ship from Spain to Philadelphia and rustication in Morrisville.

The Biddles Come to the Rescue

After Alexander Dallas set his seal upon Burr by providing a night's shelter, the Vice President came under the protection of the great merchant family of Philadelphia, the Biddles. Burr was grateful but took his own precautions, writing Theodosia not to worry: "You will find the papers filled with all manner of nonsense and lies. Among other things, accounts of attempts to assassinate me. These, I assure you, are mere fables. Those who wish me dead prefer to keep at a very respectful distance. No such attempt has been made nor will be made. I walk and ride about here as usual."[18]

Clement Biddle had been George Washington's grain broker, handling the former President's shipments to Toussaint Louverture. The head of the family in 1804 was Charles; its dauphin was Nicholas, a young man of Byronic beauty and daring. Nicholas Biddle might have been a great explorer or editor, careers he essayed with immense éclat before settling into power and money (which are, of course, the same thing) as president of the Second Bank of the United States, a role in which his great antagonist became another Burrite, Andrew Jackson. Biddle undertook his first litigation as lawyer for Burr, and during Burr's trial of 1807, Jackson wandered the streets of Richmond looking for a fight with anyone who might attack Burr's honor or his own. Jackson had his defects, but he was constant. We will find him steadfast to the last pages of this book. He said he never forgot the quality of the wine served him at Burr's residence in 1797, when he was too raw for the Virginian gentry. That taste remained in his mouth until he was able to repay Burr's hospitality thirty years later.

The prodigious Nicholas had already come to Burr's attention for some undergraduate essays in praise of Truxton. When the fugitive arrived on their doorstep, Nicholas was completing preparations for his expedition across Greece. Both Biddles were Federalists, but both remained Burrites through the subsequent din. When the father heard that some New Yorkers were bound for Philadelphia to do harm to Burr, he came in from his country house armed with his pistols and stood personal guard.[19]

Southern Hospitality

Perhaps Burr rode about Philadelphia "as usual." Perhaps he might not have been "easily taken." But things were not completely routine. A murder indictment lurked just across the border in New Jersey, and though Benjamin Rush, Alexander Dallas, and the Biddles rallied 'round, after a few days it was obvious to everyone that a place at greater remove from Weehawken might be more convenient. Owen Biddle suggested Norfolk, a port city in which both he and Burr had many friends, and, besides, it would be an adventure to contend with the Jeffersonian dragon in its lair.

Burr reported to Theodosia that the Norfolk plan seemed "good," at first, but a greater fantasy seized him, and he was led toward Florida. "My friend Butler," wrote Burr, "proposed another [plan] which pleases me better."[1]

His "friend Butler" was Pierce Butler, a power in the Southeast, who kept one foot in the United States and the other in Ascendancy Ireland. His Dublin was Philadelphia, his town house a brick mansion a block from Independence Hall, but his wealth came from the Sea Islands of South Carolina and Georgia, at the threshold of Spanish Florida. The "plan" he offered was probably only for a comfortable respite at the edge; if so, Burr's variation on it was for a foray beyond the edge.

A few precautions were necessary. Letters of introduction and pills had to be procured. The letters were to placate Spanish officials of Florida, who might not be too pleased to have Burr on their doorstep, much less over it. And pills were needed because Georgia and Florida were even more notorious as a miasma of tropical disease than the lowlands of the Carolinas. Burr got his letters and turned to Dr. Benjamin Rush for his pills. As a psychologist as well as a physician, Rush could have rendered him greater assistance, had he been asked. He and Burr had been friends since serving together during the Revolution, and Rush understood his patient. Observing Burr plunging about, considering what might be done at the extremities of place and behavior, Rush had concluded that Burr's imperatives were "directed like doctor's prescriptions by *pro re nata* circumstances." That may be true, but his circumstances did not help. So, in the face of those circumstances and placing reliance upon Rush's prescriptions, Burr wrote Theodosia on August 11, 1804, that he was in "a moment of great occupation, being on the point of embarking for St. Simons," amplifying his intentions in a note to his son-in-law that he planned "to visit the Floridas for five or six weeks."[2]

Gin, Green Seed, and Empire

Pierce Butler was not the first to direct Burr's energies toward Florida. That honor belongs to Jacob Lewis, a privateer from Marblehead, Massachusetts. At Christmastide 1803, Lewis had written Burr, urging him to pay attention to the experiments of Wade Hampton with a cotton gin and to follow the implications of those experiments all the way to Florida.

Presciently, Lewis connected the new technology of the cotton gin with increased value in the upland areas of the South, including upland Florida. The domain of King Cotton was then just a principality. Lewis had an inkling that Hampton intended to apply his gin to Florida cotton and asked Burr: "Has Col. Hamton [Wade Hampton] abandoned his plan?"[3]

Lewis came to Burr by way of Edward Greswold, the son of a New York distiller grown rich on rum from the West Indies. Greswold had

Burr in the South, 1804 and 1807

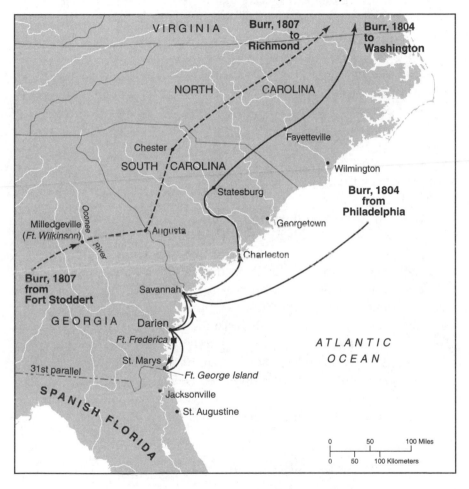

learned of the South and sugar at his father's knee, and learned a little later those skills required in the rum trade beyond chemistry and accountancy, skills akin to those of pirates and privateers. Greswold was more than a freebooter, however; he was a lawyer, combining an intellect of fine precision with a passionate heart. Burr said of him that "he was the only man he ever saw who loved the black-letter lore of the common law for its own sake," but he was diffuse in speech and undisciplined in the bedroom. He married a "lady of fortune" in Paris, left her there for several years with their daughter, but returned in 1810 to accompany Burr in his peripatetics about France and Holland.

Lewis warned Burr that "Mr. G[reswold]" should be kept under wraps, since his "projects . . . [would] excite jealousy and increase the value of property." Even in Washington, "Mr. G" was widely known to be interested in Florida and would be closely watched. Burr should not be seen with him, for if they were observed together, that would be a sign that Greswold possessed "information . . . better than theirs [other speculators] as to the probability of the province being ceded to the United States."[4]

A million years of eroding Appalachian Mountains have spread sand across the effluvial South which extends from Florida, Georgia, and Alabama northward through the Carolinas and Virginia and westward into Louisiana and Texas. For eons, that sand was of only marginal use for agriculture, though the winters were short enough to permit green-seed cotton, a subtropical shrub, to complete its life cycle. Before the gin, that sort of cotton was of no more than botanical interest, because, unlike the black-seed cotton of the barrier islands, green seeds could only be removed manually, about a pound a day. Nobody but Indians making ceremonial costumes bothered to do that. Nobody but the Yankee heroes given green-seed acres in compensation for Revolutionary services, and the Yankee tinkerers they hired as tutors.

Patriotic Gratitude and Yankee Ingenuity

With the economics of cotton production in mind, one may turn to the congenital ingratitude of state legislatures to military heroes. In the next section of this work we will see how Baron von Steuben responded to a miserly New York Assembly, which granted him only the most unappetizing of its swamp and rockland in compensation for his services to the Revolution: Von Steuben turned to the King of Spain for better treatment. General Nathaniel Greene was a Rhode Island-born hero who, more than anyone else, brought victory in the South, so Greene was given many thousands of acres which could grow nothing better than green-seed cotton. Enter Eli Whitney, a Connecticut hatpin-maker. Eli came to the Greene plantation as a tutor and remained to assist Greene's widow to find a way to give value to her upland acres. Whitney's method was to run a mechanical wire comb through the raw cotton, by means of a drum, wire teeth, wheels, and levers. He called his contraption a "gin." By springtime 1793, Whitney and the widow had demonstrated how the gin might work, and in October Whitney applied for a patent, which was so successfully pirated that Whitney received virtually nothing from it beyond fame. In the hands of others, however, the gin increased cotton exports from 138,000 pounds in 1792 to 18,000,000 in 1800.

Driven by the gin, the plantation South expanded westward and southward. Whitney repaired to New Haven, married a kinswoman of Aaron Burr (Henrietta Frances Edwards), and went into the armament business, producing muskets at Whitneyville. His plant was later converted to rifles and, after 1861, provided the North with many of the weapons it required to defeat the South. (The word "Yankee," incidentally, did not first come into use during the Civil War but in the 1790s, probably originating in Burr's New York—the Dutch diminutive for Jan [John] is "Janke.")

By 1799, Wade Hampton had been able to pirate Whitney's secret technique by placing an agent in Whitney's shop, dressed in woman's clothes. (It was assumed in the sentimental Southland that women were without the capacity for industrial espionage.) Once possessed of the secret, Hampton added an "experiment" of his own, substituting water power for horses and mules at his mill near the Alstons' summer residence in the Santee Hills of South Carolina. Even so, his machine was not as good as Whitney's, so he stooped to honesty. His letter to Whitney employed the kind of words only used by a man of his character when gripped by a very good "plan" indeed: "I will pay any price for them."[5]

Cotton became King, with Wade Hampton as its Prime Minister. Just after Burr returned to the North after his Florida foray in the fall of 1804, Hampton met Whitney in Columbia and purchased ten gins. The Spanish governors of Florida did not have Hampton's inside knowledge of cotton technology, nor did Lewis. That is why he asked Burr to find out what Colonel Hampton was planning. Then,

> if several persons would join their capital [and] employ a person in whom they had perfect confidence, send him forward and let him become a Spaniard—I am fully persuaded that cotton lands may be had of superior quality and great extent, for very little money—but all this must be done soon, or it will be too late—I speak of Sea Island cotton lands, I will add that the only good sea port in the province is round the cape which is not known [incomplete ms.] . . . You would oblige me much by giving me your opinion respecting the cession of Florida, and of the probable time etc.—has Col. Hamton—abandoned his plan—your information and advice may determine me to renew my pursuits—& *to be with you soon . . . to make a grand coupe, it's best to begin by locating . . . but all this must be done soon, or it will be too late* [his emphasis].[6]

Our fingertips can feel, in that final sentence, the heat of speculative fever. Buy now! It's cheap! Buy before it's too late! And buy before Hampton and Butler get it all!

In order to learn what to buy, Lewis suggested that Burr seek counsel from his partner in wartime privateering, John McQueen—an excellent recommendation but, it turned out, two months too late.

Lewis and McQueen were both Burr's kind of men, as Pierce Butler was not—as old General Lachlan McIntosh, the most celebrated political duelist in the borderlands, was Burr's sort, though the general's nephew John Houstoun McIntosh was not.

Had things gone differently, and had Lewis gone with Burr to Florida, the two of them might have rallied the old man and made the right sort of introduction to McQueen, and, all together, they might have had a last fling at St. Augustine. Florida! In such hands!

The Attractions of Florida

Ponce de Leon acted on the belief that life could be begun anew in Florida—the province of flowers. Three centuries later, in 1804, Aaron Burr needed a fountain of political youth—and Florida quite naturally came to mind.

Florida entered the dream world of European literature as a wild supposition, and its actualities proved that supposition to be tame. It was seen in a haze of golden aqueous sunlight, through which languidly passed birds of such outrageous plumage as to set painters to seeking new pigments, and botanists to exhausting their store of noble friends after whom to name its species. Among monsters, it offered both crocodiles and alligators. Among friendly creatures, it had both manatees and dolphins. Its parakeets and pigeons—millions and millions—were as exotic as its ungainly but beautiful ivory-billed woodpeckers. Hard men, cruel men, pirates—such as Francis Drake and John Hawkins—were moved to romantic effulgence by Florida. Their rapture was channeled into patriotic poesy by their contemporaries the astrologer John Dee and the Tudor propagandist Richard Hakluyt. For Queen Elizabeth, a Welsh princess, Dee offered the thesis that Florida had been discovered by Prince Madoc of Wales. (There was, until recently, a plaque beside Mobile Bay, once a part of West Florida, asserting that Madoc had landed there. The plaque is now in storage awaiting a Welsh revival, but the Florida mania is very much alive. The legitimate heirs to Madoc were Burr, Jacob Lewis, Henry Flagler, and the Mizener brothers.) Thomas Jefferson was of Welsh descent and sent explorers to pursue other Welsh possibilities, such as the presence of Welsh Indians in North Dakota, but Florida did not excite him to the same degree.

As for Burr, any arena for adventure would do, but Florida brought the special piquancy new technology always brings to an adventurer. In truth, without Lewis, or the gin, he might have gone to Florida anyway. In his childhood he had heard tales of it from his Ogden kin, who had explored its western extremities from their bases in Natchez and Pensacola, and when he grew up to be a land lawyer, he handled the Ogden claims in Florida which nearly bordered those of his wife's family, the Prevosts.

Burr never limited his sense of place, however, to title deeds, nor his sense of possibility to briefs. There is a story told of him—this most theatrical of the Founders—in his seventies, which explains better than any recital of precedents why he was ready for a new start in a new place. Burr had just seen a performance of *Richard III* given in New York by Charles Kemble and Kemble's daughter, Frances Anne—"Fanny" Kemble. It was late at night. The ferryboats had ceased to operate.

The weather had changed, and by the time they reached their boat, an exceedingly violent storm of wind and rain was raging and it was very dark. The waves dashed against the wharf in a manner that was not at all inviting to [his companions] . . . who advised Burr not to cross.

"Why?" exclaimed the old gentleman, as he sprang lightly into the boat, "you are not afraid of a little salt water, are you? This makes an adventure of it. This is the fun of the thing. The adventure is the best of it all."[7]

Adventure. Any adventure. In such a mood in August 1804, Burr embarked for Florida from Newcastle, Delaware. Thirteen days later, his vessel lay off Hampton, Pierce Butler's plantation on St. Simons Island. The seas were heavy. Hurricane season was approaching. Until the wind passed, two days later, it was too perilous to put a small boat into the surf. It had been Burr's intention, he wrote Charles Biddle, to remain three days, but the storm season required alterations. The plan had been to "go to St. Mary's and thence to St. Augustine, if I can find a conveyance. Traveling in this region is by water only." Burr happily put up with the delay, for "in this neighborhood I am overwhelmed by all sorts of attention and kindness. Presents are daily sent, things which it is supposed I may want, so that I live most luxuriously."[8]

(In one of those circularities commonplace in these islands, two years after the death of Burr in 1836, Fanny Kemble herself arrived at Hampton as mistress of the Butler plantation, to begin her own adventure. She was lovely—huge dark eyes, a voluptuous mouth, a pre-Raphaelite neck, a skin of the petals of a white rose—"a fine animal," Burr said of her. She was also intelligent, conscientious, witty, and a mistress of both descriptive prose and invective.)

Elsewhere, a gentleman might suffer from "the impossibility of preserving rank without a fortune, and the mortification of finding our accustomed respect in life daily diminish, and our circumstances more and more confined." But on the Golden Islands one could be "happy, independent, and in a few years rich."[9]

We arrived on Saturday evening, all well. The mail, which arrives but once a week, had just gone. An accidental opportunity enables me to forward this to Savannah. I am at the house of Major Butler, comfortably settled. A very agreeable family within half a mile. My project is to go next week to Florida, which may take up a fortnight or ten days, and soon after my return to go north-ward, by Augusta and Columbia, if I can find ways and means to get on; but I have no horse, nor does this country furnish one.[10]

The "very agreeable family" was that of Mr. and Mrs. John Cou-per, who sent him gifts to warm his heart, offering the continuous hospitality of their plantation, Cannon's Point, across an inlet from Hampton.

(Today, Major Butler's Hampton is largely owned by the Sea Island Company, which is gradually extending The Cloisters, its opulent re-sort, northward, through Major Butler's cotton lands. There are signs and surveyor's pennants and fresh fledged curbs everywhere, strips of asphalt "where once the finest cotton in the New World was grown," and roads named Fanny Kemble, Aaron Burr—and even Driver Morris. This was, after all, the plantation where Fanny Kemble learned to hate slavery *and* slavedrivers, and where Aaron Burr and his young black friend and body servant, Peter Yates, observed tropical slavery at first hand. The tabby ruins of Cannon's Point are still to be seen, looming over the shore, as one takes a boat from a marina on St. Simons to Little St. Simons Island, where Major Butler penned his recalcitrant slaves until they were "seasoned.")

The Presences of History

Burr wrote Theodosia from St. Simons on August 31, 1804, that he was "now quite settled."

My establishment consists of a housekeeper, cook, and chamber-maid, seamstress, and two footmen. There are, besides, two fish-ermen and four barge men always at command. The department of laundress is done abroad. The plantation affords plenty of milk, cream, and butter; turkeys, fowls, pigs, geese, and mutton; fish, of course, in abundance. Of figs, peaches and melons there are yet a few. Oranges and pomegranates just begin to be eatable. The house affords Madeira wine, brandy, and porter. Yesterday my neighbor, Mr. Couper, sent me an assortment of French wines, consisting of claret, Sauterne, and Champagne, all excel-lent; and at least a twelve month's supply of orange shrub, which makes a most delicious punch. Madame Couper added sweet meats and pickles. The plantations of Butler and Couper are divided by a small creek, and the houses within one quarter of a mile of each other; accessible, however, only by water. We have not a fly, mosquito, or bug. I can sit a whole evening, with open windows and lighted candles, without the least annoyance from insects; a circumstance which I never beheld in any other place. I have not even seen a cockroach.[11]

Things had improved; he could now reconsider the possibility that he would not be an embarrassment to the Alstons, though a visit to them would have to wait until it could serve as a reward for success in Florida. "God knows how ardently I wish, to return by land, and pass a week with you; but, being without horses, and there being no possibility of hiring or buying, the thing seems scarcely practicable."[12]

Burr required a boat he did not have, and, after that, horses, which he did not have either. Looking past his immediate mission, he feared that without a resolution of the horse problem, "it will be as easy for me to get to the mountains, or to the Alps, or the Andes, as to Statesburgh" (the Alstons' summer residence).[13]

Meanwhile, he was building a constituency among the Scots. On September 3, 1804, Burr wrote Theodosia that he had been to Darien, the headquarters of the clan McIntosh, who had come to Georgia under the antislavery General James Oglethorpe, twenty-two miles distant by canoe, and then to Fort Frederica, their stronghold:

You see me returned from Gaston's Bluff, now called *Hamilton's Bluff* [Burr's ironic emphasis], [*this* Hamilton being] a London merchant, partner of Mr. Couper. . . . There are now residing on the island about twenty-five white families. Frederica, now known only by the name of *Old Town*, is on the west side of the Island, and about midway between its northern and southern extremities. It was first settled by Governor Oglethorpe, and was, about fifty years ago, a very gay place, consisting of perhaps twenty-five or thirty houses. The walls of several of them still remain. Three or four families only now reside here.[14]

In the underbrush of this deeply shadowed landscape lie ruins of sugar mills, slave villages, and even great houses, most of them of "tabby," a cement stiffened with oyster shells, and everywhere there are shell buildings of considerably greater antiquity than that. On Sa-

pelo Island there is a ring more than two hundred feet across, dough-
nut or lifesaver in shape, still twenty feet high in places after much
quarrying by roadbuilders and seekers after lime. Recent calibrations
by carbon isotopes suggest that it and at least a dozen other rings in
this area were more than four thousand years old when Burr became
aware of them, as he was to become aware of the Hopewell architecture
of Marietta, Ohio—a mere two thousand years old—during the following summer.

"Fifty years ago," Frederica may have been "a very gay place"—
some of the time, but just southward was the famous Bloody Marsh,
where, in Oglethorpe's service, Lachlan McIntosh, his brother John,
and his two sons had barely defeated the Spaniards.

> In the vicinity of the town several ruins were pointed out to me,
> as having been, formerly, country seats of the governor, and of-
> ficers of the garrison, and gentlemen of the town. At present,
> nothing can be more gloomy than what once was called Freder-
> ica. The few families now remaining, or rather residing there, for
> they are all newcomers, have a sickly, melancholy appearance,
> well assorted with the ruins which surround them. The southern
> part of this island abounds with fetid swamps, which must render
> it very unhealthy. On the northern half I have seen no stagnant
> water. At Frederica and Gaston's Bluff we were convinced that
> insects can subsist on this island. Mosquitoes, flies, and cock-
> roaches abounded.[15]

Aside from insects—there were ghosts. Ghosts of men like Burr, who
had come there seeking relief from persecution, seeking renewed respectability, proud of their lineage and doubtful of their prospects,
hopeful, however, that, with one more desperate venture, all might be
restored. In this extremity of the British-American world, Scotsmen
and Irishmen and displaced Englishmen adventured together under
the tropic sun.

A few days later, bad news arrived with a hurricane. The expedition
to Florida, which had been his goal all along and had kept them apart,
was now more difficult than ever:

> On Friday last, . . . the wind . . . continued to rise and by noon it
> blew a gale from the north, which, together with the swelling of
> the water, became alarming. From twelve to three, several of the

out-houses had been destroyed; most of the trees about the house were blown down. The house in which we were shook and rocked so much that Mr. C. began to express his apprehensions for our safety. Before three, part of the piazza was carried away; two or three of the windows bursted in. The house was inundated with water, and presently one of the chimneys fell. Mr. C. then commanded a retreat to a storehouse about fifty yards off, and we decamped, men, women, and children. . . . The house, however, did not blow down. The storm continued till four, and then very suddenly abated, and in ten minutes it was almost calm. . . . The flood was about seven feet above the height of an ordinary high tide. This has been sufficient to inundate great part of the coast; to destroy all the rice; to carry off most of the buildings which were on low lands, and to destroy the life of many blacks. The roads are rendered impassable, and scarcely a boat has been preserved. Thus all intercourse is suspended. . . . [T]he effects of the storm, have defeated all my plans. To get to Florida seems now impracticable; nor do any present means occur of getting from this island in any present direction.[16]

Three Generations of McIntoshes and Slavery

In the quiet after the hurricane we can pause to supply a little background to Burr's encounters with the McIntosh clan in McIntosh County, Georgia, in Florida, and upon McIntosh Bluffs in Alabama, where great events befell him. We begin with a few pages about the relationship of the North's most notorious political duelist to the South's, Lachlan McIntosh. Both opposed slavery, and both held other opinions which set them apart from those of the next generation of McIntoshes, headed by the proprietor of Fort George Island, John Houstoun McIntosh.

In February 1733, John McIntosh Mohr, his wife, his sons Lachlan, John, and George, and a fleet of daughters, under the leadership of James Oglethorpe, landed near Savannah. They soon pressed on to Darien, in a damp, sultry, marshy lowland only a little less oppressively hot than the *first* Scottish Darien, on the Isthmus of Panama, where in 1699 the Highlanders were trained to take up machetes and abandon their claymores. Neither Darien was anything like the granite and heathery home of the McIntosh; the habits of Highland agriculture are of little better use in the marshes than those of Highland warfare. Though the McIntoshes were acquainted with herding—though "cowpens" (the name of a Revolutionary battle) came from that Scottish tradition—they knew nothing of rice paddies or indigo vats or cotton gins.

The Scottish attempt to found a colony in Panama was snuffed out by the Spaniards in 1702. Oglethorpe brought about a second attempt to colonize land claimed by Spain in 1737 and led a disastrous campaign against the Spanish at St. Augustine, in which John McIntosh was captured and locked in a Spanish prison. His son Lachlan was sent off to Savannah, to be given the best education George Whitefield could provide at the Bethesda "orphan house," and then was sent to the best business school of the times, the counting house of Henry Laurens. Lachlan's brother George was trained in architecture and made the very good marriage to which we return in discussing the even better one—financially and socially—of his son, John Houstoun McIntosh. (There was scarcely a plantation house built along the coast which did not bear the imprint of Whitefield's design—high pitched shingled roof over veranda. Two were the residence of Archibald Clark, where Burr stayed in St. Mary's, and John Houstoun McIntosh's Refuge plantation house.)

Like Burr, Lachlan McIntosh became widely known as a political duelist—he killed a Signer of the Declaration of Independence, Button Gwinnett. For our purposes, however, the affinity between the two which is most interesting is their agreement as to slavery.

John McIntosh Mohr and Oglethorpe had founded Georgia as a colony free of that blight. Together, they led the Highlanders to issue their famous antislavery Darien Resolution of 1739. Though the noble experiment of a subtropical colony of yeomen foundered twenty years later, some of the McIntosh clan, including John's son Lachlan—but not John Houstoun McIntosh—resisted the spread of slavery for another three generations.

Though the Darien Resolutions failed to deter the spread of slavery into Georgia, the institution was under attack by 1770 even in South Carolina, and even among the children of slavetraders. We have met earlier the most prominent of those sons, and the most articulate of

South Carolina's opponents to slavery—Alexander Hamilton's friend John Laurens, whose father was the employer and mentor of Lachlan McIntosh.

Together, the two young men convinced the senior Laurens to cease the traffic in slaves, and, in January 1775, Lachlan had the temerity to assume the chairmanship of a committee to produce a *second* Darien Resolution. It had a sharper bite than the first, deriding the hypocrisy of those southern delegates to the Continental Congress—such as Pierce Butler—who pretended that slavery was compatible with the concept that all men were created equal. The younger Laurens and Hamilton went even further, taking Jefferson's exalted language so literally that they proposed freeing those slaves who were willing to fight against the British.

It was hard enough for Burr, Hamilton, and John Jay to make that point in New York. But McIntosh was still advocating freeing the slaves in 1787, in *Georgia,* five years after the death of John Laurens. True, he was growing old, and had become willing to add a temporizing states' rights proviso: The northern states such as New York might "abolish slavery altogether when in their power, which however may just not be convenient for us so soon as for them, especially in a new country and hot climate such as Georgia. Let us keep the proper time for it in our own power."[17]

The proper time never quite came of their "own power." Never quite. The memory of men such as John Laurens was there, however, and Burr might have stirred that memory in East Florida in 1804. (He certainly had that effect upon West Florida in 1806.)

Family

We do not know what Burr and Lachlan McIntosh said to each other about slavery, either at Valley Forge in 1778 or in Georgia in 1804. All we know is that when Burr arrived on the doorsteps of the McIntoshes, they made it clear that he was no outcast stranger arriving unbidden. He was, as they say in Georgia, "family."

In the late eighteenth century, "family" was not a literal, biological term. It is best understood by a zoological analogy: To become "family," a man such as Burr would travel like a squirrel or some peculiarly elegant black-eyed marsupial across the canopy of the social forest until he arrived at a nest of "family." He had learned that sort of jungle travel in New York, where great families had grown up together in a trying social ecology over two centuries, grafting in the roots and at many branchings. Some of these tribes had Georgia branches, too. The Ogdens, Edwards, Daytons, and Livingstons of New Jersey were inter-married with the Bayards of New York and Delaware (who had married among the Rodneys of Delaware)—and thus, through the Livingstons and Bayards, with the Houstouns and McIntoshes of Georgia.

These connections were given greater poignancy by events during the Revolutionary War. On December 31, 1775, Burr carried the body of his mortally wounded commander, General James Montgomery, through bloody snows and under heavy fire from the walls of Quebec. This was a scene burned into the clan consciousness of many Living-stons, for Montgomery was their one genuine military hero. He was married to Janet, the sister of Robert, the clan chieftain, but Robert Livingston's Revolutionary record was anything but heroic. He had come to rebellion reluctantly, only after computing the odds and con-cluding that the family must recognize "the propriety of swimming with a stream."[18]

Two contingents of Livingston retainers led by Livingston officers did join in the defense of northern New York on Schuyler land near Saratoga, and Janet's brother Edward did don a uniform, but Mont-gomery was the hero. When the question arises as to why Burr had the support of younger members of the Livingston clan in his contest for the governorship of New York in 1804, the answer may well be found in the letters written him during and after the war by Janet Livingston Montgomery. And, commensurably, Burr's service to her husband made him a man whom Lachlan McIntosh would seek out at Valley Forge in 1778, and again in Georgia in 1804. They were kin.

Southern Communications

Burr knew the political implications of anything he might send through the mail to his daughter about meetings with the McIntoshes. He had good reason to be cautious: Gideon Granger, Postmaster Gen-eral of the United States, had engaged the services of a number of skillful melters of seals, pryers-open of envelopes, and readers of other people's mail, whose reports made Granger at once the James A. Farley and the J. Edgar Hoover of the Jefferson administration. Burr had told Theodosia to be careful in transmitting any politically important information: "Be pleased to give me name and description, in some mystical, sybilistical way, which, in case of robbery of mail, will not disclose too much. One letter may contain the name, and the other the comment. . . . I entreat that you will always enclose your letter in a blank sheet, on which is to be the seal and superscription. Health and blessings."[19]

There are signs throughout Burr's letters to Theodosia about his expedition to the South—her province—of a ripening of their relationship. He was forty-eight, she was nineteen. Here is a sampling:

> I visited Little St. Simons and several other islands; frightened the crocodiles, shot some rice-birds, and caught some trout. . . . Not having been able to kill a crocodile, I have offered a reward for one, which I mean to eat, dressed in soup, fricassees, and steaks. Oh! how you long to partake of this repast.

Burr was generally abstemious in drink, puritanical only in this regard. However, he not only drank to foolishness at this juncture but wrote his daughter while foolish.

> I had taken up another sheet to say something more, I know not what; but the appearance of a fine sheep's head smoking on the table has attractions not to be resisted. *Laissez moi diner,* "and then," &c. *Madame j'ais bien diner,* and *j'ai fait mettre mon* writing-desk *sur le table a diner.*
>
> What a scandalous thing to sit here all alone drinking Champagne—and yet—(*madame je bois* à votre santé et a celle de monsieur votre fils [his grandson])—and yet, I say, if Champagne be that exhilarating cordial which (*je bois a la santé* de Madame Sumtare) which songs and rumor ascribe to it (*a la santé* de Mademoiselle Sumtare) can there be ever an occasion in which its application could be more appropriate, or its virtues more (*mais buvons a la santé* de mon hote et bon ami, Major Butler).[20]

And who was "Madame Sumtare," whose French-accented version of her husband's name was a family joke? She was Natalie Marie Louise Stephanie Beatrice Delage de Vaolude (1782–1841), daughter of a marquis. She fled the French Revolution and, with Burr's daughter, Theodosia, attended a school established in New York by her former governess, Mme. Senat. She became a sister to Theodosia and was treated as "my adopted daughter" by Burr, who thought her at fourteen "the loveliest creature that I know in the world of her age." In 1801, Burr had found passage for her to visit France, accompanying Robert R. Livingston on his way to become American minister. Burr had also recommended Thomas Sumter, the son of a Revolutionary comrade, to be Livingston's secretary. The two young people fell in love and were married in the parlor of Fulwar Skipwith, consul to Paris, and one of the intelligence agents the Virginia Dynasty found most useful until he overstepped his instructions, made himself president of West Florida, in 1810, and was repudiated.[21]

Catching himself at the brink of an excess of boozy candor, Burr did not disclose to Theodosia the identity of a man of "sensibility and honor" who had urged him on to Florida. Considering the porosity of the mails, he decided to make use of private couriers between his base in Georgia and the Alstons in South Carolina:

> This letter goes to Savannah by a Negro, who has to swim half a dozen creeks, in one of which, at least, it is probable he may drown, and . . . if he escape drowning, various other accidents may bring it to you through the newspaper, and then how many enemies might my indiscretion create for a man who had sensibility and the honor to feel and to judge, and the firmness to avow (à la santé de Celeste un bumper toast). *La pauvre Celeste. Adieu.* A. Burr.[22]

(As to "Celeste," things are murky and unhappy. Burr opened himself to this now unknown lady in Philadelphia and acknowledged to Theodosia his full intent of offering her marriage. He wrote *of* her often, but not, as far as we currently know, *to* her. Someday we may learn that he did.)

As a result of an effort by that man of "sensibility and honor," on September 14, 1804, things brightened. Burr left Hampton Plantation, "having unexpectedly procured a boat" at the old McIntosh fortress of Frederica. From there, on the fifteenth, he wrote Theodosia in high excitement:

> I left my house yesterday afternoon, came hither by land, and proceeded in a few minutes for St. Mary's. It is possible that I may extend my tour to St. John's, and even to St. Augustine's;

but, if so, it will be very rapid; a mere flight, for I propose to be at home (Hampton, St. Simons) again in eight days.[23]

A few days later he was more specific: He would pause at St. Mary's Town on his way to Fort George, and a meeting with John Houstoun McIntosh and possibly John McQueen. There had been time for the McIntosh apparatus to bring him up to date: McQueen was still in the neighborhood, though he had sold his "fortified mansion" at Fort George to McIntosh.

Burr was rowed through the marshes of Glynn, which were planted with rice, and past islands growing a little cotton and sugar. At the southernmost tip of Cumberland Island, Burr turned westward up the broad St. Mary's River and came to dock at the little smuggling port of St. Mary's Town. It was nominally in Georgia, but "Georgia" or "Florida," "the United States" or "Spain," meant little there, for St. Mary's lay as far beyond any established polity as Tangier, Macao, or Hong Kong. Beyond the pale, it defied all rules, saluted all flags and deferred to none. Only half its population described themselves as white, and one may imagine the self-descriptions of many of the sixty-five adult (over the age of sixteen) "white" women who coped the 117 "white" males.[24]

(These islands have names now more evocative of Ward McAllister and Truman Capote, J. P. Morgan, Pierre Lorillard, Marshall Field, and Joseph Pulitzer than of Lachlan McIntosh and James Oglethorpe. Cumberland was in Burr's time rutted and disheveled after Spanish, British, French, and American occupation but after 1880 was loaded with mansions by Carnegies and Rockefellers. The island is now divided into the holdings remaining in the hands of their descendants and—with considerable unease—their new neighbors, the National Park Service. Burr's resting place in St. Mary's, the Clark residence, is a five-bay, two-story, white-painted frame building set flush upon the sidewalk, across from the sort of little white frame church every town should have to give it grace. St. Mary's is a quiet place now, but in Clark's day it was a den of smugglers.)

In St. Mary's, Burr was welcomed by the town's leading lawyer, Archibald Clark, whose grandfather had fought under Lachlan McIntosh at Savannah. The Clarks had come into Burr's life through his brother-in-law, Tapping Reeve: Archibald Clark attended Reeve's law school in Litchfield, Connecticut, where he married Rhoda Wadsworth, who sprang from a family interconnected over many generations to the Connecticut Burrs and associated with Burr himself in land speculations in western New York State.

The Clarks were all very well, in their way, of a certainty the most genteel citizens of the pirates' roost at St. Mary's, but John McQueen was the man Burr needed, and McQueen was to be found across the estuary at Fernandina, on Amelia Island, after the sale of his estate on Fort George Island, twenty miles closer to the Spanish fortress of San Marco, at St. Augustine. Though the key man was no longer in the key place, McQueen was still very much worth meeting, and so, perhaps, was McIntosh.

Fort George

In his letter to Burr extolling the glories of Florida, on December 17, 1803, Jacob Lewis urged him to seek out John McQueen as the source of "the necessary information." More than information, however, would be required of McQueen if things were to work out, for he was "second in command in this province" and would be an essential ally in a filibuster. McQueen had been born in Philadelphia, had been raised a Protestant, and might be more pliant than his superior in the Spanish service, Don Henrique (Henry) White. Though White was no more Spanish than McQueen, he was known to be a tough Irish professional soldier, loyal to the Spanish Emperor by extension of his devotion to the Roman Catholic Church. Jacob Lewis had said that he was "as inflexible as the Devil."[1]

White had observed the failure of the policy of his predecessors to garrison their frontier with Americans. He knew his Latin and owned a French commentary on the history of Rome; aware of the history of Romans and Goths, he would, no doubt, have seen Alaric in Aaron Burr. "He is extremely opposed to all persons who visit the province with a view to speculate," wrote Lewis. Unlike both Burr and White, Lewis was unlikely ever to have heard of the *foederati*. (Alaric led the sack of Rome in A.D. 410 after being welcomed deep into Roman territory as an ally of feeble emperors. His predecessors had been stationed on the frontier as components, *foederati*, of the Roman defense forces.)[2]

White could turn to more recent history and reflect upon the error of his predecessor, who had invited "foreigners to go and settle in Florida." We know, as White did not, that in 1786 Thomas Jefferson saw the welcoming of "speculators" or American mercenaries by Spain as "the means of delivering to us peaceably, what may otherwise cost us a war." Seven years thereafter, White had observed such mercenaries, in French uniforms but with American imperialism in mind, massing on the frontier under Elijah Clarke. He would not welcome Burr. But might McQueen?[3]

When Lewis wrote Burr, in December 1803, McQueen still was in possession of the strategic key to the northern defenses of St. Augustine, his "fine estate on Fort George [Island] near the mouth of the St. Johns River." And "fine" it is now, though it has lost its strategic significance. (It is governed by the National Park Service as Kingsley Plantation, the headquarters of a wildlife sanctuary, rather than by the Coastal Defense Command.) Fort George Island is not spectacular, but, as a correspondent for *Harper's* wrote in 1878,

> the view as one enters the island is one of the most enchanting in the United States, not for any one striking object, but because of the vividness of the tints, and the blending of the various elements of the picture in a harmonious whole. On the right is the encircling sea, breaking on the bar in long lines of flashing foam, and shading into the offing a deep purple under the breath of the trade-wind. . . . Overarching all is a vault of deep azure, where the blue flamingo sails and the sea-eagle soars and hovers and wheeling gracefully, swoops royally on his prey.[4]

Even today, during a migratory springtime, the sunlight shimmers with a fine glittering golden dust of warblers. In the shadows the regular denizens of the place—ibises, brown pelicans, and harsh-croaking herons—go about their business, though they are there today in only a tenth of their numbers in 1937 or even 1947, chemicals and shotguns having been active in the interim.

Some of the estate buildings remain, chief among them a headquarters on a Venetian floor plan, of the sixteenth century, to remind us that there was an efflorescence of classically derived learning and architecture in North Florida from 1763 until John Houstoun McIntosh's Patriots' Rebellion in 1810.

During the British occupation, from 1763 to 1783, and after the Spaniards returned, the Draytons and Moultries, two clans split by the Revolutionary War into Whig and Tory wings, and cosmopolitans such as White, John Houstoun McIntosh, and McQueen, lavished upon the boggy landscape in and around St. Augustine a grand Palladian mansion, Bella Vista, on the Moultrie estate down Matanzas Inlet from St. Augustine, Serlian mills, and convents and houses, a Gibbsean church, Chinese bridges, and Dutch water gardens.* This was a period of astonishing sophistication on the frontier: Aaron Burr came to another Chinese garden built at this time, complete with cross-latticed bridge, in 1805, on the Meade estate, La Chaumiere du Prairie, near Lexington, Kentucky. The governor's fortified house in St. Augustine had a gateway straight from the pages of a Spanish translation of Vitruvius.

The Fort George estate was not the most ambitious of these achievements, but it was one of the most intellectually sophisticated. From the center point of the Great Hall of the house—proportioned, like the rest of the house, to a design of Serlio—its avenue of palms led (and leads) a thousand feet to a point from which an arc is drawn, one thousand feet in diameter, upon which was laid out a precise half-circle of thirty-two shell-cement (tabby) cabins. Only twenty-three are still aboveground, but archaeology and old maps tell us of nine more.[5]

Besides the nine tabby ruins, there are other delights upon the island for archaeologists, including some of the oldest monumental architecture in North America. After much depredation, shell mining, and golf-course construction, the modern visitor can walk amid forms created at least four thousand and perhaps five thousand years ago. There are still shards remaining from the Spanish mission of San Juan, some charred from the occasion in November 1702, when the British demonstrated how little they were deterred by a cross or a mere stockade, visiting their sectarian and imperial zeal upon the mission town,

*Sebastiano Serlio (1475–1554) was a Venetian architect and popularizer who found his most celebrated employment in France, but whose published manuals effected construction in the Spanish and English colonies in Burr's time as much as those of Thomas Jefferson's beloved Palladio—who was a Venetian, too, and Serlio's competitor. James Gibbs (1682–1754) was a Scot, and is known today for his many churches, including the famously musical St. Martin's-in-the-Fields in London, from which many American churches were derived.

killing Catholic Indians as well as priests. After the British acquired the island and the rest of Florida by treaty, sixty years later, they contented themselves with kicking aside the embers of the church and replacing it with a stockade of their own, called Fort George, not for their patron saint but for their Hanoverian sovereign. After reacquiring Florida in 1783, the Spanish governors merely Hispanicized the spelling, abandoned the British fort to rot and termites, and in 1795 asked their new *alcalde* (or *seigneur*) of the upper St. Johns Valley, Don Juan McQueen, to take charge of fortifying the neighborhood against the "French" invasion of Elijah Clarke.

Jacob Lewis was right about the place. He was also right about the man. McQueen was the key. Burr's failure to recruit him was the turning point in his first Florida venture.

Don Juan McQueen

John McQueen was born in Philadelphia and educated in England. When the Revolutionary War came, he established a base at Charleston, shuttling to the northern ports as a courier for George Washington and the marquis de Lafayette, and taking prizes when he could. He had the ill luck to be in Charleston when it was captured by the British in 1780, but by that time he had made a modest fortune. After being freed from captivity, he went to Jamaica to secure sugar cane, with which he returned to Georgia and undertook experiments in its cultivation—a little early. It was twenty years before refining techniques improved sufficiently for Wade Hampton to demonstrate, in Louisiana, how profitable sugar could be.

In 1784, McQueen relieved the even more bankrupt Patrick McKay of a set of plantations McKay had gotten, at another bankruptcy, from Gray Elliot. McQueen himself was overextended, so, just ahead of his creditors, he set sail for France, to relieve himself of enough of his slaves, his mills, or his land to retain the rest.

Burnishing his relationship with Lafayette, and over suppers with Thomas Jefferson, in Paris, McQueen found buyers for seventy slaves, seven thousand acres of land (and marsh), and three mills. He also made time to visit the noble French sons-in-law of James Oglethorpe, who asked him to confirm the tale that the general's estate had a claim on portions to that same rich coastline from Savannah to Florida where

McQueen was offering property—for a price—to them and their friends. McQueen could not provide them the happy response they sought, but he did suggest other holdings which might, for a consideration, become theirs. Letters to McQueen from Lafayette show that he also made a side trip to Holland to seek financing from Dutch bankers, as Jefferson did before him and Burr afterward.[6]

With contracts for payment in hand, John McQueen returned to Georgia, pledging the contracts to his creditors. Three years had already elapsed; they wanted cash; so, in 1792, when McQueen's French clients ran into revolutionary difficulties, it became necessary for him to leave his wife and children behind and decamp across the Spanish border. (His wife later came to visit. Her shrewish report on life in Florida suggests that his motivation to put space between them cannot be explained in narrowly Marxist terms.)

Beyond the reach of wife or sheriff, McQueen began again. He was a deadbeat so charming that, even after failing to pay off a note endorsed by the hard-bitten Pierce Butler, he could confidently write Butler asking for more and receive in return an assurance that "I have never ceased to hold you as a friend."[7]

If one accepts the eighteenth-century view that gentlemen might default on the dates due on their obligations so long as they steadfastly intended to repay them, one can sympathize with both Burr and McQueen. Only those who take an accountancy view of such matters are censorious of either. Once one is willing to set aside his status as "slow pay," McQueen's letters to his family are poignant. Even after he had been forced to sell his Fort George estate and was living amid the pirates of Amelia Island, with a few pieces of silver and even fewer books, he was not embarrassed to admit a craving for music and painting.

"By this Post," he asked, "put Major Butler's friendship to the trial by asking him to lend me on McIntosh and my security fifty thousand dollars." McQueen's old notes "could be bought up at four shillings in the pound" because many of his creditors had given up. Two months later, McQueen wrote: "No answer from Major Butler—I have been offered by an agent of Colonel Hampton's thirty four thousand dollars for my Pablo lands, sawmill, and shipyard tract including Maxey's. . . . What say you, shall I take it or not?"[8]

McQueen's letter was written primarily to ask his son-in-law to obtain profiles of his family made by Raphael and Rembrandt Peale, in Savannah, and to send them to him "fixed in frames such as Peale advertises." Surely Butler, as a gentleman, would have no objection to advancing a little more to buy pictures by the Peales. In earlier years, McQueen had asked those of his family who came to visit him to bring along a pianoforte or at least a harpsichord, because the Spanish instruments available in St. Augustine were execrable.

When McQueen died in 1807, still overdue on his South Carolina obligations, he possessed hundreds of acres outside St. Augustine and a town apartment, in which he kept a fine small library (including John Marshall's just-published four-volume biography of George Washington), landscape paintings (rare anywhere in America), and an array of fine furniture and silver.[9]

(Estate sales are always melancholy and sometimes ghoulish; when they record the accumulation of the apparatus for gentility, as in the case of John McQueen, they become poignant: 1 silver pitcher, 1 silver basin, 14 silver tablespoons, 2 silver forks, 5 silver teaspoons . . . 2 iridescent epaulets (gold thread?). He was, after all, Don Juan McQueen, and a Spanish officer.

John McQueen fancied good painting, good books, good music, furniture, and silver. It is quite conceivable that he, like Jefferson, owned an edition of Serlio's work in which appeared the design for the house on Fort George in which Aaron Burr spent his Florida fortnight. It may not have been McQueen who made the measurements and made sure they were right, for Serlian models were used by the Spaniards for several public buildings in St. Augustine.

It is likely, but not certain, that the house was of McQueen's creation. His son wrote a sister, Eliza, on March 11, 1798, that, though British privateers, in their campaign against Spanish shipping, had left "the country . . . now totally broke up and in a most miserable situation . . . [t]he house at the north end [of Fort George Island] will be in the course of a month a very comfortable habitation, and in any other country a handsome situation. . . . [T]here are a great number of fruit trees of different kinds planted out."[10]

McQueen was acquainted from youth with border castles of Scotland and North England, with their little "tourettes" and hipped roofs. In the course of his marketing expeditions across France in the 1780s, he made himself familiar with its vast chateaux, similarly massed. Later, he became acquainted with the plantation houses of the West Indies, which were little closer in scale to what was built on Fort George Island,

and many of them were also of wood. Though the "fortified mansion" on Fort George Island was a mere kennel to a chateau, and to a Jamaican great house just a poor cousin, though it was a mere composite, to the eye of an architectural wayfarer, of French, Scottish, and West Indian appearance, it was remarkable for its Serlian floor plan.[11]

Most of McQueen's work was of a simpler sort: At Cowford he built a "strong, well framed . . . house, containing, below, a proper-sized guard room and, above, an airy, comfortable room for the officers"; he also constructed a magazine and "a strong squared log house . . . [for] the troops," had timbers sawed for the batteries on Amelia and at the river's mouth, and shored up the walls of the Fort San Nicolas stockade.[12]

Bowles, Slavery, and McQueen

In 1797 and 1798, Don Juan was back at the work of fortification; British privateers were back at the work of Drake and Hawkins. To oppose them McQueen installed the Queseda Battery, which by its "repeated firing . . . put those people most exposed on their guard"— including his own household. Behind the Queseda were other batteries to soften up attackers for the fort at Cowford.

Shore defenses might slow intrusions by the British, the pirates, or Americans, but not overland challengers such as the Seminoles (black and Indian) and the Creeks, who being incited to return to their warfare against all slavedriving planters by William Augustus Bowles. Bowles was one of the proto-Burrs for whom we have, in this book, only a few paragraphs of space. He was still alive, but dying slowly, in the Moro Castle in Havana, when Burr walked the paths he had walked with some of the same ideas in mind.

Bowles had been a deserter from the British army; he made himself chief of several kaleidoscopic combinations of whites, Creeks, Seminoles, and blacks, in Florida and Alabama. In 1788, 1791, and 1799, he set himself up as an independent sovereign, to the consternation of the American and Spanish governments. His most significant opponent, and that which finally brought him down, was the mercantile firm of Panton, Leslie, and Forbes. He got in the way of their land transactions with the Jefferson administration—and paid for it with his life.

Bowles had created, briefly, an independent, multiracial state in Spanish Florida and was anathema to the operators of slavedriven plantations across the border in the United States. McQueen was one of those operators, though in justice to him, he seems to have had his own ideas about slavery, albeit none so radical as those of Bowles or Burr.

Just before his death, McQueen was still sixty thousand pounds in debt and was urged by his son-in-law to bring his slaves back to Georgia. He could sell some and then start again with those he had left, this time to grow rice. McQueen declined, perhaps because he feared his surviving creditors, perhaps because, as he said at the time, he was unwilling to return "my poor Negroes" to the brutality of Georgians. The Spanish slave codes were far gentler than those transferred from the British West Indies to the Carolinas and thence to Georgia. McQueen had limits beyond which he would not go in seeking solvency. Constantly at work on new contrivances to gin cotton and mill timber by means of tide and stream, McQueen was not above smuggling slaves and, just before Burr's advent on the scene, had recourse to the last device of a Florida gentlemen of reduced fortune on that lawless coast, "wrecking": McQueen acquired a license from the Spanish government to pillage wrecks. Though he was "willing to trade Fresh Africans," he would not sell black people he knew into that kind of servitude. That may not have seemed a large distinction to anyone other than McQueen, but he sold Fort George Island instead of selling people, and at least some of his slaves were free when his grandchildren were welcomed by them to St. Augustine in 1836.[13]

As Aaron Burr was landing at Fort George Island, in 1804, John McQueen was directing the completion of the repair of the damage done to the Queseda Battery by the hurricane Burr had survived on Major Couper's island. Though it made difficult Burr's descent upon Florida and may have fatally delayed a rendevous with McQueen, the storm did provide an excuse for failing to present his credentials to Enrique White, to whom Burr sent the following apology:[14]

Having been detained here several days by the weather and hearing the roads hence to St. Augustine have been endorsed impassable by the effects of the late tempest, it is with much regret that I am constrained to forgo the pleasure of visiting that city and presenting the enclosed to you in person.[15]

221

John Houstoun McIntosh

It was in no one's interest to set in writing a record of any discussions between McQueen and Burr or among Burr, McQueen, and McIntosh. We are left to fill Burr's ten days on Fort George Island with our own suppositions.

The family portraits depicting Burr's hosts, John Houstoun McIntosh and his equally solemn lady, born Eliza Bayard, have often been used to elevate the social tone of histories of the northeastern corner of Florida. McIntosh became a chief of state of that locality thanks to James Madison's sponsorship in 1811–12, seven years after Burr's departure, and proclaimed his devotion to slavery and to the plantation system. She linked the Houstouns to the Bayards and Livingstons.

It was appropriate that Eliza imported that additional cachet, for more than any other family in the South, the Houstouns owed their eminence to an eminent female. When, in 1736, Oglethorpe found the Highlanders reluctant to emigrate to Georgia, he persuaded Captain George Dunbar to open the hearts of the McIntoshes and, after the McIntoshes, others. The captain's sister, Priscilla, was rewarded in his service with a large land grant, which was inherited by her son-in-law, an Indian-trading baronet, Sir Patrick Houstoun. Their daughter married George McIntosh and produced for him an heir, John Houstoun McIntosh, whose wife and aunt were both Bayards. His mother-in-law was Catharine Livingston. (It happens that his father-in-law, Dr. Nicholas Bayard, also had Burr connections, having studied under the Rev. Aaron Burr at Princeton.) [16]

It is pleasant to imagine the scene on Fort George Island as John Houston McIntosh, the beneficiary of all this wealth and genealogy, conversed with Aaron Burr over cigars and Madeira after dinner, observing the basking alligators and the prospecting ibises in the river. Let us rise with them, now, for an evening stroll down the palm avenue toward the slave cabins, ranged in their half-circle. Best our imaginations halt, however, before the overseers' cabins, just a little larger, at the ends of each range, for it cannot be proven that we are imagining correctly. Those cabins may not have been there. They may have been ranged in their places considerably later. The archaeological and literary evidence is inconclusive. If later, they may have been placed in that configuration by a Senegalese princess, a prospect sufficiently ingratiating as to justify an appendix, even if it takes us into the 1820s and beyond.

With the possibility in mind that Eliza Bayard Houstoun was not the last strong-minded woman to rule Fort George plantation, and that the formidable Anta Kingsley left her mark upon its architecture as well, let us return to the correspondence of Aaron Burr and Theodosia Burr Alston, which recommenced after he had left Fort George Island and had found his way to Savannah:

> I was kindly interrupted . . . by visitors, who continued in succession till dinner was announced. At the lodging-house, where rooms were provided for me, were the governor, a Scotch merchant, and a sea captain.
>
> In the evening a band of music came under the window, which I supposed to be a complement to the governor, till one of the gentlemen who accompanied it came in and said that a number of citizens at the door wished to see the Vice President. Interrupted again.[17]

Having reassured her that he was well, and well received, he tried to find horses or a larger vessel to carry him closer to her, but there were no ships or even longboats available. So Aaron Burr traveled by canoe all the way from Savannah to Charleston, and thence up the Cooper River to Stateburg, where the Alstons received him sunburnt to the color of Peter Yates—or so he said.

Burr spent ten happy days in the Santee Hills with the Alstons, and then set forth for Washington. In 1802, he had shown that he could travel that distance in twenty-four hours, when he wished to do so. In 1804, his progress was deliberate, keeping his North Carolina political roots in good tilth by caballing four days between Stateburg and Campbelltown, now called Fayetteville.

Caballing in the Carolinas with the Scots

In 1802, Burr had traveled for the first time through Campbelltown, the inland equivalent to Darien as a Scots headquarters. Its hinterland, Cumberland and Scotland counties, had manifested their preference for him over Jefferson in the previous three presidential elections. He came to the Scots, however, only after refreshing his alliances with Pierce Butler, Wade Hampton, and his son-in-law Joseph Alston, in the lower South, campaigning in Charleston and Savannah. His Federalist friend from student days, Robert Troup, ironically suggested to Rufus King that when Burr was in "Savannah [he was] doing what he could to render Jefferson more popular and promote his re-election," and that when he came to North Carolina he was not only burnishing his Scots connections but also "caballing" with the Federalists, "some of our friends . . . [thus] sending a sign to Jefferson" that he had his own following. Just before setting forth to the Southland, he had attended a Federalist birthday observance for George Washington and had toasted "the union of all honest men."[18]

Burr's North Carolina was not the North Carolina of the Research Triangle, or of the neogothic grandeurs of Duke University. Twentieth-century digicrats had not yet substituted default directories for the spittoons of earlier generations. Burr's North Carolina was rougher than Virginia or South Carolina. Between Virginia and the rich alluvia along the Cooper and Ashley rivers (forming, at Charleston, the Atlantic Ocean) there were hundreds of sandy miles, the eastern extremities of which expired in shifting banks and barrier islands, and its western in an equivalent indeterminacy of twisted valleys, laurel thickets, and fog, perpetually "Smoky." Tulip poplars, hemlocks, and oaks grew prodigiously in steep "coves" protected from the wind, sheltered and nourished by nutrients perpetually renewed by almost daily rains. Beneath these High Gothic trees lived Cherokees and Tuscaroras ferociously unimpressed by either Crowns or Proprietors. When George Washington passed through the sand plains, he pronounced them "a pine barren of the worst sort, being hilly as well as poor," a waste beyond redemption even as an appendage of Virginia, five hundred miles in extent and very thinly settled by Europeans or Indians. (There are towns in North Carolina as distant from each other as Boston and Pittsburgh. Skeptics: Measure it out!)[19]

Those plains were ultimately settled because a resourceful British governor of Scottish blood turned to the devices proposed for Georgia by his contemporary, James Oglethorpe, and solicited Highlanders to form a colony within a colony, centered upon Campbelltown.

The white population of North Carolina multiplied sixfold from 1730 to 1775, an increase largely made up of proprietors of prickly independence, prepared to achieve competencies by sweating in the hot red dirt beside their slaves. Though North Carolina lay under the overwhelming shadow of Virginia, many of its yeomen expressed an aversion to the slaveselling, land-engrossing planter-speculators of Virginia. Their antipathy was cordially and publicly reciprocated.

The very sophistication of the Tidewater intellectuals, which makes them attractive to academic historians, repelled the Scottish Highlanders resettled to North Carolina. They associated such folk with equally sophisticated enclosing lairds. These yeomen came to America with eager hearts betrayed by gentry who had driven them from home to make space for sheep. About many a North Carolina campfire was sung a requiem for the vanished Scottish system of reciprocal loyalties. In the morning, amid the full uncompromising daylight, many a North Carolina child was admonished never again to permit a proud squire in coach and four, with liveried retainers, to leave starving people in the dust of the wayside.

> When the bold kindred, in the time long-vanished
> Conquer'd the soil and fortified the keep,
> No seer foretold the children would be banished,
> That a degenerate lord might boast his sheep.[20]

Though written off by Yankee Federalists as if they were mere peasants in a "degraded condition . . . [living in a mere] miserable appendage of the Ancient Dominion," they were *truly* proud and independent yeomen, and, for a time, their leaders acted as such. There was, for example, Jesse Franklin, a great figure deserving a great biography; Franklin opposed the extension of slavery into the trans-Appalachian West, demonstrating that whatever Yankees might say, the Highlanders were *not* "destitute of national character . . . [or] self-respect."[21]

Franklin had no patience with the "abhorrent domination of the perfidious Virginians." He was known to refer to a famous man he declined to name who talked democracy and drove "a large number of slaves . . . [and professed to be] above labor himself." A squire, to suit Franklin, would "hire laboring men . . . associate with them and eat at the same table."[22]

That was Burr's reputation. Besides, he was the son and grandson of Presbyterian divines. Even at the height of the Virginian supremacy, in 1792, 1796, and 1800, the Carolinas cast electoral votes for Burr to be President of the United States. This did not please the Virginians, who scented the possibility that "in a few years, [Burr as] the leader of a popular party in the northern states . . . [might, drawing upon his upland support,] subvert the influence of the southern states."[23]

As intense as the reciprocal animosity between Virginia's Anglo-American planters and the Scots yeomen of North Carolina was that between those planters and the Scots merchants of the port cities who, in 1775, rallied to John Murray, Lord Dunmore, in 1775, joined his Tory army beside battalions of free blacks, and humiliated the Whigs in the first military action of the Revolution on Virginia's soil. Twenty-two of Jefferson's own slaves answered Dunmore's call and sought freedom. The Jeffersonians could not be expected to forget *that.* Only a last-minute action by Burr's Princeton friend John Witherspoon prevented the Continental Congress from demonstrating the planters' animosities by including in the Declaration of Independence an attack upon Scots merchants as well as upon the Hanoverian King George. All Virginia Loyalists were lumped together as "the Scotch Party"— whether city merchants or Highlanders. Jefferson's friend John Page wrote after one British defeat that George III would be distressed to learn that "seven hundred and fifty of his favorite Highlanders" had been captured.[24]

The Scots traders had little enthusiasm about theoretical schemes of independence, for few of them had any stake in those western speculations so dear to the Piedmont Whigs. Their eyes were fixed upon Bristol, not upon Kentucky, and so were the eyes of the Scots of Charleston, where merchants who opposed the political program of the planters were dismissed as "little Scotch shopkeepers of no consequence."

Merchants or yeomen, the Scots were a problem for Jefferson and an opportunity for Burr.

Burr rode the fifty miles to Raleigh on October 24, 1804, went on to Louisburg on the twenty-fifth, lavished a day in "caballing," and rode on through a snowstorm to Warrenton, North Carolina. After crossing the Virginia line, he passed the Skipwith gardens at Prestwould, of which Wade Hampton had written him, and where he may have paused to confirm Hampton's enthusiasm for the style of Capability Brown.

Once through Southside and the Jeffersonian Piedmont, Burr arrived in mercantile Petersburg on October 29, where it became apparent that Charles Biddle's "Virginia Plan" might have been a good one after all. The mayor of Petersburg called on the Vice President with an invitation from the principal citizens to a public dinner, which was attended by fifty or sixty men.

> [They] received, toasted, and listened to the Vice President with enthusiasm. After dinner, twenty of the hilarious Democrats accompanied him to the theater, where the audience rose at his entrance and cheered.[25]

"Virginia," Burr wrote to his daughter, "is the last state, and Petersburg the last town in the state, in which I should have expected any open marks of hospitality and respect."[26]

Then on for three days in Richmond, where a ceremonial banquet was held at Dodson's Tavern with thirty Virginia gentlemen present. Most of them, we may assume, were present in the city during Burr's trial, three years later, when, we are told,

> the society and elite of the town, at least, were favorable to Burr. The accused's progress to and from court each day resembled a triumphal procession. Two hundred gentlemen accompanied him as a bodyguard, breathing defiance to Government. Parties were given in his honor, and everywhere the houses of fashion and planter aristocracy were open to him.[27]

Virginia Complications

Our reference to houses of fashion needs adjustment. The sources of power in Virginia, included the houses of trade, from which many of its planters, including the Coles and Skipwiths, had but recently emerged. The doors to these houses, as well, were open to Burr, in 1802, 1804, and again in 1807, permitting us once again to engage emphatically with the canard that Burr was so discredited by the duel with Hamilton that "all doors were closed against him." As we have seen, that was not true in New Jersey, Pennsylvania, Florida, South Carolina, or North Carolina. Nor was it true in Virginia. But it was odd that when he arrived in the Old Dominion in November 1804, he was greeted by a sudden effusion of welcome from Jefferson's immediate circle. Their unwonted warmth astonished him—for a time.

Senator William Branch Giles, Jefferson's whip in the U.S. Senate, presented him with a circular letter, in which the Republicans in the Senate asked Governor Bloomfield of New Jersey to quash the indictment of Burr by the jury in Union County, where Weehawken was situated. Giles's round-robin letter was signed by Senators Bradley of Vermont, Logan of Pennsylvania, Smith and Wright of Maryland, Sumter of South Carolina, Jackson of Georgia, Anderson and Locke of Tennessee, and Smith and Worthington of Ohio.

Bloomfield had offered his opinion of Burr in a public encomium two years earlier, referring to their "intimacy in . . . youth and in the army" and stating his "confidence and esteem . . . [having] witnessed your various and uniform exertions in the cause of liberty, and the firmness and independence of your conduct on every occasion."[28]

(Giles's behavior was aberrant, for he returned to his usual Burr-bashing after Jefferson signaled a reversal of course. In 1806, it fell to Giles to go before the Senate to propose that the former Vice President be deprived of the protection of habeas corpus—so it was quite natural that the senator was one of the first proposed jurors to be challenged by Burr in Richmond in 1807.)

In the fall of 1804, however, Burr swam in Jeffersonian cordiality, which oozed over into the first two months of 1805, pouring forth from necessity. Giles and Jefferson needed Burr to preside over the impeachment trial of Samuel Chase of Maryland, whom the Republicans in the House of Representatives had voted to impeach. High Federalists asserted at the time that if Chase went down, John Marshall and William Paterson would be next. That may well have been the Jeffersonian intention, for they feverishly courted the man they had ejected from the vice presidency, and who was only a lame duck in that office. Their control of the Senate was not sufficient to produce easily either a two-thirds majority to impeach Chase or the simple majority to impose their Haitian embargo. As Vice President, Burr was to preside over the trial of Chase, and while he still held office had a tiebreaking vote which might be needed in starving out the black republic on Haiti.

(A decorous proceeding was necessary, and that decorous chamber for which the talent of Benjamin Henry Latrobe was summoned. Hamilton had brought himself to the mind of anyone with Latrobe's playwright's sense of drama because many years earlier he had issued his own extralegislative indictment of Chase, of a fervor matched only by his subsequent anathema of Burr. Burr was there, too, for he would preside over the trial in a chair of Latrobe's designing. The sexuality of the two must have been a matter of some months' ruminations to have elicited from Latrobe that essay on Jachin and Boas we quoted several chapters ago.)

In December 1804, the Senate commenced proceedings against Chase: more than six feet tall, vehement, red of mein—"bacon face," the Baltimore lawyers called him behind his back—white haired, "the living image of Dr. Johnson" according to Justice Joseph Story. Chase had been a Signer of the Declaration of Independence and served indefatigably on committees of the Continental Congress. But he occasionally slipped; on one occasion he tried to corner the supply of flour available to provision the French fleet. This discourtesy to an ally drew the wrath of Hamilton, who wrote of it so skillfully that Chase was, as Hamilton put it, "universally despised" by the end of the Revolution.[29]

He arose again in the 1780s but once again fell out of favor when he assumed two judgeships at once, an offense for which he barely missed impeachment by the Maryland Assembly; nor did he improve his position by his opposition to the ratification of the U.S. Constitution. Nonetheless, during the war he had done good service to George Washington against the Conway Cabal and was rewarded for it by appointment to the U.S. Supreme Court in 1796.

Chase turned out to be a very effective judge, whose opinions are still cited, but he increasingly used the Court as a forum for political speeches of an extreme Federalist sort and presided as a hanging judge over trials for insurrection and sedition. In a charge to a Baltimore jury in 1801, he deplored the degeneration of the Republic into a "mobocracy" just as Jefferson proclaimed his Revolution of 1800.[30]

Those were fighting words, and Chase was reported to have followed them up by speaking of the new President as "weak" and "pusillanimous." Whatever Jefferson was, those were hardly the terms for a sitting justice to use of a President. Jefferson responded by suggesting that Chase be impeached. The House did its duty as the indicting body, and the Senate was to try the case.

Burr presided with great dignity, as Luther Martin, Chase's attorney, made use of anti-Jeffersonian rhetoric he used again at Burr's own trial in Richmond in 1807. Martin had been a thorn in the side of the slaveowners since 1787 when, in the Constitutional Convention, he stated that encouraging the importation of slaves, by the inducement of giving slaveowners three-fifths of an additional vote for the Congress and for presidential electors, without a concomitant prohibition against importation of new slaves, was "inconsistent with the principles of the Revolution, and dishonorable to the American character." He had lost his argument with the southerners then and became a vehement anti-Jeffersonian, departing the Republican party for the Federalists. He wrote Burr that he could not abide the Sage, who, he said, he had been "about to say [was] the Nimrod of the times, but who has only *one* trait of Nimrod's character, to wit, that he is a hunter of *men.*" Warning Burr against this "mean, hypocritical, [and] cowardly" man, Martin told Burr that Jefferson, though feigning courtesy, had let slip against Burr "all the calumniating Dogs of Hell."[31]

At the end of 1804, with Burr in the chair, Martin convinced the Senate not to convict Chase, who remained on the Court. John Marshall was safe. Burr was no longer invited to the White House. But he was not yet as dangerous to Jefferson as he became a year later, in the West.

PART FOUR

The Great Valley

In which we come into the Great Valley of America, where Alexander Hamilton hoped for glory in 1798, and Thomas Jefferson contended with Aaron Burr in 1805 and 1806.

We survey the valley first physically, as geography. Then we add humans, placing Hamilton's plans, Burr's adventures, and Jefferson's responses within a longer sequence of high politics.

After Hamilton's death in 1804, Burr succeeded to his scheme for a military adventure against Spain and to his coconspirator, James Wilkinson. Then, as Burr began to make his own adaptations of Hamilton's design, he obtruded upon the more systematic planning of Thomas Jefferson for the West.

Jefferson had been busy in the valley, through agents, for nearly thirty years. In the 1770s, he had sent George Rogers Clark to serve Virginia's interests as far west as St. Louis. After 1802, an expedition led by Clark's brother William and Meriwether Lewis extended the reach of Jefferson's arm to the Pacific. In 1805, Burr crossed athwart Jefferson's purposes north to south, threatening to disrupt the expansion of the American plantation system.

We commence the political portion of our discussion by returning to our subthemes of secession and slavery, brought to the foreground by Jefferson's charge that Burr was seeking to dismember the Union and by the complaints of other slaveowners that Burr was becoming a threat to their economic interests. Chief among those interests was coming to be the acquisition of new land on which to plant cotton using slave labor, and the sale of slaves from exhausted eastern plan-

231

tations to those new lands. Virginia had been exhausting her thin red soil, had a surplus of slaves, and required a market in the West for that surplus. The Louisiana Purchase alleviated some of the pressure upon Virginia's planters by opening an empire to the plantation economy, but it also made inevitable a series of conflicts over whether or not some of that empire should be reserved for the use of free yeomen.

New lands? New to whom? The West was not empty of people when it was first considered as an outlet for their ambitions by Hamilton, Jefferson, and Burr. There were Indians there—as to them, as well, Jefferson and Burr had differing intentions.

Burr and the Middle Ground

As statesmen were naming mountain ranges and rivers, and allocating empires in the West among nations and powers, persons were giving names to children as they made their own, individual arrangements. Some of these denominations and arrangements, though not codified in treaties or state papers, did have political implications.

Along the routes traveled by adventurers such as Aaron Burr, a century of interaction between Europeans and Indians had made commonplace the appearance at treaty conferences of Cherokees and Muskogee chiefs named McQueen, McIntosh, MacGillivray, Ross, and Weatherford. It is worthy of note, however, that there were no chiefs named Jefferson, Randolph, or Skipwith. That was because the Scots, not the English, had a long history of merging clan to clan through marriage. A joining of clans was not the same thing as a dynastic marriage. Among the Scots and the Muskogee, the medieval practice of political intermarriage to effect merger, as distinct from alliance, was still current in the eighteenth century. (Intermarriage at the summit of the Scottish-Indian social structure was not concubinage. It was as honored a tradition as was interracial marriage among the managerial class of Spanish Florida.)[1]

Scottish-Indian mergers distinguished the southern middle ground from the borderlands west of the largely English settlements of the eastern seaboard. In the South and Southwest, clusters of villages evolved beyond the pall of settled habit, outside any grid of preestablished order, where neither bureaucrat nor lawyer, clergyman nor squire, set the tone of a myriad of adaptations without benefit of any sanction beyond necessity and preference, where no national government could keep the peace and no national sovereign assured supplies of food and water.[2]

Aaron Burr's middle ground, a composite culture of Indians and whites, had been formed during the eighteenth century around Stockbridge, in the Berkshire Mountains of Massachusetts. On the other side of the Hudson Valley, in the Catskills, blacks and whites coalesced with Indian refugees from many nations to form a composite people who might be called the Seminoles of the North. Burr grew up in Stockbridge under the tutelage of his Edwards kinsmen, who made it a family calling to minister to a succession of these middle grounds. His education in Indian relations was quite different from that of Thomas Jefferson, who, in his youth, saw parties of Indians traveling in haste past Shadwell, but never as neighbors or friends. Naturally enough, Jefferson and Burr responded to their early experience by developing different sets of ideas about Indian policy—just as their differing experience with blacks led them to propose very different policies toward them.

After 1770, a new middle ground formed between the Mississippi River and the Appalachians, shifting southward and westward as the European salient into Kentucky and Tennessee expanded into Alabama, Mississippi, Florida, and Louisiana. This continuously displaced multicultural and multiethnic area may with a little irony be called the planters' ground. The irony lies in its having been planted for a thousand years before any European seed was folded into its earth.

Aaron Burr came trained into the planters' ground, ready for Choctaws and Creeks because he had known the life of the Stockbridges and Iroquois, and was thus was well aware that all "frontiersmen" were not of one color, nor were all Indians, or whites, savages. In the Berkshires or among the Finger Lakes, one could not tell at a distance whose log-constructed villages one was entering, surrounded by fields of corn, squash, and beans.

Burr in the West, 1805–1807

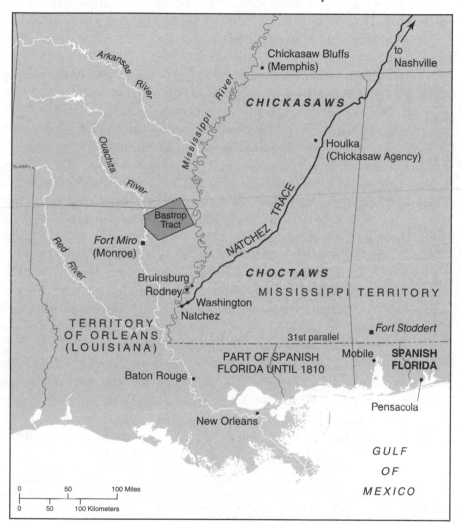

Among the Stockbridges

Stockbridge was a mission town, where Jonathan and then Timothy Edwards ministered to the Stockbridge band of "Mahicans," or "Moheaguncks."* Though few in number by the 1760s, they were survivors of a great nation of the mid-Hudson and upper Connecticut valleys. In 1609, Henry Hudson, an English captain serving the Dutch, had met the Mahicans at their village of Schotak, near Albany; by 1613, Dutch traders had settled among them at Fort Nassau. Thereafter, the swelling Dutch settlement sundered the Mahicans east from west; they broke into many small tribes ground between the colonial powers, quarreling over the fur trade, and reduced by epidemics. Many people of these remnant tribes sought refuge among the Stockbridges in the Berkshires; others went to live among their cousins in the recesses of the Catskills. Burr wrote of them all as Moheagungk, which, it seems, was their name for themselves. Others called them Stockbridges, because that is where they lived. At the end of a series of removals, a tiny remnant of the nation still bearing the name Mahican were merged, in Wisconsin, with the larger group, called by that time, even by themselves, Stockbridges.³

Along with microbes and bullets, Europeans brought religion. The New England Mahicans were visited by Moravians in the 1730s, and then by the Puritan Edwardses, who became a dynasty of missionaries among them. On the other side of the European salient, the Catskill Mahicans heeded the Moravian call and took shelter in missions. From Bethlehem they were herded to Lancaster County, and from Lancaster driven westward to Ohio by "the Paxton Boys" despite the earnest endeavors of Benjamin Franklin to defend them, and then from the Moravian towns of Ohio to the wilds of Wisconsin, where they can be found today. Experiments in interracial tolerance and comity did not

---

*American romantic literature did for the Stockbridges what French romantic literature did for the Natchez. As the novels of Chateaubriand immortalized the Natchez after they were all thought safely dead, the novels of James Fenimore Cooper treated the Stockbridges, in *The Last of the Mohicans*, as the vanished Mohicans, of whom the last, as we all know, was the immortal Uncas. Cooper's hero (the one who died attempting to save Cora Monro from evil Magua) bore a name borrowed by the novelist from a Pequot chief whose people *were* Mohicans, more or less, for the Pequots had a subnation whose name (Mohegan) sounds somewhat like "Mohican" but not very much like "Moheagunck." The Pequot-Mohegans lived in Connecticut after 1600, unlike the Mahican-Moheaguncks, who were Hudson River people, though frequently in league with coastal people and, indeed, at one time, contenders for Long Island.

last long anywhere on the frontier, but two generations of Edwardses did all they could to sustain that mutual tolerance they established with the Stockbridge Mahicans. Timothy Edwards spent his youth among the Stockbridges; as a child, Jonathan Edwards Jr. spoke better Moheagungk-Mahican than English. He was so good a linguist that his father, the evangelist, sent him off at the age of ten to live among the Iroquois. He later compiled a Mahican syllabus upon which Albert Gallatin built his more comprehensive ethnology a generation later.

By the time Aaron Burr presented himself to the authorities of Princeton University (the College of New Jersey) when he was eleven, his Edwards kinsmen had lent another theme to his life: a yearning for new starts in the West. His uncle Jonathan was working among the Iroquois. His uncles Timothy and Pierpont and his cousins Edward and Jonathan III had purchased property beyond the Iroquois lands in New York, where, shortly, Burr bought land as well. Burr's western policy was based upon a principle he learned from his grandfather and his guardian uncles: "Peace with the Indians is attainable."[4]

In 1792, at about the time Burr arrived to take his seat in the Senate, a delegation of Stockbridges and Iroquois approached Philadelphia to negotiate with the government headed by Washington, Jefferson, and Hamilton. Washington had asked that body to consent to an expansion of the army to cope with both the rebellion in Pennsylvania and the Indian war in Ohio. Burr cast his vote for Washington's new army, but with "restrictions" resented by his acquaintance of the Battle of New York, Henry Knox, who was now Washington's Secretary of the Army. Knox did note, however, that the majority came because of Burr's conditional concurrence, so an opportunity was opened for Burr to find further favor. That door was closed again as Burr needlessly provoked Washington's ire by bickering about the appointment of representatives abroad, so he had no firm ground from which to offer his support for Washington's Indian policy.

In 1783, the British and Americans had signed a treaty of peace, in which the Loyalist Indians were not represented, and the British recognized the United States as sovereign over areas previously stated by treaty as belonging to the Iroquois and Cherokee. In partial recompense, the Mohawk were provided large reservations in Ontario. This experiment commended itself to both Burr and George Washington and remained for a full generation a realistic possibility for the Ohio and Mississippi valleys, where large reservations could provide for agriculture, hunting, and fishing, according to traditional Indian ways of life. That was not, however, the way taken. There was no one in the high councils of government to reinforce Washington's capacity to treat Indians as persons worthy of treatment as he treated Alexander MacGillivray—as a peer.

Burr's experience with Indians was in the North, where the Iroquois Confederacy had broken apart during the Revolutionary War in a civil conflict contemporary to that between Whigs and Tories. Mohawks led by Joseph Brant sided with the British, joined by some Senecas and Cayugas and by most of the Onondagas. A majority of the Oneidas and Tuscaroras became allies of the Americans; Burr met with some of them in Washington's encampment at Valley Forge. After the war was over, Burr treated Brant as Washington treated another former British ally, MacGillivray, but Washington and Burr did not form an alliance. They agreed on many things, but they found each other personally repugnant. If Burr had had a father, or a grandfather, who had helped him to welcome the presence of an older man of authority, their altercation during the Revolutionary War might not have occurred. Burr might have choked down his longing for glory and been in Hamilton's place. Might have. Might have. And the Indian policy of the Washington administration might have been quite different. Nonetheless, in 1793 and 1794, Burr pressed ahead, urging the President, through Secretary of State Jefferson, to seek peace through candor.[5]

"An opinion has for sometime prevailed that peace with the Indians is attainable," he wrote, and "that the war has arisen from the belief that this government seek to dispossess them of their lands, and [that the war] will cease whenever these misapprehensions are removed." With a directness which cannot have endeared him to his recipients, he went on to point out that while there had been much talk in the capital of the Indians' fears being "misapprehensions . . . it does not appear that we have since the commencement of hostilities conveyed to them any direct assurance of our wishes and designs towards them." Driving home his point, Burr wrote that "the late attempt to negotiate through Colonel Proctor at the very time when hostile expeditions were authorized by [the] Government and actually executed by the Kentucky militia, could not have tended to conciliate."[6]

"If therefore the measure [a peaceful outcome] should be deemed in itself desirable," the Administration must act as it talked. Burr, though a freshman senator, could help in this. He had shown his values in a divided Senate. Accordingly, he suggested that he would gather support for Washington's conciliatory policy "to engage more firmly the public opinion in favor of the measures of [the] Government." He would do so if he—and the Indians—received "any intimation which shall indicate a move of access to the Indians. [That] cannot be unacceptable." Please, gentlemen, what is it that you intend?[7]

The response from Knox, Jefferson, and Hamilton was chilly. The war went on. So did the assurances of peaceful intent. No emissaries were sent to the Indians authorized to make binding commitments. How much of this stall-and-fake strategy was Washington's? How much Jefferson's, or Hamilton's? Burr did not, apparently, consider Jefferson to be irretrievably opposed to negotiation, for he recommended to him a Stockbridge chief, Aupaumut, as "a man of perfectly decent manners and deportment who has been useful to the U.S. in war and negotiation." The learned author of the *Notes on Virginia* might "consider [him] an estimable and intelligent man . . . as a desirable acquaintance . . . [of the sort who had earned from the Indians] their confidence and in whom they confide." In 1792, Burr had written of the "Stockbridge . . . remnant of the Moheagungk Tribe" that they could "be relied on" to negotiate peace with their relatives the Miamis, who were allied with the Shawnee in successfully resisting American intrusions into Ohio.[8]

Joseph Brant

At one stage in their western migration, during the 1780s, the Stockbridges sought refuge among the Oneida of the Iroquois Confederacy. The best efforts of the Edwards clan had failed to protect their client Indians from rapacious neighbors in Massachusetts, but a home might be found for them among the Iroquois. The Stockbridges, with their gift for diplomacy, achieved peace even with their traditional enemies, the Mohawk, and thus, by dint of their own necessities, became expert in the requirements of each of the tribes gathered in the Iroquois Confederacy: "The Six Nations," Burr told Jefferson, "are known to be well disposed to us . . . and . . . friendly." As evidence of this, he reported that Brant had "offered his services" as a conciliator.[9]

As noted earlier, Brant, sometimes known as King of the Mohawks, led that component of the confederacy which had remained loyal to their alliance with the British Crown and honored that alliance by fighting against the American revolutionaries. Sociable, charming, and sophisticated, he was the brother-in-law of a baronet (his sister was married to Sir William Johnson of Johnson Hall) and son-in-law of the Irish magnate of the frontier, George Croghan. Mrs. Brant, Adonwentishon, was a power on her own: As the niece of the principal sachem of the Mohawk, she presided over a council of women to select chiefs.

Brant became Burr's friend and guest in Philadelphia, and hospitality was exchanged when Burr's daughter, Theodosia, went on her honeymoon to Niagara Falls in 1801. The Alstons crossed over into Ontario, to stay with the Brants in their "palace" on Burlington Bay. It was not quite *that*, but it *was* as handsome a five-bay Georgian manor house as that of his brother-in-law the baronet with a Venetian ("Palladian") window centered above its portico—very impressive in the wilderness. Burr wrote to his daughter afterward that he had heard from Brant that the "King" was much impressed with her. She had made a conquest, said Burr: "It would have been quite in style if he had scalped your husband and made you Queen of the Mohawks."[10]

Burr could joke about Brant because they trusted each other, free of prejudices. Burr wrote Jefferson naively deploring the "host of falsehoods" being circulated to justify an "Indian War," while the Secretary of State continued his program of professing to negotiate while outfitting expeditions to ravage Indian villages—not a program which "tended to conciliate."[11]

The other alternative, channeling the expansion of the American empire to leave large tracts in which the western Indians might live in peace, required finding Indian leaders capable of working in good faith toward such agreements. That was why it was important to identify "characters who are known to many of the . . . friendly Indians[,] who possess . . . [their] confidence and in whom they confide."[12]

Washington chose MacGillivray as such a "character." Burr's choice was Brant. Jefferson and Hamilton had, however, developed toward the Indians a policy of aggression, false promises, and betrayal. Burr's proposal's being incompatible with such a program, they joined in recommending that it be refused. Nonetheless, in the Senate, Burr supported the appropriation of funds for clothing, farm animals, and tools for the Iroquois, to accompany a request that their leaders undertake the mission he had recommended.

It was too late. Before the Iroquois could reach the Miami and

Potowatami, the western Indians ceased to tolerate the intrusions of the frontiersmen and attacked their bases (generally called in our historiography their settlements). In response, federal expeditionary forces left those bases to harass the harassers. General Charles Scott boasted of having carried terror and desolation along the Wabash, and Lt. Col. James Wilkinson prided himself in having destroyed the chief town of the Ouiatanons, taking as prisoners the sons and daughters of the chief, burning their towns and crops, and leaving them without shelter or food. The Indians responded by destroying the armies sent against them by Generals Harmar and Arthur St. Clair.

A nation rich in talent trained for war, full of energy, and persuaded that all Indians were savages listened to the war-drummers subsidized by speculators in Indian lands. When Jefferson became President, he set aside the restraints established by Washington and encouraged the rush of conquest into the West. After Washington withdrew to Mount Vernon, and Burr was elbowed aside in 1804, "Indian policy" became simplified into two alternatives: removal or eradication.

By 1804, those two courses of action became ordained—one might say decreed—by a new sovereign gathering power in the South and West: King Cotton.

16

"A Country of Slaves"

If any king had a steam-powered chariot, it was King Cotton. In the late 1790s, Wade Hampton set up a battery of steam cotton gins on his plantation at Columbia, South Carolina. Thereafter, the mechanization of the plantation system proceeded at a furious pace until its arrival in the Spanish borderlands was celebrated by steam whistles at Fort Miro, Louisiana, in the summer of 1819, sounding from the first steamboat to reach the head of navigation on the Ouachita River. The *James Monroe*, it was called. Its advent so delighted the brokers and merchants of the fort, now the farthest outpost of the cotton kingdom, that on the spot they changed the name of their town to Monroe.

The Ouachita River is a vagrant, sidling stream, tangled with mats of logs and brush, clogged with sandbars, discouraging to sailing craft because of the vagaries of its fitful breezes. Only the power of steam can open such an obstructed avenue to world markets, and only steam can bring luxury goods back up such a stream. At Fort Miro-Monroe, however, the capital invested in high technology could achieve wondrous rates of return. Slaves were cheap. The lands lying north and east of the fort, known as the Bastrop Tract, are rich with the effluvia of the Bayous Bertholomew and Siard. Aaron Burr was wiser than he knew when, on July 31, 1806, he inquired of it from Albert Gallatin, in that poignant inquiry from Philadelphia quoted earlier.

Burr intended to establish his colony on four hundred thousand acres of that black soil, having purchased what he thought was the title from a man he thought was a baron. Before we come to that transaction, we should underline the role of the Bastrop Tract in the economic history of the United States. It lay at the western extremities of terrain lending itself to Hampton-sized plantations, upon which cotton could be grown on good soil. Fort Miro was, therefore, a potential market for slaves driven across the Old South from Virginia and Maryland. The tract was a prize of enormous value to planters who had capital to diversify into new lands. The most farseeing among them, Wade Hampton, understood that because of economies of scale, unit costs in the Southwest could be far less than those in the Southeast. Western land holdings—of which the Bastrop Tract was the most conspicuous—were on average considerably larger, and the number of slaves per plantation considerably greater, than in South Carolina or even in Alabama.

The *James Monroe* arrived almost precisely at the moment when a commitment to a single crop, cotton, and to world markets seemed most entrancing. Cotton exports had multiplied fiftyfold from the time Hampton applied steam to Whitney's gin and were on their way to doubling again by 1810. At the same time, the Napoleonic Wars had ensured a constant increase in cotton prices.

Sellers of cotton, and sellers of slaves to sellers of cotton, were delighted. No wonder the good burghers of Fort Miro thought it appropriate to change the name of their town. They celebrated two things at once, the ship and the Virginia Dynasty.

Turning Oglethorpe Around

Let us now turn to the racial politics of the southwestern borderlands. When Burr informed the world that he intended to settle himself on the Bastrop Tract, he was announcing to the planters that an incendiary proposed to colonize a tinderbox. There was no more sensitive spot on the frontier of the plantation system where the presence of a person with an abolitionist record would be so unwelcome. The atmosphere along the Spanish border was already so charged that Burr's mere presence was enough. He was known to have taken up Hamilton's role as an obstacle to Jefferson's program of starving out the black republic of Toussaint Louverture. He, Hamilton, and Jay had led New York to abolish slavery. And now he was staking out a role for himself in a place set aside in 1797 by the Spanish government as a colony, within a colony, without slaves.

The Bastrop Tract was to have been divided into yeoman holdings of farm, not plantation, size, in an equivalent to James Oglethorpe's original concept for Georgia. The Spaniards had proposed to establish on a frontier an apparatus of yeoman garrisons like those Oglethorpe had proposed to John McIntosh Mohr and his son Lachlan.

There was a problem. There already were slaves along the Ouachita. Under those circumstances, Fort Miro could not resound with sweeping antislavery pronouncements like those of McIntosh and Oglethorpe at Fort Frederica. To reach that point it was necessary to revive another idea, a Spanish royal decree encouraging slaves to set themselves free.

If Oglethorpe's Georgia, in the 1730s, was the model for the first part of a resolution of the problem, Spanish East Florida provided the second.

Seminole

The history of slaves cannot be written only from the point of view of those who own and sell them. Slaves had minds of their own. The American language confuses that. The word "Seminole" is derived from "cimarron," meaning "wild" or "runaway," by way of the Muskogean *simano'li*. No one is quite certain when the form "Seminole" was first used, or whether it was first applied to fugitive slaves or to Indians. All agree, however, that the word means "refugee" or "one who escaped." Spanish records as early as 1503 mention "Cimarrones" on Hispaniola mixing with the Indians. Joshua Giddings, the abolitionist, wrote that it was first used by English-speaking people in the early eighteenth century to mean runaway black slaves—not Indians. By that time, Florida was already a sanctuary for black Seminoles, under a Spanish policy which, in 1687, began systematically subverting the British system by offering freedom to "British" slaves.

Eight Negro men, two women, and a child had escaped from Carolina and sought sanctuary in Florida. At first they were merely added to the supply of slaves in Spanish hands, but, in 1693, their larger utility emerged, and the King of Spain freed them, to encourage others who might be drawn out of the Carolinas or Georgia. The results were impressive: At the siege of St. Augustine in 1702, the British were defeated by a mixed force of 174 "regulars," who were largely white, 44 white militiamen, 123 Indians, and 57 blacks. This coalition went roaring back into the Carolinas in 1715, in the "Yamassee War."

The most distinguished military leader of that war was a Mandingo war-chief who bore the Spanish name Francisco Menendez. The Muslim Mandinga were famous as cavalrymen, and, from the time of Menendez, the Spanish black militias were famous horsemen, too. Muslims of dark skin had long served Spain, and Spanish Catholics had made provision for them. The theology of Spanish Catholicism affirmed a personhood of blacks and Indians about which British Protestantism was by no means so emphatic. The experience of Spaniards with Moorish and Jewish intellectuals brought them to a more respectful view of the capacity of people of darker skins did the upbringing of Anglo-Saxons.

With an ideology, a theology, and a set of experiences to guide it, and with a resourceful population of blacks accessible to add energy to its devices, the Spanish empire drew upon its cadre of devoted sons of the Church to oppose the Anglo-Americans along the southern fringes of the continent. As Enrique White defended East Florida, François Louis Hector, baron de Carondelet, undertook the task with equal zeal in Louisiana.

Carondelet became governor in 1791, just before he turned thirty. He was a Burgundian nobleman, one of many in the "Spanish" colonial service. The Spanish Bourbons had inherited this cadre of officers from the house of Hapsburg after the descendants of Charles V who had become dukes of Burgundy also became Kings of Spain. The mother of Carondelet, Rosa Plunkett, was descended from the Dunsanys of County Louth who had been exiled from Ireland after the rising of 1641.

Spanish subversion of American officers, such as George Morgan, Baron von Steuben, and James Wilkinson, operated at a higher level than Carondelet operations, for he was only after the foot-soldiers, the yeomen, to garrison his Ouachita frontier. To attract them, he sought out two fellow royalists, the "baron" Bastrop and the marquis de Maison Rouge.

Carondelet was a genuine baron. Bastrop was not. He was a cashiered Dutch tax collector born in Surinam. But he was a fellow Burgundian, very tall, very handsome, very convincing, and Carondelet saw in him qualities he could use. Though Bastrop was a magnificent fraud, given further instruction while sojourning in Kentucky in the special arts required on a frontier by the archfraud, James Wilkinson, Carondelet provided him with a contract—only a contract, to sell land within what came to be known as the Bastrop Tract. This transaction was no more a grant than Bastrop was a baron, though not until forty years passed did that become clear, after Aaron Burr, Edward Livingston, and Stephen Girard had all made the mistake of thinking it was. For nearly a century, Bastrop's deliberate confusions of a *right to seek* with *ownership* drew even shrewd lawyers like Burr to buy from him. They got nothing but litigation. Only when the matter was brought to the U.S. Supreme Court by the trustees of Girard College was this difference clearly defined—to the chagrin of the trustees, who had been endowed with claims on the "Bastrop Grant" by their philanthropic founder, Stephen Girard. Girard had purchased those claims from the successors to Aaron Burr.

Bastrop was to encourage settlers to take up portions of eight hundred thousand acres set aside along the Ouachita River, between the present cities of El Dorado, Arkansas, and Bastrop, Louisiana. Bastrop did not get *title* to the land; his profit was to come from an exclusive right to mill the settlers' wheat and to sell the ensuing flour in Havana and New Orleans. The Spanish government would transport the newcomers to Louisiana and provide, to each, 336 acres of land, sufficient to grow wheat but not an economic unit on which to mobilize slaves producing sugar, indigo, or, later, cotton. Carondelet issued a similar contract to the marquis de Maison Rouge, apparently a real marquis. It was also on the Ouachita, just south of Bastrop's tract. A portion of the Maison Rouge claim was purchased by Fulwar Skipwith at about the time Burr and Edward Livingston acquired their portions of the Bastrop claim.

Carondelet and Servile Insurrection

The creation by Carondelet of these wheat-growing yeomanries to stiffen his own frontier was the first of his devices against the advancing Americans. The second was the revival of the royal decree providing sanctuary for slaves. If they could follow the "underground railroad" leading to Spanish Florida or Spanish Louisiana, they were to have freedom, land, and the consolations of the Roman Catholic religion.

So Aaron Burr, an abolitionist in word and deed, had found himself a hot spot. He was proposing to locate, at a terminus of an "underground railroad," a colony of people coming there mainly from Pennsylvania, Ohio, and other slave-free states of the North, to be housed in buildings to be designed by the well-known abolitionist architect, Benjamin Henry Latrobe.

In the imaginations of the owners and sellers of slaves, a Burrite colony on the Ouachita River became an impregnable fastness, more threatening as an obstacle to the spread of their system than the bypassed free states above the Ohio, as the southern support for the Northwest Ordinance demonstrated. It was common knowledge that slave-grown staple crops such as rice, tobacco, and cotton did not grow well in the North, but, as Carondelet had feared, they throve along the Ouachita. Without impediment, the plantation system would quickly absorb the Louisiana sand plains. Behind it was all of Mexico, where Spain proposed to erect a society without slavery, while in the meantime, populating the Ouachita with whites rather than blacks to diminish the risk of further slave revolts in Louisiana. That was important, also, to Carondelet, because for forty years Louisiana had been in continuous insurrection. To diminish the turbulence there, Carondelet set about to reduce the incentives to revolt by abating the brutality of Louisiana's servile system.

As early as 1732, French Louisianans had developed the quaint custom of placing the heads of executed slaves on posts along the public roads of the province at the center of insurrectionary danger, an area, it happens, called Pointe Coupée. The "cutoff point" was 150 miles north of New Orleans, and about a hundred from Burr's Bastrop Tract. It was almost an island, created by a change in the course of the Mississippi. Upon this exposed position two thousand whites lived in perpetual fear amongst seven thousand subjugated blacks, whose most recent rising had occurred in 1791, four years before Carondelet and

Bastrop worked out their understanding. After it was suppressed by troops from Baton Rouge, Carondelet was urged to signalize success with another head-posting. He refused and, instead, issued a regulation requiring better food, clothing, and working conditions for slaves, reminding the French planters that the King of Spain regarded blacks as humans deserving treatment as such.

He had courage: The Haitian rebellion was underway, and New Orleans was teeming with refugee whites horrifying the local planters with tales of rape and massacre. In the face of cries for curfews, militia musters, and ceremonial hangings, Carondelet continued his attempts to ameliorate the condition of blacks already in servitude, while seeking to change the racial mix by encouraging settlement by white yeomen through arrangements such as that with Bastrop and confronting the slavetraders by closing Louisiana to importation of slaves from the French islands. In 1795, he terminated the slave trade from anywhere. In 1796, after another outbreak, this time on the "German coast," he forbade bringing blacks, free *or* slave, into his dominions. Not until 1799 was slave importation renewed—after Carondelet was no longer in power.

Brissot's government of France had announced the abolition of slavery in 1794, and thereafter Les Amis des Noirs served for a time both the philanthropic purposes of those who opposed slavery and the political purposes of the French regime. Just as Kentucky might be brought to secession from the United States, and East Florida conquered, Louisiana might be recovered with the aid of the blacks. French agents were sent to Louisiana to stimulate slaves to revolt. This aspect of the policies of Les Amis des Noirs was not advertised by Brissot to Jefferson, but, when it became known, it added a further incentive to a Louisiana Purchase, because France had now joined Spain as a power posing a danger to the expansion of the plantation system. When Aaron Burr appeared, he added an American threat.

In April 1795, Carondelet was informed that the blacks of Pointe Coupée were planning another rising, this time coordinated with Les Amis des Noirs in Natchez. He managed to contain this outbreak as well, and without much violence; then, outraging the planters desiring more heads on poles, he issued another plea for decent treatment.

After the departure of Carondelet, repression returned. In response, the slaves went into continuous revolt. While Burr was reconnoitering East Florida in 1804, there were more outbreaks in Louisiana; while he was in New Orleans in 1805, a French abolitionist named LeGrand was arrested for inciting the slaves to rise. When Burr reappeared in the next year, there were rumors of risings everywhere.

(After Burr was gone, in 1811, Pointe Coupée erupted once again. At least two hundred slaves, crying, "On to New Orleans!" went into battle against the U.S. Army. Wade Hampton had artillery and defeated them in a pitched battle, after which sixty-six more heads went onto the road posts.)

Militia Matters

Jefferson had appointed to the governorship of Louisiana a Virginian named William C. C. Claiborne, who upon appointment proceeded to disband Carondelet's racially mixed militia and to replace it with a whites-only force, whose task was to keep down the slaves. The regular army, under Wilkinson, was to stand by to help if needed. In New Orleans it became settled doctrine that "the greatest of human calamities" was not a foreign invasion but "a formidable insurrection . . . among the blacks . . . carrying in its train fire, murder and pillage." That was why so few troops were available to respond to the British invasion of 1814, and why the administration had to turn to two Burrites: Andrew Jackson, with his Tennessee militia, and John Adair, who had emerged from imprisonment to lead the Kentuckians. Jackson was told by the Secretary of War, "The militia of Louisiana will be less effective for general purposes from the dread of domestic insurrection, so that on the militia of Tennessee your principal reliance must be."[1]

Claiborne confirmed that understanding by ordering additional militia units to be prepared to resist any Negroes attempting to rise in concurrence with the British, while the Commander-in-Chief of the U.S. Army relieved nearly all the southern militias except those of Kentucky and Tennessee from a duty to defend the nation against the external enemy. The lesson was not lost on the British. The occupation force sent against Pensacola included hundreds of Negro troops; Wilkinson reported three hundred more at Mobile; and Sir Alexander Cochrane's first proclamation on assuming the North American Command was to renew the offer of freedom and sanctuary to escaped slaves issued in 1776 by Lord Dunmore.[2]

The magnitude of Claiborne's task of racial management in Louisiana becomes clearer in the light of the first census data taken in New Orleans after he became governor: There were 2,108 white males over the age of twenty, 2,781 females, 2,312 free men and women of color, and 8,378 black slaves. Claiborne's whites-only policy for the militia was explained to Madison on the ground that there was present in the city a "large corps of people of color ... [who] should be carefully watched." Claiborne's biographer explained that he was forced to reverse the policies of Carondelet because otherwise he "might anger a large segment of the nation's population and destroy some of the principles upon which the safety of the South rested."[3]

Claiborne had the virtue of candor: In the "Southern concept of the principal functions of the militia," he said, "it was to be the major agency in suppressing slave insurrection." The ability of a mixed system "to perform its duties" was, he said, doubtful because "the loyalty of free blacks could ... be questioned." That was a new note: The Spaniards had found the mixed militia very loyal in campaigns against the Chickasaw, the British, the French, and the Americans.[4]

In February 1804, Claiborne and Wilkinson announced a policy of screening out politically "undesirable" blacks, free or slave. As shipments of "raw" slaves from Africa continued, the troops of the regular army under Wilkinson's command were offered bounties to add to their conventional responsibilities the recovery of fugitive slaves. In September, while Burr was sounding out the situation in East Florida, Claiborne ordered the army to patrol the streets of New Orleans with their weapons charged.[5]

In November, a rumor of a "slave plot" in Natchitoches reached the governor. Nine slaves broke into a house, found weapons and horses, and made for the Sabine River and Spanish territory. Another slave, wounded by a patrol, turned informer and asserted that a Spaniard named Martinez had stimulated the rising. The escapees were on their way to Spanish Nacogdoches, "where they apparently expected to receive sanctuary, and it was feared that others might follow." A former French officer, who had defected from the Spanish garrison at Nacogdoches, swore to the Americans that he had seen the royal decree lying open in his commander's office, with the words displayed offering "a free and friendly asylum ... in the dominions of his Catholic Majesty, to such slave or slaves as shall escape." Furthermore, Samuel Davenport, Indian trader and double agent, reported that the decree had been thrice publicly read and that the commander at Nacogdoches was promising to follow His Majesty's orders.[6]

"The trouble was attributed to the proximity of the border between American and Spanish territory"—trouble which might become doubly troublous with the "proximity" of a Burrite colony on the Ouachita. In August 1804, Jefferson's agent for the frontier, Dr. John Sibley, reported that "all of the officers at Natchitoches were non-Jeffersonians."[7]

Claiborne increased the garrison at Natchitoches, instructing its commander to "quiet" the citizens—not the slaves—with "promises of protection and justice." Simultaneously he lodged protests with Carondelet's successor, who was still in New Orleans and replied that he would send a remonstrance to the commander at Nacogdoches, which he did. His action was endorsed by Jacobo Ugarte at the second level of the local bureaucracy, but Ugarte's superior, Governor Nimecio Salcedo, reversed them both, ordered the decree enforced, suspended Ugarte for having used troops to retrieve fugitive slaves and return them to Louisiana, and increased the size of his own garrison facing the Americans.[8]

Calming Mr. Jefferson

Meanwhile, at Monticello, the Spanish minister, the marques de Casa Yrujo, was calming President Jefferson with assurances that reports of Salcedo's actions "and others relating to escaping slaves" should be received "with great circumspection." Surely, just because Spain was assisting slaves to escape, the Americans should not escalate their military activity. Jefferson nodded. Casa Yrujo departed. As soon as his carriage was out of the driveway, orders were sent for more regular troops to assume "the regular function" of the militia in keeping the slaves repressed.

In September 1806, one of the agents of the governor of Spanish West Florida wrote him that the word on the streets of Baton Rouge and Pensacola was that Burr would command "ten thousand Kentuckians, three thousand men from Tennessee, eight or ten thousand militia from Louisiana, [and] five thousand slaves who will be given their freedom." The governor passed a somewhat amplified version of this along to the Viceroy of Mexico: "They will raise a corps of five thousand blacks, who will be taken from the plantations and declared free." Perhaps the governor was somewhat persuaded by Wilkinson, who had written him to propose a joint expedition against Burr on the ground that otherwise "his first attack will probably be made on Baton Rouge . . . and the slaves will furnish him as many men as he may have occasion for."[9]

That was the line Wilkinson had also taken with Jefferson.

Aaron Burr proposed to locate his possibly abolitionist colony of people in a territory in which the slaves were rested and being encouraged in restlessness already. At this late date, we cannot prove that Burr would have behaved in either Florida or Louisiana as he had in New York. But we have ample testimony, in statements made at the time by Wilkinson, Granger, Charles Claiborne, Stephen Minor, and Silas Dinsmoor, that there was widespread apprehension among the slaveowners that he might, and that their fears reached the ears of their President.

For King Cotton to acquire his new province in Louisiana, a labor force of slaves had to be containable there. Therefore, it was not merely the potential loss of the Ouachita lands which was to be feared but also the presence of Burr and, behind Burr, of a regime in Mexico that welcomed slaves into freedom.

From December 1803 onward, Wilkinson rang the firebell in the night. The phrase became famous after Jefferson made use of it during the controversy over attempts in Congress in 1819 to limit slavery in Missouri. Jefferson did not employ the term as we might anticipate, to mean a bell rung when slaves were in rebellion, setting things afire. That was surely the "firebell" most southerners feared most. He used it, instead, to refer to a bell rung to warn of political disunion if southerners were deprived of their right to hold, buy, and sell slaves. Psychologists may find his transposition of some interest.

As Wilkinson was stroking the fears of "armed blacks and mulattoes, officered and organized," he asked Jefferson for more troops and fewer restraints, proposing that Claiborne turn the government of Louisiana over to him under martial law. "Only with extraordinary powers," he insisted, could he "withstand the desperation and superiority of numbers opposed to you, and the brigands provoked by the opposition, might result to the dreadful expedient of exciting a revolt of the Negroes."[10]

Claiborne was at first unwilling to bow to a military government, but he did send a message in French to the leaders of the New Orleans militia that their troops should be made "ready to march; that the slaves should be watched, and that guards be mounted."[11]

On the proposition that the "Creoles of color in the city of New Orleans" were about to carry off a coup, Wilkinson got his martial law. John Graham, Jefferson's personal agent in New Orleans, wrote James Madison that he considered "this country as in a state of constant danger . . . requiring the presence of a considerable military force," not because of any foreign threat but because "we are in a country of slaves." "I am not a friend to standing armies in a free country," wrote Graham, but "masters must be protected against their slaves."[12]

On the other side of the border, Spanish officials were less fearful of that eventuality than they were of an American invasion. To them, it was not important whether or not Burr was an Ami des Noirs. He was a famous American colonel, renowned as a leader of soldiers. To cope with him, they summoned, out of retirement, José Vidal, their executioner of Philip Nolan and their most experienced secret agent. Nolan is often presented as a mere wrangler, but like Philip Augustus Bowles, he was a proto-Burr. Spain had its reasons to want Burr as dead as Nolan. Thomas Jefferson, and the planters he represented, seldom made use of violent means to cope with their political enemies, but they had their own devices. We turn to those techniques next, and to the history of their development in the West.

PART FIVE
The Expedition

In which we follow Aaron Burr in 1805, 1806, and 1807, as he adventured along the Ohio and Mississippi rivers to the border of Spanish West Florida. At the same time, we keep an eye on events in Washington: On November 27, 1806, Jefferson issued a presidential proclamation of another filibuster being prepared against the Spanish dominions in violation of George Washington's Neutrality Act of 1794. He did not name Burr, nor did he assert there to be any "conspiracy" against the Union.

Five days later, Jefferson's Annual Message to the Congress repeated these unspecific assertions, adding the suggestion that he might have to invoke the laws of the nation to prevent an "enterprise . . . against the United States." Only after the Congress required that he explain himself did the President charge Burr with the treason of arming citizens to seek separation of its western from its eastern states and with the misdemeanor of planning an attack on the possessions of Spain.[1]

We observe Burr's response to Jefferson's attack and to his betrayal by Wilkinson, his flight, his capture, his imprisonment in a wheeled cell, his trial in Richmond, the failure of Jefferson's effort to obtain a conviction, and the success of Jefferson's campaign against Burr's reputation, driving him into exile in 1808. Having brought our story to an end, we attempt a final evaluation of the character of each of our four protagonists, bringing to bear some informed judgments and some belated apologies.

Intentions, 1800–1805

John Adams was not an unpopular President. He probably received more popular votes for reelection in 1800 than did his challenger, Thomas Jefferson, whom he had defeated for the office four years earlier. The nomination of Aaron Burr to be Jefferson's companion on the ticket proceeded from a calculation that without him the party could not gain New York and that without that state the Republican would lose. The margin of victory for Jefferson in 1800 was provided by two discordant factors: the counting of humans held in bondage in the South as three-fifths persons in allocating electoral votes, and the presence on the ticket of Burr, whose antislavery position brought to him the votes of free blacks in key precincts in New York City.

The Virginians had first considered as their vice presidential candidate the elderly governor of New York, George Clinton, who could also deliver votes and had no energetic position as to slavery. Clinton was rejected because he had vociferously opposed the Constitution and was less competent and popular than Burr. By 1802, however, Jefferson had had enough of Burr, resolved to rid himself of him, and summoned Clinton to teeter onto the national scene to ready himself in 1804 to be his new Vice President. In that year, Burr sought election to the governorship evacuated by Clinton but was opposed by a coalition of a revivified Clinton interest under the former governor's tough and ambitious nephew De Witt, by the older members of the still powerful Livingston clan, and by Federalists inflamed against him by Hamilton. Though neither Burr's ally against slavery, John Jay, nor Hamilton's brother-in-law the patroon Stephen van Rensselaer joined the alliance against him, Burr was defeated.

In the summer of 1804, Burr killed Hamilton in their duel. Baffled and destabilized by the hubbub aroused against him after the duel, Burr resolved first to try his luck in the Florida expedition we have recounted earlier and, failing to find there a fit partner, set forth to the borderlands fronting upon Spanish West Florida and Texas. He had heard tales of western investments and adventures from his boyhood, but only in the spring of 1805 was he able to explore the area on his own.

Burr arrived at Blennerhasset's Island, in the Ohio off the coast of what is now West Virginia, paused to take counsel with its proprietor, and went on to Cincinnati, where he met with his kinsman Senator Jonathan Dayton of New Jersey and Senator John Smith of Ohio. Dayton had invested in the "Jersey Settlements" near Natchez, Mississippi, and Smith claimed thousands of acres in West Florida.

This book will be big enough without an extended inquiry into the Burrites as a group, but it is worth noting at this point that Dayton was a Federalist from a slave state (New Jersey) who, unlike most northern Federalists, was all for the expansion of the plantation system, with slaves, into the Southwest. He did, however, oppose a fugitive slave law which might operate in the Northwest Territory. Dayton became a major liability to Burr. John Smith was an antislavery Republican from Ohio, a state which had become more firmly opposed to slavery after the arrival of Thomas Worthington, a Virginian who acted upon Jefferson's stated principles, manumitted, and migrated.

In 1807, Smith was brought before the Senate on charges of conspiring with Burr, though Burr had just been discharged from his Richmond Trial. Smith was acquitted in a proceeding managed by John Quincy Adams and Jesse Franklin. Both were opposed to slavery (though Adams was only privately so at the time), and an entirely fresh look at their actions is required to determine what actually was done, for what is currently in print about the process simply does not make sense in the light of what else we know about them. Like Burr after Richmond, Smith knew that his reputation had been irreparably damaged despite the legal outcome and resigned his seat.

Absurd Reports

Many people, at the time and thereafter, believed that Burr coupled such an expedition against Spain with the separation of the western from the eastern states. The reasons are already before us: A succession of military adventurers, including George Rogers Clark, had publicly paired the two ideas for two decades. The Danville Convention had been full of such talk, and so had the "conspiracies" of Sevier and Blount. In his correspondence with Hamilton in 1798 and 1799, Wilkinson had written that the possibility of conjoining secession and filibustering was old hat. It was, therefore, easy for Stephen Minor, in the interest of Spain, to ignite a prairie fire of supposition to blaze up around Burr in 1805.

As Daniel Clark wrote Wilkinson from New Orleans: "Many absurd and wild reports are circulated here, and have reached the ears of the officers of the . . . Spanish government, respecting our ex vice president. . . . I believe that Minor, of Natchez, has a great part in this business, in order to make himself of importance—he is in the pay of Spain." Clark knew that Wilkinson, too, was on the Spanish payroll and that Wilkinson also had proposed filibustering *against* the Spanish possessions and was plainly indictable for treason and breaches of the Neutrality Act of 1794. The two had cooperated when the wind was right, but now it was blowing dangerously for Clark. He wished to warn Wilkinson that he should not be trifled with. It was essential to his safety when he was in Vera Cruz on business that the Spanish government not think him an enemy. In dealing with the American government, Clark wished to differentiate preparations for assaults upon Mexico (of which he was guilty) from separatist schemes (of which he was probably not). As an Irish immigrant exposed to the animosities revealed in the Alien Acts, he must be judicious in avoidance of that sort of thing. As we noted earlier, filibustering was merely a misdemeanor, and armed secession carried a death sentence.[1]

Clark went on to put the onus on Minor and on the possibility that

Burr had been garrulous: "Perhaps finding Minor on his way, and endeavoring to extract something from him [as Burr had from the Spanish and British representatives in the national capital], he has amused himself at the blockhead's expense, and then Minor has retailed the news to his employers. . . . The tale is a horrid one. . . . But how the devil I have been dragged into the conspiracy . . . is to me incomprehensible." His reconnaissances of Mexico, which had taken him to Vera Cruz, had been "cursedly hurt at the rumors, and might, in consequence of Spanish jealousy, get into a hobble I could not easily get out of."[2]

Quite so. Translation: Please tell your Spanish employers, or your American employers, or whichever you write next, that Daniel Clark is no threat to the one or to the other. As for Burr: "Amuse Mr. Burr with an account of it." Translation: If you have the decency, warn Burr not to confide in Minor. With proper recognition that decency was not Wilkinson's long suit, Clark sent a copy of his letter to Burr, who replied: "I love the society of that person [Minor], but surely I could never be guilty of the folly of confiding to one of his levity anything I wished not to be repeated." So Minor had made himself important without any help from Burr, who went on to say: "Pray do not disturb yourself with such nonsense." It would have been better for Burr if he had disturbed himself to consider who else had an interest in propagating "such nonsense." Once Minor had set the prairie aflame, it would blaze because of Wilkinson's old conspiracy in Kentucky, where the Federalists would have every reason to believe that anyone dealing with him would couple filibuster with separatism. And then there was Jefferson. His work was largely done for him by Stephen Minor. All he had to do was to set his seal upon Minor's story, as amplified by Wilkinson, and the world would believe it.[3]

What Jefferson believed and what Burr intended has been debated ever since. But perhaps the best summary of the debate is to be found in an editorial note commencing at page 919 of the *Papers of Aaron Burr,* in which the editors reach the convincing conclusion that, having been somehow disappointed in East Florida, he went without any more detailed plan than, as he said, "first, the revolutionizing of Mexico, and second, a settlement in what was known as the Bastrop lands."

The Manic Burr Goes West

During the late summer of 1806, Burr was induced by his new and persuasive acquaintances in Kentucky to make his new speculation in what he thought to be his four hundred thousand acres of the Bastrop Tract.

Had he not been so diverted toward the horizon, he might have made a new career In Kentucky or Tennessee. Burr was urged to do so by Matthew Lyon, a former congressman from Vermont who had taken that step himself. Once more, however, Burr could not grasp what came to his hand, but persisted, instead, in galloping toward the horizon, away from Kentucky, toward Louisiana and Texas.

Throughout his life, his friends wondered at Burr's strange incapacity to focus upon what was close at hand. He was a precise technician and tactician in the legislative process, but the subject matter of legislation was not himself. Upon that subject, he was incapable of deliberation or planning. He was forever vaulting into the saddle before he knew where he was going. Far from being cold, he was impetuous, warmhearted, loyal, and easily distracted by the enthusiasms of others from his own self-interest. Andrew Jackson knew Burr well and wondered at this: "He is as far from a fool as I ever saw," said Jackson, "and yet is as easily fooled as any man I ever knew." Another friend, Benjamin Henry Latrobe, put it another way. Burr was, he said, "two most opposite characters . . . the most sanguine and the most suspicious. . . . [C]areless of his interest, and even of public opinion, he is cautious to a degree of folly."[4]

The terms "schizophrenic" and "manic depressive" were not available to Jackson or Latrobe, but they did observe in Burr opposite characters appearing in sequence. Sometimes he was phlegmatic, sometimes preternaturally active. It is essential to our understanding of his behavior in the West that we give this matter a few further paragraphs, though, in doing so, we must retrace our steps to the early 1780s, when Burr wrote his friend William Paterson that he could not pull himself out of a depression lasting many months—"I am often a little inclined to *hypo*"—but wrote in the opposite mood to his brother-in-law, Tapping Reeve, that he was considering a madcap venture "in the Carolinas . . . a pretty rational one, for a madman."[5]

In 1806, Burr lay surrounded by enemies on the Bayou Pierre under observation by Cowles Mead, a dispassionate observer. Meade—no kin, it seems, to the Kentucky Meades—was governor of Mississippi Territory, under orders from Jefferson to treat Burr as Alcibiades and his sixty followers as a host. Mead had opportunity to assess the character of his quarry and concluded that Burr was derangedly optimistic when he had every reason to despair. Then, too, in Richmond in 1807, Burr had even more reason to abandon hope but was, instead, "as gay as usual" and spoke of the spirit in his prison rooms as "a scene of uninterrupted gaiety." This was not Chesterfieldian reserve or Epictetian grace. Epictetus might endure disaster with dignity but not necessarily chortle over it, and Chesterfield enjoined his sons *never* to be gay—in the eighteenth-century sense.[6]

On to the Hermitage, New Orleans, and the Clergy

Though loath to settle in for a campaign for Congress, Burr was prudent enough to attempt to protect his rear. He was a shareholder in the canal which might be built around the falls of the Ohio, so he made a hasty inspection of the route proposed for it by Benjamin Henry Latrobe, then proceeded to Frankfort and Lexington for conversations with Henry Clay, John Brown, the former associate of Innes and Wilkinson and now a senator, and Lyon. His next stop was Nashville, where he was greeted by former Senator Andrew Jackson. After resting at the Hermitage, he continued his ceremonial progress to Natchez and New Orleans, floating downstream in a partying procession of boats large and small, received by the gentry as a celebrity.[7]

New Orleans was especially hospitable, for the Crescent City likes its rakes even when their rakishness is overrated. In this way it was then, as now, a Caribbean city. Burr wrote his daughter that he regretted that it was not closer to her and his grandchild in South Carolina; instead, it looked across the steamy Gulf toward Mexico, and silver, and the empire of Cortez. Burr made careful inquiries about political conditions in Mexico from members of the city's Mexican Society, among whom the most prominent were the great merchants who shared the name Daniel Clark. They were uncle and nephew, and occupied the same status in New Orleans as the Biddles in Philadelphia.

There were other forces in New Orleans that could not be solicited by appeal to economics. While the city was, by Puritan standards, raffish in its sexual mores, and more eclectic in its race relations than was conventional in the inland South, it had its own deep-seated traditions, the most important of which was maintained by a Creole clergy like that which had developed, over several centuries, a role in the politics of Latin America. Ecclesiastically and theologically, New Orleans, like St. Augustine and Santa Fe, was a middle ground. The clergy mattered, as they mattered in New England, but in a very different way.

In such a place, the appearance of a man trained in theology, and springing from the most celebrated family of theologians in North America, was news beyond politics. Aaron Burr, in particular, brought to the Catholic frontier personal relationships that could not be matched by any other of the Founding Fathers of the American Republic, including those, like Charles Carroll of Carrolton, who were famously but not assertively Catholic.

Lest a grave portentousness fall over us in all this parsing of religious associations, let us return to Burr's own style to offer two examples of why he was beloved by many Catholics. When he served in the New York legislature, in 1799, it was dominated by Federalists in the nativist and anti-Catholic mood which gave rise to the Alien and Sedition Acts. On February 6, a motion was offered to single out the Rev. Mr. O'Brien from the eight or more chaplains to the Assembly and to dispense with his services. After it passed, 59 to 33, Burr promptly offered a killing amendment, dispensing with Drs. Ellison, Johnson, Bassett, Nott, Braun, and Jefferson as well. "Killing" is not the right word in this instance, except in the way that word was used in the 1920s to mean something unusually funny. We may assume that the Rev. Mr. O'Brien remained as a chaplain, and that other Catholics had paid attention.

History first became aware of Burr's Catholic connections in Canada, in 1775, when he demonstrated that a theologically trained, Latin-speaking American could establish his authenticity among Catholic clergy of a culture very different from that of New Haven or Princeton. Burr and his ragged detachment, having completed their winter expedition across Maine into Canada, sought contact with the main army under General Montgomery. Burr volunteered to get to Montgomery, through territory thought to be hostile, "disguised as a Catholic priest." "In this order of men," he told Matthew L. Davis, "he was willing to repose confidence," and they were willing to repose confidence in him. "He knew that the French Catholics were not satisfied with their situation . . . especially the priesthood. Feeling no apprehension for his own safety from treachery he proceeded to a learned and reverend father of the church, to whom he communicated frankly who he was, and what was his object."[8]

And how was this done? As a result of both his years at Princeton and his subsequent theological studies, "Burr was a master of the Latin language, [though he] . . . had an imperfect knowledge of the French. The priest was an educated man, so that a conversation was held without difficulty." After trying to talk Burr out of a mission that would bring death on discovery, the priest conceded to his "settled purpose [and] procured him a confidential guide and a cabriolet. . . . Without interruption, he was conducted in perfect safety from one religious family to another, until he arrived at Three Rivers . . . and reached Montgomery."[9]

A second tale told of Burr's Catholic connections is more ambiguous in its complications: When he was in Natchez, in 1806, he walked to his meetings with potential followers by following "a rural path . . . trellised with vines and shaded by evergreens. . . . Burr's daily resort . . . [was] a little vine-covered cottage," inhabited by "a widow lady from Virginia whose small farm and two or three slaves were all that remained of a large fortune. . . . She had but one child, Madeline . . . a miracle of beauty."[10]

Whene'er the words "vine-covered cottage" and "miracle of beauty" appear, we are forewarned that a nineteenth-century historian is about to produce a tragic lady to be seduced by satanic Aaron Burr. Cottages, miracles, and virgins are strewn like faded rose petals across accounts of his career, though seldom with citations to sources earlier than a generation after his death. Miraculous Madeline was contributed in 1879 by J. F. H. Claiborne. She may have existed. On the chance she did, let us doff our hats, as we pass along the path to the trellised cottage toward the more likely possibilities buried in Claiborne's sentimental twaddle—possibilities which, unlike Madeline's, were confirmed by eyewitness accounts.

> The family were Catholics, and there Colonel Burr went to meet . . . one of his numerous agents and correspondents, the Abbe Viel, a Jesuit priest . . . [Viel had been] born in New Orleans . . . studied in Paris, and became a member of the Congregation of the Oratory. . . . [H]e returned to Louisiana . . . [and] returned to France. I find among the papers of Colonel Burr, (left at Colonel Osmun's,) several pages of a hexameter version of Telema-

chus, in the handwriting of the Abbe, in Latin . . . and the following fragment.[11]

The "fragment" has been submitted to Father Ed Bodnar of
Georgetown University and has received from him both a translation
and a judgment that, as poetry, it is "wretched." Nonetheless, the
abbé, if that is what he was, leads us backward first, into Burr's youth,
and then forward, into the commencement of his dealings with the
clergy of Louisiana and Mexico. The step toward his past is necessary
to emphasize Burr's long-standing association with Catholic clergy
committed to the overthrow of regimes they felt to be oppressive. That
association, as applied to Latin American politics, lasted until the week
in which he died.

Finally, let us observe Burr at work upon his connections to the
higher clergy, in the New Orleans middle ground. By 1805, his French
was much improved from that available to him in Canada. He
was received by Madame Xavier Tarjon and the Ursuline nuns of
New Orleans both as a cosmopolitan and as a representative of the
American regime that, through the Louisiana Purchase, had rescued them from a French Emperor who had been most unkind to the
Pope.

Besides, Burr liked women. He wrote to his daughter that while he
had been "received with distinction" by the gentry of the town, "the
mark of attention with which I have been the most flattered is a letter
from the holy sisters, the Ursuline nuns. . . . [I]t was intimated to me
that the saints had a desire to see me. The bishop conducted me to
the cloister." Burr and the ladies first talked through the grates, but
when he passed whatever subtle test was put to him, he was admitted
and found "none of the calm monotony which I expected. All was
gaiety, wit, and sprightliness. I was conducted to every part of the building. All is neatness, simplicity, and order. At parting, I asked them to
remember me in their prayers, which they all promised with great
promptness and courtesy—Saint A. with earnestness."[12]

This is a pleasant account, written, as usual, to inform, and to accommodate as well the curiosity of those in the postal service. We need
not believe that all was "wine, fruit, and cakes." Did the "bishop" leave
Burr standing before the grate? Some member of the higher clergy
had escorted him there, and Burr may well have thought him a bishop,
possibly because Daniel Clark so designated him. Clark was also, no

doubt, the source for the following tantalizing tidbit, which found its way into Matthew L. Davis's *Memoirs of Aaron Burr:*[13]

> The Catholic bishop . . . was also consulted, and prepared to assist the enterprise [of revolutionizing Mexico]. He designated three priests . . . as suitable agents, and they were accordingly employed. The bishop was an intelligent and social man. He had been in Mexico, and spoke with great freedom of the dissatisfaction of the clergy in South America. The religious establishments of the country were not to be molested. Madame Xavier Tarjon, superior of the convent of the Ursuline nuns at New Orleans, was in the secret. Some of the sisterhood were also employed in Mexico.[14]

One may have doubts about the depth of Aaron Burr's commitment to many things, but not to the cause of liberating the people of Mexico, Texas, and Florida from the rule of the Kings of Spain. He found common cause with the clergy both because they and he agreed as to that objective and because he was a born ecclesiastical politician, naturally drawn to clandestine operations and the encrypted life of private understandings. In New York, he had vied with the Clintons for support from Catholic interests, especially those of the Irish artisans of the Society of St. Tammany, and one may assume that he came to Madame Tarjon with the correct letters of introduction.

Casa Calvo, Grand Pré, Morales, and Recruiting

Having renewed his clerical relations, Burr was ready to negotiate with the officials of the Spanish civil service who might be willing to listen to a proposition. The most eminent and accessible of them was the marquis de Casa Calvo, who had been charged with handing over New Orleans to the Americans after the Louisiana Purchase and was still lurking about the city. Exquisite, perfumed, without official status, a master of intelligence and sponsor of amiable young men, this Hiberno-Hispanic aristocrat was very tough, taking the same hard line with regard to American colonists as Henry White of Florida. So Burr detoured Casa Calvo.

It seems, however, that he found means to communicate with two other Spanish officials who, though feuding with each other, gave signs that they might be interested in a new order along the Gulf. Carlos de Grand Pré commanded at Baton Rouge and had been receiving a stream of warnings against Burr from both Governor Vincente Folch of West Florida and James Wilkinson (in his role as unofficial adviser to the Spanish military). When Burr appeared on his doorstep in 1806, Grand Pré "preserved a mysterious silence . . . [having] neglected to carry out Folch's suggestions for strengthening that part of the province." Somewhat later, Folch came to the view that a Burrite emergence might not be a disaster for Spain. In both 1805 and 1806, the mails and newspapers were full of rumors about western separatism. From a Spanish point of view, a divided United States would threaten Spain less than one truly united. According to Isaac Cox, who read his way through all Folch's orders and reports, "he was prepared to support the insurgents if they asked for aid, and now advised Grand Pré to observe a neutral attitude between them and the United States."[15]

Completing a possibly complaisant trio was Juan Ventura Morales. Morales also resided in New Orleans, though he was charged with governing Mobile and Pensacola. He was rich, actively in partnership with Daniel Clark, and made no secret of his views:

> [He] preferred to sell the province [Florida] to the Americans . . . [having assessed the] expense of maintaining a hopeless front against these restless neighbors, with no local revenues, and uncertain subsidies from Mexico, with fortifications in ruins and no possibility of increasing their defenders. . . . Pensacola and Mobile could not support their combined population of about fifteen hundred, including soldiery. . . . Baton Rouge . . . was so enclosed by neighboring American territory as to be defenseless.[16]

Which Spanish officials were on which side? And what, indeed, was a "Spanish" official? The multinational colonial bureaucracy of the Spanish empire was increasingly impatient with the incompetence of the Spanish court and willing to consider alliances with the Americans to head off France and Britain.

In 1798, Gayoso de Lemos, then governor of the Province of Louisiana and chief of the regional Spanish intelligence, had written another Spanish official that if there were a joint American-Spanish venture to create an independent state in Mexico, resistance would quickly crumble. In 1805, newspapers in Mississippi Territory reported that an unnamed "Spanish officer from Pensacola had visited Burr at the town of Washington" and that "the second in command at Baton Rouge was reported to be involved with Burr"—that could be Grand Pré, for he was second to Folch. Burr's companion, Robert Ashley, later told the American authorities that "Morales was awaiting Burr . . . [in Pensacola], where the local officials were expecting him."[17]

At the end of May 1805, having completed his interfaith discussions, Burr ascended the Natchez Trace to Nashville. In September he joined Wilkinson in St. Louis, where, according to Jackson, they "settled the plan for an attack on Mexico." It appears that Wilkinson provided maps drawn by one protégé, Philip Nolan, and written accounts gathered for another, Zebulon Pike, who, at the time, was on a mission toward the Colorado Rockies and Santa Fe.[18]

For a conquest of Mexico, Burr would need recruits. From St. Louis, he retraced the route of George Rogers Clark across Illinois to Vincennes, where he attempted without success to convince William Henry Harrison to join him. At the end of November 1805, he was back in Washington for a two-hour private conversation with Jefferson. It cannot have been a clubby session, and we have no firsthand account of what they discussed. Afterward, however, Burr reported to Henry Clay that "my views have been fully explained . . . to several principal officers of the government. . . . [They] are well considered by the administration and seen by it with complacency." Some authorities offer the hypothesis that Jefferson told Burr that the immediate prospect of war with Spain had receded, though Burr implied to Senator Smith of Ohio that this surcease was only temporary and that[19]

> if there should be a war . . . I shall head a corps of volunteers and be the first to march on the Mexican provinces. If peace be proffered . . . I shall settle my Wichita lands, and make society as pleasant as possible.[20]

The meeting with Jefferson had occurred as the President was preparing what was in effect a war message, threatening to "throw away the scabbard" against Spain, which he sent the Congress in December 1805. "With Spain our negotiations have not had a satisfactory issue. . . . Propositions for adjusting amicably the boundaries of Louisiana have not been acceded to." The Spaniards had invaded American territory, Jefferson charged, seizing citizens and plundering property. "I have therefore found it necessary . . . to give orders to our troops on that frontier to be made in readiness . . . and to repel by arms any similar aggressions in future." The "boundaries" to which he referred had been moved ahead in February 1804, when he claimed Spanish West Florida for the United States by signing John Randolph's Mobile Act. The seizures and plunderings were no doubt those north of the thirty-first parallel in response to Reuben Kemper's south of it. One man's "aggressions" were another's "readiness to repel" aggressions.[21]

Small wonder Burr expected war and thought he had Jefferson's acquiescence to his plans. He failed to understand that it was not a matter of whether but of whom. Filibustering, in defiance of the Neutrality Act of 1794, was not the issue. It was, instead, who would have the administration's support in filibustering. Somebody would lead an attack on Mexico. As Jefferson wrote, afterward, to his man in Madrid, "so popular is an enterprise on that country . . . that we had only to be still, and [Burr] could have had followers enough to have been in the city of Mexico in six weeks."[22]

There is a tantalizing passage in a letter Burr wrote to General Edward Tupper which suggests that Albert Gallatin may inadvertently have set the bait:

> I am authorized in saying that it is the wish of Government that American settlers should go to the country west of the Mississippi in the Orleans Territory. Indeed a man high in office and in the confidence of the President told me that I should render a very great service to the public and afford pleasure to the administration, if I should take ten thousand men to that country—(I wish it was in my power).[23]

The probability that this high official was Gallatin arises from the fact that in the previous July Burr made his inquiry of Gallatin about the Bastrop Tract, giving the administration another clear indication of the direction in which he was heading. If it was not Gallatin—who would not purposely bait a hook for an old friend—then it might have been Gideon Granger. It is easy to imagine him, delighted, salivating, placing the bait; and such a picture is provoked by certain inferences in his blackmailing correspondence with Jefferson, to which we will come in time.

In November 1805, in any case, Burr borrowed trouble in Kentucky by appearing among associates of Wilkinson—and Bastrop—in Lexington. The Federalists, of course, charged him with reigniting the old Wilkinson-Innes-Brown conspiracy. Apparently somewhat bewildered,

Burr insisted upon a grand jury proceeding to clear his name. The jury accommodated, but the stain upon Burr's garments did not wash off. There had been a "Burr conspiracy." Conspiracies are clandestine. For fifteen months, Burr trumpeted his intentions to find a new career in the West, telling every statesman who would listen that he planned to go to his Bastrop Tract and hope for a bully war against Spain.

La Chaumiere du Prairie

For two weeks, as Burr awaited the jury's completing its deliberations and affirmations, he had the pleasure of rusticating at La Chaumiere du Prairie, surely the most interesting estate in America at the time. His hosts were a family which, if not so brilliant as the Adamses, was more urbane and considerably more witty. The Meades were old-fashioned, Whiggish gentry—in costume, habit, horticulture, financial profligacy, landscape design, and speech. But like Burr, they were considerably ahead of their time in racial matters.

Let us pause, therefore, with Burr, quieting politics amid the eleven Meades. If we require a reason, let us content ourselves with the saw that it is not foolish to inquire into the company a person keeps. Guilt by association is a dangerous procedure in criminal proof, but we all look to association as one guide to character: Charm may be commonplace, and reputation may be purchased, but we trust a man or woman who has long-lasting friendships among people of taste, intelligence, discrimination, and a sense of the absurd. David Meade II was such a friend, and another reminder of why it was that Aaron Burr commended himself to us for reexamination. Along with Meade, Burr's friends included John Jay, Albert Gallatin, William Paterson, Robert Troup, Charles Biddle, Edward Livingston, Andrew Jackson, Benjamin Henry Latrobe, Eric Bollmann, Julien de Pestre, Luther Martin, and Pierpont Edwards. These were people of discriminating taste, and so, in their own ways, were others we will meet shortly: Silas Dinsmoor, Peter Bruin, and Robert Ashley, who also demonstrated an enduring fondness for Burr.

David Meade II was the creator of two of the five earliest grand-scale landscape plans in America—the others being Jefferson's at Monticello, the Middletons' at Middleton Place in South Carolina, and Andrew Hamilton's Woodlands in Philadelphia. Meade created his first at Maycox, Virginia, across the James from Westover, in the 1770s, and his second in central Kentucky, on Catnip Hill Road, just off the Harrodsburg Pike, eight miles south of Lexington. That was in 1796, after his disaffection with things in Virginia induced him to bring his wife and nine children to a new life in the West.

The Meades are an old Virginia family, though their most celebrated member, General George Meade, was on the other side at Gettysburg. They descend from Thomas Cromwell, who succeeded Cardinal Wolsey as chief minister to King Henry VIII. Those who saw the Cromwell family portraits on the walls at La Chaumiere, beside the Reynoldses, Sullys, and Hudsons, and who saw David Meade II walk past, were prone to speak of how similar he was to Oliver Cromwell, but only, one supposes, until he spoke. For his nature was not Puritan. It expressed instead the other side of the family, from County Cork—a good thing indeed.

The first eminent American Meade was David I, who married Susannah Everard, whose father had been royal governor of North Carolina. Three of the sons of this union, including David II and Richard K., attended Harrow, in England, and went on to achieve other distinctions. Richard K. Meade served on George Washington's staff during the Revolution, and his son the celebrated Bishop William Meade resuscitated the Episcopal Church of Virginia after Jefferson's disestablishment and the defection from America of all but one or two of its clergy. The bishop's uncle David sent his son David III to Princeton, where he became a friend of Burr's.

The marquis de Chastellux reported of David Meade II, while he was expending three inherited fortunes on Maycox, that he was "a philosopher of a very amiable but singular turn of mind . . . uncommon in Virginia, since he . . . cannot prevail upon himself to make his Negroes work. He is even so disgusted with a culture, wherein it is necessary to make use of slaves, that he is tempted to sell his possessions in Virginia and remove to New England." George Washington expressed the thought that Meade's circumstances in Virginia became incompatible with his character, as he could no longer stomach the slave system, so he went to Kentucky, taking with him enough of the family fortune to place in a gentle valley "the first lordly house in Kentucky" amid "the most fabulous estate ever to be erected in the Blue Grass."[24]

As one came along Catnip Hill Road, one saw first an archway of stone, which, when entered, led to a second gateway, the columns for which were inverted tree trunks. If one were on foot, the house could be reached along a mile-long serpentine walk, bordered by flowering hedges, which choreographed movement past a little artificial lake with a Chinese Bridge (like that of the Moultries at Bella Vista, in Florida) and a Grecian temple (like the Biddles' in Philadelphia). There was a "haw-haw" avenue (meaning a stone-lined ditch to keep the cattle off the lawn without an obtrusive wall, hedge, or fence), a "bird-cage walk," cut through a wild plum thicket flowering white and sweet in the early spring, a pagoda "among the maple and ash trees, and broad stretches of velvet turf on which a small company of Negro children were kept continually employed picking up leaves and twigs."[25]

The senior Meades costumed themselves in an eighteenth-century mode. Well into the 1820s, the squire wore embroidered waistcoats with silver buttons bearing the family arms, knee britches, and slippers with silver buckles, "while on dress occasions the silver ornaments were replaced by gold." His lady favored black satin with lace, "a standing ruff about her neck, and a high-crowned muslin cap."[26]

Meade was quoted as saying that the most beautiful thing in his life was the sight of twenty or more young ladies, clad only in white, scudding across his greensward. Since he and his wife had nine children, and each of them entertained frequently, he often had that pleasure. Meade was no fool; he loved landscape and saw no need to pursue the pretensions of his brick-and-white-trim neighbors in either Virginia or Kentucky. His residence at Maycox was plain, and in Kentucky he and his brood lived in an assemblage of cabins of stone, log, wood, and brick, centered upon a grand rectangular dining room paneled in black walnut with scarlet curtains. Behind the dining room was a brick octagonal ballroom, which is the only remnant of all this grandeur to survive.

The affectionate memoirs of his grandchildren of the antebellum generation elevated certain elements of the life of David Meade II they wished to recall as pleasantly eccentric and repressed those they and their contemporaries thought dangerously radical. It was undeniable that, like his own Virginian contemporaries Edward Coles and Thomas Worthington, Meade manumitted all his slaves who could support themselves on his death and provided for the others. And it was further admissible to say of him that "he had a greater respect for the courteous Negro of the old time [whatever that may mean] than for the unfortunately ill-bred white."[27]

From this account of a bucolic idyll, we must now tear ourselves away to travel eight miles to town—to Lexington, James Wilkinson's town.

Wilkinson's Fidelity

Sometime prior to October 25, 1806, Wilkinson decided that Jefferson was a better choice as a sponsor than Burr and entered into communication with Gideon Granger. Minutes of a cabinet meeting of that date record a discussion of Burr's activities and the conclusion of those assembled that, whatever Wilkinson and the Federalists had charged, the evidence indicated that Burr was "committing no overt act against the law." At the same time, however, the government's own provocations against Spain were to be continued. "Marines . . . to reinforce, or take [the] place [of?] . . . the garrison of New Orleans, with a view to Spanish operations! Offensive or defensive?" What did that question imply? Was the cabinet in doubt as to the purposes of Spain? Or as to its own purposes? And how did such doubts bear upon Burr's activities and Wilkinson's? Minutes of a meeting three days earlier, on October 22, 1806, in the President's own hand, referred to some information brought them by Granger about statements made to him by General William Eaton:[28]

> General Wilkinson being expressly declared by Burr to Eaton to be engaged in this design [meaning: Eaton had said that Burr had said to him that Wilkinson was engaged in Burr's design] as his lieutenant, or first in command, and suspicion of infidelity in Wilkinson being now become very general, a question is proposed what is proper to be done with him on this account as well as for his disobedience of orders received by him June 11 at St. Louis to descend with all practical dispatch to New Orleans . . . and then repair to take command at Natchitoches, on which business he did not leave St. Louis till September.[29]

Somewhat earlier, some thoughts were offered as to the distinction between assigning guilt by association and judging character by taking account of company kept and of agents used. Bearing those general principles in mind, it will not make pleasant reading to observe the alacrity with which General Eaton was taken up by the Postmaster General of the United States, Gideon Granger. It is not altogether surprising that he was compatible with James Wilkinson, because Eaton first came to some notoriety for being suspended from his army command as a speculator in government stores for sale to his own soldiers. Thereafter, his chief distinction had been a filibustering expedition into the desert of Tripoli, where he had installed a puppet on the throne of one of the Barbary States. For years thereafter, he toured the taverns from Boston to Richmond wearing an Arab costume of his own invention, regaling all who would listen with tales of his exploit, and pursuing a congressional grant of ten thousand dollars for quelling Tripolitanian piracy. The Congress demurred; and so, for a time, did President Jefferson. Eaton had not yet developed a product Jefferson wanted to buy.

During the winter of 1805–6, Eaton found his product—tales derogatory to Aaron Burr. He began retailing a story that Burr sought him out to propose a coup d'état, including the assassination of President Jefferson, the dismissal of Congress, and the seizure of the Treasury and navy. Eaton tried this farrago upon the upright Federalist William Plumer, but Plumer was not buying. However, when Eaton gave Gideon Granger a performance in Massachusetts, the postmaster sent a rave review to Jefferson. Of course Eaton would have to do a little editing, for he had implicated Wilkinson alongside Burr. That would never do. But Eaton might be useful, so the President provided him a private discussion, in Washington, in February or March 1806. And that is how, as Jefferson wrote, "in 1806 he [Granger] gave us the first effectual notice of Burr's Western projects by which we were enabled to take specific measures to meet them." That "first effectual notice" came from the Hero of Derne.[30]

We may anticipate a little: When Burr was brought to trial in Richmond, in August 1807, Eaton was the administration's lead-off witness, having trimmed his story of Wilkinson's role and some of its more ludicrous details. Now he merely charged Burr with treason, proposing to separate the West from the East. That was the core of the administration's case. And "almost immediately after Eaton placed his deposition in Jefferson's hands, Congress suddenly authorized the payment to him of $10,000 on a doubtful claim which had been before

it for years, and which it had shown no previous disposition to honor."
William Eaton spent his bribe on clothes and liquor.[31]

To understand how such a man gained the President's ear, we must
appreciate the devices of his sponsor, Gideon Granger, and that requires us to draw upon Granger's own account of how he and Eaton
managed matters, rendered several years later. When James Madison
became President in 1809, he inherited Granger from Jefferson and
found that the Postmaster General, thinking of himself more in the
line of a judge than a political fixer, was organizing a bid for appointment to the Supreme Court of the United States. Writing Jefferson as
his "political father," in 1810, Granger assured the former President
that he was fully prepared to assume the "sober, steady, prudent life
which a judge must lead." As for his "qualifications," he offered his
role as "principal agent in affecting the political revolution of the western part of New Hampshire . . . and I formed the republican party . . .
in . . . Hampshire County . . . Massachusetts." As for his role as a lob-
byist for speculators in western lands, he would abstain from any more
of that: "If I have rights, they will not be lost by delay."[32]

Granger claimed Jefferson's gratitude for intelligence operations in
1805–6, when he had become the Washington manager of the affairs
of De Witt Clinton, who wished Burr and Jefferson to be at each other's
throats. "You, sir," he wrote Jefferson, "know that I gave you authentic
information of Burr's conspiracy and how I got that information. You
also know, sir, that it was by your advice and for what purpose I allowed
the Federalist [sic] to assume a free intercourse with me. It was to aid
my country and you." It seems that this "free intercourse" led Granger
into some dubious transaction "on the advice of General Dearborn
[Secretary of War at the time] . . . when I sacrificed my own character
and feelings to preserve the feelings and character of others [Wilkin-
son?], who were dear to you and to me. My conduct was equally correct
and honorable in 1808. I cannot be more particular." He did not need
to be. That was the year in which Jefferson saw to it that Dearborn
protected Wilkinson against the charges of treason brought by Daniel
Clark and Edward Livingston. By protecting Wilkinson, Dearborn was
protecting Jefferson. Lest the point be lost, Granger added a whiff of
blackmail: He had means by "publicity . . . to give my vindication to
the world. . . . You will not believe that with everything in my hands
I had not the means of explanation to *myself* [my emphasis] highly
honorable."[33]

Was there ever so persuasive an application for a seat on the nation's ultimate court of justice? Thomas Jefferson responded by writing his successor, James Madison, that if the leading candidate, Levi Lincoln, should be

> out of the way I should think Granger prominent for the place. His abilities are great, I have confidence in his integrity, though I am sensible that J. R. [John Randolph] has been able to lesson the confidence of many in him. But I believe he would soon reconcile to him. . . . Granger and Morton [a third candidate] have both been interested in Yazooism. The former however has long been clear of it.[34]

To his credit, Madison was unmoved and appointed another New Englander, the thirty-two-year-old Joseph Story. Story had been specifically mentioned by Jefferson as disqualified by his failure to commit political suicide in Massachusetts by supporting Jefferson's embargo.

Granger remained Postmaster General but went into skulking opposition to Madison. There is strong evidence that he conspired with Clinton to replace the President in 1812, but until 1814 Madison still deferred to Jefferson's expressed confidence in Granger. In that year, however, the Postmaster went into outright revolt, appointing Madison's political enemies to lucrative postmasterships. Madison had had enough and threatened to fire him. Granger turned again to blackmail. First he attempted to terrify Madison himself with disclosures about his wife. While Dolley Madison was a widow in reduced circumstances, Burr may have been only a friend, but, Granger let it be known, others had been more than friends, and he had letters to prove it. Blackmail is not pretty. Granger was induced to send to the Madisons copies of the blackmailing documents. The Madisons destroyed them, and Granger's heirs told posterity that his papers did not include the originals at his death. Given the sensitivity of Burr's relationship to Dolley Madison, we are left wondering what went to the flames. It is not that we might expect any authentic disclosures of mind-shattering significance. The interest these documents might have would be merely a demonstration that Granger was as capable of forgery as James Wilkinson, his sometime partner in politics and land speculation. It would be interesting to know how imaginative he could be.

Madison refused to be blackmailed; Granger turned again to Jeffer-

son on February 22, 1814, writing: "Though I possess the evidence.
. . . I think to publish them at large would not be pleasing to you and
would be distressing to me," and proposing that Jefferson put in writing whatever version of his relationship to Burr that might please them
both. Jefferson's response was a model of pious incorruptibility, as he
summarized it to Madison on March 10: "Mr. G . . . mentioned . . . that
a state of things existed which probably would oblige him to make a
solemn appeal to the public, and he asked my testimony to certain
specific facts . . . related solely to charges against him as a Burrite, and
to his agency in dismissing prosecutions in Connecticut under the Sedition Law. [No reference to this aspect of the matter appears in the
published correspondence, and Jefferson did not refer to it again.]
The facts alleged as disproving his Burrism were 1. That he through
Erving in 1800 put Virginia on her guard against the designs of Burr.
2. That in 1802 at my request he communicated to DeWitt Clinton
Burr's aspiring to the government of New York. 3. That in 1806 he
gave us the first effectual notice of Burr's Western projects by which
we were enabled to take specific measures to meet them. 4. His mission
to Mr. Pease on the route to N[ew] Orleans to expedite [!] the mails
and remove suspected agents [!] of the Post Office. These appeals to
my very defective memory are very painful . . . but of justice to him
personally for his conduct towards me was ever friendly and faithful,
and I on several occasions used his services to the advantage of the
public. . . . [Finally, an] expression in Mr. G.'s letter gave me ground
to advise him to confine his vindication to its important points whatever they might be and not let his passions lead him into matters which
would degrade himself alone in the public opinion, and I have urged
it in such terms as I trust will have effect."[35]

Granger's biographer, Arthur Hamlin, characterized Jefferson's response as "a most friendly letter in which he fully confirmed Granger's
conduct." Few of us would welcome the following admonition from a
friend, or "political father," who was clearly squashing an annoying,
blackmailing, blackguard who had once been of use, and was no
longer:

> With respect to the first article mentioned in your letter, in which
> I am neither concerned nor consulted, I will yet as a friend, vol-
> unteer some advice. I never knew anything of it, nor would ever
> listen to such gossiping trash. Be assured, my dear sir, that the

dragging such a subject before the public will excite universal reprobation, and they will drown in their indignation all the solid justifications which they would otherwise have received and weighed with candor. . . . You may give pain where perhaps you wish it, but be assured it will re-act on yourself with double though delayed effect, and that it will be one of those incidents of your life on which you will never with satisfaction. . . . Be advised then; erase it from your memory, and stand erect before the world on the high ground of your own merits, without stooping to what is unworthy of your or their notice. . . . I have suggested with frankness other considerations . . . because I wish you well, and I add sincere assurances of my great respect and esteem.[36]

Granger remained quiet. Madison dismissed him, and he finished his life as a country squire in Canandaigua, New York, speculating with great success in Ohio lands. But the exchanges among the Madisons, Granger, and Jefferson reopened an old wound. We will deal with that wound, but not quite yet. When we are ready, it will be because the course of events forces upon us a recognition that the women in our story have been insufficiently considered. They, too, affected the circumstances now before us. They, too, inform us of aspects of the character of each of our principal subjects which would otherwise be drowned out in the noise.

Wilkinson's Estimates

With Granger in place, we can get on with our tale. In November 1806, James Wilkinson's "infidelity" should have come as no surprise to Mr. Jefferson's cabinet. No one, except his first wife, seems to have aroused in Wilkinson any fidelity whatever. While talking to Alexander Hamilton in 1798–99, and to Aaron Burr in 1805, he was derisive of Thomas Jefferson, deploying all his powers of persuasion to convince them that Jefferson was a weakling and that Spain would be a pushover. His motivation was not complex: If Hamilton or Burr were to lead invasion forces against Spain, he wanted to be in on the swag. Later, when he was beguiling Jefferson in 1806, he presented Spain as a formidable antagonist, and thus justified that "disobedience" to which the cabinet referred. For a traitor, disobedience could be remunerative. Wilkinson's Spanish employers paid him well and used the time provided by his delay to make more credible his estimates of their strength by assembling, on the Sabine frontier, their forces against his own army. Thereafter, their presence became the excuse for him again to disobey the instructions of his Commander-in-Chief and to negotiate with the Spaniards an unauthorized separate peace, collecting from them pay beyond his usual retainer.

To provide some explanation for the cabinet's puzzlement at the time, we must drop back two years, to follow Wilkinson to the point at which he, Granger, Eaton, and some Kentucky Federalists all offered themselves to Jefferson as paladins against Burr. In 1803–4, Daniel Clark, the old Etonian who had become the preeminent New Orleans merchant, had turned on Jefferson and was urging Burr to come to that city and meet with Clark's Mexican Association. Wilkinson was then offering Clark what Clark wanted to hear—derisive comments about Jefferson and about Jefferson's appointed governor of Louisiana, William C. C. Claiborne. On April 30, 1803, Wilkinson sent Clark "under cover . . . in the most sacred confidence, a literal extract from a letter written" him on March 6 by Jefferson. As if with an incredulous sneer, Wilkinson provided that extract to confirm what Clark had previously told Wilkinson about an evening in which he and a group of congressmen, at the President's House, heard Jefferson discourse about the ease by which Spain could be defeated and Louisiana enlarged. Since Wilkinson's new game, with both Jefferson and Clark, was to make that outcome appear difficult, he made Jefferson's disingenuousness appear ludicrous,

> giving lessons to certain members of a great assembly. The puerility and weakness of this extract is perhaps unequaled but by the spirit which dictated it. Those who do not know how to preserve peace, or to make war, surely are unfit for exalted station or public confidence. Another courier has gone down [from the President to Governor Claiborne], which the Gr calls highly important, and that we shall certainly know what we have to expect in twelve days. God of Heaven!—that our honor, interests and safety should be confided to such hands.[37]

Among the others for which Wilkinson expressed disdain was Claiborne, at whom he smiled each morning and with whom he dined on many an evening: "W.C.C. . . . is a mass of duplicity, meanness, envy, ignorance, and cowardice," he wrote Clark. He moderated his language only a little in confiding to the solemn John Quincy Adams that "Claiborne gives great dissatisfaction . . . in his office . . . is hooted at by the very old women, whom he has heard to exclaim, 'Quel Commandant!' 'Quel Gouverneur!' 'quelle bête!' ''[38]

Not even Granger seems to have suggested that the cabinet rely upon Wilkinson and Eaton, so the utterly reliable John Graham, of Mason's Neck, Virginia, was sent to gather a truthful account of the circumstances in the West, "to inquire into Burr's movements, put the governors on their guard, [and] to provide for his [Burr's] arrest if necessary." Always there were two agendas: the apprehension of Burr and the carrying forward of operations against Spain. To move both of these purposes forward, the cabinet agreed that letters were to be written to the governors of Louisiana and Mississippi.[39]

(Graham was their best equivalent to Patrick O'Brian's Stephen Maturin. One of the innumerable reasons to read O'Brian's Maturin-Aubrey novels is that they provide a real sense of the intelligence operations available to governments that had no quick mode of communication with which to instruct agents, who were, therefore, left to their own considerable resources. So reliable was Graham that we are free to believe that the puzzling reference to operations "offensive or defensive" meant that he might be entrusted with a decision as to whether the administration's policy should be offensive or defensive.)

Jefferson Recomputes the Odds

A sudden change occurred in Thomas Jefferson's behavior in the middle of November 1806, as it became apparent that, however he himself might have assessed the threat represented by Burr, he had recalculated what *others* might think. He had been saying that he had not trusted Burr since the middle 1790s and had warned James Madison against him, so his change of course in November could not have been occasioned by any sudden revulsion at Burr's character. Nor could it have arisen from any new discoveries, since he had been told Burr's intentions in detail, had permitted Burr to believe he approved of them, and had withheld any sign of disapproval. For fifteen months he had been apparently willing to permit his former Vice President to take a role in his *own* program of provocation against Spain.

Though no new data had arrived, in mid-November Jefferson suddenly turned his entire network of intelligence agents and that portion of the apparatus of the Republican party loyal to him, together with the full power of the government of the United States, toward the defeat of Burr's plans. It is likely that he was prompted by these concurrent appraisals:

First, Jefferson assessed the state of the inflammation of patriotic public feeling induced by the rumors circulated against Burr, some of them put into currency by himself. In November, rumor-induced fever reached a degree of intensity permitting the calculator to conclude that public opinion—or enough of it—would permit him to deal with his rival as he had probably intended to deal all along.

Second, Jefferson took account of the intensity of dread among his fellow slaveowners that Burr, loose in the West, might be dangerous to the plantation system. (We earlier reviewed testimony as to the level of anxiety in the South on this score.)

Third, Jefferson had to come to an opinion as to how much truth there was in what he had been told by Granger, Eaton, and Wilkinson. He may actually have believed, some or all of the time, some or all or what they reported. Perhaps, despite his later denials of any anxiety, he may have feared that Burr intended to wrest from him the benefits of his imperial dreams and to separate Louisiana and the West from the East.

Scholars divide in their conjectures as to what Jefferson really thought or believed, according to their disposition to believe what he said he thought. No one has found it easy to penetrate the mystery of the American sphinx. All that can be said with certainty is that from time to time, Jefferson acted *as if* he believed Burr to have had such an evil intent. If he had any constant feeling, it was probably a hunger for evidence of something loathsome to believe of Burr.

A fourth recalculation was necessary on Jefferson's part because the international climate had altered radically. During the escalation of the President's campaign against Spain, William Pitt had been Prime Minister of Great Britain. A British fleet under orders from Pitt was a friendly fleet, for Pitt had supported American independence and shared some of Jefferson's affinities to the French Republic. In January 1806, Pitt died. His successor, Charles James Fox, discouraged interventionist schemes, though he was friendlier than Pitt to the Americans; there was a chance he might come around, but he, too, died, in the summer of 1806, depriving Jefferson of any hope of a British co-belligerent and of easy conquests of Spanish territory. The odds against success for an aggressive foreign policy were further diminished by the reappearance of Napoleon in American affairs. The Emperor announced that France would go to war alongside Spain if the Americans, with or without British aid, provoked a confrontation on the Louisiana-Texas border. The Bonaparte brothers, Napoleon and Joseph, had their own designs upon a Spanish empire; Napoleon was in the process of placing Joseph upon the throne of Spain.

At the same time, the Spaniards themselves were showing unwonted spunk, as power within their colonial bureaucracy shifted to a new generation hoping to rekindle that vitality in their North American empire which Bernardo Galvez had ignited at the end of the 1770s. Napoleon and Talleyrand encouraged this revitalization, seeking to establish a "wall of brass" between the Anglo-Americans and the silver mines of Mexico.

Thus it was that in an autumnal efflorescence of vigor, the Spanish empire placed a thousand men on its northern frontier. Thereafter, the Spaniards faced down, in sequence, all of Mr. Jefferson's expeditions of science and espionage except that of Lewis and Clark—which escaped only because the Pawnee missed them. Wilkinson had urged the Spaniards to have Lewis and Clark massacred and also recommended the assassination of old Daniel Boone, who was then settling himself in Missouri.[40]

18

Whose Valley?

The Great Valley is shaped like an oak leaf. Its three lobes, each veined by thousands of miles of river, come together near St. Louis to form the stem of the continent, into which other great rivers bring the surplus moisture of the grasslands and savannahs of the Midwest and the sparse runoff of the dry Great Plains. Most of the moving water of the continent flows through this immense hydraulic apparatus into the Gulf of Mexico.

The western lobe of the system is the basin of the Missouri, two thousand miles long, the sources of which were claimed in 1806 for Virginia, by the conventional European process of naming them. That is why these streams and the three broad-shouldered, white-maned ranges through which they forced their way are called respectively the Jefferson, the Madison, and the Gallatin. Thomas Jefferson was the President of the United States who bought the entire western half of the valley from Napoleon. James Madison was the Secretary of State who did not quail at arrangements more than doubling the size of the national territory at a cost exceeding five times the total annual national budget. And Albert Gallatin, the Secretary of the Treasury, found the money.

These ranges and rivers were provided these patronymics by two Virginian explorers named Meriwether Lewis and William Clark, as imperial proclamations to posterity. That message has diminished in impact subsequently as it has become less important that all three statesmen were also Virginians: Jefferson and Madison were born in the Old Dominion, and Gallatin first became an American citizen while in residence there. Three Forks, Montana, where Lewis and Clark proclaimed the Missouri to begin, is a long way from Charlottesville or Richmond, but the ambitions of the Virginians were very large, extending even beyond the boundaries of the Louisiana sold to Jefferson by Napoleon. The watershed of the Missouri is ample, but Virginian energy rushed with Lewis and Clark across the Continental Divide, down its western slope, and into the basin of the Columbia River, which even Napoleon had neither claimed nor claimed to sell. When they reached the Pacific, Lewis and Clark asserted that the United States owned everything they had traversed, and, for a time, neither the British, Russians, Spanish, nor Indians, all of whom had better title, were in a position to dispute them.

The boldness, one might say the effrontery, of all this naming and claiming is often underrated in our schoolbooks. We do not emphasize the fact that the Lewis and Clark Expedition set forth down the Ohio toward St. Louis and the West before there had been a Louisiana Sale and Purchase. It was still being negotiated in Paris as they got underway, and though it ultimately made legitimate their presence on the *north* bank of the Missouri, even then the government of Spain took the view that Louisiana was considerably smaller than Napoleon (and Jefferson, as his successor-in-interest) contended. The *south* bank, according to the Spaniards, was theirs, and so the route imagined by Jefferson, mapped by Gallatin, and traversed by Lewis and Clark trespassed upon Spanish territory every time they turned left, so to speak, to walk the mud flats or to hunt deer and antelope through the willows on the Spanish bank.

Accordingly, the Spanish authorities sent an Indian detachment to drive away the trespassers, but in the vastness of the plains the Pawnee detachment and the expedition passed each other by. That could easily happen, for in North Dakota one tributary of the Missouri is difficult to distinguish from another. Rivers hide in folds in a gently swelling prairie, with only cottonwoods to mark their courses. That is not saying much, for the Missouri Valley cottonwood is not a stately tree like an

English oak or a German linden or the white pine of Maine. It does not age into a "giant of the forest," becoming instead a disheveled, battered old poke of a tree.

As Lewis and Clark wandered upward and westward, things might have been unpleasant had the Spanish-sponsored Indians found them, but the explorers had assumed that risk. Though Jefferson was himself a homebody, he placed in equal peril four other expeditions which he had under way shortly. According to Jefferson's grand geopolitical scheme, four more detachments of troops and scientists, each profess- ing scientific purposes, invaded territory claimed by Spain and occu- pied by Indians. He had come to the presidency to head an uneasy alliance of states. Though professing devotion to a diffident style of management, he enlarged the sway of a nation the name of which he himself had written as a plural, using the lower case "the united states," and made of it, through an indeterminate but enormous acquisition, an imperial power. By the time he was done, it was spoken of with a rising inflection, in the singular. And it was written in capital letters: "these united states" had become "The United States."

Meanwhile, the old rivers kept rolling along. It would not be fair to leave the impression that because the Missouri can uproot a cotton- wood in spring runoff, it is the sort of river which looks very impressive year round for its first thousand miles or so. It sidles northeasterly for a time, then southeasterly, then south. It acts as if affrighted by the first hardwood forest it enters, starting directly eastward as if to find company, drawn by the sound of the Mississippi through the trees. Regaining its confidence in the center of the state of Missouri, it acts like a grown-up river like the Rhine, to which it was often compared by German emigrants who planted their vineyards upon its bluffs and placed on a summit a colossal statue of the hero of the Battle of the Teutoburger Wald. He was Arminius to the Romans, and Hermann to Missourian Germans. Until then, the Missouri is not at all Wagnerian. In Montana and the Dakotas, its banks are mere clay layers two or three feet above its surface, crumbling and plopping into its muddy waters. Even when it joins the big rivers, it is shallow by the standards of the Rhine or Rhone.

Out of the eastern lobe of the Mississippi Basin comes the Ohio, carrying more water than the Missouri though it is less than half as long, having been joined by the Monongahela, Allegheny, Miami,

Scioto, Muskingum, Kanawha, Wabash, Kentucky, Cumberland, and Tennessee as it descends twelve hundred miles from western New York, Pennsylvania, and West Virginia.

The central, or northern, lobe of the Mississippi Basin is drained by the Mississippi itself, which travels a distance to the meeting place about as great as the course of the Ohio. It is difficult to say where the Mississippi begins, and not easy to tell where it ends. It may seem strange that something so large should be so vaguely placed, but that is the way it is, and has been since the question agitated three generations of pirates and scientists, engineers and archaeologists—some of whom were the same people—in the time of Jefferson, Hamilton, and Aaron Burr.

We deal first with its indeterminate origin. The Mississippi arises in a bog of muskeg, frequented by mosquitoes and visited by occasional moose; the land lies so flat that springs ooze from it within a few miles of each other, sending waters northward, eastward, and southward; droplets formed in Koochiching County may eventuate in Hudson's Bay by way of the Churchill River system, the Atlantic via the St. Lawrence, or the Gulf of Mexico borne southward by the great river itself. As these interdigitated origins suggest, northern Minnesota is a frontier, where one has to be careful not to be too emphatic about what is water and what is land.

It is a sort of delta in vitro. The "land" is largely a ridge of residual granite, ground smooth by the coming and going of glaciers. If one thinks of sandpaper, with fifty-foot boulders acting in place of grains of sand, one can get some sense of the fierceness of that abrasion, but the waters which fill every depression among these ridges are dense with nutrition. Muck-rooted tubers of starchy arrowroot have kept many a wanderer alive and thus able to enjoy both the taste and sight of the edible blossoms of white and yellow lilies, often made to quiver by the passage, just underneath, of schools of mobile protein. Between the lily leaves, one can see flitting and darting sunfish turn with the precision of Japanese middle managers, while, hovering in deeper pools, the potbellied, belligerent bass, the Colonel Blimps of the Boundary Waters, open and close their mouths in continuous indignation against affronts to their dignity, and, sometimes, the imperturbable passage of a sixty-pound muskellunge causes all other fish to swim aside.

These were the fishing grounds of the Cheyenne and the Sioux when they were north-woods people, before they learned to become prairie hunters. Long before many of them saw a bison, they hunted moose, browsers of the shallows, and deer, browsers of the glades, to supplement the protein gathered from the water itself.

Seen from above, in winter, the green of pines, spruce, and hemlock is often surrounded by a dispirited brown wreath of tamarack. During the region's brief summer, the tamarack appears to be coniferous, but in winter it gives up all pretenses and shivers bare beside the white birch and brittle aspen. These tentative leaf-bearers never grow large; they are the mere skirmishers for the lords of the Big Woods, the oak and elm and maple, which, since the glacier withdrew, have dominated the moist, deep-soiled region interposed between the conifers and the prairie.

There is little left, now, of the old-growth pinewoods or hardwoods—an island or two of pine in the Boundary Waters Park of Minnesota and Ontario, a stand here and there in northern Wisconsin and northern Michigan, where fishing clubs stood off the lumbermen's final campaign during the Second World War. There is a strip of roadside giant pines along the Gunflint Trail; Hartwick Pines, near Grayling, Michigan, is there, about as extensive as the patch of the Big Woods near Northfield, Minnesota. Far up on the headwaters of the Wisconsin, within the borders of upper Michigan, near the village of Watersmeet, there is still a twenty-seven-thousand-acre reserve called the Sylvania Tract, much of which is old growth. The rest of the big trees have gone to build Minneapolis, Milwaukee, Chicago, and the other prairie towns, to heat them afterward, and to compose sidewalks, boardwalks, ties, and piers.

Nature itself places limitations on large trees; they cannot outgrow their tensile strength and their allotted time, though some bristlecone pines last four millennia. In the prairie, no trees survive except those close to the rivers, as James Monroe observed to his disgust, and there are no trees very close to the Arctic. As one paddles northward through Saskatchewan, the tree-line becomes a scraggly row of bushy veterans of ten-month winters, two or three feet off the ground, which is itself a sponge whose surface is no more than a foot or two above the level of the sea and of the endless northern lakes.

A Garden with a Past

Before George Washington and Aaron Burr, the most appreciative observers of the Great Valley were the French, who saw in it "exceeding great fertility and beauty . . . meadows, which need not to be grubb'd up but are ready for the plow and seed . . . vast fields of the best land in the world," and forests like orchards: "oak trees, elms, chestnut-trees, walnut-trees, apple-trees, plum-trees, and vines which bear their fine cluster up to the very top of the trees, upon a sort of ground that lies as smooth as one's hand."[1]

In the 1770s, while New England was still regarding the West as wilderness beyond the hedge, Jean Bernard Bossu described it as if it were the sunny valley of the Loire: "The soil is so fertile that, almost without cultivation, it produces European wheat and all kinds of fruit and vegetables." Pere Marquette reported that as far north as the Falls of St. Anthony "no better soil can be found either for corn, for vines, or for any other fruit whatever"; and one-armed Henri Tonti, companion of La Salle, told the world that the Lower Valley, the region in which, in 1805, Burr proposed to settle, was "the most beautiful country in the world."[2]

When La Salle came to the neighborhood of Natchez, he entered precincts where a sun-worshiping principality was still building mounds. La Salle's negotiations with its chiefs took place on or near the immensity of Emerald Mound, nearly eight hundred feet in length and as tall as a six-story building, and the huge complex of Anna, only now (1998) receiving full archaeological attention.

By the time it passes Natchez, the Mississippi itself is a wonder. Though not much broader at Baton Rouge or New Orleans than at St. Louis or even at St. Paul, it is much, much deeper—a great battering ram of silt and water. The Nile is too tranquil a comparison; one should see the Mississippi as a vastly greater Rhone, so powerful that, like the Rhone, it might have its way with the Alps.

But the Mississippi, while powerful, is subtle. Below Memphis, it returns to its indeterminate youth, hesitates, meanders, turns from side to side through half of Arkansas, a third of Mississippi and all of Louisiana, changing its course whimsically, leaving bayous, oxbows, and half-circular "false rivers" to confuse air travelers, to infuriate engineers, and to bankrupt highway departments. These caprices leave bridges bridging nothing, ruptured levies and gasping ripraps. In the

1990s, the Mississippi was threatening to return to an earlier course, leaving New Orleans a backwater town and Vicksburg or Natchez, upon their bluffs, looking out in summer upon quaking mud-plains turning to elephant-hide crust and then to dust. Not so long ago, the Mississippi ran through the valley of the Yazoo and the Sunflower. It could, if it willed, go back. Or it might be amused to strike out in the other direction, to reclaim its Arkansas meanders. If, in some ebullient springtime, it were to gather itself for such an assault, all the devices of modernity would avail for little against it, though it be assaulted by nuclear weapons.

There is an old map yellowing away in the dim light of the museum at Marksville, Louisiana, which shows where the Mississippi has taken itself over the last two or three thousand years. It once flowed and coiled through what is now relatively dry land in a variety of courses twining about each other like spaghetti.

Burr's Lost Paradise

A hundred miles west of Natchez, along the Ouachita River, two hundred thousand acres of a lost paradise awaited Aaron Burr in 1805. This was Caddonia, a favored place since six thousand years earlier the Indians created there the most ancient monumental architecture in North America. In Burr's time, this valley of ruins had become a vast aviary. It still takes pride in its white egrets; they still peck flies from the backs of lazy cattle, but in 1805, egrets and ibises seemed poor pale creatures when the valley was visited by ivory-billed woodpeckers, nearly two feet long, brilliantly colored and raucous, feasting upon grubs. The grubs, in turn, had grown fat decomposing the fallen trees of an immense hardwood forest.

In the woods, cardinals whistled. Great white herons rose from the bayous pulling their long legs behind them through the air as if they were Indians carrying duffle on travois. Mississippi kites, black of bill and tail feather, heads bluish white, bodies lead-colored, swooped down upon frogs and caught electric-green dragonflies in midair. In the woodland, wild turkeys strutted, and on the prairies, bobwhite quail rose in flurries as buffaloes lumbered past. Black bear were so numerous in the woods that one tributary of the Red was called "the river of bears." The peasantry of the air, blue jays and crows, celebrated, in their vulgar ways, events noted more elegantly by chuck-will-willows and innumerable species of warblers.[3]

Opossums clamored over fallen oaks and hickories which had grown too huge and ancient to stand upright; flocks of screaming Carolina parakeets moved like schools of yellow fish through the treetops. From time to time, a pileated woodpecker would careen past, with its brilliant scarlet topknot, its crow-sized bulk, and its maniacal laughter.

Wild strawberries turned the meadows red in April, encrimsoning the shanks of herds of wild horses. For a century, stallions and mares set loose by raiding Indians, or having declared their own independence, proliferated in the grasslands. It was the great age of wrangling. In the course of driving thousands of horses from the Texas plains to Natchez, the greatest of wranglers, Philip Nolan, had created maps showing Aaron Burr how to reach the Rio Grande. His cartographic equipment had been provided by Andrew Ellicott, probably the same instruments Ellicott had earlier shared with Benjamin Banneker.

The Indians had already made use of the horses set loose upon the plains to become the best light cavalry in the world, trained for woodland tactics as well as open-field maneuvers in the savannahs of their own creation. For thousands of years, they had been making changes in this landscape in other than architectural ways. To grow their corn, squash and beans, and to offer browse for deer, they burnt out the underbrush from horizon to horizon, and in the eighteenth century there suddenly appeared flocks of passenger pigeons so numerous that the ground below their assemblies became as dark as if beneath a canopy of branches.

In those days "a canopy of branches" was an expression having meaning, for beside the Ouachita the great trees were as high as ten-storied buildings. Yet this was an ecological frontier as Minnesota was, for only a few miles away the prairie began. The difference, of course, lies in the vehemence of color and in the exotic juxtapositions of animals to be found in Arkansas. Louisiana's pink sprays of mimosa and Spanish moss appear beside Nebraska's cottonwoods. Alligators up to ten feet in length lay in the Ouachita. When they chose to move, they sent blue-wing teal careening terrified into the air and hurried the peregrinations of gar and catfish.

And new animals—new to science—were appearing all the time. While Burr was lingering in Natchez, preparing to ascend into Caddonia, mankind learned from science for the first time of the existence in the Ouachita of the three-and-a-half-foot-long, eel-like, three-toed amphibiuma.[4]

Empire, Sanctuary, and Speculation

In 1783, after the French, Dutch, and Spaniards had assisted thirteen of the fifteen North American colonies of Great Britain to achieve independence, peace was negotiated. It was possible that the cession of the Great Valley by France to Britain, in 1762–63, might be reversed. But the French fell into a miscalculation of immense consequence, turning their backs upon North America. Only after it was too late did Brissot and Volney rediscover the Great Valley. They succeeded in making it so interesting, however, that in the late 1780s "nothing was talked of in every social circle but the paradise that was opened for Frenchmen in the western wilderness, the free and happy life to be led on the blissful banks of the Scioto."[5]

No such thoughts of bliss led Napoleon to conclude his negotiations to recover from Spain the empire foregone in 1762 and forsaken in 1783. As we observed earlier, he had other things in mind. Disappointed in them, however, and pressed for cash, he disposed of Louisiana to the government of the United States in 1803. The British statesman Edward Canning correctly allocated the credit:

> It is not difficult to apportion the credit for this transaction. Napoleon, for reasons having nothing to do with the United states, suddenly determined to get whatever he could for whatever title to Louisiana he had. He threw the province, so to speak, at Livingston, Monroe, Madison and Jefferson; and they share between them—equally—whatever credit there was in catching it and holding it—that is all.[6]

19

Mr. Jefferson's Colleagues

Without Pitt or Fox as an ally, and bereft of any illusions he might have had about Napoleon, Jefferson abandoned his schemes for war against Spain and set about reigning in his former Vice President. With a Spanish war deferred, Burr, who might have been marginally useful in such a war, now had no utility. That computation was, no doubt, made contemporaneously by both Jefferson and Wilkinson, who announced their conclusions characteristically. Jefferson acted quietly at first, getting his Virginian agents in place and making certain that he had the military force at hand to make his will fact. Wilkinson preferred melodrama—informing his new ally, the President, through letters secreted in the shoes of a Virginian who was his own chosen instrument. When the commander of the largest assembly of military force in the West so assured Jefferson that he was ready to abandon Burr and to take up, instead, a commission to eliminate Burr as a rival, Jefferson abruptly changed his game. Free of the risk that Wilkinson might lead his army in support of Burr, the President took a high moral ground previously imperiled by Wilkinson's presence on his flank.

By the end of November 1806, Wilkinson and Gideon Granger became the principal instruments in Jefferson's campaign to rid himself of his rival. Acting together, Wilkinson and Granger provided forged and perjured evidence to support the fable of a Burrite "conspiracy." As Wilkinson turned his army away from the Spanish frontier toward New Orleans, Granger mobilized his network of Post Office employees to seek out private correspondence which might incriminate Burr or his followers; for example, a "Mr. Pease [was sent] on the route to New Orleans to expedite [!] the mails and remove suspected agents [of Burr] of the Post Office."

Granger was able to do this because he had already established that role which made him famous in the lore of the postal service; as the initiator of its spoils system, he systematically removed from its rolls not only all "suspected agents" of Burr but all free black mail carriers. The *Dictionary of American Biography*, in accrediting the first of these feats—Granger was, it tells us, "a pioneer in the practice of separating political opponents from the post-office payroll"—diminishes it only a little by adding that "during his service the spoils system was still somewhat rudimentary."[1]

As to the second Granger "reform," we have commentary in the from of a printer's exclamation mark. The official history of the Post Office Department published in 1879, written by one D. D. Leech, carries this passage:

> A suggestion which this administrator [Granger] succeeded in having incorporated into the revised postal law of 1810, and which was not repealed till 1865—though doubtless well intended, would have found latterly few advocates in Congress— the provision prohibiting Negroes from employment as mail carriers. He was of the opinion that they could not be safely trusted with such a duty, as it would enable the more intelligent of them to form schemes for the communication of intelligence detrimental to the whites.[2]

At this point in the text, the printer—who, one hopes, was a Negro— inserted in the margin an exclamation point.

Acting in concert, Granger and Wilkinson played upon Jefferson's fears and saw to it that his cabinet considered "Burrism" and slave revolt as conjoined in Louisiana. It was not necessary that they believe their own propaganda, for each had his own reasons to want Burr out of the way, but only with maximum distracting drama. They had both made speculations in the Yazoo frauds, real estate transactions illegal in origin and sustained in corruption, requiring the wholesale purchase of Georgia legislators. While a member of Jefferson's cabinet, Granger acted as paid agent to secure the ratification of the Yazoo interests by the Congress. His bullying style was too much for John Randolph of Roanoke, whose breach with Jefferson widened as he observed Granger turn upon the legislative branch the methods by which he had corrupted the executive. Randolph mobilized and deployed upon Granger that gift for invective which has been matched by no one in the history of American politics. (No, not even John L. Lewis or Ignatius Donnelly, though they, too, were masters.) Here is Randolph's view of the Postmaster General and chief of Thomas Jefferson's domestic intelligence system:[3]

His gigantic grasp embraces on one hand the shores of Lake Erie and stretches with the other to the bay of Mobile. Millions of acres are easily digested by such stomachs. Goaded by avarice, they only buy to sell, and sell only to buy. The retail trade of fraud and imposture yields too small and slow a profit to gratify their cupidity.

. . . They buy and sell corruption in the gross, and a few millions more or less is hardly felt in the amount. . . . [T]he game and the stake which is set upon their throw, is nothing less than the patrimony of the people. . . . This same agent is at the head of an executive department of our Government . . . inferior to none in the influence attached to it. This officer, possessed of how many snug appointments and fat contracts, . . . having an influence which is confined to no quarter of the Country . . . with offices in his gift amongst the most lucrative . . . this officer presents himself at your bar, at once a party and an advocate. . . . Is it come to this? Are heads of executive departments of the government to be brought into this House with all the influence and patronage attached to them, to extort from us now what was refused at the last session of Congress? . . . [I]f they are, and if the abominable villainy practiced upon, and by, the legislature of Georgia, in 1795, is now to be glossed over, I . . . ask . . . what . . . they can offer. [Is] it . . . necessary to give the Cerberus of corruption, this many-headed god of Hell a sop . . . to pacify him:— and this sentiment is re-echoed by his yells. Good God, Sir![4]

Seeking any means to draw attention from the putrescence of the Yazoo frauds, and having correctly assessed the troubled mind of the President, Wilkinson and Granger rightly concluded that he could be relied upon to protect them. First they kicked up the dust; after it settled, their swag in the Delta might still be collected.

Neutral Ground

On November 5, 1806, Wilkinson concluded what was essentially a treaty with himself. The Neutral Ground Agreement provided that the American army he commanded, and the Spanish army he advised, both would withdraw a safe distance from the disputed frontier between their respective claims to Texas. Surely no one in American history ever so amply earned the term "neutral" as Wilkinson: he was on the payroll of both sides and loyal to neither. He did not, however, permit himself much leisure to enjoy his neutrality, for another theatrical gesture was required to demonstrate his repudiation of Burr. Omitting the agreement's final ceremonies, Wilkinson departed at daybreak for New Orleans, telling his military aide that he must return to stand off a Burrite invasion of Louisiana. The Spanish agents observing his behavior were much relieved; until that point they could not be sure that Wilkinson was not deliberately staging the confrontation on the frontier in order to keep his army together for a joint venture with Burr.

After the general reached New Orleans, he made use of every means short of a firing squad to eliminate witnesses who might testify as to his complicity with either Burr or Spain. He suborned perjury, intimidated potential witnesses, and attacked judges, in defiance of the Bill of Rights. On January 12, 1807, the Louisiana legislature sent the governor a memorial (soon to be echoed by the grand jury of Mississippi):

> Nothing can justify . . . these violent measures. . . . [N]o foreign enemy or open domestic foe was then or has yet been proved to have been within our walls. . . . The acts of high-handed military power to which we have been exposed [are] acts too notorious to be denied, too illegal to be justified, too wanton to be excused.[5]

On June 21, however, Jefferson demonstrated that he was undeterred, sending a letter to Wilkinson urging him neither to repent nor to relent:

> Your enemies have filled the air with slanders and your mind with trouble on that account. The establishment of their guilt will let the world see what they ought to think of their clamors; it will dissipate the doubts of those who doubted for want of knowledge, and will place you on higher ground in the public estimate and public confidence. No one is more sensible than myself of the injustice which has been aimed at you. Accept, I pray you, my salutations and assurances of respect and esteem.[6]

Once again, Mr. Jefferson's esteem. Burr had been assured of it once. Wilkinson's claim upon it was reasserted often over the ensuing three years, through three congressional investigations and two more courts-martial.

In the Shoes of Thomas Adam Smith

Gideon Granger may have given Jefferson "the first effectual notice of Burr's intentions," but Wilkinson was not slow in following up. On November 25, 1806, a messenger appeared before the President of the United States, opened the secret compartment in his shoe, and drew forth documents on the strength of which, Jefferson later asserted, he concluded that he must warn the nation against "persons . . . confederating . . . to set on foot . . . a military . . . enterprise against the dominions of Spain." Because of those letters, many of which we now know to have been forgeries, Jefferson ordered Henry Dearborn, the Secretary of War, to "frustrate" such persons.[7]

The messenger with the compartmented shoes was Thomas Adam Smith, another young Virginian, the nephew of Jefferson's political lieutenant Meriwether Smith. Other members of Smith's family within the Monticello circle were Governor William Smith, his cousin, and Congressman Peter Early, his brother-in-law (later also governor). When Thomas Smith performed his first chores for Wilkinson and Jefferson, he was a mere lieutenant, but thereafter he was promoted rapidly. After he had become a lieutenant colonel, he offered an affidavit as to his initiation into the secret service:

> Sometime between the 15th and the 20th October, 1806, General Wilkinson communicated to me, under the strictest injunctions of confidence, the communication he had received from Aaron Burr through Mr. Swartwout. He said it was necessary to send a confidential letter to the President and decided that I should be the bearer of it. . . . To prevent suspicion as to the object of my journey I must tender my resignation which he would accept in orders, but would have the matter understood at the War Office. The General mentioned the names of many persons of high rank as being concerned with Burr, and furnished me with a cipher to communicate to him any information I might receive on the journey. He also required me to take an oath to conceal from all persons the object of my journey. I delivered his letter to the President, having it concealed between the soles of my slipper which I opened to the General's order, in his [the President's] presence.[8]

During the Richmond Trial, Wilkinson was forced to acknowledge that he had forged at least parts of a letter allegedly written him by Burr, and delivered by Smith to Jefferson, but it was his own covering letter, nestled between the soles of the plainclothes lieutenant's shoe, which, said Jefferson, convinced him to go after Burr in earnest. At first, the means were left to Wilkinson, as Jefferson's agent, and it would no doubt be unfair to attribute them to the President. Jefferson was not a bloodthirsty man. But it is fair to observe that the subagent, Smith, returned promptly for other assignments from Wilkinson. By January 28, 1807, he had been sent on an extraordinary mission under the command of Captain Moses Hooke. The detail also included Lieutenants Mulford and Peter and—curiously enough—two military surgeons, Drs. Davidson and Carmichael. They were to disguise themselves in civilian clothes, to arm themselves with pistols and dirks, and to seek out and "seize Burr and bring him to New Orleans on one of the armed boats. They had no civil warrants, and no crime was charged against Burr in their orders."[9]

We will come upon these gentlemen shortly, in their disguises and bearing their weapons, wading about in the flooded lowlands along the Arkansas side of the Mississippi, but they will then move so fast that we will not be able to pause for a graceful leavetaking from Thomas Adam Smith. Let us note here, therefore, that six years later he was serving his President in another subtropical swamp, charged with bringing to an end John Houstoun McIntosh's sponsored filibuster, the East Florida "Patriots' Rebellion." Smith had the sorry task of mopping up after the failure of McIntosh to capture the Castillo San Marcos or anything else of note, after being goaded into trying to do so by George Mathews, the former governor of Georgia, who in turn had been directed by James Madison. By the time Smith reached Florida as a full colonel, he had been thoroughly broken in, having gone in and out of the uniform of the U.S. Army as regular officer and as secret agent to convenience his betters. Always his behavior was honorable, however, which is more than one can say for other agents of the administration.

George Morgan for the Prosecution

With honor in mind, we turn back now to follow that portion of Burr's western adventures which took him from his idyll with the Meades to Natchez, and thus within reach of Wilkinson, Moses Hooke, Mulford, Peter, Davidson, Carmichael, and Smith.

Burr left Frankfort on December 10, 1806, and reached Nashville on the thirteenth. There, in the presence of Andrew Jackson, he reiterated his oath of allegiance to the United States, the same assurance he had given Henry Clay and William Henry Harrison. Proceeding down the Cumberland, he spent New Year's Day 1807 at New Madrid. This Tangier of the West had been founded as the product of the sedition, two decades earlier, of George Morgan.

Morgan had retired from Revolutionary service in 1779, having seen no noteworthy action but complaining of being insufficiently appreciated. In 1789, he secured a land grant from the Spanish government on the understanding that he would garrison it with American officers and troops. Like his friend Wilkinson, Morgan swore fealty to the King of Spain against all enemies—including those who might follow them down the Ohio from the United States.

In Morgan's case, these sentiments were imprudently put in writing, in damning detail. It became clear that Morgan was for sale. Though he was never quite asked to take up arms against his country, his readiness to do so was no deeper secret in the West than Wilkinson's service to Spain. After the King proved insufficiently generous, Morgan turned to Thomas Jefferson. Action by the federal government was required to clear the titles for certain land speculations in Indiana. Morgan was getting on, and his sons had become "rather light and to say the least equivocal in point of credit."[10]

The same might be said of Morgan's own reputation, yet when not crediting Gideon Granger with convincing him to go after Burr, Thomas Jefferson wrote that Morgan gave him the "first" concrete news of Burr's conspiracy. This could only have occurred in September 1806, when he received from Morgan an account of conversations he asserted he had with Burr a month earlier, when Burr called upon his Princeton classmate at Morganza, the estate near Pittsburgh to which Morgan reverted after the failure of his scheme for New Madrid. As soon as Burr departed, Morgan wrote Jefferson with a florid tale, offering to relate whatever parts of it the President might find useful. There was, of course, to be a little reciprocity: With miraculous speed, Morgan's Indiana claims were reopened and approved. During the trial of Burr in Richmond, Mr. Jefferson's prosecutors had no difficulty in leading the Morgans into attributing to Burr a project like Morgan's of twenty years earlier, though they did not have the boldness to attribute to Burr a willingness to become a mercenary of the King of Spain.[11]

John Adams and the "Lying Spirit" of the Virginians

On December 22, 1806, John Randolph prevailed upon the House of Representatives to inquire what was behind the President's still vague proclamation of an "illegal combination of private individuals against the peace and safety of the Union." Jefferson responded by naming Burr for the first time, alluding to his "pretended purchase ... of a tract of country on the Wichita, claimed by a Baron Bastrop ... as a pretext for all his preparations, an allurement for such followers as really wished to acquire settlements ... and a cover under which to retreat in the event of a ... discomfiture ... of his real designs." The

President had spoken, and across the political landscape, people began airing for disinfection any clothing that might spread the contagion of Burrism.[12]

Skeptics such as William Plumer discounted Jefferson's charges: "I am too well acquainted with the man [Burr] to believe him guilty of all the absurdity ascribed to him. He is a man of first rate talents. He may be capable of much wickedness, but not of folly." And many whose careers were over and who were thus past ambition, such as John Adams, looked beyond personalities to the constitutional questions raised by a presidential indictment.[13]

Adams was still raw from the bruising he had received when the Jeffersonians accused him of abusing presidential power during the Sedition Act crisis. Abuse of power, he growled; what about guilt by presidential proclamation! Where was process, arraignment, indictment, trial? Adams was not so much concerned with Burr as an individual as with the absence of constitutional safeguards in the West. Not only was Burr vulnerable to the abuse of his rights, but so was anyone else living in the territories of the West. In Adams's view, their exposure arose from the ruling of the Supreme Court that they were living in territories not parties to the original compact creating the Union. In this view, the Constitution did not protect those unlucky enough to reside where a territory had not yet been organized into a state.

Until March 1805, the administration had marched into this cavernous opportunity by concentrating all governing power in Louisiana in its appointed governor and his appointed council. Only then did it get around to permitting Louisiana an elected Assembly, and, in Adams's interpretation, no Bill of Rights inhibited Jefferson in Mississippi, where he sought to take Burr into custody.

Adams did not like what he saw; besides, he had his own experience with the veracity of those who were proclaiming Burr's guilt. So Adams wrote Benjamin Rush that "the lying spirit" of the Virginians was "at work concerning Burr" and that if Burr's guilt *were* "as clear as the noonday sun . . . the first magistrate ought not to have pronounced it before a jury had tried him."[14]

Even Adams, however, did not anticipate the lengths to which the administration's whip in the Senate would go. During a secret session, William Branch Giles proposed that in dealing with Burr, the right of habeas corpus be suspended, supporting his case with certain mysterious documents. At the time they were said to have been presented

James Wilkinson, the Finished Scoundrel, as he was beginning to run to fat. Artist unknown.

George Rogers Clark, as he wished to be seen, as Revolutionary hero, by James Barton Longacre. NATIONAL PORTRAIT GALLERY, SMITHSONIAN INSTITUTION, WASHINGTON, D.C.

Winthrop Sargent, Federalist official in Ohio and Mississippi, by Charles Balthazar Julien Fevret de Saint-Memin. NATIONAL PORTRAIT GALLERY, SMITHSONIAN INSTITUTION, WASHINGTON, D.C.

A recent photograph of a portion of the Natchez Trace not yet paved over and much as it was when traversed by Aaron Burr. COURTESY OF THE NATIONAL PARK SERVICE.

Benjamin Henry Latrobe, architect, playwright, and friend to the mighty, who was asked by Burr to be the architect for his Ouachita colony. ARCHITECT OF THE CAPITOL.

An imaginary portrait of Toussaint Louverture, probably as close to his appearance as we are likely to get, judging by its conformity to written description. It is worthy of remark that we have many portraits from life of statesmen of considerably less importance. PICTURE COLLECTION, THE BRANCH LIBRARIES, THE NEW YORK PUBLIC LIBRARY.

The Meades' Chinese Garden at Le Chaumiere des Prairies, Kentucky, sketch by Anna Maria von Phul. COURTESY OF THE MISSOURI HISTORICAL SOCIETY, ST. LOUIS.

Gideon Granger, Postmaster General in the Jefferson Administration, who expelled Free Blacks from the U.S. Postal Service and inflamed fears that Aaron Burr would arouse a slave revolt if permitted to settle in the Mississippi Valley. COURTESY OF THE UNITED STATES POSTAL SERVICE LIBRARY.

A nineteenth-century imaginary impression of the arrest of Aaron Burr at McIntosh Bluffs, Alabama.

Andrew Jackson as Backwoods
Bonaparte. THE HISTORIC NEW
ORLEANS COLLECTION, ACCESSION
NO. 1974.25.5.75.

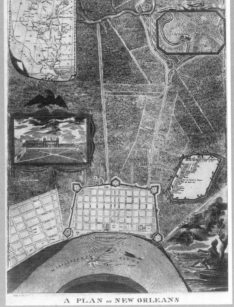

A PLAN of NEW ORLEANS

New Orleans as imperial city and
fortress; an eighteenth-century
image. THE HISTORIC NEW ORLEANS
COLLECTION, ACCESSION NO.
1958.41.

Justus Eric Bollmann, inventor, would-be rescuer of Lafayette and, later, of Burr. COURTESY OF THE NEW YORK PUBLIC LIBRARY.

John Marshall as young lawyer and Federalist politician, after a painting by J. Paul.

John Randolph of Roanoke in a quiet moment, by John Wesley Jarvis. NATIONAL PORTRAIT
GALLERY, SMITHSONIAN INSTITUTION, WASHINGTON, D.C. GIFT OF MRS. GERARD B. LAMBERT.

John H. I. Browere's portrait
bust of James Madison in
1825. COURTESY OF THE NEW
YORK STATE HISTORICAL ASSO-
CIATION, COOPERSTOWN, NEW
YORK.

John H. I. Browere's portrait bust of Dolley Madison in 1825. COURTESY OF THE NEW YORK STATE HISTORICAL ASSOCIATION, COOPERSTOWN, NEW YORK.

Aaron Burr as an elderly gentleman, by James Van Dyck. OIL ON CANVAS, 86.4 x 63.5 CM. 1834/1882. GIFT OF MR. AND MRS. ARTHUR FLEISCHMAN. PHOTOGRAPH © THE DETROIT INSTITUTE OF ARTS.

John Quincy Adams as elder statesman, by George Caleb Bingham. NATIONAL PORTRAIT GALLERY, SMITHSONIAN INSTITUTION, WASHINGTON, D.C.

by Samuel Smith of Maryland, and they may have been further letters from Wilkinson or Granger—they were soon conveniently lost. Burr was correct in the apprehensions about secret sessions he had stated in 1792.[15]

Meanwhile, in Bruinsburg

On January 10, 1806, oblivious to the orchestrated crescendo rising about him, Burr arrived fifteen miles north of Natchez at the dock below the plantation headquarters of Judge Peter Bruin, at Bruinsburg. Judge Bruin's colleague on the bench of the Territory of Mississippi, Judge Thomas Rodney, was proprietor of the nearby settlement of Rodney. From his bluffs, Rodney observed Burr's little flotilla, and reported it to be

> ten boats, about one hundred men and not a gun apiece for them—a mighty force to erect a new and independent empire. If one were to believe the President's assertion of Burr's felonious intentions, then Burr . . . [is] the greatest Don Quixote.[16]

That he was. That he was. For those who hold him in affection, it is sorrowful that when he came to Natchez he was not the cynical creature he appeared to be. Instead, he was still the enthusiast he had always been, utterly unprepared for the trap awaiting him.

Life was going to be such a lark! Another triumphal procession down the Mississippi—then a little jog to the west—and up the Ouachita.

> We are now going through a settled country [he wrote his daughter. For] about three hundred miles, I shall take breakfast and dinner each day at the house of some gentleman on shore. I take no letters of introduction; but, whenever I hear of any gentleman whose acquaintance or hospitalities I should desire, I send word that I am coming to see him, and have always had a most cordial reception.[17]

Burr had returned to a setting compatible with his somewhat old-fashioned ways of thinking and acting. The Mississippi Territory had entered the nineteenth century only chronologically. Burr had killed a political opponent in a duel. The same might be said of a score, or more, of well-regarded gentlemen he met on the streets of Washington, Mississippi's territorial capital, or in Nashville, New Orleans, or, for that matter, Washington, D.C.[18]

Duels were frequent but rarely lethal, and witty men of ambition were welcomed. Had Jefferson, Claiborne, and James Wilkinson not changed his plans, Burr might have lingered in these Mississippi villages for a graceful gathering of his followers before proceeding to their adventure up the Ouachita. He had every reason to believe that his colonization project, the most widely advertised "conspiracy" in history, had the support of Wilkinson and the acquiescence of Jefferson, as he made a private contribution to the array of probes by the Spanish borderlands then underway at Jefferson's orders.

In Judge Bruin, Burr had a friend sympathetic to his somewhat desperate adventuring and not at all impressed with Jefferson. Born in 1754, Bruin joined the Eleventh Virginia Regiment and served with Burr in Canada, where both were wounded. Captured during the retreat from Quebec, he contracted smallpox but survived, was released, and reenlisted under General John Sullivan for a campaign against the Iroquois. Bruin served with the French in their Rhode Island campaign and was with the Virginia Continentals in the siege lines around Yorktown to witness the surrender of Cornwallis. Like George Morgan, George Rogers Clark, and Baron von Steuben, Bruin saw greater opportunity in the thinly settled Spanish West than in the East, but unlike the others, Bruin worked out a dignified arrangement with the Spanish authorities.

Without any promises except to keep the peace, Bruin received a grant of 1,450 acres along Coles Creek, eighteen miles above Natchez, and, in the fashion of medieval Spain, was commissioned an *alcalde*—judge, sheriff, and leader of the militia. Clark attempted unsuccessfully to recruit Bruin for his expedition against the Spanish in New Orleans, but Bruin wanted no part of French plots. Summoning his militia, he marched to New Orleans to protect the city. After his return to his tobacco-raising latifundium at Bruinsburg, the old soldier became the beloved if boozy patriarch of the neighborhood. In an alcoholic age, his frequent drunkenness, like that of Clark, was a subject of regret though not of wonderment.

Bruin's son-in-law, Dr. John Cummins, became one of the most resolute of Burrites after being introduced to Burr through their mutual friend Benjamin Rush, from whom Cummins had learned his medicine in Philadelphia. So, when Burr arrived at Bruinsburg, he was a welcome guest.[19]

Captain Hooke

For a time. Then, one dark morning, Bruin received a confirmation of Wilkinson's defection, and Burr became a dangerous guest. Bruin knew Wilkinson. Violence could be expected. Bruin may have heard of Captain Hooke's commission, but it is likely that he took comfort from the fact that Hooke, Thomas Smith, the two surgeons, and the others were officers of the U.S. Army. Though subject to Wilkinson's command, they were unlikely to accept his standards of behavior. They were not thugs like those Wilkinson had hired along the Ohio and like those to whom he next turned for service on Coles Creek. And, it turned out, Hooke and his men did have their scruples. When informed by the civil authorities of Mississippi that Burr was in the custody of Judge Rodney, with a warrant against him issued by Judge Harry Toulmin, Hooke and his men emerged from their swamp and stationed themselves in Natchez, asserting that they could not obtain the gunboats they needed to convey their prisoner to New Orleans.

The freshwater navy, like the saltwater navy, was still John Adams's and Thomas Truxton's navy. Like the Federalist gentry of Natchez, the officers of the navy were forming up for Burr. We need only recall Truxton's point of view to imagine what his fellow officers told the disguised detail purporting to act under Wilkinson's orders. "Hooke ... therefore was unwilling to use violence, especially as the naval officers refused their cooperation."[20]

Disappointed in Hooke and the navy, Wilkinson engaged "twenty men well armed," with "orders ... in writing and peremptory." They could be observed "hovering about Colonel Burr's camp for four hours, had ascertained his situation [that his small party was almost entirely unarmed and vulnerable] and that they had with one consent agreed to ambuscade and cut off some of his party on the beach, if possible."[21]

And what were Wilkinson's orders?

It is my wish to have them [Burr and his chief of staff] arrested and carried off. . . . If you fail, your expenses shall be paid. If you succeed I pledge the government to you for five thousand dollars.[22]

If Wilkinson spared Burr's life, Jefferson would not spare him another trial. After acquittals in Kentucky and Tennessee, Burr's enemies were closing in for the third time. Fortunately for Burr, Bruin and Cummins had assembled their own men to defend Bruinsburg and were readying their guest to make any trial more exciting than any solemn ratification of Jefferson's allegations.

20

The Thinking Part of the People

There was, however, another judge to sit beside Bruin at any such trial, Thomas Rodney. Rodney had once been a man of vigor and conviction, but age had rendered him both pusillanimous and capable of stealthy misfeasance to please the powerful. By nature indisposed to question higher authority, he had become peculiarly desirous of avoiding offense to Thomas Jefferson. His son Caesar Augustus Rodney, after five years of loyal service to the party of Jefferson in the House of Representatives, was about to be elevated to the office of Attorney General of the United States.

Otherwise, our story might have had another outcome. Rodney was aware that Wilkinson had turned upon Burr and, having served with Wilkinson during the Revolution, knew he was not to be trusted. It was widely believed in Natchez, Rodney wrote at the time, that Wilkinson had sold himself to Spain and was engaged in "a project, which, whether he succeeds in it or not, must render him execrable in the view of all mankind, for all mankind despise traitors." Though some of mankind excused Wilkinson on the ground that he was merely reviving the efforts of the Kentuckians and Tennesseans of the 1780s and 1790s to protect themselves against Spain, Rodney's response had

Burr in Mississippi Territory

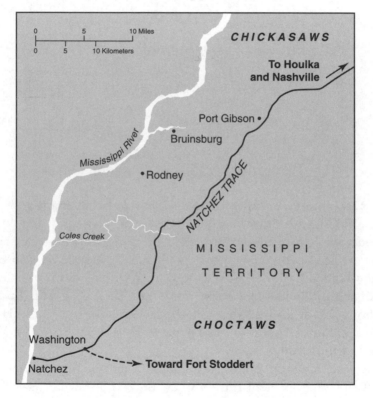

been that Louisiana was now a part of the United States and that Wilkinson's separatism was "not the project of a people laboring under tyranny, but the project of restless individuals ambitious to aggrandize themselves."[1]

That was the right language for a Rodney, for the Rodneys were patriots. Their patriarch, the father of Thomas, had been a Signer of the Declaration of Independence, and Thomas himself had served as a soldier of the Revolution. His uniform, "Old '76," was ready in his closet, yet even after evidence accumulated of Wilkinson's role in one conspiracy or another, Rodney wrote that it "has been hard for me to believe that Genl W. an old Revolutionary soldier and now enjoying the highest favor of government would engage in a project so adverse to the government he is serving."[2]

Could it be true, Rodney asked his son, that the Jefferson administration did not know what a loathsome creature Wilkinson was? Had "our superior officers . . . become too elevated to have any connection or correspondence with the distant officers of government, or . . . become regardless of [come to disregard] these distant parts of our country"? Lest he be ignored, however, he added: "Inferior officers have as much right to judge of the conduct of superior officers, as these last have of theirs."[3]

As a still proud member of the squirarchy of Delaware, though removed to Mississippi, Rodney felt the right to question those to whom "the constitution has confided the supreme guardianship and protection of the country" and, at the highest pitch of his indignation, proclaimed that if Wilkinson "should attempt to remove his [Burr's] person out of Mississippi Territory, prior to his trial," he would don again " 'old '76' and march out in support of Col. Burr and the Constitution."[4]

On November 6, 1806, Rodney reported directly to Jefferson that Wilkinson had removed arms and ammunition from the Natchez district, "the only part of the western country where the firm friends of the United States could immediately make any resistance to the operations of the conspirators." He added that Wilkinson's placing the Mississippi militia directly under his own command "either to influence them to act with him[,] or at least to prevent their acting against him[,] . . . [gave] suspicion at least of his being concerned in the conspiracy—indeed such an attempt could have no prospect of success without his concurrence." Therefore, the old soldier implored

Jefferson to depose Wilkinson, for "without such conduct there is danger of . . . losing this country."[5]

Later, having heard of Wilkinson's reign of terror in New Orleans, Judge Rodney wrote his son:

> All is military bustle, and the Constitution and laws are forgotten. . . . How many thousand agents and emissaries has France[,] Spain[,] and England spread over our country to blow up these windy storms and confusion. . . . Is it not to frighten us into discord and extravagant and unconstitutional conduct—Will not the arbitrary conduct of our high officers on the pretext of supporting government give the constitution a more dangerous shock than Burr or any other man could do at the head of ten thousand men in open rebellion?[6]

Rodney went on to report that the gentlemen of Natchez were all aware that Burr had assembled only "a trifling force. . . . The mountain has surely brought forth a mouse."[7]

Cowles Meade, the acting governor of Mississippi Territory, sent orders to William Shields, commander of the Natchez militia, to try to bring Burr in but to avoid bloodshed. Shields and Meade then asked Burr to abandon Bruin's protection and come to the territorial capital to explain himself. Burr replied that he would do so but, with an eye on the strange activity in the canebrake and underbrush, was "desirous of being protected pending his visit." Colonel Fitzpatrick of the Mississippi militia, who reported to the governor and not to Wilkinson, complied by clearing the way of Wilkinson's thugs.[8]

From Bruinsburg, and a measure of safety, Burr descended the river and placed himself under the protection of Fitzpatrick, Shields, Rodney, and Meade. Rodney looked him over, and wrote:

> He does not appear to me to possess a mind in condition and competent to plan or execute such an enterprise as has been talked of—his aspect appears that of distress not one prompted by the strong genius of certain success.[9]

The Jury Convenes at Jefferson College

In a small brick building on the campus of Jefferson College, east of Natchez, during the first week of February 1807, Judges Bruin and

Rodney assembled a grand jury of the Territory of Mississippi to hear Jefferson's charges and his evidence against his former Vice President. For the first (and, fortunately, the last) time in American history, a President had indicted a citizen by presidential proclamation. His agents had offered a reward of five thousand dollars for Burr's apprehension, never mind the absence of a warrant. What was an honest citizen such as Philander Smith, foreman of the jury, to think? Fortunately, we know what he thought, for Smith disclosed his perceptions in a letter to his father, Jedediah.[10]

The addressee must have been his father, because Philander's *brother* Jedediah was only nine years old at the time. Though that celebrated "mountain man" and explorer was precocious—he became a clerk on a Lake Erie freighter at thirteen and a veteran of the Rocky Mountain fur trade by the time he was twenty-five—it is unlikely that even a preternaturally apt nine-year-old would catch the ironies with which the foreman's letter is laden. Smith told of the mobilization of the militia to intercept Burr's "ten boats and about 100 [assembled by] this formidable hero . . . without arms and military stores. [After] the militia returned in triumph . . . [they] illuminated their houses in the city; a stranger would have supposed that a victory equal to Lord Nelson's [at Trafalgar, in 1805] had been obtained. However the thinking part of the inhabitants felt indignant at the ridiculous force."[11]

"The thinking part of the inhabitants" was well represented on the grand jury, a "very respectable one." In Natchez, that description was likely to mean that they were gentry of a Federalist bent, "a majority" of whom, according to Smith, "looked upon Burr as the murderer of Hamilton and believed him capable of committing the crimes that he was accused with, (or greater, if it flattered his ambition) but this was not sufficient for them to find him guilty without proof of his guilt." These citizens of Adams County, Mississippi, shared the view of John Adams, who wrote that he was "anxious to see the progress of Burr's trial: not from any love or hatred I bear the man, for I cannot say that I feel either. . . . [Burr's actions] could be instigated only by his own ambitions[,] avarice[,] or revenge. But I hope his innocence will be made to appear, and that he will be fully acquitted."[12]

Senator Plumer Reports

As these events were transpiring in Washington, Mississippi, Senator William Plumer of New Hampshire was keeping a diary in the District of Columbia. Plumer was a Federalist, but a frequent guest at the Jefferson White House. After one such visit, Plumer expressed surprise at the ardor of the President's expressions of admiration for Wilkinson and denunciations of Burr:

> If Wilkinson's communications are correct, Burr either discovers want of talent, discernment and prudence—or a mania, a frenzy, has seized his mind. W. is not an accurate correct man.[13]

These impressions were gathered during a dinner with Jefferson followed by coffee and "a glass or two. . . . I do not mean that the President is under the influence of wine—for he is very temperate . . . [but] even two glasses of wine ofttimes renders a temperate man communicate." *This* temperate and cagey man *wished* to communicate. Plumer was told that

> governmental agents are in possession of full evidence to convict [Harmon Blennerhasset] . . . of being engaged in the conspiracy. But he thought not enough against the arch traitor Burr. . . . That Gen. Wilkinson was at that date . . . at New Orleans fortifying the city—and that he had ordered his army to follow him [from their deployment on the Spanish frontier]—That the General apprehended the city would be attacked by Burr—by land—and on water by vessels suited to such an enterprise. I asked the President who was to supply the naval force. He replied he could not tell . . . but that W. seemed to intimate Miranda.[14]

"W." was placing Miranda in the role Wilkinson and Hamilton had developed for him in 1799, as Plumer may well have recognized. In any case, this senator's doubts of Wilkinson's loyalty and integrity made him wonder at Jefferson's insistence "that there was no room to doubt of the integrity, firmness and attachment of Wilkinson to our government. And as little room to doubt the loyalty and attachment of the western people to the Union."[15]

Jefferson was either inconsistent in what he was telling people or changing and rechanging his mind. On January 24, 1807, he told Plumer that "he knew of no evidence sufficient to convict him [Burr] of either high crimes or misdemeanors." Yet, only a little later, he denounced Burr to Plumer as an "arch traitor" endangering the Union. Then again, on April 2, 1807, Jefferson wrote James Bowdoin, his minister in Madrid, that the danger was past, asserting that though Burr's purpose had earlier been to dissever the Union, he had by April become a mere filibuster again, to be prosecuted for a mere misdemeanor. Bowdoin was instructed that[16]

> no better proof of the good faith of the United States could have been given [Spain] than the vigor with which we acted ... in suppressing the enterprise meditated lately by Burr against Mexico, although at first he proposed a separation of the western country ... yet he very early saw that the fidelity of the western country was not to be shaken and turned himself wholly toward Mexico.[17]

During Burr's trial three months later, his letter to Bowdoin was one of the diplomatic dispatches Jefferson was unwilling to permit the grand jury in Richmond to see. It would have blown out of the water his treason indictment. Nonetheless, after Burr was acquitted, Jefferson wrote Madrid again. Now he wanted "our Ministers at Paris, London, and Madrid ... [to] find out Burr's propositions and agents there," as if the conspiracy were worldwide in its scope and huge in scale.[18]

The Charge of Filibustering

Jefferson's presidential proclamation had charged someone—Burr was as yet unnamed—with violation of Washington's Neutrality Act of 1794; armed men had been assembled, said the President, to invade the colonial possessions of Spain. To prevent this misdemeanor, Jefferson alarmed the nation, called up the militia, summoned the fleet, and rallied the regular army. As he amplified his charge to include treason he interrupted trade, disrupted the national defenses, ruptured his constitutional authority, and failed to reprimand his notorious subordinate, Wilkinson, for proclaiming martial law and creating a deputy dictatorship in New Orleans.

And he irrecoverably injured his reputation among those who

perceived inconsistency in his professing a passion to protect Spanish possessions from Burr while sending his own armies of provocation into the same territories, heavily armed though wearing the lineaments of scientific inquiry. Peter Custis, Freeman, Hunter, Dunbar, Pike, the Wilkinsons father and son, Lewis, and Clark were deep into territory claimed by Spain, on Jefferson's orders, with private armies of Mississippians and Georgians and Floridians standing by to support them if their probes found weakness on the Spanish side.

Jefferson's professions of pacific intentions were not persuasive, for he had a longer record as a war hawk against Spain than did either Hamilton or Burr. He had proposed war against "the Dons" in 1790, 1792, 1793, 1795, and 1802. In his Annual Message of 1805, he was at it once again: "The spirit and honor of our country require that force be interposed to a certain degree." In 1806, he wrote Du Pont de Nemours that force might be required to "take or obtain our just limits," and in 1807 he rejoiced that "our southern defensive force can take the Floridas, volunteers for a Mexican army will flock to our standard, and rich pabulum will be offered to our privateers in the plunder of their commerce and coasts. Probably Cuba would also add itself to our confederation." Hamilton's "squint" at Cuba had become a glare.[19]

Adams refused to be put off by any laying off against Burr of responsibility for the tension on the frontier: "War or no war? That is the question," he wrote. "Our monarchical, Anti-republican administration conceal from us the People, all that information which I a zealous Republican was always prompt to communicate."[20]

The letter is interesting in another way: Adams could not resist contrasting Jeffersonian policies toward two sets of runaways, fugitive slaves and impressed seamen. When slaves escaped, Jeffersonians insisted that federal authorities be sent after them to return them to their owners. Yet the Jefferson government recruited deserters from the British navy to serve on American ships, protesting at the same time that American honor required that the U.S. Navy *protect* from "impressment," meaning recapture, by the British. "Our people have such a predilection for runaways of every description except runaway Negroes that I suppose that Congress would think it too unpopular to abridge this right of man [running away from impressment]."[21]

Mr. Jefferson's Private Armies
and the Opinion of Another Jury

However conscientiously they might seek to penetrate the misinformation and disinformation communicated to them from the seat of government, neither Adams nor any other representative of "the thinking part of the people" outside the inner circle of the Virginia Dynasty was likely to discover an essential part of the puzzle of that dynasty's strategy for the Spanish borderlands in 1806–7. We have observed Jefferson's expeditions of exploration and science, but there was yet another range of plans so secret that they only became known after 1917, when Isaac Cox found correspondence in the archives of the War Department referring to a "plan of intervention," hatched by Governor W. C. C. Claiborne and James Madison. Sponsored filibusters were to intervene in Spanish West Florida, organized and equipped by the government of the United States without any pretensions to science, precisely at the time when other elements of the governmental apparatus—its army, navy, and judicial system—were deployed to punish Aaron Burr for proceeding independently. There is, of course, a vast difference between "liberation," carried forward by your friends, and "imperialism," conducted by your enemies, though the terrain, method, and results may be the same. Freelancers are seldom encouraged.[22]

It may be argued that the Virginians were merely acting to supplement the territories of the United States and to secure the mouth of the Mississippi. That is what they said they were doing. "Force [was being] . . . interposed to a certain degree" by people directed to do so by a resourceful President and by his successor, James Madison, though Madison was neither so resourceful nor so hypocritical. In 1806, they may actually have feared that Burr intended to set himself up as an independent actor athwart the critical path of their territorial supplements.

Whatever may have been the motivation of Jefferson, the gentry of Mississippi Territory took sufficient cognizance of the turmoil in the background and of the inexplicable behavior of the administration's agents in the foreground. Philander Smith's Mississippi Territory grand jury emerged from its review of the evidence before them and announced themselves to be disgusted with the conduct of the officers of government in this business. . . . The grand jury of the Mississippi Territory, on a due investigation of the evidence brought before them, are of the opinion that Aaron Burr has not been guilty of any crime or misdemeanor against the laws of the united States, or of this Territory; or given any just cause of alarm or inquietude to the good people of the same.[23]

That might have been enough for a modern grand jury, but these were gentlemen of the generation that had produced the Declaration of Independence with its syllabus of despotic acts charged against George III. Once launched upon opinion-writing, and with a revolutionary wind at their backs, the Mississippians responded to an unprecedented presidential indictment with an unprecedented counter-indictment:

> A military expedition [was] unnecessarily . . . fitted out against the person and property of the said Aaron Burr. . . . [It had destroyed] the personal liberty . . . [of Burr and of Burr's friends through] military arrest made without warrant, and . . . without other lawful authority; and they do sincerely regret that so much cause has been given to the enemies of our glorious Constitution, to rejoice at such measures . . . as, if sanctioned by the Executive of our country, must sap the vitals of our political existence, and crumble this glorious fabric in the dust.[24]

The Mississippi Federalists

Let us probe a little deeper into the musculature of this Mississippi grand jury: They were men of a Federalist city that remained Unionist between 1860 and 1865; Natchez never officially flew the Confederate flag. In 1806, it was not a place that would welcome someone bent upon disrupting the Union. That game might be played in Lexington, Knoxville, or Nashville, but it would not be played in Mississippi until Natchez was overwhelmed by Jefferson Davis's "new men" in the 1850s, after the "old men" were gone, including such fierce Federalists and Unionists as Winthrop Sargent.[25]

Sargent served his apprenticeship in territorial government as secretary of the Hamiltonian colony of Marietta, Ohio, and was sent to take charge of things in Mississippi by President John Adams. After arriving in Natchez, Sargent used his powers as territorial governor to build among its numerous settlers from New Jersey and New England a severe kind of Cincinnatian Federalism. There was symbolic importance in the naming of Adams County and Pickering County next door, as there was in Claiborne's renaming Pickering County as Jefferson County, thereby engulfing Sargent's enclave between Jefferson County and Wilkinson County.

Governor Sargent differed from his closest ally, Andrew Ellicott, the Maryland Quaker, in that Ellicott was an explicit abolitionist and Sargent merely made it difficult for slavetraders to use Natchez as their base. Sargent's first code for Mississippi prohibited the importation of slaves from the Spanish possessions, as he struck up an alliance with the planters who had held power under Spain to place men of their persuasion in command of the militia, increasing the probability that in Mississippi, as in Louisiana, the militia might continue as a mixed force of whites and blacks in the Spanish pattern. Militias held great power in the South. A biracial militia could have been as important a political force as the free black precincts were, at the time, in New York.

A Federalist-Quaker coalition came close to bringing Mississippi Territory into the Union on the same antislavery template as the Northwest Territory. Their efforts were defeated in 1798 only because of the effects of the three-fifths clause in creating a proslavery majority in the Congress, the same clause that two years later determined the outcome of the presidential election of 1800. Soon thereafter, Sargent was sacked by Jefferson, despite an appeal to Burr. Why Burr? Because, we may assume, Sargent believed he would be more responsive than Jefferson.

The second major figure to establish the climate of Burrite Natchez was Ellicott. Until the advent of Jefferson's corps of explorers, provocateurs, and scientists, he was the chief agent of official American expansion in the Mississippi, but, unlike them, he had been warned against James Wilkinson. In his saddlebags next to a letter of introduction from Burr, Ellicott bore another, from President George Washington, admonishing the friends of the Federal Union in the West not to trust Wilkinson, known to the President as a deceitful and faithless officer during the darkest days of the Revolution. Washington had heard the seditious talk emanating from Kentucky and went so far as to put in writing to Ellicott that Wilkinson might well be among those "improperly connecting themselves with the Spanish government."[26]

In 1796, Washington had asked Ellicott to keep him apprised, personally, of any relevant information adduced in the West. It would have been better for everyone (except Wilkinson) had Ellicott taken that responsibility more seriously. He made several efforts to act as a collector of such intelligence but failed to knit together what he had learned before he left the West at the end of 1799.[27]

A letter sent at the same time by Burr to Isaac Guion, a companion of the march to Quebec in 1775, establishes another connection to Ellicott. In December 1797, Guion commanded a small, but sufficient, detachment that arrived in the nick of time to support Ellicott, who had arrived in Natchez to find Spaniards indisposed to hand it over to the Americans under the requirements of Pinckney's treaty of the year before. After becoming in effect the town's military governor, Guion protected the Spaniards from Ellicott, and (though Guion may not have been aware of the need, at the time) Ellicott from Wilkinson. That became necessary because the old Quaker had showed to friends of the general copies of the derogatory reports he had sent to Washington, and then, in a moment of effulgent indiscretion, had gone so far as to tell Wilkinson himself of his suspicions.[28]

Thanks to two Indian agents, John McKee and Silas Dinsmoor (of whom we will have more to say shortly), many of the neighboring Choctaws were still well disposed toward high officials of the American government and were traditionally wary of Spain. Ellicott, William Blount, Aaron Burr, and, after them, Andrew Jackson at the Battle of New Orleans counted on Choctaw support. While clinging to his handhold in Natchez before Guion's arrival, Ellicott sought aid not only from the Anglo-American citizens of Natchez but also from the Choctaws. Whether on a routine caper or in response to Ellicott, a band of warriors descended upon the town and threatened a violent end to Spanish rule at the moment Guion arrived to settle things down. The Choctaw departed, and Guion ordered the chief local Spanish intelligence agent out of town. (He was Jose Vidal, who reappeared to manage the extermination of Philip Nolan in 1801 and to shadow Aaron Burr in 1806.)[29]

The Choctaws, twenty thousand strong, were a political force far more significant than Guion's few hundred when the total nonnative population of Mississippi Territory, slaves and all, was less than seven thousand. Let us meet Silas Dinsmoor, the agent who sustained their friendship to his own government for twenty years, until Jackson had them forcibly "removed" to Oklahoma—and let us recall that this is a book about character tested by circumstance.

Silas Dinsmoor

Dinsmoor was sent among the Choctaws in 1802, after a stint as agent to the Cherokees, and thenceforward was hard pressed to preserve his character while at the same time serving a corrupt social and political system. He was conscientiously opposed to slavery and, when he could, acted against it, but was only strong enough to do so on the margins of a life of accommodation. Assigned by his government to serve as agent to the Choctaws during a period in which they were being forced aside by the plantation system, like many others Dinsmoor purchased slaves to do his labor.

Dinsmoor's superior officer, Secretary of War Henry Dearborn, had served beside Burr, Peter Bruin, Isaac Guion, and James Wilkinson in the Quebec campaign of 1775 and may have been a silent partner in Wilkinson and Burr's early plans in 1805. However, after Wilkinson joined Jefferson against Burr, Dearborn panted along behind them, issuing orders to subordinates like Dinsmoor to close ranks in the dust. When told by another officer that it could be proven that Wilkinson was in the pay of the Spanish, the Secretary of War replied that "there might be an enquiry after the present bustle was over, but at present, he [Wilkinson] must and would be supported." To this sentiment, Attorney General Rodney added the comment: "What would be the result if this should be proven?" That is, why should that evidence be produced? "It would turn the indignation of the people from Burr on Wilkinson; Burr would escape, and Wilkinson take his place."[30]

The character of these two members of Mr. Jefferson's cabinet having been established, we turn now to the effect of such a political ecosystem upon lesser figures such as Silas Dinsmoor and, after him, his friend and predecessor as Choctaw agent, John McKee. We do so at some length because it is often said of Aaron Burr that he was forced out of public life because the society of gentlemen within which he moved did not feel him to rise to their level of character, whereas people such as Dearborn or Rodney or Thomas Jefferson did. At a recent discussion of Burr's character in New York, one of the leading scholars of the period so stated, adding as examples the opinions of Burr given by Hamilton and Jefferson. We have indicated earlier that there were many people of unassailable character, such as Stephen van Rensselaer and John Jay as late as 1804, and Albert Gallatin apparently so late as that, who joined John Adams and John Marshall in expressing judgments of Jefferson and Burr in which neither appeared as more or less a moral paragon than the other.

Now we turn to a group of lesser-known persons of good character who knew Burr in crisis circumstances as late as 1807 and failed to respond to him with the aversion we might expect if he was, in fact, the black sheep among the Founders. He has become that. The instances before us suggest that he was not so perceived by all gentlemen until Jefferson's machine, including such saints as James Wilkinson, Gideon Granger, George Morgan, Henry Dearborn, and Caesar Augustus Rodney, bore down on him. Let us see how Silas Dinsmoor, Robert Ashley, Isaac Guion, and even the pliant John McKee behaved when asked by that cabal to cast Burr out from virtuous society.

Silas Dinsmoor might be expected to follow where power pressed him. Both he and Guion made their adjustments to the slave system, though Guion had been born in Westchester County, New York, and Dinsmoor in New Hampshire. After his retirement from his command, in the summer of 1802, Guion bought himself some slaves and settled onto a cattle ranch and plantation near Natchez. That was also the year in which Dinsmoor, having recovered from a wound suffered in a duel, took his station at the Choctaw agency. It was not until 1806 that he followed Guion's lead and made himself a part-time planter and rancher, with slaves to do his hot work. At the end of 1805, he had reported to the War Department on his treaty-making with the Choctaws, then spent the spring and summer of 1806 in New Hampshire to marry Miss Mary Gordon. She remained there for a time, while he took ship to Charleston, to "purchase some Africans." Dinsmoor's state of mind is manifest in a letter to his new wife, in which he reported that on Friday night, October 10, he got thoroughly drunk. On Sunday, October 12, he "went three times to meeting. Monday began a horrid traffic of purchasing Negroes. I never felt meaner in my life and because I was obliged to have intercourse with the most unprincipled people." He went "twice to church on Sunday the 19th" and on "Saturday 25 . . . shipped my flock of black sheep, sixteen in number. At 11 o'clock we set sail for New Orleans.[31]

In the leaden humidity of the previous July, Burr traversed the pasture into which Dinsmoor intended to place his "black sheep." Burr wrote Theodosia that the Trace, which passed Dinsmoor's door, the "road . . . you will see laid down . . . on the map . . . as having been cut by the order of the minister of war[,] . . . is imaginary; there is no such road." The region between Washington, Mississippi, and the Choctaw domain was, Burr reported, "a vile country, destitute of springs or of running water—think of drinking the nasty puddle water, covered with green scum, and full of animaculae—bah! . . . [H]ow glad I was to get [into the high country,] all fine, transparent, lively streams, and itself [the Tennessee] a clear, beautiful, magnificent river."[32]

But there had been some political work to be done, despite the animaculae. On July 23, 1805, Silas Dinsmoor presided over a ball attended by both Burr and McKee at the Chickasaw Agency House, near the hamlet now known as Houlka, Chickasaw County, Mississippi. McKee said of Burr:

> He speaks so much of the disadvantage that results to the western country from their not making themselves heard on the floor of Congress that I cannot help thinking western popularity and power may be his pursuit at present—what he means to do with it let those who know him guess.[33]

At the end of November 1806, Wilkinson was turning against Burr and arrived in New Orleans from his most recent round of Spanish negotiations just as Dinsmoor was returning through that port from New Hampshire. Neither left an account of what they discussed, but it may well have proceeded from an observation by the commanding general, possibly with a cash offer attached, that the Vice President was likely to be returning to Natchez from Nashville through the defiles of that "imaginary" road without any larger escort than his ally General John Adair of Kentucky. All we have is a tantalizing letter abstract in the National Archives marked as from Dinsmoor, presumably acting under Wilkinson's orders—or was it from Wilkinson, and misfiled?— to Dearborn, advising the remittance of two thousand dollars "in favor of G W Morgan." There are no other indications of Dinsmoor having anything to do with George Morgan, who was in the process of collecting favors from the Jefferson administration for betraying Burr. Perhaps the settlement of Morgan's Indiana land claims was not enough, in Wilkinson's opinion. Perhaps two thousand dollars in a War Department draft was needed to turn the trick.[34]

On December 4, Wilkinson wrote to Dinsmoor, apparently putting in writing another cash offer—five thousand dollars (four times the annual salary of an Indian agent) to "cut off" Burr and Adair:

> To cut off the two principal leaders, would in my opinion be to discomfit the sinister design, and gain time for preparation to resist successfully the baneful plot. . . . [I]t is my wish to have them arrested and carried off from that place. To be delivered to the Executive authority of the Union. . . . I believe you competent to the enterprise, and pray of you to undertake it. If you fail, your expenses will be paid. If you succeed I pledge the government to you for five thousand dollars.[35]

Lest anyone doubt what Wilkinson had in mind, it is well to recall his record with regard to hiring assassins. Five years before his assassination plot against Anthony Wayne, he had rented his conscience to the British in double occupancy with the Spaniards. During the course of 1788, he managed to demonstrate his fidelity to Dr. John Connolly, his British counterpart, by providing to him a bodyguard to produce a stand-off with killers Wilkinson had himself hired on behalf of Spain. Dinsmoor's refusal to rush to serve Wilkinson's behest required the commanding general to turn to Captain Hooke and, after Hooke lost his verve, to the wharf rats of Natchez Lower Town.

Having received Wilkinson's first proposal (if our supposition is correct) on November 25 or 26, and having been prodded along on December 4, Dinsmoor did nothing. On the eighth he wrote his wife that he had been in New Orleans "about three weeks" and said that "tomorrow," the ninth, he would travel by land to Natchez. He had arrived by the thirtieth, for he wrote from there to Dearborn that he was on his way to his agency, but, with strange lassitude, was still in Natchez on January 7, 1807. On that date he wrote his friend John McKee: "We are all in a flurry here hourly expecting Colonel Burr and all Kentucky and half of Tennessee at his back to punish General Wilkinson, set the Negroes free, rob the banks and take Mexico. Come and help me laugh at the fun." Burr arrived, finally and by water, on January 11, having shared a thought, in retrospect, with Ellicott: He asked

Lieutenant Jacob Jackson, at Chickasaw Bluffs, how many warriors McKee "could raise." Perhaps Burr actually did contemplate a polyglot force against the Spaniards.[36]

McKee came down to Natchez to meet Dinsmoor; there he introduced Burr to some friends from the West Florida border. He and Dinsmoor shared a room after January 17, when Burr surrendered to the authorities of Mississippi Territory. McKee went to some pains to stay on good terms with the commanding general, writing Wilkinson on the twenty-fifth that "I have little doubt that ere this you will have set me down as a Burrite, and as little that you will believe me when I assure you that as yet I am not; and I must know the object and the means better than I do before I can be." Like Guion and Dinsmoor, McKee was not ready to write Burr off. The three of them may have worked together to sort things out, for when Dinsmoor was invited by Burr to a meeting, he appeared with others. He wrote later that he only saw Burr "in company. . . . [Burr] solicited no private interview, and I had none with him." After Burr determined that even with the support of some steadfast friends he could no longer risk staying within the reach of Wilkinson's thugs, Dinsmoor rode into Natchez on February 5, to bring the news to Captain Hooke that the Vice President had escaped.[37]

By February 8, Burr was deep into Choctaw territory. Wilkinson now tried to see what might be done with McKee: "If you want to distinguish yourself, and tax the government beyond denial, go alone and seize Burr." McKee responded blandly that "nothing could have given me greater pleasure" and added two barbs. "In the strange distant reserve of some of my friends in this quarter" he detected proof that Wilkinson had shared with others McKee's "not yet" note of the twenty-fifth. "I must have been very unfortunate in expressing myself," McKee went on. "I never was a Burrite, nor can I ever give myself up to schemes of lawless plunder. . . . I might have engaged in any honorable enterprise, however hazardous, but the late one, such as it has been represented is such as I hope no friend of mine will ever suspect me of favoring." It is a joy to encounter such precision of language: "such as it has been represented." Indeed. And then the other barb, delivered to a man many knew to be on the Spanish payroll: "May your purse keep pace with your heart, and may you live a thousand years." McKee was a man willing to take certain "hazards."[38]

As we shall see, Burr was arrested again, on the West Florida frontier, on February 19, 1807. It is unlikely that word of his capture had reached Natchez by the twenty-third, when Dinsmoor was writing Dearborn that ever since Wilkinson solicited his aid in New Orleans, he had been exerting himself to be useful, having "kept up a regular communication with the general . . . and should have done so with you also had not strong suspicions existed that the mails were examined." Indeed again. Like McKee, Dinsmoor was letting the mighty cats know that while the mice had little power to resist, and would deny any desire to escape their fate, they retained a grim sense of humor. The mails were Gideon Granger's. The Postmaster General and the Secretary were on the same side.[39]

Like McKee, Dinsmoor assured Dearborn that as soon as he heard that "Col. Burr had escaped from the civil authority," he had ridden "express to the Upper Choctaws, employed runners to intercept all the passes through the country, and on the 12th [of February] returned to Natchez." So that was where he wanted it thought he had gone after delivering the news to Captain Hooke, though he did have the temerity to add: "There are strong reasons to believe he [Burr] is still in this territory." Since the Vice President had made his way southeasterly, through the territory of the Six Towns Choctaws, toward Florida, rather than northward along the Trace, through the Upper Choctaws, it is entirely possible that Dinsmoor knew some of those "strong reasons." He knew the route toward the Tombigbee better than anyone and may have been choosing his words carefully; perhaps he did not ride north but went instead at least part of the way southward, with Burr and Robert Ashley, through the lands of his Choctaw charges.[40]

On the first of March, the governor of Mississippi Territory, Robert Williams, wrote Dinsmoor ordering him out of Natchez, or Washington, next door, to Fort Stoddert, on the Tombigbee, where Burr was being held, to "convey him safely to the City of Washington . . . and . . . submit him to the order of the President." Williams followed up by ordering the commander of Fort Stoddert to hand Burr over to Dinsmoor, confirming that instruction to Secretary of State Madison, who had every reason to think Dinsmoor to be Wilkinson's agent. Dinsmoor apparently reached Fort Stoddert about the tenth, but by that time Burr was gone. Bounties had been paid. Other entrepreneurs had seen fit to make names and purses for themselves.[41]

At Burr's trial in Richmond, at the end of September 1807, many of the people who had been with him in Natchez came together again.

Those, like Dinsmoor, who earned their livelihood from the administration and had been subpoenaed by it to testify against Burr, did all they could to avoid perjury and at the same time give no offense to the winners. Dinsmoor wrote his wife that "the farce play grows more farcical every day. Such iniquity was never before practiced in this iniquitous world." He said nothing to implicate Burr, and his cross-examination by Burr drew only one spark: When Burr asked him whether or not he had assiduously followed Wilkinson's instruction to cut him off, Dinsmore replied that he had done so "as far as was practicable and expedient." That brought Jefferson's lead counsel, William Wirt, to his feet to ask what he meant by "expedient." Dinsmoor cooly responded: "I meant that if I should have found him at large, I should have taken him, but not out of the hands of civil authority."[42]

> WIRT: "Were there not officers sent up to take him?
> ANSWER: Yes, and I was instructed to cooperate with them; but he being exactly where General Wilkinson wanted him, in the hands of the civil authority, I advised the officers to return, and they separated.
> COL. BURR (cross-examining): Were you to seize me privately?
> ANSWER: Yes, if practicable.
> BURR: Was I not reputed to be at the head of an army, by General Wilkinson?
> ANSWER: Yes, and by others, too.
> BURR: How, then, were these men to take me?"

Burr then asked Dinsmoor a series of questions about Wilkinson's professed doubts as to the patriotism or firmness of the militia, the citizens of New Orleans, the judges, Governor Claiborne, and Cowles Mead, acting as governor in the absence of Governor Robert Williams, Dinsmoor responded solemnly to this chain of inquiries that Wilkinson, always pure and patriotic himself, expressed doubts about them all. The list was lengthening when Wirt once more objected, legitimately, that Dinsmoor was not an expert on Wilkinson's opinions. But the damage was done, without Dinsmoor being discomfited by doing it. Wirt and Wilkinson had his future in their hands; he was still a War Department employee. He had gone as far as he could go.

There was little doubt that sooner or later Dinsmoor would lose his agency, but there were bigger fish for the administration to catch after he finally returned to his post a year later, situating his wife and two children on 120 acres he purchased in Washington, Mississippi. He was back in the spotlight, however, in 1811, when he reappeared at Fort Stoddert to spoil a filibuster against the Spaniards. This time it was no Burrite who was in the saddle but Reuben Kemper, who was among the government-sponsored filibusters against Spanish Florida. It appears that Dinsmoor was unwilling to permit Kemper, whoever were his sponsors, to use a base in Choctaw territory in 1811 to violate Washington's Neutrality Law of 1794, since Burr had been prosecuted under that law. Such consistency has not endeared Dinsmoor to those to whom a willingness to serve the expansion of the plantation system is the universal test of virtue. Kemper served that system, and Dinsmoor did not.[43]

Dinsmoor and Robert Ashley—who, in our construction of events, was Burr's other companion in his escape from Natchez—are instructive Burrites. We can learn from them what sort of people Burr attracted. So let us dig a little deeper into the history of Dinsmoor's relationship to the expansion of slavery. As we have already observed, he participated in that expansion, though it cost him five church services and many a hangover (we have omitted a further series of references to his getting drunk in disgust). Nonetheless, his ambiguous relationship to slavery and his loyalty to the Choctaws continued throughout the rest of his life, as we learn from Robert Remini's biography of Andrew Jackson. In the year after throwing himself in the path of Reuben Kemper, 1812, "one Silas Dinsmoor," Remini tells us, was keeping an "agency house" where he "used to detain every slave traveling with a white man." "Detain" is an interesting word.[44]

> Jackson decided to interfere and teach Dinsmoor his duty. . . . Dinsmoor was very tolerant of runaways. Worse, he required each master to show documentary proof of ownership before he would let him pass with his slaves. If proof were lacking, he took the slaves into custody. Obviously there were many complaints to the Secretary of War about the highhandedness of this official. At the time, Jackson was an inactive partner of a business firm that traded in slaves. . . . [He resolved] to instruct Dinsmoor in the proper execution of his duties.[45]

Dinsmoor happened to be away when his instructor in duty arrived, and returned only after Jackson had departed, leaving behind him threats. Undismayed, Dinsmoor continued his mischief, impounding slaves—and, perhaps, setting some at liberty. When Jackson heard that he had been ignored and that another "outrage" had occurred, he provided a classic contribution to the inadvertent humor of slaveocracy: "My God! Are we freemen, or are we slaves? Is it real or is it a dream? . . . Can the Secretary of War [Dinsmoor's employer] . . . retain the idea that we will permit this petty tyrant to sport with our rights?"[46]

Dinsmoor, who opposed the use of alcohol by traders to beguile Indians into land sessions and to lubricate swindling them in trade, next appears in Remini's account in 1820, when "he supposedly had asserted that 'the policy of our government towards the Indian tribes' [forced removal along the Trail of Tears] was a harsh one." Jackson and Dinsmoor met at a gathering of the Choctaws; Jackson, says Remini, found an occasion to summon "all the sternness of manner for which he was famous, [and] devastated the unfortunate man with a blast of contempt. 'No, sir,' he barked, 'I never go where I have no business.' "[47]

A little farther on in his text, Remini remarks that Dinsmoor was denied a claim for a farm on some land in the Choctaw Session of 1820, in compensation for personal property taken by Choctaws over the preceding years. So much for a loser. Dinsmoor stood in the way of Jackson's trade in slaves and also resisted Jackson's policy of Indian "removal." Is it really likely, though, that he was "devastated," or that he was surprised to be told that he had no "business" appearing in Jackson's camp to protest the harshness of forcing the Choctaws from their homes?[48]

No business, perhaps. But a great deal of courage—of the kind he had displayed toward Wilkinson, fourteen years earlier.[49]

Robert Ashley

Silas Dinsmoor first came to our attention because he did not dry-gulch Aaron Burr on his way into Natchez. Major Robert Ashley is the man who got Burr safely out again. The Vice President could hardly have had a better bodyguard; Ashley had escaped the Spanish assassination of Philip Nolan in 1801, provided stallions to Judge Bruin and Dr. Cummins thereafter, and reappeared to do what he could to rescue Aaron Burr.

The earliest documents bearing Ashley's name are in Spanish records of the hearings held in 1795 by Bruin, soon after the judge had returned from leading the Coles Creek militia to New Orleans to stand off the threatened invasion by George Rogers Clark. Bruin's interrogation was directed at determining what part, if any, Ashley had in the plans of Clark. To catch the nuances in their dialogue, one must bear in mind that Clark and Citizen Genêt had been repudiated by the southern planters, who had discovered that the Girondist government the two men represented was abolitionist. From Ashley's responses to Bruin's interrogatories, it appears that while living in Georgia or South Carolina, he had given protection to an "ill-used" slave then called Jack, whom Ashley renamed "Smart" for having run away from his master. It was charged that Ashley told Smart that "he would never want for victuals and clothes, and that he would give him a horse." When Smart's owner "was not willing" to assent to the "sale," Ashley parted with another horse "and thereby obtained his consent."[50]

(Horses were stock-in-trade for the Ashleys of Georgia: The strait-laced Indian agent James Seagrove wrote Governor Henry White of Spanish Florida that, in the Ashley settlement of St. Patrick's—later given its present name of St. Marys—on the border of Georgia and Florida, the patriarch, Nathan Ashley, and two of his freebooting sons, William and Ludovic, were "harboring all the vagabonds and horse thieves that come into the country.")

Ashley and Smart then took out for the West, first to Nashville, then down the Tennessee to the Ohio, working their way toward Natchez. Unlike Mark Twain's Huck and Jim, however, they did not travel alone. Other "Smarts" joined them, with angry former owners in pursuit.

> BRUIN: Were you not pursued by a party as far as Diamond Island, on the Ohio . . . on account of the Negroes you had in your possession?
>
> ASHLEY: I did understand . . . that a party was coming . . . to take me, but on what account I know not. But being conscious of not having transgressed the laws of any country, I should not have removed in the manner I did, if I had not been well-informed that they were a lawless, blood-thirsty set, who were in pursuit of me.[51]

So far, Ashley's testimony offered no problems to Bruin: the royal decree had established the policy on the part of the Spanish authorities that sanctuary might be provided for escaped English or American slaves. The next part was more delicate: Bruin asked Ashley if it were true that he had accepted the rank of captain in Clark's revolutionary army and had recruited men for an invasion of the Spanish possessions. Ashley denied that but admitted traveling with Peter Tardeveau, who had been engaged to serve as interpreter for André Michaux to "encourage and forward their business." Then why were a regimental uniform and a commission in the French army found in Ashley's baggage?

> General Clark is my uncle by marriage, and he insisted (much against my inclinations) that I should wear a regimental coat which he had made for me, at the same time he offered me money to raise men and told me I was entitled, at any rate, to the privilege of wearing a uniform coat, having once been an officer in the Georgia militia. On this principle I received the coat, but refused to take any money for the purpose of training men or having any agency in the enterprise.
>
> I did show . . . Tardeveau the commission that had been offered me by General Elijah Clarke, of Georgia, and which til then had remained in my possession, though I had never acted under it, and in my answer to General Clark [George Rogers Clark] declared I never would.[52]

Professing satisfaction of all his curiosity, Judge Bruin released Robert Ashley on January 24, 1795. That is why Ashley was available in 1806, and why he found Silas Dinsmoor and Burr compatible.

Thomas Rodney and Old '76

With the "thinking portion" of the people of Natchez on his side, and with the support of experienced frontiersmen like Robert Ashley, Aaron Burr awaited the response of Thomas Rodney to the grand jury. Would Rodney now don Old '76? He would not. His sword had rusted in its sheath; he could no longer wrench it free to act against "the express orders of the general government." For this sometime revolutionary, "the constitution . . . [had] confided the supreme guardianship and protection of the country" to Jefferson's administration, however unconstitutional might be its actions. He was rewarded: On April 25, 1806, Jefferson wrote James Madison: "I enclose you a warrant for $5,000 for Mr. Rodney in the form advised by Mr. Gallatin." Thereafter Rodney was willing to go beyond acquiescence. Under his direction, the jury's verdict was stricken from the record, with the notation that he disapproved of their "particular impropriety in censuring their [the government's] conduct."[53]

Having taken his money, on January 12, 1807, Thomas Rodney amended the stipulations under which Burr and his attorneys had put up a heavy bond, secretly adding, after they had gone, a requirement that though the jury verdict was in, Burr must remain in the neighborhood indefinitely, at the discretion of the judge. Weeks later, Burr was taken into captivity for violating an amendment he did not know existed.[54]

Wilkinson's thugs were still lingering in Natchez Lower Town and in the underbrush below Bruinsburg. "There were several gunboats stationed here," wrote foreman Smith, "and it was believed that they had orders to take him [Burr] as soon as he was discharged by the court." Rodney had placed a leash on the Vice President where the arm of Wilkinson might reach at any moment. His only choices were to defy "illegal incarceration" or to risk "private assassination." Cowles Mead was scrupulous in following the orders of the President who had appointed him but began at this point to make his own assessment of the public danger created by Burr's little flotilla of nine unarmed houseboats and "one hundred men and the major part are boys or young men just from school," concluding that the grand jury was correct. Jefferson's "mighty alarm (with all its exaggerations)" had been unnecessary.[55]

Though Mead did what he was told to do, proclaiming that there was a plot to dissever the Union, he declined to identify Burr as its originator. Jefferson's response was to write Madison: "I expect we shall have to remove Mead" and rely entirely upon John Graham, who had just arrived in Natchez to give his employer an appraisal of the state of the public mind in Mississippi Territory. But Graham's assessment was no more consoling than Mead's:

> I am sorry to say that since my arrival . . . I have met with many people who either openly or indirectly attack the government for not countenancing Colonel Burr in the invasion of Mexico, for

it is generally considered here that that was his object. . . . Most of his followers were of this opinion.[56]

And so, it seems, were enough influential citizens of Natchez to open a barn door, for Smith informed his father that "while the motion was pending Burr made his escape."[57]

John McKee

While Burr was attending the hearing of the Mississippi grand jury, early in January 1807, his host was another of the New Jersey settlers, Colonel Benijah Osmun. Osmun had served beside Isaac Guion, Burr, and Bruin in the New Jersey Continentals and was Guion's neighbor. "With these two, and other influential gentlemen, . . . [Burr] had daily consultations." Though Mexico may have been the ultimate prize, in the meantime a safe haven was needed, and West Florida was available. It then encompassed all the terrain between Mobile and Baton Rouge not claimed by the Choctaw. Ninety percent of the European population of this vast area had come there from the former English colonies, and, if we are to judge by the number of its gentry who joined Osmun, Guion, and Burr in that exceedingly busy rose-covered cottage, Burr could expect a warm welcome among them. Their leaders included Lemuel Henry, James Caller, and Colonel John McKee.

McKee later testified that it was Caller who aroused Burr's enthusiasm for the possibilities of West Florida. Westward ventures had been cut off by Wilkinson's army, but the way through the woods to the east was open. If Burr had gone directly

> to the Tombigbee settlements and told the people that his enterprise was a secret one against Spain which had the sanction of the Government he might have procured enough men to take Mobile, where he would have found sufficient arms and ammunition and armed vessels to convey his troops to wherever place he pleased. Burr replied that the Government had neglected these people and under the Constitution they had a right to erect a new government for themselves or to seek protection of another government. Burr stressed "constitutional right."[58]

Burr stood in well with the 'Bigbee gentry because he had been receptive to their needs. Though the Louisiana Purchase had freed the

Mississippi to carry inland commerce, that did not help the planters on the upper reaches of the Tombigbee system. Spanish authorities in Mobile continued to cut them off from the Gulf, repeating the sphincter tactics used on the Mississippi. While he was agent to the Choctaws, as predecessor to his friend Dinsmoor, McKee had become the specialist in the peculiar politics along the Tombigbee.

The eastern states had demonstrated that they were no more disposed to help people deep in Alabama than they had been to help Harry Innes's Kentuckians or John Sevier's Tennesseans; Burr told his visitors that he "had seen, with regret, the memorial of the inhabitants of that part of the country treated by Congress with contempt; that he was surprised that they had not made a concerted attempt to release themselves." When these gentlemen called on him again, in Natchez, Burr added an expressed desire "to give you the Floridas." As earnest of his intentions, Burr provided them forty or fifty muskets and bayonets from his small store of arms "at a third of their value."[59]

The shadow of John McKee upon this scene reminds us that if Burr was to "give" anyone the Floridas, he would have to get the Floridas from someone first. McKee had been Alexander Hamilton's advance man for that task; he was a cousin of Sam Houston's, born as Houston was in Rockbridge County, Virginia. After a thorough education at the institution now known as Washington and Lee University, he joined William Blount as early as 1792 to assist with his undertakings with the British, the Cherokee, and Choctaw. Though he was then only in his early twenties, McKee was important to Blount's arrangements. He was an able man, about whom one must not assume too little. We find McKee next in Natchez, in 1797, where he aroused the suspicions of Ellicott, and then in Pensacola, having switched parties. Now he was acting as agent for "the Federalist war party" headed by Hamilton, during Hamilton's flirtation with Wilkinson. It is likely that McKee's conversations with Panton, Leslie, and company were intended to "pave the way for the conquest of Florida."

It is not without significance that McKee . . . was under the orders of Secretary of War McHenry, and that Secretary of State Pickering was privy to the purpose of his mission. When Andrew Ellicott wrote from Natchez that McKee, on passing through that place, had been suspiciously intimate with Blount's adherents,

Pickering replied that the government was informed of McKee's activities and fully satisfied of his loyalty.[60]

The Federalist government was, it appears, using McKee to detach from their Spanish alliance the British traders of Pensacola, especially the great trading house of Panton, Leslie, and Forbes, and thus to reduce the danger of an Indian attack upon the flank of Hamilton's contemplated descent of the Mississippi to New Orleans. This was to be achieved by removing William Augustus Bowles and his Creeks from the path of expansion of the plantation economy. A deal was struck, described five years later by McKee as a "promise made by the government *through me* [his emphasis] in the summer of 1797 that they [Panton, etc.] might reasonably look forward to such indulgences as would greatly facilitate the effectual and prompt collection of their debts within our Indian Nations."[61]

That accomplished, by 1806 McKee had extended his travels, perhaps as far as Santa Fe, for he began corresponding with a new client—Wilkinson—referring to Santa Fe as if from personal acquaintance. He added another potential patron, encouraging Burr to advance either in the direction of New Mexico or to Pensacola, where, we may assume, his friends Panton, Leslie, and Forbes had worked out contingency plans. When Burr failed in his attempt to reach Pensacola (see below), those with whom he (or Hamilton) might have established a regime there were still willing to use McKee as an intermediary to the American government. In 1810, Governor Vincente Folch asked McKee to convey to the Secretary of State a proposal that the United States acquire West Florida along the lines which could have been rehearsed with Burr in 1807. Writing to McKee as if he were a friend, Folch asked him to explain to the American government why an honorable Spanish civil servant might take such a proposition, acknowledging the weakness of his position and his patriotic preference that West Florida go to the Americans rather than to Napoleonic France—as Louisiana had.

> From having been an eye witness to all that has passed in this part of the province and the adjoining countries, you can give information respecting the alarm which reigns among its inhabitants, of the influence which the French agents in Louisiana exercise in these disturbances, and the risk which that province runs in being involved in the disorders which have had their birth in

Florida, as well as the fatal consequences which may follow if the evil is not stopped in its beginning.[62]

McKee was not in fact, a friend; he wrote Monroe describing Folch as "constantly vacillating betwixt avarice and ambition with a puerile fondness for parade." But the governor was in a position to deliver a valuable province—as the former intendant at New Orleans, Jean Ventura Morales, seems to have been three years earlier. If the transaction was to be between Hamilton and Folch, Burr and Morales, or Folch and Monroe, McKee would have a role.

It is now apparent that Burr did not ride out from Natchez into an unfriendly wilderness, nor did he go without a plan. Between Natchez and Pensacola was a forest, but not a wilderness. And, at the other end, there was adventure.

21

The Wheeled Cell and the Trial

In the final days of 1806, Robert Ashley and Aaron Burr departed Natchez, riding eastward in disguise. Dr. Cummins, the son-in-law of Peter Bruin, came along a few days later, entrusted with Burr's precious maps of the Gulf Coast, and began a long career vindicating Mississippi's judgment in favor of Burr. Cummins probably outfitted Burr with that disguise subsequently described with such malicious delight by Jefferson: "an old white hat, a pair of Virginia cloth pantaloons, and old Virginia leggins, and an old Virginia cloth coat."[1]

A disguise was necessary, because a Virginian President had made Burr a hunted man. Believing that Burr had knowingly violated Judge Rodney's post-hoc parole, Cowles Mead joined the pack against him, adding an additional two thousand dollars to Wilkinson's bounty. It is sometimes said that Burr "went into hiding," a phrase tinged with implications of "conspiracy," but the editors of the Burr Papers put it better:

Contemporary investigators found willing witnesses to almost every aspect, real or imagined, of his activities before the second week of February, but no one could be located who was willing to give evidence on AB's travels through 200 miles of wilderness to Wakefield, in present-day Washington Co., Ala. where he appeared on 18 Feb. He could not have made the journey without friends willing to give him lodging and fresh mounts; but the Mississippians who aided him in that desperate flight proved more loyal and discreet than the followers he had chosen elsewhere.[2]

As Burr and Ashley rode through the winter woods of the Choctaw Cession toward the McIntosh Bluffs on the Tombigbee, they were also riding into the ambitions of two young men who grasped the magnitude of the opportunity approaching them, Nicholas Perkins and Edmund Gaines.[3]

Appointments, promotions, and careers could be built by doing Thomas Jefferson's bidding, especially if one were born in Virginia and lucky. Gaines was from Culpeper County and was congenitally fortunate, particularly in being stationed, in 1807, as lieutenant in charge at Fort Stoddert. Perkins was an impecunious young lawyer, serving as clerk of the court in the remote 'Bigbee settlements protected by the fort.

We owe our detailed knowledge of the events of the next month to the meticulous Albert James Pickett, whose *History of Alabama, and incidentally of Georgia and Mississippi* was compiled from the testimony of many eyewitnesses. Pickett interviewed Gaines forty years later, along with Thomas Malone, who, when a muscular young man, had been recruited by Gaines and Perkins. Malone had done some clerking, too, in North Carolina, but, since he was not yet a member of the bar, was easily abashed by Perkins, who was. Pickett's other three witnesses were Mrs. John Hinson, who received Burr at her cabin on the Tombigbee, Lieutenant Gaines's brother George, an Indian trader, who lay ill at Fort Stoddert, and a Mrs. Howes, who observed Burr, after he was captured, passing by canoe up Lake Tensaw.

According to these accounts, about ten o'clock on the night of February 18, 1807, Perkins and Malone were playing backgammon in their cabin in the hamlet of Wakefield, when two mounted travelers came to their door and asked the road to Colonel Hinson's house. One was Burr, in the costume Jefferson found so ludicrous: the floppy, wide-brimmed hat (once white, now stained to a tobacco color), homespun trousers, and a long frontiersman's jacket with a hunting knife slung theatrically over his shoulder and a tin cup hanging from his belt.

Interviewed forty years later, the eyewitnesses asserted that anyone would know *what* he was if not *who* he was. No homespun, they said, could disguise a gentleman who wore fine leather boots and bestrode a fine horse—one of Philip Nolan's best, no doubt. Malone later insisted that he knew the man was a gentleman by the way he sat upon that horse.[4]

Perkins scented the possibility of profitable patriotism. The gentleman on the fine horse was redeemable in bounty money, since, judging from Cowles Mead's description, he had to be Burr. Though Malone declined to badger such a visitor, Perkins was a natural badger in some ways, but unlike badgers, he did not like solo engagements. Off he went for help from the local sheriff, Theodore Brightwell, whose cabin was nearby. Brightwell agreed to follow Burr as far as the residence of Colonel and Mrs. Hinson. The colonel had journeyed to Natchez to discuss matters with Burr; had such a powerful squire accompanied Burr back to the 'Bigbee settlements, things might have come out differently. But Burr's luck was out. Like Cummins, Hinson was delayed. Burr and Ashley came alone.

Mrs. Hinson was providing a midnight supper to them when Perkins and Brightwell came to the edge of the Hinsons' clearing. Brightwell went to the house while Perkins remained outside in the cold. Having introduced himself, the sheriff was invited to join in the meal. Exposed to Burr's bright black eyes and treated as a peer, he was recruited; he either forgot, or chose to forget, the eager Perkins. After two hours shivering in the February night, the clerk of court abandoned his post and rode off toward Fort Stoddert, to gather up Gaines.

Early on the next day, Gaines and Perkins, accompanied by a squad of soldiers, caught up with Burr, who was now accompanied by Sheriff Brightwell. (Ashley was off somewhere, probably seeking to complete a rendezvous.) As Burr and Brightwell descended the bank of the Tombigbee, Gaines, Perkins, and their men rushed to surround them, threatening Burr with their weapons. Brightwell professed surprise that it was Burr, and Burr protested that the soldiers had no right to arrest him. Gaines asserted to Pickett that he had given a response which seems a little melodramatic: Though young, he recalled himself saying, he knew his duty, and his duty was to do what Mr. Jefferson and Mr. Jefferson's governor required. Whatever he really said, his men had their pistols ready, and the lesson was plain. Burr nodded his head and turned his horse, conceding defeat.

Burr's first imprisonment was a week in custody in Fort Stoddert, while Gaines sought instruction from Wilkinson and a promotion. He got both. Those birds in hand, he could afford to turn Perkins loose to reap for them both shares in the two thousand dollars of additional pelf which would only be paid for delivery of the prisoner fifteen hundred miles away in Richmond, the capital city of Jefferson's Virginia.

Rousing the Neighborhood

Burr's tenure in Fort Stoddert might have been longer had Burr's bodyguard not roused the neighborhood, where he and Hinson had many friends. When Ashley was picked up by Gaines's troopers and grilled at Fort Stoddert, he displayed the skill which had bemused Peter Bruin so many years before: He testified that "he had met Col. Burr by accident, found him a pleasant traveling companion and had come with him to that place." Ashley was popular, local, and, therefore, released, though Gaines later asserted that he feared he might "assuredly find the inhabitants such as they [Ashley and Burr] could wish." (And so they might. Shortly afterward, many of those "inhabitants" signed a memorial to the government like that of the grand jury in Natchez, deploring the treatment accorded Burr.) Even after Burr had been hustled away under an armed guard, Gaines acknowledged to Wilkinson that "Ashley has made a wonderful effect on many of them—the plans of Burr are now spoken of in terms of approbation, and Burr in terms of sympathy and regard. I am convinced that if Burr had remained here a week longer the consequences would have been of the most serious nature."[5]

Haste. Haste. On the nineteenth, Gaines urged Perkins along:

It strikes me as . . . indispensable . . . for the security of this settlement [presumably the place, not the pelf] and the tranquility of the Western country generally, to send the Col. direct to Washington City and leave the place at all events by the 22nd of the present month."[6]

Before the twenty-second, as Ashley's "wonderful effect" was accumulating against them, Gaines was visited by a "Spanish officer, who *I think* he said commanded a Spanish armed vessel called Louisa, and who had been up the river, *as I was told* [italics mine] to purchase sea stores or some things that were necessary for a cruise that he was about to undertake."[7]

Gaines's careful disavowal of personal knowledge of the mission of this officer has misled some scholars into accepting the implication of "a cruise" to mean that Burr planned to travel somewhere by sea from Pensacola. This is doubtful. Why should he not travel overland? Gaines wrote that he felt that even his fort and garrison were insufficient to keep Burr—"Our Great Prisoner"—from rescue. If loose in the woods, with Ashley's and Hinson's friends about him, there was no reason for him not to ride comfortably, even grandly (having changed clothes) into Pensacola, where McKee and Morales might have prepared the way. Was it not Morales who was represented by that mysterious "Spanish officer"?

Perkins attempted to question that gentleman, but, professing to speak no English, the visitor asked to be permitted to converse with Burr, who spoke Spanish. Gaines asked Perkins "whether it was proper." Perkins said it was not, so Gaines went alone into Burr's cell.

> [He returned] into the room where the Spanish officer and myself [Perkins] were, holding a piece of paper in his hand, on which was some writing. He said to the officer it was improper he should see Col. Burr . . . and . . . then said, as well as I can recollect, Col. Burr sends his compliments to Morates [Morales] and his daughter and requests that he would send him some wine, and I think some articles but I do not remember what, and then gave the paper to the Spanish officer who started off down the river toward Mobile in a short time, at which Lieutenant Gaines appeared to be alarmed, and told me he was suspicious that the Spaniard would endeavor to rescue Col. Burr, and that he was unable to defend himself, as his pickets [his palisade?] were pulled down and some of his men were unfit for duty.[8]

As a soldier rather than a lawyer, Gaines was inadvertently confusing, somewhat, the subsequent case against Burr. An allegation that Burr and the Spanish authorities were conspiring together toward an "endeavor to rescue Burr" would not square with the misdemeanor charge that Burr planned an "assault against" those authorities. Of course it was not necessary that Burr have agreement from all Spanish officers to engage in such an "endeavor," only from enough of them. But such jurisprudential niceties were not of much importance at Fort

Stoddert, either to Gaines or to Burr. Gaines had the firepower. Burr was trapped. He could hardly encourage his visitor with Gaines and Perkins peering over their shoulders. So he jotted down an apparently innocuous note, asking politely for some wine, and handed it to the emissary, without bothering to inconvenience Gaines or Perkins by folding the paper.

What he desired, no doubt, was a garrote for Gaines, a stout rope for Perkins, and a battalion of grenadiers.

Benjamin Hawkins

Holding Burr at pistol-point, Gaines summoned three men picked for their burly resistance to charm, and assigned them to join Perkins's bounty hunters. The squad so composed was to convey the Vice President from Fort Stoddert along the "Three Chopped Way" to Fort Wilkinson, in Georgia, the first long leg of their journey to Richmond.

The "Three Chops" were the blazes left by Gaines's men on the trees along a track they built to permit horses to travel single file through the forest from the head of navigation on the Tombigbee watershed, a widening called Lake Tensaw, to the forts and settlements in Georgia, on the Oconee River. It was Gaines's highest achievement to date, permitting the mail to be carried to and from the fractious 'Bigbee settlements. It followed an Indian pathway, past the abandoned French Fort Toulouse, and the ruins of the trading posts of the McIntoshes and MacGillivrays, to the Creek agency, where, awaiting them, crouched Benjamin Hawkins, the government's chief representative among the Muskogee.

(Gaines ascended rapidly thereafter. He was a general in the War of 1812 and fought the Creeks and Seminoles in Alabama and Florida and the Sacs and Foxes in Wisconsin. In 1819–20, he served as Jackson's deputy in the seizure of Florida, thereby completing—without acknowledgment—the work as discussed between Burr and Jackson in 1805.)

President Jefferson could count on Hawkins, a North Carolina politician steadfast in devotion to any President in power, whose career as a magnetized particle commenced as an adherent to George Washington. After his Federalist years, Hawkins was assisted into Jeffersonian ranks by his North Carolina colleague Nathaniel Macon, "Jefferson's dispenser of federal patronage." Among the "better known and most influential Federalists . . . [who might respond to] an understanding between Macon and Jefferson," Hawkins was approached in June 1801 and offered a commission to "negotiate" with the southwestern Indian tribes for land, choice pieces of which might be "cherry picked" by the commissioners. "Hawkins at once accepted and was thereafter lost to the Federalist party." And what was won? "Hawkins was won," writes another historian specializing in the intricacies of patronage, "and he was continued many years in the lucrative office of Indian Commissioner to the Creek Nation."[9]

Unlike his counterparts Silas Dinsmoor and James Seagrove, Hawkins would do nothing to risk that fat opportunity, so, as soon as he heard of Burr's "arrest near Tombigbee," he wrote his agents down the road to look out for him.

> The officer having him in charge should deliver him only to the orders of the President . . . [N]o person but a commissioned officer [should] be permitted to have any conversation with him and . . . he be not permitted to write any letters to any person.[10]

There had been no judicial proceeding. Yet a former Vice President was to be allowed neither conversation nor opportunity to communicate. No indeed! Hawkins asserted that his model was "the order of General Wilkinson in the case of Doctor Bollmann and I think a proper one."[11]

The Case of Bollmann

That reference makes it easy for anyone acquainted with the history of heroism and technology in the early years of the American Republic to decide what to think of Benjamin Hawkins. Hawkins had chosen his side. Justus Eric Bollmann (1769–1821) was a physician, trained at Göttingen, who became an engineer, waterworks promoter, artificial-flower manufacturer, and friend to Burr and to Benjamin Henry Latrobe. He first became famous for his role in a harebrained but magnificent effort to liberate Lafayette from an Austrian prison at Ollmutz.[12]

When that attempt failed, Bollmann himself was captured and imprisoned for the first time—the second was by Thomas Jefferson, for

helping Burr. Bollmann came to the United States in 1796 and pros-
pered supplying the American forces against France in the Quasi-War.
Heeding a request from Lafayette, Jefferson offered him the role on
Haiti which Edward Stevens had performed for Hamilton. Bollmann
declined and in 1805 was given, instead, the Indian agency at Natchitoches, possibly as one of the last-minute accommodations given Burr
just before the trial of Justice Chase.

Bollmann was active in soliciting settlers for the Bastrop Tract and,
in the process had the misfortune to carry one of the letters from Burr
to Wilkinson which the latter altered and interpolated with forgeries,
making it appear that there was a conspiracy afoot. Presumably to keep
him quiet, Wilkinson had him locked up in New Orleans without warrant. When a federal judge freed him under habeas corpus, Wilkinson
defied the court, seized Bollmann and Samuel Swartwout, placed them
on board a ship, and shipped them off to Virginia under the con-
straints which seemed so commendable to Hawkins. The judge in New
Orleans was so appalled by Wilkinson's brand of propriety that he
refused to meet with his court while Wilkinson reigned.

As soon as Bollmann reached Washington, he was brought under
guard before the President of the United States, to be interrogated
personally. Given every encouragement to join the list of government
witnesses, he insisted that Burr had planned nothing beyond another
expedition against Spain. In the presence of other government officers, Jefferson assured Bollmann that any statement he might compose
of the details of his conversations with Burr would never leave the
President's hands. Swartwout and Bollman then engaged counsel to
petition the Supreme Court for habeas corpus, and the high court set
them free.

Jefferson proceeded to break his promise to Bollmann, whose statement was conveyed to the prosecution, together with a sheaf of blank
pardons to be issued to him, or to anyone else willing to offer testimony favorable to the President's case. So confident was the prosecution that George Hay, Jefferson's lead lawyer, entered into this
exchange with Bollmann: "Categorically then I ask you, Mr. Bollmann,
do you accept your pardon?" But Bollmann would not be bought: "I
say no!"[13]

Bollmann persisted with the same answers he had given earlier and
was thereafter barred from further federal employment. Nonetheless,
he remained a patriotic American. In 1815, he returned from the Con-

gress of Vienna bearing "special dispatches to our government." Latrobe reported that "his views . . . would be immediately seized . . . if
prejudice and passion, and collateral views did not govern the world,
to the exclusion of every proper motive."[14]

"The case of Doctor Bollmann" was a case of picking the losing
side in 1807 and remaining adamant against bribes and bullying. Not
so the case of Hawkins, who eagerly sent for approval by Secretary of
War Dearborn the instructions he had issued to his subagents, with
this cringing addition:

> The party having him [Burr] under guard, skulked through, un-
> der fears from the exaggerated reports of the numbers who ad-
> hered to him, that it was possible he might be rescued. [But not
> in Hawkins's agency. Oh my, No!] . . . there is not one man in
> the agency who would have joined him, or given the least coun-
> tenance to him, and his projects.[15]

If that were true, why all the fuss? On that frontier no possibility
can be dismissed as absurd: Let us recall two celebrated rescues of his
time. The first was the heisting of John Sevier from a treason trial in
Morgantown, Tennessee, in 1788. As we saw earlier, Sevier's Franklin-
ites, despairing of help from the feeble Confederation, communicated
to Spanish officials in New Orleans and Pensacola that "they wished
to place themselves under the protection of the King of Spain."[16]

The governor of North Carolina, Samuel Johnston, promptly declared "that John Sevier, who styles himself as Captain-General of the
State of Franklin, has been guilty of high treason" and had him cor-
ralled by a posse. In Tennessee, the rest of the story goes this way:

> The chivalry of the country gathered together . . . armed to the
> teeth . . . determined to rescue their beloved commander. . . .
> Their plan was to obtain his release by a stratagem, and if that
> failed, to fire the town, and in the hurry and confusion, burst the
> prison doors by force, and make their escape. . . .
> [T]he rescue party, bringing with it Sevier's celebrated race
> mare, saddled and ready to ride, entered Morgantown quietly,
> one by one, and sauntered calmly into the court room, where
> they found Sevier . . . firm and undaunted. . . . Meanwhile, a
> member of the party, named Evans, had brought the racehorse
> to a place which could be seen from the courtroom door, and,

catching Sevier's eye, let him know that his rescuers had come and were ready to ride. Sevier, so the story goes, immediately dashed from the room, jumped into the saddle, and with his party, made a mad dash for the mountains—and home.[17]

Sevier was never tried. He became the first governor of the new State of Tennessee, elected to that office three times, and was still serving in 1798, when William Blount, his ally and Tennessee's U.S. senator, lapsed into his negotiations with Great Britain. Blount was indiscreet. He entrusted his thoughts to the mails and became the first senator to be expelled from that August conclave under threat of impeachment, but Blount was *not* disgraced in Tennessee. When the Senate sergeant-at-arms, James Mathews, came thence to bring Blount back to the national capital for trial, Mathews was "entertained with apparently sincere hospitality for several days. When he finally decided it was time to leave with his prisoner, "a body of horsemen appeared and told him pleasantly that they would ride out with him to start him on his way—but that he could not take William Blount off of Tennessee soil. . . . Mathews made the rest of his journey alone. Eventually, for a variety of legal reasons, the impeachment charges were dismissed."[18]

In Tennessee, given a good horse or two, one could lasso the English common law and bring it to the ground like a steer in a rodeo.

The situation was much the same in upcountry Georgia and South Carolina. Pickett's *History* tells us that Perkins and his posse skulked through every settlement and fort along the way, taking special care in such places as Buzzard's Roost, where the backwoods men outnumbered the military.

Gaines's forest track had neither bridges nor ferries. It was February. Even in Alabama, February is cold. Occasionally there were canoes in which the prisoner and his guard could travel while the horses swam alongside, but often Burr was made to swim frigid streams between armed men or to ride across shallows as high as the girth of his horse.

Hundreds of Indians . . . thronged the trail, and the party might have been killed in one moment. . . . In the journey through Alabama the guard always slept in the woods, near swamps of reed, upon which the belled and hobbled horses fed during the night. After breakfast, it was their custom again to mount their horses and march on, with a silence which was sometimes broken by a remark about the weather, the creeks, or the Indians. . . . Though drenched for hours with cold . . . rain, and at night extended upon a thin pallet, on the bare ground, yet, in the whole distance to Richmond, this remarkable man was never heard to complain that he was sick, or even fatigued.[19]

Elijah Clarke and His Trans-Oconee Ruins

West of the Oconee, the Perkins party traversed the strip of land secured from the Creek Nation by the Forbes "Purchase" of 1805, made possible by the removal from the scene of the proto-Burr William Augustus Bowles. Then they came amid the charred remains of the little forts and villages, overgrown by brush and poison ivy, of the Trans-Oconee Republic established in 1794 by another proto-Burr, Elijah Clarke. At each fort and hamlet, Burr was crossing over the experience of others who had attempted some of the things he tried, but with quite different results. Bowles, too, had been kidnapped at McIntosh Bluffs, only five years before Burr was taken into custody, and had suffered the fate Wilkinson might have provided Burr: an obscure death while in custody.

Clarke preceded Burr to the Oconee by nearly a decade, but his case was even more precisely comparable. He was a Revolutionary patriot rather than a Tory like Bowles, and though he succeeded in setting himself up as an independent sovereign just beyond the limits of land governed by the United States, as Burr might have done in Texas, he had been brought up short by the federal government, acquiesced, collapsed his republic, and went home. As a patriot, he no more contemplated civil war than did Burr. In 1807, the offense charged against Burr was one Clarke had committed, yet Clarke was permitted to live out his years on a Revolutionary pension as an honored old gentleman. Though Burr was declared *not* guilty of treason, and the Virginia allegation of a misdemeanor was never brought to trial, his Revolutionary pension was withheld from him until Andrew Jackson restored it when it was almost too late to be of use.

Fort Wilkinson

Fort Wilkinson, one of several Wilkinson named as monuments to himself, was a pleasant little post. Its garrison of thirty could bring their families to live in cabins outside the walls, and the commander, Colonel Boot, had created a vineyard along the river with vines sent him by Lafayette—or so it is said in Milledgeville, the city that has grown up around it.

After a breakfast below the ramparts of Fort Wilkinson, at the house of William Bivins, Burr and his captors set off toward Augusta. Perkins redoubled his precautions, having been warned by an incident at Fort Wilkinson that Burr was not without a potential following. Burr's captors had risked the shelter of a tavern, arousing the curiosity of its host, who began asking questions about the prisoner. James Parton, Burr's biographer, tells us what ensued:

> Burr, who was sitting in the corner near the fire, raised his head, and, fixing his blazing eyes upon the unsuspecting landlord, said, "I am Aaron Burr—what is it you want with me?"
>
> The poor landlord, amazed at the information, and struck with the majestic manner of the man, stood aghast, and without a syllable of reply, glided about the house, offering the party the most obsequious attentions.[20]

From Fort Wilkinson to Augusta, there were no further incidents. But "two days later brought them to the confines of South Carolina, where Burr from old had been a popular favorite."[21]

Perkins did not dare to risk the main road, taking instead the backwoods route for the village of Chester, where a stone monument on the main street memorializes the next series of events.

> Perkins . . . changed the order of their march, placing two men in front of the prisoner, two more behind, and one on each side of him. In this manner they . . . passed near a tavern, before which a considerable number of persons were standing, while music and dancing were heard from within. Here, Burr threw himself from his horse, and exclaiming in a loud voice, "I am Aaron Burr, under military arrest, and claim the protection of the civil authorities." Perkins snatched his pistols from his holster, sprang to the ground, and in an instant was at the side of his prisoner. With a pistol in each hand, he sternly ordered him to remount. "I will not!" shouted Burr . . . Perkins, unwilling to shed blood, but resolute to execute the commission intrusted to him, threw his pistols upon the ground, caught the prisoner

round the waist . . . and threw him into the saddle. One of the guard[,] seizing the bridle of Burr's horse[,] led him rapidly away, and the whole party swept through the village in a mass, and disappeared.[22]

Malone later told listeners avid for tabloid detail that, when the party paused to regroup a few miles out of town, he found Burr weeping in anger and frustration, and others of the party, Malone included, weeping in sympathy. From that point onward, "Perkins . . . watched his prisoner more closely than ever, for in this State lived Colonel Joseph Alston—a man of talents and influence, afterwards governor—who had married the only daughter, and, indeed, the only child of Burr. Afraid that the prisoner would be rescued at some point in this State, he exhorted his men to renewed vigilance."[23]

Lest vigilance be insufficient, a means to convey his prisoner in secret was found; Perkins sneaked back into Chester, where he purchased a closed carriage. With Burr penned safely out of sight, the unhappy band made their way through the back roads of South Carolina on a trail leading northwest, away from the Alstons' enclave around Camden and Stateburg. Burr's daughter and her husband may actually have been less than seventy miles away, at their summer residence, worrying about Burr and wondering where he was. They did not learn that he had been spirited past until he was beyond their aid.

Once across the border in North Carolina, the peril of rescue came from the Scottish settlements lying along the upper reaches of the Cape Fear River and athwart the customary route of travel. Burr's caballing of 1802 and 1804 had left many a friend among the Highlanders of Scotland County and Cumberland County, friends whose folk life demanded of them that they rescue fallen political leaders: Every child had learned tales of Bonnic Prince Charlie, of the '45 and Flora MacDonald; the myth of rescue of fallen princes was engraved upon the soul of these people, superseding the rescue of a damsel in distress. And in 1807, into their midst, came a state prisoner, guarded by hired agents of the "court" of the rulers of the nation. So, lest the Scots seek to rescue another fallen prince, Perkins led his party off to the northward for another hundred and fifty backwoods miles, until, finally, in the carriage converted into a wheeled cell, their explosive captive was smuggled into Virginia.

As the cavalcade arrived beside the Staunton River, Burr was released to finish the journey to Richmond on his own horse. John Randolph peered from the window of his plantation at Roanoke and sought a glimpse of him as he and his guards rode past. On March 25, 1807, Randolph wrote Joseph Hopper Nicholson of Maryland: "Col. Burr (quantum mutatus ab illo!) passed by my door the day before yesterday under a strong guard." Five years earlier, it might have been otherwise, for Randolph had invited Burr to visit him at Roanoke, so that he might have "the pleasure of accompanying him through Virginia," and six months later, Randolph had his opportunity to set Burr free.[24]

22

Precedents and Justice

We have come to the climax of our story. Thomas Jefferson's charges against the character of Aaron Burr will be placed before judge and jury in a courtroom in Richmond, Virginia, in March and April 1807. And the character of Jefferson will be tested by the way he chooses to proceed. Not only will the matter be settled in the capital city of Jefferson's Virginia; three of his Virginian kinsmen will take key roles in settling it. The judge is John Marshall, Chief Justice of the United States. The foreman of the grand jury is Representative John Randolph of Roanoke. Another cousin, Edmond Randolph, formerly Attorney General of the United States, is one of Burr's attorneys.

The current Attorney General, Caesar Augustus Rodney, had achieved that eminence on January 20, 1807. When Burr was finally brought to trial on May 22 of that year, Rodney's appearance against him was remarkably brief and tepid. There was a quiet, apologetic speech, acknowledging, by implication, that public furor in the newspapers had prejudiced the public against the defendant.

> For my part, I wish nothing but that justice may be done. . . . I do not desire to take advantage of the reports which have resounded

through the newspapers . . . , and so strangely have agitated the public mind. . . . I rejoice that . . . men of talents and liberality have been found of sufficient independence of mind to come forward to defend the prisoner, notwithstanding the general opinion of his guilt.[1]

Then the Attorney General departed, maintaining a strange silence thereafter.

(It is worth noting that his subsequent career indicates that he became capable of considerable independence of the Virginia Dynasty. In 1820 Rodney vigorously and publicly opposed the expansion of slavery into Missouri and the West, which Jefferson endorsed. This conduct becomes somewhat more explicable in the light of what Rodney had learned in 1806 and 1807, and when we recall that his political base was in Delaware, a slave state but one which was demonstrating the fallacy of the Virginian argument that free blacks and whites could not coexist. By 1820, three quarters of the black population of Delaware was free, a reversal of the proportions of 1790.)

While they did not have roles in the formal workings of the court, two later southern presidents reflected upon the Burr trial, one of them a Virginian, and, implicitly, both rendered their judgments upon Jefferson's presidential role in it. When Woodrow Wilson stood at Burr's grave, he murmured: "How misunderstood—how maligned!" And during the trial itself, Andrew Jackson demonstrated his belief that Jefferson had maligned Burr; Jackson stormed about the city, picking fights with Jefferson's friends, challenging his star witness, James Wilkinson, to a duel, and proclaiming Burr innocent. "As easily fooled as any man I ever knew," Jackson called Burr, because the fooler, as Jackson knew from experience, was Wilkinson.[2]

Jackson learned to keep his opinion of Thomas Jefferson more carefully hidden, but there was never much doubt what it was. While passing through Virginia after his victory at New Orleans in 1815, Jackson received the congratulations of the Sage at a public dinner but wrote a friend: "I am glad the old gentleman has plucked up courage enough to at least attend a banquet in honor of a battle."[3]

John Marshall needed no help from Jackson to sort out his opinions of Jefferson, Burr, or Wilkinson. Marshall's father had emigrated to Kentucky and had for years informed his son about separatism and the reports that the general so favored by Jefferson was a traitor. Though he was a junior lieutenant to Brigadier General Wilkinson at Valley Forge in 1778–79, Marshall had heard what was said in the camp about his opinions of Marshall's hero, George Washington. So, when Wilkinson vomited upon the hearing in Richmond his gallimauferous perjury, the Chief Justice evidenced his incredulity as clearly as did both Randolphs.

The Burr trial at Richmond, in 1807, has been described and dramatized many times. We will not do that work again but will merely bring together, in Richmond, a number of earlier themes in our story. Before we do that, however, we must provide the terminus of a tale left unfinished earlier and explain why it was that one witness did not appear in Richmond.

James Wilkinson was there, as commander of all the American forces in the West, confidante of the President of the United States, and star witness against the defendant, Aaron Burr. Robert Newman was not. Anthony Wayne's special agent sought out Wilkinson to elicit from him some explanation of his separatist activity, as well as his plot against Wayne. Nothing in the whole history of Wilkinson's beguilements is so astonishing as his ability to convince Newman not to come forward and support Burr by discrediting the general. Here is what Newman wrote of that occasion:

> General Wilkinson . . . gave the whole of the transactions in the western country such a turn, that, in spite of myself, I have been in part deceived. . . . But General Wilkinson, in Richmond, admitted to me he had held a correspondence with the Spaniards on the subject, but declared most solemnly that he never seriously designed the dismemberment of the Union; and that his only object was to cheat the Spaniards of their money, and that he had cheated them out of half a million dollars for himself and his friends.[4]

So much for Newman.

Let us return to the two charges made against Aaron Burr by Thomas Jefferson: the misdemeanor of violating George Washington's Neutrality Law of 1794 by planning an expedition against the possessions of Spain, a nation with which the United States was at peace; and treason. Jefferson's presidential proclamation of 1806, his explanation to Congress that it was Burr against whom that proclamation had been issued, and his subsequent accusations leading to the Richmond Trial all charged Burr with assembling an army (and a very small navy) to separate the western states and territories from the Union.

Memories of the Whiskey Rebellion, ten years earlier, were reignited in Richmond. During the intervening years no President had nationalized the militias of several states, nor had justices of the Supreme Court been summoned to preside over a treason trial. Furthermore, Jefferson's attorneys made much of the definition of treason propounded in the trials of the Whiskey Rebels by Justice Paterson, which seemed to open the way to a broad indictment, like that made presidentially by Jefferson. There was language in Paterson's charge which might make it possible to indict a defendant though the act alleged to have been treasonable had not been observed, as the Constitution required, by two credible witnesses. It was essential to Jefferson's case that some way be found around the constitutional standard, for no one could be found to testify that Aaron Burr had been present at any time when armed men assembled to disrupt the orderly process of government. It would have been a convenience if Paterson had provided that detour, for Marshall was known to admire Paterson as a judge and as a man.

Recalling a Real Rebellion

It became important, therefore, to recall to everyone in the courtroom who Paterson was and enough of the circumstances of the Whiskey Rebellion to permit a comparison of those before Paterson to those before Marshall. Having risen through the New Jersey governorship and the U.S. Senate, Paterson had been appointed to the U.S. Supreme Court by George Washington in 1793 just in time to preside over the Whiskey Rebellion trials, the first to deal with treason in American history.

It was interesting, though not germane, that Paterson had been Burr's mentor in the law and his friend from childhood. It is probable that both Burr and Marshall also knew that Marshall's predecessor, Chief Justice Oliver Ellsworth, had expressed apprehension that if Paterson left the Court to take a diplomatic post, John Adams might appoint Burr to his place. Ellsworth was an even fiercer Federalist than Marshall.

Let us recall the circumstances leading to Paterson's definition of peacetime treason. In 1794, an insurrection, centered in Pennsylvania, extended into Kentucky, western Virginia, and New York. Thousands of rebels marched into Pittsburgh, threatening to create a separate state. They destroyed the operations of the courts and revenue system and required President Washington and Secretary Hamilton to raise an army to restore order. Jefferson had expressed sympathy for the rebels, disaffection from the actions of the President, and derision for the role of Hamilton.

The prosecutor in the Whiskey Rebellion case, William Rawle, defined treason to mean "raising a body of men to obtain, by intimidation or violence, the *repeal* of a law [emphasis added]." To seek repeal of a law by force was nullification carried to its logical extreme. When it was done by a group of individuals, it was, therefore, "an act of levying war," whatever it might be if done peacefully by a state legislature. Rawle's definition made violence and intimidation, on the part of all or part of a body of men, the factor which made treasonous what otherwise would be a constitutionally protected assembly. That right, Paterson agreed, was limited to peaceable assembly.

It remained, however, of importance to a democratic society. Neither Rawle nor Paterson proposed that it be abrogated unless the intention to be violent was demonstrated—and seen to be demonstrated by two credible witnesses—by the presence of weapons among the assembled crowd and by subsequent behavior of force or intimidation. The only exception to these requirements was that rebels would be guilty of treason if they either carried arms or were so numerous that their intimidation was sufficiently threatening without arms. There was no difficulty in finding witnesses to both the weapons and the magnitude of the mob.

That being true, Paterson permitted himself to refer to certain British precedents extending the implication of treason to include those conspiring with others, or inducing others, to commit armed defiance of law, though not all of them were armed or were present when the induced behavior reached violence. It became obvious that if one could be proved to have defiance in mind, then one should avoid gathering together with others if any of them carried a weapon.[5]

What if one could be proved to have consorted with such people before they came to such an assembly? Had Paterson meant to set the halter about all such persons? John Marshall had to sort out that question, because Paterson's language was indistinct. It was helpful that the differences between the circumstances of 1794 and those of 1804 were very clear.

John Mitchell, the defendant of 1794, was a bellicose brawler who had assembled with others, in arms, for the assault on Pittsburgh. He had joined in an attack upon a tax collector's house in which people were killed. He had robbed the mails to disrupt the government's communications. In each of these actions, he was seen by scores of people. Aaron Burr had done none of these things, so, naturally enough, no one could say he had seen Burr do them. That left Paterson's charge to the jury about what the twentieth century called "guilt by association." When that language was laid before Marshall by Jefferson's lawyers, he responded that "Judge Paterson required the constitutional proof of two witnesses to the same overt act." What if Paterson had permitted the detour of the Constitution requested by the government's case against Burr? That, Marshall said with some heat, would have been to say "that Mitchell was constructively present, and might, on the straining of legal fiction, be found guilty of treason." What then? "Had he [Paterson] given this opinion, it would have required all the correctness of his life to strike his name from that bloody list in which the name of Jeffreys is enrolled."[6]

Marshall's words were carefully chosen, and they could be clearly heard in Washington. The First Baron Jeffreys, also known as "the infamous Jeffreys," had presided over the "Bloody Assizes" and was responsible for the judicial murder of Algernon Sidney in one of a series of political trials during the reign of King James II. The reference was clear. A sovereign, James, had been so eager to rid himself of political enemies that he had found a judicial executioner in Jeffreys. Marshall had no intention of joining the "bloody list" to suit Thomas Jefferson.

Comparing the "circumstances" of the Whiskey Rebels "to Burr's case," wrote the Chief Justice, "the prisoner at the bar was neither legally nor actually present at Blennerhasset's island [where an allegedly armed crowd had assembled in 1806] . . . and . . . the overt act laid in this indictment cannot be proved."[7]

In 1806, there was no insurrection. In 1794, Washington and Hamilton felt themselves required to raise an army of nine thousand men to restore order. Even if one were to accuse them of overreacting to deal with the two thousand rebels who marched into Pittsburgh, what is one to say of Jefferson's mobilizing fleets and armies against Burr's sixty adventurers with their sporting rifles? Washington's rebels took Pittsburgh. Burr's friends could not have taken Bruinsburg, if they had been so inclined. In any case, they came as guests and quietly submitted to Jefferson's gunboats, cavalry, and infantry.

Consolation Prizes

Once Justice Marshall made it clear that Jefferson could not have Burr's head by the use of the methods of Justice Jeffreys, that the Constitution's definitions had superseded British concepts of constructive treason, Jefferson's case fell apart. The Virginia jury concurred with those of Kentucky and Mississippi, and for the third time Burr was acquitted of treason. Indeed, the Virginians declined even to hold him in custody on the misdemeanor charge.

Nonetheless, the fever of hate which had seized Thomas Jefferson did not so quickly disperse. John Marshall had refused the role of either Judge Jeffreys or Judge Lynch, so Jefferson went after him next with a threat of impeachment. Burr's management of the case of Justice Chase, and Luther Martin's bulldog arguments for both defendants, had set the limits to the removal of judges for their political opinions. Jefferson had to content himself with ordering the U.S. marshal in New Orleans to seize property owned by Edward Livingston, who had made no secret of his affinity to Burr. Going after Livingston was a mistake, for he turned out to be more resilient than Burr himself and responded with his own suit against Jefferson for exceeding his powers. We are left to wonder what would have happened if Burr had done the same.

However, as Martin had warned in 1804 that he would do, Jefferson had a media plan. Gideon Granger's Post Office renewed its printing contracts with publishers of local political newspapers, and the word went out: Burr was really guilty. The Constitution was a mere technicality. Marshall was out to get Jefferson. Burr won in court and lost in the newspapers.

In major ironic measure, this was because the public had come to trust what Presidents said. Washington had trained them, and the craggy, uncompromising integrity of John Adams had not betrayed Washington's majestic example. Jefferson was the first President to make to the people assertions he later admitted were not true. He proclaimed that Aaron Burr constituted a threat to the unity of the United States, then later said that only a madman would believe that was the case.

However, belated acknowledgment that false witness has been borne is throwing a life jacket on the site of a drowning. Jefferson drowned Burr in calumny. After 1807, many who knew the truth, people such as Albert Gallatin and John Quincy Adams, kept silence. Burr was a poor risk. They could not help much anyway. And both had thirty years of public life before them. So, despite the Chief Justice and the grand jury, enough of the people have been fooled enough of the time to require of each new generation a reappraisal of the characters of Aaron Burr, Thomas Jefferson, and, to a lesser extent, Gallatin and Adams.

After the trial and Burr's subsequent self-imposed exile, his followers took what was left of his boats and provisions to New Orleans, sold them, divided the proceeds, and then dispersed into the region around Natchez, becoming "school masters, singing masters, dancing masters, clerks, tavern keepers, and doctors."[8]

There were of course, more eminent casualties. When Burr arrived at Cincinnati, in 1805, he had met with Senator John Smith of Ohio, an antislavery Republican. Ohio had recently acquired another opponent to the spread of slavery with the arrival of Thomas Worthington, a "man of his time" from Virginia, who had acted upon Jefferson's stated principles and manumitted his slaves. In 1807, Smith was brought before the Senate on charges of conspiring with Burr, though Burr had just been discharged from his Richmond Trial. Smith was acquitted in a proceeding managed by John Quincy Adams and Jesse Franklin. It has seldom been noted that they, too, were opposed to slavery (though Adams was only privately so at the time). If one takes this factor into account, a fresh look is required at their actions in the Smith case.

French Accessories

While reappraisals are going forward, we may permit ourselves to be reminded of our earlier flash forward to 1810 for the purpose of debriefing M. Roux, the enthusiastic minion of Napoleon's duc de Cadore, as he reported to his chief on his interrogation of Aaron Burr as to his intentions for the West. M. Roux and Cadore provoke us to reflect upon the story of French participation in American affairs. Though it is not conventional to put as much emphasis as we have placed upon Genêt, Volney, Brissot, Michaux, Collot, and Moreau, the power of France has been felt throughout this tale. That is scarcely surprising. France was the dominant military power in the world; only by chivvying together a series of coalitions against the French were the British able to hold Napoleon at bay.

According to John Adams, Thomas Jefferson was never happier than in Paris, in the ancien régime. Certainly Burr was never unhappier than in Paris in 1810, except when death struck his family. Scarcely any sequence of events in these pages transpired without being affected by French people of one political stripe or another. That was true of Burr's western expedition as well. It is entirely possible that it was urged upon him by his friend General Moreau. We know an expedition into the Spanish borderlands was in Burr's mind as early as 1796, when he discussed it first with John Jay, and James Wilkinson pressed the idea as soon as his first choice, Alexander Hamilton, fell from grace. It seems likely that Moreau talked about the idea in 1804, before Burr went to reconnoiter East Florida.

In any case, it was not a novel notion: It had been discussed in Flanders in 1793–94 by Miranda and by Americans serving in the French army, among them Colonel Eleazar Oswald, Lieutenant John Cox, and John Skey Eustace. Eustace had already reconnoitered Venezuela before he rose to become a general in the French service under Moreau. Their scheme became common currency, as Joel Barlow submitted to the French government a plan to "take Louisiana at no cost to the nation." (Louisiana was still in Spanish hands.)[9]

When he returned in 1806 to visit Moreau, Burr had been to East Florida and was ready to think seriously about Louisiana. Another visitor, Paul Henry Mallet Prevost, a cousin of Burr's wife, saw a map of the Spanish frontier on Moreau's table and asked Burr about it. The reply was that as soon as hostilities commenced between Spain and the United States the people of the West would rise to join in the liberation of Mexico, and Prevost should join in the fun. Prevost, a prudent Swiss, declined, but Burr wrote Charles Biddle to summarize what he and Moreau had in mind.

A number of gentlemen of the first respectability . . . wished him [Burr] to form a settlement on the Mississippi of military men; that the Spaniards he knew were ripe for revolt, and would make the fortunes of all those revolutionizing that country. . . . He would have collected a number of military men round him near the lines, formed a barrier between us and the Spaniards which would have prevented their ever disturbing us.[10]

In 1807, after the collapse of Burr's plan and his trial in Richmond, Moreau decided to make a foray into the West on his own. After a jolly dinner in Philadelphia with Erich Bollmann, Burr, John Cummins of Natchez, Harmon Blennerhasset, and Vincent Nolte (whose memoirs were fictionalized in the novel *Anthony Adverse*), Moreau set forth for New Orleans with Nolte and Bollmann. Their arrival convulsed the Spanish authorities, who not only recalled William Augustus Bowles and Philip Nolan but summoned as well the ghosts of Hamilton and Burr. Now a French hero might substitute for an American. Madrid demanded written explanations from any colonial official who had the temerity to converse with Moreau, but, as he had shown in Paris, there was no need for worry. Moreau was not constituted for conspiracy. Having concluded that he could not succeed where Burr had failed, he returned to New Jersey.

Five years later, after he was persuaded that only an allied victory would restore to France a republican government, Moreau was on the field at Dresden, giving advice to the Czar, as Russians, Austrians, and Prussians in their hundreds of thousands were arrayed against Napoleon in the "Battle of the Nations." On the twenty-seventh of August, 1813, Moreau was struck by a cannonball and mortally wounded. As he died he was heard to say: "Soyez tranquilles, messieurs; c'est mon sort."[11]

It was a sentiment one might expect from Burr under similar circumstances—and in French, a language he used often—had fate provided Alexander Hamilton with a steadier hand or a better set of eyeglasses.

Among the many French emigrés who gathered in the neighborhood of Moreau and befriended Aaron Burr was Colonel Julien de Pestre. De Pestre had served as a colonel under the Bourbon flag of France, and had settled in Saint Domingue, where he married into the de Mun family. In France the de Muns were only minor nobility, but in the colonies they were nabobs. Nabobery did not last long in the sugar islands, however; de Pestre and the de Muns were driven from the island by the revolution of Toussaint Louverture. De Pestre settled across the Delaware from Moreau "with the wreck of an immense fortune," but he was not a man to repose in a wreck. In 1806, he sold the New Jersey farm and became Burr's chief of staff in the West. His brother-in-law Louis de Mun became one of Latrobe's draftsmen, working with Robert Mills on the designs for shallow-draft boats designed to carry Burr's expedition down the Ohio and Mississippi.[12]

Though Latrobe and de Pestre were both ordered by Jefferson to come to Richmond for Burr's trial in 1807, they made themselves unappetizing to the prosecution by insisting upon the same truth asserted by Thomas Truxton. They insisted that Burr had contemplated neither treason nor division of the western from the eastern states. Recalling a conversation with de Pestre, Latrobe wrote:

> He laughed at the idea of separation, as being entertained by Mr. Burr. Dep[estre] had viewed the lands on the Ohio and had a good idea of the advantages and disadvantages of a settlement to the westward [into which to reinvest the proceeds of selling his New Jersey farm]. . . . As to Colonel B. his opinion was, that he would make some exertion to retrieve the loss of character and fortune he had suffered, but certainly had no intention of attempting a dismemberment of the Union.
>
> Of Col. Burr he spoke as being *bien aimable,* and as a man of great genius, and enterprise, but too sanguine, and who probably would fail from precipitancy, in any thing he might undertake.[13]

De Pestre and de Mun had seen enough of revolution, war, and harebrained heroics. They followed Burr loyally until convinced of his folly. Even then, however, like Truxton they refused to lie about him, though this required of them an even more robust code of honor than that demonstrated by Truxton. He was a rich man. All that Jefferson could deny to *him* was another command at sea. De Mun, though a nobleman, was poor; his employer, Latrobe, was a notoriously improvident genius. So when de Mun was among those suborned to perjure themselves against Burr, his proud rejection of the offer, as recounted by Latrobe, was especially telling:

> Col. de Pestre informed me that his brother-in-law, a promising young man of various merit, had been turned out of his place as

Clerk in the War Office, because he could not accuse the Col. of Burr-ism; and afterward, some honorable friends of the government had the delicacy to insinuate how handsomely the Col. might be provided for in the army, if his principles or engagements were not adverse to the administration.[14]

After the Burr trial, de Mun went into exile once again, joining his brothers in Cuba. Later, having listened once more to echoes of the ambitions of 1806–7, he returned for the mainland, and in 1816 he was reported to be "engaged in a great land concern west of the Mississippi."[15]

Before we leave the New Jersey French, let us leap ahead once more, to savor another set of coincident circumstances, though, it must be admitted, they do not much illuminate character: When Jacob Lewis of Marblehead introduced Aaron Burr to Florida, he was only Captain Lewis. Two years later, it seems that on the strength of his acquisition of another ship he was called "commodore" by de Pestre, who is our source for the report that Commodore Lewis was to convey a group of French junior officers on his ship *Emperor* from New York to New Orleans to join Burr. In 1815, Commodore Lewis recognized Joseph Bonaparte the brother of *the* Emperor, at a fashionable boardinghouse in New York. Joseph, who had himself briefly been Emperor of the Spanish dominions, had escaped the British at the time his brother Napoleon was packed off to St. Helena. Lewis took pride in chivalrously refusing to reveal his identity to the others in the house, though one may doubt that he was the only person present to note Joseph's family resemblance to the most recognizable man of the time. In any case, Joseph expressed gratitude and accepted residence with the Lewises before taking a lease on a Hudson River property. He soon moved on to Burlington, New Jersey.

We return, now, to our serious business.

23

Groundsprings of Wrath

In 1808, Jefferson rid himself of Aaron Burr. His campaign to achieve that outcome reached back, we can now be fairly certain, as far as 1794. During the interval Jefferson used Burr, from time to time, to serve political necessity, but never, he said, because he liked him. The reasons for Jefferson's settled animus are the subject of our inquiry in this chapter, which is written in full acknowledgment of the difficulty of descrying the motivations of anyone, living or, especially, dead; more especially, of a dead politician; and most especially, of Thomas Jefferson.

Let us start with the stipulation that Jefferson did not welcome competition and that Burr was a real competitor. Hamilton, who is often placed as the statue opposite Jefferson, really was not fully competitive. He was too volatile, too impolitic, too much the victim of his own resentments. Though contending with Hamilton was a formidable intellectual challenge, he was not, as a politician, a rival to either Jefferson or Burr. Though John Jay once considered appointing him to the U.S. Senate, he was never elected to an office under the Constitution he so ably advocated. And, as we noted in Chapter Three, he never received a vote in the electoral college, while Burr was being seriously considered for the presidency in 1792, 1796, and 1800.

Hamilton would not have been a rival to Jefferson in real politics even if he had not been a foreigner, like Gallatin. That may be one reason why the Jeffersonians assumed he would have to ride to the White House on a white horse, at the head of an army. Burr, on the other hand, could get there by election and was descended from the true American aristocracy, the gentry of the cloth and the mind.

Doing in a competitor is an outcome as devoutly to be wished in politics as in business, but it is seldom either necessary or desirable to hate that competitor. Hatred inflames the mind and congests its passages. It is not easy to think while hating. The evidence is overwhelming that Jefferson hated Burr and also that he did not think clearly when dealing with him. The ferocity of his feelings is greater than we would expect from so cool a practitioner if his antagonist could be dismissed merely as a clever scamp. Burr must have been more than that, worse than that, to him or he would have not pursued him as he did. And unless he both hated and feared Burr, his meticulous calculating brain would not have permitted him to give preferment at public expense to the array of characters he employed against Burr, including the despicable Wilkinson, Granger, Eaton, and the Morgans. He would not otherwise have exposed his reputation to contamination from them.

Those who have paid attention to Jefferson's choice of agents against Burr wonder at his lack of fastidiousness, and wonder as well at the absence of finesse in his tactics in dealing with everyone associated with Burr: Bollmann, Swartwout, Ogden, Adair, John Smith, and Harmon Blennerhasset were dealt with very sloppily. Even Jefferson's language became imprecise and verged on the vulgar.

West by Southwest

There must have been something in Aaron Burr which drove Thomas Jefferson a little mad. . . .

No. That is not quite right. Like Hamlet, he was not mad in all points of the compass—only west by southwest. When Burr entered the southwest of his mind, Jefferson became unjeffersonian. Why was he so sensitive in that quarter? What was it that Burr might do there which was of such intense importance to him?

Let us begin the search for answers by grounding ourselves in the patent fact that the southwestern borderlands were of intense geopolitical importance to any American statesman, Jefferson or Burr included. The military capacity of the Indian nations, if they assembled in a strategic alliance in that quarter, was considerably greater than that of the forces the United States could put there. Though Spain was not able to assemble such an alliance to stand between the Americans and Mexico, Britain and France had both sustained long-standing relationships to the native nations and might renew their coalition-building. Had the British invasion of Louisiana at the end of 1814 occurred two years earlier, while Andrew Jackson was fighting it out with the Creeks, it is entirely likely that the War of 1812 would be known today as the Great Creek and British War, with an outcome hideous for American patriots to contemplate.

Jefferson had every reason to fear disruptions of the fragile defenses his government had in place in 1808, and his acute observation of the deficiencies in Spain's attempted use of American settlers to garrison its borders led him shrewdly to propose the opposite deployment once Burr was gone. Americans would garrison the American frontier—but not with Burr in command. Jefferson addressed to the Senate the following proposal early in 1808:

> It is now, perhaps, become as interesting to obtain footing for a strong settlement of militias, along our southern frontier, east-ward of the Mississippi, as on the west of that river. . . . The consolidation of the Mississippi Territory, and the establishment of a barrier of separation between the Indians and our southern neighbors, are also important objects.[1]

To this manifestation of the continuity of his views from the 1780s onward, Jefferson added his genius as a sharpener of actionable language. He had created many a phrase—such as "all men are created equal," "a New Order in the Ages,"* and "the Empire of Liberty"—that had, like other weapons, their own imperatives. He was required to take them seriously.

---

*The Latin phrase on the Great Seal of the Republic, "Novo Ordo Saecularum," could also be read as "New Order in the Universe"—denoting either time or place.

The proposition as to the equality of humankind was placed by Jefferson into the Declaration of Independence. It was linked to the high aspiration stated in the Great Seal to hold the founding of the United States to a new standard among nations, a "new birth of freedom," as Abraham Lincoln put it. And the Louisiana Purchase was to provide, in liberty's empire, a new birth, with a renewed intention to produce a society dedicated to the proposition that all men are created equal.

Jefferson could not escape the knowledge that after issuing a call to conscience in 1776, and after proclaiming both a New Order of the Universe and an Empire of Liberty, he had done very little to resist the infestation of that New Order and its Empire by the old sin of slavery.

For slaves, there would be no benign new order, and in the Southwest, no Empire of Liberty. In fact, it would have been better for them if the arrival of the Americans had sustained the old order, because the French and Spanish slave codes were not philanthropic, but they were considerably less brutal than the system imported into the American South from Barbados and then extended across the Mississippi toward Texas.

In 1803, Jefferson presented his countrymen with a second New Order, a renewed opportunity in the Mississippi Valley, with his Louisiana Purchase, raising afresh the entire question of slavery. Yet after that occasion was presented, he stood by while liberty and equality of opportunity were once more forfeited to the imperatives of slavery. Worse. He became an active participant in the degradation of the second grand opportunity he himself had offered his countrymen when, declaring moral bankruptcy, he sold off his own obstreperous slaves to be "disciplined" in Louisiana cane fields.

Having doubled the size of the United States through the Louisiana Purchase and having announced it as the Empire of Liberty, Jefferson observed it becoming, instead, the empire of slavery—and did nothing to prevent that outcome. And there, *there*, in Louisiana, Aaron Burr threatened to establish his own base and to reestablish *his own* reputation.

It was a question of both reputation and character. Is it possible that a man of Jefferson's imaginative breadth and subtle intelligence would have seen it otherwise? And, having seen it, how could he possibly abide the presence of a sly, mocking enemy within the space he had provided, moving within the intellectual and moral climate he, more than any other man, had created?

Jefferson had offered the charter in the Declaration and the space with the Purchase. He had failed in every test of his professed principles: failed in 1784 when he did not press for the Federalists' concept of a wall at the Appalachians against slavery; failed in 1787–89 when, even from Paris, he might have spoken out against the fugitive slave clauses of the Northwest Ordinance and of the Constitution itself; failed when Kentucky entered the Union as a slave state in 1792, joined by Tennessee four years later and by Mississippi Territory in 1798. As we assess what was possible for him, and what he believed himself to represent, beyond "the people," meaning the slaveowning people, of whom he wrote Brissot and Volney in 1789, we must recall how narrowly slavery won its triumphs while Jefferson was at his most influential and his most ambitious.

It was not inevitable that Kentucky would enter the Union with a slaveowners' constitution, nor that the planters of the Nashville Basin would triumph over the yeomen of East Tennessee on the question of slavery. Mississippi might have been the bulwark against slavery if men like Andrew Ellicott, Winthrop Sargent, and Silas Dinsmoor had had Jefferson's support. And in 1805–6, when the future of slavery within the Louisiana Purchase was debated, Jefferson was utterly silent.

The reader who has come this far with us may well ask: And was not Hamilton silent, as well? And Burr? They had taken up the cause of slaves in New York, and, as Secretary of the Treasury, Hamilton sought to convince President Washington not to deploy the moral force of the U.S. government to recover slaves freed by the British navy. But after Jefferson's victory in 1800, both fell silent. They cannot be excused merely because they had not invited the attention of the world to the creation of a New Order or of an Empire of Liberty. All three failed the test, Jefferson most conspicuously because Louisiana was the place where his failure to strive to achieve either, for persons enslaved, was most obvious.

And, if we believe him to have been a sensitive and moral being, the most painful to him. If it was not painful, what does that say? If it was, could he have been expected to welcome Aaron Burr into the aura of that distress? From the time of their shadow play over the presidency in 1800, and certainly after their open break in 1803, the insufferable mocking sotto voce of his Vice President echoed through the boardinghouses frequented by Burr and the antislavery members of Congress. Burr was always "caballing," while Jefferson, never a man for hobnobbery, could not, as President, go about town wrapped in a cloak, answering malicious laughter by picking up from boardinghouse tables copies of Gilbert Imlay's extended analysis of the disharmony between his antislavery professions in *Notes on the State of Virginia* and his actual behavior. The northern Federalist press was unsparing on the subject.

Burr did not risk much by private mockery; but however little we may admire his adaptation to the predominant political forces of his time, it was too much to expect Jefferson to tolerate amiably the abolitionist who had not been his preference for his Vice President in 1800. Burr had been placed on the ticket only because without Vice President Burr there would have been no President Jefferson.

The process of getting rid of him began the day after the electoral college voted. If Hamilton was Hotspur to Jefferson's Bolingbroke, Burr was to Jefferson both Falstaff and Prince Hal. He was witty, irreverent, and also a rival for power. Was Jefferson, who put up with Gideon Granger and James Wilkinson, morally affronted by Burr? Not likely. We must assume, instead, that Jefferson disliked him not so much for his lack of purity—he was a rogue—but for his lack of hypocrisy.

There is no way for us to learn whether or not Jefferson actually believed what Gideon Granger and James Wilkinson told him of Burr's plans to free the slaves in Louisiana. Yet even if he did not accept their story, their floating it was useful to him in rallying opposition to Burr in the South and detaching from Burr Wade Hampton, as much a power in Louisiana as in South Carolina. It is noteworthy that though Hampton loathed Wilkinson, he did not assist Burr.

It is said that Jefferson hated Burr. The statement is probably imprecise. He hated, that is true. But what he hated was what Burr *was for him*. That is how it was with Hamilton, and with many others in many other cases. Hating a comment in the form of a person is not rare, but it is seldom so manifest as in this instance.

Let us recall that while the inflammations of his brain were at their height in 1806–7, Jefferson put the armed forces of the United States on a wartime footing and insisted that "our Ministers at Paris, London, and Madrid . . . find out Burr's propositions and agents there," in his search for a worldwide conspiracy of terrifying scale. Though he later assured Du Pont de Nemours that anyone who had taken seriously Burr's chances of mobilizing a formidable force "must be perfectly ripe for bedlam," madness had been in the air. It was not, however, Burr's. When he was asked, many years afterward, if he ever contemplated separating the West from the East, he replied: "No, I would as soon have thought of taking possession of the moon."[2]

Let us bring back into the record the moment in 1807, after the verdict in the trial at Richmond, when, as if seized once more by wrath, Jefferson directed his lawyers not only to seek to impeach Marshall but also to see to it that no witness should be allowed to depart Richmond until he submitted an affidavit of his testimony, which was "now more important than ever!" (Jefferson's exclamation mark).

> The criminal is preserved to become the rallying-point of all the disaffected and worthless of the United States, and to be the pivot on which all the intrigues and conspiracies which foreign governments may wish to disturb us with, are to turn. If he is convicted of the misdemeanor, the judge must in decency give us respite by some short confinement of him.[3]

A respite? From what? Burr was done for. The question once more arises: Why did Jefferson so demean himself? He as an attorney and thus an "officer of the court." As master draftsman of the Declaration of Independence, he proclaimed a new society free of the capricious tyranny of a sovereign. As President, he was sworn to preserve and protect the Constitution. Yet this intelligent man, fully familiar with his obligations as lawyer and as President, offered to eager, impressionable William C. C. Claiborne—to whom he was more than Sage, he was demi-God—the counsel that in dealing with Burr and Burrites, the "strict line of the law" should be no barrier to a conscientious public servant.[4]

As we asked at the outlet, what was it about Burr which led the Sage of Monticello, generally so admirable a man, to become careless about due process? Why was Burr so infuriating as to lead Jefferson to expend his moral capital in rewarding and protecting from justice traitors and scoundrels, merely because they could help in his vendetta against Burr?

Did Jefferson in fact fear Burr's challenge? His response to that threat may have been disproportionate, but he was not alone in crediting Burr with remarkable resilience. So powerful had Burr's presence been among the Founders that, despite all Jefferson had done, despite the squalid Paris years, we may recall as well John Adams's question: "Colonel Burr; Attorney General Burr; Senator Burr; Vice President Burr; almost President Burr . . . What is to be his destiny?"[6]

At the outset of this narrative we set forth a determination to accept Adams's implicit injunction to seek the opinions of other public people—men and women—as to how the themes of "emulation, rivalry, and ambition" may be followed through the careers of Burr, Hamilton, and Jefferson.

When Jefferson roused the nation and issued his presidential proclamation of Burr's guilt, he may, for the moment, have believed it. He certainly believed in his own mission to lead the nation and in the mission of the Republican party he had brought together. Burr was worse than a threat. He was out of harmony with the principles of that party—remonstrances are often felt as betrayals. Let us give Jefferson the benefit of an assumption that he was *not* deliberately deceiving the nation merely to rid himself of a rival. Let us stipulate that he believed, enough of the time, that Burr was a threat to the Union. Let us follow with a leap of further faith: that he accepted as true what he was told by Granger, the Morgans, Wilkinson, and William Eaton, finding these gentlemen more credible than Andrew Jackson, Henry Clay, Thomas Truxton, Charles Biddle, Alexander Dallas, and Edward Livingston. He was, then, merely protecting his machismo from Du Pont.

On the other hand, we need not be quite so sympathetic to Jefferson. It is equally likely that he already detested Burr, wanted him out of the way, and calibrated very precisely the nature of Burr's threat to the Empire of Liberty. Whose liberty, the unsympathetic may ask? The liberty of "those whom I serve," among them those who had slaves to sell into an expanding plantation system.

All this may explain what Jefferson did—antagonism to a rival, embarrassment at having failed to make the necessary exertions to bring about a true Empire of Liberty, class and sectional interest, and a statesman's sense that no risks could be run on a frontier so exposed to British or French or Indian coalitions. None of these, however, nor all of them together, tell us why he was so ardent in doing it. And there is nothing historical research can do to resolve that question to everyone's satisfaction. All we can stipulate is that when that sort of passion is discerned in most humans, it emerges from volcanic depths within the psyche beyond the reach of analytical spelunking—that is to say, beyond the sort of analysis outsiders can do. When a man as composed as Jefferson flares and explodes, we may legitimately look for volcanism beneath political advantage or even political necessity. As early as February 15, 1794, Jefferson had his private reasons for disliking Burr—and would have had them had Burr never entered politics.

Cherchez les Femmes

The adage opening this section has remarkable vitality in the criminal justice system. It remains a very good prescription for solving difficult cases.

Leaving the cases of Maria Cosway and Sally Hemings as amply aerated elsewhere, it is apparent that the other four women who were most important to Thomas Jefferson were his mother, with whom he lived until he was nearly thirty, his wife, his daughter, Martha, and Dolley Payne Madison, the wife of his best friend. His mother, wife, and daughter had nothing to do with his antipathy to Burr. What of Dolley?

She had been one of the women Burr befriended when they were in need, all of whom, Malice always insisted, were his lovers. As Dolley Payne, she was an impecunious widow, and he a widower on the loose in Philadelphia. However, in the tone and content of their correspondence there is no fragment, no shadow, of confirmation of any such dirty little secret, nor was any asserted at the time by anyone who knew them well enough to have a worthwhile opinion. She called Burr "her trusted friend and adviser" and named him as the guardian of her vagrant son by her first marriage. Burr had lived in her mother's boardinghouse like many other senators while Philadelphia was the national capital.

In 1794, Burr introduced Dolley to "the great little Madison," as she called him. "The great little Madison" was forty-four. He had never married, having had only a brief engagement ten years earlier, terminated by the lady in question. (Apparently this incident so embarrassed Madison that in old age he laboriously excised or blackened over all references to her in his correspondence.)[7]

Once exposed to Dolley's bosomy, smiling warmth and wit, he courted her, won her, and they were married. It is passing strange that so little attention has been paid to the chain of events beginning with Burr's relationship to Dolley through his introduction of her into the intimate space between Jefferson and Madison. Jefferson had himself come late to marriage and became a widower at thirty-eight, in 1782. Over the next fourteen years, he and Madison achieved a bachelor partnership without parallel in American public life. Then, because of Burr, Jefferson received the third great shock of his life, after the deaths of his mother and his wife—Dolley entered that partnership, and forever altered its terms.

"His [Burr's] conduct very soon inspired me with distrust," said Jefferson. "I habitually cautioned Mr. Madison against trusting him too much." That required some exertion, for Madison was not only Burr's college friend, he had shown an uncomfortable degree of respect for Burr in the same summer in which he and Dolley were married, rec- ommending him to President Washington for the coveted post of min- ister to France. Because of his animosity to Burr, Washington had no need of any third party to induce him to withhold the prize, awarding it instead to James Monroe, but it is noteworthy that Jefferson does not tell us that he bothered to warn *Monroe* against Burr, for during the 1790s Monroe was even closer to Burr than Madison. The two gossiped about the Madisons' marriage, and, when Monroe was chal- lenged to duel by Hamilton, he asked Burr to be his second. But, of course, Jefferson never displayed anything but a professional affinity for Monroe and had no psychological inducement to warn him. Mon- roe was neither politically nor emotionally within the circle which, be- fore Dolley, contained only Madison and Jefferson.[8]

Fourteen years is a long time for two brilliant and lonely men to work together. When interveners enter such mutual dependencies, they do so at their peril. Burr intruded. That alone could explain Jef- ferson's "distrust" of him. As time went on, that distrust settled into something like hatred. After Hamilton was removed from the scene, Jefferson became a sort of alternative host to Hamilton's malignancy.

Hatred? Malignancy? Indeed. There lay behind Jefferson's porcelain mask a more vehement emotion than simple distrust—Burr loomed larger in his psychological ecology than any mere rascally scamp. If Burr had been only George Dangerfield's "adventurer—nothing more," Jefferson's behavior toward him would be inexplicable.

Jefferson was destabilized by Burr—as Hamilton had been, but for entirely different reasons. But, as John Marshall said when they were all old men—Marshall seventy, Burr sixty-eight, Jefferson eighty, Madison seventy-three—Jefferson was "among the most unforgiving of men." He forgave Burr least of all; that we can say with some assurance, though we must concede that we cannot be sure why characters long dead behaved as they did.

While acknowledging the difficulties of direct assault upon the secrets of the motivation of historic characters, courtroom practice suggests that we may do better if we seek the opinions of their contemporaries. That of course requires us to go through a second round of characterization, like the process of qualifying witnesses. We need not bother with everybody's impressions, especially because we know how easily impressions can be created. Nor need we here again browse through the many good books written about the careers of the reputations of Alexander Hamilton, Aaron Burr, and Thomas Jefferson in the nineteenth and twentieth centuries. Here we will content ourselves with a postscript in which some attention is directed at two of those who contributed nearly as much to the opinions held of Burr by their fellow citizens after Burr's death as did Alexander Hamilton and Thomas Jefferson while he lived: Harriet Beecher Stowe and John Quincy Adams.

At the end of our narrative, however, we may, here, bring Burr back together with Andrew Jackson, the public man who probably understood him best, and understood Jefferson quite well also.

When Jackson was President, in the 1830s, he made his comment on Burr, characteristically, in action. It was generally known that the old man wished to be remembered as a hero of the Revolution in which Jackson and he were both wounded. As he sat in the White House, or at the Hermitage, reflecting upon the vagaries, brutalities, and injustices of life, Jackson may have recalled the story of Burr's dealing with the mutineer at Valley Forge with his saber, and that may have recalled to Jackson another saber, used less gloriously. The ugly realities of the War of Revolution were known to him as poignantly as they were to Burr. In the hideous backcountry guerrilla bloodletting of the Carolinas, "men hunted each other like beasts of prey, and the savages were outdone in cruelties to the living and indignities to the dead." As Banastre Tarleton was chasing Jefferson from Monticello, Lord Rawdon was detaching other cavalry units to burn out the houses of other Whig leaders in the mountains of South Carolina. Jackson was fourteen years old and in uniform when he was among the rebels captured by one such troop. He was brought under guard to another, larger force, as it was trashing the house of his cousin Thomas Crawford. He was ordered by a British officer to clean his boots. Jackson retorted that he was a prisoner of war. The officer swung his saber and cut into Jackson's head, and as the boy sought to protect himself, he nearly lost several of his fingers.[9]

Remembering all this, President Jackson instructed his Secretary of the Treasury, Roger B. Taney, to award to Burr that Revolutionary pension denied to him for fifty-one years.

Postscript

John Quincy Adams, Harriet Beecher Stowe, and Other Women

Someday soon one may be able to attend a seminar on the character and presidency of William Jefferson Clinton without devoting most of one's time to Monica Lewinsky, a seminar on Thomas Jefferson without an exclusive focus on Sally Hemings, on Alexander Hamilton without attending to Mrs. Reynolds, or on Aaron Burr without passing through another tedious recital of charges that Burr was an adulterous, profligate libertine. In the 1980s, we could wonder at how important Burr's sexuality seemed to be to the writers of the Victorian age, but at the end of the 1990s we wonder no more. It appears that in an era of commercial prurience passing for journalism, and journalism passing as history, we have had enough keyhole-peeping to fill the nation's quota for another century.

We add this extended postscript not to provide further salacious detail but to bring together the two themes of Burr's private character as it fascinated Hamilton and his public character as it obsessed, for a time, Thomas Jefferson. Our method will be to bring to bear upon these two studies the opinions of their contemporaries, especially their female contemporaries. In this way we may be able better to make our own judgments of all three.

A fascination with Burr's physical life, which seemed disproportionate to that accorded that of others, until recent years has overwhelmed a due appreciation of his intellect, his achievements in the struggle for the civil rights of people of color, his efforts on behalf of Indians, and his fervent feminism. These, too, are elements of his character, as their presence or absence in the lives of his great antagonists are aspects of theirs.

The sustained power of the derogatory view of Burr expressed by Hamilton and Jefferson may well be due to the late adherence to the Hamilton-Jefferson position taken by two influential people of the next two generations, Harriet Beecher Stowe and John Quincy Adams. These were powerful witnesses against him. How could Burr the abolitionist be taken seriously when his enemies included the author of *Uncle Tom's Cabin* and the advocate of the rebels of the *Amistad?*

What did these two paragons of virtue have to say of Burr? Why was it that Adams was so furtive in admitting that he might have been unfair in what he said and ignoble for saying it?

Let us start our enquiry with the aspects of Burr's life which Stowe made the points of leverage to turn the plot of her novel *A Minister's Wooing*. According to Benjamin Henry Latrobe, Burr "indulged in amorous excesses without disguise" after the death of his wife, "but he carried unhappiness into no man's family." That judgment by a contemporary squares with that of every serious scholar who has inquired into the matter: There is not a single proven instance in which Burr disregarded the laws of matrimony, either as a married man by having extramarital affairs, or as a single man intruding upon the marriage of others. On the other hand, both Hamilton and Jefferson admitted doing so. The recently reignited discussion of Jefferson's relationship to Hemings properly focuses upon the relationships of master and slave, father and children, but it is also of some significance that she was not married at the time and neither was Jefferson. Before he was married, he made an unsuccessful effort to seduce Mrs. Walker, the wife of a friend absent on patriotic business, and his amorata Mrs. Cosway was only nominally *Mrs.* Cosway. Hamilton's lengthy description of his affair with Mrs. Reynolds was one of many (we recall what Latrobe and John Adams had to say of him). He felt it necessary to explain himself in that instance only to assert that adultery was less shameful than the possibility that her compliant husband might have found him useful politically.[1]

Then why is Burr thought to be the libertine of the three? Hamilton was not so convincing a propagandist as to have achieved that triumph of transference unassisted. Mrs. Stowe finished the job. She used Burr as a Mephistophelian device to provide zest to her otherwise tepid account, and after the duel with the saintly Hamilton there were many who elided fiction and fact. There was some irony in the fact that Stowe and Burr were both the children of influential Calvinist clergymen and that Burr's evangelical grandfather, Jonathan Edwards, could match in profundity, though perhaps not in popularity, Stowe's brother Henry Ward Beecher. *A Minister's Wooing* was published in 1859, seven years after her celebrity with *Uncle Tom's Cabin.*

Stowe's diabolic Burr is not of much interest. Latrobe, and witnesses James Parton assembled for the defense, to be heard next, can give us the truth about him. But as we also turn to women of Burr's generation to help us understand him, we can learn from Stowe what to avoid in our qualifying of them as witnesses. Hers is not an image of womanhood that can be useful to us. It comes to us by way of her image of a ladylike relationship to Burr, in *A Minister's Wooing:*

> Burr was one of those men willing to play with any charming woman the game of those navigators who give to simple natives glass beads and feathers in return for gold and diamonds,—to accept from a woman her heart's blood in return for such odds and ends and clippings as he can afford her from the serious ambition of life.
>
> . . . We have been told, in extenuation of the course of Aaron Burr, that he was not a man of gross passions or of coarse indulgence, but, in the most consummate and refined sense, a *man of gallantry.* This, then, is the descriptive name which polite society has invented for the man who does this thing![2]

Victims. Impulsive, unguarded, angelic, noble, pure—and stupid. They flew as high as heaven above men, presumably because they flew unweighted by brains. Stowe did not originate this idea of women; it was already abroad when Burr and the Theodosias, mother and daughter, regretted the absence of an audience for Mary Wollstonecraft. Regret might have become lamentation had they lived on to observe the troops of preening acquiescents who attended every syllable uttered on the lecture platform by Harriet Beecher Stowe. Burr had had the candor to say that he was not drawn to passive-aggressive females. He limited his attentions to those who met him "half way." That thought was repeated in horror by Stowe, presumably because it implied active sexual engagement by a woman. Hamilton, the hypocritical philanderer, began the process of fixing upon Burr his own projected character; she finished the job. No one other than Jefferson has been so effective in blackening his character as she.

Stowe's view of ladylike behavior was formed in the household in which each of Lyman Beecher's children was set to spying on the others. Though all were to be pure, only the boys could be great. How different it was in the household of Aaron and Theodosia Burr; purity was a matter of what became known in the 1970s as "situation ethics," and greatness was encouraged in their daughter, as it was in her son. One cannot imagine Burr writing of the early promise of his daughter as Beecher wrote of Harriet: "Hattie is a genius. I would give a hundred dollars if she was a boy."[3]

We now come to Matthew Livingston Davis, to whom Burr entrusted his private papers, and who thereafter sought to rehabilitate his own reputation by chinning himself on Burr's. In the first biography published of Burr, which he rushed to the printers after Burr's death, Davis asserted that he had found in the old man's apartments a "mass of letters . . . indicating no very strict morality in some of his female correspondence," so he had "committed to the fire all . . . not a vestige now remains."[4]

Having destroyed the evidence, Davis was free to tell us that "in his intercourse with females he [Burr] was an unprincipled flatterer, ever prepared to take advantage of their weakness, their credulity, and their confidence. She that confided in him was lost. . . . His conduct was most licentious."[5]

Here she is again, "she that confided in him," that weak and credulous, ladylike victim. And here he is again, Hamilton's profligate. Unlike Hamilton in his deathbed self-reconstruction, and unlike Jefferson in his *Anas*, Burr never attempted a systematic response to his critics, either on this score or as to his politics. In his old age, in response to questions, he would offer such remarks as that upon which Stowe pounced: "I never had an amour in my life in which I was not met half way. I would be the last man on earth to make such advances where they were not welcome." A real question to be asked in a society in which thousands of mulatto children roamed plantations in which "inferiors" were exploited sexually is whether or not we may take seriously Burr's affirmation that "a man who will so much as look with lustful eyes upon a servant is no gentleman; and if he does it in the house of a friend, he dishonors that house and insults the friend."[6]

James Parton Attempts a Rescue

James Parton took Burr seriously and sought out those who could tell him whether or not Burr's behavior squared better with his professions of belief than Jefferson's or Hamilton's. In the same year that Stowe was bringing *A Minister's Wooing* to press, Burr's second biographer completed his questioning of Burr's "friends and relatives, most of whom knew him better than Mr. Davis," and published his conclusions. Parton found that Burr did, in fact, behave as a "gentleman" toward those vulnerable to him and that Davis's comments to the contrary "convey ideas ludicrously at variance with the truth." Burr had not made Parton's task easy, for, though he was himself poor, until the very end he insisted upon giving support to women who had been his friends, despite what Malice would say. Parton reported that Burr was contributing to the support of ten old ladies at one time and that the biographer had been "assured . . . by four individuals, each of which stood nearer to Burr than Davis ever did, . . . that not one of these women had ever borne to him the relation which the . . . world would infer from the fact that he gave them money."[7]

Parton did bow to midcentury morality by conceding that "in the mind of the moralist, Burr must stand condemned. . . . [H]e was guilty toward women—he who should have inaugurated the new morality . . . of . . . ideal virtue!" If ideal virtue is not too ambitious a standard for Burr, perhaps we should have an equivalently Alpine expectation for Jefferson with regard to what he might have achieved, at great political cost, by sustaining his opposition to slavery in the Mississippi Valley.[8]

The Falling Man

That brings us to public life, and to John Quincy Adams. It has been justly said of Adams that he was no paragon in the debates over slavery in 1806, though with equal justice one must admit that neither Burr nor Jefferson (in their very different stations) acted a noble part at the time. Burr could have done so, surely, if he had wished to make of his western adventure the antislavery campaign charged against him and take the predictable consequences. But Burr was not John Brown. For Jefferson, the price would likely have been the end of his influence over his "country," Virginia, and with "those I represent." For Adams, the case was not so hard. He represented an antislavery state in the Senate, as did those colleagues who did propose a cessation of both the interstate commerce in slaves and of slavery itself in new territories. But his ambitions were not bound by the Senate; Adams was on his way to his one-term presidency from 1824 to 1828, at the sufferance of the Virginia Dynasty to which he succeeded. That presidency was as unhappy as his father's, and, his ambitions shriveled, Adams returned to the fray as a member of the House of Representatives. He reached the actual apogee of his career not as President but in 1841, making an eight-hour argument to the U.S. Supreme Court on behalf of the freedom of a group of slaves who had rebelled from their captors aboard the Spanish ship *Amistad*.

Jefferson had died in 1826, Burr in 1836. Because Adams had known the two since the 1790s, two passages relevant to our story leap from the pages of his pleadings of the *Amistad* case and his diary.

In the course of his speech to the Court, Adams offered a strange interpolation—a rumination upon what should constitute virtuous conduct when a great man falls from eminence. The most eminent man he had known who had such a fall was Burr; it is probable that what he had to say was a commentary upon his own behavior—his own *lack* of virtue—when Burr fell. The context was a disquisition on slavery. As to that subject, and as to his conduct toward Burr, Adams was traveling a lifelong process of redemption. The scriptwriters of the film *Amistad* chose most of the words for their version of Adams's 1841 speech from what he had confided only to his diary after he had walked home with John C. Calhoun in 1819, after a discussion in President James Monroe's cabinet about the extension of slavery into Missouri. Neither in the conversation with Calhoun nor in the cabinet discussion had he expressed himself with the fervency of his diary entry.

From the diary came that portion of his filmed argument in which Adams asserted that the Court should be moved by the "all men are created equal" clause of the Declaration of Independence, to give it precedence over the treaties and statutes which might have sent his clients back to slavery. That clause had special meaning to Adams. He had enjoyed—and suffered from—a special relationship to its author.

Adams's diary was written as he was emerging in private from the shadow of the Virginia Dynasty, a shadow which had provided the necessary ecology within which his own ambition could flower. Adams was a shade-tolerant plant—no, a shadow-requiring one. Had he appeared earlier as a professed antagonist to slavery, his prospects for the presidency would have withered.

After Adams's defeat in 1828, his successor, Andrew Jackson, gave succor to the aged, poverty-stricken Aaron Burr in an act of charity requiring courage, for Jackson's ascent had been slowed by his association with Burr twenty years earlier. Adams, on the other hand, had joined the jackal pack against Burr. On the last day of 1807, after the Richmond Trial completed Burr's fall from power, he had shown how uncontaminated by Burrism he was by taking the floor of the Senate to heap obloquy upon the falling man, introducing a motion referring to "the conspiracy of Aaron Burr and his associates against the peace, union, and liberties, of the people of the United States."[9]

That was why it was so revealing for him to interpolate into his *Amistad* argument a scene from Shakespeare about the dismissal of Cardinal Wolsey from the service of King Henry VIII. Wolsey was sent to disgrace, impeached, and his estates forfeited in 1529. What had his fall to do with African slaves in 1841? Not nearly so much as with the fall of Aaron Burr in 1807, and with Adams.

[The scene was that which] . . . exhibits in action the sudden . . . fall from unbounded power into irretrievable disgrace of Cardinal Wolsey, by . . . dismission from the service of the King [Henry VIII] . . . in the presence of Lord Surrey and of the Lord Chamberlain; at the moment of Wolsey's humiliation . . . , Surrey gives vent to his long suppressed resentments for the insolence and injuries which he had endured from the fallen favorite while in power, and breaks out into insulting and bitter reproaches, till checked by the Chamberlain, who says:

'Oh! My Lords;
Press not a falling man too far: 'tis VIRTUE.'[10]

The *Amistad* case was an admiralty matter, having to do with slaves and treaties utterly unrelated either to Cardinal Wolsey or to virtue in public life. A disquisition on falling men would not help Adams's clients. It erupted into the courtroom as if forcing itself through a rupture in the membrane between Adams's conscience and his lawyer's mind—a phenomenon not unknown in court.

(If we were to stretch to seek something making Wolsey germane to the *Amistad* rebels, we might touch with our fingernails an ironic intention by Adams to play to the two Justices who shared his loathing for Martin Van Buren, telling them ironically how much he regretted having to utter a critical syllable about the Magician of Kinderhook. But it does not read like a little joke to draw discreet smiles. Besides, Van Buren was not a falling man. He retained a powerful political organization in New York and was a presidential possibility for another decade.)

Adams explained his outburst by telling the Court that he had "carried . . . an impression" of the scene of Wolsey's fall "with me through all the changes of my life," from "an early period." If so, that impression was in his mind on that last day of 1807 when he was forty and played Surrey to Burr's Wolsey, exclaiming to the ravening crowd that Burr had "no religious principles, and little, if any sense of reverence to a moral Governor of the Universe." How could even an Adams purport to know such a thing? John Quincy Adams's theologically trained father would have been aware that one makes a statement about the state of another person's soul at great peril to one's own.[11]

Quincy Adams's fulmination against "the conspiracy of Aaron Burr and his associates against the peace, union, and liberties of the United States" had been offered after the decisions of Chief Justice Marshall and the Richmond grand jury on August 31, 1807, for the purpose of expelling John Smith of Ohio from the Senate for his part in such a nefarious scheme. Senator Hillhouse of Connecticut, who had suffered from Adams's defection from the antislavery cause in the Louisiana debates of the previous year, a cause which had then been supported by Smith, rose in reply:

> Where . . . is the evidence whereon we can ground . . . a vote which is to disrobe a Senator from his office and of his honor? . . . Nothing but jealousy, that jealousy which frequently attaches itself to a charge of treason . . . and must in this case have taken hold of the mind of the gentleman from Massachusetts.[12]

Then, once more, William Branch Giles of Virginia surprised his colleagues. He had led those who, in 1804, proposed that the governor of New Jersey acquit Burr of the indictment for murdering Hamilton. His action then may be dismissed as only an expression of Jefferson's instructions to buy Burr's support against Justice Chase. But after Adams and Hillhouse had their say, Giles was on his feet to vote against

Adams's persecution of Smith "solely from the conviction of the innocence of the accused."[13]

Adams, Abolition, and Jefferson

The conduct of Adams toward Burr entirely justifies the verdict of Ralph Waldo Emerson that he was a "bruiser." But he had another side: He could be exceedingly compassionate in his assessment of those who shared his own frailties, one of whom was Thomas Jefferson.[14]

President and son of a President, John Quincy Adams wrote a diary as much intended for the instruction of posterity as Jefferson's *Anas* or Burr's lost journals. In that diary, Adams has his say about his relationship to Jefferson and about their relationship to slavery, often commenting upon himself by commenting upon Jefferson—and others. Some have read his rhetoric in the *Amistad* argument about Jefferson's Declaration as a play for headlines or as a solicitation of the admiration of posterity after a lifetime of trimming. Yet it seems to have burst forth from the same spring of feeling as his "falling man" cadenza, a source of energy becoming available to Adams only after, his ambitions spent, he could listen to his better angels.

The positions taken by Adams as to slavery while he was a senator and while he was Secretary of State were required of him if he were not to lose the support of Jefferson and other slaveowners for his higher ambitions. In 1838, only two years before the *Amistad* case brought the abolitionists into common cause with Adams, they had grown tired of his temporizing and had run a candidate against him for his seat in the House. Though Adams had fought the gag rule (by which the House refused to hear abolitionist petitions), he steadfastly asserted that he was merely arguing for any citizen's constitutional right to present such documents, implying no support for their content. This may not seem much of a distinction to us, but it set a gulf between him and those who were petitioning. While Adams sheltered himself behind such distinctions, they were being stoned and lynched for *acting* to free slaves.

Adams missed his opportunity to obstruct the progression of the slave system into Louisiana during the Hillhouse Debates of 1806, as nearly all his Federalist colleagues from New England sought to abolish the intrastate and international slave trade in the newly acquired territories. He would say only that "slavery is in a moral sense an evil; but as connected with commerce it has important uses."[15]

"I am opposed to slavery," he added, "but I have . . . voted against the provisions introduced to prohibit and lesson it . . . on two principles, 1. That I am opposed to legislating at all for that country [Louisiana]—2. I think we are proceeding with too much haste on such an important question."[16]

Too much haste. Always, for forty years, too much haste. In 1819, he had guarded his true feelings from Monroe's cabinet, even when provoked by his rival, William H. Crawford, then Jefferson's candidate to succeed Monroe in the presidency. Crawford attempted to draw forth from Adams disqualifying remarks such as those he made to his diary, but Adams cannily declined to oblige even when Crawford, while arguing that the administration should disregard the Northwest Ordinance line against slavery, denounced the ordinance itself. It had been a mistake, he said, to deprive the slaveowners of the right to introduce their system into Ohio, Indiana, and Illinois territories.

Though Adams told his diary that he found that assertion "sickening to my soul," he "did not reply. . . . [T]o have discussed it there would have been useless, and only have kindled in the bosom of the Executive the same flame which had been raging in Congress and in the country." He then buried in his diary that line which the writers for the motion picture *Amistad* made the climax of his speech to the Court: "If the Union must be dissolved, slavery is precisely the question upon which it ought to break."[17]

Adams and Jefferson

For forty years, Adams's sickening soul was held in thrall to his ambitions for the presidency. Like Jefferson, he was suspended between necessity and ambition, and, like Jefferson, he knew it. Adams was a profoundly introspective bruiser, constantly checking the vital signs of his own performance of duty as well as that of others. He recorded the crossings over and the tensions between his, and their, ambitions for public life and ambitions for moral life. Situated, as he was, upon an eminence from which he might judge others living through these complexities and tensions, he was able to do justice—and thus to practice "virtue"—toward *some* of those others. Though Aaron Burr was beyond his empathetic reach, Thomas Jefferson fell comfortably within it.

According to Adams, Jefferson "saw the gross inconsistency between the principles of the Declaration of Independence and the fact of Negro slavery" but was never able to resolve that inconsistency in his own behavior. The Declaration might have been irrelevant to the *Amistad* decision, but it was not irrelevant to an assessment of Jefferson. "All his life a slave-holder . . . he has published opinions . . . blasting to the very existence of slavery" but acted in accordance with those "opinions" only until 1784 or so. After that, wrote Adams, Jefferson's dilemma had been demonstrated in one significant *inaction* and two *actions*. What Jefferson did *not* do was to originate the "positive good" argument for slavery: "He could not, or would not prostitute the faculties of his mind to the vindication of that slavery which from his soul he abhorred."[18]

There it comes again, that wondrous certitude about the contents of another man's soul. We note it. And pass it by. Lacking a commensurate confidence, we can catch up with Adams at the point at which he observed another man's actions. In 1776 and 1784, Jefferson made his attempts at diminishing the power of slavery—in both instances, without success. In the first, "he would have introduced a flaming denunciation of slavery into the Declaration of Independence, but the discretion of his colleagues struck it out." Enough general rhetoric was left in the Declaration, however, to constitute a problem for the slave-owners: "With the Declaration of Independence on their lips, and the merciless scourge of slavery in their hands, a more flagrant image of human inconsistency can hardly be conceived."[19]

Adams observed as well that in 1784 Jefferson proposed to keep slavery out of the western territories, though his colleagues defeated him once again. The moral silence that ensued thereafter was justified by Adams on the ground that "Mr. Jefferson did not have the spirit of martyrdom." Indeed so. Adams knew the price of martyrdom, and he also knew the offsetting price of accommodation, the first to be paid publicly, the second privately, the former suffered noisily, the other in silence. As Jefferson had said in Paris: "Those whom I serve have never been in a position to lift up their voices against slavery."[20]

Burr, on the other hand, apparently had felt himself in a position to lift up *his* voice against slavery at least as late as 1799. His friends must admit that thereafter he, too, lacked the spirit of martyrdom, except when breaking the tie on the Logan Bill. Like Quincy Adams, Gallatin, and Jefferson, he knew that if his view toward slavery became too audible he would cease to be a candidate for national office. Perhaps he might have raised his voice again in the West. Perhaps.

It is to the credit of John Quincy Adams that, as he *finished* his public career in the 1840s, he achieved the same moral level, as to slavery, at which Hamilton and Burr *commenced* theirs—in the 1790s. That being true, we might love Adams more had he then acknowledged that they had preceded him in virtue, as William Lloyd Garrison admitted. Adams might have completed purging his equivocal past with a generous reassessment of those he had attacked as they were falling.

The Worst and the Best

What if? What if the mother of John Quincy Adams had broken through to her husband's understanding in 1775? What if the Founders had actually remembered the ladies—the women, in general—and followed Aaron Burr's lead toward at least some of the reforms advocated by his wife and Mary Wollstonecraft? Theodosia Burr died before she could press her husband further, and their daughter died before she could take up the work. But women were there, all along. Let us heed what they had to say.

Abigail Adams expressed herself earlier in this narrative as to the relative merits of Burr and Thomas Jefferson. Dolley Madison and Hannah Gallatin shared her high opinion of Burr, and there is a possibility that once Jefferson had left the White House and was succeeded by Madison, they used their influence to moderate the ferocity of the treatment accorded Burr.

When Burr was in penniless exile in Paris, Theodosia Alston turned to the women he had befriended. She began with Hannah Gallatin, asking whether or not the obvious role of the administration's subsidized editors' "expressions calculated to enliven every spark of animosity [to Burr] which exists in the country," meant that

> my father's return to this country would be productive of ill con-
> sequences to him, or draw on him further prosecution from any

branch of the government[?] ... Must he ever remain excommunicated from the participation of domestic enjoyments and the privileges of a citizen ... ? It must be evident to the worst enemies of my father, that no man, situated as he will be, could obtain any undue influence, even supposing him desirous of it.[21]

Next, Theodosia tried Dolley Madison:

Why is my father banished from a country for which he has encountered wounds and dangers and fatigue for years? Why is he driven from his friends, from an only child, to ... exile, and that too at an age when others are reaping the harvest of past toils?[22]

There was no response. Or so it seemed. But these were women of character, and they may in fact have done something for their old friend. Mysteriously, in July 1811, an unknown woman in Paris acted as the intermediary between Hugues-Bernard Maret, duc de Bassano, Napoleon's man for such matters, and the American chargé d'affaires, Jonathan Russell, carrying instructions to Russell that he should not refuse Burr a passport. With equal suddenness, Bassano paid Burr's debts and gave him an advance to enable him to leave France with a little money in his pocket. No one has yet discovered the identity of that lady, or for whom she acted. But Russell was quick to act on her request.[23]

There is an aspect of those years of degradation which troubles many who otherwise find much in Burr to admire, and that is what one thoughtful writer has called "his quirky relationship to his daughter," as manifested in his "odd" letters from Europe in which he "chatted about his sexual exploits on an ongoing basis."[24]

There is no denying the revolting content of some of the journal entries Burr sent Theodosia covering the winter months of 1810–11, before he escaped from Paris. That is not, however, because they present his sexual desperation as a series of "exploits," or because that is all he reported to her. He did not ask that she approve of what he was doing, and his catalogues of sexual encounters were only incidental to little essays on the conditions of the poor, on architecture, stove design, politics, and gossip. She did not approve, but she did not admonish, either, for she knew what he was doing. He may have thought he was drinking life to its dregs, yet even then this astonishing woman wrote her father that he would never reach the bottom of the cup: "Believe me, you do not yet know the world."[25]

What can explain Burr's accountant's notations of sexual encounters for pay? He was a man famous for his appeal to women, Beau Burr, elegant, impeccably tailored, witty, charming, fastidious—now driven to extremity. In poverty, hunger, and exile, shivering and unable to pay for a bath or a crust, he wrote to the woman who had always stood beside him, whatever he was. "Yes," he was saying, "yes, this is what I have become—a hideous parody of a gallant. 'The black-eyed charmer!' Here I am, in stained and tattered clothing, dirty linen, smelling like a drover, buying whores' favors to be taken in doorways." Even his body was failing him; his teeth were abscessing, and his wartime intestinal infliction had returned: "A sick man is an object of contempt," he wrote. Valentino with diarrhea.[26]

"Love me now!" he cried out to his daughter, "love me, even thus, even now!"

Burr required of himself, and sent to his daughter, as the custodian of his flickering sense of self, a precise accounting of his payments for sex, as an alcoholic might keep a ledger of his payments for bottles, or a master his purchases of slaves to keep him in guilty comfort. Are we to be appalled at this? Only if we have never known good men and women who drink themselves into the gutter with money cadged from friends and who tell all this to those who they hope may love them anyway—until they stop doing it. Burr borrowed money to purchase sex and told his daughter what he had done—until he stopped doing it.

There is a long gap in these journals, nearly four months. The exact dating of events is garbled. But there was a night on which he walked and walked and walked, on swollen and infected feet, until he came to the Pantheon, "without knowing where I was going. I stood some minutes to discover who I was. In what country I was. What business I had there. For what I came abroad. And where I intended to go."[27]

In the spring, he was released from this circle of Hell, thanks in part, at least, to a woman. There will be those who will find all this merely disgusting, who have never been so tried, and who cannot imagine being so. Impeccable in their tailoring, their laundry, their deodorants, and their sexual restraint when drunk or sober, stiff in upper lip, they may never have never craved a daughter's approval of themselves, or anyone's approval. Yet when Burr returned to health, and sanity, and home, Theodosia hastened to welcome him, and she was no fool.

There were others who welcomed him as well. Among the fragments remaining to us of Burr's correspondence are letters from a woman who can relieve us of any need to speculate about how those who knew him intimately, in good times and bad, felt about him. Rebecca Smith Blodget was practical. She had to be. She knew the great ones, and she made her judgments. When she was Rebecca Smith, she was beautiful. When she was Mrs. Blodget, she was wise and courageous. To her dying day she was witty and loyal, despite a hard life. Like her husband's competitor, Benjamin Henry Latrobe, she knew both Jefferson and Burr.

Rebecca Smith was the daughter of the provost of the University of Pennsylvania. When she was fifteen, in 1787, she first met Burr. He was married and not available. Eight years later, she married Samuel Blodget, who had made a fortune in the East India trade and was already combining the profession of real estate speculation with the sort of amateur interest in architecture which was displayed to greater effect by Dr. William Thornton and Thomas Jefferson. Blodget was an early speculator in Washington, D.C., doing occasional architectural work such as a truly dreadful design entered in the competition for the U.S. Capitol. It was not accepted, so one of its aspects was developed into Blodget's Hotel, which was the District of Columbia's first grand hostelry. Blodget had already drawn upon the talent of a newly arrived Irish immigrant, James Hoban, for the design of the First Bank of the United States, in Philadelphia, the first monumentally marble structure in North America. (In tribute to the romance then going on between Ireland and the new American Republic, the bank was—and remains—a reduced version of the Dublin Merchant's Exchange.)

Paris, too, had its effects upon Blodget as it had upon Jefferson. Both were struck by the huge semilaminated struts supporting the dome of the Paris Grain Market. In 1797, while Jefferson was underway with his own somewhat reduced and considerably more successful version of the Grain Market—the dome at Monticello, Blodget reported that he had made an enlarged replica, 247 feet in diameter.

At the end of the 1790s, things did not go well for Samuel Blodget. He and the beautiful Rebecca separated. She went to live in

Philadelphia, where she became a companion to Dolley Madison. Blodget was caught in a whirlpool of lotteries and ever more frantic speculations, which finally deposited him in a debtor's prison.[28]

In 1808, after the Richmond Trial, Rebecca Blodget offered Burr refuge in her house in Philadelphia. It appears that he remained there for several months before he took ship for Europe. There is no certainty as to their relationship, except that she loved him enough to put herself at risk of the wrath of the Jefferson administration—the President had instructed government agents that "it was now more important than ever" to bring Burr to heel. Jefferson was going out of office, however, and the Madisons were about to be President and First Lady. After the former Vice President escaped to Britain, Rebecca Blodget joined in Theodosia Alston's campaign to persuade them to "drop the persecution against him." Though on most other occasions charming, she was not tactful when she told the Madisons that she ascribed to Burr her self-esteem—"whatever is valuable in myself" she owed to him, she wrote—"heaven forbid that I should ever place myself in the light of an inferior to Thomas Jefferson."[29]

The political principles of the Sage of Monticello, she said, were "weak" and "wicked," and his character was that of a "shifting, shuffling visionary, an old woman in her dotage! A wretch without nerve!" She was writing Madison! "Pardon me, Sir." This was a message even less likely to bring a response than Theodosia's, but Rebecca Blodget was a woman of spirit, as she demonstrated again after Burr's return, and her husband's death. In 1814, following her principles of candor, she told Burr she loved him "more than all the rest of the world" and asked him to handle her tangled legal affairs. They were too much for both of them working together, and by 1823 things had declined for them both. She wrote him that she was living in a boardinghouse, without heat, "rolled up in a blanket." Until then, she had never before asked him for money, because she had sought to avoid "laying myself under an obligation . . . which could . . . render my professions of friendship doubtful." Now, she recalled how, in 1815, he had offered to give her support. She had "refused it, though I fear I pained you by doing so—but I could do without . . . but now I am facing life—ill—without flannel or money for my winter's wood. . . . If you can oblige me I know you will—if not, your silence . . . will afflict on my heart the pang of knowing that *you* are *without the means.*" Was this the letter of a woman who felt herself seduced?

If you were rich I should . . . unashamedly ask you for every thing unless, which is highly probable, you prevented me by giving it before I could ask it—but not being rich, believe me, I have felt really as much for your difficulties as for my own. . . . [B]y the constancy of my friendship of nearly 35 years . . . when I tell you of my distresses, it is because it is a relief to my heart.[30]

Let us complete our tale by bringing forward two final witnesses, a man and a woman, not to tell us how they felt about Burr but, instead, to permit us to discern his character in the way he treated them, and they him. First, there was his daughter's rich husband, Joseph Alston. Dark, bearded, intelligent, muted in manner, as prone as Burr himself to fits of black, debilitating depression, Alston had many advantages and many virtues. He inherited an array of rice plantations around the port of Georgetown and served in the South Carolina legislature almost continuously from 1802 until he became governor of South Carolina in 1812—despite his association with Burr. But in June of that year, his son, Aaron Burr Alston, died, and on December 31, about noon, his wife bade him farewell.

After Theodosia's death, Alston went on with life but sank slowly into despair. Burr sought to shake him out of it in November 1815, urging him to head a national effort to draft Andrew Jackson for the presidency. Jackson, Alston, and Burr were united in a common disdain for "the Virginia Junto . . . this vile combination which rules and degrades the U.S."[31]

As if writing to himself in the doldrums seven years earlier, Burr exhorted Alston: "It is time that you manifested that you had some individual character—some opinion of your own—some influence to support that opinion—Make them fear you and they will be at your feet—thus far they have reason to believe that you fear them."[32]

Then, in an intensity of feeling he had seldom before placed on paper, Burr raged at the Virginians, at fate, and at the leaden depression which weighed down his son-in-law, as its equivalent had destroyed his own career: "Emerge from this state of nullity—You owe it to yourself—You owe it to me—You owe it to your Country—You owe it to the memory of the dead."[33]

There was no reply in December. Or January. Then, on February 16, Alston replied that he was ill, so ill that he had been unable to attend the fall session of the legislature. He had not "the spirit, the energy, the health necessary to give practical effect to sentiment. All are gone. I feel too much alone, to entirely unconnected with the world, to take much interest in anything.''[34]

Alston, too, was dead by the end of the year. He was barely thirty-seven. Burr, in old age, remained sly, charming, implying mischief, and even in his seventies it once again became conventional to call him a gallant, even a cold, Chesterfieldian, exploiter of women. He was always better than that, as he was better than a political adventurer. When not in extremis and a friend to no one, least of all himself, he was a friend to women, and to the very end of his life they were friends to him, whatever might be said against them for being so.

As Burr was nearing death, paralyzed and frail, his landlady, the widow of a British officer, came to him and said:

> ''What do you think I've heard this morning, colonel? They say I'm your daughter.''
>
> ''Well,'' he responded, ''We don't care for that, do we?''
>
> ''Not a bit! But they say something else, colonel, they say I was your mistress.''
>
> ''Do they? I don't think we care much for that, either, do we? . . . But . . . (taking her hand in both his, and lifting it to his lips, his hands shaking with paralysis) I'll tell you something they might say that would be true! Let them say this of you: She gave the old man a home when nobody else would!''[35]

Finally, he was able to express himself plainly, without being ''coy.'' If ever there was a tragedy of manner, it was Burr's. In an effulgent age, he had always been constrained. While others cultivated an apparent openness, he was covered, appearing to be naturally conspiratorial, always hiding a secret. Once Thomas Jefferson grasped that truth, he knew what to do.

Appendix

Biases and Apologies

Herewith the promised statement of the biases brought to this conversation, biases arising, as most people's do, from my experience. Foremost among them is a sympathy for losers and for the underappreciated. One friendly reader has suggested that my treatment of winners and the excessively celebrated is symmetrically unsympathetic. It is true that my ancestors transmitted to me both curiosity about what lies hidden under the hedge and deep skepticism about what is proclaimed to be truth by the landlord. To their prejudices I have added the rueful consequences of living as I have, enjoying some victories in the course of half a century in or near public life, and smarting from losses described in the press releases of the winners. As journalism has become hastier and lazier, those releases have been so often swallowed whole that I no longer take any comfort whatever in received wisdom, whether as to the past or as to the present, until I have checked it myself.

The library of the big house is seldom constructed around the records left by losers. Losers seldom walk from the battlefield laden with any documents at all, nor do they grow often prosperous enough to select what they wish posterity to believe. The importance of losers' history is not however limited to the recovery of the significant and neglected. The flaming-up of a fresh appreciation of an overshadowed character can illuminate the stage well beyond the shadows that surrounded him or her. "New light" can give dimension, depth, and breadth to the winners. In the case of Aaron Burr, most of what he hoped to provide his biographers was lost at sea, with his daughter. He had no close family to guard his papers or his reputation, and his tragic final years reached their nadir as his few archives were entrusted to a hypocritical Tammany sachem, Matthew Davis, who had neither taste nor wit. But there are two volumes, and some microfiches of his Papers, which, like other great archives, provide us documents in their original form—and illumination in the medieval sense, as they are given color and ornament in the form of notes. Likewise, the Papers of Alexander Hamilton, those of the presidential Founders and of that sharp critic of presidents, Benjamin Henry Latrobe, also give great joy.

Many of us who live outside great university towns and travel without steamer trunks full of books make it our practice to cite for each other the most accessible and portable versions of the standard works we use. We do so to direct colleagues—all readers are colleagues—to clean texts, some of which are readily to be found in an airport bookstore. That is why in this work I have often cited someone else's use of a frequently quoted passage of a classic; that way the likelihood increases that a reader who becomes interested in an idea may have another conversation about it. Surely it is foolish to cite an inaccessible original merely to seek to create the appearance of never having read what somebody else has written about an interesting subject. This urge toward accessibity also explains why I have adjusted for clarity to a contemporary reader both spelling and punctuation, except when the original meaning would thereby be obscured.

Once upon a time, we could follow up leads found in a book within the Library of America by repairing to the stacks of the Library of Congress to see what other books generations of readers had thought it wise to place on shelves next to the Big Texts. That epoch is over—I do not dispute the no-browsing rule, but I do lament its causes. Nonetheless, the other mode of checking, going where the action occurred, is still available, though not sufficiently honored in the academy. Academicians are by nature sedentary, seldom honoring field notes so much as footnotes. Literary history needs field notes. That is something one learns as director of the Park Service or of a national history museum. History, to be true, must be grounded in real places and real objects. Curators and rangers have a predilection toward the tangible. They are skeptical of literary sources taken alone, knowing that literature is by definition hearsay. As any police-court reporter knows, things in place are the best evidence. In the course of editing the twelve volumes of the Smithsonian's *Guide to Historic America* and introducing a reissue of volumes of the great old *WPA Guides*, my desire to touch and to see things in the round became reinforced into a passion for place. I like to know where things happened and what those places are like now.

As to the political biases brought to this work: My mother announced in her ninety-fifth year that she was born a Republican and a Presbyterian and intended to die one. As she passed one hundred, she seemed to be less certain about the Republican part. My father was Roman Catholic, Irish—his father had a fine brogue—and I am sure would today be a Democrat. He was in the sporting goods business, which was a good thing because people hunted and fished all during the depression years of the thirties. The depression was not yet over when I entered military service in the Second World War. I emerged unheroically but with some understanding of those who had been heroes and who, like my best friend, died in their country's service. It is possible that my veneration for those who have put their lives in peril for patriotic reasons biases me unduly toward Aaron Burr and against certain others.

In 1948, I attended my first national political convention, accompanying my college roommate, who was the son of a losing contender for the Republican presidential nomination. After college and during law school, I was elected successively precinct chairman, ward chairman, and district chairman in the Minnesota Republican party, and in 1952 I won my first and last election toward a national office—a primary for the U.S. Congress. In the process I had the experience of campaigning along the Minnesota-Iowa border with two representatives of an earlier age: Dwight D. Eisenhower and a man named Julian Kirby, who had spoken on the same platform with William Jennings Bryan, fifty years earlier, before the age of microphones and deodorants. I confess that more than a decade passed before I came to understand what great men were the Prairie Populists like Bryan; Ignatius Donnelly could give us all instruction in deflationary economics. I admire those who dirty their hands with politics and those who dare to think for themselves.

I was taken to Washington as a lawyer and assistant by Warren E. Burger, then Assistant Attorney General and later Chief Justice. My "political education"—in my friend Harry MacPherson's phrase—

entered a harsher phase as I was given for review a set of files demonstrating how two administrations disregarded the civil liberties of a
number of citizens, including Owen Lattimore. After leaving the Justice
Department, I took up journalism for the National Broadcasting Company and various magazines, reporting from the White House and elsewhere, working on television documentaries such as *Victory at Sea* and
a series of my own on network radio. While engaged in all this glam-
our, I was brooding about justice denied, justice deferred, and the
Lattimore case. I went to work on the matter, on my own, and learned
the cheerful lesson that truthful writing can improve the likelihood
that justice ultimately will be done.

Appalled by the assaults of the 1950s upon constitutional liberty, I
joined a group of young lawyers and a great judge, Luther Youngdahl,
who stood against the Senate Internal Security Subcommittee, survived
the defection of a group of craven bleacher-sitters, and won. An eminent and prosperous Washington lawyer—and mariner—who was then
Youngdahl's clerk has recently suggested that I should warn my readers
of my lack of enthusiasm for cloistered critics who rat on those who
put themselves at risk. Done!

During the same period, the mid-1950s, I took a second assignment
in the Eisenhower administration, working under Oveta Culp Hobby
toward the delivery of the Salk polio vaccine. Thereafter, I returned to
NBC for brief celebrity followed by abrupt dismissal: Management
changed; I was an insignificant and unintended victim. After a stint in
regional television, I got outrageously lucky and met a rancher's grandchild from the bleakest corner of Texas, who is working on her own
book across this room at this instant.

Shortly thereafter, a call came from the Labor Department to become a special assistant to Secretary James P. Mitchell, with an assignment to work on housing for migrant farm workers. They were then
kenneled in places more appropriate for farm animals than for people.
Harvest of Shame ensued. So did an infuriated response from the Nixon
White House, and I was out again. Perhaps I overuse the word "betrayal" as a consequence.

Requiring an occupation, and it being late, I thought, for law or
television, I became a banker in St. Paul, Minnesota. I have been recently assured by former customers that I was not a bad one, and it
seems so: After a decade, the bank was considerably bigger, and I was
chairman of the executive committee and a director. But I was also a

problem for the management of the holding company. As a redeveloper of portions of the city without "urban renewal," as a founder of the Guthrie Theater, of which I was the first board chairman, and as a writer of two books about regional history (one of them, *Men on a Moving Frontier*, was published by Wallace Stegner and Tom Watkins and won a prize), I did not fit. It was also thought strange that I took time off to return on a special assignment to the Nixon administration to work on the creation of the student loan program.

The ceiling to eccentricity seemed impermeable, but, it turned out, there was kindness in the neighborhood. I was asked, one day, by the president of the regional Federal Reserve Bank if it were not true that I would be happier doing something else. So I went to the University of Minnesota to run its foundation, manage its finances, teach, and write—and got lucky again. The ensuing altercations with brokers and bankers whose relationships with the university had been excessively cozy and profitable led to sufficient national notoriety to draw the attention of the greatest leader I have ever known, McGeorge Bundy, then president of the Ford Foundation. Bundy was not perfect. He was wrong on some things. But he took the responsibility for acting on his convictions. Many who criticize him never left the bleachers to get on the field. There's another bias.

Bundy suggested that I come to the foundation as its chief financial officer, sell off the Ford stock, and diversify the consequences. That went well, so I was made vice president for the arts as well—and, implicitly, for the humanities. With the latter franchise we launched the redevelopment process for 42nd Street now unfolding (after a needless delay of twenty years occasioned by the pusillanimity of Mayor Ed Koch). We launched as well the American Literary Classics, as a testimonial to Bundy. When he retired, so did I, or thought so. Earlier, President Carter had asked me to chair a committee about what the National Endowment for the Humanities might do and about the sort of man who should head it. That work reexposed me to public education in the humanities and led me toward the Smithsonian Institution. For fourteen years thereafter, I directed a museum but was free to do other things. The museum had been called the National Museum of History and Technology but operated as the Museum of All Other. We made it a Museum of American History and, I think, something of greater interest. More books came along in the ensuing fourteen years—*American Churches; Architecture, Men, Women, and Money; Orders from France; Greek Revival America; Rediscovering America; Mission;* and *Hidden Cities.* There were several television series, and a decent financial practice on the side.

I retired from the Smithsonian in 1992. Then, to my surprise—an Indian summer. In 1993, I became director of the National Park Service, transported back to the whole-souled patriotic world of my father's youth before the First World War, amid a corps of men and women who still believe in simple verities like the trusteeship of Mr. Lincoln's "Great Estate"—the land we inherited. The people of the Park Service are remarkably loyal to each other, and they know a great deal about teaching about place *in* place. Together we first survived a "downsizing" foolishly required by an administration and Congress unwilling to ask the American people to pay for what that nation says it cares about, and then, after 1994, we had to survive attacks by a new Congress possessed by militant ignorance. At the same time, we had to endure the obstructionism of environmental groups lacking any affirmative ideas, and we learned once again the lesson that those who merit the respect of history get off the grandstand and onto the field. When that set of battles was done, however, an educational agenda was being carried forward within an intact system and service. Of that I am proud. And for me, in 1996, there was, for the third—or was it fourth—time, retirement. Which hasn't lasted. I hope it won't.

Notes

Notes to Chapter One

1. Burr on his error, Parton, *Burr*, Vol. I, p. 276.
2. Leveling principles, ibid., Vol. II, p 226.
3. Ibid., p. 277.
4. Adams on Burr's descent, etc., ibid., Vol. I, p. 235.
5. Hamilton to Morris, given in *Hamilton Papers* Vol. XXV, p. 554, given there as February 29, 1802. Or was it really 1800? Quoted also in the Schneidmans, p. 178, fn. 50. The deathbed Hamilton cited in Freeman, "Dueling," p. 317, fn. 110, with further citations. The opinion of Henry Adams, probably salvaged from his lost biography of Burr, appeared in his *Jefferson Administration*, Vol. II, p. 189.
6. The quotations are from the summary of the recent opinions of psychobiographers in the Schneidmans, pp. 159–60.
7. Hosack quoted p. 403, fn. Allan Hamilton, *Hamilton*.
8. Hamilton's public statement on the duel, Allan Hamilton, *Hamilton*, pp. 381–83.
9. Hamilton on Burr, to John Rutledge, Jan. 4, 1801, quoted in ibid., pp. 386 ff.
10. Hamilton and Burr being vindictive, quoted in Beard, *Economic Origins*, p. 405.
11. Hamilton on trapping Burr, ibid.
12. Jefferson on Hamilton, up to the familiar reference to corruption, quoted in Schachner, *Hamilton*, p. 303, and the succeeding passage from Kenin and Wintle's anthology, with its citations, p. 354.
13. Parton on Chesterfield, *Burr*, Vol. I, p. 132. He follows Davis, *Burr*, pp. 224–26, and is followed by Schachner, *Burr*, 74–75, and Lomask, *Burr*, Vol. I, p. 69. Rogow, in *Fatal Friendship*, shows admirable skepticism about this tradition.
14. As Harold Nicholson has pointed out, not even an insolent lord without "consideration" would seek in such contemptible lessons "to instil into young Philip . . . the principles of ethics and religion or even the foundations of a liberal education." Chesterfield had "left such instruction to several tutors. His aim was to assist Philip, exiled to France, in acquiring "the air, the address, the graces and the manners of a man of fashion . . . at

the court of France . . . French manners, rather than . . . English manners." Nicholson *Good Behavior,* p. 199.

15. Burr to Theodosia, Sept. 17, 1795, *Correspondence,* pp. 36–37.
16. Latrobe on Burr, Hamlin, *Latrobe,* p. 591; Burr on himself, and others' comments, Lomask, *Burr,* Vol. I, pp. 94, 96.
17. Latrobe on Burr and Hamilton, Hamlin, *Latrobe,* p. 591.
18. Oliver and, by implication, Hamilton, Allan Hamilton, *Hamilton,* p. 429.

Notes to Chapter Two

1. Hamilton as Creole at The Grange, see *Hamilton Papers,* ed. Syrett, Vol. XXV, pp. 481–82. This paragraph is a précis of pp. 108–30 in my *Orders from France.*
2. After Burr was bankrupted and exiled, John Jacob Astor subdivided the property into 25-by-100-foot lots and began the flattening of the terrain to its present featureless condition. The Richmond Hill estate is now a maze of warehouses and boutiques in the West Village, but, while Burr owned it, the mansion was the most distinguished private residence in Manhattan, more admired than Archibald Gracie's "Mansion" in the upper 80s on the East Side. Dr. Hosack's nursery occupied the site of Rockefeller Center.
3. Jefferson on Burr, Oct. 17, 1808, quoted in Parton, *Burr,* Vol. II, p. 166 fn.
4. Jefferson to Hay, quoted in ibid., Vol. II, pp. 158–59. The exclamation mark is Jefferson's.
5. Ibid.
6. John Adams to Samuel B. Malcolm, Aug. 6, 1812, in the Gilder Lehrman Collection at the Morgan Library, catalogue number GLCO5262.
7. My account of Adams's flirtation with Burr, and these quotations from Adams, are drawn from Samuels, *Adams, Middle Years,* pp. 204–14.
8. The quotation comes from my *Orders from France,* p. 306, in a section devoted to Burr and Jefferson, the revision of which led to the creation of this book. There were too many conclusions drawn there which I now feel to be overdrawn to permit them to stand.
9. Burr on Burr, Burr to Paterson, Davis, *Burr,* p. 194, Burr to Ogden (in a different context), p. 52. Allan Hamilton, in *Hamilton,* p. 43.

Notes to Chapter Three

1. Burr on leveling principles and expounding the Constitution, Parton, *Burr,* Vol. II, p. 262.
2. Ibid.
3. I am grateful to a remarkable work of research and synthesis by Joanne B. Freeman both for this anecdote of Hamilton (which she uses for quite a different effect) and for the count of Hamilton's affairs of honor. Ms. Freeman presents the Burr-Hamilton duel as

a ritual drama and provides for the first time a full statement of the requirements of that ritual, with admirable examples from other duels. She does not, however, seem to support the view that Hamilton was psychologically driven to make Burr his executioner, as I do. Freeman, "Dueling as Politics: Reinterpreting the Burr-Hamilton Duel."

4. Burr coy about theology, quoted in Parton, *Burr*, Vol. II, p. 330.

5. Hamilton and Christian Constitutional Society, see Kerber, *Federalists in Dissent*, note on p. 164.

6. Adams on Burr, Parton, *Burr*, Vol. I, p. 235.

7. Latrobe on Hamilton and Burr, *Papers*, pp. 331–32.

8. Court in Flexner. *Hamilton*, p. 23.

9. The best source for study of Edward Stevens is Stacy B. Day, *Edward Stevens* (Cincinnati: Cultural and Educational Productions, 1969). I have done my best for him in *Orders from France*, pp. 146–64. Lodge's treatment appears in his *Hamilton*, pp. 286–87.

10. Quotations from Hamilton's early writings in Schneidman and Levine-Schneidman, with an excellent bibliography. See p. 163 and footnotes.

11. Schneidman and Levine-Schneidman discovered, or, rather, collated, the instances of "A.B." rather than "A.H." See their p. 165 and bibliography. I am grateful to Joanne Freeman for rescuing me from repeating the theory that Hamilton, under strain, was wont to sign documents "A.B." instead of "A.H." Freeman tells us that using the first two letters of the alphabet instead of one's own signature was commonplace. Too bad. A lovely Freudian opportunity is lost to us.

12. Hamilton on himself, and the description, from Flexner, *Young Hamilton*, p. 41.

13. Burr's appearance, Lomask, Vol. I, p. 89.

14. The Hamilton family position is stated by Allan Hamilton, *Hamilton*, pp. 380–81.

Notes to Chapter Four

1. Hamilton to Stevens, on war, quoted in Flexner, *Hamilton*, p. 35; and his cannon, Allan Hamilton, *Hamilton*, p. 42; Burr in military, Parton, *Burr*, Vol. 1, p. 66.

2. Burr on Arnold, ibid., p. 78.

3. "Electric Burr," Parton, *Burr*, Vol. I, p. 82.

4. Burr and Hamilton on Washington, ibid., p. 83.

5. Washington on Hamilton, Schachner, *Hamilton*, p. 151.

6. Hamilton to Washington, New Winsor, Nov. 10, 1777, draft in Hamilton's hand, *Papers*, 1st series. Hamilton to Putnam, Dec. 9, 1777, *Works*, Vol. IX, pp. 120–21.

7. Hamilton to James Duane on Gates, Sept. 6, 1780, *Hamilton*, ed. Morris, p. 39.

8. Royster on Lee and Jefferson, *Light-Horse Harry Lee*, p. 224.

9. The Signers who did military service were the following: Benjamin Rush was present in Washington's New Jersey campaign as a military surgeon of the Philadelphia militia, not an activity for the squeamish in those preanaesthetic days. Josiah Bartlett of New Hampshire did the same for General John Stark's New Hampshire militia at Bennington. Oliver Wolcott saw action as a major general of the Connecticut militia as it fended off Governor

Tryon's assaults upon the coast. Thomas Nelson, while serving as an officer of the Virginia militia, ordered his own house shelled when the British used it during the Yorktown campaign. The records at Independence Hall show that John Hancock, Thomas Hayward Jr., Arthur Middleton, Thomas McKean, Lewis Morris, Thomas Nelson, Caesar Rodney, Edward Rutledge, George Walton, and Thomas Whipple all saw military service. Hancock was not a success as a major general of the Massachusetts militia, failing to take Newport in his one active campaign, but he tried. Morris served as a major general in the New York militia. Rodney saw action as a major general in the Delaware militia. Walton served as a colonel in the Georgia militia and was wounded and captured during the siege of Savannah in 1779. Whipple was a brigadier general in the New Hampshire militia, serving vigorously in the northern campaigns. Middleton, Hayward, and Rutledge served with the South Carolina militia in the defense of Charleston in 1780, were captured by the British, and suffered nearly a year's imprisonment in St. Augustine.

I am indebted to Coxey Toogood and Laurence Addicott of the National Park Service for review of the Independence National Park's archives to determine the fruits of research into the records of the Pennsylvania Cincinnati, and to Myers, *Liberty without Anarchy*, which is the semiofficial history of the society. The librarian of the society at its headquarters in Washington could find no additions to this list.

The rules for admission to the society varied from state to state, but the intention was to be inclusive of those who had actually served, plus a few who had contributed to the success of the Revolution in other ways. Standards varied from state to state, but in general the requirement of three years' service in the Continental Army was extended to those who served as officers of the state forces as well, together with those who did not put in the full three years if their units were "deranged" by the Congress.

10. Beveridge, *Marshall*, Vol. I, pp. 126 ff. Jefferson had explained his departure from national affairs by "the situation of my domestic affairs." As Beveridge noted: "In his Autobiography, written forty-four years afterward (1821), Jefferson declares that he resigned from Congress and went to the State Legislature because 'our [State] legislation under the regal government had many very vicious points which urgently required reformation and I thought I could be of more use in forwarding that work.' "

11. Valley Forge quotations are from Ward, *Revolution*, Vol. II, p. 544.

12. The mutiny at the Gulf quoted from Davis, *Burr*, Vol. I, pp. 119 ff.

13. Jefferson's band, Malone, *Jefferson the Virginian*, pp. 288–89.

14. Washington quoted in ibid.

15. Ibid.

16. Malone, ibid., p. 290 fn. Beveridge, *Marshall*, Vol. I, p. 126 ff.

17. Ibid., p. 330.

18. Ibid., p. 358.

19. Jefferson's Mazzei letter, quoted in Smith, *Marshall*, p. 14 fn.

20. Marshall on Jefferson, quoted in Beveridge, *Marshall*, Vol. II, p. 537.

21. Ibid.

22. On p. 18 of his Marshall biography, Dr. Smith properly warns us not to take all that Albert Beveridge has to say about Marshall or Jefferson as gospel and presents an array of citations to scholars who think Beveridge unfair to Jefferson. Among them was Richard

Hooker, who, in 1948, found that Beveridge had omitted a "not" from a quotation from Marshall about Jefferson, reversing his meaning. Smith produces an array of other scholars to dismiss as too "generous" and charitable Dumas Malone's suggestion that Beveridge, writing before 1919, may merely have erred by using "an incorrect text of the latter," though these scholars should have known Professor Hooker did not bring the correct copy to light until 1948. Marshall on Jefferson, quoted in Beveridge, *Marshall*, Vol. II, p. 537. On his p. 64, Smith expresses the view that "it strains credulity to believe that as a beleaguered twenty-two-year-old company commander, he [Marshall] would have fretted about Jefferson's absence." Does it? Jefferson was worth fretting about. He was the author of the Declaration of Independence, about to be selected as governor of Virginia, and as eminent in the councils of that commonwealth as his admirers have always claimed.

Notes to Chapter Five

1. The Hermitage, the home of Theodosia Bartow Prevost Burr, remains in Ho-Ho-Kus, New Jersey, which is near Ridgewood, which, in turn, is just north of Paterson. The house, in which she and Burr were married in 1782, was engulfed two generations later by a Gothic Revival shell, designed by William Ranlett. The official guide gives the date of that remodeling as 1804, though 1844 is more likely. The house is owned by the State of New Jersey and maintained by the Friends of the Hermitage. The false front of Burr's Hermitage is less flamboyantly false than that fronting the other Hermitage, Andrew Jackson's residence near Nashville, Tennessee.
2. Parton on the families, *Burr*, Vol. I, p. 169. The Schuyler house is maintained and explicated by the National Park Service near Saratoga, New York.
3. Hamilton on truth, ibid.
4. Burr to Theodosia, Feb. 8, 1793, quoted in Davis, *Burr*, Vol. I, pp. 361–62.
5. Ibid.
6. Burr on women, and Wollstonecraft on women, quoted in Lomask, *Burr, Princeton Years*, pp. 161, 194.
7. Jefferson on women quoted in Brodie, pp. 447–48; each of us may read what he or she will into Jefferson's letter to David Humphreys reporting that "all the handsome young women . . . are for the Tiers Etat, and this is an army more powerful in France than the two hundred thousand men of the King." Jefferson to Washington and Humphreys, Dec. 21, 1788, March 18, 1789, in Sarah Randolph, *Domestic Life*, pp. 158–59.
8. Jefferson to Gallatin, on women, Stevens, *Gallatin*, p. 283.
9. Adams and Abigail, in Ferling, *Adams*, p. 172; Abigail on Burr quoted in Smith, *Adams*, Vol. II, p. 1061.
10. Burr to Theodosia, Feb. 16, 1793, quoted in Davis, *Burr*, Vol. I, p. 363. Before she met and married Godwin in 1797, Wollstonecraft had the misfortune to have fallen under the spell of Gilbert Imlay when they were both in Paris during the Terror, in 1792. Imlay was a notorious philanderer who was also, among other things, Daniel Boone's literary

agent in Europe. He nearly brought ruin to Wollstonecraft, but he achieved immortality to Boone by bringing the Kentucky "b'ar skinner" to the attention of Lord Byron, who immortalized him. Imlay had come to know Boone on the Kentucky frontier when he was there preparing "copy" as a prospectus writer for land speculators in the 1780s, as one of the Wilkinson circle in Lexington. Before he turned his skills from real estate puffery to biographical puffery, in Paris and London, Imlay had come to Burr's attention as the author of a *Topographical Description* of the Ohio Valley, which contained a merciless dissection of the racism of Jefferson's *Notes on Virginia* as well as an enthralling account of the monumental architecture of the Ohio Valley Indians. Having brought Boone to Byron, and Ohio's Hopewell culture for the first time to a large international audience, Imlay became the father of Wollstonecraft's daughter, Fanny, half-sister of Godwin's daughter Mary, who became the wife of Percy Bysshe Shelley.

11. Burr to Theodosia, Feb. 8, 1793, ibid., pp. 361–62.

12. Burr to Theodosia, July 10, 1804, *Correspondence*, pp. 168–70.

13. Burr to Theodosia, Feb. 8, 1793, Davis, *Burr*, Vol. I,. pp. 361–62.

14. After Burr became a senator, he began to demonstrate that though he was disinclined to self-explanation he did have ideas, many of them well ahead of his time. One distinction between the political opinions of Schuyler and Burr was that Burr, then and thereafter, opposed secret sessions of legislatures, especially in the foreign policy deliberations of the U.S. Senate, while Schuyler insisted upon "excluding the vulgar public from the deliberations of a body that felt itself to be the American House of Lords." The quotation is drawn from the biography of Burr (Vol. I, p. 179) by James Parton, who dismissed the matter as "one of the great little questions of the day" and failed to pay sufficient heed to the effects of the Founders' failure to resolve that "little question."

Many of their least admirable actions were hidden in the deep shadow of secret sessions. Those of us who were exposed to committees of the Senate operating in secrecy during the 1950s do not take Parton's blithe view of star chambers, whether judicial or legislative. Burr was right. The threat of secret despotism is not a "little" one. In 1806–7, the niceties of public proceedings and due process became important to Burr himself. Jefferson proclaimed him guilty of treason without public presentment, indictment, or trial and despite an oath of office to uphold the Constitution, ordered Burr and an array of witnesses who might testify for him to be abducted by force, held in secret confinement, and denied access to counsel or to the press.

15. I am indebted to Jack Warren, of the *Washington Papers*, for Jay's letter of January 27, 1792, to Washington, Washington's response of March 6, a letter on the secret-session leak by Benjamin Hawkins, dated January 27, 1792, of whom more anon, and the explanatory notes. Mr. Warren suggests that there was something more nefarious than mischievous in Burr's action. I don't read it so.

16. Adams on Burr and Hamilton, quoted in Webb, "Fateful Encounter," p. 47.

17. My quotation and Malone's comment are to be found in his magisterial *Jefferson the President: Second Term*, p. 300. One is reminded that Jefferson—after proclaiming Burr to be guilty of treason, personally dishonest, and utterly without integrity, and after having harried him into exile—wrote that "against Burr, personally, I never had one hostile sentiment." Jefferson's averral elicited even from the admiring Malone the demurrer

that "this assertion may be questioned as being too much to be believed," hastily adding that "but there is abundant evidence that, previously, he had been notably tolerant of one he had good reason to regard as a troublemaker." One does not always use the presidency to condemn troublemakers as traitors. Hamilton on Burr, ibid., pp. 265–85.

18. Otis's letter and a fragment of Hamilton's response appear in *The Papers of Alexander Hamilton*, Vol. XXV, pp. 259–60, 271. The Gilder Lehrman file number is transcript GLC 496.028. I am grateful to Paul Roman, curator of that collection, for calling it to my attention.

19. Hamilton on Jefferson and Burr, ibid., and quoted in Lomask, *Vice President*, p. 281.

20. Hamilton on Burr, Gilder Lehrman text cited in note 18, and in Lomask, ibid.

21. Gilder Lehrman text cited in note 18. The full text of this letter was recently discovered in the Gilder Lehrman Collection in the Morgan Library; there is only a snippet in the Hamilton Papers.

22. Bayard and Smith quoted in Schachner, *Burr*, p. 207.

23. Jefferson quoted, amid an excellent discussion of the ebb and flow of events in 1804, in *Burr Papers*, pp. 852 ff.

24. Ibid., p. 823.

25. Armstrong on Burr, ibid., p. 823.

26. For Burr and Church, see Lomask, *Burr*, Vol. I, pp. 218 ff. I do not know that Hamilton himself criticized Burr amid these ambiguities. It is true that Burr did serve a private client's interests while a member of the Assembly and was paid for it. There was nothing unusual about this practice at the time, however.

27. Hamilton, Monroe, and the friend in Virginia, quoted in Schachner, *Hamilton*, pp. 369 ff.

28. Ibid.

29. Ibid.

30. Freeman provides an exemplary account of the Hamilton-Monroe provocations, "Dueling," pp. 300–301.

31. Adams on dueling, to Samuel B. Malcom, Aug. 6, 1818, in Gilder Lehrman Collection at the Morgan Library, file no. GLC 5262.

32. Monroe on Adams, quoted in Freeman, "Dueling," p. 298; Madison to Jefferson, ca. Feb. 18, 1798, ibid., p. 299.

33. Henry Adams on Jefferson's courage, quoted in Samuels, *Adams*, p. 49.

34. The Greene-Washington story appears in Gamble, *Savannah Duels*, pp. 73–76.

35. Cooper, in the Schniedmans, p. 170.

36. Burr on rumors, draft of June 26, 1804, quoted in Syrett and Cooke, *Interview*, p. 91. I am indebted to Joanne Freeman not only for a careful reading of my text, and corrections to it, but also a willingness to permit me to draw my own conclusions from the facts upon which we agree, though those conclusions are not the same as hers.

37. Pendleton's Second Report, June 25, 1804, ibid., p. 81.

38. As is the case throughout this work, texts quoted are usually adjusted to twentieth-century practice for ease of reading, but in this instance the dashes may have some psychological significance. Those skilled in eighteenth-century orthography may find the spelling or the capitalization indicative of something which has escaped me, but the original docu-

ments are there for them, as modified in the cited sources, which present, of necessity, a sort of midway between manuscript and the practice of the contemporaries of the editors. First Report, June 25, 1804, in writing of Pendleton, ibid., p. 75.

39. Burr to Hamilton, Parton, *Burr*, Vol, I, p. 343. Neither Parton nor Webb is wholly reliable in his analysis of the events leading up to the duel, nor can Parton be relied upon as to the facts. But their accounts do provide a useful compendium of relevant passages from the correspondence. Webb, "Fateful Encounter," pp. 47 ff.

40. Ibid.

Notes to Chapter Six

1. Chapter epigraph, Allan Hamilton, *Hamilton*, pp. 389–390.
2. Hamilton on fame and on Burr's ambition, quotations in fn. 35 on p. 180 of the Schniedmans' compendium. The quotation on temper is from William Plumer's account of a conversation between Hamilton and Jonathan Mason in Brown, E., *William Plumer's Memorandum*, p. 584.
3. Hamilton's apologia, quoted in ibid., p. 51.
4. Latrobe on Burr and Hamilton, Hamlin, *Latrobe*, p. 591; Hamilton on Burr the voluptuary, Allan Hamilton, *Hamilton*, p. 386.
5. Adams on Hamilton, quoted in Flexner, *Hamilton*, p. 62; Angelica to her sister, quoted in Schachner, *Hamilton*, p. 230. The town of Angelica, New York, is named for her; nearby there is her villa, Belvedere, which, after several visits, seems to me Latrobian, though it is my guess that, contrary to local legend, Latrobe never saw it. Angelica flirted with him, too, and he probably gave her a table-napkin design, to be executed by others.
6. Latrobe on Hamilton and Burr, *Latrobe Papers*, Vol. II, pp. 331–32.
7. Latrobe on Burr, Hamilton, and phallic statues, to John Lenthall, Jan. 7, 1805, ibid., p. 6.
8. Hamilton to Laurens, quoted in Flexner, *Hamilton*, p. 260. Jefferson paid attention to the length of noses as well. In a slightly scatological letter to Maria Cosway, he referred her to the chapter in *Tristram Shandy* in which a whole village turns out to inspect the wondrous nose of a visitor. Though she was not easily shocked in person, perhaps she did not like to see such things in print. Or perhaps she had no sense of humor, failing to have so high an opinion of therapeutic laughter as Burr, who said toward the end of his life that if he had read more of *Tristram Shandy* and less of Voltaire, the world would have been capacious enough for both him and Hamilton.

The subject of noses as repositories, or expressions, of masculine pride is addressed by students of dueling as well as students of humor. "For Southern men of honor," we are told by one such student, Kenneth Greenberg, "the nose was part of the face that preceded a man as he moved in the world. It was the most prominent physical projection of a man's character and was exposed before the eyes of others. Little wonder that men of honor should regard the nose as the most important part of their bodies."

Greenberg repeats a tale told by "one antebellum Southern writer, as follows: a man 'with a most extravagantly protuberant nose [that] moved to and fro like a pendulum [decided to have it trimmed by a doctor.] . . . I saw him afterwards and did not recognize him. I do not recognize him now, nor do I intend to. His individuality, his whole identity is lost'. . . . The liver, the heart, the penis, and the stomach were not even possible as candidates of great significance. A man's character was expressed in what could be publicly displayed, not in what was hidden under clothes or skin. . . . Thus it makes sense that one of the grossest insults for a man of honor was to have his nose pulled or tweaked.''

Greenberg proceeds to give the particulars of the "extraordinary nose-pulling incident . . . and attack upon the most highly venerated nose of the age—that of President Andrew Jackson." Greenberg, "The Nose, the Lie, and the Duel in the Antebellum South," pp. 57 ff.

9. Apparently this was the sort of physiological joshing Hamilton enjoyed; Edward Stevens wrote him from London, on May 8, 1778 (Hamilton, *Works* p. 484):

Mon cher Ami,

Comment vous portez vous? & comment vous etes vous porte dupuis que je n'ai eu le plaisir de vous voir? Si vous etes en bonne sante tout est bien avec vous; j'en suis sure. Qui pourrait avoir imagine mon Ami qu'un homme do votre *grandeur* [Stevens's emphasis], de votre delicatesse de constitution, & de votre tranquillite aurait brille tant, & en si peu de temps, dans le Champ de Mars, que vous l'avez fait.

10. Burr at Hamilton's performance, Allan Hamilton, *Hamilton*, p. 389–90.
11. Pendleton to Van Ness, 26 June 1804, in Syrett and Wallace, p. 94.
12. Burr's determination to fight, quoted in Freeman, "Duel," p. 310.
13. Parton on Burr as friend of Hamilton, *Burr*, Vol. II, pp. 264–65.
14. Ibid.
15. Ibid., pp. 265–66.
16. Ibid.
17. Ritual duels, Freeman, "Dueling," p. 294.
18. Burr's contempt, Parton, *Burr*, Vol. II, p. 266. Parton gives the "convicted felon" version. Burr himself wrote of Hamilton's "conscious guilt" in his letter to Charles Biddle of July 18, 1804, quoted in Freeman, p. 316. Freeman says that Hamilton's "facial expression was his final testimony to the complexities of the affair of honor." I think that it expressed complexities greater than status and reputation, that he was anxious to restrain a political rival and at the same time convinced that he was acting in the public good, and that he felt twinges of religious faith, personal morality, and familial responsibility. "Hamilton was a duelist who refused to fire." But he did fire. Freeman was not attempting, and perhaps would not favor attempting, an inquiry into Hamilton's relationship to Burr outside politics. She was simply telling us more about the ritual quality of their duel, and of others at the time, than anyone else has told us.
19. Hamilton quoted in Schachner, *Hamilton*, p. 428.
20. Van Ness quoted in Freeman, "Dueling," p. 311.
21. While many details of the duel are disputed, I believe I am recounting only those to which there is agreement among all contemporary accounts, as restated by Webb and in

considerably greater technological detail by Merrill Lindsay, the firearms expert who discovered the hidden hair triggers by examining the pistols, which had been reposing in the vaults of the Chase Manhattan Bank. Lindsay in *Smithsonian Magazine*, Webb in *American Heritage*. The quotations are from Lindsay.

22. Hamilton and second fire, quoted in Schachner, *Hamilton*, p. 428.
23. Burr's account given in Parton, *Burr*, Vol. II, p. 266; Hamilton's words, Webb, p. 52.
24. Ibid.

Notes to Chapter Seven

1. There have been a number of detailed studies of emancipation of slaves in New York. My percentages are taken from a review by Steve Rosswurm, *Journal of Urban History*, Vol. XXI, no. 4, (May 1995): pp. 505–10, reviewing Shane White's *Somewhat More Independent* (Athens: University of Georgia Press, 1991).

   Anthony Gronowicz stated in 1998, with a multitude of citations, that in the early eighteenth century "New York City became the principal depot for the North American market in slaves. . . . Its European-American citizenry took advantage of this bounty; in 1703, 43 percent owned one or two slaves [or, one assumes, more]. . . . The most prominent New York families, like the Livingstons, established their fortunes as slave traders." Gronowicz, *Race and Class*, p. 9 and endnote 25 on p. 203.

   The emphasis in these paragraphs is upon the concentration of slaves in the lower Hudson Valley and in New York City, not upon total figures for the entire state or colony. The total population of slaves in the colony was counted at 19,883 in 1771 and was probably still about that in 1786, though many blacks had left with the British. The ratio of slaves to whites in 1771 was one to seven. See citations by McManus, p. 172.

2. My statistics are drawn from William P. McDermott, "Slaves and Slave Owners in Dutchess County," *Afro-Americans in New York Life and History*, Vol. XVIV, no. 1 (1995): pp. 17–41.

   When the chancellor, Jefferson's most powerful ally in the North, composed a memorandum to Talleyrand and Napoleon to dissuade them from interest in Louisiana, he addressed them as men of his world, who would understand that investment in slaves brought to its unbounded vastness would be riskier than on an island in the West Indies, where the sea could act as a moat. With the Catskill "maroon" colonies on his horizon, he could sympathize with the complaints of his relatives in West Florida and Jamaica. And in West Florida they had to cope with the interracial counterparts to the Catskill "maroons," the "Seminoles." Today, however one does not need to look all the way to the Catskills for evidence of the slaveowning past of the Hudson River merchant-squires; through the window of Franklin Roosevelt's study at Hyde Park, one can see, discreetly beyond a hedge, the slave quarters.

3. Hamilton on blacks, to John Jay, March 14, 1779, in *Papers*, Vol. II, pp. 17–18; Hamilton and degraded slaves, quoted in Flexner, *Young Hamilton*, p. 39.

4. Lomask on Burr and slavery, *Burr*, Vol. I, pp. 119–20.

5. Garrison was also the source of a strange tale that in 1831 Burr journeyed to Boston to seek to persuade him to cease his abolitionist activity, including publication of the *Liberator*, which he had just then begun. The tale is full of self-congratulatory comparisons of Garrison to Burr, leaving one very curious as to what actually transpired between the two. It is not inconceivable that Garrison's tribute to Burr in 1858 was offered for the same reasons of distressed conscience as John Quincy Adams's "fallen man" cadenza (see Chapter 30). Perhaps Garrison had, all the while, been retailing a version of the Boston visit which made him look better by making Burr worse and felt badly about the matter, though not so badly as to admit that the despised Burr actually urged him on. See Lomask, *Burr, Conspiracy*, pp. 403–4.

6. Samuel Flagg Bemis on Jay, *Dictionary of American Biography* (hereafter called *DAB*), Vol. IX, pp. 7 ff; Lodge on Burr, in his *Hamilton*, pp. 244–45.

7. Cheetham on Burr and blacks, *Burr Papers*, p. 837.

8. Adams on Burr, Parton, *Burr*, Vol. I, p. 235.

9. Jay on Jay, Dangerfield, *Livingston*, p. 46; Dangerfield on Jay, ibid., p. 225; Burr on Burr, Parton, *Burr*, Vol. II, p. 234.

10. Van Gassbeck to Burr, *Burr Papers*, Vol. I, p. 104.

11. Flexner on Hamilton and slavery, *Young Hamilton*, p. 39.

12. Hamilton and the Manumission Society, McManus, pp. 170–71.

13. Ibid.

14. Higginbotham, *Matter of Color*, pp. 142–43.

15. See Jay, *Correspondence*, Vol. IV, item 430, Nov. 17, 1819.

16. Washington and the West, see *Hidden Cities*, pp. 97–114, with citations.

17. Hamilton, speaking to the New York Ratifying Convention, June 20 and 22, 1788, quoted in Syrett, *Hamilton Papers*, Vol. III, p. 654. There is a lively debate about Hamilton's bona fides as historians display varying degrees of cynicism about his motives. See footnote 32 in Weston, "Alexander Hamilton and the Abolition of Slavery," pp. 31 ff.

18. The duc de Rochefoucauld-Liancourt responded to another aspect of Hamilton's character, his tenderness: "He united dignity and feeling, and much force and decision, delightful manners, great sweetness . . . infinitely agreeable." Hamilton and the French, Allan Hamilton, *Hamilton*, pp. 34 ff.

19. Jefferson and the Friends of the Blacks, quoted in Fay, p. 242.

20. It is worth noting that others have dealt with the problem of Jefferson's refusal to join with Les Amis des Noirs by ignoring it. The justly celebrated biography of Jefferson by Dumas Malone includes two volumes on this period. Their titles are *Thomas Jefferson, the Virginian* and *Thomas Jefferson and the Rights of Man*. Neither carries in its index a reference to Les Amis des Noirs or to Brissot.

21. The Library of America edition of the *Writings* of Jefferson has this quotation at p. 1202.

22. My quotation and much of this discussion are drawn from Dixon Ryan Fox, "The Negro Vote in Old New York."

23. Burr and Tammany, McManus, p. 175, fn. 58; Tammany and Negro emancipation, *New York Evening Post*, Oct. 31, 1846. As I was rewriting these pages I came upon Anthony Gronowicz's *Race and Class Politics in New York City before the Civil War*, a new (1998), thorough, and well-written scrutiny of the process by which "democratic republicanism

. . . rationalized inequality" (p. xi). Gronowicz has produced a classic to be set next to Dixon Ryan Fox's work of two generations earlier on the shelves of every serious scholar of the relationship among race politics, class politics, and ethnic politics in the United States.

24. McManus, ibid. It is not quite fair for Gronowicz to write that Thomas Jefferson "did more to guaranty slavery's growth than any other president." Nor is it fair for him to write that "no public official, including Hamilton and Burr, dared speak up about integrating the ex-slave into the social or economic mainstream." Burr did "speak up" often enough, as the steps *of* slaves *toward* the mainstream were facilitated by the removal of manacles. And Burr, with Hamilton, helped to prevent a new set of manacles from being placed upon blacks by their reenslavement by slave-stealers from the South or by former masters from Haiti. (Gronowicz, quoted from his p. 21.)

25. I cite the Virginia and Kentucky Resolutions from the extended—and admirably clear—account by Elkins and McKittrick, pp. 719 ff.

26. Burr and discretion, Lomask, *Burr*, Vol. I, p. 233.

27. Jay quoted in Schachner, *Hamilton*, p. 394.

28. Munro to Burr, Bedford, April 18, 1804, *Burr Papers*, Vol. II, p. 866.

29. Jefferson on free blacks, quoted in Miller, *Wolf by the Ears*, p. 218, in the midst of a brilliant discussion of Jefferson's differences with John Marshall; the book of fate is opened in a passage from *The Writings of Thomas Jefferson*, ed. Lipscomb (Washington, 1904), Vol. I, pp. 72–73.

30. The Kentucky Abolition Society proposal appears in an excellent discussion of this subject in D. W. Meinig, *Continental*, p. 301.

Notes to Chapter Eight

1. For titles given the Watauga Association, see Robert E. Corlew, *Tennessee* (U. of Tenn., Knoxville, 1981), p. 49.

2. Thomas Marshall in Abernethy, *South*, p. 68.

3. Wilkinson to Carondelet, quoted in Abernethy, ibid., and in the Innes Papers. Brown, in Abernethy, *South*, p. 52.

4. Marshall's letter is printed in Green, *Conspiracy*, pp. 250 ff.

5. Allen on Innes, ibid., pp. 255–65.

6. The *Dictionary of American Biography* does well by James Innes. I have paraphrased its report and have taken my quotations from it. "Innes, James," Vol. IX, p. 487.

7. Innes on revolt, Green, *Conspiracy*, p. 83.

8. Innes declines, Abernethy, *South*, p. 215. Innes and Nicholas to Power, Sept. 14, 1797, in Clark, *Proofs*, p. 195.

9. Hamilton on French, Kline, *Hamilton*, Vol. I, p. 283.

10. Ibid., p. 284.

11. Jefferson to Monroe on the breach, quoted in Schachner, *Hamilton*, p. 318.

12. Lewis, "Jefferson and Virginia's Pioneers," pp. 573, 577.

13. Ibid.
14. Ibid., p. 579.
15. James, *Clark*, p. 236.
16. Clark on the infirm United States, Van Every, *Ark*, p. 176.
17. Jefferson to Innes, letter dated March 7, 1791.
18. *The Alcoholic Republic* is the title of an excellent book on the subject by W. J. Rorabaugh. Washington's remarks are in Flexner, *George Washington and the New Nation*, pp. 302–3.
19. Clark on certainty, ibid., p. 290.
20. In the early 1780s, Michaux had botanized along the Tigris and Euphrates, in modern Iraq. After his return from the espionage work in the United States, he went out to Madagascar, in 1801–2. Lest it be thought that he only engaged in spying, historians of botany tell us that Michaux was a conscientious scientist; his *North American Sylva* still has value today. It is one of Jefferson's virtues that he preferred to use as intelligence agents people who practiced good science as well.
21. I have followed the account of Abernethy, *South*, 1976 printing, pp. 102 ff., and the quotation comes from p. 115.

Notes to Chapter Nine

1. Genêt, quoted in Elkins and McKitrick, p. 350.
2. Malone on Jefferson and connivance, in his *DAB* entry on Jefferson, Vol. X, p. 25; Jefferson's memorandum of July 5, 1793, quoted in Sharp, p. 107.
3. Jefferson to Washington, quoted in Patrick, *Fiasco*, p. 50.
4. Ibid.
5. Nicholas to Madison, Nov. 15, 1793, quoted in Abernethy, *South*, pp. 122–23.
6. Washington's proclamation of March 1794, Sharp, p. 107.
7. Wilkinson to Nolan, quoted in Claiborne, p. 157 fn.
8. Wilkinson to Brown, August 28, 1794, James Wilkinson Papers, special collections, Chicago Historical Society, Vol. I, p. 29, quoted in Rusche.
9. Wilkinson's famous expatriation declaration is to be found in Rusche, in *Littell's Political Transactions*, Vols. CXXXVII-CXXXIX, and in any of Wilkinson's biographies written since the Spanish archives were opened.
10. Wilkinson's correspondence with the British is reported in Simcoe, Vol. II, p. 243. Rusche has found a letter confirming this process from Wilkinson to Robert Elliot, dated April 15, 1794, among the Anthony Wayne Papers in the Philadelphia Historical Society, Vol. XXXIV, p. 13.
11. Rusche, in "The Battle of Fallen Timbers: Securing America's Western Frontier," a senior thesis, University of Pennsylvania, April 1997. I am indebted to Michael Zuckerman, Rusche's adviser, for bringing this work to my attention.
12. I am following Rusche's account, based upon an exposition by Newman in the Anthony Wayne Papers in the Philadelphia Historical Society, Vol. XXXVIII, p. 79.
13. Rusche makes a persuasive case that Newman was not a deserter from the American

forces trying to save his skin by implicating Wilkinson, the theory of Wiley Sword in *President Washington's Indian War* (1985). Newman was apprehended, and given his chance to get to Wayne with his story, on his way back to the American army at Fort Washington. If one did not know what Wilkinson was later willing to do in the Southwest, Newman's story would be less credible. Rusche followed the lead offered in British doubts of Newman's bona fides as a deserter in the Simcoe Papers.

14. Nolan to Wilkinson, May 6, 1797, in *Wilkinson Papers*, Vol. I, p. 90, in the Chicago Historical Society.
15. Wayne to Knox, Jan. 29, 1795, in Rusche.
16. Ibid.
17. Hamilton to McHenry, ibid.
18. Washington's reply, ibid. Some of Wilkinson's biographers, followed by the otherwise admirable Thomas Abernethy, place Washington's reply as a propos to the 1791, not the 1799, appointment. But Washington's letter is dated June 25,1799. See *Works*, Vol. V, p. 277.
19. McHenry to Hamilton, quoted in Hendrickson, p. 483.
20. Though these founders knew that the unity of the Great Valley, with its watery trunk spreading into two great limbs to the west and east, the Missouri and the Ohio, could not be divided in parts without destroying all hope of a united and vigorous nation, none but Jefferson seems to have contemplated the extension of the Republic beyond that valley. Jefferson, Madison, and Monroe stated the Rocky Mountains to be the limit, and Washington does not seem to have thought beyond the great plains. The leaders of the next generation, Gallatin, Crawford, and Clay, agreed. Thomas Hart Benton suggested a statue of "the fabled god Terminus should be raised upon. . . . [the] highest peak [of the Rockies], and if a government *should* be formed beyond it, that government should separate from the mother Empire as the child separates from the parent at the age of manhood (Merk, pp. 315–16). For Hamilton and the British, see Boyd, *Number 7;* Hamilton on New Orleans, *Papers*, Vol. V, p. 484, Vol. VII, p. 112, Vol. XXVI, p. 72.
21. Jefferson to Burr, cited supra.
22. Hamilton to King, quoted in Schachner, *Hamilton*, p. 384.
23. Hamilton and South America, ibid.
24. Hamilton to Miranda, quoted in Abernethy, p. 227. The inference is my own.
25. Wilkinson to Hamilton, August 1799, Wandell and Minnigerode, *Burr*, Vol. II, p. 15.
26. Adams on Hamilton, Hendrickson, supra.
27. Jefferson on New Orleans, quoted in Merk, *Westward Movement*, p. 141.
28. Jefferson to the British Ambassador, and Pichon, quoted in Wandell and Minnigerode, Vol. II, pp. 20–21.
29. Hamilton to Wilkinson, draft dated Oct. 31, 1799, in Hamilton's hand, quoted in Morris, *Hamilton*, p. 117.
30. Hamilton on his rivals, Parton, *Burr*, Vol. I, pp. 256, 280.
31. Adams on Hamilton, ibid., p. 258.
32. Hamilton's will, Wolcott, etc., in Allan Hamilton, *Hamilton*, pp. 426 ff.
33. My quotations are drawn from Linda Kerber's account, in her *Federalists in Dissent*, pp. 153 ff.

34. Ibid., p. 44.
35. King on Griswold's conversation with Burr, April 5,1804, *Burr Papers*, pp. 862 ff.
36. There is not enough space in this book to rehabilitate the characters of all those unfortunate enough to have stood at the edge of the road as the juggernaut sent against Burr has rolled through the decades. The intrepid and incorruptible Justus Eric Bollmann comes first to mind, but there were many other innocents swept into the ditch almost incidentally, as historians invoked "the maxim: . . . 'noscitur ex sociis.' " It was dangerous to be a friend of Burr's, for any friend had to be denigrated lest, indeed, one would know him *better* by his associates. A few scholars have gone to the edge of the road, looked in the ditch, and brought forth a rehabilitated character. One of these independents was Bill Brunson, who turned his attention to Samuel Swartwout, concluded that "if one were to make a list of the twelve—or even of the six—most maligned men in American history, surely Samuel Swartwout would be on the list," and gave in great detail his reasons for saying so. He had the pleasure of offering another list—that of eminent historians who had their facts entirely wrong about Swartwout, in detail. See Brunson, "Samuel Swartwout." My quotations come from pp. 180 ff.
37. Burr on secession, *Papers*, p. 1105.
38. Ibid., pp. 1116–17. The documents in question are the series of notes taken by a middle-level French official, Louis Roux, dated March 13, 14, and 19, 1810, and transmitted to his chief, the duc de Cadore. The first portion of the March 13 memorandum offers a credible, and possibly close to verbatim, account of what Burr may have said. Those of March 14 and 19 were written later, as afterthoughts.
39. For a good, cool review of the debate on Burr's discussions in Paris, see Mary-Jo Kline and the other editors of the *Burr Papers*, pp. 1099 ff.; for a somewhat warmer view, see Milton Lomask, *Burr, Conspiracy and Exile*, pp. 334 ff; for Walter McCaleb in full heat, see his *New Light*, pp. 137 ff. The Cadore letter appears at p. 150.
40. Ibid.
41. Ibid.
42. Burr's conversations with Jay, Davis, *Burr*, Vol. II, p. 376. Davis guessed that the subject was South America, but this is most unlikely, and Davis can seldom be trusted even as to events he himself observed.

Notes to Chapter Ten

1. Duff Cooper on Talleyrand and Hamilton, *Talleyrand*, pp. 73–74.
2. Talleyrand on Hamilton, quoted in Flexner, *Young Hamilton*, p. 449; for extended discussion of the interrelationships of Burr, Talleyrand, and Hamilton, see *Orders from France*.
3. Hamilton to Washington, April 18, 1792, quoted in Morris, *Hamilton*, p. 281.
4. Washington on the condition of roads, quoted in Slaughter, p. 79; the lady, p. 63.
5. Ibid.
6. Washington on the Ohio Valley, entry for Oct. 4, 1784, *Diaries*, pp. 317 ff, as printed in Cleland, *George Washington in the Ohio Valley.*

7. Jefferson and new colonies, *Papers*, ed. Boyd, Vol. 1, pp. 362–36.

8. Jefferson in Slaughter, p. 42.

9. Jefferson to Brown, May 26, 1788, *Works*, ed. Ford, Vol. X, p. 6.

10. Jefferson to Madison, Jan. 30, 1787, *Writings*, p. 882.

11. Jefferson on blessing them both, quoted in Wandell and Minnigerode, *Burr*, Vol. II, p. 39.

12. Gallatin's Insurrection, quoted on p. 32 of Jerry Clouse's fine short summary of the Whiskey Rebellion for the Pennsylvania Historical and Museum Commission, with an excellent bibliography.

13. Walters on Gallatin and Burr, *Gallatin*, p. 169.

14. Tracy and Allen of Connecticut, ibid., pp. 119–20, 136.

15. Dumont and Bentham on Burr, Parton, *Burr*, Vol. II, pp. 168–69.

16. Jefferson to Gallatin, Aug. 1823, and comment on that letter, *Hidden Cities*, p. 151.

17. Remonstrance of 1791, Clouse, p. 32.

18. Gallatin on the resolutions, ibid.; on his sin, Walters, p. 69.

19. Washington's reaction of Aug. 1792, in Clouse, p. 32.

20. Malone on Jefferson and Whiskey Rebels, *Jefferson and the Rights of Man*, p. 479.

21. Gallatin to Badollet, Feb. 1, 1794, quoted in Stevens, *Gallatin*, pp. 56–57. The Terror had meted out what Gallatin admitted to be "its dreadful executions . . . [y]et, upon the whole, as long as the combined despots press in upon every frontier, and employ every engine to destroy and distress the interior parts [of France], I think they, and they alone, are answerable for every act of severity or injustice, for every excess, nay for every crime, which either of the contending parties in France have committed."

22. Talents, quoted ibid., p. 70.

23. Tully letter, quoted ibid., p. 87.

24. Dallas on Gallatin, ibid., p. 90.

25. Hamilton quoted in Slaughter, *Whiskey Rebellion*, p. 219.

26. Walter on Bradford, *Gallatin*, p. 71.

27. Those who wish to follow the bibliography of duck soup may find it in *Hidden Cities*, p. 313, fn. 4, and in Thomas Slaughter's much more extended discussion of this point in his *Whiskey Rebellion*. I have used Slaughter's research at greater length in both *Orders from France* and *Hidden Cities*.

28. Jefferson to Madison, Dec. 28, 1794, quoted in Abernethy, *South*, p. 224.

29. Bowers, *Jefferson and Hamilton*, pp. 250–56.

30. Ibid.

31. Collot as quoted, in an extended context, in *Hidden Cities*, p. 111.

32. Ibid.

33. Jefferson to Burr, quoted in Lomask, *Burr, Princeton Years*, p. 158.

34. Washington and integrity, quoted ibid., p. 183.

35. Ibid., p. 184.

36. Adams quoted in Dangerfield on Livingstons and Clintons, *Livingston*, pp. 298–99. Dangerfield was busy rehabilitating the reputation of the subject of his biography, Chancellor Robert Livingston. Henry Adams's approving citation of Gallatin was an impediment to that end, so Dangerfield wrote: "Nobody doubts the honesty of Gallatin's politics or the

keenness, in general, of his observation: but how he reached this conclusion, it would be difficult to say. . . . One disagrees with Henry Adams (or, for that matter, with Albert Gallatin) only with the utmost diffidence: yet to lump all three factions together is almost to miss the point." Dangerfield would grant to Burr only that he "was an adventurer and nothing more: he came of a good Calvinist family, his manners were unexceptionable, he had a great deal of charm, and he was a most dangerous associate." Dangerfield quotes Adams in his *Livingston*, p. 298.

37. Nicholson to Gallatin, May 7, 1800, Walters, p. 125.

38. Jefferson to Burr, ibid.

39. For Burr on Virginians, see Walters, p. 125; for Jackson, see Chapter Four, above.

40. Jefferson to Burr, Dec. 15, 1800, ibid., p. 126.

41. Burr to Jefferson, Feb. 12, 1801, quoted in Lomask, *Princeton Years*, p. 287.

42. Howell's account, ibid., p. 288.

43. Ibid. Lomask does not develop the point or relate it to other instances of temporizing. He and I do not precisely agree in our interpretations of these events.

44. Burr to Gallatin, Feb. 12, 1800, ibid., pp. 128–29.

45. Gallatin quoted in Walters, *Gallatin*, p. 129 fn.

46. Burr and Gallatin, ibid., pp. 164–65. All these ibids. may encourage a reader to recognize that I have been following Walters's generally excellent account of their interchange. But my interpretation flows from quite a different view of the character of Burr, and thus of Jefferson, than that of either of Gallatin's biographers, Stevens or Walters. Stevens puts the entire onus for their rupture on Burr and ties it to this patronage dispute. As noted in the main text, Walters follows his account with this remarkably mild statement: "The President's perhaps unconscious [!] but certainly pronounced efforts to isolate and weaken Burr politically had placed" Gallatin in an "ambiguous position."

47. Gallatin to Harrison, May 1809, ibid., p. 221.

48. Gallatin to his wife on the duel, Walters, pp. 166–67.

49. Burr to Gallatin, July 31, 1806, *Burr Papers*, p. 992.

Notes to Chapter Eleven

1. Jefferson to Burr on cannibals, Feb. 11, 1799, *Burr Papers*, Vol. I, p. 390.

2. French pay, Gallatin to Hannah, Dec. 7, 1798, in Adams, *Gallatin*, pp. 222–23. It must be acknowledged that Henry Adams's dutiful life of Gallatin is duller than anything he might have done for Burr.

3. Jefferson to Monroe and his fears of contagion are presented in a larger context in *Orders from France*, pp. 152 ff.

4. Gallatin's Black Speech, ibid.

5. Lear's letter of February 7, 1802, is cited along with other dispatches of a similar tenor in Tim Matthewson's "Jefferson and Haiti," to which additional reference, some of it critical was made earlier.

6. Jefferson to British and the Congress, ibid., pp. 233–34.

7. Egerton, *Gabriel's Rebellion*, p. 161.
8. The *Hamilton Papers*, in Vol. XXV (April 1800–April 1802), pp. 413 ff., have provided what little is known about this incident, with excellent notes. Someone could do a dandy thesis on the subject.
9. Gallatin on Louisianans, Walters, *Gallatin*, p. 180.
10. Gallatin's letter is properly emphasized by Matthewson, who found it in the Gallatin Papers, and to whom we owe a debt for that discovery. But he places its full text only in a footnote (p. 240) which diminishes the effect of its embarrassed tone, and permits the inference that Gallatin was offering a legitimate excuse.
11. Ibid.
12. Eppes and the Treasury are quoted in Egerton's elegant account of these events, *Gabriel's Rebellion*, p. 171.
13. The documentary history of this event in the life of Aaron Burr is exceedingly difficult to disentangle. Here is all that I have been able to learn: In Senator Robert C. Byrd's *The Senate* (Washington, D.C.: USGPO, 1993) only three tiebreaking votes by Burr are given, those of January 26, 1802, January 27, 1802, and February 9, 1802. These three had to do with the repeal of the Judiciary Act, not with diplomacy. However, in the last days of the 8th Congress and of his term as Vice President, Burr did preside over the debate on the Clearance Bill of 1805 on February 19, 1805, and there was action. The tradition is that there was a tie, and a tiebreaking vote by Burr, against the bill. The amended bill was returned to the House on February 22, and only after conference and Burr's departure was there agreement, on March 2, on a bill which controlled supplies of arms and provisions to the West Indian rebels (*U.S. Statutes* 2:342–43).

Milton Lomask, in his scrupulous *Aaron Burr*, Vol. I, p. 365, wrote: "He (Burr) was not taken in by the unprecedented flow of warmth from the Jeffersonians. How little that affected his thinking is shown by an incident in late February when for the last time he was called on to give his casting vote in the Senate. The bill before the body was one that the Administration wanted. A political maverick to the end, Burr blandly voted against it." Mr. Lomask's characteristically copious citations are not broken out by paragraph or page, and I have not been able to find in them precise identification of which bill it was, since Byrd's listing does not contain a vote against the administration as I read them. As I have indicated elsewhere, Lomask did not give much space to Burr's views on slavery.

It would be unmannerly to suggest why Senator Byrd and his assistants have failed to help us confirm the inference which led me, in *Orders from France* (p. 154), to state that Burr broke the tie which sent the Logan antitrading bill back to the House. Lamentably, I had not then seen the Byrd version of his tiebreaking record and did not keep the source notes which led me to my assertion.

It is possible that my account is mistaken, though for several years I have badgered archivists and friends in an effort to get it right. I must emphasize that these are my interpretations only; the state of the record leaves the precise sequence of events unclear. Marilyn Parr of the Library of Congress, and the staff of the National Archives, have done their best to bring greater clarity to the matter. Neither OCLC FirstSearch nor

Eureka helped the resourceful Ms. Parr, who, after all she could do, gently informed me that "this particular field appears to have generated little recent interest" (personal note of July 6, 1996).

Notes to Chapter Twelve

1. The two Clinton affairs of honor are reported in Lomask, *Aaron Burr*, Vol. I, p. 307.
2. Morris on Burr, quoted in Schachner, *Hamilton*, p. 431; Morris on Clarkson, quoted in Freeman, "Ducling," p. 316.
3. Burr on the duel, *Papers*, Vol. II, p. 887.
4. Burr to Theodosia, Aug. 3, 1804, *Correspondence*, p. 172.
5. Burr on South Carolina, *Correspondence*, pp. 179–81.
6. Ibid.
7. Burr to Alston on exile, quoted in Waddell and Minnegerode, *Burr*, Vol. I, p. 305.
8. Truxton on half-wars, etc., DeConde, *Quasi-War*, pp. 128–29.
9. Truxton on Hamilton, quoted in Parton, *Burr*, vol. II, pp. 17–18.
10. Ibid.
11. This is how I interpret Truxton's scrawl to be found among the *Burr Papers*, pp. 677–78. The editors of those papers have it this way: "You must take care of Alexander Hamilton. King—Pinckney and Patterson—besides all those at the head of Departments."
12. Truxton of March 19, 1804, ibid., pp. 856 ff.
13. Truxton, first in a letter to Joseph Alston and then in testimony, quoted in McCaleb, *Conspiracy*, p. 285.
14. Truxton's testimony and its tone, *Papers*, p. 990.
15. With eyes beguiled by red ripening berries thirty miles farther to the southeast of the Princeton upland, one set of Burr biographers, Waddell and Minnegerode, has this town as "Cranberry." Sad to say, it was named not for the fruit of the bog but for Lord Cranbury.
16. Burr on the streets, Parton, *Burr*, Vol. II, p. 18.
17. Moreau and Bonaparte, quoted in Pratt, *Road to Empire*, p. 335.
18. Burr to Theodosia, *Letters*, p. 173.
19. Biddle's Grecian expedition, his conflict with Andrew Jackson, and his contributions to the American Greek Revival are discussed in *Architecture, Men, Women, and Money* and in *Greek Revival America*. I am grateful for the kind words about those works expressed by R. A. McNeal in his *Nicholas Biddle in Greece*, p. 12.

Notes to Chapter Thirteen

1. The coproponent of the "better" plan was Charles Williamson, a Scots officer from Stirling, where his brother Lord Belgray later became of aid to Burr during his Scottish wanderings. Williamson seems to have been in Philadelphia in the spring of 1804 and

may have emphasized to Burr the importance of the Scottish associations in Georgia, especially among the McIntoshes and Clarks.

Williamson had come to the United States in 1791 as agent for investors in New York lands. He became a citizen of the United States and settled in the Genesee Valley beside the Wadsworths. That allocates him to another volume, which might be an account of Burr's New York associations, though it is worth noting here that the Scottish Clarks, of St. Mary's, Georgia, who befriended Burr there, were connected with the Wadsworths through introductions by Burr's brother-in-law, Tapping Reeve, who trained the younger Clark in the law and lived in a nest of Wadsworths.

2. Burr and Rush, *Papers*, Vol. II, p. 891; to Theodosia and Joseph Alston, pp. 893–94 fn.

3. Lewis to Burr, Dec. 17, 1803, *Burr Papers*, pp. 809–11, with elegant notes by the editors.

4. Ibid.

5. Hampton to Taylor, Sept. 30, 1799, quoted in Bridwell, *Hampton*, p. 408; Hampton to Whitney, Feb. 8, 1805, ibid.

6. Lewis to Burr, Dec. 17, 1803, *Papers*, p. 809 and notes.

7. Burr's theatrical adventure, in Parton, *Burr*, Vol. II, p. 284.

8. Burr to Biddle from Hampton, ibid., p. 894.

9. Preserving rank, from "An Exhortation to Gentlemen of small fortunes to settle in East Florida," quoted in Bailyn, *Voyagers*, pp. 434–35.

10. Burr to Theodosia, *Correspondence*, pp. 174–75.

11. Burr to Theodosia, ibid., pp. 175–76.

12. Ibid., p. 177.

13. Ibid.

14. Frederica, ibid., pp. 180–81.

15. Ibid., p. 181.

16. Wednesday, Sept. 12, 1804, ibid., pp. 181–84.

17. Jackson, *McIntosh*, pp. 24–25, fn. 14, and quotation on p. 146.

18. Livingston's stream, he had said, "is impossible to stem. . . . I long ago advised that they should yield to the torrent if they hoped to direct its course—you know that nothing but well-timed delays, indefatigable industry, and a minute attention to every favorable circumstance could have prevented our being exactly in their [the Livingstons' Tory kinsmen of Pennsylvania] situation." Livingston to William Duer, June 12, 1777, quoted in Staughton Lynd, *Class Conflict*, pp. 40–41.

19. Burr to Theodosia about ciphers, Feb. 21, 1802, *Correspondence*, p. 177. A friend suggests that kinder words may be in order about Gideon Granger. Let it be said, then, that he knew a good architectural plan when he saw one—see *Orders from France*. Richard R. John has fairly treated him in his *Spreading the News*.

20. Burr to Theodosia, *Correspondence*, pp. 184–85. Burr's playfulness in the face of Gideon Granger's postal inspectors is infuriating to historians seeking to learn what he had in mind for Florida, though it was no doubt good for his political health. It did, however, lead his first professional biographer, James Parton, into inserting a name into Burr's text without indicating to the reader that he had done so. Where Burr had written "he," in the following sentence, Parton inserted the name "Major Butler."

By-the-by, you have no idea—how should you have, seeing that you never heard a word about it?—you have no idea, I was going to say, of the zeal and animation, of the intrepidity and frankness with which *he* [my italics] avowed and maintained. . . .

It is possible that Burr meant Butler. He had just toasted him. But "zeal and animation"? "Intrepidity and frankness"? Is this the host who had saved himself from contamination by remaining in Philadelphia while Burr visited Georgia. *Someone* had gained Burr's admiration for avowing and maintaining something—something, we may assume, such as affection, or respect, or an assertion of Burr's innocence of any breach of the gentleman's code, or perhaps something such as willingness to *do* something in the light of such an avowal and assertion. That does not sound like Butler, who never permitted enthusiasm to outrun advantage.

Forewarned by Parton's excess of interpretation, it would no doubt be prudent to eschew any further guesses, but let us take the risk: Burr was adverting to some unstated "he," someone in the neighborhood, someone who *did* display the qualities of zeal, animation, intrepidity, and frankness, someone who, perhaps, *had* joined him for a few drinks and Revolutionary reminiscence. Such a person might have offered from his own experience in Florida some thoughts to elevate Burr's aspirations higher than bushes of long-staple cotton. Perhaps on that evening—à votre santé—Burr was told of a project appealing to adventurers, a project attempted a score of times before him and attempted three times after him, until it was brought to success in 1819 by Andrew Jackson—the seizure of Spanish Florida by a filibustering expedition.

Who, possessing zeal, animation, intrepidity, and frankness, *who*, sympathetic to military commanders of the Revolution, *who*, wholly of Burr's mind with respect to dueling with political rivals even to the death, *who*, a veteran of attempts against St. Augustine, *who* was at hand? General Lachlan McIntosh.

21. For Ms. Sumter, see *Burr Papers*, pp. 280 fn., 580 fn.
22. Ibid. I do not suggest that Granger felt any special malice toward Burr. The Burr Papers contain amicable correspondence between the two early in the administration of 1800 on patronage matters. All that is necessary to know of Granger is his eagerness to be of service to Burr's enemies, especially to his archenemy, Thomas Jefferson. The evidence of that eagerness will be set forth shortly.
23. Burr from Frederica, St. Simons, Sept. 15, 1804, ibid., pp. 185–87.
24. My population figures are drawn from Patrick, *Fiasco*, p. 44.

Notes to Chapter Fourteen

1. Lewis to Burr, ibid. White had grown "inflexible" in a lifetime of defending the remaining portions of the empire of the Catholic Majesty to which he, and many another Irish Catholic gentleman devoted to the Stuart cause, had sworn fealty. He had done service in Hungary and Silesia, before transferring to the Hibernia Regiment from the Royal Walloon Guards. After stints in Algeria and assisting the American Revolution, he settled into the governorship of East Florida, where he stood ready to cope with either

an armed invasion or any stratagem hatched by such a man as Lewis. And, probably to Burr's dismay, he had successfully recruited McQueen to be his military and judicial deputy.

2. Politics aside, it is a pity that White and Burr did not meet, for they might have found each other interesting. White was a civilized man; his library included Andrew Ellicott's *Journal* and the *Gazetteer* of Jedediah Morse, "A Letter to Joseph Priestley," *Peter Pindar*, William Prist's *Journey to the United States*, Doctor Johnson's *Dictionary*, treatises on war in Spanish, English, and French, a Latin dictionary, books on Ireland and a French history of the House of Stuart, works of economics, a volume of sketches, an English *New Testament*, and a French history of the Emperors of Rome. Andrew Jackson did not have a library like that. (The endlessly resourceful Charles Tingley of St. Augustine provided me with a copy of James Gregory Cusick's 1993 dissertation, "Ethnic Groups and Class in Late Colonial St. Augustine," which contains White's inventory as Table A-4.)

3. Jefferson to Washington, quoted in Patrick, *Fiasco*, p. 50.

4. William S. Coker found in the East Florida Papers at the University of Florida the documents pertaining to Aaron Burr in Florida in 1804 and generously provided to me photocopies by letter dated June 2, 1994. The documents (Reel 40, Legajo 105A9) are the letter of introduction from Casa Trujo to White, dated August 9, 1804, and another letter from Casa Yrujo to White, dated August 12, 1804.

   An unsigned letter, almost certainly from White to Casa Trujo, acknowledges Casa Trujo's of August 12 and states that Burr was staying at "la Ysla de Fuerte George" about fourteen leagues from St. Augustine, the residence of John Houstoun McIntosh. This letter is in Reel 40, Legajo 105A9.

5. The *Harper's* article cited below says there were originally thirty-five cabins.

6. The McQueen archive assembled by Hartridge contains invitations to family suppers with the Jeffersons.

7. For McQueen as a friend, Bell, *Legacy*, p. 50.

8. McQueen to Robert Mackay, March 4, 1804, *Letters*, xliii; McQueen to Mackay, May 6, 1804, *Letters*, xliv.

9. For McQueen's estate, the Library of Congress is one good source. I am indebted, however, to Charles Tingley of the St. Augustine Preservation Society for pointing out to me, in its copies of that inventory, a listing of McQueen's library, paintings, and furniture. Lamentably, the listing of books holds no Castell or Ware (see below). If it did, we could pronounce the architectural historian's equivalent of "pounce." But the other works on gardening and the arts are what one would expect to find in a gentleman's shelves beside either Ware or Castell—and several entries are unintelligible in their Spanish translations.

10. Hartridge, *The Letters of Don Juan McQueen to His Family*, Vol. XXX, pp. 30, 44.

11. Politicians at the end of the eighteenth century and the beginning of the nineteenth could afford to gratify a gentleman's interest in architecture. Architecture, for Thomas Jefferson, was more than a gentleman's diversion. Jefferson expressed in architecture many of the feelings he did not put into words, including his patriotism.

12. McQueen as military builder, Ward and Snodgrass, *Old Hickory's Town*, pp. 89 ff.

13. McQueen, ibid., pp. 56, 63.

14. McQueen's building activity in 1798, Ward and Snodgrass, n.p.
15. Burr's letter to White from "McIntosh's—St. Johns," dated September 22, giving the excuse that he could not get to St. Augustine because of storm damage, is in Reel 42, Legajo 108E9.
16. Here again is how the rhizomes connected this skein of Livingstons, Bayards, Houstouns, and McIntoshes:

   Robert Livingston, first Lord of Livingston Manor (1654–1728), was a Presbyterian Scot whose father took him to Holland at the age of nine to escape the furious Episcopalians. This connection was significant to the Presbyterians among the Livingstons, many of whom went to Princeton and whose intellectual chief was Aaron Burr Sr.

   Philip Livingston (1686–1749), second Lord of the Manor, had a brother, Judge Robert of Clermont (1718–75). Janet Livingston Montgomery, the wife of Burr's commander in Canada, was the daughter of *Judge* Robert Livingston. Her brothers were Edward (1764–1836) and the *chancellor* Robert.

   Philip the Second Manor Lord married Caterina van Brugh. Their son Peter van Brugh Livingston (1710–92) was the father of the Catharine, born in 1742, who married Nicholas Bayard (1736-?) in 1762.

   Nicholas and Catherine Livingston Bayard had two daughters: Eliza married John Houstoun McIntosh, and Mary married his uncle William Houstoun (1757–1812), son of Sir Patrick. William Houstoun's sister, the aforesaid mother of John Houstoun McIntosh, was Anne Priscilla Houstoun. The Bayards arrived in Nieuw Amsterdam with Peter Stuyvesant. They divided thereafter into the New Jersey branch, which grew rich from owning the terrain upon which was built the city of Hoboken, and a Maryland-Delaware branch, from which sprang that James Bayard who made Thomas Jefferson, rather than Aaron Burr, President in 1800.

   The Livingstons and Bayards had a cadet branch almost everywhere Aaron Burr wandered; when those clusters acted in concert, they comprised the most powerful aggregate of family interests with which either Burr or Thomas Jefferson had to come to terms. In the North, the family interest had been founded by the first patroon, during Dutch days. The Philip Philip [*sic*] branch of Livingstons were on Jamaica. The Florida Livingstons were based in Pensacola, where Philip Livingston Jr. served unhappily as secretary to the British governor of West Florida but managed to facilitate two grants of twenty-five thousand acres each to Peter Van Brugh Livingston and his associates, and thus to that branch of the family closest to the Bayards and McIntoshes. After 1802, the New Orleans Livingstons were established by the family's presiding intellect and Burr's steadfast friend, Edward Livingston.
17. Burr to Theodosia, Oct. 1, 1804, *Correspondence*, p. 188.
18. The banquet, Hamilton to King, March 4, 1802, *Hamilton Papers*, Vol. XXV, p. 600; Troup to King, May 6, 1802, *Burr Papers*, p. 720.
19. Washington is quoted in Smith, *Patriarch*, p. 102.
20. Keep and sheep, quoted in Meyer, *Highland Scots*, p. 37.
21. North Carolina's degraded condition, William Richardson Davie quoted in Kerber, *Federalists*, p. 31.

22. "Abhorrent domination" is Oliver Wolcott's phrase, quoted ibid., p. 32; the Yankee vs. planter quotation is drawn from the Raleigh, N.C. "Minerva", ibid., p. 27.
23. Anonymous Virginian quoted in Lomask, *Burr, 1756–1805*, p. 190.
24. I am following Meyer's account, from which the quotations are taken. See *Highland Scots*, p. 150.
25. Burr in Petersburg, Parton, *Burr*, Vol. II, p. 21.
26. Ibid.
27. Burr in Richmond, Schachner, *Burr*, p. 422, citing the Blennerhasset Papers.
28. Bloomfield to Burr, *Papers*, p. 737.
29. The quotation and my summary are drawn from the neat little biography of Chase in the *DAB*.
30. Ibid.
31. Martin, of March 27, *Burr Papers*, pp. 861–62.

Notes to Chapter Fifteen

1. The Spanish tradition provided for marriages of prominent men of European origin to women of African descent. Florida's multiracial culture was like that of Brazil, or Mexico, or of New Orleans, under Spanish rule. In the case of the Kingsleys, the lineage of the wife was more distinguished than that of the husband, which may also have been true of the African wife of Kingsley's overseer, Abraham Hannahan. Their neighbor James Erwin was married to an African wife named Molly, and George Clarke's two African wives were both received as prominent ladies of the area. The wives of Francis Richard, Francisco Xavier Sanchez, and other leaders of early Florida, raised their interracial children as families, according to Daniel Schafer, the expert in north Florida's social history and biographer of Anta Kingsley. Schafer generously provided me with a copy of the chapter entitled "Shades of Freedom" from his forthcoming biography of *Anta Kingsley*, in its prepublication and unpaginated version, in 1996.
2. The concept of "middle grounds" was contributed by Richard White to our understanding of our history, in a study largely focused on the Great Lakes region. Since 1991, when White showed us where to look and what to look for, we have had less than a decade to consider how distinct was each of the Middle Grounds forming along the western reach of European American control and how different were the responses of each of the Founding Fathers to this phenomenon of the frontier.
3. The consolidated tribes were assembled from many groups, not all speaking the same now-extinct Munsee dialect of the Algonquian stem. "Mahicans" has also been spelled "Mohicans" and "Mohegans."
4. Burr's principle that peace was attainable was stated in a letter to George Washington, dated March 13, 1792, for the text of which I am most grateful to Jack Warren of the Washington Papers.
5. Once more I acknowledge the aid of Jack Warren (see above), who provided the full text of Knox's letter of February 18, 1792, as well as Burr's of March 13, 1792, from the Washington Papers.

6. Burr's of March 13, 1792, ibid.
7. Ibid.
8. Burr to Jefferson, March 13, 1792, is also to be found in *Burr Papers*, p. 102 ff., with wonderfully helpful footnotes. Burr to Jefferson on Aupaumut, April 6, 1798, ibid, p. 341.
9. Ibid.
10. For Brant and Burr, see Kelsay, p. 576; Burr to his daughter, ibid., p. 623.
11. *Burr Papers*, pp. 101–3, with the usual exemplary notes.
12. Burr to Jefferson, *Burr Papers*, pp. 102 ff.

Notes to Chapter Sixteen

1. Slave insurrection, quoted in Bridwell, p. 575; Tennessee militia, in Tommy Young, "U.S. Army," p. 212.
2. Free black militia, Young, "U.S. Army," p. 204.
3. Claiborne to Madison, Dec. 27, 1803, Claiborne, *Official Letter Books*.
4. Free black militia, quoted in Young, "U.S. Army," p. 204.
5. Ibid.
6. Ibid., pp. 205–6.
7. Officers in Natchitoches, Cox, "Frontier," pp. 36–37.
8. Jefferson and Yrujo, ibid., p. 42.
9. Anonymous to Folch, quoted in McCaleb, *New Light*, p. 88.
10. Wilkinson to Dearborn, Dec. 20, 1803, quoted in ibid., p. 19; Wilkinson and Claiborne, quoted in Schachner, *Burr*, p. 366.
11. Claiborne, Dec. 9, 1806, in his journal as quoted in McCaleb, *Conspiracy*, p. 175.
12. Ibid., pp. 206–7.

Note to Part Five Introduction

1. Jefferson's proclamation, with excellent analysis, in Schachner, *Burr*, pp. 354 ff.

Notes to Chapter Seventeen

1. Clark to Wilkinson, Sept. 7, 1805, quoted in Waddell and Minnigerode, *Burr*, pp. 48 ff.
2. Ibid.
3. Ibid.
4. Jackson on Burr, quoted in Lomask, Vol. I, p. 151; Latrobe on Burr, *Orders from France*, p. 341.
5. Burr to Paterson, Davis, *Burr*, Vol. I p. 194; Burr to Reeve, quoted in Wandell and Minnigerode, *Burr*, Vol. II, p. 267.

6. Burr and gaiety, in Wandell and Minnigerode, *Burr*, Vol. II, p. 266.

7. Burr asked Latrobe to travel to Louisville in April 1805, when he himself would be in the area, to survey a canal on the Indiana side of the Ohio, around the falls. Later that year, the Indiana legislature incorporated a company with such a purpose, naming Burr as a director. With federal assistance, a canal was built in the 1820s on the Kentucky side. Burr's offer of the ten thousand acres came on October 26, 1806.

8. Burr in Canada, Davis, *Burr*, Vol. I, pp. 67–68.

9. Ibid.

10. The miracle of beauty is offered by Claiborne in his *Mississippi*, p. 287. Claiborne was not so excellent a writer as Pickett of Alabama and was writing in 1880, thirty years later. By that time only Henry Adams was still holding out against that torrent of abuse and rumor about Burr which Pickett resisted and to which Claiborne succumbed. Deferring to Jefferson, Claiborne preferred the testimony of Wilkinson to that of Burr and wrote too early to be informed of the documentation of Wilkinson's treason and perfidy produced in the Spanish archives by Isaac J. Cox.

11. Ibid., p. 287 fn.

12. Davis, *Burr*, Vol. II, p. 371.

13. Bishop he was not, any more than the priest in the rose-covered cottage was likely to have been an abbé. There is a sort of "grade-creep" in these accounts, as that term is understood in the military. That wonderful Sulpician and friend to architecture, Louis-Guillaume-Valantin Du Bourg (later known as William), a refugee from Saint Domingue and former leader of Georgetown and Saint Mary's Colleges, had not yet arrived in New Orleans as apostolic administrator. He was roughly treated in a schismatic city and went on to St. Louis, where he built the splendid cathedral which stands beneath the shadow of the Lewis and Clark arch. See *Orders from France*, pp. 296, 378.

14. Ibid., p. 382; Davis is not reliable, but this passage has the ring of at least partial truth.

15. Cox on Folch, *West Florida*, p. 200. We must remember that Cox was antithetical to Burr.

16. I am quoting the summary of Morales's views, ibid., pp. 211–12.

17. This account is Abernethy's, *Conspiracy*, pp. 223–24. Perkins's own account does not speak of a conversation with the Spanish officer, but perhaps Abernethy's research in local newspapers led to this additional embellishment, for one may surmise that while Perkins and Gaines were alive every passing reporter asked them for details.

18. Jackson on Burr's plans, Lomask, *Conspiracy*, p. 82.

19. Abernethy, *Conspiracy*, p. 37, tells us that Burr's hopes for a war were "completely crushed." Abernethy was hostile to Burr and apparently relied upon one of Wilkinson's "coded letters," dated December 12, 1805, about which the editors of the Burr Papers express appropriate skepticism on p. 948. Burr's letter to Clay, quoted in Lomask, *Conspiracy*, p. 96, does not read as crushed. And Lomask concludes that he "was telling the truth."

20. Burr to Smith, quoted in Lomask, *Conspiracy*, p. 112.

21. Jefferson to the Congress, quoted in Wandell and Minnigerode, pp. 28–29.

22. Jefferson to Bowdoin in Madrid, ibid., p. 40.

23. Burr to Tupper, ibid., p. 93.

24. For Washington and slavery, see especially *Hidden Cities*, p. 97. The best account of the Meades is to be found in *The Age* (Louisville, Kentucky), Feb. 8, 1879, pp. 81–84. Other accounts omit the embarrassments of Meade's view of slavery or of his friendship for Burr. It is fairly typical of the contaminated state of local histories attempting to find positions pleasant to admirers of Jefferson, and shrinking from Burr, that two or three other accounts garble David II's custodianship of Harmon Blennerhasset in 1807— Meade escorted Blennerhasset to the Richmond Trial—with Burr's happy visit to the Meades in 1805, when he was not only *not* in custody but was a local celebrity, being vindicated by a jury with the assistance of Henry Clay.

25. My description comes from Rexford Newcomb, *Architecture in Old Kentucky*, from which comes the line about fabulous estates, on p. 47; from *The Age*, supra, and from Elizabeth Simpson, *Bluegrass Houses*, with the quotation about Negro children.

26. The Meades' costume, in Simpson, p. 95.

27. I am quoting from *The Age*, as in note 24.

28. Jefferson memorandum, Oct. 22, 1806, quoted in McCaleb, *Conspiracy*, p. 91.

29. Jefferson on Eaton, ibid.

30. Jefferson's notes on the importance of Eaton's transmittal through Granger are reprinted in Lomask, *Burr, Conspiracy*, pp. 176–77. Jefferson to James Madison on Granger's role, letter dated March 10, 1814, reprinted by Hamlin, pp. 47–48.

31. Eaton, discussed by Schachner, *Burr*, pp. 315–16.

32. Granger to Jefferson, Sept. 27, 1810, quoted in Hamlin, pp. 41–43.

Granger's letter is an anthology of coded references to events in the lives of Jefferson and Burr for which we have lost the decoding keys. "It may be said that a cloud of suspicion has overshadowed me. . . . I have been accused of Burrism." What might that mean? No one has ever managed to connect Granger and Burr more closely than the coincident presence of Burr's cousin Pierpont Edwards and Granger among the organizers of the Republican party in Connecticut, and subsequent correspondence between Burr and Granger on patronage questions early in their administration. What else was there? In his letter to Jefferson, Granger asserted that in 1800 he had betrayed Burr's confidence by sending "Mr. Erving to go to Virginia to warn your electors" that a deadlock was impending, and "in the winter of 1804 I acted in concert and in confidence with you," presumably to arrange the replacement of Burr by George Clinton. Something must have gone awry, for though "I was denounced to you in the spring of that year, you knew that the denunciation was void of truth."

Denunciation of complicity with Burr and the Federalists, perhaps? Surely not by De Witt Clinton, for Granger's connections to him persisted to his dying day. Then, perhaps, by Chancellor Robert Livingston, increasingly estranged from the Virginians after unpleasant experiences with them in Paris, as they purloined credit from him for the Louisiana Purchase. "I have long known . . . the person who set that vile business on foot—he knew better, and happy will it be for him, if with all his importance he lingers two years without appearing as Burr did on the disclosure of his intrigue in 1800." Aha! Another intrigue with the Federalists! That might be Livingston: Granger went on—in this application for a seat on the Supreme Court of the United States—to write the former President: "I am not given to create suspicions [!] I know what I write and know that intrigue did not go to Europe with Burr—she has a haunt between Richmond and New Haven." Bisecting the two, one gets Livingston Manor.

33. Ibid.

34. Jefferson to Madison, Oct. 15, 1810, ibid., p. 44.

35. Granger to Jefferson, February 22, 1814, and Jefferson to Madison, March 10, 1814, quoted in Hamlin, pp. 47–48.

36. Hamlin, ibid., pp. 47–48 Jefferson to Granger, March 9, 1814, quoted ibid., pp. 48–49.

37. Wilkinson to Clark about Jefferson, Clark, *Proofs*, p. 196.

38. Wilkinson on Claiborne, ibid., pp. 197, 365.

39. Cabinet minutes, Lomask, *Conspiracy*, p. 178.

40. I have been unable to find out why Wilkinson felt it necessary to go after Boone. This episode in his sequence of perfidies is told in an extended footnote in *Hidden Cities*, pp. 324–25, which also deals with his associate Gilbert Imlay, the cad who brought unhappiness to Mary Wollstonecraft and also was the first novelist to present Thomas Jefferson as a racial hypocrite.

Notes to Chapter Eighteen

1. French views of the West quoted from largely French sources in John Logan Allen, pp. 3–4.

2. Bossu in Allen, p. 3; Marquette in De Voto, p. 234; De Voto, p. 134.

3. This and the surrounding paragraphs are tributes to Custis's meticulous notes and to Flores's remarkably intelligible and extended notes on those notes.

4. Alligators in abundance, Custis quoted in Flores, p. 226.

5. Comte de Volney, quoted in Sibley, p. 25.

6. Canning quote in Dangerfield, *Livingston*, p. 369.

Notes to Chapter Nineteen

1. Granger in *DAB*, Vol. VII-VIII, p. 483.

2. Granger and Negroes, Leech, *Post Office*, p. 14.

3. Granger admitted his membership in the Yazoo company in a long letter to Jefferson, Sept. 27, 1810, reprinted in Hamlin, *Granger*, pp. 40–43.

4. Randolph on Granger and Yazoo, quoted in Kirk, *Randolph*, pp. 308–9.

5. Orleans Legislature, quoted in McCaleb, *New Light*, p. 60.

6. Jefferson to Wilkinson, June 21, 1807, quoted in H. Adams, *Jefferson*, p. 917.

7. Proclamation and instruction to Wilkinson, Lomask, *Conspiracy*, pp. 180–82.

8. Smith's affidavit is to be found in Claiborne's *Mississippi*, p. 268; Claiborne did not identify Smith or mention him again.

9. Smith's assignment is summarized by Abernethy, *Conspiracy*, p. 218. Abernethy spells the captain's name "Hook," which is a little too close to Peter Pan; I. J. Cox, citing correspondence from Hooke himself, says "Hooke." See *West Florida*, p. 682.

10. The description of Morgan's sons was by Burr, writing on July 25, 1807, to Jonathan Rhea asking confirmation by other people of Princeton of what he had been told was known by Rhea, Daniel Agnew, John Hamilton, and William Hight. Letter in Gilder Lehrman Collection at the Morgan Library, file no. GLC 1544.

11. Morgan the first, see Burr, *Papers*, p. 978. This does not square with Abernethy's statement that Jefferson "passed over" Morgan's account (*Conspiracy*, p. 193). But Jefferson said different things at different times, and Abernethy, otherwise a master of this field, was not at his best in his Burr book.

12. Jefferson on Burr's plans, quoted in Lomask, *Conspiracy*, p. 199.

13. Plumer on Burr, quoted in Schachner, *Burr*, p. 388.

14. Adams on Burr, Lomask, *Conspiracy*, p. 200.

15. Adams, ibid.

16. Ibid.

17. Burr on the way to New Orleans, quoted in Parton, *Burr*, Vol. II, p. 40.

18. Mississippi's most celebrated and reprinted historian of the Victorian age, John F. H. Claiborne, must be read cautiously except as a writer of descriptive prose, but he was acquainted with Washington, Mississippi, when it was

> rich, elevated and picturesque. . . . The society was highly cultured and refined . . . a gay and fashionable place. The presence of the military had its influence . . . ; punctilio and ceremony, parades and public entertainments were the features of the place. . . . [It was] famous for its wine parties and dinners, usually enlivened by one or more duels directly afterward.
>
> Such was this now deserted and forlorn looking village. . . In its forums there was more oratory, in its salons more wit and beauty than we have ever witnessed since— all now moldering, neglected and forgotten, in the desolate graveyard of the ancient capital. (pp. 259–60)

   Claiborne's history of Mississippi, published in 1879, bears the impress of the middle years of the Victorian era, having been expunged of the vigor of its counterpart for Alabama, that of Albert James Pickett, which reached its publishers in 1851. Naturally enough, these two works differ in their views of Aaron Burr. Burr's refusal to offer to the general public an effusive churchiness was as offensive to Claiborne as his opposition to Jefferson and Jefferson's man, James Wilkinson, whom Claiborne defended to the end. Alabama's Pickett made a cool judgment of the evidence as to Burr and Wilkinson and, fifty years before proof of Wilkinson's perfidy was discovered in the Spanish archives, concluded that the former spoke truth and the latter falsehood.

19. William F. Coker, the expert on Bruin, has kindly corrected a number of errors derived from other authors, and some beauties of my own creation, which might otherwise have found their way into these pages. Coker, private communications and in "Peter Bryan Bruin of Bath," *West Virginia History*, Vol. XXX, no. 4 (July 1969).

20. Cox on Hooke, *West Florida*, p. 203, citing Hooke's report to Wilkinson.
21. Ambuscade, Shields letter, Feb. 26, 1807, quoted in Claiborne, *History*, p. 285.
22. Ibid., p. 378.

Notes to Chapter Twenty

1. *Pennsylvania Magazine of History and Biography*, hereafter designated as *PMHB*, Vol. XLIV (1920), pp. 297–98.
2. Ibid.
3. Rodney to his son, ibid.
4. Old '76 and Rodney, Lomask, *Conspiracy*, p. 214.
5. Rodney to Jefferson, Nov. 21, 1806, *PMHB*, Vol. XLIV (1920), pp. 295–96.
6. Rodney to his son, ibid., p. 300.
7. Rodney to his son, *PMHB*, Vol. XLIV (1920), pp. 295 ff. and see below.
8. Ibid.
9. Rodney to his son on Burr, *PMHB*, Vol. XLIV (1920), pp. 300–301.
10. Philander Smith to Jedediah Smith, April 14, 1807, in the Gilder Lehrman Collection in the Morgan Library, file no. GLC 4601. I am grateful to Sandra Trenholm for bringing it to my attention. I cannot prove that we have the right Jedediahs and Philanders, but the Yankee Federalism inherent in this correspondence has the right tone for the upstate Smiths.
11. Smith to Smith, ibid.
12. Smith on the jury, ibid.; Adams to Benjamin Rush, Sept. 1, 1807, in the Gilder Lehrman Collection at the Morgan Library, file no. GLC 4879.
13. Plumer, p. 584.
14. Ibid.
15. Plumer, p. 544. The offer to Blennerhasset was made by William Duane, speaking for the administration; see Davis, *Burr*, Vol. II, pp. 294–95.
16. Jefferson on no evidence, quoted in Schachner, *Burr*, p. 388. The entry in Plumer's *Memorandum* is for July 4, 1807.
17. Jefferson to Bowdoin, April 2, 1807, Wandell and Minnigerode, *Burr*, Vol. II, p. 178.
18. Jefferson to Madison, May 1, 1807, quoted in McCaleb, *New Light*, p. 105.
19. Jefferson as war hawk against Spain, see Reginald Stuart, *Half-Way Pacifist*, quotations on p. 41.
20. Adams, ibid.
21. Adams to Benjamin Rush, Sept. 1, 1807, in Gilder Lehrman Collection at the Morgan Library, file no. GLC 4879.
22. Cox on Claiborne's success, *West Florida*, p. 330.
23. Ibid.
24. Ibid., pp. 379–80.
25. These references to a later period are necessary because we must seek for truth about what was happening in Mississippi between 1804 and 1807 through a scrim created fifty

years thereafter, a scrim of Confederate history. Events before "the War Between the States" were examined after 1865 to justify the Confederate side of that war. Whether in 1807 or in 1857, those on the side of states' rights, nullification, and slavery—or who seemed through southern eyes to be so, such as Thomas Jefferson—were nobly treated by most southern historians (there were remarkable exceptions, such as Alabama's Pickett). Those who opposed them were presented as proto-carpetbaggers, especially if they were, in fact, Yankees, such as Winthrop Sargent.

The apologist-in-chief for the plantation system was J. F. H. Claiborne, as noted earlier. Claiborne's uncle was selected by Jefferson to extirpate as much as he could of the effects of Sargent's governorship. Claiborne the historian expressed vehement disapproval of Ellicott and an only slightly moderated aversion to Sargent, the modification possibly arising from Sargent's accommodations late in life to slavery.

Claiborne expressed particular horror that Yankee Federalists had attempted to promulgate for Mississippi the legal system developed for the Northwest Territory, citing with evident approval the local slaveowners' protest to Congress that the "two sections in their people and institutions [were] entirely dissimilar" (Claiborne on slaveowners' petition, in *Mississippi*, pp. 211 ff.).

26. Washington to Ellicott about Wilkinson, quoted in Wilson and Jackson, p. 121, fn. 5.

27. It is easy to dismiss Ellicott as a knave, a fool, or a dupe, for that is how Claiborne treats him. But we can make better judgments of him if we recognize that Ellicott had earned the hostility of slaveowners while laying out the District of Columbia, by having the temerity to bring into his work, as a peer, the African-American engineer Benjamin Banneker. Thomas Jefferson expressed doubt of Banneker's ability to handle complex calculations, apparently miffed by the mere presence of such a man in a supervisory role, where it might be demonstrated that blacks were fit for nobler tasks than hoeing tobacco or cotton.

The bad press accorded Ellicott in southern histories does not square with an assessment by Benjamin Henry Latrobe—consistently the best judge of character of any of our witnesses to these events—or that offered by Latrobe's son, the great railroad engineer John H. B. Latrobe. The younger Latrobe, who studied under Ellicott at West Point, was as unsentimental a character as any produced during the great age of engineering. So the opinion expressed of Ellicott by these two skeptics is of value. "When he died," wrote John to his father, "and was buried with full military honors, and I was one of the escort that fired over his grave, I felt that a good and true man had passed away, and that I had lost a warm and kind hearted friend" (Latrobe, on *Papers*, Vol. III, p. 1033).

It has rightly been written of Ellicott:

Although not a Houston or a Frémont, he played a similar part in American expansion. Finding himself in disputed territory which his government greatly desired; surrounded by an unsettled population, most of whose elements were eager for American control; facing officials of an expiring regime . . . he furthered every effort to stimulate a revolt against the Spaniards. (Cox, *West Florida*, p. 41)

With these judgments of Ellicott in mind, we come to Claiborne's introduction of him and his companion, James Seagrove:

In 1791, Andrew Ellicott, a Pennsylvania quaker [*sic*], who had some reputation as a mathematician and astronomer, had been sent . . . to run the line between the State of Georgia and the Creek Indians. He was accompanied by James Seagrove, a foreigner [Seagrove was Irish—like Governor George Mathews of Georgia and Pierce Butler of South Carolina, neither of whom was described by Claiborne as "a foreigner"] who by some strange influence [that of George Washington] had been appointed Superintendent of Indian Affairs on that frontier—a position of great delicacy . . . demanding circumspection, forbearance and vigilance, and a thorough knowledge of the Southern people and of the circumstances of the savages. [His job was to keep the slavedriving planters from illegally occupying more Indian land.] Seagrove was of an irritable and suspicious temperament . . . [and] occupied himself in fomenting misunderstandings between Georgians and the Indians, and misrepresenting the State authorities to his employers. . . . Ellicott remained with Seagrove, a willing and mischievous co-adjutor. He [Ellicott] brought with him, from his prim and semi-saintly home in Pennsylvania, the bitterest hatred of the southern slave-holder, studiously disguised under a sedate exterior, but, like the treacherous moccasin, ever ready to strike. (Claiborne, *Mississippi*, p. 161)

28. Burr, excusing himself to Guion, *Papers*, p. 938. Thanks to Jack Elliott Jr. of the Mississippi Department of Archives and History, I have made use of Guion's own letter book, as printed in the Seventh Annual Report of that department (Oct. 1, 1907, to Oct. 1, 1908), Appendix, pp. 25 ff.

29. Dinsmore insisted that those who spelled his name "Dinsmore" were "miscalling" him; he never wrote it as "Dinsmore." The Dinsmoor Papers at Dartmouth have it right; the Dinsmore Papers in the Arizona Historical Society don't. Jack Elliott is the expert on this embattled question and provides the citation to Dinsmoor's own view on pp. 470–71 in Leonard A. Morrison's *History of Windham in New Hampshire, 1719–1883* (reprinted by Phoenix Publishing, Canaan, N.H.).

30. Dearborn to Major Bruff, on Wilkinson, and Rodney to Bruff, quoted in Schachner, *Burr*, p. 399.

31. Dinsmoor's letter to his wife of October 26, 1806, reposes in the Dinsmoor Papers in the Baker Library, Dartmouth College. All further references to Dinsmoor's correspondence came from the same source unless otherwise noted, and in every instance are before you because of Mr. Elliott's generosity. In due consciousness of the infirmities of reading a state of feeling at a distance in time, Mr. Elliott has admonished me (letter, Feb. 11, 1999) that Dinsmoor also got drunk twice in late September 1806, in Philadelphia, and "it seems that it would have been unlikely that they [these two "drunks"] were produced in anticipation of purchasing slaves the following month." Who knows?

32. Burr to Theodosia, quoted in Davis, *Burr*, Vol. II, p. 373. I have altered the sequence of his remarks to provide a little clearer exposition, indicating the alterations by the triple dots. During the summer of 1805, Rush Nutt passed along the Trace within a week of Burr's transit, leaving in his journal (in the hands of the National Park Service—copies available from its Natchez Trace unit) the best description available to us of the Trace itself, the Chickasaws, the agents stationed among them, and the archaeology of the

region. Nutt's baptismal name was Rushford, but he changed it to Rush in admiration for Benjamin Rush; he and Dr. Cummins of Bruinsburg were both students of Rush in Philadelphia. Burr and Nutt may have known each other through Cummins or Rush.

33. McKee on Burr at Chickasaw Agency Ball, in microfilm copy of his diary in the Mississippi Department of Archives and History. Thanks to Jack Elliott Jr.

34. RG 107, M22, roll 3, p. 88, in the National Archives.

35. Dinsmoor and Wilkinson, in Abernethy, *Conspiracy*, pp. 218–19; Wilkinson to Dinsmoor, Dec. 4, 1806, quoted in McCaleb, *Conspiracy*, p. 230.

36. The dates are important and emerge from Dinsmoor's letter to his wife of Dec. 8 in Box 1 of the Dinsmoor Papers; from *American State Papers*, Miscellaneous, Vol. I, p. 601 (his departure date); and his letter to the secretary of 12/30 (RG 107, M22, roll 3, p. 88, in the National Archives). Jackson's report, Abernethy, *Conspiracy*, pp. 116–17.

37. McKee to Wilkinson, *American State Papers*, Miscellaneous, Vol. I, p. 595; Dinsmoor summoned to Burr, etc., ibid., p. 600.

38. Wilkinson to McKee, and reply, ibid., pp. 593, 595.

39. Dinsmoor to Dearborn, RG 107, M22, roll 6, abstract in RG 107, M22, roll 3, p. 88, in National Archives.

40. Ibid.

41. Williams to Dinsmoor, RG 2, Vol. XXVIII, no. 745, Miss. Dept. of Archives and History. Williams to Lieutenant Edw. P. Gaines, ibid., no. 743. Williams to Madison, ibid., no. 746. Dinsmoor refers to arrival at Fort Stoddert in letter to his wife, Dinsmoor Papers, Dartmouth College, Box 1. These, like all the other references in this section to this point, were kindly provided by Jack Elliott Jr.

42. Dinsmoor to his wife, Oct. 1, 1807, Dinsmoor Papers, Dartmouth College, Box 1; the testimony at the trial, *American State Papers*, Miscellaneous, Vol. I, pp. 600 ff.

43. Dinsmoor was introduced by J. F. H. Claiborne as an "accomplished but mischief-making man." The particular instance of mischief-making which affronted Claiborne was Dinsmoor's role in bringing to an end Kemper's government-sponsored filibuster against Spanish Mobile.

Toward Burr, Claiborne assured us, Judge Toulmin did right in applying Washington's Neutrality Proclamation of 1794, and, of course, there had been Jefferson's presidential proclamation. As to Kemper, however, Toulmin and Dinsmoor perpetrated an "uncalled for proceeding . . . [and] officious . . . [because, unlike Burr,] Kemper was regarded everywhere as a liberator and hero . . . [and] Mississippi has commemorated his name in one of her finest counties." Kemper County is not far from Wilkinson County. Both counties are, indeed, fine, but Dinsmoor deserves a county, also—perhaps renamed from Wilkinson County. Claiborne on Dinsmoor and Kemper, *Mississippi*, p. 308. I. J. Cox quotes Claiborne with approval; Cox, *West Florida*, p. 483.

Those to whom Mr. Jefferson was an unsullied hero, Burr a villain, and the expansion of a slave-based plantation system a patriot's duty tend to be the same people, though, of course, one need not hold all three views at once.

44. Dinsmoor in Remini, *Jackson and Course of Empire*, pp. 162–64. The specialist on the matter is Bette B. Tilly, who gives a good account in her "The Jackson-Dinsmore Feud: A Feud in a Minor Key," *Journal of Mississippi History*, Vol. XXXIX (May 1977): pp. 117–31.

45. After the War of 1812, Remini tells us, Jackson, "hero of the war and a considerable influence in the War Department," saw to it that Dinsmoor was removed from his post. That isn't quite the case, according to Jack Elliott: Dinsmoor was removed earlier, on April 30, 1814 (National Archives RG 75, M15, roll 3, p. 167) and, after being replaced by John McKee, received the rank of lieutenant colonel for having recruited the Choctaw detachment that fought under Jackson at the Battle of New Orleans. Remini goes on: "Dinsmore was reduced to wandering in poverty among the Indians he had tried to protect." Elliott tells us that that, too, isn't quite right (letter, Feb. 11, 1999). Dinsmoor remained at the agency, living with McKee and his family until early 1816. Early in that year, "he had a keelboat constructed on the Pearl River . . . and loaded with his family and possessions." Down the river to the Gulf, and thence to the booming little town of St. Stephens, of which Dinsmoor owned one sixth. He was an incorporator "of the St. Stephens Steamboat Company, which built the first steamboat in Alabama. During the early 1820s he served as Deputy Surveyor for the GLO and later moved to Kentucky."

46. Remini on Dinsmoor and Jackson at Doak's Stand, in his *Jackson and Course of Empire*, pp. 392–93.

47. Thomas D. Clark and John D. W. Guice, in their celebrated *The Old Southwest, 1795–1830* (1996 paperback reissue), are unsympathetic with what they describe as "the appeasement policies" of Washington and Adams toward the Indians, avid in their support of Jefferson's, and dismissive of Aaron Burr as an adventurer seeking troubled conditions in which to breed more trouble. At page 256, they assert, without offering evidence, the old saw that "Burr and James Wilkinson merely represented the best known of frontiersmen who entertained plans to achieve fame and fortune by establishing an independent nation on the flanks of the young Republic." They do, however, clearly approve of Dinsmoor, whom they describe as "venerable," "sensitive," "witty," "good-natured," and "popular." For appeasement, see p. 30; for Burr, pp. 56, 256; for Dinsmoor, pp. 29, 30, 33, 35, 36, 43, 135, 197, 201, 241, 256.

48. The expert on Dinsmoor's entire career is Jack Elliott of the Mississippi Department of Archives and History, with whom I discussed the matter in January 1999. Elliott rescued me from the assumption that Dinsmoor was in 1805-6 in his later location along the Trace. His agency was, instead, at what is now Quitman, Mississippi, while he maintained a residence in the capital city of Washington.

49. The statement is described as a "curious paper" by J. F. H. Claiborne, who is often cited by later writers. Claiborne characteristically took Ashley's exchange with Bruin with a straight face, and gives the name of Burr's companion as "Chester Ashley." (Claiborne's reprint of the affidavit is on pp. 152–53, his reference to Chester Ashley on p. 288.)

Claiborne became careless and confused (as all historical writers do under the influence of passion) when dealing with Burr, northerners, abolitionists, or Roman Catholics. His account of Burr's adventures concludes with a riff on the nasal singing of northern choirs and the music sung in the churches of New England: "They now give us, every Sabbath, the latest opera airs, and the man who cannot buy a ticket to the theater, may go to church to hear the music, but unfortunately, no poor man can buy a seat in the church!" (*Mississippi*, p. 292)

50. Ashley deposition, Claiborne, *Mississippi*, pp. 152–53.

51. Ibid.

52. Ibid.

53. Jefferson to Madison, April 25, 1806, quoted in McCaleb, *New Light*, pp. 80–81; Rodney on censuring a government, Claiborne, p. 285.

54. Schachner's interpretation of these events (*Burr*, p. 380), squares with mine and with Burr's own, in a letter to Robert Williams, Feb. 12, 1807, *Papers*, pp. 1022–23. The editorial note accompanying that document is kinder to Judge Rodney but, I believe, does not take sufficient account of the collapse of Rodney's enthusiasm for the spirit of '76.

55. Boys with Burr, Schachner, *Burr*, p. 376.

56. Jefferson to Madison, April 25, 1806, quoted in McCaleb, *New Light;* Graham, ibid., p. 385.

57. Smith to Smith. See n. 10, supra.

Between Natchez and the thirty-first parallel lay the "Jersey Settlements." When Aaron Burr was a boy, he had heard tales of this pine-and-palmetto borderland in the household of his guardians, Timothy Edwards and Rhoda Ogden Edwards. Their Ogden kin were then exploring possibilities coming to them from cousin Captain Amos Ogden, whose prowess against the French in the 1750s had been rewarded with twenty-five thousand acres in Florida and lower Mississippi. As justice of the peace in Pensacola, Ogden was able to assure protection to kinsmen and retainers who might settle his acreage. And so—the Jersey Settlements. In 1806, Burr was foremost among the military heroes of New Jersey. His father and grandfather had been its leading intellectuals. His Ogden kinfolk were interrelated with the Daytons, and his ally in western speculation was Jonathan Dayton, U.S. Senator from New Jersey. In 1804, Burr had taken steps to refurbish the southwestern Dayton-Ogden connection, arranging to be met in New Orleans by Peter Ogden, nephew of his aunt Rhoda Ogden Edwards and son of his boyhood chum Matthias Ogden. (After Burr's failure, Peter Ogden joined his older brother George and established a mercantile firm in New Orleans.)

Beyond the Jersey Settlements were clusters of log cabins inhabited by clients of Winthrop Sargent, villages bearing Federalist names such as Pinckneyville and Fort Adams, and a Connecticut colony founded by Burr's mentor "Old Put," General Israel Putnam, and the Lymans of Connecticut. They were also related to the New Jersey Burrs, Edwardses, and Ogdens. General Phineas Lyman became military governor of Havana after leading four thousand Yankees beside a British army to conquer that Spanish city in 1762. When Havana was exchanged for Florida, a year later, Lyman exchanged his governorship for twenty thousand acres along the Mississippi, south of the Jersey Settlements.

58. Burr and McKee, quoted in Abernethy, *Conspiracy*, p. 215.

59. Burr's giving the Floridas, Gaines to Wilkinson, March 4, 1807, quoted in McCaleb, *Conspiracy*, p. 234; sales of muskets, Abernethy, *Conspiracy*, p. 215.

60. Whitaker on McKee, *Mississippi*, pp. 125–26.

61. Ibid.

62. Folch to McKee, Dec. 2, 1810, in McKee Papers, quoted in Abernethy, *South*, pp. 362–36.

Notes to Chapter Twenty-One

1. The description was contained in a letter from Jefferson to George Morgan, expressing pleasure in Morgan's testimony against Burr. Morgan was not clever. Jefferson was, and knew he was safe in a malicious twist at the end of an apparently friendly missive. Only a watchful eye would catch the reference to the days in which Jefferson's Virginian, George Rogers Clark, contended successfully against Morgan the Pennsylvanian, while the two states were barely sustaining their cobelligerency against the British. Morgan had been with Edward Hand and Daniel Brodhead among Clark's most recalcitrant opponents, and Virginia's. But the exultant Jefferson could not resist writing that when Burr was captured his costume was Virginian. Jefferson to Morgan, March 26, 1807, quoted in McCaleb, *New Light*, p. 110.
2. Burr's flight, *Papers*, Vol. II, pp. 1025–26.
3. I have been instructed by Peter Kastor that Gaines's role in the matter may best be understood by perusing the correspondence between him and the War Department to be found in two microfilm collections, both in Record Group 107 of the National Archives: Letters Received by the Secretary of War: Registered Series, and Letters Sent by the Secretary of War to Officers.
4. Perkins's manuscript is in the Tennessee State Historical Collections.
5. Ashley's statement in *Burr Papers*, p. 1026; Gaines to Wilkinson on Ashley, quoted in McCaleb, *Conspiracy*, p. 234.
6. Gaines to Perkins, Feb. 19, *Burr Papers*, Vol. II, pp. 1026–7 fn.
7. Gaines to Perkins, Feb. 9, 1807, "The Capture of Aaron Burr," *American History Magazine*, Vol. I (April 1896): p. 147.
8. Perkins on Gaines's behavior, ibid., pp. 145–46.
9. Hawkins and Jefferson, Wagstaff, *Federalism*, p. 40, and Dodd, *Nathaniel Macon*, p. 171, quoted in Pound, *Hawkins*, p. 139.
10. Hawkins's instructions, *Hawkins Letters*, Vol. II, p. 515.
11. Ibid.
12. I must confess a bias in favor of Bollmann, about whom I have written several times before. He was born in the ancestral home of Clara Von Hoya, the little river town of Hoya, near Emden, in North Germany. She was my great-great-grandmother, the first of a series of businesswomen in the family, or at least the first of whom we have certain knowledge. She became the first and, so far, the only woman to become an industrial magnate in Pittsburgh, after arriving there in the 1830s as a widow with six children. Before she was done, she owned a bank, an insurance company, two horsecar lines, a brewery, and a cold-storage company—and wrote good verse. I like to think she was related to Justus Eric Bollmann, though other family members think it more important that her forebears included a Queen of Sweden and that another Von Hoya was that Bishop of Munster whose ineptitude provoked the Protestant revolt immortalized in Meyerbeer's *Les Huguenots*.
13. Bollmann at the trial, Lomask, *Burr, Conspiracy*, p. 251.
14. Latrobe on Bollmann, *Papers*, Vol. III, p. 718 fn.

15. Hawkins to Dearborn, *Letters*, Vol. II, p. 515.
16. Sevier and the King of Spain, quoted in Corlew, *Tennessee*, p. 79.
17. Sevier's escape, from various accounts synthesized in Caldwell, *Tennessee*, pp. 181–82.
18. Blount's rescue, ibid., p. 217.
19. Perkins on the transit through Alabama, "Capture," *American History Magazine*, Vol. I (April 1896): p. 497.
20. Burr in Fort Wilkinson, Parton, *Burr*, Vol. II, p. 100.
21. Ibid.
22. The event at Chester, ibid.
23. Vigilance, Pickett, p. 498.
24. Randolph to Nicholson, quoted in Schachner, *Burr*, p. 386.

There may be some slight danger that a reference to Nikolai Lenin might be misunderstood at this juncture, though the character of Aaron Burr had nothing in common with that of the founder of the Russian dictatorship. Yet at one key occasion in the lives of each, their circumstances were those for which Winston Churchill provided the perfect image in his *The World Crisis*. In 1807, Jefferson's political prisoner was contained in a mobile prison so that he might be shipped across Indian Country and the Carolinas to Virginia, where he could be eliminated as a rival by imprisonment or exile. Thomas Jefferson no doubt had motives as noble as those of the German High Command, which saw to it in 1917 that Lenin was contained from Switzerland, through Germany, into Russia, where he might disrupt Russian resistance to German arms. In Churchill's words, "they transported Lenin in a sealed truck like a plague bacillus."

Notes to Chapter Twenty-Two

1. Rodney's statement is most conveniently at hand for those without law libraries in Elliott and Hammett, *Charged*, pp. 83 ff.
2. Jackson on Burr, ibid., p. 310.
3. Jackson quoted in Rogow, *Fatal Friendship*, p. 50.
4. Newman on Wilkinson in Richmond, quoted in Clark, *Proofs*, p. 198.
5. Treason and Paterson, quoted in Clouse, *Whiskey Rebellion*, p. 41. The case law is to be found in Criminal Case Files of the U.S. Circuit Court for the Eastern District of Pennsylvania, 1791–1840, reel 1, A. J. Dallas. Reports of Cases Ruled and Adjudged in the Courts of Pennsylvania, I (New York, 1882), pp. 334–58.
6. Marshall's opinion, Aug. 30, 1807, printed in full in Elliott and Hammett, *Charged*, pp. 318 ff.
7. Ibid.
8. Lomask on the Burr survivors, p. 221.
9. For more on the Flanders discussions, see *Orders from France*, pp. 313 ff.
10. Biddle on Burr's plans, *Papers*, Vol. II, p. 972.
11. Moreau's dying statement, quoted in *Encyclopedia Britannica*, 11th ed., Vol. XVIII, p. 827.
12. De Pestre described in *Latrobe Papers*, Vol. II, p. 295 fn.

13. De Pestre on Burr, in Latrobe's statement, *Latrobe Papers*, Vol. II, p. 293.
14. Blennerhasset's story of the attempted suborning of de Pestre as quoted in Lomask, *Burr, Conspiracy*, pp. 253–54.
15. De Mun's western scheme, *Latrobe Papers*, Vol. 1, p. 535.

Notes to Chapter Twenty-Three

1. Jefferson to Senate, 1808, quoted in Clark and Guice, *Old Southwest*, p. 38.
2. Jefferson to Madison, May 1, 1807, quoted in McCaleb, *New Light*, p. 105; Dupont, quoted with citations in *Orders from France*, p. 334; Burr's response quoted on p. 325.
3. Jefferson to Hay, quoted in Parton, *Burr*, Vol. II, pp. 158–59.
4. Jefferson to Claiborne, in Schachner, *Burr*, p. 392.
5. Thomas Jefferson on Burr, Oct. 17, 1808, quoted in Parton, *Burr*, Vol. II, p. 166 fn.
6. John Adams to Samuel B. Malcolm, Aug. 6, 1812, in the Gilder Lehrman Collection at the Morgan Library, file no. GLCO5262.
7. Dolley's friendship with Burr, quotation from Lomask, *Burr, Princeton Years*, pp. 161–62.
8. Jefferson on Burr, in his *Anas* for Jan. 26, 1804, quoted in Burr *Papers*, Vol. II, p. 822.
9. The description quoted in Remini, *Jackson, 1767–1821*, pp. 19–21.

Notes to Postscript

1. Latrobe on Burr, *Latrobe Papers*, Vol. II, pp. 331–2; Adams on Hamilton, Flexner, *Hamilton*, p. 62.
2. I am using the Library of America edition of Stowe's works. This is from pp. 666–68.
3. Stowe on Hattie, quoted in the entry on Stowe by Robyn R. Warhol in Benét's *Reader's Encyclopedia* (1991), p. 1022. I do not profess to be an expert on Stowe, and perhaps in my interpretation of her I have done her some injustice.
4. Davis, *Burr*, Vol. I, pp. v-vi.
5. Davis, quoted in Parton, *Burr*, Vol. II, pp. 296–97.
6. Parton on Davis and Burr, ibid., pp. 306–7.
7. Parton on old ladies, ibid., p. 302.
8. Parton, ibid, p. 303. Parton's exclamation mark.
9. Adams's resolution, quoted in Abernethy, *Conspiracy*, p. 263.
10. Adams and Shakespeare, "Argument," p. 5.
11. Adams on Burr, quoted in Kenin and Wintle, p. 122.
12. Hillhouse and Giles in the account of Wandell and Minnigerode, *Burr*, Vol. II., p. 227 ff.
13. Ibid.
14. Emerson on Adams, quoted in Miller, *Arguing*, p. 297.
15. Adams in Hillhouse Debates, in Brown, *William Plumer's Memorandum*, pp. 114, 126.
16. Ibid.

17. Adams on the debate in Monroe's cabinet, *Diary*, March 1, 1820, p. 7.

18. John Q. Adams on Jefferson and slavery, *Memoirs*, Dec. 27, 1819, and Jan. 27, 1831.

19. Adams and lips and scourges, quoted in Miller, *Arguing*, p. 530.

20. Jefferson and the Friends of the Blacks, quoted in Fay, p. 242.

21. Theodosia to the Gallatins, quoted in Lomask, *Burr, Exile*, pp. 323–24.

22. Theodosia to Dolley Madison, ibid., p. 323.

23. The lady in Paris, *Burr Papers*, p. 1133 n.

24. The welcome suggestion that Burr's embarrassing letters to Theodosia from Paris could not be omitted from a full account of their relationship, though written after the primary period presented in our study, came from Joanne Freeman in a private communication dated December 23, 1998. I have placed my thoughts about those letters here, at the end, where I also include other late correspondence, as a final discussion of their relationship.

25. Theodosia to Burr, May 31, 1809, quoted in Lomask, *Burr*, Vol. II, p. 347.

26. Burr to Theodosia, ibid, p. 345.

27. Burr to Theodosia on the moment in the Pantheon, Lomask, *Burr*, Vol. II, p. 345.

28. I have followed the chronology in the biographical sketch of Blodget in the *DAB*. Milton Lomask says that her half of her correspondence with Burr suggests that they met first "about" 1787 (*Conspiracy*, p. 378). Arnold Rogow puts the date at 1794 (p. 282). In either case, Burr was already a married man when they met.

29. Rebecca Blodget to the Madisons, Madison, *Papers*, Presidential Series, pp. 33–34.

30. Blodget to Burr, quoted in Lomask, *Conspiracy*, pp. 379–80.

31. Burr to Alston, Nov. 15, 1815, *Burr Papers*, pp. 1165 ff.

32. Ibid.

33. Ibid.

34. Alston to Burr, Feb. 16, 1816, ibid., p. 1169 n.

35. Burr and his landlady, as told by Parton, *Burr*, Vol. II p. 325.

Bibliography

Abernethy, Thomas P. *The South in the New Nation, 1789–1819.* Baton Rouge: Louisiana State University Press, 1976.

———. *Western Lands and the American Revolution.* New York: D. Appleton-Century, 1937.

Ackerman, James S. *The Villa: Form and Ideology of Country Houses.* Princeton: Princeton University Press, 1990.

Adams, Henry. *The Life of Albert Gallatin.* New York: Peter Smith, 1943.

———. *Second Administration of Thomas Jefferson.* New York: Library of America, 1986.

Adams, John Quincy. "Argument of John Quincy Adams Before the Supreme Court of the United States in the Case of the United States, Appellants, vs. Cinque, and Others, Africans, Captured in the Schooner Amistad, by Lieut. Gedney, Delivered on the 24th of February and 1st of March, 1841." New York: 1841.

———. *Memoirs.* Ed. Charles Francis Adams. 12 vols. Philadelphia: Lippincott, 1874–77.

———. *Writings of John Quincy Adams.* Ed. Worthington Chauncey Ford. New York: Greenwood, 1968.

Agar, Herbert. *The Price of Union.* Boston: Houghton Mifflin, 1950.

Allen, John Logan. *Passage through the Garden.* Urbana: University of Illinois Press, 1975.

Ambler, Charles. *George Washington and the West.* Chapel Hill: University of North Carolina Press, 1936.

American Philosophical Society. *Documents Relating to the Purchase and Exploration of Louisiana* [2 reports, one by T. Jefferson and one by William Dunbar]. Boston: Houghton Mifflin, 1904.

Ammon, Harry. *James Monroe: The Quest for National Identity.* Charlottesville: University Press of Virginia, 1990.

Andrews, Kenneth. *Trade, Plunder, and Settlement: Maritime Enterprise and the Genesis of the British Empire, 1480–1630.* New York: Cambridge University Press, 1984.

Arthur, Stanley Clisby. *The Story of the West Florida Rebellion.* St. Francisville, La.: St. Francisville Democrat, 1935.

Ashe, Geoffrey. *Land to the West: St. Brendan's Voyage to America.* New York: Viking, 1962.

Aubry, Octave. *Napoleon: Soldier and Emperor.* Philidelphia: Lippincott, 1938.

Bacarisse, Charles A. "Baron de Bastrop." *Southwestern Historical Quarterly,* Vol. LVIII, no. 3 (Jan. 1955).

Bailyn, Bernard. *Voyagers to the West: A Passage in the Peopling of America on the Eve of the Revolution.* New York: Vintage, 1988.

Bailyn, Bernard, and Philip D. Morgan, eds. *Strangers within the Realm: Cultural Margins of the First British Empire.* Chapel Hill: University of North Carolina Press, 1991.

Bannon, John Francis. *The Spanish Borderlands Frontier, 1513–1821.* Albuquerque: University of New Mexico Press, 1988.

Bartlett, Thomas, and Keith Jeffery, eds. *A Military History of Ireland.* Cambridge: Cambridge University Press, 1996.

Bartram, William. *The Travels of William Bartram.* Ed. Mark Van Doren. New York: Dover, 1955.

Beard, Charles A. *An Economic Interpretation of the Constitution of the United States.* New York: Macmillan, 1957; first pub. 1913.

Bedini, Silvio. *Thomas Jefferson: Statesman of Science.* New York: Macmillan, 1990.

Beeman, Richard, Stephen Botein, and Edward C. Carter II, eds. *Beyond Confederation: Origins of the Constitution and American National Identity.* Chapel Hill: University of North Carolina Press, 1987.

Bell, Malcolm, Jr. *Major Butler's Legacy: Five Generations of a Slaveholding Family.* Athens: University of Georgia Press, 1987.

Bemis, Samuel F. *Pinckney's Treaty.* Baltimore: Johns Hopkins University Press, 1960.

Bennett, Charles E. *Twelve on the River St. Johns.* Jacksonville: University of North Florida Press, 1989.

Berkeley, Edmund, and Dorothy Smith Berkeley. *The Life and Travels of John Bartram: From Lake Ontario to the River St. John.* Tallahassee: University Presses of Florida, 1982.

Berman, Eleanor. *Thomas Jefferson among the Arts.* New York: New York Philosophical Library, 1947.

Berns, Walter. "The Constitution and the Migration of Slaves." *Yale Law Journal* 78 (Dec. 1968).

Berthoff, Rowland. *An Unsettled People: Social Order and Disorder in American History.* New York: Harper and Row, 1971.

Beveridge, Albert J. *The Life of John Marshall.* Vol. IV. New York: Houghton Mifflin, 1919.

Blackburn, Joyce. *James Edward Oglethorpe.* Marietta, Ga.: Mocking, 1994.

Bodley, Temple, ed. *Reprints of Littell's Political Transactions in and Concerning Kentucky and Letter of George Nicholas to his Friend in Virgina: Also General Wilkinson's Memorial.* Louisville, Ky.: John P. Morton, 1926.

Bonner, James C. *Milledgeville: Georgia's Antebellum Capital.* Athens: University of Georgia Press, 1978.

Boorstin, Daniel J. *The Americans: The Colonial Experience.* New York: Random House, 1958.

———. *The Lost World of Thomas Jefferson.* Chicago: University of Chicago Press, 1993.

Bos, Harriet P. "Barthelemy Lafon." Master's thesis, Tulane University, 1977.

Bourne, Henry E. "The Travels of Jonathan Carver." *American Historical Review,* Vol. XI, no. 2 (Jan. 1906).

Bowers, Claude. *The Young Jefferson.* Boston: Houghton Mifflin, 1945.

Boyd, Julian P. *Number 7: Alexander Hamilton's Secret Attempts to Control American Foreign Policy.* Princeton: Princeton University Press, 1964.

Brackenridge, Henry Marie. *Early Discoveries by Spaniards in New Mexico, Containing an Account of the Ruins of Cibola.* Pittsburgh: Henry Miner, 1857.

———. *History of the Western Insurrection, 1794.* New York: Arno and New York Times, 1969.

———. *Recollections of Persons and Places in the West.* Philadelphia: Lippincott, 1868.

Brant, Irving. *James Madison: Secretary of State, 1800–1809.* Indianapolis: Bobbs-Merrill, 1953.

Bridwell, Ronald E. *The South's Wealthiest Planter: Wade Hampton I of South Carolina, 1754–1835.* Ann Arbor, Mich.: University Microfilms, 1980.

Brooks, Van Wyck. *The World of Washington Irving.* New York: Dutton, 1950.

Brown, C. Allan. "Poplar Forest: The Mathematics of an Ideal Villa." *Journal of Garden History,* Vol. X, no. 2 (1990).

Brown, Everett Somerville, ed. *William Plumer's Memorandum of Proceedings in the United States Senate, 1803–1807.* New York: Macmillan, 1923.

Brown, Lloyd Arnold. *Early Maps of the Ohio Valley.* Pittsburgh: University of Pittsburgh Press, 1959.

Brown, Stuart E. *Virginia Baron.* Berryville, Va: Chesapeake, 1965.

Brunson, Bill R. *"The Adventures of Samuel Swartwout in the Age of Jefferson and Jackson."* In *Studies in American History,* Lewiston, N.Y., and Queenston, Ont.: Edwin Mellen, 1989.

Buley, R. Carlyle. *The Old Northwest.* 2 vols. Bloomington: Indiana University Press, 1950.

Burr, Aaron. *Correspondence of Aaron Burr and His Daughter Theodosia.* Ed. Mark Van Doren. New York: Covici-Friede, 1929.

———. *Political Correspondence and Public Papers.* 2 vols. Ed. Mary-Jo Kline. Princeton, N.J.: Princeton University Press, 1983.

Burrows, Edwin, "Notes on Settling America: Albert Gallatin, New England, and the American Revolution." *New England Quarterly,* Vol. LVIII, no. 3 (1985).

Caldwell, Mary French. *Tennessee: The Dangerous Example.* Nashville: Aurora Publishers, 1974.

Cashin, Edward J. *Lachlan McGillivray, Indian Trader: The Shaping of the Southern Colonial Frontier.* Athens: University of Georgia Press, 1992.

Caughey, John W. *McGillivray of the Creeks.* Norman: University of Oklahoma Press, 1938.

Cayton, Andrew R. L. *The Frontier Republic: Ideology and Politics in the Ohio Country, 1780–1825.* Kent, Ohio: Kent State University Press, 1986.

Churchill, Winston S. *Maxims and Reflections*. Arr. Colin Coote. Boston: Houghton Mifflin, 1949.

Claiborne, J. F. H. *Mississippi as a Province, Territory, and State*. Vol. I. Ann Arbor: Cushing-Malloy, 1964.

Claiborne, W. C. C. *Official Letter Books*. 5 vols. Ed. Dunbar Rowlands. 1917.

Clark, Daniel. *Proofs of the Corruption of Gen. James Wilkinson, and of His Connexion with Aaron Burr*. Philadelphia: Wm. Hall, Jun. & Geo. W. Pierie, 1809.

Clark, Thomas D., and John D. W. Guice. *The Old Southwest, 1795–1830*. Norman and London: University of Oklahoma Press, 1996 paperback reissue.

Cleland, Hugh. *George Washington in the Ohio Valley*. Pittsburgh: University of Pittsburgh Press, 1955.

Clemens, Samuel Langhorne (Mark Twain). *Life on the Mississippi*. Boston: Osgood, 1883.

Clouse, Jerry A. *The Whiskey Rebellion*. Harrisburg: Bureau of Historic Preservation, Pennsylvania Historical and Museum Commission, 1994.

Coker, William S. Editor. *John Forbes' Description of the Spanish Floridas, 1804*. Pensacola: Peridido Bay, 1979.

Cole, Frank. "Thomas Worthington of Ohio." *Old Northwest Genealogical Quarterly*, April 1902.

Coleman, Kenneth. *Colonial Georgia: A History*. New York: Charles Scribner's Sons, 1976.

Collot, Victor. *A Journey in North America*. 3 vols. New York: AMS reprint, 1974.

Coming, Alexander. "Travels." *Tennessee Historical Magazine*, Vol. V (1919).

Cooper, Duff. *Talleyrand*. New York: Fromm, 1986.

Copeland, Pamela C., and Richard K. MacMaster. *The Five George Masons: Patriots and Planters of Virginia and Maryland*. Charlottesville: University of Virginia Press, 1975.

Corlew, Robert E. *Tennessee: A Short History*. Knoxville: University of Tennessee Press, 1981.

Coulter, E. Merton. "Elijah Clarke's Foreign Intrigues. . . . " Mississippi Valley Historical Association, *Proceedings*, Vol. X (Pt. 2, 1919–21).

Cox, I. J. "Hispanic-American Phases of the Burr Conspiracy." *Hispanic-American History Review* 12 (1932).

———. "The Louisiana-Texas Frontier." *Southwestern Historical Quarterly*, Vol. X, Vol. XVII (1913).

———. *The West Florida Controversy: A Study in American Diplomacy*. Gloucester, Mass.: Peter Smith, 1967.

Crane, Verner. *The Southern Frontier, 1670–1732*. New York: Norton, 1981.

Craven, Avery. *The Coming of the Civil War*. Chicago: University of Chicago Press, 1957.

Cunliffe, Marcus. *George Washington, Man and Monument*. New York: New American Library, 1982.

Cusick, James Gregory. "Ethnic Groups and Class in an Emerging Market Economy: Spaniards and Minorcans in Late Colonial St. Augustine." Ph.D. dissertation, University of Florida, 1993.

Dangerfield, George. *Chancellor Robert R. Livingston of New York, 1746–1813*. New York: Harcourt, Brace, 1960.

————. *The Era of Good Feeling.* New York: Harcourt, Brace, 1952.

Davis, D. B. *The Problem of Slavery in the Age of Revolution, 1770–1823.* Ithaca: Cornell University Press, 1975.

Davis, Matthew L., ed. *Memoirs of Aaron Burr.* 2 vols. New York: Harper and Brothers, 1836, 1837.

Davis, T. Frederick. *Macgregor's Invasion of Florida, 1817; Together with an Account of His Successors.* Jacksonville: Florida Historical Society, 1928.

Deagan, Kathleen, and Darcie MacMahon. *Fort Mose: Colonial America's Black Fortress of Freedom.* Gainsville: University Press of Florida, 1995.

DeConde, Alexander. *The Quasi-War: The Politics and Diplomacy of the Undeclared War with France, 1797–1801.* New York: Charles Scribner's Sons, 1966.

Devine, T. M. *Clanship to Crofter's War: The Social Transformation of the Scottish Highlands.* Manchester, Eng.: Manchester University Press, 1994.

DeVoto, Bernard. *The Course of Empire.* Cambridge, Mass.: Riverside, 1952.

DeWitt, John. "Journal of John Sevier." *Tennessee Historical Magazine,* Vol. V, no. 3 (1919).

Dowd, Gregory Evans. *A Spirited Resistance.* Baltimore: Johns Hopkins University Press, 1992.

Doyle, David Noel. *Ireland, Irishmen, and Revolutionary America, 1760–1820.* Dublin: Mercier, 1981.

Drinnon, Richard. *Facing West: The Metaphysics of Indian-Hating and Empire Building.* New York: Meridian, 1980.

Dunn, J. P. *Indiana: A Redemption from Slavery.* Boston: Houghton Mifflin, 1905.

Egerton, Douglas R. *Gabriel's Rebellion: The Virginia Slave Conspiracies of 1800 and 1802.* Chapel Hill: University of North Carolina Press, 1993.

Egnal, Marc. *A Mighty Empire: Origins of the American Revolution.* Ithaca: Cornell University Press, 1988.

Elkins, Stanley, and Eric McKitrick. *The Age of Federalism: The Early American Republic, 1788–1800.* New York: Oxford University Press, 1993.

Elliott, John Carroll, and Ellen Gale Hammett. *Charged with Treason, Jury Verdict: Not Guilty.* Parsons, W. Va.: McClain, 1986.

Fairbanks, Charles H. "The Kingsley Slave Cabins in Duval County, Florida." *Conference on Historical Archaeology Papers 1972,* no. 7 (1974).

Fay, Bernard. *The Revolutionary Spirit in France and America.* New York: Cooper Square, 1966.

Faye, Stanley. "Privateersmen of the Gulf and Their Prizes." *Louisiana Historical Quarterly,* Vol. XXII, no. 4 (Oct. 1939).

Fehrenbacher, Don E. *Slavery, Law, and Politics: The Dred Scott Case in Historical Perspective.* New York: Oxford University Press, 1981.

Ferling, John. *John Adams: A Life.* Knoxville: University of Tennessee Press, 1992.

Filson, John. *The Discovery and Settlement of Kentucky.* Ann Arbor: University Microfilms, 1966.

Finkelman, Paul. *Slavery and the Founders: Race and Liberty in the Age of Jefferson.* Armonk, N.Y.: Sharpe, 1996.

Fischer, David H. *Albion's Seed: Four British Folkways in America.* New York: Oxford University Press, 1989.

Fitzpatrick, J. C., ed. *The Diaries of George Washington, 1748–1799.* Boston: Houghton Mifflin, 1925.

Fleming, John. *Robert Adam and His Circle: In Edinburgh and Rome.* London: John Murray, 1962.

Flexner, James T. *George Washington and the New Nation: 1783–1793.* Vol. III. Boston: Little, Brown, 1970.

———. *George Washington: Anguish and Farewell.* Vol. IV. Boston: Little, Brown, 1972.

———. *George Washington: The Forge of Experience.* Vol. I. Boston: Little, Brown, 1965.

———. *Washington: The Indispensable Man.* New York: Signet, 1984.

———. *The Young Hamilton: A Biography.* Boston: Little, Brown, 1978.

Flores, Dan, ed. *Jefferson and Southwest Exploration: The Freeman and Curtis Accounts of the Red River Expedition.* Norman: University of Oklahoma Press, 1984.

Forbes, James Grant. *Sketches, Historical and Topographical, of the Floridas; More Particularly of East Florida.* New York: C. S. Van Winkle, 1821.

Formwalt, Lee. "Benjamin Henry Latrobe and the Revival of the Gallatin Plan of 1808." *Pennsylvania History,* Vol. XLVIII, no. 2 (1981).

Foote, Shelby. *The Civil War, a Narrative.* New York: Random House, 1986.

Fox, Dixon Ryan. *The Decline of Aristocracy in the Politics of New York.* New York: AMS, 1976.

Freeman, Joanne B. "Dueling as Politics: Reinterpreting the Burr-Hamilton Duel." *William and Mary Quarterly* 53 (April 1996).

Gallatin, Albert. *Correspondence of Jean Badollet and Albert Gallatin.* Ed. Gayle Thornbrough. Indianapolis: Indiana University Press, 1963; Ind. Hist. Soc. Pubs., Vol. XXII.

———. *The Papers of Albert Gallatin.* Ed. Carl E. Prince and Helene W. Fineman. Philadelphia: Philadelphia Historic, 1969, 46 reels of microfilm, with *Guide* by Prince, 1970.

———. "Synopsis," *Proceedings of the American Antiquarian Society,* Vol. II, 1838.

———. *The Works of Albert Gallatin.* Ed. Henry Adams. 3 vols. Philadelphia: Lippincott, 1879; rpt. New York: New York Antiquarian Society, 1960.

Gamble, Thomas. *Savannah Duels and Duellists, 1733–1877.* Savannah, Ga.: Review, 1923.

Garraty, John, ed. *Quarrels That Have Shaped the Constitution.* New York: Harper and Row, 1962.

Gibson, Jon. "Earth Sitting: Architectural Masses at Poverty Point, Northeastern Louisiana." *Louisiana Archaeology* (1986).

———. "The Poverty Point Earthworks Reconsidered." *Mississippi Archaeology* 22 (Dec. 1987).

———, and J. Richard Shenkel. "Louisiana Earthworks: Middle Woodland and Predecessors." *Archaeological Report,* Vol. XX (1988).

Gienapp, William E. *The Origins of the Republican Party.* New York: Oxford University Press, 1987.

Gilbert, Bil. *God Gave Us This Country: Tekamthe and the First American Civil War.* New York: Doubleday, 1989.

Girouard, Mark. *The Return to Camelot: Chivalry and the English Gentleman*. New Haven: Yale University Press, 1981.

Govan, Thomas Payne. *Nicholas Biddle: Nationalist and Public Banker, 1786–1844*. Chicago: University of Chicago Press, 1959.

Graff, Mary B. *Mandarin on the St. Johns*. Gainesville: University of Florida Press, 1953.

Graham, James. *The Life of General Daniel Morgan*. New York: Derby & Jackson, 1856.

Grant, C. L., ed. *Letters, Journals, and Writings of Benjamin Hawkins: Volume II, 1802–1816*. Savannah, Ga.: Beehive, 1980.

Gratz, Simon. "Thomas Rodney." *Pennsylvania Magazine of History and Biography*, Vol. XLIII-XLV (1919–21).

Green, John C. *American Science in the Age of Jefferson*. Ames: Iowa State University Press, 1984.

Green, Thomas Marshall. *The Spanish Conspiracy*. N.p., 1891.

Greenberg, Kenneth S. "The Nose, The Lie, and the Duel in the Antebellum South." *American Historical Review*, Vol. XCV (1990): 57–74.

Gregory, Jack, and Rennard Strickland. *Sam Houston with the Cherokees, 1829–1833*. Norman: University of Oklahoma Press, 1996.

Griffith, Benjamin W., Jr. *McIntosh and Weatherford Creek Indian Leaders*. Tuscaloosa: University of Alabama Press, 1988.

Griswold, Ralph E., and Frederick Doveton Nichols. *Thomas Jefferson: Landscape Architect*. Charlottesville: University Press of Virginia, 1978.

Gronowicz, Anthony. *Race and Class Politics in New York City before the Civil War*. Boston: Northeastern University Press, 1998.

Haggard, J. Villasana. "The House of Barr and Davenport." *Southwestern Historical Quarterly* Vol. LXVIX (July 1945).

Hale, Edward Everett. *Memories of a Hundred Years*. Vol. I. New York: Macmillan, 1902.

Hamilton, Alexander. *The Papers of Alexander Hamilton*. Vol. XXV. Ed. Harold C. Syrett. New York: Columbia University Press, 1977.

Hamilton, Allan McLane. *The Intimate Life of Alexander Hamilton*. New York: Charles Scribner's Sons, 1910.

Hamilton, Kathryn Ruth. "Villains and Cultural Change: Aaron Burr and Victorian America." Master's thesis, California State University, Fullerton, 1985.

Hamlin, Talbot. *Benjamin Henry Latrobe*. New York: Oxford University Press, 1955.

Harnsberger, Douglas. "In Delorme's Manner." *Association for Preservation Technology Bulletin: Journal of Preservation Technology*, Vol. XIII, no. 4 (1981).

Harrison, Ida Withers. "Chaumiere du Praire." *Journal of American History* (1915).

Hartridge, Walter C., ed. *The Letters of Don Juan McQueen to His Family*. Columbia: Bostick and Thornley, 1943

Hawes, Lilla M., ed. *Lachlan McIntosh Papers in the University of Georgia Libraries*. Athens: University of Georgia Press, 1968.

Hay, Robert. "The Pillorying of Albert Gallatin." *Western Pennsylvania Historical Magazine*, Vol. LXVII, no. 3 (1982).

Hay, Thomas, and M. R. Werner. *The Admirable Trumpeter: A Biography of James Wilkinson*. Garden City, N.Y.: Doubleday, Doran, 1941.

Hendrickson, Robert A. *The Rise and Fall of Alexander Hamilton*. New York: Van Nostrand Reinhold, 1981.

Higginbotham, A. Leon, Jr. *In the Matter of Color, Race, and the Legal Process: The Colonial Period*. New York: Oxford University Press, 1978.

Holmes, Jack D. L. "The Abortive Slave Revolt at Pointe Coupée, Louisiana, 1795." *Louisiana History*, Vol. XL (1970).

Hudson, Charles. *The Juan Pardo Expeditions: Explorations of the Carolinas and Tennessee, 1566–1568*. Washington: Smithsonian Institution Press, 1990.

———, and Carmen Chaves Tresser. *The Forgotten Centuries: Indians and Europeans in the American South, 1521–1704*. Athens: University of Georgia Press, 1994.

Hudson, Joyce Rockwood. *Looking for DeSoto: A Search through the South for the Spaniard's Trail*. Athens: University of Georgia Press, 1993.

Hunter, George. *The Western Journals of Dr. George Hunter*. Ed. J. F. McDermott. *Transactions of the American Philosophical Society*, new series, Vol. LIII, pt. 4 (1963).

Imlay, Gilbert. *Topographical Description of the Western Territory of North America*. New York: Johnson Reprint, 1968.

Insh, G. P. *Scottish Colonial Schemes, 1620–1686*. Glasgow: Maclehose, Jackson, 1922.

Jackson, Donald, ed. *Letters of the Lewis and Clark Expedition*. Urbana: University of Illinois Press, 1978.

———. *Thomas Jefferson and the Stony Mountains: Exploring the West from Monticello*. Urbana: University of Illinois Press, 1981.

Jackson, Harvey H. *Lachlan McIntosh and the Politics of Revolutionary Georgia*. Athens: University of Georgia Press, 1979.

Jackson, Henry H. "The Darien Antislavery Petition." *William and Mary Quarterly*, Vol. XXXIV (1977).

Jacobs, James Ripley. *Tarnished Warrior*. New York: Macmillan, 1938.

Jacobs, Wilbur. *Dispossessing the American Indian*. Norman: University of Oklahoma Press, 1972.

James, D. Clayton. *Antebellum Natchez*. Baton Rouge: Louisiana State University Press, 1968.

James, James A. *The Life of George Rogers Clark*. New York: AMS reprint, 1970.

Jay, John. *The Correspondence and Public Papers of John Jay, 1763–1826*. Ed. Henry P. Johnston. New York: Da Capo, 1971.

Jefferson, Thomas. *Autobiography*. In *Thomas Jefferson, Writings*. New York: Library of America, 1984.

———. *Notes on the State of Virginia*. Chapel Hill: University of North Carolina Press, 1954.

———. "Notes on the State of Virginia." *The Complete Jefferson*. Ed. Saul K. Padover. New York: 1943.

———. *The Papers of Thomas Jefferson.* 27 vols. Ed. Julian Boyd. Princeton: Princeton University Press, 1950–1997.

———. "Writings." In *Literary Classics of the United States.* New York: Viking, 1984.

———. *Writings.* Ed. A. A. Lipscomb and A. E. Bergh. Washington, D.C., 1903–4.

———. *Writings of Thomas Jefferson.* Ed. Saul K. Padover. Norwalk, Conn.: Easton, 1967.

Jennings, Francis. *The Invasion of America: Indians, Colonialism and the Cant of Conquest.* New York: Norton, 1975.

Jennings, Jesse. "Nutt's Trip to the Chickasaw Country." *Journal of Mississippi History,* Vol. IX (1947).

———, ed. *Ancient North Americans.* New York: Freeman, 1983.

Johannsen, Robert W. *To the Halls of the Montezumas.* New York: Oxford University Press, 1985.

John, Richard R. *Spreading the News: The American Postal System from Franklin to Morse.* Cambridge, Mass.: Harvard University Press, 1995.

Jones, George F. *The Georgia Dutch: From the Rhine and Danube to the Savannah, 1733–1783.* Athens: The University of Georgia Press, 1992.

Jones, Howard. *Mutiny on the Amistad.* Rev. ed. New York: Oxford University Press, 1987

Kee, Robert. *The Most Distressful Country.* New York: Penguin, 1972.

Keller, William. *The Nation's Advocate: Henry Marie Brackenridge and Young America.* Pittsburgh: University of Pittsburgh Press, 1956.

Kelsay, Isabel Thompson. *Joseph Brant, 1743–1807: Man of Two Worlds.* Syracuse: Syracuse University Press, 1984.

Kenin, Richard, and Justin Wintle, eds. *The Dictionary of Biographical Quotation.* New York: Knopf, 1978.

Kennedy, Roger G. *Architecture, Men, Women, and Money.* New York: Random House, 1985.

———. *Greek Revival America.* New York: Stewart, Tabori and Chang, 1989.

———. *Hidden Cities: The Discovery and Loss of Ancient American Civilization.* New York: Free Press, 1994.

———. "Jefferson and the Indians." *Winterthur Portfolio,* Vol. 27, nos. 2/3, (Summer/Autumn 1992).

———. *Orders from France: The Americans and French in a Revolutionary World.* Philadelphia: University of Pennsylvania Press, 1990.

———. *Rediscovering America: Journeys through Our Forgotten Past.* Boston: Houghton Mifflin, 1990.

Kerber, Linda K. *Federalists in Dissent: Imagery and Ideology in Jeffersonian America.* Ithaca: Cornell University Press, 1970.

Ketcham, Ralph. *James Madison: A Biography.* Charlottesville: University Press of Virginia, 1990.

Ketchum, Richard. *The World of George Washington.* New York: American Heritage, 1974.

Kimball, Fiske. "A Landscape Garden on the James in 1793." *Beginnings of Landscape Gardening,* Vol. VII (July 1917).

———. *Thomas Jefferson, Architect.* New York: Da Capo, 1968.

Kimball, Marie. *Jefferson: the Scene of Europe 1784 to 1789.* New York: Coward-McCann, 1950.

Kirk, Russell. *John Randolph of Roanoke.* Indianapolis: Liberty, 1951.

Knepper, George W. *Ohio and Its People.* Kent, Ohio: Kent State University Press, 1989.

Kolchin, Peter. *American Slavery, 1619–1877.* New York: Hill and Wang, 1993.

Lancaster, Clay. *Vestiges of the Venerable City: A Chronicle of Lexington, Kentucky.* Lexington: Lexington-Fayette County Historic Commission, 1978.

Landers, Jane. *Fort Mose. Gracia Real de Santa Teresa de Mose: A Free Black Town in Spanish Colonial Florida.* St. Augustine: St. Augustine Historical Society, 1992.

Langhorne, Elizabeth, K. E. Lang, and W. D. Rieley. *A Virginia Family and Its Plantation Houses.* Charlottesville: University of Virginia Press, 1987.

Latrobe, Benjamin Henry. *The Correspondence and Miscellaneous Papers of Benjamin Henry Latrobe.* 3 vols. New Haven: Yale University Press and Maryland Historical Society, 1984–88.

Lawrence, Alexander A. "General Lachlan McIntosh and His Suspension from the Continental Command during the Revolution." *Georgia Historical Quarterly,* Vol. XXXVIII (June 1954).

Leech, D. D. T. *History of the Post Office Department, 1789–1879.* Washington: Judd and Detweiler, 1879.

Levy, Leonard W. *Jefferson and Civil Liberties: The Darker Side.* Chicago: Ivan R. Dee, 1989.

Lewis, Anthony Marc. "Jefferson and Virginia's Pioneers." *The Mississippi Valley Historical Review,* Vol. XXXIV, no. 4 (March 1948).

Lewis, Thomas A. *For King and Country.* New York: HarperCollins, 1993.

Lincoln, Abraham. *Speeches and Writings.* New York: Library of America, 1989.

Lindsay, Merrill. "Pistols Shed Light on Famed Duel." *Smithsonian,* Vol. VII–VIII (Nov. 1976): 94–98.

Lobell, Mimi. "Special Archetypes." *Revision* 6 (Fall 1983).

Lodge, Henry Cabot. *Alexander Hamilton.* New York: Chelsea House, 1980.

Logan, Marie. *Mississippi-Louisiana Border Country: A History of Rodney, Miss., St. Joseph, La., and Environs.* Baton Rouge: Claitor's, 1970.

Lomask, Milton. *The Conspiracy and the Years of Exile.* Vol. II of *Aaron Burr.* New York: Farrar, Straus and Giroux, 1982.

———. *The Years from Princeton to Vice President.* Vol. I of *Aaron Burr.* New York: Farrar, Straus and Giroux, 1979.

"Louisiana-Texas Frontier." *Quarterly of the Texas State Historical Association,* Vols. X and XVII (July and October 1913).

Lynd, Staughton, *Class Conflict, Slavery, and the United States Constitution.* Indianapolis: The Bobbs-Merrill Co., Inc., 1968.

Macaulay, James. *The Classical Country House in Scotland, 1660–1800.* London: Faber and Faber, 1987.

MacDermot, Frank. *Theobald Wolfe Tone and His Times.* Tralee, Ireland: Anvil, 1980.

Mackey, James P. *An Introduction to Celtic Christianity.* Edinburgh: T. & T. Clark, 1989.

Mackintosh, Margaret. *The Clan Mackintosh and the Clan Chattan.* Orange, Ca.: Macdonald; distributed by KM Enterprises, 1982.

Malone, Dumas. *Jefferson and the Rights of Man.* Vol. II. Boston: Little Brown, 1951.

———. *Jefferson the President: First Term, 1801–1805.* Vol. IV. Boston: Little, Brown, 1970.

———. *Jefferson the President: Second Term, 1805–1809.* Vol. V. Boston: Little, Brown, 1974.

———. *Jefferson the Virginian.* Vol. I. Boston: Little Brown, 1948.

———. *The Sage of Monticello.* Vol. VI. Boston: Little Brown, 1981.

Mannix, Richard. "Albert Gallatin and the Movement for Peace with Mexico." *Social Studies* 60, no. 7 (1969).

Martin, Peter. *The Pleasure Garden of Virginia: From Jamestown to Jefferson.* Princeton: Princeton University Press, 1991.

Masterson, William H. *William Blount.* Baton Rouge: Louisiana State University Press, 1954.

Matson, Cathy D., and Peter S. Onuf. *A Union of Interests: Political and Economic Thought in Revolutionary America.* Lawrence: University Press of Kansas, 1990.

Mayo, Robert. *Political Sketches of Eight Years in Washington.* Baltimore: Fielding Lucas Jr., 1839.

McCaleb, Walter Flavius. *The Aaron Burr Conspiracy* and *A New Light on Aaron Burr.* New York: Argosy-Antiquarian, 1966.

McColley, Robert. *Slavery and Jeffersonian Virginia.* Urbana: University of Illinois Press, 1973.

McCoy, Drew R. *The Last of the Fathers: James Madison and the Republican Legacy.* New York: Cambridge University Press, 1989.

McDermott, John Francis, ed. *The French in the Mississippi Valley.* Urbana: University of Illinois Press, 1965.

———. *The Spanish in the Mississippi Valley, 1762–1804.* Urbana: University of Illinois Press, 1974.

McFaul, John. "Expediency vs. Morality: Jacksonian Politics and Slavery." *Journal of American History,* Vol. LXII, no. 1 (June 1975).

McIntosh, Lachlan. "The Papers of Lachlan McIntosh, 1774–1779." *Georgia Historical Society Collection,* Vol. XII (1957).

McKay, A. G. *Houses, Villas, and Palaces in the Roman World.* Ithaca: Cornell University Press, 1975.

McManus, Edgar J. *A History of Negro Slavery in New York.* Syracuse: Syracuse University Press, 1966.

McNeal, R. A., ed. *Nicholas Biddle in Greece: The Journals and Letters of 1806.* University Park: Pennsylvania State University Press, 1993.

Meinig, D. W. *The Shaping of America, Vol. 2: Continental America, 1800–1867.* New Haven: Yale University Press, 1993.

Merck, Frederick. *History of the Westward Movement.* New York: Knopf, 1980.

Meyer, Duane. *The Highland Scots of North Carolina, 1732–1776.* Chapel Hill: University of North Carolina Press, 1961.

Millar, John F. *Classical Architecture in Renaissance Europe, 1419–1585.* Williamsburg, Va.: Thirteen Colonies, 1987.

Miller, John Chester. *The Wolf by the Ears.* New York: Macmillan, 1977.

Miller, Kerby. *Emigrants and Exiles: Ireland and the Irish Exodus to North America.* New York: Oxford University Press, 1985.

Miller, William Lee. *Arguing About Slavery.* New York: Random House, 1995.

Mitchell, Jennie O'Kelly, and Robert Dabney Calhoun. "The Marquis de Maison Rouge, the Baron de Bastrop, and Colonel Abraham Morhouse, Three Ouachita Vally Soldiers of Fortune. The Maison Rouge and Bastrop Spanish Land 'Grants.' " *Louisiana Historical Quarterly,* Vol. XX, no. 2 (April 1937).

Monette, John Wesley. *History of the Discovery and Settlement of the Misissippi Valley.* New York, 1846.

Morris, Richard B., ed. *Alexander Hamilton and the Founding of the Nation.* New York: Dial, 1957.

Murdoch, Richard K. *The Georgia-Florida Frontier, 1793–1796: Spanish Reaction to French Intrigue and American Designs.* Berkeley: University of California Press, 1951.

Myers, Minor, Jr. *Liberty Without Anarchy: A History of the Society of the Cincinnati.* Charlottesville: University Press of Virginia, 1983.

Nash, Gary. *Red, White, and Black: The Peoples of Early America.* Englewood, N.J.: Prentice-Hall, 1974.

Nash, Gary B., and Jean R. Soderlund. *Freedom by Degrees: Emancipation in Pennsylvania and Its Aftermath.* New York: Oxford University Press, 1991.

National Museum of American History and Foundation for Prussian Cultural Property, Berlin. *Steuben: Secret Aid for the Americans.* Washington: National Museum of American History, 1981–82.

Neuman, Robert. *An Introduction to Louisiana Archaeology.* Baton Rouge: Louisiana State University Press, 1984.

———. *Melanges: An Archaeological Assessment of Coastal Louisiana.* Baton Rouge: Louisiana State University Museum of Geoscience, March 21, 1977.

Nevins, Allan. *The Emergence of Lincoln.* New York: Scribners, 1950.

The New Handbook of Texas. Austin: Texas State Historical Association, 1996.

Newcomb, Rexford. *Architecture in Old Kentucky.* Urbana: University of Illinois Press, 1953.

Nicholson, Harold George. *Good Behavior: Being a Study of Certain Types of Civility.* Gloucester, Mass.: P. Smith, 1969.

Nolte, Vincent Otto. *Fifty Years in Both Hemispheres.* New York: Redfield, 1854.

Orrmont, Arthur. *Diplomat in Warpaint: Chief Alexander McGillivary of the Creeks.* New York: Abelard-Schuman, 1968.

Osgood, E. S., ed. *The Field Notes of Captain William Clark.* New Haven: Yale University Press, 1964.

Owen, Thomas McAdory. *Annals of Alabama.* Spartanburg, S.C.: Reprint Co., 1988.

Owsley, Frank Lawrence, Jr. *Struggle for the Gulf Borderlands: The Creek War and the Battle of New Orleans, 1812–1815.* Gainesville: University Press of Florida, 1981.

Padgett, James A. "The West Florida Revolution of 1810, as told by the Letters of John Rhea, Fulwar Skipwith, Reuben Kemper, and others." *Louisiana Historical Quarterly*, Vol. XXII (Jan. 1938).

Pakenham, Thomas. *The Year of Liberty: The Story of the Great Irish Rebellion of 1798.* New York: Granada, 1982.

Parkman, Francis. *LaSalle and the Discovery of the Great West.* New York: Modern Library, 1985.

Parton, James. *The Life and Times of Aaron Burr.* 2 vols. New York: Chelsea House, 1983.

Patrick, Rembert W. *Florida Fiasco.* Athens: University of Georgia Press, 1954.

Patterson, Richard S., and Richardson Dougall. *The Eagle and the Shield.* Washington: Department of State, 1976.

Pearce, Roy. *The Savages of America: A Study of the Indian and the Idea of Civilization.* Baltimore: Johns Hopkins University Press, 1953.

Peet, Henry J. *Chaumiere Papers Containing Matters of Interest to the Descendants of David Meade, of Nansemond County, Va., Who Died in the Year 1757.* Chicago: Horace O'Donoghue, 1883.

Peter, S. W. K. *Private Memoir of Thomas Worthington, Esq.* Cincinnati: Robert Clarke, 1882.

Picket, Albert James. *History of Alabama.* Spartanburg, S.C.: Reprint Co., 1988.

Pitt, Arthur. "Franklin and the Quaker Movement against Slavery." *Friends Historical Association Bulletin*, Vol. XXXII, no. 1 (Spring 1943).

Pound, Merritt B. *Benjamin Hawkins, Indian Agent.* Athens: University of Georgia Press, 1951.

Pratt, Fletcher. *Road to Empire: The Life and Times of Bonaparte the General.* New York: Doubleday, Doran, 1939.

Prussing, Eugene. *The Estate of George Washington, Deceased.* Boston: Little, Brown, 1927.

Randall, E. O. "Washington's Ohio Lands." *Ohio Archaeological and Historical Quarterly*, Vol. XIX (July 1990).

Randall, Henry S. *The Life of Thomas Jefferson.* Philadelphia: Lippincott, 1865.

Randolph, Sara. *The Domestic Life of Thomas Jefferson.* Charlottesville: University Press of Virginia, 1990.

Reiter, Edith. *Marietta and the Northwest Territory.* 9th rpt. Marietta, Ohio: Hyde Bros., 1986.

Remini, Robert V. *Andrew Jackson and the Course of American Democracy, 1833–1845.* Vol. III. New York: Harper and Row, 1984.

———. *Andrew Jackson and the Course of American Empire, 1767–1821.* Vol. I. New York: Harper and Row, 1977.

Reps, John W. *The Making of Urban America: A History of City Planning in the United States.* Princeton: Princeton University Press, 1965.

Rice, Otis. *The Allegheny Frontier.* Lexington: University of Kentucky Press, 1970.

Riley, Carroll. *The Frontier People.* Albuquerque: University of New Mexico Press, 1987.

Rochester, Junius. *Little St. Simons Island on the Coast of Georgia.* Little St. Simons, Ga.: Little St. Simons Press, 1994.

Rodney, Thomas. "Arthur St. Clair." *Pennsylvania Magazine of History and Biography*, Vol. XLIII (1919).

———. "Cincinnati and Marietta." *Pennsylvania Magazine of History and Biography*, Vol. XLIII (1919).

———. "Natchez." *Pennsylvania Magazine of History and Biography*, Vol. XLIV (1920).

Rogers, George C., Jr. *The History of Georgetown County, South Carolina.* 5th printing. Spartanburg, S.C.: Georgetown County Historical Society, 1995.

Rogin, Paul. *Fathers and Children: Andrew Jackson and the Subjugation of the American Indian.* New York: Vintage, 1975.

Rogow, Arnold A. *A Fatal Friendship: Alexander Hamilton and Aaron Burr.* New York: Hill and Wang, 1998.

Rorabaugh, W. J. *The Alcoholic Republic: An American Tradition.* New York: Oxford University Press, 1981.

Rowland, Mrs. Dunbar. *Life, Letters, and Papers of William Dunbar.* Jackson, Miss.: Press of the Mississippi Historical Society, 1930.

Royster, Charles. *Light-Horse Harry Lee and the Legacy of the American Revolution.* Cambridge: Cambridge University Press, 1981.

Rusche, Timothy. "The Battle of Fallen Timbers: Securing America's Western Frontier." Senior thesis, University of Pennsylvania, April 1997.

Samuels, Ernest. *Henry Adams: The Middle Years.* Cambridge: Belknap Press of Harvard University Press, 1958.

Sargent, Winthrop. *Memoirs of the American Academy of Arts and Sciences*, new series, Vol. V (1853).

Sauer, Carl. *Sixteenth-Century North America.* Berkeley: University of California Press, 1971.

Saum, Lewis. *The Fur Trade and the Indian.* Seattle: University of Washington Press, 1965.

Savelle, Max. *George Morgan: Colony Builder.* New York: Columbia University Press, 1932.

Schachner, Nathan. *Aaron Burr: A Biography.* New York: Barnes, 1961.

———. *Alexander Hamilton.* New York: Appleton-Century, 1946.

Schelbert, Leo. "Albert Gallatin, 1761–1899," *Swiss American Historical Society Newsletter*, Vol. XVIII, no. 1 (1982).

Schlesinger, Arthur, Jr. *The Age of Jackson.* Boston: Little, Brown, 1947.

Schneidman, J. Lee, and Conalee Levine-Schneidman. "Suicide or Murder: The Burr-Hamilton Duel." *Journal of Psychohistory*, Vol. VIII (1980–81): 159–81.

Schultz, Christian. *Travels on an Inland Voyage . . . Made in 1807 and 1808.* New York: Issac Riley, 1810.

Schwarz, Philip J. *Slave Laws in Virginia: Studies in the Legal History of the South.* Athens: University of Georgia Press, 1996.

Sears, Alfred. *Thomas Worthington: Father of Ohio Statehood.* Columbus; Ohio Historical Society, 1958.

Sharp, James Roger. *American Politics in the Early Republic.* New Haven: Yale University Press, 1993.

Showalter, Joseph. "The Travels of George Washington." *National Geographic,* Vol. LXI, no. 1 (Jan. 1932).

Sibley, William. *The French Five Hundred.* Gallipolis, Ohio, 1933.

Simpson, Elizabeth M. *Bluegrass Houses and Their Traditions.* Lexington, Ky.: Transylvania, 1932.

Slaughter, Thomas. *The Whiskey Rebellion.* New York: Oxford University Press, 1986.

Smith, Henry. *Virgin Land: The American West as Symbol and Myth.* Cambridge: Harvard University Press, 1978.

Smith, Jean Edward. *John Marshall: Definer of a Nation.* New York: Holt, 1996.

Smith, Joseph Burkholder. *James Madison's Phony War: The Plot to Steal Florida.* New York: Arbor House, 1983.

Smith, Page. *John Adams, 1784–1826.* Vol. II. Garden City, N.Y.: Doubleday, 1962.

Smith, Richard N. *Patriarch: George Washington and the New American Nation.* Boston: Houghton Mifflin, 1993.

Smith, Thomas. *The Mapping of Ohio.* Kent. Ohio: Kent State University Press, 1977.

"Some Notes on British Intrigue in Kentucky." *Register of the Kentucky State Historical Society,* Vol. XXXVIII (1940).

Spalding, Phinizy. *Oglethorpe in America.* Athens: University of Georgia Press, 1984.

Sparks, William H. *The Memories of Fifty Years.* Philadelphia: Claxton, Remsen and Haffelinger, 1870.

Sprague, Marshall. *So Vast, So Beautiful a Land; Louisiana and the Purchase.* Boston: Little, Brown, 1974.

Squier, E. G., and E. H. Davis, "Ancient Monuments of the Mississippi Valley," *Smithsonian Contribution to Knowledge,* Vol. I (Washington, D.C., 1848).

Stagg, J. C. *Mr. Madison's War.* Princeton: Princeton University Press, 1983.

Stanley, Samuel. "The End of the Natchez Indians." *History Today,* Vol. XXVIII (1978).

Stark, Terry. "The Face of Philip Nolan." *Texas Studies,* Vol. I (1994).

Stegmaier, Mark. "Zachary Taylor versus the South." *Civil War History,* Vol. XXXIII, no. 3 (Sept. 1987).

Stephens, A. Ray, and William Holmes. *Historical Atlas of Texas.* Norman: University of Oklahoma Press, 1989.

Stevens, John A. *Albert Gallatin.* New York: Houghton Mifflin, 1972.

Stoddard, Amos. *Sketches, Historical and Descriptive, of Louisiana.* Philadelphia, 1812.

Stowe, Harriet Beecher. *The Minister's Wooing.* In *Three Novels* by Harriet Beecher Stowe. New York: The Library of America, 1982.

Stuart, Reginald, *The Half Way Pacifist: Thomas Jefferson's View of War.* Toronto: University of Toronto Press, 1978.

Sturdevant, Rick. *Quest for Eden: George Washington's Frontier Land Interests.* Ph.D. dissertation, University of California, Santa Barbara, 1982.

Sullivan, Buddy. *Early Days on the Georgia Tidewater: The Story of McIntosh County and Sapelo.* Darian, Ga.: McIntosh County Board of Commissioners, 1990.

Sword, Wiley. *President Washington's Indian War: The Struggle for the Old Northwest, 1790–1795.* Norman: University of Oklahoma Press, 1985.

Syrett, Harold C.. and Cooke, Jean G., eds. *Interview at Weehawken.* Middletown, Conn.: Wesleyan University Press, 1960.

Tanner, Helen. *Atlas of the Great Lakes Indian History.* Norman: University of Oklahoma Press, 1987.

Tavernor, Robert. *Palladio and Palladianism.* London: Thames and Hudson, 1991.

Thwaites, Reuben, ed. *Travels and Explorations of the Jesuit Missionaries in New France: The Voyages of Marquette.* Cleveland: Burrows Brothers, 1966.

Truettner, William H., ed. *The West as America: Reinterpreting Images of the Frontier, 1820–1920.* Washington: Smithsonian Institution Press, 1991.

Turner, Frederick Jackson. *The Frontier in American History.* Ed. Ray Billington. New York: Holt, Rinehart and Winston, 1962.

Twain, Mark. *Life on the Mississippi.* Boston: Osgood, 1883.

Tyler, Lyon G. "David Meade." *William and Mary Quarterly,* Vol. XIII (1905).

Usner, Daniel H., Jr. *Indians, Settlers, and Slaves in a Frontier Exchange Economy.* Chapel Hill: University of North Carolina Press for Institute of Early American History and Culture, Williamsburg, Va., 1990.

Van Every, Dale. *Ark of the Empire: The American Frontier, 1784–1803.* New York: Quill, 1963.

———. *Forth to the Wilderness.* New York, Morrow, 1961.

Vidal, Gore. *Burr.* New York: Bantam, 1974.

Viola, Herman. *After Columbus: The Smithsonian Chronicle of North American Indians.* Washington: Smithsonian Institution Press, 1990.

Viola, Herman, and Carolyn Margolis. *Seeds of Change: Five Hundred Years Since Columbus.* Washington: Smithsonian Institution Press, 1991.

Volney, comte de (Constantin-François Chasseboeuf). *A View of the Soil and Climate of the United States of America.* Facsimile of Philadelphia 1804 edition. Ed. George W. White. New York: Hafner, 1968.

Von Hagen, Victor W. *Highway of the Sun.* London: Gollancz, 1956.

Walker, Karen Jo. "Kingsley and His Slaves: Anthropological Interpretation and Evaluation." *Volumes in Historical Archaeology* 5 (1988), ed. Stanley South.

Walters, Raymond, Jr. *Albert Gallatin: Jeffersonian Financier and Dipolmat.* Pittsburgh: University of Pittsburgh Press, 1957.

Wandell, Samuel H., and Meade Minnigerode. *Aaron Burr.* Vol. II. New York: G. P. Putnam's Sons, 1925.

Ward, Christopher. *The Revolution.* 2 vols. New York: Macmillan, 1952.

Ward, J.R., and Dena Snodgrass. *Old Hickory's Town.* Jacksonville: Florida Publishing Company, 1982.

Washington, George. *The Diaries of George Washington.* Ed. John Fitzpatrick. Boston: Houghton Mifflin, 1925.

———. *Writings.* 39 vols. Ed. John C. Fitzpatrick. Washington, D.C.: USGPO, 1931–65.

Webb, James R. "The Fateful Encounter." *American Heritage,* Vol. XXVI (Aug. 1975): 45 ff.

Wellman, Paul. *The Indian Wars of the West.* Garden City, N.Y.: Doubleday, 1956.

Weston, Rob N. "Alexander Hamilton and the Abolition of Slavery in New York." *Afro-Americans in New York Life and History,* Vol. XVIII (1994).

Whitaker, Arthur Preston. *The Mississippi Question, 1795–1803.* New York: Appleton-Century, 1934.

White, Shane. *Somewhat More Independent: The End of Slavery in New York City, 1770–1810.* Athens: University of Georgia Press, 1991.

Williams, Gwyn. *Madoc: The Legend of the Welsh Discovery of America.* New York: Oxford University Press, 1987.

Williams, Stephen. "Aboriginal Location of the Kadohadacho and Related Tribes." *Explorations in Cultural Anthropology* (1965). Ed. Ward Goodenough.

———. *Fantastic Archaeology: The Wild Side of North American Prehistory.* Philadelphia: University of Pennsylvania Press, 1991.

———. "Nineteenth-Century Perceptions of Cahokia and its Meaning." Paper read at the Cahokia Symposium, SAA Meetings, April 26, 1991.

Wills, Garry. *Cincinnatus: George Washington and the Enlightenment: Images of Power in Early America.* Garden City, N.Y.: Doubleday, 198.

Wilson, Maurine T., and Jack Jackson. *Philip Nolan and Texas.* Waco: Texian Press, 1987.

Wittkower, Rudolph. "English Neoclassicism and Palladio's 'Quatro Libri.' " In *Palladio and English Palladianism.* London: Thames and Hudson, 1974.

Wood, Gordon S. *The Creation of the American Republic, 1776–1787.* New York: Norton, 1972.

Wood, Peter, Gregory Waselkov, and M. Thomas Hatley, ed. *Powhatan's Mantle: Indians in the Colonial Southeast.* Lincoln: University of Nebrasks Press, 1989.

Young, Tommy R. "The United States Army and the Institution of Slavery in Louisiana, 1803–1815." *Louisiana Studies* (Fall 1974).

Index

NOTE:

Page numbers followed by a n. refer to endnotes.

Page numbers in italics refer to maps or illustrations.

Page numbers in parentheses denote the original text to which the endnotes refer.

Readers will find limited information about any of the three central figures under main entries. The bulk of information about Burr, Hamilton, and Jefferson will be found throughout the index. In entries that refer to all three men, the three will be referred to as "subjects."

Aaron Burr (Lomask), 412–13n. 13
    (181–182)
abolition. *See also* slavery
    Burr's work for, in New York
      Assembly, 30, 89–90, 164,
      401n. 26 (68)
    Hamilton's views on, 97–98
    John Jay's views on, 88, 90
    Kentucky Abolition Society, 109
    Manumission Society, 91–92, 97–98,
      101–2, 103, 180
    views of Burr and Hamilton on, 92–
      93
acquittal of Burr, 309, 353
Adair, Douglas, 12
Adair, John, 249, 319
Adams, Abigail, 61, 167, 382
Adams, Henry, 26–27, 166, 411n. 36
    (166), 420n. 10 (264)

Adams, John
    on Burr, 9–10, 95, 309
    as described by Hamilton, 140
    on dueling, 69–70
    on Hamilton, 75–77
    Hamilton's interference with
      political goals of, 56
    popularity of, 108
    vice presidential tie-breaking vote of,
      63
Adams, John Quincy
    Amistad case, 180, 375–79
    on Burr, 318
    on Collot's travels west, 164
    compared with Jefferson, 379–
      82
    concern for Jefferson's abuse of
      office, 300
    on Jefferson, 318

Adams, John Quincy (*continued*)
  obtaining commission for Wilkinson,
    135–36
  plantation owners influence on,
    100
  popularity of, as president, 257
  refusal to support Haitian embargo,
    180
  silence in Burr matter, 354
  on slavery, 375–80
  tie breaking vote of, 181
  in trial of John Smith, 258
  as witness against Burr, 369, 372
Adams, Samuel, 165
Addicott, Laurence, 399–400n. 10
    (61)
Adonwentishon (Mrs. Brant), 240
adultery. *See* sex lives of subjects
Alabama, 330
Albany Register, 72
alcoholism, effect on military of, 124–
    25
Alexandria Gazette, 117
Alien and Sedition Acts, 105, 106–7,
    154, 159
Allen, John, 117
Alston, Aaron Burr, 62, 387
Alston, Joseph, 183, 224, 345, 387
Alston, Theodosia Burr (Burr's
    daughter)
  attempts to rally support for Burr of,
    382–83
  Burr conveyed near home of, 345
  Burr's letters to, 60, 187–88, 203–4,
    210, 211, 223, 227
  Burr's respect for, 61–62
  death of, 62, 387
  relationship with Burr, 383
  visit with Brant, 240
ambition, 4, 309
Amistad case, 180, 375–79
Angelica, New York, 402n. 5 (77)

apologies, Hamilton's, 13–14, 68–69,
    80, 84–85
appeasement policies, 428n. 47 (325)
archeology, 121–22, 205, 216, 288
architecture. *See also* Latrobe,
    Benjamin Henry
  design of Belvedere, 402n. 5 (77)
  of Fort George Island, 219–20
  of The Hermitage, 399n. 1 (58)
  Hopewell architecture of Marietta,
    Ohio, 205
  Jefferson's interest in, 417n. 11
    (220)
  of Ohio Valley Indians, 399–400n.
    10 (61)
Armstrong, John, 68
army, racism in militias, 250
Arnold, Benedict, 45
arrests of Burr, 30, 297–98, 303–4,
    308, 309, 321–22, 335
Arthur, Gabriel, 177, 179
Ashley, Robert, 268, 270, 324, 325–
    27, 333, 336
assassins, Wilkinson's history with, 320
Astor, John Jacob, 396n. 2 (22)
Attorneys General commenting on
    trial, 347–48
Augusta, Georgia, Burr in, 344
Aupaumut (Stockbridge chief), 239

backgrounds of subjects compared, 29–
    30
Bahamas, 145
Bancroft, George, 113
bankruptcy, 16, 396n. 2 (22). *See also*
    finances
Banneker, Benjamin, 425–26n. 27
    (316)
Barlow, Joel, 355
Bartlett, Josiah, 397–98n. 9 (49)
Bastrop, "baron," 246
Bastrop Tract, 235

Bastrop's acquisition of, 246
Bollmann's role in soliciting settlers
    for, 340
Burr's desire to settle, 170, 243–44,
    261
role in economic history of U. S.,
    242–43
Bayard, Eliza, 222
Bayard, James, 64, 66, 141
Bayard, Nicholas, 222
Belgray, Lord, 414n. 1 (195)
Bella Vista, 216
Belvedere, design of, 402n. 5 (77)
Bentham, Jeremy, 156
Benton, Thomas Hart, 408n. 20 (136)
Berkshires, mixture of races in, 234
Beveridge, Albert, 398–99n. 22 (55)
biases of author, 389–94
Biddle, Ann, 131
Biddle, Charles, 226–27, 270
Biddle family, 193–95
biographers of Burr, 26–27, 62, 374,
    375
Bivins, William, 344
Black Corps, 110
Black Republic, 178
Black Speech, Albert Gallatin's, 158,
    177–78
blackmail, Granger's attempt to, 275–
    76
Blennerhasset, Harmon, 310, 421n. 24
    (271)
Blodget, Rebecca Smith, 385–87
Blodget, Samuel, 385–86
Bloody Assizes, 352
Bloody Marsh, 205
Bloomfield, Joseph, 187, 228
Blount, William, 117–18, 125, 128,
    134, 342
Blue Ridge, Washington's survey of,
    149
Bodnar, Ed, 265

body guard, Ashley as Burr's, 325–27
Bollmann, Justus Eric, 270, 339–43,
    409n. 36 (142), 430–31n. 12
    (339)
Bonaparte, Joseph, 358
Bonaparte, Napoleon
  alliance with Jefferson, 172–73
  Burr's dislike for, 175–76
  Federalists' dislike for, 142
  Jefferson's cooperation with, 138
  Napoleonic War's effect on cotton
    market, 243
  reintroduction of slavery to French
    West Indies, 102
  on slavery, 179–80
  Talleyrand on, 148
Boone, Daniel, 399–400n. 10 (61),
    422n. 40 (282)
Bossu, Jean Bernard, 288
bounty for Burr, 309, 322, 333
Bowers, Claude, 162
Bowles, William Augustus, 220–21,
    331, 343, 356
boycotts of the Manumission Society,
    97–98
Brackenridge, Henry, 159
Braddock's Field, demonstrations at,
    159
Braddock's Road, military significance
    of, 163–64
Bradford, David, 161–63
Brant, Joseph, 154, 238, 239–41
Breckinridge, John, 130
bribery
  Jefferson's, of Eaton, 274–75
  Wilkinson's attempts at, 319–20
Brightwell, Theodore, 335
Brissot de Warville, Jacques Pierre,
    102–3, 105, 119–20, 248
Brodhead, Daniel, 122–23, 430n. 1
    (333)
Brown, John, 116, 117, 118, 262

Brown, Lancelot (Capability Brown), 226
Bruin, Peter, 270, 301, 302–4, 325, 336
Brunson, Bill, 409n. 36 (142)
Burger, Warren E., 391
Burlington Bay, 240
Burr, Aaron. *See* Alston, Theodosia Burr (Burr's daughter); character; charges against Burr; exile, Burr's; Hamilton, James; Jefferson, Thomas; trial, Burr's; Wilkinson, James
Burr, Aaron Sr., 222, 417–18n. 16
Burr, Theodosia Bartow (Burr's wife), 17–18, 58–60, 78, 399n. 1 (58)
Burr, Theodosia (Burr's daughter). *See* Alston, Theodosia Burr (Burr's daughter)
Butler, Pierce
    background of, 195–96
    Burr's visit with, 202–3
    financial matters of, 218
    reference to, in Burr's correspondence, 415n. 20 (210)
    on slavery, 208
    support for Burr of, 183
Byrd, Robert C., 412–13n. 13 (181–182)
Byron, 399–400n. 10 (61)

Caddonia, 289
Cahokia, medieval ruins at, 121–22
Calhoun, John C., 376
Callender, James, 69
Caller, James, 329
camp, Burr's, 303–4
Campbelltown, North Carolina, 223, 224
career, death of Burr's, 27, 30
Carmichael, Dr., 297

Carondelet, 247–49
Casa Calvo, marquis de, 266
Casa Yrujo, marques de, 251, 416n. 4 (215)
Catholicism, Burr's relationship with, 263–65
Catskill "maroon" colonies, 404n. 2 (92)
Cayuga Indians, 238
census of New Orleans, 250
character
    Burr and Hamilton's personalities compared, 19
    Burr's
        acceptance of other races, 21
        aristocratic demeanor, 9–10
        commented on by Woodrow Wilson, 348
        coyness, 388
        distractibility, 261–62
        gallantry, 373
        general character described, 8–12, 30–32
        generosity, 16–17, 19–20
        impulsiveness, 261–62
        integrity, 63
        lack of hypocrisy, 364
        lying, 11–12
        passivity, 31
        reputation, 317–18, 372–74
    charity, 16–17, 19–20
    defending by dueling, 83
    defined, 16
    Hamilton's, 4, 8–12, 34, 78–79, 93, 405n. 18 (103)
    Jefferson's, 8–12, 32, 35, 51, 363, 400n. 17 (64)
    Latrobe as a judge of, 425–26n. 27 (316)
    manners, 9–10
    "pretensions to," 15–16

subjects summarized and compared, 3–5

use of paid character assassins, 94

charges against Burr

of conspiracy, 255, 269–70, 274, 299–301, 311

Hamilton's allegations, 76–77, 80

refutation of, 143–44

treason and violation of Neutrality Law, 111, 349–50

Charles V, 245

Chase, Samuel, 228–30

Chasseboeuf, Constantin-François (Volney), 105–6

Chateaubriand, François-Auguste-René, Vicomte, 236n

Cheetham, James, 81, 94

Cherokee Indians, 224, 233, 237

Chesterfield, 17–18, 395–96n. 14 (17–18)

Chickasaw Indians, 427n. 32 (319)

Chief Justice, 347

childhood

Burr's, 42

Hamilton's, 29–30, 38

Choctaw Indians, 234, 316–17, 321

Church, Angelica, 76–77

Church, John Barker, 68, 115

Churchill, Winston, 431n. 24 (346)

civil rights movement, 88

Claiborne, Charles, 252

Claiborne, John F. H., 264, 423–24n. 18 (301–302), 425n. 25 (314), 427–28n. 43 (324), 428–29n. 49 (325)

Claiborne, William C. C., 249–51, 253, 279, 313

Clark, Archibald, 207, 212

Clark, Daniel, 259–60, 262, 267, 275

Clark, George Rogers

dislike of Wilkinson, 134

invasion of New Orleans, 326–27

military service of, 121–26, 231

reference to, in Jefferson's correspondence, 430n. 1 (333)

Clark, William, 123–25, 231, 284–85

Clarke, Elijah, 125, 128, 215, 217, 327, 343

Clay, Henry, 262, 268

Clearance Bill, 412–13n. 13 (181–182)

clerk, Burr assigned as a, 45–46

Clinton, De Witt, 105, 169, 185, 258, 275, 421–22n. 32 (275)

Clinton, George, 64, 96, 166, 170, 257, 421–22n. 32 (275)

Clinton, Henry, 79

Clinton family, 63, 68, 91–92, 94

Clopton, John, 181

Coker, William S., 416n. 4 (215)

Coles, Edward, 109

College of New Jersey, 40

Collot, Georges, 144, 163–64

communication, Burr prohibited from, 339

confinement of Burr, Jefferson's demands for, 365

consolidated tribes, 419n. 3 (236)

conspiracy, Burr accused of, 255, 269–70, 274, 311

Constellation, 189, 190

Constitution of the United States

concerning slavery, 101

Conway, Thomas, 115

Conway Cabal, 229

Cooper, Charles D., 72, 77

Cooper, Duff, 147–48

Cooper, James Fenimore, 236n

correspondence

anonymous letters by Hamilton, 160

insecurity of, 209–10, 293, 322

Cosway, Maria, 60, 77, 367

cotton
  cotton gins, 110, 184, 199, 242
  effect of steam power on exports of,
    243
  greenseed cotton, 198
  influence on southern economy of,
    183–84
Cotton Whigs, 90
Couper, John, 203–4
Cox, Isaac Joslin, 27, 267, 313
Cox, John, 355
Cranbury, New Jersey, 192
Crawford on expansionism, 408n. 20
  (136)
Creek Indians, 220
criticisms
  Burr's lack of response to, 374
  of Jefferson, 140, 229–30
Croghan, George, 240
Cromwell, Thomas, 271
Cruger, Nicholas, 29
Cumberland Island, 212
Cummins, John, 302, 304, 325, 333
Custis, George Washington Parke, 27–
  28
Custis, John Parke, 117
Cutler, Manasseh, 99

Dallas, Alexander, 161, 192, 193, 195
Danton, Georges Jacques, 147
Danville Convention, 125, 259
Darien, Georgia, 206–7
Darien Resolution of 1739, 207
daughter of Burr. See Alston,
  Theodosia Burr (Burr's
  daughter)
Davenport, Samuel, 250–51
Davidson, Dr., 297
Davis, Jay, 409n. 42 (146)
Davis, Matthew Livingston, 105, 169,
  266, 390

Dayton, Jonathan, 165, 185, 187, 258,
  429–30n. 57 (329)
Dearborn, Henry, 275, 317
Declaration of Independence, 48–49,
  381
Dee, John, 201
defenders of Burr, 300, 333–34, 354,
  357
defense, Burr's refusal to offer, 7–8,
  308
denial, Burr's request for Hamilton's
  denial of allegations, 72–73
Dinsmoor (Dinsmore), Silas
  Burr and Wilkinson's opinion of,
    428n. 47 (325)
  courage of, 325
  meeting with Burr, 321
  opposition to Kemper's filibuster,
    427–28n. 43 (324)
  recognized as a friend of Burr, 270
  relations with Native Americans, 316–
    18
  removal of, from military post,
    428n. 45 (324)
  on response to Burr's plans in
    Louisiana, 252
  role of, in arrest and trial of Burr,
    320–25
  role of, in westward expansion, 318–
    25
  spelling of name, 426n. 28 (316)
diplomacy skills of the Stockbridge
  Indians, 239
disguise, Burr's use of, 333, 334
documentation, Jefferson's prolific
  records, 8
Drake, Francis, 201
Drayton, 101
dueling
  Burr versus Church, 68
  Burr versus Hamilton, 72–74, 82–86,

258, 396–97n. 3 (34–35), 403–4n. 21 (83), 403n. 18 (82)
Burr's return to scene of, 81
culture of, 69–72, 82–83, 302, 396–97n. 3 (34–35), 403n. 18 (82)
defending character by, 83
Eacker *versus* Hamilton, 68
Hamilton's expectations of, 42–43
Hamilton's intention to throw away the first fire, 14, 42–43, 43, 84, 85
Hamilton's last writing on Burr, 13–15
Hamilton's provocation for, 76, 79–80
Hamilton's religious aversion to, 37
Jefferson on, 70–71
Lee *versus* Laurens, 48
pistols used in Burr and Hamilton's duel, 83–84, 403–4n. 21 (83)
political response to, 170, 185, 186–87
suicidal nature of, 12–15, 84
Wilkinson, 115, 348
Dumont, Pierre-Étienne-Louis, 156
Dunbar, George, 222
Dunbar, Priscilla, 222
Dunmore, Lord, 226, 249

East Florida Republic, 129
Eaton, William, 273–75
economics, inadequacy of, to explain politics, 178–79
education of subjects, 29, 39–40
Edwards, Henrietta Frances, 199
Edwards, Jonathan, 373
Edwards, Jonathan, Jr., 237
Edwards, Pierpont, 95, 270, 421–22n. 32 (275)
Edwards, Rhoda Ogden, 429–30n. 57 (329)

Edwards, Timothy, 95, 236, 237, 429–30n. 57 (329)
Egerton, Douglas, 179
election of 1800, 164–68, 257
Ellicott, Andrew, 315–17, 330–31, 425–26n. 27 (316), 425n. 25 (314)
Elliot, Gray, 217
Elliot, Matthew, 133
Elliott, Jack, 426n. 28 (316)
Ellsworth, Oliver, 350
emancipation, studies on, 404n. 1 (91)
embargo of Haiti, Burr's role in, 181–82, 228
Emerson, Ralph Waldo, 379
emotion
    Burr's aversion to public, 42
    Burr's expression of, 81–82, 261–62, 345
    Jefferson's objectivity contaminated by, 360–61
envy, Hamilton's envy of Burr, 31–32, 37
Eppes, John W., 181
equality
    Burr and Hamilton's belief in, 92
    Jefferson's disbelief in, 92
    John Quincy Adam's on, 376
Erwin, James, 418n. 1 (233)
escape
    Burr's attempted, 344–45
    Burr's successful, 321, 329
espionage, British, 133
estate sale, John McQueen, 219
estates of subjects, 21–23
Eustace, John Skey, 355
evidence against Burr, 310–11
exile, Burr's, 30, 62, 144, 255, 382–83
expansionism
    alternatives to, 240
    differing views on, 408n. 20 (136)

expansionism (*continued*)
  Ellicott's role in, 425–26n. 27 (316)
  Hamilton's ambitions of, 28
  slavery as factor encouraging, 174
expedition, Burr's 1796 plans for, 355

factions, political, 23–24
family
  Burr's, 29–30, 36, 41–42 (*see also*
    Alston, Theodosia Burr (Burr's
    daughter); Burr, Theodosia
    Bartow (Burr's wife))
  Hamilton's, 17
Fawcett, Mary, 38
The Federalist, 23, 58
Federalists, 24, 140–41
  Burr's alliance with, 90
  dislike for Napoleon, 142
  foreign policy of, 172
  resistance to French politics, 106
  on Scottish settlers in North
    Carolina, 225
  value of Hamilton to, 77
feminism, Burr's, 21, 59–62
"Fenno," anonymous letters by
    Hamilton, 160
field notes, 390–91
filibusters
  Burr's failure to get support for, 269
  Burr's possible contemplation of,
    321
  Clarke's alleged, 343
  etymology of word, 111–12
  French involvement in, 119–21
  Jefferson's support for, 128, 129
  Jefferson's warning of, 255
  penalty for, 259
  Virginia party's covert plans for, 313
finances
  bankruptcy of subjects, 16, 396n. 2
    (22)

  of Burr, 258, 375
  in eighteenth century, 218
  of Hamilton, 75–76
Finger Lakes region, mixture of races
    in, 234
firearms, Burr's provision of, to
    Alabama residents, 330
Flagler, Henry, 201
Flexner, James Thomas, 97
Florida
  Burr's attraction to, 200–203
  Burr's departure for, 202
  Burr's views on independence of, 144
  cotton lands in, 200
  importance of, to French, 144–46
  Jacob Lewis on, 214
  McKee's designs on, 330–31
  multiracial culture of, 418n. 1 (233)
  Seminole Indians in, 244–46
Folch, Vincente, 267, 331
foreign policy, 172, 400n. 14 (63)
forged documents incriminating Burr,
    293, 296–97
Fort Adams, 429–30n. 57 (329)
Fort Frederica, 204–5
Fort George, 214–17, 222–23
Fort Miro, 129, 243
Fort Necessity, 149
Fort Stoddert, 336
Fort Wilkinson, 338, 343–46
fortitude of Burr, 342–43
Fox, Charles James, 281–82
France
  Hamilton's relations with, 102
  influence on American politics of,
    354–58
  involvement in filibustering and
    secessionism, 119–21
  role of French in slave revolts, 248
  Spain resisting the imperialism of,
    331–32

franchise
  blacks deprived of, 90–91, 105
  requirements for, 104
  three-fifths rule, 174–75, 230
Frankfort, Kentucky, 118–19
Franklin, Benjamin, 236
Franklin, Jesse, 225, 258
Franklin and Armfield (slave trading
    company), 101
Free State of Muskogee, 130
Freeman, Joanne B., 396–97n. 3 (34–
    35)
Frémont, John C., 128–29
French National Assembly, Hamilton's
    honorary membership in, 103
French Revolution, 102, 120
French secret service, on Burr and
    Florida, 144–45
friends of Burr, 270, 339–43
frustration of Burr over repeated
    attacks, 80–81
fugitive slave laws, 180, 258

Gaasbeck, Peter van, 96
Gaines, Edmund, 334–38
Gallatin, Albert
  biographies of, 411n. 46 (169)
  Black Speech, 177–78
  Black Speech of, 158
  on Burr and Jefferson, 318
  charges of French influence on, 176
  charges of treason against, 113
  compared to John Jay, 155
  connection with Whiskey Rebellion,
    154, 161–63
  Dangerfield on, 411n. 36 (166)
  at demonstrations at Parkinson's
    Ferry, 160
  on dueling, 170
  ethnology, 237
  on expansionism, 408n. 20 (136)

feminist views of, 61
  on former slave owners, 180
  as friend to Burr, 270
  influence of plantation owners on,
    100
  involvement in Amistad case, 180
  as Jefferson's agent against Burr,
    269
  on Jefferson's embargo of Haiti, 180–
    81
  meeting Washington, 150
  negotiating with Britain, 142
  political positions held, 173
  poor hygiene of, 156–57
  resistance against Toussaint regime
    in Haiti, 176–77
  role of, in election of 1800, 164–68
  service in U. S. Senate, 159
  service to Jefferson, 24
  silence of, on Burr's problems, 354
  on slavery, 158, 168–70, 181
Gallatin, Hannah, 382–83
Gallatin (Stevens), 410n. 21 (158)
Gardoqui, Don Diego de, 114
Garrison, William Lloyd, 93, 382, 404–
    5n. 5 (93)
Gates, Horatio, 47–48, 115
genealogy
  Bayard family, 417–18n. 16 (222)
  Kingsley family, 418n. 1 (233)
  Livingston family, 417–18n. 16 (222)
Genêt, Edmund-Charles, 120–21, 125–
    26, 126, 127, 129
Gibbs, James, influence on American
    architecture, 216n
Giddings, Joshua, 244
Giles, William Branch, 227–28, 300,
    378–79
Girard, Stephen, 246
Godwin, William, 60
Golden Islands, 202–3

Gordon, George, 399–400n. 10 (61)
government's representatives,
    Benjamin Hawkins, 338–39
governorship, Burr's sabotaged bid
    for, 67–68, 258
Graham, John, 253, 280, 328–29
grand jury, 308–9, 313–14
Grand Pré, Carlos de, 267
Granger, Gideon
  association with Wilkinson, 273, 275–
    78, 292–94
  attitude toward Burr, 415n. 22 (211)
  coded correspondence of, 421–22n.
    32 (275)
  creation of spoils system, 35
  as Jefferson's agent against Burr,
    269, 274–75, 292–93
  John Randolph on, 294
  patronage matters of, 169
  publicizing the Burr case, 353
  racial politics of, 104–5
  on response to Burr's plans in
    Louisiana, 252
  theft of Burr's correspondence, 209–
    10, 415n. 20 (210)
grave of Burr, 212
The Great Valley, 231, 283–87, 408n.
    20 (136)
Greenberg, Kenneth, 402–3n. 8 (78–79)
Greene, Nathaniel, 199
Gregoire, Abbé Henri, 103–4
Greswold, Edward, 196–98
Griswold, Roger, 141–42
Gronowicz, Anthony, 404n. 1 (91)
Guion, Isaac, 316, 329
Gwinnett, Button, 207

habeas corpus
  proposed suspension of, 300
  Wilkinson's abuse of, 340
Haiti
  constitution of, 175

  embargo on, 180–82
  French policy regarding, 136
  immigration from forbidden, 179
  rebellion in, 248
  repression of Toussaint regime, 176,
    177–78
Hakluyt, Richard, 201
Hamilton, Alexander. See also dueling;
    Jefferson, Thomas; political
    offices; Wilkinson, James
  admission of guilt to wife, 77
  animosity toward Burr, 24
  anonymous letter's by, 160
  attempting to impede Burr's
    political goals, 63–64
  on Burr's ability to serve as
    president, 65–66
  Burr's belief that, would not fight,
    69
  compared to Burr, 40–41
  criticisms of Burr, 15, 75–76
  fascination with Burr, 75
  friendship with Burr, 42
  legitimacy gained through marriage,
    59
  relationship with Jefferson, 359–60
  religious duty to oppose Burr, 36–
    37
  sponsors of, 29, 35
  Western ambitions of, 28
Hamilton, Henry, capture of, 122
Hamilton, James, 38
Hamilton, Mrs., 140
Hamilton's Bluff, 204
Hampton, Wade
  battle at Pointe Coupée, 249
  development of cane sugar industry,
    217
  experiments with cotton gin, 196
  influence on cotton industry, 242–
    43
  lack of assistance for Burr, 364

piracy of cotton gin design, 199
  rise of, in southern agriculture, 183–
    84
Hancock, John, 397–98n. 9 (49)
Hand, Edward, 122, 430n. 1 (333)
Hannahan, Abraham, 418n. 1 (233)
Harper's, on Fort George Island, 215–
  16
Harrisburg convention, Gallatin's
  participation in, 157
Harrison, William Henry, 169–70, 268
Hartford Convention, criticisms of
  Madison administration, 142
hatred of Burr, 12, 43, 360, 368
Hawkins, Benjamin, 338–39, 400n. 15
  (63)
Hawkins, John, 201
Hayward, Thomas Jr., military service
  of, 397–98n. 9 (49)
health
  Burr's failing, in exile, 384
  Hamilton's, 13
Hector, François Louis, 245
Hemings, Sally, 103, 367
Henry, Lemuel, 329
The Hermitage, 399n. 1 (58)
hero, wartime, 48
Hidden Cities, 422n. 40 (282)
Higginbotham, Leon, 98
Hilhouse, (senator), 378
Hillhouse Amendments, 29
Hillhouse Debates, 100
Hinson, John, 334
Hooke, Moses, 297, 303
Hooker, Richard, 398–99n. 22 (55)
Hopewell architecture of Marietta,
  Ohio, 205
horses, 326
Houston, Sam, 128
Houstoun, Patrick, 222
Howell, Benjamin Betterton, 167
Howell, David, 57

Hudson, Henry, 236
Hudson Valley, concentration of slaves
  in, 404n. 1 (91)
hurricanes, 205–6

Imlay, Gilbert, 399–400n. 10 (61),
  422n. 40 (282)
immigration from Haiti forbidden,
  179
impeachment
  threat for Hamilton, 69
  trial of Samuel Chase, Burr's role in,
    228
imperialism
  Jefferson's desire to take land from
    Spain by war, 312
  Virginia party's covert plans for, 313
impressment contrasted with runaway
    slaves, 312
Indian adoption of European names,
  233
Indian nations, military capacity of,
  361
Indian policy
  Burr and Jefferson compared on,
    234
  Burr's influence on, 237–39
  Jefferson's, 241
Innes, Harry, 116–18, 131, 143
Insurgente, 189
intermarriage, 233–34, 418n. 1 (233)
intrigue, Jefferson's adeptness for, 32
Iroquois Indians, 234, 237, 238, 240–
  41

Jackson, Andrew
  architecture of The Hermitage,
    399n. 1 (58)
  on Burr, 261, 369–70, 377
  on Burr's candidacy for Vice
    President, 167
  Burr's roll in presidency of, 387

Jackson, Andrew (*continued*)
  character of, 193–94
  decline of, in southern agriculture, 183
  filibustering in Florida, 415n. 20 (210)
  military resistance to British, 249
  nose of, 402–3n. 8 (78–79)
  opinion of Burr, 348
  removal of Dinsmoor from military post, 428n. 45 (324)
  support of Burr, 270, 348
Jackson, Jacob, 321
Jacobin leveling principles, 8–9
Jacobins, 102, 120, 158–59, 163
James Monroe (steamboat), 242, 243
Jay, John
  Burr's relationship with, 63, 68, 94–96, 108, 146, 258, 270, 318
  compared to Gallatin, 155
  opinions on separatism, 152–53
  religious beliefs of, 95
  support of abolition, 88, 90
  writing of *The Federalist*, 23
Jefferson, Thomas. *See also* character; charges against Burr; military; political offices; trial, Burr's
  apprehending Burr, 297, 311–12, 340, 364
  change in attitude toward Burr, 280–82
  compared to Burr, 143–44
  as described by Hamilton, 140
  hatred of Burr, 24–27, 360–61, 366–69
  inconsistency concerning Burr, 310–11
  relationship with Burr considered, 359, 362–64
  resolve to rid himself of Burr, 257
Jefferson the President: Second Term (Malone), 400–401n. 17 (64)

Jersey Settlements, 429–30n. 57 (329)
Jews' influence on Spain, 245
Jim Crow period, 88, 104
Johnson, William, 240
Johnston, Samuel, 341
Jones, James, 185
Jones, Strother, 50
Journal of Urban History, Vol. XXI, no. 4 (Rosswurm), 404n. 1 (91)
journalism, quality of, 371
judge, 26, 347
Judiciary Act, 412–13n. 13 (181–182)
jury, 328, 347

Kemble, Charles, 201
Kemble, Frances Anne "Fanny," 201–2
Kemper, Reuben, 129, 269, 324, 427–28n. 43 (324)
Kentucky
  Burr in, 269–70
  secessionism in, 113–17, 151–52
  slave owners' constitution, 100, 363
  violence in, during Whiskey Rebellion, 161
Kentucky Abolition Society, 109
Kentucky Resolution, 106–7, 154
Kill, Arthur, 188–89
King, Rufus, 137, 138, 179, 224
King Cotton, 196
Kingsley, Anta, 223
Kingsley Plantation, 215
Knox, Henry, 46, 62, 131, 133–34, 237
Knox, Hugh, 39–40

La Chaumiere du Prairie, 216, 270
La Salle, René-Robert Cavelier de Sieur, 288
La Venveance, 190
Lafayette, Marie Gilbert du Motier, 102

language
  Jefferson's creation of phrases, 361
  multilingualism of Burr, 264
  Munsee dialect, 419n. 3 (236)
The Last of the Mohicans (Cooper),
    236n
Latrobe, Benjamin Henry
  on Burr, 19, 261, 372
  design of Belvedere, 402n. 5 (77)
  design of Ohio River Canal, 420n. 7
    (262)
  fame as architect, 247
  as a friend of Burr, 270
  as judge of character, 425–26n. 27
    (316)
  on sexuality of Burr and Hamilton,
    78
  at trial of Samuel Chase, 228–29
Latrobe, John H. B., 425–26n. 27
    (316)
Lattimore, Owen, 392
Laurens, Henry, 48, 207
Laurens, John, 78–79, 110, 208
Lavien, Peter, 38–39
Lavien, Rachel Fawcett, 38
law practices, Burr and Hamilton's, 57
League of Franco-American
    Friendship, 102
Lear, Tobias, 178
Lee, Charles, 48
Lee, Richard Henry, 48–49
Lee, Robert E., 110
LeGrand (French abolitionist), 249
Lemos, Gayoso de, 267–68
Lenin, Nikolai, 431n. 24 (346)
Les Amis des Noirs, 102–3, 125–26,
    248, 405n. 20 (103)
Lewis, Anthony Marc, 122
Lewis, Jacob
  interest in Florida, 196–98, 214
  on John McQueen, 217
  naval service of, 358

speculation on Florida cotton lands,
    200
  warning about Greswold, 198
Lewis, Joseph, 181
Lewis, Meriwether, 123, 170, 231, 284–
    85
Lexington, Kentucky, 119
Liberty Without Anarchy (Myers), 399–
    400n. 10 (61)
libraries, 416–17n. 9 (219), 416n. 2
    (215)
Library of Congress, 412–13n. 13 (181–
    182)
Lincoln, Abraham, 181
Little Democrat, 125–26
Livingston, Brockholst, 185
Livingston, Catharine, 222
Livingston, Edward
  Burr's relationship with, 68, 168,
    270
  charging Wilkinson with treason,
    275
  on Hamilton, 185
  impeachment trial of, 353
  swindling of, by Bastrop, 246
Livingston, Maturin, 185
Livingston, Robert R., 68, 208, 211,
    411n. 36 (166), 414n. 18
    (209), 421–22n. 32 (275)
Livingston, William "Billy," 187
Livingston family
  architecture of, 153
  history in slave trade, 91–92, 404n.
    1 (91)
  Jefferson's association with, 94
  support of Burr, 68
Livingston Montgomery, Janet, 208
Lodge, Henry Cabot, 94
Logan, George, 181, 412–13n. 13
    (181–182)
Lomask, Milton, 168
losers, author's bias for, 389–90

Louis XVI, Washington's response to execution of, 158–59
Louisiana Purchase
  effect on plantation economy of purchase, 232
  effect on slavery of purchase, 100
  factors encouraging purchase of, 248, 291
  financing of purchase, 158, 421–22n. 32 (275)
  history of insurrection in, 247
  Jefferson on slavery in, 363
Louisiana Territory, 235
Louverture, Toussaint. See Toussaint Louverture, Pierre Dominique
Lucayes Islands, 145
lying, Hamilton and Burr's, 11–12
Lyman, Phineas, 429–30n. 57 (329)
Lyon, Matthew, 261, 262

MacGillivray, Alexander, 238, 240
Macon, Nathaniel, 338–39
Madison, Dolley Payne, 276, 367–68, 383
Madison, James
  compared to Jefferson, 313
  criticisms of, 142
  on dueling, 70–71
  on expansionism, 408n. 20 (136)
  Granger's attempts to blackmail, 276
  involvement in filibustering, 112
  Jefferson's relationship with, 276, 368
  views on slavery, 98
  writing of The Federalist, 23
Madoc, Prince of Wales, 201
Mahican Indians, 236, 236n, 419n. 3 (236)
mail, insecurity of, 209–10, 293, 322
Maison Rouge, Marquis de, 246

Malone, Dumas, 398–99n. 22 (55)
Malone, Thomas, 128, 334–35
manic depressive tendencies, Burr's, 261
manumission, Burr's work for, 164, 401n. 26 (68)
Manumission Society, 91–92, 97–98, 101–2, 103, 180
maps
  Burr's travels, 197, 235
  Natchez Trace, 306
Maret, Hugues-Bernard, 383
Marietta, Ohio, Hopewell architecture of, 205
Marietta, origin of town name of, 120
"maroon" colonies, 404n. 2 (92)
Marquette, Pere, 288
marriage of Alexander Hamilton, 59
Marshall, John
  connection to Chase impeachment, 228, 230
  distrust of Jefferson, 53–55
  on Jefferson and Burr, 167, 318, 348–49
  Jefferson's attempts to impeach, 26, 353, 365
  military service, 52–53
  on Wilkinson, 348–49
Marshall, Thomas, 116–17
martial law, Wilkinson imposing, on New Orleans, 307–8
martial law, Wilkinson imposing on New Orleans, 311
Martin, Luther, 229–30, 270
Mathews, George, 129
Mathews, James, 342
Mazzei, Philip, 54
McCaleb, Flavius, 27
McHenry, James, 135–36, 140, 330–31
McIntosh, George, 207, 222
McIntosh, John Houstoun

arrival in Florida, 206–7
Burr's visit with, 212
filibusters of, 184
lineage of, 222–23
support of Jefferson and Madison, 128–29
McIntosh, Lachlan, 200, 205–8, 415n. 20 (210)
McIntosh family, 204, 206–9, 222
McKay, Patrick, 217
McKean, Thomas, 397–98n. 9 (49)
McKee, John, 316, 317, 321, 329–32, 428n. 45 (324)
McQueen, John, 200, 212–14, 217–20, 221, 416–17n. 9 (219), 416n. 1 (214)
McWilliams, William, 115
Mead, Cowles, 261–62, 308, 328, 333
Meade, David, 109
Meade family, 270–73, 421n. 24 (271)
Memoirs of Aaron Burr (Davis), 266
Menedez, Francisco, 245
Mero District, 114
Mexico
  Burr's interest in, 266
  Mexican War, 181
  Spain's interest in, 247
Miami Indians, 239
Michaux, André, 125, 406n. 24 (105)
"middle grounds" concept, 233–34, 418n. 2 (234)
Middleton, Arthur, military service of, 397–98n. 9 (49)
military
  effect of alcohol on, 124–25
  Jefferson's avoidance of service in, 4, 49–53
  service of author in, 391
  service of Burr in, 4, 44–48, 50
  service of Hamilton in, 4, 44, 46–47, 50

service of subjects in, 4, 50
service of the Declaration of Independence signers in, 397–98n. 9 (49)
strength of Indian nations, 361
militias, in the south, 315–17
Minor, Stephen, 252, 259–60
Miranda, Francisco de, 192, 310, 355
Miró, Esteban Rodriguez, 114
Mississippi, slavery in, 100, 363, 425n. 25 (314)
Mississippi (Claiborne), 420n. 10 (264), 425–26n. 27 (316)
Mississippi river
  Burr's travel down, 301
  described, 288–89
  failure to open through diplomacy, 153
  importance of, to French plans in North America, 106
  origins of, 286
  role of, in secessionist movements, 119
Mississippi Territory, *306*
Mississippi Valley
  Collot's visit to, 164
  reservations in, 237
  Washington's investments in, 149–50
Mitchell, John, 352
Mizener Brothers, 201
Mobile Act, 269
Mohawk Indians, 239
Moheagunck Indians, 236, 236n, 419n. 3 (236)
Mohegan/Mohican Indians. *See* Mahican Indians
Mohr, John McIntosh, 206
monarchism, Hamilton's alleged, 15–16
Monmouth, defeat at, 48

Monroe, James
appointment as minister in London, 179
appointment as minister to France, 165
confrontation with Hamilton, 69
drinking bout with Wilkinson, 115
on expansionism, 408n. 20 (136)
opposition to creation of the Constitution, 23
relationship with Burr, 368
Monroe, Louisiana, naming of, 242
Montgomery, James, 209
Montgomery, John, 134
Moorish influence on Spain, 245
Morales, Juan Ventura, 267, 337
Moravians, 236
Moreau, Victor Marie, 189, 192, 355–56
Morgan, George, 122, 245, 298–99, 319–20, 430n. 1 (333)
Morris, Gouverneur, 90, 165, 186–87
Morris, Lewis, 397–98n. 9 (49)
Muhlenberg, Henry, 168
Mulford, (Lieutenant), 297
Mun, Louis de, 356–58
Murray, John, 226
musicians, Jefferson's desire for, 51
Muskogee Indians, 233
mutiny, Burr's handling of, 50–51

Napoleon. See Bonaparte, Napoleon
Napoleonic Wars, effect on cotton market, 243
Nashville, Burr's arrival in, 268, 298
Natchez
Burr's arrival in (1807), 320
Burr's departure from, to Pensacola, 332
Burr's travel through, 289–91
political make up of, 314–17

Natchez Indians, 236n
Natchez Trace, 235, 306, 427n. 32 (319)
National Archives, 412–13n. 13 (181–182)
National Park Service, 212, 215, 397–98n. 9 (49)
navy
confrontation with Jefferson over Black Republic, 178
naval battles, 189–90
refusal to cooperate with arrest of Burr, 303
support of Toussaint regime, 176–77
Nelson, Thomas, military service of, 397–98n. 9 (49)
Nemours, Pierre-Samuel Du Pont du, 312, 365, 366
Neutral Ground Agreement (1806), 295
Neutrality Law of 1794. See also filibusters
Act signed into law, 130
Burr charged with violating, 111, 349, 427–28n. 43 (324)
Hamilton's violation of, 137
Jefferson's charge of violation of, 255, 311
Jefferson's violation of, 184
lack of enforcement, 134
New Madrid, 298
New Orleans, Louisiana
Burr's travels in, 262–63
Hamilton's planned expansion to, 331
importance of to western expansion, 150–51
Jefferson on importance of, 139
plans to take from France, 136
role of, in seccssionist movements, 114–15

role of in secessionist movements,
119

New York, 89–91, 404n. 1 (91)

New York Assembly, Burr's service in,
164, 401n. 26 (68)

Newman, Robert, 132, 133, 349,
408n. 13 (133)

Nicholas, George, 119, 130

Nicholson, Hannah, 61, 159

Nicholson, James, 24, 166

Nicholson, Joseph Hopper, 346

Nolan, Philip
assassination of, 325
as cartographer, 268, 290
misrepresentation of, 253
split with Wilkinson, 133

North American Sylva (Michaux), 407n.
20 (125)

North Carolina, 224–27

Northwest Ordinance, 100, 101

"The Nose, the Lie, and the Duel in
the Antebellum South"
(Greenberg), 402–3n. 8 (78–79)

noses, significance of, 402–3n. 8 (78–
79)

Notes on Virginia (Jefferson), 102, 103,
399–400n. 10 (61)

nullification, 107, 425n. 25 (107)

Nutt, Rush, 427n. 32 (319)

O'Fallon, James, 131

Ogden, Aaron, 187

Ogden family, 429–30n. 57 (329)

Oglethorpe, James, 204, 206–7, 222,
224, 243–44

Ohio, 239, 420n. 7 (262)

Ohio Valley
architecture of Native Americans,
399–400n. 10 (61)
reservations in, 237
Washington's survey of, 149–50

Old Town (Fort Frederica), 204–5

Oliver, Frederick Scott, 19–20

Oneida Indians, 238, 239

Onondaga Indians, 238

oration skills of subjects, 9, 19

Order of the Cincinnati, 49, 79, 183

Ordinance of 1784, 57, 126

orthography, 401–2n. 38 (73–74)

Osmun, Benijah, 329

Oswald, Eleazar, 355

Otis, Harrison Gray, 65

Otis, Samuel, 63

Ouachita River, 242

Ouiatanon Indians, 241

Page, John, 226

Paine, Thomas, 107, 124–25

Palladio, Andrea, 216n

Panama, attempts to establish colony,
207

Panton, Leslie, and Forbes (mercantile
firm), 220

Papers of Aaron Burr, 260

pardons offered in exchange for
statements against Burr, 340

Parkinson's Ferry, demonstrations at,
159–60

parole, Burr's, 328, 333

Parr, Marilyn, 412–13n. 13 (181–182)

Parton, James, 17–18, 81, 344, 375,
400n. 14 (63), 402n. 39 (74),
415n. 20 (210)

Paterson, William, 228, 261, 270, 350–
52

Patriot's Rebellion, 216

patronage, dispute over, 411n. 46
(169)

Paxton Boys, 236

Peale, Rembrandt, portraiture of
McQueen family, 218–19

Pendleton, Nathaniel, 73

Pennsylvania, secessionism in, 160
Pennsylvania Assembly, 157, 161
Pennsylvania Turnpike, 160
pension, Burr's Revolutionary, 343, 370
Pequot-Mohegan Indians, 236n
perjury, Wilkinson's, 293, 295
Perkins, Nicholas, 334, 335–38, 420n. 17 (268)
Pestre, Julien de, 270, 356–57
Phelps, Oliver, 67
philanthropy, 16–17, 19–20
physical attributes of subjects, 40–41, 78–79
Pickering, Timothy, 134, 175, 181, 330–31
Pickett, Albert James, 334, 423–24n. 18 (301–302)
Pike, Zebulon, 131, 268
Pinckney, Charles Cotesworth, 139
Pinckney, Thomas, 153
Pinckney's Treaty, 119
Pinckneyville, 429–30n. 57 (329)
piracy, 111, 124
Pitt, William, 281
plantation system, 425n. 25 (314)
Plumer, William, 300, 310
Plunkett, Rosa, 245
Pointe Coupée, 247–49
political offices
    Burr as Attorney General of New York, 58
    Burr's career death, 27, 30
    Burr's sabotaged bid for governorship, 67–68, 258
    careers of subjects summarized, 4
    Hamilton's appointment as brigadier general, 63
    Hamilton's elected offices, 34
    Hamilton's presidential potential of, 33

Jefferson's appointment as Secretary of Treasury, 58
Jefferson's governorship of Virginia, 53
Jefferson's presidency secured by Hamilton, 65–66
political career of Jefferson, 48
political service of Jefferson during the war, 49–53
political parties, absence of, 23
Ponce de Leon, Juan, 200
Power, Thomas, 114–15, 131
Presbyterian party, 95
President Washington's Indian War (Sword), 408n. 13 (133)
presidential elections, 33, 54–55, 67
presidential proclamations, use of to indict, 309
press
    Burr's guilt announced by, 353–54
    use of, as paid character assassins, 94
Prevost, Paul Henry Mallet, 355
Princeton University, 40
"private war" of the American merchants, 178–82
prostitution, Burr's use of, 384
public opinion of Burr, 34, 281, 328–29
public speaking, subjects' abilities, 9, 19
punctuation conventions, 390
Puritan influence, 10, 236
Putnam, Israel, 45, 47, 429–30n. 57 (329)

Quakers opposition to slavery, 123
Quasi-War, 153, 175–78
Queseda Battery, 220, 221

Race and Class Politics in New York City before the Civil War (Gronowicz), 405–6n. 23 (105)

racial integration, 234, 236–37
racism
  Burr's lack of, 21
  in militias, 250
  racial prejudice of Jefferson, 103,
    108, 399–400n. 10 (61)
Randolph, Edmond, 347
Randolph, John, 181, 294, 299, 346,
  347
Randolph, Thomas Mann, 101
Ranlett, William, 399n. 1 (58)
Raphael, portraiture of McQueen
    family, 218–19
Rawden, Francis, 370
Rawle, William, 351
Reeve, Tapping, 212, 261, 414n. 1
    (195)
religion
  Burr's coyness concerning, 36, 95
  Burr's relationships with other
    denominations, 37, 263–65
  convictions of Alexander Hamilton,
    36–37
  European influence on Mahicans,
    236
  in New Orleans, 262–63
  religious influences on Spain, 245
  subjects' attitudes toward, 17
Rensselaer, Stephen van, 64, 68, 258,
  318
Republic of Watauga, 113
Republicans, 24
reputation of Burr. See character
rescues
  captor's fear of Burr's, 337–38, 342,
    344–45
  John Sevier's, 341–42
resting place of Burr, 212
Revolution of 1800, Jefferson's, 162
reward offer. See bounty for Burr
Reynolds, Mrs. James, 69
Richmond, Virginia, 227, 345–46

Richmond Hill estate, 396n. 2 (22)
Rio Grande river, Burr's travels to,
  290
rivalry, Jefferson and Burr's, 366–67
Rockefeller Center, 396n. 2 (22)
Rodney, Caesar Augustus, 317, 347–
  48, 397–98n. 9 (49)
Rodney, Thomas, 301, 305–9, 327–29
Roman Catholic Church, 214
Roosevelt, Theodore, 113
Roux, Louis, 144, 354–55, 409n. 38
    (144)
Royster, Charles, 49
Rusche, Timothy, 132
Rush, Benjamin, 195, 196, 300, 397–
  98n. 9 (49), 427n. 32 (319)
Russell, Jonathan, 383
Rutledge, Edward, military service of,
  397–98n. 9 (49)

Saint Domingue, 179
Salcedo, Nimecio, 251
salvage of ship wrecks, 221
San Juan, Spanish mission at, 216
Sanchez, Francisco Xavier, 418n. 1
    (233)
Sancho, 179
Santee Hills, 223
Sapelo Island, 204–5
Sargent, Winthrop, 314–15, 425n. 25
    (314), 429–30n. 57 (329)
Schafer, Daniel, 418n. 1 (233)
Schuyler, Elizabeth, 59, 77
Schuyler, Philip, 24, 59, 93, 400n. 14
    (63)
Scott, Charles, 241
Scottish settlements
  Highlanders resettlement to North
    Carolina, 225
  influence in Georgia of, 414n. 1
    (195)
  threat of Burr's rescue from, 345

Seagrove, James, 425–26n. 27 (316)
secession
  Burr on, 143–46
  compared to separatism, 113–14
  Federalists involvement with, 141–42
  French involvement in, 119–21
  Georges Collot, 163
  Jefferson on, 162
  and the Ordinance of 1784, 57–58
  penalty for, 259
  political implications, 231–32
  relationship to slavery issue, 173
  in Virginia and Pennsylvania, 160
  Washington's struggles against, 117
secret sessions of legislatures, 400n. 14
    (63), 400n. 15 (63)
Sedgwick, Theodore, 165
Seminole Indians, 220, 244–46
The Senate (Byrd), 412–13n. 13 (181–182)
Seneca Indians, 238
separatism
  background of in volonies, 88
  Burr compared to Jefferson, 143–44
  fragmentation in the Union, 123
  Hamilton's views of north vs. south,
    149
  Jefferson's opinions on, 152
  John Jay's opinions on, 152–53
  of Kentucky, 151–52
  Ordinance of 1784, 126
  racial, 108–9
  rumors of, 267
Serlio, Sebastiano, 216n
Sevier, John, 114, 117, 125, 128, 134,
    341
sex lives of subjects, 76–79, 264, 372–74, 383–84
Shakespeare quoted by J. Q. Adams,
    377
Shawnee Indians, 239

Shelby, Isaac, 119, 127
Shields, William, 308
Short, Peyton, 119
Short, William, 119
Sibley, John, 251
Sidney, Algernon, 352
Sierra Leone, 179
Sieyès, Emmanuel Joseph Comte, 193
signature of Alexander Hamilton,
    397n. 11 (50)
sincerity of Hamilton compared to
    Burr, 10–11
The Six Nations, 239
Skelton, Martha Wayles, 58
Skipwith, Fulwar, 129, 211, 246
slavery. See also abolition; manumission
  Burr's position on, 29, 89, 281, 381
  foreign and domestic implications,
    173–74, 231–32, 243–44
  founder's intentions concerning,
    100–101
  freeing of slaves, 326–27
  Hamilton's position on, 89
  Jefferson's position on, 23, 28, 100,
    104, 168–70, 362, 380–82,
    406n. 24 (105)
  John Quincy Adams's position on,
    375–80
  in Mississippi, 100, 363, 425n. 25
    (314)
  in New York, 89–91
  opposition to, 101–2, 123, 168–70,
    271, 347–48
  as origin of Seminole indians,
    244
  runaway slaves, 312, 324–25
  slave codes, Georgian vs. Spanish,
    221
  slave revolts, 248, 249–51
  slaves' service in Revolutionary War,
    226
  support for, 100, 324–25

in Tennessee, 100
three-fifths rule, 174–75, 230
westward expansion of, 27–29, 57–
58, 99
Smilie, John, 156–57
Smith, John, 258–59, 354, 378
Smith, Philander, 308–9, 313
Smith, Rebecca. *See* Blodget, Rebecca
Smith
Smith, Samuel, 168
Smith, Thomas Adam, 296–98
Somewhat More Independent (White),
404n. 1 (91)
song, Hamilton's provocation of Burr,
79–80
South African Homeland, comparison
to Kentucky proposal, 109
South Carolina, violence during
Whiskey Rebellion in, 161
southwestern borderlands, strategic
importance of, 361
Spain
Burr and the liberation of Mexico
from, 266
Burr's intentions concerning war
with, 268
considering alliances with the U. S.
against France and Britain, 267
cultural influences on, 245
influence of, on American slave
system, 100
policy towards American slaves, 244–
45
spelling conventions, 390
spoils system of Granger, 293
St. Augustine, Florida, 129, 245
St. Clair, Arthur, 241
St. Martins-in-the-Fields, influence on
American architecture of, 216n
St. Mary's Town, 212
St. Stephens Steamboat Company,
428n. 45 (324)

Stanhope, Philip, 18, 395–96n. 14 (17–
18)
State of Franklin, 113–14, 341
steamboats, 242, 428n. 45 (324)
Stephens, Thomas, 29
Steuben, Baron von, 198–99, 245
Stevens, Edward, 39, 44, 79, 175, 178,
403n. 9 (79)
Stevens, Thomas, 39
Stockbridge Indians, 154, 236, 236n,
239
Story, Joseph, 229
Stowe, Harriet Beecher, 109, 369, 372–
74
strategic awareness, Burr's lack of, 31
Stuart, David, 117
Stuyvesant, Peter, 64
suffrage. *See* franchise
suicidal nature of Hamilton's death,
12–15
Sumter, Thomas, 183, 211
surrender of Burr to governor of
Mississippi, 308
Swartwout, John, 185
Swartwout, Robert, 142
Swartwout, Samuel, 105, 189, 340,
409n. 36 (142)

Talleyrand, Charles Maurice de, 139,
147, 148, 404n. 2 (92)
Tammany, 9, 34, 105
Taney, Roger B., 370
Tarjon, Madame Xavier, 265–66
Tarleton, Banastre, 370
taxes, resistance to excise taxes, 157.
See also Whiskey Rebellion
Tennessee, 100, 113–17, 363
Thacher, George, 100
Three Chopped Way, 338
three-fifths rule, 174–75, 230. *See also*
franchise

tie-breaking votes, 412–13n. 13 (181–182)

Tingley, Charles, 416–17n. 9 (219)

tobacco economy in Virginia, 183

Tombighee River territory, 329–30

Tonti, Henri, 288

Toogood, Coxey, 397–98n. 9 (49)

Topographical Description (Boone), 399–400n. 10 (61)

Toulmin, Harry, 303, 427–28n. 43 (324)

Toussaint Louverture, Pierre Dominique, 156, 173, 175–77

Townsend, Peter, 167

Tracy, Uriah, 141, 154

trade, development of, on frontier, 150–51

Trail of Tears, 325

Trans-Oconee Republic, 130

translation issues, 401–2n. 38 (73–74)

Transylvania Colony, 121

travels of Burr, 21

treason
  Burr charged with, 349
  charge of, 7-, 274
    against Burr, 255
  charged against Burr, 111, 112
  defined, 351
  evidence of, 27

treaties between France and Spain, 153

trees of the west, 287–88

trial, Burr's
  Attorneys General commenting on trial, 347–48
  Burr's case compared to Whiskey Rebellion, 350–53
  evidence against Burr, 310–11
  grand jury, 308–9, 313–14, 347
  Jefferson's attempt to impeach the judge, 26
  Jefferson's demand for Burr's imprisonment, 26
  Jefferson's reactions to acquittal, 365
  participants in, 347
  prosecution's examination, 323
  in Richmond (1807), 322–23
  testimony of Truxton, 191
  verdicts of, 30, 328
  Wilkinson's perjury, 293

Tristram Shandy, 402–3n. 8 (78–79)

Troup, Robert, 224, 270

Truxton, Thomas, 188, 189–92, 357

Truxton family, 188–92

Tucker, St. George, freeing of slaves, 109

"Tully," anonymous letters by Hamilton, 160

Tupper, Edward, 269

Tuscarora Indians, 224, 238

Twain, Mark, 187

Ugarte, Jacobo, 251

underground railroad, 109, 247

United States, naming of, 285

United States Congress, Gallatin's election to, 161

United States Highway 30, site of old Indian track, 160

United States Postal Service, monitoring Burr's mail, 209–10, 293, 322

upland cotton, 184

Ursuline nuns, Burr's encounter with, 265

Valley Forge, winter of 1778–79, 53

Van Buren, Martin, 378

Van Ness, William, 67

Vaolude, Natalie Marie Louise
    Stephanie Beatrice Delage de,
    210–11
Vice Presidency of Burr, 24, 64–65, 87
Vidal, José, 253, 316
Viel, Abbe, 264
Vincennes, capture of, 122
Vindication of the Rights of Women
    (Wollstonecraft), 59–60
violence, 44, 303
Virginia
    Burr's reception in Richmond, 227
    as exporter of slaves, 174
    politics in, 227–30
    secessionism in, 160
    slavery in, 231–32
    western expansion, 151
Virginia Plan, 226–27
Virginia Resolution, 106–7, 154
Volney (Constantin-François
    Chasseboeuf), 105–6
Von Hoya, Clara, 430–31n. 12 (339)
votes, tie-breaking, 412–13n. 13 (181–
    182)

Wadsworth, Rhoda, 212–13
Walker, William, 112
Walters, Raymond, 155
Walton, George, military service of,
    397–98n. 9 (49)
War of 1812, 142, 158
Warren, Jack, 400n. 15 (63)
Washington, George
    appeasement policies of, 428n. 47
        (325)
    assistance from Albert Gallatin, 155
    blocking Burr's appointments, 63
    Burr and Hamilton serving as a
        clerks under, 46–47
    Burr's discussion with (1805), 268
    Burr's opinion of, 46
    cabinet of, 23
    commenting on Jefferson's absence
        in war, 52
    differences with Federalists, 52
    distrust of Wilkinson, 315–16
    on dueling, 71
    freeing of slaves, 109
    Hamilton advising, 62–63
    Hamilton and Burr's relationships
        with, 24
    as Hamilton's sponsor, 29
    on North Carolina, 224
    opposition to Gallatin's plans, 158
    opposition to slavery late in life, 99
    orders against filibustering, 112
    ownership of slaves, 27–28
    political sophistication of, 154
    reaction to Whiskey Rebellion, 162
    role of in birth of U. S., 147–49
    struggles against secession, 117
    on western settlers, 163
Washington, Justice Bushrod, 186
Washington, Mississippi, 423–24n. 18
    (301–302)
Watauga Association, 113
Watauga-Franklin, 130
Wayne, Anthony, 124, 126, 131–35,
    320, 349
West Florida Republic, 129
West Indies, control of arms supplies
    to, 412–13n. 13 (181–182)
Whipple, Thomas, military service of,
    397–98n. 9 (49)
Whiskey Rebellion, 112, 135, 154, 161–
    62, 350–53
Whiskey Tax, reactions to, 157
White, Don Henrique, 214–15, 416n.
    1 (214), 416n. 2 (215), 416n.
    4 (215)
White, Enrique, 221–22, 245
White, Richard, 418n. 2 (234)

White Plains Convention (1776), 90
Whitefield, George, 207
Whitney, Eli, 199
wife
  of Burr (*See* Burr, Theodosia Bartow
    (Burr's wife))
  of Hamilton (*See* Schuyler,
    Elizabeth)
  of Jefferson (*See* Skelton, Martha
    Wayles)
Wilkinson, James
  abuse of habeas corpus, 340
  acquisition of arms and militia, 307
  association with Burr, 231, 269–70
  association with Hamilton, 135–39
  attempt to seize martial leadership
    of Louisiana, 252–53
  attempted payoff of Dinsmoor, 319
  at Burr's trial, 349
  challenged by Andrew Jackson to
    duel, 348
  Claiborne's defense of, 423–24n. 18
    (301–302)
  commission in army, 117–18
  confrontation with Boone, 422n. 40
    (282)
  connection with Spain, 126, 130–35,
    138, 278–80
  cooperation with Bastrop, 246
  encouragement of Kentucky
    separatists, 143
  fame of, 428n. 47 (325)
  forgery of incriminating documents,
    297
  history of assassination attempts, 320
  imposing martial law on New
    Orleans, 307–8, 311
  as Jefferson's agent against Burr,
    274–75
  Jefferson's defense of, 310
  as key to understanding Burr, 27

Neutral Ground Agreement, 295–96
  perjury of, 293, 295
  representatives of, waiting for
    release of Burr, 328–29
  role in capture of Burr, 321
  testimony of, 420n. 10 (264)
  Thomas Rodney on, 305–7
  violation of Neutrality Law, 259
  war with indians, 241
  warning Folch against Burr, 267
  Washington's warnings about, 315–16
  working with Granger against Burr,
    293–94
Williams, Robert, 322
Williamson, Charles, 414n. 1 (195)
Wilson, Woodrow, 348
Wirt, William, 323
Witherspoon, John, 226
witnesses. *See also* trial, Burr's
  affidavit of testimony demanded of,
    365
  discretion of, 333–34
  requirement of two, 350
  Wilkinson eliminating, 295
Wolcott, Oliver, 140, 397–98n. 9 (49)
Wollstonecraft, Mary, 59–60, 399–
  400n. 10 (61), 422n. 40 (282)
women
  role of, in Burr's life, 382–87, 388
  significant, in Jefferson's life, 367
  subjects attitudes toward, 60–61,
    388
Worthington, Thomas, 109, 258, 354
"wrecking" (salvage of ships), 221

xenophobia, 106, 108. *See also* Alien
  and Sedition Acts

Yamassee War, 245
Yankee, origin of term, 199
Yates, Peter, 189, 203